Capital Markets in Central and Eastern Europe

Edited by

Christian Helmenstein

Department of Economics & Finance
Institute for Advanced Studies, Vienna

Edward Elgar

Cheltenham, UK • Northampton, MA, USA

Published by
Edward Elgar Publishing Limited
Glensanda House
Montpellier Parade
Cheltenham
Glos GL50 1UA
UK

136 West Street
Suite 202
Northampton
Massachusetts 01060
USA

A catalogue record for this book
is available from the British Library

Library of Congress Cataloguing in Publication Data
Capital Markets in Central and Eastern Europe / edited by Christian
  Helmenstein.
    "Papers included in this book were presented at the conference
    'Capital Markets in Emerging Economies – Central and Eastern Europe'
    that was held in Vienna at the Institute for Advanced Studies,
    February 14–15, 1997"—Acknowledgments.
      1. Capital market—Europe, Eastern—Congresses. I. Helmenstein.
    Christian. II. Institut für Höhere Studien, Wien.
    HG5430.7.A3C36 1999
    332'.042'0947—DC21   99–17043
                                                                 CIP

ISBN 1 85898 498 X

M|L Printed and bound in Great Britain by MPG Books Ltd, Bodmin, Cornwall

Contents

List of figures   viii
List of tables   x
Acknowledgements   xvi
Contributors   xvii

Introduction   1
Christian Helmenstein

Part I   COUNTRY PROFILES

1.   Albania   13
     Rexhina Bajraktari and Ermira Brahja

2.   Bulgaria   38
     Todor Balabanov, Tatiana Houbenova and Borislav Vladimirov

3.   Croatia   67
     Velimir Šonje

4.   Czech Republic   89
     Oldřich Rejnuš and Radek Schmied

5.   Hungary   109
     István Ábel

6.   Macedonia   129
     Gordana Bival and Vladimir Gligorov

7.   Poland   148
     Ryszard Kokoszczyński

8.   Romania   163
     Ion Drăgulin and Daniela Grozea-Helmenstein

Contents

9. Slovak Republic   184
    Jarko Fidrmuc, Viliam Pálenik and Ladislav Unčovský

10. Slovenia   214
    Gordana Bival and Vlado Dimovski

11. FR Yugoslavia   239
    Vladimir Gligorov

Part II SELECTED TOPICS

12. The Role of Central Bank Independence for Seigniorage:
    A Study of Transitional Economies   251
    Eduard Hochreiter, Riccardo Rovelli and Georg Winckler

13. Collusive Trade Credit and Stabilization Policies   270
    Enrico Perotti

14. Banks in the Czech Republic: Current State and Prospects   283
    Petr Zahradník

15. Establishing and Cooperating With Promotional Banks
    in Central and Eastern Europe   301
    Norbert Irsch and Heike Wiegand

16. Privatization: A Comparative Experiment –
    Poland, the Czech Republic and Hungary   318
    Lina Takla

17. RM-System Slovakia   371
    Viliam Pálenik

18. Managing Central European Financial Risks –
    With a Case Study on the CECE Index Family   381
    Günther Schiendl

Contents

19. The Extent of Efficiency in Central European Equity Markets   392
    Randall K. Filer and Jan Hanousek

20. Modeling Polish Stock Returns   417
    Martin Scheicher

21. Foreign Debt Settlements in Bulgaria, Hungary and Poland
    1989–1996   438
    Jérôme Sgard

Index   461

Figures

Figure 1.1	The consumer price index and inflation	17
Figure 1.2	Interest rates 1993–1995	31
Figure 2.1	Internal credit to the government and non-government sectors	41
Figure 2.2	The Reuters All-Bulgarian Stock Index (RABSI)	53
Figure 2.3	Term structure of government securities	56
Figure 2.4	EMBI+ for Bulgarian Bradies	64
Figure 3.1	International reserves and US$ equivalents of M1 in US$ millions	68
Figure 3.2	Exchange rate of the Croatian Kuna (end of month)	70
Figure 3.3	Rate of reserve requirements and the share of NBC bills in M1	71
Figure 3.4	Average monthly trading volume on the Zagreb Stock Exchange	82
Figure 4.1	Exchange rate CZK/US$ and CZK/DEM	92
Figure 4.2	Prague Stock Exchange Index PX50	101
Figure 4.3	Change in foreign portfolio investment between 1994 and 1995	104
Figure 7.1	The US$-Zloty exchange rate	152
Figure 7.2	Warsaw Stock Exchange Index and main market turnover	160
Figure 8.1	Refinancing interest rate and inflation rate	165
Figure 8.2	Interest rates applied by banks	166
Figure 8.3	Real exchange rate and current account balance	168
Figure 8.4	Companies in the mass privatization program by branches	174
Figure 8.5	Market capitalization and turnover on the Bucharest Stock Exchange	178
Figure 8.6	Imports versus foreign direct investment	181
Figure 10.1	Exchange rates SIT/DEM in Slovenia	217
Figure 10.2	The Ljubljana Stock Exchange market capitalization	235
Figure 13.1	Adjustment under a credible program	273
Figure 13.2	Adjustment under a program with low credibility	273
Figure 13.3	Adjustment as a function of credibility	275

Figures

Figure 16.1	Sector breakdown of ownership transformation type as a percentage of total	344
Figure 16.2	Size breakdown by ownership transformation type as a percentage of total	344
Figure 17.1	Regional Structure of RM-System Slovakia	373
Figure 17.2	RM-S Indices	378
Figure 19.1	Capitalization of equity markets/GDP	396
Figure 20.1	The Warsaw General Index	419
Figure 20.2	Returns of the WGI	422
Figure 20.3	Returns of the DAX	422
Figure 20.4	Normalized estimated unconditional distribution of the WGI	423
Figure 20.5	Normalized estimated unconditional distribution of the DAX	423
Figure 20.6	20-day volatility of the WGI	426
Figure 20.7	20-day volatility of the DAX	426
Figure 20.8	GARCH volatility of the WGI	429
Figure 20.9	GARCH volatility of the DAX	429
Figure 21.1	Emerging market yields	450

Tables

Table 1.1	Structure of interest rates	20
Table 1.2	Structure of interest rates in the bond market	31
Table 1.3	The dynamics of the Lek/US$ exchange rate	32
Table 1.4	Foreign Direct Investment in Albania 1992–1995	33
Table 1.5	The dynamics of foreign financing	35
Table 2.1	Growth of broad money	40
Table 2.2	The top five Bulgarian banks	45
Table 2.3	Prices of selected OTC securities as of July 1996	51
Table 2.4	Prices of stock exchange and over-the-counter traded securities of selected non-financial stock	52
Table 2.5	The ZUNK market from January to October 1995	57
Table 2.6	BGL and US$-denominated ZUNK bonds	58
Table 2.7	Features of Bulgarian DISCs, FLIRBs and IABs	61
Table 2.8	Daily spot prices for Bulgarian Brady bonds, as a percentage of their face value	62
Table 2.9	Returns on Bulgarian Brady bonds	65
Table 3.1	Structure of the NBC balance sheet (percentages)	72
Table 3.2	End-period annual interest rates and financial ratios (percentages)	73
Table 3.3	Ownership structure of the banking sector	76
Table 3.4	Results of privatization 1995	80
Table 3.5	Foreign investments through the privatization process 1991–1995	84
Table 3.A	Balance of payments (US$ million) and related indicators 1993–1996	87
Table 3.B	Most active shares by turnover during January–September 1996	88
Table 4.1	Economic and financial indicators	92
Table 4.2	Average interbank depository offer rate (PRIBOR)	92
Table 4.3	Number of commercial banks in the Czech Republic	94
Table 4.4	Comparison of domestic banks, according to various criteria	95
Table 4.5	Results of privatization (CZK billion end of 1995)	97
Table 4.6	Selected indicators of the Prague Stock Exchange	105

Table 4.7	The capital account in US$ million	106
Table 5.1	Market share of groups of banks	111
Table 5.2	Total balance sheet by groups of banks in Hungary 1995	111
Table 5.3	Ownership structure of banks in Hungary	112
Table 5.4	The privatization of MOL	115
Table 5.5	Privatization of the electricity sector	117
Table 5.6	Budapest Stock Exchange listing requirements	120
Table 5.A	Main figures of the Budapest Stock Exchange	126
Table 5.B	Turnover of the Budapest Stock Exchange	127
Table 6.1	Money supply (M1) growth and inflation (CPI) dynamics	131
Table 6.2	Discount and interest rates in Macedonia (by end of period)	132
Table 6.3	Privatization process by sectors	137
Table 6.4	Macedonian current account 1990–1995	139
Table 6.5	The first three months of trading on the Macedonian Stock Exchange	144
Table 7.1	Polish banks by ownership structure	154
Table 7.2	Market share of major bank groups in assets, loans and deposits	155
Table 8.1	Monetary indicators 1996	167
Table 8.2	Prudential rules	170
Table 8.3	Share price dynamics on the Bucharest Stock Exchange	178
Table 8.4	External sector (eop)	181
Table 8.A	Selected macroeconomic indicators 1990–1996	182
Table 9.1	Minimum listing conditions on the Bratislava Stock Exchange	196
Table 9.2	Securities listed on the Bratislava Stock Exchange	197
Table 9.3	Trading volumes on the Bratislava Stock Exchange	198
Table 9.4	SAX index component stocks	199
Table 9.5	Development of the SAX Index	200
Table 9.6	Total trading volume on the Bratislava Options Exchange	202
Table 9.7	Trade volume as a percentage of GDP	203
Table 9.8	External finance and foreign debt in Slovakia	205
Table 9.A	Instruments of interest rate policy	210
Table 9.B	The currency basket of the SKK as of 14 July 1994	211

Tables

Table 10.1   Bills issued by Bank of Slovenia   216
Table 10.2   The top five Slovenian banks by total assets as of
              30 June 1996   219
Table 10.3   Summary balance sheet structure of the banking
              sector   221
Table 10.4   The Ljubljana Stock Exchange listing requirements   227
Table 10.5   Openness of the selected sectors for foreign
              investment   236
Table 10.6   The most important foreign investors
              (as of December 1995)   236
Table 10.7   Foreign financial assistance by international
              financial institutions   236
Table 11.1   Indicators of bank performance   246
Table 12.1   Central banks: liabilities and assets, 1993
              (ratio to GDP, percentage points)   258
Table 12.2   Seigniorage earning liabilities and imputed central
              bank seigniorage (1993)   259
Table 12.3   Appropriation of central bank seigniorage
              (ratio to GDP, %)   260
Table 12.4   Central bank legislation relevant to the generation
              of seigniorage   269
Table 14.1   Market shares of the largest Czech banks
              (%, 31 December 1995)   285
Table 14.2   Market shares of the largest Czech banks
              (billion CZK, 31 December 1995)   285
Table 14.3   Concentration in the Czech banking industry by
              market shares (%, 31 December 1995)   285
Table 14.4   Concentration in the Czech banking industry by
              assets and liabilities
              (billion CZK, 31 December 1995)   286
Table 14.5   Moody's ratings of Czech banks   289
Table 14.6   IBCA ratings of Czech banks   290
Table 14.7   Average interest rates from primary deposits
              compared with the rate of inflation (in %)   291
Table 14.8   Structure of the money aggregate M2
              (in %, end of period)   291
Table 14.9   Total volume and development of credits in the
              banking sector (in billion CZK)   293
Table 14.10   Banks by market capitalization   297

Tables

Table 14.11	Banks by total assets	298
Table 16.1	The share of the state sector in the Czech Republic, Hungary and Poland	320
Table 16.2	Ownership and legal form structure of industrial companies at the onset of reform	321
Table 16.3	Initial macroeconomic conditions	324
Table 16.4	Debt cross-country comparisons 1989	326
Table 16.5	Subsidies outcome in Poland, Hungary and the Czech Republic in the first years of transition	330
Table 16.6	Privatization plans in the Czech Republic, Hungary and Poland in mid-1991 compared to privatization outcomes	335
Table 16.7	Summary of the progress of privatization (cumulative number of enterprises eop)	339
Table 16.8	Distribution of shares by end 1995	343
Table 16.9	Employment distribution of Polish state enterprises, 30 June 1994	345
Table 16.10	Employment distribution of Polish joint stock companies, end 1995	346
Table 16.11	Sales revenues from privatization	346
Table 16.12	Distribution of shares by 31 December 1993	349
Table 16.13	Privatization of stocks	350
Table 16.14	Approved privatization projects in the Czech Republic in the two waves	350
Table 16.15	State-led restructuring as part of the privatization program	352
Table 16.16	Importance of vouchers and other privatization methods in the first privatization wave	354
Table 16.17	First wave results – the importance of funds	356
Table 16.18	Structure of NPF ownership after the first wave of privatization at the end of 1993	357
Table 16.19	Distribution of shares by the end of 1993	358
Table 16.20	Revenues from privatization SPA/SHC separate accounts 1990–1994 Q3	359
Table 16.21	Revenues from privatization SPA/SHC joint accounts 1990–1995 (HUF billion)	359
Table 16.22	Incidence of state ownership in Hungary December 1992	365
Table 16.23	The role of the state: State Property Agency (SPA)	366

xiii

Table 16.24	Changes in ownership structure	367
Table 17.1	Results of trading at RM-S	374
Table 18.1	Number of banks and brokers	381
Table 18.2	Number and volume of mutual funds	382
Table 18.3	Foreign trading places for Central and Eastern European shares	385
Table 18.4	Prominent emerging markets index families	386
Table 18.5	Local equity indices for Central and Eastern European markets	387
Table 18.6	The CECE index family	390
Table 18.7	Key data on the CECE indices	390
Table 19.1	Extent and liquidity of equity markets (1997)	397
Table 19.2	Variance-ratio tests of random walk hypothesis. Monthly returns variance ratio	402
Table 19.3	Variance-ratio tests of random walk hypothesis. Weekly returns variance ratio	403
Table 19.4	Distribution of returns in Central European equity markets	405
Table 19.5	Runs tests of weak form efficiency	406
Table 20.1	Unit root tests	420
Table 20.2	Statistical properties of returns	421
Table 20.3	Autocorrelations of returns	424
Table 20.4a	GARCH-t with AR(1)	427
Table 20.4b	Integrated GARCH-t	428
Table 20.4c	Properties of standardized residuals	428
Table 20.5	GARCH-in-mean	431
Table 20.6	EGARCH-t with AR(1)	432
Table 20.7	Poisson jump process	434
Table 21.1	Debt indicators, 1985–1995	440
Table 21.2	Debt settlements since 1981	445
Table 21.3	Contributions to variations in the debt-to-GDP ratio 1989–1994	453
Table 21.A	Growth in real gross domestic product (percentage change year-on-year)	457
Table 21.B	Short-term interest rates (treasury bill rates) (in percentage p.a., end of year)	457
Table 21.C	US$ exchange rates (end of year)	458
Table 21.D	Inflation (consumer price index) (percentage change year-on-year)	458

Tables

Table 21.E   General government balances
              (in per cent of gross domestic product)   459
Table 21.F   Current account and trade balances
              (in per cent of gross domestic product,
              1996, estimated)   459
Table 21.G   Foreign direct investment
              (net inflows recorded in the balance of payments,
              in US$, estimated)   460
Table 21.H   Current account and trade balances
              (in per cent of gross domestic product,
              1996, estimated)   460

* Rounding errors may prevent equalization of table sums.

Acknowledgements

Most of the papers included in this book were presented at the conference 'Capital Markets in Emerging Economies – Central and Eastern Europe' that was held in Vienna at the Institute for Advanced Studies, February 14–15, 1997. I am grateful to Andreas Wörgötter for co-organizing the conference, and to the Institute for granting financial and logistic support. Acknowledgements are extended to Beatrix Krones who ensured the smooth functioning of the conference with her customary spirit and efficiency. In editing this book, I particularly thank my wife (and colleague), Daniela Grozea-Helmenstein, for her precious help and inspiring wit.

I am indebted to a number of individuals for their cooperation in reviewing the contributions to this book, notably Todor Balabanov, Gordana Bival, Jarko Fidrmuc, Oliver Grabherr, Adelina Gschwandtner, Ioan Haiduc, Miloslav Hoschek, Peter Huber, Jan Stankovsky, Werner Varga, and Christine Zulehner.

Moreover, I gratefully acknowledge editorial guidance by Dymphna Evans, Julie Leppard, Francine O'Sullivan, and Valerie Polding at Edward Elgar Publishing.

Christian Helmenstein
Vienna, Austria

Contributors

István Ábel
Budapest University of Economics and National Bank of Hungary,
Budapest, Hungary

Rexhina Bajraktari
Bank of Albania, Tirana, Albania

Todor Balabanov
Institute for Advanced Studies, Department of Transition Economics,
Vienna, Austria

Gordana Bival
AlphaInspect, Vienna, Austria

Ermira Brahja
International Commercial Bank of Albania, Tirana, Albania

Vlado Dimovski
Center for International Competitiveness, Ljubljana, Slovenia

Ion Drăgulin
National Bank of Romania, Bucharest, Romania

Jarko Fidrmuc
Institute for Advanced Studies, Department of Transition Economics,
Vienna, Austria

Randall K. Filer
City University New York, USA, and CERGE-EI (a joint workplace of
Charles University and the Academy of Sciences of the Czech Republic),
Prague, Czech Republic

Vladimir Gligorov
Vienna Institute for Comparative Economic Studies, Austria

Daniela Grozea-Helmenstein
Institute for Advanced Studies, Department of Transition Economics,
Vienna, Austria

Jan Hanousek
CERGE-EI (a joint workplace of Charles University and The Academy of
Sciences of the Czech Republic), Prague, Czech Republic

Eduard Hochreiter
Austrian National Bank, Vienna, Austria

Tatiana Houbenova
Bulgarian Academy of Sciences, Sofia, Bulgaria

Norbert Irsch
German Bank for Development (KfW), Frankfurt/Main, Germany

Ryszard Kokoszczyński
National Bank of Poland, Warsaw, Poland

Viliam Páleník
Slovak Academy of Sciences, Bratislava, Slovakia

Enrico Perotti
University of Amsterdam, The Netherlands

Oldřch Rejnuš
Mendel University, Brno, Czech Republic

Riccardo Rovelli
Innocenzo Gasparini Institute for Economic Research (IGIER) – Bocconi
University, Milan, Italy

Martin Scheicher
University of Vienna, Austria

Günther Schiendl
Vienna Stock Exchange, Austria

Radek Schmied
Mendel University, Brno, Czech Republic

Jérôme Sgard
Centre d'Etudes Prospectives d'Informations Internationales (CEPII), Paris,
France

Velimir Šonje
National Bank of Croatia, Zagreb, Croatia

Lina Takla
London Business School, United Kingdom

Ladislav Unčovský
Economic University, Bratislava, Slovakia

Borislav Vladimirov
Institute for Advanced Studies, Department of Political Science, Vienna,
Austria

Heike Wiegand
German Bank for Development (KfW), Frankfurt/Main, Germany

Georg Winckler
University of Vienna, Austria

Petr Zahradník
Patria Finance, Prague, Czech Republic

/C, and E, Europe)

P24 F32
P33 L33
P34 G21
     E52

BK Title:

Introduction

Christian Helmenstein

Since the lifting of the Iron Curtain, Central and East European countries have faced complex reform needs at each stage of their economic transition. In particular, the rebuilding of capital markets in Central and Eastern Europe took place under conditions that differ in kind rather than degree from those that characterize the capital market environments in North America, Western Europe or Asia. Tailor-made responses to the challenges of transition were called for since quite often textbook solutions either were unavailable or non-applicable. In many cases policy makers had no recourse to well-tried blueprints and had to forge compromises to accommodate divergent objectives, as reflected by the rich variety of individualistic transition paths documented in this book.

Moreover, despite the (visible) hand of international organizations and the proliferation of information, the policy response was cumbersome. Thus, to a considerable extent, the prevailing level of – broadly defined – capital market development in the region is the result of trial-and-error processes. Specific and comparative information, as provided in the first part of this book, could have helped avoid especially for the latecomers among the countries in transition the costly trials and the repeated errors of the frontrunners.

In spite of the pitfalls, several countries have come a long way in their institution-building and mechanism-design. To allow both the progress and the disappointments to be presented on a comparable basis, five key areas of financial market development that represent the core financial activities presently pursued in the transitional economies are selected for close analysis: the conduct of monetary policy and its role in monetary stabilization; the characteristics of banking in Central and Eastern Europe; the transfer of corporate ownership through privatization; the dynamics of exchange-related trading; and the importance of international funding. Each of these key inquiries addresses in a similar manner all the countries reviewed in the earlier part of the volume, while still attending to specific country issues.

The cumulative research effort of this book produces key insights as to the characteristics of the capital markets that were developed and the variation of these characteristics across countries.

MONETARY POLICY

In all eleven countries under consideration, at the outset of transition in the early 1990s, the banking system was monolithic by its very nature. One of the first steps to be taken, therefore, was to create a two-tier banking system with a strict separation of central from commercial banking. With regard to the role of the central bank, an issue that deserves particular attention is that of its independence. Rather as an exception to the rule, there was a blueprint available for designing a successful central bank – success being measured in terms of long-term average inflation rates. However, a legal framework similar to the one under which the German Bundesbank conducts monetary policy has either not been implemented or has not been translated into adequate action in many of the countries under consideration. In some cases gaps, such as missing stipulations on the conditions for the resignation of central bank governors, have contributed to an overly permissive monetary policy. In other examples over-ambitious regulations are in place which have proved vulnerable to being overruled by budget legislation. An inquiry into who benefits from not embarking on a stricter legislation might reveal how to improve the performance of central banks.

In many regions a turbulent political environment has spilled over into the economic sphere. This has raised issues hardly ever encountered outside wartime or revolutionary eras. For example, the monetary concomitant of Slovenia and Croatia emerging as independent states in the aftermath of the breaking-up of former Yugoslavia is nothing less than the incarnation of a central banker's nightmare. The monetary sovereignty of Slovenia and Croatia commenced and evolved despite the initial absence of foreign reserves in the central bank's treasury. Nevertheless, in retrospect the issuing of their own currencies proved a successful undertaking.

BANKING

The installation of a two-tier banking system was the precondition for the emergence of a market economy-type financial system of banks and other kinds of financial institutions. Although in the early years of transition access to banking licences was wide open, endeavors to preserve insider interests and, in some instances, a lack of interest on the part of foreign investors caused the financial sector to persist with a high degree of supply side concentration. The long-established players retained a dominant market position in both volume (the gross corporate customer base remained intact) and value terms.

From the experience of several Central and Eastern European countries it has become clear that the widespread non-performing loans problem is not a synonym for an inherited loans problem. The bad debts problem was aggravated by the over-ambitious growth targets of banks, which caused the number and the volume of credits to rocket. Even worse, ex post some newly established banks appear to have been founded primarily to extend credit to their own (corporate) shareholders whose last thought was to service their debts. This way, these banks served as the vehicle to turn otherwise unpromising companies into a goldmine for their (non-corporate) owners at the expense of the soundness of the banking sector as a whole. It hardly comes as a surprise that such 'profitable' businesses soon found imitators elsewhere.

Pyramid schemes are an example of another activity that, like a contagious disease, spread throughout Central and Eastern European countries wherever it was not stamped out during its early stages. The high-grade virulence of these fraudulent undertakings manifested itself when Albania slid into an economic, social, and political catastrophe. Country-specific capital market imperfections, however, helped for a long time to blur the progress of the catastrophe. Among these factors were the lack of investment opportunities, the scarcity of credit in the formal financial sector, the combining with apparently solid business activities, as well as the large inflow of remittance money from abroad which allowed real sector returns to become separated from financial sector returns.

In the course of recent privatizations, foreign investors have acquired stakes in various state-owned banks. This policy has fostered competition in the industry, accelerated the transfer of knowhow and promoted the diversification of banking products. Upon entry, within a short period of time foreign banks have established a supremacy in certain niches. In some cases, however, economic policy may merely have viewed allowing in foreign capital as the lesser of two evils. Faced with the constraint that foreign banks could start operations only if they invested in an existing bank, foreign investors gained access in exchange for their participation in the restructuring of the domestic banking sector, *inter alia* by improving the financial status of troubled banks. In tandem with the tightening of capital requirements and banking supervision the main objective of this approach was to avert systemic risk.

PRIVATIZATION

The routes pursued in the privatization of firms are almost as diverse as the macroeconomic performance of the economies under consideration. Some countries have opted for implementing a mass privatization programme. Prior to its split-up, the former Czechoslovakia led the way with large-scale voucher privatization which caused its successor states to feature, in percentage terms, an extraordinarily high degree of corporate ownership by private households. In the case of the Czech Republic, market capitalization relative to GDP has already approached the level of (other) OECD countries. However, several investments in Czech mutual funds have moved from light into shadow. In the wake of heavy losses on mutual fund participation certificates, the confidence of private households in the financial markets has been shaken. For many years to come the appropriation of assets by insiders due to insufficient legal provisions (the so-called 'tunneling') may dull the appetite of private households for investments in the stock market.

Various transitional countries have opted for management–employee buy-outs (MEBO) and direct sales to foreign investors as their main privatization tools. Already in 1990 Hungary was choosing to sell its productive assets instead of giving them away, so that privatized enterprises were blessed with fresh money from the outside which could be used for investment projects. The Hungarian approach came at the cost of slow privatization, however, and only recently has the process accelerated. By contrast, Polish firms subject to privatization underwent prior restructuring and consolidation. A mass privatization program was finally initiated in 1997 but comprised only about 500 companies. In retrospect, it appears that voucher privatization has led to blurred ownership structures which has resulted in a lack of effective corporate control, thus facilitating mismanagement and, in aggregate terms, delaying restructuring, whereas privatization on a case-by-case basis has turned out to be more successful.

EXCHANGE-RELATED TRADING

Contrary to widespread anticipation, according to statistical criteria the characteristics of Central and East European equity markets are similar to the equity markets of far more developed countries. An obvious question suggests itself. Why are market results so much alike? *Inter alia*, the attractiveness of an equity market stems from its 'investibility' and the growth potential of the real economy. Taking it for granted that the growth potential of most Central and East European economies is intact, such frequently used, operational sub-criteria as market capitalization and the size of individual issues are used to determine the degree of investibility. In the more advanced transitional economies market capitalization relative to per capita income reaches a level that is comparable to the level of some G7 countries. In some, but not all, cases this comparatively high market capitalization is a result of mass privatization which in this respect appears to be the main instrument for rapid catching-up. Due to the privatization of large state-owned companies which in many countries during the pre-reform period were the sole suppliers of their respective goods and services, large equity issues with a sufficient free float are generally available. Furthermore, human resource commitments for market research and trading by banks and brokers from outside the Central and Eastern European countries are large relative to the invested capital. The ensuing competition between domestic and foreign institutions, facilitated by the trading of stocks from the region and of stock index derivatives on foreign exchanges, has contributed to an enhanced degree of market efficiency. In essence, the intriguing development of equity markets stands in sharp contrast to the relative underperformance of the banking sector in Central and Eastern Europe to date.

Furthermore, the dynamics of equity trading in the Czech and the Slovak Republics as well as in Romania and Bulgaria may be meaningful with respect to the evolution of trading platforms in Western Europe. It is no longer the case that companies alone compete for investors' sympathy, but rather that traditional marketplaces themselves face harsh competition from both established and newly emerging electronic marketplaces. For the most endangered exchanges in the future EMU member countries, it may be of interest to study the survival strategies pursued by their counterparts in Central and Eastern Europe.

INTERNATIONAL FUNDING

Given the low savings rates throughout Central and Eastern Europe, international funding, by supplementing the domestic capital pool, plays an important role since it allows for higher investment rates than would otherwise be possible. In contrast to the post-World War II situation, however, the availability of large amounts of international funding makes a 'Marshall Plan' unnecessary for reforming countries. It is clearly more important for Central and Eastern European countries to obtain access to funds on affordable terms.

As a rule, in Central and Eastern Europe it seems to be the case that a potential debtor with a passable financial status but without a recent credit record is less attractive to lenders than a weaker but well-known debtor – that is, some countries find it difficult to obtain international financing because of the low level of their inherited liabilities or the brevity of their existence. A case in point is Romania. Due to its virtual absence on the international capital market for many years prior to the reforms, the country was not covered at all by the international rating agencies. This, in turn, caused international lenders to be reluctant to extend credit to the country despite its low level of foreign debt at the beginning of reforms.

By contrast, Bulgaria, Hungary and Poland had entered the transition period with high per capita levels of foreign debt. In the early 1990s, Bulgaria and Poland concluded arrangements with the London Club and the Paris Club which allowed for the reduction of debt. While Poland managed gradually to reduce its foreign debt, Bulgaria found itself confronted with new economic calamities that were worsened by the volatility associated with international funding. To restore confidence in its policy, Bulgaria resorted to the introduction of a currency board.

In Hungary the burden of foreign debt servicing had a negative impact upon its economic performance in the first half of the 1990s. The need to generate inflows of foreign capital even had repercussions on the methods of privatization chosen. In retrospect, direct sales across the board (including public utilities) have contributed to accelerate restructuring and may be viewed as a blessing in disguise. In sum, international funding may aggravate the adverse consequences of an unsustainable policy stance through credibility crises. In contrast, if coupled with sound economic policy, foreign financing appears to act as catalyst for a more rapid convergence towards European Union income levels, thus paving the way for EU Eastern enlargement.

The second part of the book consists of in-depth analyses focusing on specific issues. **Eduard Hochreiter**, **Riccardo Rovelli**, and **Georg Winckler** examine the relations between central banks and other macro sectors in the Czech Republic, Hungary and Romania, with respect to the creation and distribution of seigniorage, using Austria and Germany as reference countries. In economies in transition, transfers of seigniorage from the central bank to the government or to the banking sector may appear as a natural way to soften their financial constraints. The authors propose a simple analytical framework for the analysis of central bank seigniorage, based on the opportunity cost approach, and measure both the amount and the allocation of seigniorage for the five countries in 1993. Central bank seigniorage appears to reach approximately four times the benchmark value in Hungary, and thirty times in Romania (the latter due to the high level of inflation tax). In Hungary and Romania most seigniorage is expropriated (as an interest rate subsidy) by the government; in Romania a large part also goes as a subsidy to the financial sector. For none of the five countries (with the possible exception of Romania, with the appreciation of the gold reserves in terms of the domestic currency) do the authors find that central banks retain an excessive amount of seigniorage for reserve accumulation or for current expenditures.

The paper by **Enrico Perotti** has the purpose of illustrating the potential for a collusive creation of financial arrears, arising from the temptation even for potentially profitable firms to collude against a centralized imposition of credit discipline. The reason for this is that, in the face of a large number of value-subtractors, a tight initial credit stance will subtract more liquidity than the corporate sector may generate by internal restructuring. Lack of liquidity forces firms with no alternative sale outlet to accept trade credit from their traditional buyers. Easily available trade credit in turn encourages collusive resistance to restructuring, by ensuring supply of inputs to illiquid firms. There are serious potential costs associated with a high volume of arrears. First, there are significant imbalances across sectors and enterprises: thus the likely failure of direct enforcement of credit will result in illiquidity and financial rationing for viable enterprises, redistributing liquidity from the better to the worse firms. Secondly, involuntary or collusive trade credit to uncreditworthy enterprises leads to a loss of information about the true financial position of individual firms, challenging the development of independent financial intermediaries and hindering privatization.

The reform of the banking sector in a transitional economy features as the main subject of **Petr Zahradník**'s article. In the first part of the article the author traces the dynamics of the Czech banking sector. With regard to the safety and soundness of its banking sector as a whole, the Czech Republic was an investment-grade, long-term rating (A) – the best in the region. On the level of the individual banks, the average rating was considerably lower, however. In particular, the ratings suffered from inadequate mechanisms for internal control and audit, the lack of (reliable) financial information and a shortage of experience in risk analysis on the part of the banks. Moreover, the ratings of individual banks reflected a frequently observed bias. It is implicitly assumed that if a large bank gets into financial distress, the state will intervene to prevent a 'domino effect' of bank failures. Being considered too large to fail, the largest banks receive a comparatively better rating. This overstates their intrinsic financial strength on a stand-alone basis. In the second part of the contribution, particular attention is paid to the prospects of the Czech banking sector. *Inter alia*, Zahradník considers the creation of non-performing loans, the adequacy of reserves, bank privatization prospects, and the international exposure and competitiveness of the sector.

The highly specific field of promotional banking is addressed in the contribution by **Norbert Irsch** and **Heike Wiegand**. To ensure that a promotional bank performs its main task successfully – that is, to foster reconstruction and development – a canon of constituent principles has to be implemented. According to the authors, among these are the following: shareholders should mainly consist of the state or state institutions since a promotional bank's purpose is not to maximize profit; a high degree of professionalism and independence is required in its internal decision-making processes; to perform its refinancing function on the international capital markets at low cost, the promotional bank should be endowed with a sufficient start-up capital and a state guarantee to provide an excellent credit rating; through tax-exemption and the waiving of dividend payouts the bank should be in the position to generate an autonomous promotion potential; however, to prevent a crowding-out of commercial banks, the promotional bank should not be mandated to offer finance if sufficient funding from commercial banks can be obtained, and it should channel its loans through the commercial banking system. A promotional bank so structured will feature the attractive political implication that a government will find it easier to withstand pressure for subsidized credits from particular-interest groups when financial support is being offered through a promotional bank rather than directly by the government. During recent years the promotion of small and medium sized enterprises has become a key factor in the promotional activities of the German Bank for Development. In the second part of their article, through the use of case studies, the authors provide examples of the consulting activities of the German Bank for Development in Central and Eastern Europe.

An in-depth analysis of the aims, processes and outcomes of privatization is conducted by **Lina Takla**. Based on a comparative assessment of privatization in the Czech Republic, Hungary, and Poland, she shows that privatization methods, as perceived in the earliest plans, all encompassed a mass privatization element. Privatization outcomes in all three countries, by contrast, exhibit a mixture of methods. Takla argues that, in effect, the Czech Republic experienced mass privatization (in association with the emergence of funds), while Poland saw the emergence of employee ownership as a *de facto* outcome. Hungary, by contrast, opted for a gradualist approach through a systematic sale of assets.

In the field of securities trading, **Viliam Pálenık** presents the Slovak RM-System as an off-exchange electronic stock market that was established in connection with the Slovak voucher privatization. Besides the twin Czech RM-System, the Romanian Association of Securities Dealers Automatic Quotation (RASDAQ) constitutes another off-exchange trading platform in the region, whereas with OFEX and Tradepoint similar institutions have also been established in the United Kingdom. Nevertheless, from an institutional point of view the RM-System is unique in relying on a non-membership approach that allows everybody to trade shares by entering RM directly or indirectly through banks, brokers, investment companies or funds. To implement this idea technically, a nationwide system of trading desks has been established. It is not too fanciful to expect that the RM-S may be a forerunner of new Internet trading platforms, with its explicit emphasis on computer networking and computer algorithm-based trading.

Randall Filer and **Jan Hanousek** investigate the efficiency of the Central European equity markets. While there is a widespread belief that they can be manipulated by insiders who have ample incentive to attempt to appropriate assets in the privatization process, the markets in these countries are similar in that they do not appear markedly less efficient than far more developed equity markets. Provided that these preliminary results hold up as more sophisticated tests become possible, it will provide strong evidence of the power of markets to achieve proper pricing even in the most difficult of circumstances.

A similar outcome is derived by **Martin Scheicher** who studies the econometric properties of returns from the Warsaw Stock Exchange in comparison with returns from the Frankfurt Stock Exchange. Viewed from an option-pricing perspective, upon which the most advanced Central and East European markets are already embarking, it demonstrates that the Black–Scholes world of returns drawn from a normal distribution with constant returns is inappropriate. It emerges from the study that the GARCH model is superior to a Poisson jump process in fitting the data.

The contribution by **Günther Schiendl** may provide clues to explain the high degree of efficiency to be found on the Central and East European capital markets reported above. The widespread attention and massive coverage provided by financial analysts has quickly eroded the opportunities for excess returns, and in this sense the (brief) history of exchange-related securities trading in Eastern Europe may provide a major example of how an adequate institutional design along with decentralized decision-making by individual market participants enhances efficiency.

The experience of three Central and Eastern European countries with regard to debt management and debt-service reduction programs is analysed by **Jérôme Sgard**. Drawing upon the cases of Bulgaria, Hungary, and Poland, all of which were heavily in debt at the beginning of the reforms, he assesses the impact of debt reduction in terms of the solvency and macroeconomic performances of the three countries. Hypothetically, three factors apparently account for the medium-term impact of debt write-offs in transitional economies: the transfer problem, the Ricardian effect, and their potential for a real appreciation of the exchange rate. It appears that in the case of Poland the debt write-off, along with the ensuing strong recovery of the economy, a real appreciation, and the highest household savings rates in Central and Eastern Europe, helped the economy to rapidly pull itself free from debt. In the case of

Bulgaria, by contrast, the impact of debt write-offs is overshadowed by the poor performance of the real economy through insufficient macroeconomic and institutional adjustment as well as capital inflows (mostly interest capitalization). By not implementing a sharp devaluation of its currency, Hungary managed to contain the foreign indebtedness on the initial real level but, because the country did not embark on debt renegotiation, the impact of a large public debt overhang depressed domestic savings, contributed to fiscal deficits, and resulted in slower growth.

Overall, striving for the most comprehensive coverage of the region, the present volume also comprises European transitional economies whose capital market developments have not been included in an assessment so far. The present volume constitutes a reference collection on the emerging capital markets of *all* Central and Eastern European transitional countries except for the Baltic states and Bosnia-Herzegovina.

PART I

Country Profiles

G-28
G-21 E52
P34 P33
P24

1. Albania

Rexhina Bajraktari and Ermira Brahja

INTRODUCTION

From central planning Albania inherited a banking system that was under-developed and highly centralized. The abolition of old mechanisms and structures and the creation of new ones by mid-1992 marked the beginning of the transition period. The new Albanian government, resulting from the 22 March 1992 elections, compiled a short-term program for 1992–1993, which was then supplemented by a medium-term program for 1993–1996. In order to achieve macroeconomic stabilization and to build a market economy, a radical transformation process was necessary. Crucial to accomplishing the objectives on the macroeconomic level was, and still is, the ongoing reform of the banking and financial systems.

The approval of the law on the Bank of Albania (BoA) and the law on the banking system in April 1992 was the most important first step towards the restructuring of the banking system. This legislation established the necessary legal framework on the basis of which Albania adopted the two- tier banking system. The task of formulating and conducting monetary policy in Albania was assigned to BoA. Meanwhile the banks of the second level were trans-formed into commercial organizations which could collect deposits and grant credits for enterprises and individuals.

This contribution is organized as follows: The first part deals with monetary policy and its instruments used by BoA under the constraints of a high-inflation environment. The second analyses the progress of reform in the banking system. The third focuses on the developments in the money and the capital markets. In the fourth part we elaborate on the sources of external finance, in particular foreign direct investment and foreign aid.

MONETARY POLICY

Central Bank Independence

The widespread notion that central banks should have independent control over monetary policy, on the basis of legal and economic independence, is difficult to assess at this early stage of Albanian economic reforms, where no relevant experience exists. The two laws mentioned before laid the foundations of the banking system. They were the preliminary steps necessary to a total reform of the financial and institutional system, which, *inter alia*, includes establishing the necessary legal framework, increasing the autonomy of the Central Bank, improving the payments system, and fostering competition in the banking sector.

In April 1992, the recently-created Bank of Albania defined as its main goal 'the preservation of the domestic and external value of national currency' (Law for the Bank of Albania, 1992). The choice of a floating exchange rate regime, however, implies a larger degree of sovereignty for Albanian monetary policy, since it gives the Bank of Albania full responsibility for domestic inflation.

The revision of the law on BoA, approved by Parliament on 22 February 1996, paved the way to a further enhancement of central bank independence. The independence of the Bank rests on four bases: first, the law on BoA stipulates that 'price stability' is the major objective to be pursued in the formulation and implementation of monetary policy for the performance of which BoA has been made responsible. Secondly, BoA rather than the government has to account for the conduct of monetary policy to parliament. Furthermore, every six months BoA has to deliver and publish a banking policy statement to the Council of Ministers. Thirdly, the appointment of the governor overlaps with the electoral cycle, which reduces the possibility that government will find it easy to interfere with monetary policy by appointing a governor of its own choice. The governor of BoA is appointed by the President for a term of seven years. Moreover, only the first deputy governor is appointed by the Council of Ministers, while the second one and the four other members who compose the Supervisory Council are appointed by Parliament.[1] Lastly, by reducing the obligation of BoA to finance the budget deficit by the purchase of

---

[1] The governor is proposed by the Supervision Council, while the deputy governors are proposed by the governor.

treasury bills in the years 1996, 1997, 1998 to 10%, 6% and 2%, respectively, central bank independence has been further strengthened.[2]

Targets

According to its main objective, *viz* price stability, BoA intends to promote the development of the foreign exchange system, the internal financial market, and the payments system. The main targets of the BoA (according to the law of BoA) are:

- the formulation and conduct of monetary policy, that is, the creation and sustainment of the market for foreign exchange;
- the issuing of currency;
- the licensing and supervision of the activity of commercial banks and financial institutions, thereby assuring the stability of the banking system;
- performing operations linked to the crediting of the banks and the government;
- the development of international relationships;
- the creation of institutions for the trading of securities.

BoA is also responsible for the foreign exchange reserves of the country and compiles the balance of payments. It serves as the official depositor of the state and organizes the cash management of the state budget operations through the commercial banks. The supervision of commercial banks was mandated to the central bank (rather than creating a separate institution) which is now empowered 'to take all necessary actions for ensuring the stability of the banking system' (Law for the Bank of Albania, 1992). BoA is entitled to set rules regulating different banking operations, including the issuing of licenses for banking activities. In implementing these functions the central bank has wide-ranging rights.

Instruments

The implementation of a tight monetary policy relied mainly on direct instruments of monetary control – a policy which was conditioned by the low level of banking system development and the poor state of national credit. The whole banking system in Albania was undergoing a restructuring process, as was the BoA. Faced with the urgent necessity to counteract the rapid expansion of the money supply, these instruments were initially considered appropriate but later

---

[2] A step towards less government intervention was the separation of the salary system from strong state control. The state put a ceiling on the wages paid in the banking sector which limited a possible wage drift.

on were deemed too drastic. Hence, in parallel with direct instruments such as deposit ceilings and interest rates,[3] BoA increasingly relied on indirect instruments such as reserve requirements, interventions in the interbank money and the treasury bills markets, and the setting-up of adequate refinancing terms.

How did these instruments work during the transition process? The collapse of the socialist system late in 1990 led to the loss of state control over revenues and expenditures. The resulting inactive budget policy led to an increase in the money in circulation without any corresponding increase in GDP. During the period 1990–1991 government expenditures rose significantly due to wage increases and social protection pressure as enterprises were still state-owned and employees and trade unions pressure on the government was high.

At the same time, the 80% rule was adopted – that is, employees in the state-owned enterprises received only 80% of their wages due to a standstill in manufacturing, resulting from the lack of raw materials or of orders. The total enterprise subsidy represented 13.9% and 17.8% of GDP for 1991 and 1992, respectively. The price subsidies for some consumer goods such as cereals, meat, flour, childrens' wear, etc., and also fertilizers reached 2.5% of GDP in 1991 and 3.6% in 1992. Total subsidies included in current government expenditures reached 33%, while government revenues actually decreased due to tax collection difficulties. As a result the budget deficit reached 44% of GDP by the end of 1992.

This deficit was financed through printing money, while GDP declined further. Money supply grew by 152% in 1992 compared with 1991. The highly inflationary environment contributed to a contraction of GDP by 10% in 1990 and 27% in 1991 relative to the previous years. In 1991 industrial and agricultural production fell by 37% and 21%, respectively. Unlike agricultural production, which increased by 18% in 1992 because of the privatization of agricultural land, industrial production declined further by 60% in 1992 compared to the previous year.

The contraction of GDP came to a halt in mid-1992, thanks mainly to an increase of 18% in agricultural production and in construction (which is estimated by the IMF at about 30% in real terms) and services (private commerce) by 5%. From the extremely low 1992 level, GDP grew by 11% in 1993, but was nevertheless still 30% lower than in 1989 (International Monetary Fund, 1994).

The credit given by commercial banks to state enterprises and farms was another cause of the expansion of money supply. By mid-1992, the outstanding

---

[3] Credit ceilings, by contrast, were used only in the beginning of the banking reform and later replaced by other instruments such as the refinancing rate.

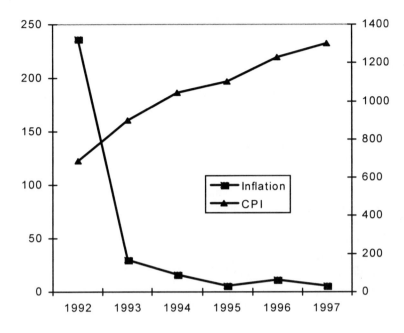

Source: Bank of Albania, 1996.

Figure 1.1. The consumer price index and inflation

credit amounted to 33% of GDP, 'most of which was either nonperforming or considered unlikely to be repaid' (International Monetary Fund, 1994).

The monetary policy implemented by the BoA was aimed at decreasing the level of budget deficit financing and the crediting of the economy by commercial banks as the main factors affecting the overhang of the money supply in the country. Tighter monetary policy, supported by fiscal policy, resulted in a fall in inflation to 6% by the end of 1995 (Figure 1.1). Fiscal policy was more effective in reducing expenditure, mainly through a tighter wage policy. As a result, the budget deficit was reduced to 7.6% of GDP in 1995 from 8.3% in the previous year. 4.2% of the budget deficit was financed in 1995 through foreign financing.

In parallel, BoA managed to control money supply by determining the maximum quarterly credit which commercial banks were allowed to grant, and after that by setting credit ceilings. This instrument also affected the credit expansion for state-owned enterprises and farms. This restrictive credit policy thus proved to be an efficient instrument during the price stabilization process.

In the future, its gradual replacement by indirect measures will contribute to the creation of a standard, competitive market environment.

Interest Rate Policy

Interest rate policy is considered as one of the most important instruments which BoA uses in its monetary policy. For that reason, BoA ensures that interest rates stay in line with the desired inflation rate. During 1991 BoA attempted to bring about a change in the interest rate structure. Interest rates between 3.5% and 8% for deposits and between 8% and 12% for credits were established, replacing ones that previously ranged from 0.5% to 3%. The latter interest rates had been determined administratively, left unchanged for a period of more than 15 years, and no longer fulfilled a steering role. The system of interest rates is now composed of:
- a discount window rate;
- a minimum deposit rate;
- a remuneration rate (13.5% in 1994, 5% in 1995, 0% in 1996);
- a credit ceiling rate.

At the beginning of the economic reforms, BoA had defined the following rates:
- refinancing (from July 1992 onwards, subject to basic and penalty rates);
- deposits;[4]
- credits.[5]

Commercial banks are free to change interest rates on credits and deposits. In practice commercial banks use minimum rates for deposits and maximum for credits. At the same time, BoA implemented a very tight credit policy which in fact restricted the freedom of banks to operate in the credit market and to allow market mechanisms to establish the interest rates. Commercial banks were confronted with difficulties resulting from the high demand for credit and the credit ceiling policy followed by the BoA. This led to a wide spread of

---

[4] After mid-1992 BoA set the interest rates which had to be implemented by the commercial banks. Subsequently, in July 1993 it lowered deposits and lending rates by 400-900 points, and in order to support the restructuring of the banking system, foster more competition and at the same time improve the level of self-regulating action through the credit and deposit policy, BoA announced a bandwidth of 200 basis points within which interest rates could fluctuate, defining afterwards only the minimum deposit rates.

[5] Until 1993 there was an interest rate ceiling for credits and since then an interest rate floor for deposits and an interest rate ceiling for credits have been in operation.

deposit and credit rates, which reached 980 basis points in November 1995.[6]

In July 1992 BoA used, for the first time, an indirect instrument of monetary policy, namely refinancing rates. Commercial banks, faced with the need for liquid funds, were able to borrow from BoA as the lender of last resort. The high refinancing rates of 40% for the first tranche and the proportional increase of the rates to 45–50%, respectively for the second and third tranches were intended to control the expansion of money supply. Comparing the ratio of refinancing tenders with the total liabilities of the commercial banks, it becomes clear, however, that this instrument is far from being fully utilized in the conduct of the monetary policy.

Interest rates for deposits are divided into non-term deposits and term deposits, and the latter ones are subdivided according to maturities, *viz* 3-months, 6-months, and annual deposits.

By raising interest rates, BoA intended to increase the attractiveness of deposits as an instrument to fight inflation. As a result, demand deposits rose by approximately 34% and term-deposits by 541% (end of 1992), which also reflected the tendency towards long-term deposits and thereby changed the relative growth rates of the individual money aggregates.

Although the interest rate for long-term deposits was raised to a historically high level of 32%, real interest rates remained highly negative. At the end of 1992 they reached -61% on a yearly basis, which was partially due to the continuous price liberalization in the consumer goods sector leading to permanent upward price pressures. Notably, real interest rates were negative during the bread price liberalization with monthly inflation amounting to about 45%. By the end of 1993 it fluctuated in a range of -0.7% and -4.6%.[7]

BoA started applying interest rates for foreign currency deposits late in 1992. The inflow of foreign currency consisted mainly of remittances from migrants working abroad. High domestic inflation and the large degree of uncertainty caused by price and exchange rate liberalization added to their attractiveness.

The foreign currency deposits increased 44 times by the end of 1992 compared to the previous year-end. This tendency, however, came to an abrupt halt at the end of 1993 and eventually turned into a decrease of foreign exchange deposits and an increase in holding national currency.

---

[6] This shows the difference of the weighted average rates of new lending and deposits with 12 months maturity.

[7] Real credit rates were -0.7% in December 1993 for the 12 months which is calculated for the year on year inflation rate.

Table 1.1. Structure of interest rates

Interest rates	1986–1990	1991–06/1993	07/1992–05/1993	06/1993–12/1993	Since 01/1994
Refinancing rates	–	–	40.0	34.0	32.0
Basic rates	–	–	45.0–50.0	39.0–44.0	37.0–44.0
Deposit rates	0.5–3.0	3.0	3.0^1	3.0	3.0
3 months	–	3.5–5.0	18.0^1	14.0^2	10.0^2
6 months	3.0	4.0–7.0	25.0^1	19.0^2	16.0^2
12 months	–	5.0–8.0	32.0^1	25.0^2	22.0^2
Lending rates					
3 months	$1.0–2.0^3$	$8.0–12.0^4$	25.0^5	20.0^2	17.0^2
6 months	$1.0–2.0^3$	$8.0–12.0^4$	25.0^5	26.0^2	22.0^2
12 months	$1.0–2.0^3$	$8.0–12.0^4$	39.0^5	30.0^2	26.0^2

Notes:
[1] Minimum rates;
[2] Plus or minus 200 basis points, lower end of band of imposed minimum;
[3] Interest rate doubled for overdue credits, tripled if financing for inventory or stocks;
[4] Interest rate was 30.0–35.0% for Albanian Commercial Bank loans to individuals or private enterprises, interest rate on all overdue loans is 1.5 times the base rate;
[5] Guideline rates.
Source: Bank of Albania, 1996.

Two factors account for this development: first, interest rates for deposits in Albanian Leks turned highly positive; and, secondly, exchange rate volatility had decreased considerably. At the end of 1993 the Lek started to appreciate against the leading foreign currencies, thereby mirroring the successful disinflation process. In spite of the Lek stability, the foreign exchange deposits started to increase again by about 50% in 1995, compared with 27% and 50% increases in 1993 and 1994.

Although term deposits are still growing rapidly, their growth rates slowed down from 146% (1993) to 60% (1994) and 50% (1995), reflecting the reluctance of the banking system to offer attractive terms. As a consequence, with interest rates many times higher than the ones offered by banks, the informal deposit market is thriving.

The remuneration rates have a transitive role. They were introduced in 1994 to stimulate the large excess reserves of the SB in the BoA. The opportunities for this bank to grant credit were limited by the credit ceiling defined by the BoA and the poor state of the interbank market. BoA stopped financing remuneration rates in January 1996 in order to allow more freedom for the commercial banks.

Interbank Money Market

The transition from credit supply determination to the credit ceiling approach provided the opportunity to trade excessive or shortage positions of liquidity. In general, however, the interbank money market is still in its infancy.

The direct trading of the liquidity excess (caused by savings deposits belonging to the public) in the Savings Bank (SB) is undertaken through the channelling of these deposits to the National Commercial Bank (NCB) and Rural Commercial Bank as investments. Before 1992 the Albanian Banking System consisted of the State Bank of Albania as a central and commercial bank, Savings Bank as a depository institution for household savings deposits, and the State Agriculture Bank which granted credits for the cooperatives and the state farms. In January 1991 the Albanian Commercial Bank was established. After the establishment of the two-tier system in mid-1992, SBA was renamed BoA and undertook the central banks' responsibilities, while its commercial activities were transferred to NCB which was merged with the Commercial Bank of Albania. For that reason SB as a household depository company had large deposits but limited opportunities for credit. At the same time, NCB was an investment bank with large credit potential, but which suffered from a shortage of liquidity.

Due to poor management within NCB the liquidity shortage became chronic (International Monetary Fund, 1994), and, even worse, a stoppage in interest payments for these deposits led to the suspension of these interbank operations. Between mid-1992 and early 1993 the SB deposited household savings at BoA in the form of excess liquidity. Since that time only minor transactions have been performed under the supervision of BoA. BoA is currently striving to increase the attractiveness of the interbank money market for the commercial banks as it provides a relatively cheap source of financing and reduces the role of the refinancing policy. In fact, in 1994 the interbank money market started functioning under the supervision of the BoA, providing limited funding for short periods from 1 to 3 months.

Reserves Policy

At the beginning of economic reforms in late 1991 the level of reserves was negligible. Their subsequent growth has been aided by programs conducted by international financial institutions, in particular the International Monetary Fund, the G-24, and IDA. At the end of 1993 foreign reserves increased to about 2.3 weeks of imports, at the end of 1994 to about 12.7 weeks of imports, and at the end of 1995 to about 18.5 weeks of imports as against only 1.4 in 1991.

The intervention of BoA in the foreign exchange market played an important role in the conduct of the reserves policy. While the central bank implemented a floating exchange rate regime, with the external stability of the currency as one of its main objectives, BoA repeatedly intervened in the foreign exchange market in order to eliminate the large and abrupt fluctuations. For example, BoA intervened at the end of 1994 to damp down a further appreciation of the Lek caused by an increased supply of foreign currency resulting from illegal activities in connection with the UN embargo on FR Yugoslavia.

The approval of the new law on the BoA in February 1996 marked a qualitative change in the reserves policy. In order to build up a sustainable level of reserves, BoA has established the accumulation of safe and liquid foreign assets as one of its primary objectives. Simultaneously, BoA is working to improve the asset composition of its reserves, by holding gold, different foreign currencies, and securities issued or guaranteed by foreign governments, central banks or international organizations. Sixty per cent of the total amount of reserves are currently denominated in US Dollar.

Exchange Rate Policy

A floating exchange rate regime was considered the most appropriate in order to curb the upward inflation tendency. The main factors influencing the choice of this regime were: the level of foreign debt; the poor state of foreign currency reserves; and the support received from different international organizations. BoA began by implementing the full internal convertibility of the national currency.

The exchange rates are freely determined on the domestic bank market which competes with the very active street market where traders with and without licenses and bureaux de change conduct business. During the initial development of the foreign exchange market, with weak control over the open positions of commercial banks and the practical absence of capital control, the street market traders had a significant impact on the exchange rates. The demand for foreign currency was better and more quickly satisfied by the street market, which offered more competitive rates, while banks offered these services in a very ineffective and bureaucratic way. The poor state of BoA's reserves and commercial banks' poor management facilitated speculations and contributed to fluctuations.

Moreover, after 1993 when the central bank reserves improved, the exchange rate policy was considered an important part of monetary policy, intended to bring about exchange rate stability through intervention in the market to prevent excessive fluctuations (see also Table 1.4).

PRIVATIZATION

In the medium-term program of the Albanian government the restructuring of the state-owned enterprises is considered an indispensable condition for achieving reform. For that reason the Enterprise Restructuring Agency (ERA) has been established. Following the completion of the first and the second phase of the Albanian privatization program including the privatization of the small and medium-sized enterprises, the privatization process passed through the following phases:

- In 1991, the Law on Privatization was approved.
- Before March 1992, the privatization of trade and services, handicraft and transportation sectors was completed. The privatization of the retail outlets (including furniture) was conducted through former employees, which bought them for cash.
- In April 1993 the Law on Land Restitution and Compensation was approved.
- In May 1993 the privatization of houses, ownership of which in fact was transferred to their owners, was completed.
- In June 1993 all small and medium-sized trade, services, enterprises, which had less than 300 workers and whose assets did not exceed 500,000 Leks, were privatized by auctions.

In mid-1995 began the mass privatization to be performed through vouchers[8] and 'privatization Leks' which are given to former political prisoners. First, the enterprises will be converted into joint-stock companies and then privatized through 'share' auctions. It is anticipated that the mass privatization will finish by the end of 1997. All Albanian citizens above the age 18 who live in urban areas and have not benefited from land privatization or restitution claims are entitled to get privatization bonuses (issued by SB), which can be exchanged for shares in one of the auctioned enterprises.

The distribution of the privatization bonuses in 1995 resulted in the establishment of an informal market for privatization bonuses. On this market bonuses were sold at about a quarter of their value. Usually the price varied between 30% and 10–11% of their par value. (For example, if the privatization bonus was worth 100,000 Leks – the maximum share value – it was sold on the market for 30,000 Leks). The rate continued to decrease because supply was high and demand low due to the poor state of the big enterprises, mostly of which are non-profitable and with old capital stock.

---

[8] The Lek-privatization and privatization bonuses are tools for redistributing national wealth. The mass privatization is realized through vouchers.

This had also an impact on the macroeconomic situation. The demand for cash increased the currency in circulation (by 52% in 1995), but without having an inflationary effect.

Foreign Debt

Albania entered the process of transformation towards a market economy in a weak position caused by inherited foreign debt, amounting to US$ 592 million or about 68% of GDP in December 1992 (International Monetary Fund, 1994). The accumulated debt consisted of short-term debt with international organizations, commercial banks and bilateral creditors. The position of a net debtor with 30 foreign banks led to major difficulties, including the suspension of further financing.

With support from the IMF and the World Bank new negotiations were carried out with the Paris Club. In June 1995, Albania agreed with the crediting banks to consider the debt outstanding taking in consideration its incapacity to pay. The foreign debt was reduced to US$ 264.4 million equivalent, or 1.8% of GDP.[9] US$ 224 million of principal obligations were substituted by a zero-coupon, 30-year par bond, fully collaterized by US Treasury bonds and the rights to an income fund.

THE BANKING SECTOR

Regulatory Framework[10] and Supervision

The reform of the banking system in parallel with its recapitalization is considered a crucial support for economic reforms in Albania and the achievement of the macroeconomic objectives set in the medium- and long-term programs.

The Law on the Banking System in Albania, in conjunction with the Law on the Bank of Albania, stipulates the creation of a two-tier banking system, comprising the BoA on the first level and the commercial banks on the second one. At present, the second level is composed of:
• 3 state-owned commercial banks (National Commercial Bank, Savings

---

[9]The ratio is calculated on the basis of the GDP in 1995.

[10] The Banking System in Albania operates on the basis of:
• The Law on the Banking System approved by the Parliament in 22 February 1996;
• The Internal Regulation of the Bank of Albania compiled by the Supervision Department.
To date there is no Law on deposits insurance and bankruptcy.

Bank and Rural Commercial Bank) which have been established on the basis of the existing banks;

- 2 joint-venture banks (one with Italian and Albanian capital and the other one with Arab and Albanian capital);
- 1 private bank (Dardania Bank from Kosovo).

The joint venture banks and Dardania Bank perform only limited operations in the market. The approval of the new Law on the Banking System established favorable conditions for opening new private, domestic and foreign banks, and for the consolidation of existing ones. By the provisions of the law on the banking system, the banks can be established on the model of joint-stock companies or, for the first time, as cooperatives (under the Law on Commercial Association).

The law does not stipulate any limitation regarding the participation of foreign capital in local banks. On the basis of the Regulation on Licensing banks may be established with 100% of foreign capital participation, or as joint ventures. However, in order to increase investment opportunities for Albanians through the establishment of Albanian private banks, the required minimum capital is higher for foreign than for domestic banks. The law stipulates that banks should be managed by persons with the necessary qualifications and expertise. BoA is authorized to remove top executive bank managers from office if they do not meet the requirements of the law. In general, this law laid the foundations for the development of a banking system that is capable of meeting the demands of an emerging economy.

The supervision of the banking system to ensure its stability and development is defined in the Law as one of the central bank's functions. For the achievement of this target BoA has compiled regulations regarding capital requirements, credit policy, and lending procedures as well as foreign assets positions.

The supervision of BoA is in the process of transformation. In order to support the restructuring of the banking system, BoA has compiled a detailed reporting system which is in the process of revision. The new Reporting System approved in 1995 replaced the one that existed after 1992.

The rapid privatization of the state-owned banks in conjunction with the establishment of new banks will increase competition in the banking system. The agreement on a bankruptcy law for banks, however, is still missing. The main consequence of this is a lack of efficiency reflected particularly in the poor quality of the services offered, an inadequate payment system, a high level of overdue loans, a lack of incentive to increase the level of deposits through interest rates which are not market-oriented, unqualified staff, overstaffing, etc. The Bankruptcy Law was submitted in the Parliament in mid-1995 and was expected to be approved by the end of the year. However, this has not yet taken place.

Reserves Requirements

BoA has used minimum reserve requirements as a mean of controlling money supply since its establishment as a central bank. Since the middle of 1992, BoA has requested a – since then unchanged – reserve requirement of 10% on all deposits in domestic and foreign currency. The reserves are in the form of non-interest-bearing deposits for the commercial banks. The monitoring of the reserves is carried out monthly on the basis of the balance sheets presented to BoA by the commercial banks.

In November 1993 BoA increased the level of the reserves by 139% compared with 1992, while at the end of 1994 and 1995 the growth was 20% and 34%, respectively, reflecting the increase in the level of deposits.

Given the situation of a non-functioning interbank market and the absence of other investments possibilities, excess of assets (mostly by the Savings Bank) were deposited in the BoA in the form of excess reserves, which were remunerated. These rates were changed by BoA in order to bring them into line with the changes in deposits rates and the inflation rate. By the end of 1993 the excess reserves reached about Lek 9 million and remained almost constant throughout 1994, showing a downward trend in 1995 because investment possibilities in the treasury bills market increased. Thus, compared with the previous year, excess reserves decreased by 41% by December 1995.

Adequacy Ratios

Two Regulations on the Licensing and Capital Adequacy issued by the BoA regulate the supervision of the central bank regarding adequacy ratios. In these are specified the requirements for capital base and capital adequacy. The Banking Regulation on Licensing contains a minimum capital base requirement of:
- Lek 100 million (about US$ 1 million) for domestic banks;
- Lek 200 million (or about 2 US$ million) for foreign and joint ventures banks.

The issue of capital adequacy is treated in the Regulation on the Capital Requirements (27 June 1994) which sets out the rules for defining capital base value and the general adequacy ratio, which should not be lower than 8%. BoA supervises the capital adequacy of the commercial banks and requires that the banks fulfill the requirements of the Regulation.

Assets and Liabilities [11]

Under the law governing the banking system each person having more than 10% of the capital is considered a participant, which is a way of promoting small shareholders. Banks are obliged to deposit the capital amount, which varies and is defined by the BoA according to the particular internal regulations. The required capital amount is expressed as a percentage of the assets considered as risk-weighted ones. The minimal capital required is defined on the basis of the banking activities to be performed, in accordance with the legislation following prior approval by the BoA.

The law governing the banking system lays down that banks need the permission of the BoA to:
- decrease their capital by repurchase of shares or distribution of reserve assets;
- purchase shares or become a partner in aggregate amounts to more than 10% of a company's capital.

In carrying out credit transactions, banks shall comply with principles of risk avoidance, diversification and liquidity, as well as the directives and instructions issued by the BoA. According to the law governing the banking system, the assets are classified in four groups : free, low, average, and high-risk (in figures 0%, 30%, 50% and 100%, respectively).

Non-performing Loans

Non-performing loans are an important problem that banks have been faced with ever since the beginning of the transition period. Bad debts were inherited from the past and they were augmented during the deep economic crisis in the first years of the transition period.

By the end of 1992, bad debts amounted to Lek 11 billion. Debtors are exclusively state-owned enterprises, farms, and cooperatives. The standstill in manufacturing and production has led to an inability to repay credit loans. Trade liberalization makes it difficult for producers to sell their products in the country and abroad. They have been unprepared and unable to adapt themselves to the newly created situation. Exporters also were unused to the floating

---

[11] BoA issued its provisions regarding the:
- Regulation on the Licensing and establishment as a Private Bank in Albania (after the enactment of the new Law on the Banking System all internal regulations are being improved);
- Regulation on the Position of banks;
- Regulation on Adequacy Ratios;
- Regulation on foreign exchange market;
- Regulation on the domestic loans.

exchange rate. They worked under domestic prices which were fixed and unrelated to foreign exchange. Also, the high proportion of non-performing loans caused by the disruption of the exports to CMEA countries, the poor management of banks, staff difficulties, the lack of unitary book-keeping procedures, the continued payment of wages and salaries to workers during production stoppages, all combined to weaken the banks' portfolios.

Taking into consideration the detrimental effect of non-performing loans for the future development of the Albanian banking system, the government decided to cover the losses. It issued government bonds with a value of Lek 4.3 million to clear the balance sheet of the National Commercial Bank of bad debts, as well as Lek 2.9 million for the Rural Commercial Bank, with a maturity of 15 years and a floating interest rate. Their ownership is transferable and they can be traded in a secondary market in which private investors and companies are allowed to participate.

In the period 1993–1995, the structure of the credit system has changed to the benefit of the private sector where consolidation has been achieved. By the end of 1993, the ratio of private-sector financed as against the total amount of outstanding credit reached 54.5%, rising to 75% in 1994, and 89% in 1995 – that is, 89% of the total amount of outstanding credit.

Nevertheless, the problem of the bad debts with which the balance sheets of the commercial banks are burdened is still evident. By the end of 1994 the bad loans reached 26.6% against 16% at the end of 1993, and in 1995 the amount of the overdue credit was estimated at 30.4%, reflecting the underdevelopment of the banking system and the blocking of the privatization process.

Inter-enterprise Arrears

The state-owned enterprises which were on the verge of bankruptcy were unable to pay their commercial partners because of the standstill in production. As a consequence inter-enterprise arrears amounted to about 33% of GDP at the end of 1992 (International Monetary Fund, 1994). The implementation of a prepayment system to replace the post-shipment system curtailed the progress of debt accumulation, while the banks froze the accounts of these enterprises in order to force them to pay their debts. To solve the problem of inter-enterprise arrears, the government budget took over the burden of cleaning up an amount equal to Lek 131 million.

EXCHANGES

Recently, monetary policy has sought to establish alternatives to refinancing by the central bank through increasing capital-raising opportunities for the commercial banks. The development of the domestic capital market is now considered to be of strategic importance. This will help the establishment of a new institutional environment.

In parallel, the BoA is working to replace the old direct instruments of monetary policy such as credit ceilings with other more indirect instruments. The development of the Albanian financial market began during the second half of 1994 with the issuing of treasury bills. At present, the Albanian financial market conducts only a small number of operations, but this is the only dynamic part of the Albanian financial market.

Bond Trading

Treasury bills, as an important financial instrument of the money market, are widely used in the market economies because of their high level of liquidity, the comparatively low degree of risk associated with them and the short duration of their maturity.

The government securities market in Albania, which only became active in the second half of 1994, consists of securities trading in treasury bills which are issued by the Ministry of Finance in order to finance the budget deficit. The realization of financial operations based on the activity of buying and selling of treasury bills in the primary market follows a policy decision by the Administration Committee of Domestic Loans (ACDL).

The ongoing auctions are being organized by a team of three, two of whom are employees of the BoA, while the third is affiliated to the Ministry of Finance. The auctions are carried out at least once a month. In exceptional cases, and with the special permission of the Ministry of Finance, BoA can organize auctions in which the banks and the institutions specified in the decision can participate.

Regular participants in the treasury bills market are:

- BoA, in accordance with the terms and conditions defined by its Board Committee under non-competitive conditions. It is the first buyer of the requested amount and the remaining part is shared between competitive and non-competitive requests by the ratios defined in the ACDL decision.
- NCB, SB, RCB, etc., and non-banking institutions such as the Insurance Institute.
- Private firms, joint-stock companies, and individuals which must present to the Bank of Albania the statement of the bank's deposit opened and blocked in the amount equivalent to their auction's request.

The treasury bills are tradable and they can be bought and sold before the maturity date only under the terms defined by the Bank of Albania and only by the Bank. At the beginning treasury bills were issued with a maturity of 90 days, but since May 1995 newly issued treasury bills have a maturity of one year. The issuing of treasury bills with one year maturity is linked to the desire to foster the development of a bond market and attract private investors away from the informal market to the formal one. The main buyer of the bonds is the Savings Bank because of its excess liquidity. Since the government bond market was not sufficiently attractive to private investors, the BoA increased the interest rates by two percentage points (200 basis points) for treasury bills against the annual rate for deposits in May 1995. A month later the bond rates were 900, 500, and 350 basis points higher than the respective rates for 3-month, 6-month and 12-month deposits. The first step towards the establishment of the secondary market was taken by the opening of a securities exchange in May.[12] The securities exchange is opened only two days a week and its activities are mostly limited to treasury bills auctions.

The treasury bills are of the discounted type, so the buyers earn the interest as the difference between the nominal value of the bills and the price paid at purchase. The minimal amount to be purchased is 100,000 Leks and it can be increased in steps of 25,000. The treasury bills market is the most important channel through which the budget deficit is financed: at the end of 1995 63.7% of the total fiscal deficit is financed this way, while another 32% is financed by bank credit, compared with 88% at the end of 1994. This shows that BoA took up this instrument in order to implement monetary policy goals.

To summarize, the bond market in Albania is composed of:

- *government bonds* which were traded since October 1992. These bonds were issued to replace loans which were considered unlikely to be paid;
- *treasury bills* which were issued in mid-1994 with 3-month and 6-month maturity, in order to finance the budget deficit. Also, the Ministry of Finance issued 12-month treasury bills with attractive interest rates in order to attract large private investors to participate in the bond market.

The lack of a secondary market development, however, left this process in a rudimentary state.

---

[12] The securities exchange functions on the basis of the Law on Securities approved by Parliament on 29 April 1994 and the Regulations on:
- The functioning of securities retailing in Albania (treasury bills);
- The listing requirements on the securities exchange;
- The trading procedures on the Securities Exchange of Tirana.
There is as yet no Law governing the Securities Exchange.

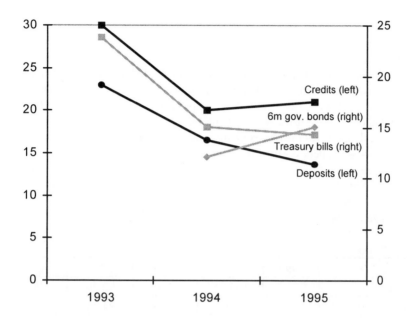

Figure 1.2. Interest rates 1993-1995

Table 1.2. Structure of interest rates in the bond market

	1993	*1994*	*1995*
Treasury bills* 3-month	–	10	14.7
6-month	–	12.1	14.9
12-month	–	–	15.1
Government bonds	23.8	15.1	14.3

Note: * The weighted average rate of accepted bids for treasury bills during the last auctions of the period.
Source: Bank of Albania, 1996.

Currency Exchange

The currency exchange was the first and is still the most active financial market operating in Albania. Given the large bid/ask spreads in the exchange market, interest rate differentials did not play such an important role as expected for the portfolio choice of agents. Instead, foreign currency holdings are considered a safe haven for a part of household savings. Strong fluctuations in the exchange rate further contributed to their massive build-up. Given these conditions, the BoA's intention to control these fluctuations through continual interventions is, however, constrained by the low level of foreign currency reserves.

The foreign exchange market consists of a market for exchange bureaux (a retail market) and a more active and competitive street market. The retail market, by contrast, does not generate large volumes, and up to now BoA has granted only 15 licenses. An interbank market does not yet exist.

The dynamics of the Lek exchange rate against the foreign currencies shows a downward tendency, reflecting the appreciation of the Lek. Since May 1992, during the period of the monetary expansion when the US Dollar was 130 Lek, it appreciated almost non-stop. The appreciation of the Lek reached its peak in August 1994 when the exchange rate was equivalent to 84 Lek/US$. On average the rate fixed was 92.8 Lek/US$.

Table 1.3. The dynamics of the Lek/US$ exchange rate

Lek/US$	1992	1993	1994	1995	Aug. 1996
Average	75.03	102.06	94.68	92.79	108.84
End of period	102.09	98.68	95.39	94.24	108.47
Difference	+ 27.06	- 4.38	+ 0.71	+ 1.45	- 0..37

Source: Bank of Albania, 1995 and 1996.

In addition, the expansion of economic activity during the last three years has caused a significant increase in foreign trade turnover. While the current account deficit persists, it was nevertheless halved to 8.3% of GDP from 16% in 1994. The generally increasing degree of macroeconomic stability is thus reflected in greater exchange rate stability. The spread has now shrunk to 7.27 Lek (the largest difference in the currency exchange rates during 1995).

The evolution of the Lek/US$ exchange rate in the years 1992–1995 shows an Albanian peculiarity. The Lek appreciates during the summer time because of short supply, and depreciates in January (after the New Year celebrations). The main factors determining this pattern are:
- import activities which influence the supplies of foreign exchange and are different in the summer and the winter;
- capital inflows due to remittances from Albanian migrants abroad.

Nonetheless, after a period of three years the appreciation of the Lek came to a halt and was finally reversed. During the first four months of 1996, CPI showed an increase of 5.4% mainly through bread and flour price liberalization. On the other hand, there is an increase of currency in circulation because of the budget deficit and wage increases, all of which have led to an inflationary environment.

The depreciation of the Lek continued up to October 1996, the period in which some charitable foundations which were established on the basis of pyramid schemes changed their interest rates. They offered excessive rates which persuaded almost 25% of the population to deposit their savings in these foundations, participating as 3-year members. The investment of personal savings only in Leks increased the supply of foreign currency (mainly US$) in the market, causing the temporary appreciation of the Lek.

SOURCES OF EXTERNAL FINANCE

Foreign Direct Investment

Albania, like several other East European countries, was characterized by a centralized state trade system. Several foreign trade enterprises had the right to conduct export-import business while direct foreign investment was forbidden. With the dawning of the market economy, foreign direct investment began to be considered essential to help Albania utilize its potential of human, physical, and institutional assets.

In October 1993 to foster foreign direct investment, the parliament approved the Law on Foreign Investments, under which foreign investors can freely invest in Albania. The law allows all foreign investors to repatriate all funds including profits as well as contributions in kind related to their foreign investments. Furthermore, foreign investors are allowed to participate in the privatization process under the same conditions as the Albanian public.

The Law on Tax and Custom Duties has been amended to support capital inflows to Albania in the form of foreign direct investments through tax exemptions for the import of machinery and equipment by domestic or foreign firms.

Political and economic stabilization together with the liberalization of foreign trade and exchange rates liberalization have been the main factors in inducing foreign direct investment to increase (see Table 1.4).

Table 1.4. Foreign Direct Investment in Albania 1992–1995

1992	*1993*	*1994*	*1995*
20	58	53	70

Note: US$ billion.
Source: Office of the Prime Minister, 1996.

Foreign direct investment was concentrated in light industry, the construction sector, and the services sector, and recently also in mining and heavy industry.

FOREIGN AID AND FOREIGN FINANCIAL ASSISTANCE

In 1992 the Albanian economy reached a state of emergency, with income per capita the lowest in Europe or 50% relative to the average international level,[13] an extremely difficult payment position, with large external debts, a shortage of essential consumer goods, and the decline of productive activity in most of the state enterprises. Foreign aid in the shape of the grants or loans was vital to support the economic reform and stabilization program. After macroeconomic stabilization has made some progress, foreign aid and financial assistance components now play an important role in generating a surplus in the capital account.

Foreign financing is considered as the chief financial support for the implementation of the general reform program undertaken by the new Albanian government after the elections of March 1992. The main donors were: the World Bank, which granted a loan for the financing of the critical imports; the International Monetary Fund, through a stand-by agreement; and the G-24 through emergency assistance and support such as food aid. Although high in 1991 (87% in total aid) and 1992 (71%), its share decreased to 43% in 1993, 11% in 1994, and 1% in 1995. These figures reflect both the improving economic situation and a qualitative shift in foreign aid towards more aid for project development (7% in 1992, 23% in 1993, 23% in 1994, and 48% in 1995) since the restructuring of the manufacturing sector is considered essential for Albania's economic development.

The financing for the production sector, economic and social infrastructure has increased over the years from 7.2% and 14.5% in 1991 and 1992. It reached a level of 58% and 75% of total aid, in 1994 and 1995, respectively.

Commodity aid, by contrast, has a share of about 8% in 1995 without showing large fluctuations over the relevant period but with a projected reduction to 2% in the future.

Moreover, the balance of payment deficit represents another area in which foreign aid is needed to maintain and improve the future development of Albania's economy. At the end of 1995 the share of balance of payments (BoP) financing by the European Union/G-24 reached 21%, while in 1992 BoP financing was only 13% of the total aid. Emergency aid in 1992 was 70% of total aid, and in 1991 it was 87%.

Under the financing structure of the period 1991–1993, 64% of total funds were grants, while the remaining 36% were made up of credit. Nevertheless,

---

[13] Per capita income at current exchange rates was US$ 760 compared with US$ 314 in 1992.

for some time foreign financial support will be important for preserving a minimal level of consumption and for enhancing investment. In the medium term, however, one of Albania's main objectives is to decrease its dependency on emergency assistance.

The government's intention is to develop industrial production disrupted after 1990 as well as agricultural through the support given by foreign financing. Foreign financing is now mainly used to develop the physical and administrative infrastructure of particular sectors, such as agriculture, energy, trade, local community, public administration, and transportation.

Foreign projects which are currently being pursued are aimed at putting the labor force to work and improving their economic conditions through the creation of self-employment schemes (through the granting of small-scale credits in both urban and rural areas) or the improvement of the economic and social infrastructure.

Table 1.5. The dynamics of foreign financing

1991	1992	1993	1994	1995
Base year	140%	-30%	0%	-17%

Source: Bank of Albania, 1996.

In 1992 foreign financing increased considerably, ensuring the financial viability and support for the implementation of economic reforms. The fluctuations in foreign financing are due to agreements based on short- and medium-term strategic plans.

CONCLUSION

The Albanian economy has recovered and increased its viability. Economic reforms have been fairly successful for macroeconomic stabilization but there is still a long way to go in terms of microeconomic restructuring. There is hardly any other economic sphere that reflects the present state of reform as much as the financial sector. Albanian financial markets are confined to forex trading and treasury bills auctions, while the banking system consists of just six commercial institutions with the Bank of Albania at the head. Although a securities exchange has been founded, the necessary accompanying legal and institutional infrastructure for capital market development such as investments funds hardly exists. The activity on the securities exchange consists mainly of financial bureaux performing a very limited number of over-the-counter trades.

There is no legislation covering securities exchanges as yet, so that activity on the exchange is based on the Law on Securities and the regulations approved by BoA.

This situation imposes severe restrictions on the activities of the banking system, which is confined to very limited fields of activity. The main factors that affect the performance of banks are the lack of competition among banks due to the small number of new market entrants, and the persistent segmentation in commercial banking due to the high degree of specialization among banks, which further restricts competition. The Savings Bank has collected 85% of personal savings and given only 7% of total credits, while the National Commercial Bank has given 71% of all credits to firms and 90% of all credit to the economy, and the Rural Commercial Bank which dominates the financing activities in the agricultural section.

In future a more independent central bank together with a competitive banking system and the continued development of financial institutions, resulting in the transfer of informal market activity to established marketplaces, will pave the way for the development of a capital market in Albania. BoA will increase the minimum level of deposits to assets, putting pressure on banks to behave in a more market-oriented manner. The full liberalization of prices through raising the price ceilings for flour and bread, together with the elimination of subsidies, the replacement of the turnover tax by a value added tax, and the further modernization of customs arrangements will have inflationary effects in the short term. Hence, inflation is expected to rise to 11% in 1996. For 1997 the inflation target is 6% according to the IMF medium-term strategy for Albania.

Thus, the restructuring of the banking sector and the fostering of competition among banks through new market entrants, together with the completion of the privatization process, remains a crucial task for the successful development of the Albanian capital market.

Moreover, the existence of a very active informal market, in which large parts of the population have been inveigled through promises of astronomically high monthly returns,[14] is an obvious danger to the future of the banking system and the macroeconomic stabilization of the country as a whole.

---

[14] There are some private companies, such as Vefa, Cani, Kamberi, Silva, Gjallica, which finance their economic activities using household and corporate deposits, and some bogus charities which offer interest of up to 50% per month which in the case of default would cause turmoil.

REFERENCES

Bank of Albania (1996): *Quarterly Statistical Report*, June, Tirana.
Bank of Albania (1995): *Quarterly Statistical Report*, various issues, Tirana.
Bank of Albania (1994): *Quarterly Statistical Report*, December, Tirana.
Law on the Bank of Albania April 22, 1992.
Law on the Bank of Albania February 22, 1996.
Law on the Banking System April 22, 1992.
Law on the Banking System February 22, 1996.
Law on Foreign Investments October 1993.
Law on Custom Duties and Turnover Tax.
International Monetary Fund (1994): *Economic Review Albania*, Washington, D.C.

G21 P33
G28 P34
L33
P24 F34

2.   Bulgaria

Todor Balabanov, Tatiana Houbenova and Borislav Vladimirov

INTRODUCTION

For the first five years of transition (1990–1995) the development of Bulgarian capital markets lagged significantly behind those of Central European countries. The main reasons for this are related to the slow pace of privatization which prolonged the existence of a large number of heavily indebted, state-owned enterprises. These are still being financed, in line with old central-planning practices, via non-collaterated bank loans. The protected market for banking services and the liberal licensing policy of the central bank, as well as the significant share of the state-owned banks operating in the country, not only resulted in market inefficiencies but generated a heavy banking crisis. This actually dissolved the savings of a significant part of the population and led to increasing social and political tension within the country. Alternative sources of financing and investment such as the stock markets remained under-developed in comparison with their counterparts in Budapest, Warsaw, Ljubljana and Prague. The limited significance of the stock exchanges was a result of the lack of know-how, of a legal basis and of credibility in the stock issuing companies.

The financial difficulties of Bulgaria have a history starting in the end of the 1970s which went on through the 1980s, when the country accumulated more than US$ 10 billion of foreign debt, mainly through the huge losses amassed by the state-owned enterprises (SOEs). These apparently specialized in the creation of a 'negative value added', as their input costs, valued at world prices, exceeded the value of output sold at the COMECON internal prices. Another critical moment was the 1990 moratorium on foreign debt repayments imposed by the government of Lukanov, which has cut off the country from private foreign financing for the past six years. At present the country is plagued by a deepening banking crisis, with 15 of the 47 state and private banks being under central bank supervision with the prospect for liquidation, and an increasing distrust among the population of both the local currency and the financial institutions.

1996 was a difficult year not only for the Bulgarian financial sector, but also for the economy as a whole. Although the 1995 GDP figures were pointing to a slight growth of 2.6%, by now it has become clear that this has been achieved at the expense of a sharp rise in governmental internal and external indebtedness and a significant increase in inter-enterprise arrears, both leading finally to a soaring bank crisis. The simple prime interest rate went up from 108% in May to 300% per year in September 1996, which in late October was reduced to 240%. For the first ten months of 1996 the Bulgarian Lev (BGL), depreciated from 70 BGL/US$ in January to around 340 BGL/US$ by mid-November. It was not too much of a surprise, therefore, that the IMF had difficulties in releasing the subsequent tranches of the negotiated emergency credit. The figures released in October 1996 by the National Statistics Institute (NSI) are also quite gloomy, e.g. for 1996 the GDP is expected to fall by 10.5% with an annual inflation rate that could climb up to 520%. The good news is that the share of the private sector is rising – in 1996 it created 49.4% of the GDP which is up from around 40% in 1995.

During 1996, acceding to the political pressure of state enterprise and state banking management as well as facing rising dissatisfaction among the population, the socialist-dominated government together with the Central Bank pursued a policy of subsidization leading to regular increases in the budget deficit, as they persisted in covering the debts of the banking sector and the loss-making, state-owned enterprises by budgetary means. Consequently, the economically harmful government financing to the real sector was redirected by the Central Bank to the major state-owned banks which from their side were extending non-collaterated credits to the SOEs. Thus the young and undeveloped banking system was increasingly burdened with bad debts in their portfolios. A second process which contributed to the increase in the banks' bad debts was the rapid capitalization of the emerging private sector. Many private firms took advantage of the poorly regulated banking system, which lacked efficient control mechanisms, to amass non-performing loans. As a result of these two processes the indebtedness of the banking system became the main source for financing the losses of the SOEs and the bad debts of the private firms. Thus, aggregate banking losses during the first six months of 1996 were Leva 64 billion (US$ 675 million), about 5% of the gross domestic product, an estimated 75% of bank loans are bad (that is, non-performing) and all but one bank, Bulbank, do not have adequate provision for their bad debts, etc. The banks in turn were financed by the budget, so that they could cover the credits extended to the state-owned enterprises. One of the worst elements of this policy was that the debts were written off in portions, at particular intervals of time, thus creating incentives for debtors to expect the future cancellation of their debts and for banks to expect state financing for extended loans.

What follows is an attempt to provide an overview of the policies and economic processes which have been experienced by Bulgaria for the past three years and have been relevant for the developments in the Bulgarian capital market. Discussing the limited scope and importance of the country's stock exchanges so far we focus on the internal and external debt markets as the most significant of the country's financial sector at this stage of economic transition.

MONETARY POLICY

According to figures released by the Bulgarian National Bank (see Table 2.1) the broad money grew by 39.6% in 1995, and by 64.3% for the period July 1995 – June 1996 and the foreign exchange rose by 16.42% during 1995. At the end of 1995 the total amount of foreign exchange in Bulgaria's currency circulation was US$ 2.246 billion.

Table 2.1. Growth of broad money

June 1996	1.4%
July 1995 – June 1996	64.3%
1995	39.6%
1994	71.8%
1993	47.0%
1992	51.0%

Note: End of period except first two figures.
Source: OMRI Economic Digest, Vol. 2, No. 42, 17 October 1996 (part II)

Narrow money (on current accounts and extra-bank) showed the steepest rise during 1995, i.e. from BGL 68.6 billion to 107.9 billion, or by 57%. Individuals hold the bulk of time deposits: BGL 233 billion, up 49% over the year. State-owned enterprises hold BGL 10.2 billion on such deposits, and private enterprises BGL 12.4 billion. Private individuals keep another BGL 57.8 billion in savings deposit accounts, up from BGL 40.9 billion at the beginning of the year.

The bulk of foreign-currency deposits are also held by members of the public, US$ 885 million at the beginning of 1995 and US$ 1.243 billion at the end of the year. State-owned enterprises cut back their forex savings from US$ 739 million in January to US$ 526 million in December. Private companies held US$ 310.5 million at year's start and US$ 353.6 million at year's end. The

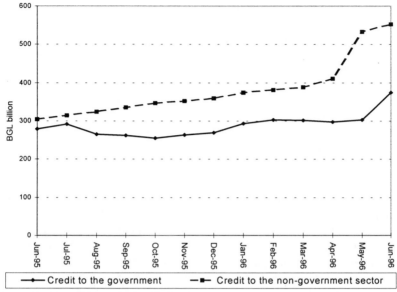

Source: Banker weekly, no. 38, 23–29/09/1996, p. 11.

Figure 2.1. Internal credit to the government and non-government sectors

foreign currency deposited with banks by businesses and individuals increased from US$ 1.993 billion to US$ 2.123 billion last year. Members of the public have saved a total of BGL 471 billion in national and foreign currency, up 89% from the previous year. In the banking system as a whole, one-month deposits paid 42.39% weighted average interest for the year 1995.

Instruments

The main policies the BNB used to control the monetary base are the changes in its refinancing policies and, recently, its open market operations. However, the BNB is not capable of controlling the processes related to the government deficits and the crises on the foreign currency markets, which both have unfavourably influenced the monetary base. The crisis period in the early summer of 1996 resulted in rapid increases in internal credit both to the government – up 23.24% from May to June 1996, and to the non-government sector – up 29.55% from April to May 1996 (Figure 2.1).

As mentioned in the introduction, the basic obstacles to the monetary control have been:
1. the state enterprises' losses;

2. the banks' slack financing and debt management policies,
3. insufficient bank supervision;
4. the pressure created by the unregulated forex market.

Interest Rates

The main reason for both the present and medium-term financial destabilization remains the high price of money. As the economy's interest rates are
closely related to the basic interest rate (BIR) determined by the Central Bank
(BNB), it is in the policy of the Central Bank where one should seek an answer
to the ongoing financing and debt crisis. The Central Bank failed to suppress
the mounting inflationary expectations of economic agents and to implement
a policy of real, gradual depreciation of the Lev. On the contrary, it used to
exploit foreign exchange reserves in order to support an artificially appreciated
exchange rate. Besides causing the exhaustion of the forex reserves, this policy
led to unexpected forex market crashes which further decreased confidence in
the domestic currency. The above mentioned increase in the BIR, aimed at
restoring the attractiveness of Lev deposits, had a negative effect on the earning
capacity of a sorely troubled banking system. Commercial banks' interest rates
have so far been following closely the movement of the BIR and the BNB's
interest policy. With the increase in the simple monthly BIR to 25% in
September 1996, subsequently reduced to 20% at the end of October, the
commercial banks began to offer 10% monthly interest rate on deposits. For
this reason, most of the depositors preferred to invest either in government
securities or to exchange their free Levs for dollars.

The high interest rate charged by BNB on overdrafts, unsecured deposits,
foreign-currency loans, etc. quickly intensified the tendency towards bank
decapitalization. It undermined the bank's liquidity and profitability (especially
through the narrower margin between lending and deposit rates). The
commercial banks tend to raise their deposit rates more slowly than their
lending rates.

Another adverse trend is the persistence of negative interest rates on Leva
deposits. It may be suggested that until 1997 the real interest rate will remain
negative: from -19% in 1994 to +0.4% in 1995, -12% in 1996 and -7% in
1997. Implementing a restrictive monetary policy is the only way to reduce
negative real interest rates and to encourage savings in Leva, especially with
better support for the monetary stabilization from foreign-exchange policy.

Foreign Exchange Policy

For the past four years the movement of the BGL exchange rate has emerged as a source and indicator of major macroeconomic disequilibria, strengthening the tendency towards a nominal and real depreciation of the Lev. This deeper depreciation has confronted the Central Bank with considerable difficulties in maintaining a floating exchange rate. During 1994 and 1995 the Central Bank had to make extensive use of monetary tools to sustain the exchange rate despite the depressing effect of such a policy on the real economy.

The increased instability in the foreign-exchange sector mainly stems from: (a) inflation pressure for Lev depreciation in nominal and real terms; (b) the liberalized foreign-exchange transactions helping the speculative pressure on the market; (c) the relatively low level of foreign-exchange reserves weakening the credibility of the National Bank's interventions on the currency market. As a result, the measures of monetary policy were insufficient to alleviate the pressures on the forex market. Therefore, the restrictive monetary policy had to be tightened by the introduction of stricter foreign currency controls.

The stabilization of the BGL exchange rate in 1995 was largely due to the increase of the forex reserves, from US$ 899 million in January 1995 to US$ 1206 million at the beginning of 1996. The rapid depletion of forex reserves during January – April 1996, down to US$ 600 million, reaching their lowest point at US$ 506 million in September, together with the uncertain timing of the new standby agreement with the IMF, unleashed a process of rapid currency devaluation. BNB used some US$ 250 million net of its foreign exchange reserves to intervene on the forex market in the first half of 1996. Net foreign currency sales of US$ 249.7 million to local banks contributed to a fall of 38% in central bank reserves. Nevertheless, the Lev continued its slide down from 70 per dollar in January 1996 to 350 per dollar by the end of November 1996. Reserves fell by a total of US$ 663 million to US$ 573.4 million in the first half of the year due to payments on foreign debt and net foreign currency sales to local banks. This, as well as the forthcoming external-debt repayments, makes the years 1996–1997 critical ones in respect of the stabilization process. The level to which the Lev has fallen in November 1996 shows that, within the present exchange control mechanism, foreign-exchange policy is finding it difficult to act as a buffer against inflation.

During their meeting with the Bulgarian government in November 1996, the IMF urged the adoption of special measures to prop up the rapidly devaluating national currency. The complete distrust in the value of the Lev among the public intensified the process of the 'dollarization' of savings. The government declared their intention to resort to extremely severe restrictions to achieve a quick restoration of confidence in the Lev, similar to the measures applied in Estonia, Lithuania and Argentina. These three countries introduced currency boards with help from the IMF to boost credibility in their national currencies. Under a currency board system, the amount of national currency in circulation must be matched by the Central Bank's hard currency reserves. But it also deprives the bank of the usual tools of monetary management, such as market interventions and interest rates.

The flaws in the existing institutional and regulatory framework, combined with the liquidity and solvency crises suffered by a number of banking institutions, has reduced the confidence of the investors in the banking system and has led to capital outflows. According to Western bankers[1] between US$ 3 and 5 billion have been drained out of Bulgaria during the past four years. This process has resulted inevitably in a restricted access to private and public forex deposits, thus further destabilizing the monetary system.

THE BANKING SECTOR

In Bulgaria a two-tier banking system existed from 1989, but the related legal framework was introduced only in 1992 with the enactment of two laws: The Law on the Bulgarian National Bank of June 1991 and the Law on Banks and Credit Activity of March 1992. The first establishes the independence of the Central Bank and defines its functions and objectives with regard to providing the internal and external stability of the national currency. The Central Bank has really maintained an independent restrictive monetary policy through 1994 and 1995 which had to be eased in 1996 because of the collapse of the Lev (BGL) and the declining demand for government securities. The second law defines the range of financial transactions that banks can engage in, permits foreign participation and allows domestic investors to purchase shares in commercial banks. It also gives the Bulgarian National Bank the regulatory and supervisory authority over the other banks. This law, however, could not prevent the registration of a number of private banks owned by the ex-*nomenclatura*, which soon became insolvent because of their inadequate reserves and corrupt lending practices. In this way, the problems of a few banks generated a general panic, which spread among the depositors of otherwise stable banks and affected the whole banking system. Under pressure from the International Monetary Fund (IMF) by September 1996 the Central Bank put 15 of the 47 private and state-owned banks into liquidation, freezing the accounts of a large proportion of companies and individuals. This followed the following sequence: (1) on 17 May 1996 the Central Bank effectively closed Parva Chastna Banka (First Private Bank) and the state-owned Mineralbank; (2) on 18 June 1996 it shut down Agrobiznesbank, Kristalbank, and First

---

[1] As quoted in the article 'Sofia: Old Guard Stung', *International Herald Tribune* of 29 October 1996.

Agricultural and Investment Bank; (3) on 23 September nine more banks were closed, including TSBank, Balkanbank, Stopanska banka, Biznesbank, Elit Bank, Slavyani Bank, Yambol Bank, and Dobrudzha Bank.

Table 2.2. The top five Bulgarian banks

	Tier one capital, BGL mn	Total assets, BGL mn	Pre-tax profit, BGL mn	Profit/ capital	Staff	Number of branches
Bulbank (31/12/95)	24754	219733	5672	22.9%	1266	24
State Saving Bank (31/12/95)	12481	191556	10384	83.2%	7807	209
First Private Bank* (31/12/94)	2146	38667	894	41.7%	3100	76
First East International Bank (31/12/95)	1659	19496	14	0.8%	n.a.	39
Economic Bank* (31/12/95)	1467	32756	-6525	-444.8%	1006	29

BGL/US$=70.86 (12/95); 65.978 (12/94)
Note: * First Private Bank and Economic Bank are now under receivership.
Source: Showdown in Sofia, *The Banker*, October 1996.

The liquidity difficulties of most of the banks and the insolvency crisis of some of them create obstacles in the way of the accomplishment of the still delayed program of reform and restructuring.

On the positive side the number of licensed branches of foreign banks has increased to nine, including ING Bank, Société Générale, Bayrisch-Bulgarian Handelsbank, Raiffeisen Investment, Xios bank, Ionian bank, BNP-Dresdner-Bulgaria, National Bank of Greece, and the Bulgarian-American Credit Bank.

The restructuring by consolidation of the existing state banks is to be organized and carried out by the Bank Consolidation Company (BCC), registered at the beginning of 1992 as a joint-stock company. BCC aims at the creation of an efficient banking system by managing the stocks acquired by it and by consolidation of the state-owned banks. BCC's capital includes 49.7% from transferred participation shares of the BNB in the form of the capital of the commercial banks, 7% from the Foreign Trade bank and 42.7% from the Council of Ministers representing the state enterprises' shares. Recently, BCC acquired the commercial bank shares held by all state-owned enterprises. In this way it pooled 80% of the shares in the state banking system. BCC has acquired capital shares in the commercial banks, which allows for its participation in the management and privatization of these banks.

The restructuring of state banks has been envisaged in two stages. The first is the consolidation of the banks, and the current purging process is perhaps the most substantial and painful step in the restructuring of the banking sector. The next step envisaged is the privatization of state-owned banks. These measures will, however, contribute to the improvement of financial discipline and market-consistent behaviour only if the Central Bank ceases its practice of the generous refinancing of the banking system and if the loss-making SOEs are either privatized or liquidated.

PRIVATIZATION

Small-scale Privatization

The small businesses belonging to the public sector concentrate mostly on trade, services, transport and construction. They are comparatively small-scale and readily accessible to small and medium-sized investors. The purpose of the privatization of municipal property is to restructure it and rid the municipalities of atypical activities.

By 31 December 1995 procedures for 3,132 privatization deals had been opened, 169 for whole enterprises, and 2,963 for parts of enterprises. A total of 1,650 transactions had been concluded, of which 31 were for entire enterprises and 1,619 for only certain assets of enterprises. Among the projects were shops, studios, kiosks, restaurants and parts of industrial and construction companies. Auctions (682) and direct negotiations (652) were the prevailing methods for transferring ownership, followed by tenders (148). The successfully concluded transactions brought total proceeds exceeding BGL 4.5 billion.

Privatization by Restitution

A considerable number of enterprises were reprivatized by restitution in the period 1992–1995. From the enactment of the laws on restitution in February 1992 up to the end of September 1995, some 22,155 units had been reprivatized, including shops, restaurants, hotels, warehouses, and manufacturing enterprises. Some 87% of those units are situated in towns and 13% in villages.

While the restitution of commercial property was quite a rapid process, housing may take years to be returned to the lawful owners. There is an ongoing argument concerning the restitution of the accumulated value (including the forgone profit) of the productive assets as against simply returning the decaying property. One of the solutions is to compensate former owners by providing them with mass privatization vouchers whose face values corresponds to a recent valuations of their former property.

Mass (Voucher) Privatization

Bulgarian authorities, like the authorities in the other reforming economies, realized that the only way to effect economic transformation and privatization quickly was to transfer ownership into private hands on a large scale. A proven way to transfer ownership to a large number of shareholders is through the use of vouchers and auctions, as a part of a mass privatization program. Bulgaria's mass privatization program is similar in many ways to the other voucher programs that have been implemented in Eastern and Central Europe, but it has specifically followed the Czech model.

The mass privatization was launched at the beginning of the registration period on 8 January 1996 and aimed at selling 6.3 million voucher books with a face value of BGL 25,000, called Investment Bonds, to Bulgarian residents. By the end of the first term, 8 April 1996, around 1,650,000 sets of vouchers had been claimed and purchased, mostly at discount, by retirees and military personnel. The second term expired on 8 May, with around 3 million vouchers changing to private hands. Those who have registered participated in the next stage, the transfer period (Summer 1996), when they had to choose between three options: to entrust the booklets to a specific fund, to a relative, or to a chosen representative. During the next stage the individual participants and the privatization funds were ready to bid for company shares at each of the three centralised auctions (autumn 1996). The program is scheduled to continue throughout the rest of 1996 and conclude in 1997.

After Parliament's adoption of laws providing the framework for mass privatization, the Council of Ministers issued decrees on the details of mass privatization not covered in the other laws. The following institutions are involved in the mass privatization program:

- The *Centre for Mass Privatization (CMP)* is in charge of managing the entire mass privatization process.
- The *Ministry of Finance* prints the list of eligible citizens, divides it by collection region, and distributes these sub-lists to the regional centres.
- The *Securities and Stock Exchange Commission (SSEC)* has a set of responsibilities similar to securities commissions in the West, and its main role is to regulate the securities market. For the mass privatization program, the SSEC is responsible for regulating activities of privatization funds.
- The *Auction Commission* is responsible for regulating the three voucher auctions.
- The 28 *Regional Centres* established by the CMP are responsible for distributing the lists of citizens that go from the Ministry of Finance to the local post offices.
- *Privatization Funds* are the financial intermediaries of the mass privatiza-

tion program. They are entitled to collect Investment Bonds from the population, acquire shares in enterprises subject to mass privatization, and manage the shares.
- The *Registration Bureaux,* housed and staffed by local post offices, issue voucher booklets and process the transfers and bids.

Through the mass privatization program Bulgarian citizens will become shareholders in 1,063 of Bulgaria's largest and most important firms. Of the country's flagship enterprises, 200 will offer under half of their capital. Another 346 enterprises will privatize between one-half and two-thirds of their capital; and more than two-thirds of the capital will be privatized in the remaining 517 companies.

At present, 81 privatization funds (PFs) have been registered by the Securities and Stock Exchange Commission. The PFs have collected Investment Bonds from the population and are exchanging them for shares of privatized companies at Investment Bond auctions. Beside participation in auctions the PFs are also entitled to acquire other tradable securities, including government bonds, corporate bonds, and company stock. According to privatization fund legislation, funds can:
- act as the main financial intermediaries for the transfer of state-owned companies to the population;
- improve corporate governance by actively monitoring the companies in their portfolios;
- ultimately, once the mass privatization auctions have ended, help raise capital for further restructuring efforts.

The PFs will have significant freedom of choice when investing in listed securities, but are restricted in investing in possibly riskier assets such as real estate and unlimited liability partnerships.

Cash Privatization

The cash privatization program started with the enactment of the Law on Transformation and Privatization of State-Owned and Municipal Enterprises on 23 April 1992. In June 1994 the law was supplemented with regulations regarding mass privatization by investment vouchers.

The law divides the responsibility for the implementation of privatization among the different authorities:
- Branch ministries and committees for state-owned enterprises with a book value of fixed assets up to around BGL 70 million (US$ 1 million).
- The Privatization Agency – for state-owned enterprises with a book value of fixed assets exceeding BGL 70 million (US$ 1 million).
- The Privatization Agency, following the approval of the Council of

Ministers for some of the state-owned core companies.
- The Municipal Councils for privatization of municipal enterprises on their respective municipal territory.
- The Center for Mass Privatization responsible to the Council of Ministers for privatization by investment vouchers.

This model aims at opening parallel strata for privatization deals as well as ensuring relative independence in negotiating specific contracts.

The following methods are applied to the transfer of ownership: public offering of shares, auction, tender or negotiations with potential buyers. Foreign investors can participate using flexible schemes such as:
- purchasing a company by themselves;
- joint purchase with Bulgarian investors;
- joint purchase with employee/management partnership.

In conformity with Bulgarian legislation, up to 20% of the shares and stakes of a company are to be offered initially to the employees and management, but in practice the preferential purchasing right over those stakes is not always fully utilized.

The privatization price is determined by the downpayment, the investment commitments, and the liabilities assumed over or settled by the buyers of the company. In negotiating the price of a transaction, the Privatization Agency attempts to secure the resources for the future restructuring and development of the privatized company.

The present Bulgarian legislation offers an implicit subsidy to investors in privatization, by the use of debt swaps. Bulgarian Brady bonds and internal ZUNK bonds can be used as instruments for such payments. The amount of a swap, however, is restricted to 50% of the privatization deal. From the Brady bonds, DISCs are accepted at their nominal value, while the FLIRBs are accepted at half of their nominal value. ZUNKs can serve with 140% of their nominal value as a means of privatization payment. At their current market price of about 90% of the nominal, this gives a 36% advantage of paying with ZUNKs compared with the 50% advantage of paying with the Brady bonds. Despite the fact that there is no restriction on the proportion of ZUNKs in the privatization payment so that they can finance the whole deal, foreign investors usually prefer a combination of cash and Brady bond payment.

The Law for Transformation and Privatization of State-owned and Municipal-owned Enterprises and the Law for Foreign Investments provide various options for investments in the country, such as privatization, green-field investment, various forms of cooperation, joint ventures and portfolio investment. According to the Foreign Investment Agency, foreign direct investments (FDI) within the period 1991 – 15 December 1995 amounted to US$ 531 million. FDI in the three quarters of 1996 was US$ 484 million, bringing the cumulative total since 1991 to around US$ 1 billion. According to this account, Germany is the largest investor, followed by Switzerland, Belgium, Greece, and the US.

FINANCIAL MARKETS

Equity Markets

Up to the middle of 1995 the financial markets served not only the monetary, fiscal, and budgetary policies but also the needs of the banking sector with regard to financial intermediation, credit availability, and the refinancing of economic agents.

The penetration of local private capital into the financial market has been supported by different forms of financial intermediation. Starting from exchange bureaux and financial houses, private capital expanded into the creation of private banks, financial holding groups, investment funds, and private stock exchanges incorporated as shareholding companies under the Commercial Law.

During this initial period of capital market formation many securities trading rules were based upon self-regulatory schemes which caused the trade with securities to be plagued with high risks and uncertainties. A typical example of the risks involved in such unregulated trading is the loss suffered in 1995 by more than 100,000 people as a result of their financial involvement in speculative pyramidal structures.

The lack of legislation concerning the above activities has been corrected by new restrictions on trade in securities and on financial intermediaries, introduced in 1995. Under these provisions a Securities and Stock Exchange Commission (SSEC) was established in January 1996 to supervise the operations and regulate the institutional environment of privatization. The high capital requirements set by the Securities, Stock Exchanges and Investment Companies Law forced the existing 14 private stock exchanges to merge, so that by the middle of 1996 the all-Bulgarian Stock Exchange located in Sofia was inaugurated. At present a computerized securities trading system is being installed so as to be ready for the expected trading of 'mass privatized' company shares later in 1997.

Despite the existence of a regulatory framework for stock exchanges during 1996 there has been a sharp decline in trading. The lack of investors' interest can be explained, among other factors, by bank bankruptcies. The growing riskiness of equity investments increased the buy-sell margin on the over-the-counter market by 80%–200% for all shares. For many of the shares the prices range between 50% and 10% under the nominal par value (Tables 2.2 and 2.3).

Table 2.3. Prices of selected OTC securities as of July 1996

Bank	Par value, BGL	Over-the-counter prices, BGL (selected financial brokers), as of 15 July 1996					
		Lady VSM		Benefis		Vi-Vesta	
		Buy	Sell	Buy	Sell	Buy	Sell
Balkanbank*	1000	n.a.	1500	500	1100	980	1280
Biochim	1000	n.a.	800	600	950	780	1050
United Bulgarian Bank	1000	720	900	600	790	780	930
Economic Bank*	1000	n.a.	1300	700	1200	1050	1430

Note: *Banks put into liquidation on 24 September 1996.
Source: Capital Press, July 1996.

The companies in the non-financial sector are the ones which are regularly traded, not only over-the-counter but also on the country's stock exchanges. The buy – sell margin for these companies varies between 10 and 200% . What is noticeable, however, is the significant difference between the sale prices and the par value of the shares, which indicates a credibility failure on the part of the companies who have issued the stock.

The Reuters All-Bulgarian Stock Index (RABSI) starting at a 100 base (see Figure 2.2), and established on the secondary market-traded stock of eight financial and non-financial companies, has been in a continuous decline since February 1996, reaching 41.23 points in mid-July, which is the lowest rate since it was initiated.

Contrary to the basic capital market rule that the interest on an investment rises with its risk, company stock was far surpassed in returns by government securities. This can be explained by the low trading volumes of company stocks caused by very high real interest rates. Specifically, in order to be able to pay a dividend equal to the basic interest rate, which in mid-1996 was 108%, and after paying a profit tax of 36%, the company would have to finish the year with a profit before tax equal to 168%. For this reason listed companies are unwilling to issue new stock, or to increase their capital, hence diverting potential investment away from the private sector.

Table 2.4. Prices of stock exchange and over-the-counter traded securities of selected non-financial stock

Company	Stock exchange prices (July 95 – July 96)		Over-the-counter prices (BGL, selected brokers, 15 July 1996)					
			Lady VSM		Benefis		Vi-Vesta	
	min	max	Buy	Sell	Buy	Sell	Buy	Sell
Grand Hotel Varna (100)	50	90	80	85	75	n.a.	70	78
Trakia Commerce 2nd issue (100)	36	75	n.a.	40	10	25	55	65
IF Razvitie 2nd issue (100)	70	103	n.a.	115	50	75	n.a.	93
IF Razvitie 3rd issue (100)	30	100	24	51	25	39	n.a.	80
TBS Hotels 1st issue (1000)	100	550	75	200	79	n.a.	110	160
TBS Hotels 2nd issue (1000)	100	600	75	200	79	n.a.	110	160

Note: Par value in brackets (in BGL).
Source: Capital Press, July 1996.

In order to be able to accommodate the significant trading of shares expected to be generated by the mass privatization program, the current system of trading on the stock exchange is being regulated and restructured.

The Securities and Exchange Commission (SSEC) has set clear rules for the first auction of the mass privatization which is to be carried out before November 1996. At the end of October 1996 the SSEC made some efforts to impose a degree of discipline on the stock markets before the trade with privatization shares began. Following the failure by listed public companies to comply with the regulation to submit to the SSEC a detailed report on the size and distribution of their capital and shareholders, the Commission suspended floor trading on corporate stocks until the requirement was met.

During the second half of 1996 the Government, the Central Bank and the SSEC established a Central Depository, having as its main function the registering of property transfers during the privatization process and the recording of all stock transactions thereafter.

The main traders at the mass privatization auctions will be the registered 81 Privatization Funds. Active trading is expected to take place before the end

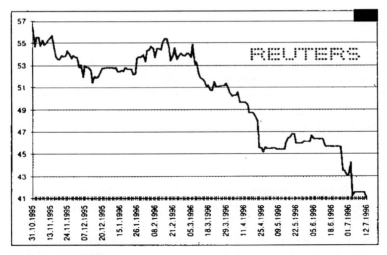

Source: Kapital, No. 28, 1996.

Figure 2.2. The Reuters All-Bulgarian Stock Index (RABSI)

of 1997 as both individuals and funds are not allowed to trade shares for six months after the end of the last voucher-based auction.

For the time being both the slow development of the privatization process and the increased indebtedness of the economy is directing the activities at the capital markets predominantly towards the financing of the government's internal and external debt and of the budget deficit.

Bond Markets

Government securities are the most common debt instruments transacted on the Bulgarian market. Their characteristics – low risk because of the Treasury guarantee and an unusually high yield – make them suitable for various purposes, e.g. financing of the national budget deficit, manipulation of the money market through the injection and extraction of liquidity, securing loans, etc. Government securities proved to be the only opportunity for private and institutional investors to place their savings at a positive interest rate.

The shortage of foreign financing and the limited domestic market for government bonds has severely narrowed the government's options for financing the budget deficit. The budget is therefore also financed through transfers from the Bulgarian National Bank (BNB) and loans from domestic banks. The limited financing options available place increased importance on containing the budget deficit in order to reduce inflationary pressures and on the role of the markets for government securities.

The issue of government securities and their purchases by the banking and non-banking institutions as well as by the public have become the main sources of funds to cover the net credit needs of the government. This has substantially increased the domestic public debt. The total public debt reached 122.3% of GDP by the end of 1995. The domestic debt has two main components: the bad loans and losses of state-owned enterprises; and payments related to the accumulated budget deficit.

The primary market for government securities was initiated in 1991 by the sale of government securities at auctions organized by the National Bank. The development of the government securities market went through three main stages:

1. The issue of short-term treasury bills that were sold par nominal at 8–10 points higher than the primary interest rate in order to make them competitive with the interest deposits offered by the relatively stable banks at that time. Towards the end of 1991 short-term liabilities in the Treasury bills increased to 10.6% of the domestic debt.

2. As of the beginning of 1992 the Ministry of Finance kept its minimum offer for the treasury bills (t-bills) at a rate below the primary one. Because of the unfavourable interest rates the commercial banks did not purchase them and the issues were absorbed solely by the State Savings Bank (SSB), i.e. it has been reported that around 70% of its portfolio consists of t-bills. The public's saving deposits are concentrated in the SSB as it is the only state-owned bank where these deposits are insured, hence the public's deposits through the Savings bank have been directly involved in financing both the state budget deficit and the domestic public debt.

3. During 1993–1995 interest rates on the t-bills were increased in an attempt to make them attractive to the commercial banks and by effectuating a 'secondary market' to foster the resale of securities to the general public.

For example, in mid-1996 the government securities traded on the stock exchanges offered a monthly interest rate of between 10.73% and 13.30%, which was 1.73% to 4.30% higher than the base interest rate fixed by the Central Bank and attracted investors' interest to a low-risk instrument with relatively good returns. An additional impetus came from the banking crisis which so reduced private investor's confidence in the banking system that they redirected large amounts of savings to the purchase of government securities. As a result, during June 1996 private investors bought government securities for BGL 5.8 billion and companies have bought government securities for BGL 41.5 billion.

Express issues

The express issues are of three types: three-month t-bills (discount) and six- and twelve-month t-bills (interest-bearing). The yield of the last two is linked to the base interest rate. At the end of the first and the beginning of the second quarter of 1996 the most popular issues were the discount, fixed-yield bills. This was because of fears (which were realized) that base interest rates would be lowered. In August 1996 six-month issues were selling best because of the tax concessions to which sole trading companies are entitled. Foreign investment in Bulgarian government securities amounted to BGL 3 billion at the end of August 1996. Since the period of internal instability and exchange rate fluctuation in September, this amount has diminished by 10% to BGL 2.7 billion.Since most of the securities were bought at an exchange rate of 190 BGL per US$, the Lev's depreciation to 230 at the end of September resulted in 20% losses for foreign investors.

The collapse of the state-owned enterprises' (SOE) manufacturing output and the accumulation by them of both non-performing loans and inter-enterprise arrears, with the attendant fall in tax revenue, is leading to a considerable erosion of government revenues. The accumulated losses of SOE and private enterprises for the period 1992–1995 reached BGL 387.7 billion (US$ 2 billion at the exchange rate as of 1 September). In addition to the need to cover SOE losses, the reform of the financial sector will cost the budget an estimated US$ 1.7 billion. The budget will be burdened by interest payments on government bonds issued to replace the banks' bad liabilities. A further burden was imposed by the increases in the simple base interest rate, first to 25% per month in September 1996, then reduced to 20% in October, in a bid to curb inflation and support the local currency. Following the rise in the base rate, the first placement by the Finance Ministry of coupon t-bills at par value of BGL 3.016 billion has taken place on 2 October 1996. The yield to maturity on 23 December 1996 was set by the National Bank of Bulgaria (BNB) at 68.24%, and the average accepted price was BGL 99.50.

This sharp rise in the base interest rate has resulted in a corresponding leap in interest in the portfolio instruments of companies and individuals. This temporary relief of the government budget's debt will, however, place unbearable pressure on the budget at the time of the bonds' maturity if these interest rates are maintained at the same level for a long period.

Internal debt: ZUNK bonds

The first attempt at the management of the internal debt crisis and stabilization of the banking system came at the end of 1993, with the adoption of the Law for Settling the Non-performing Credits incurred up to December 1990 (with

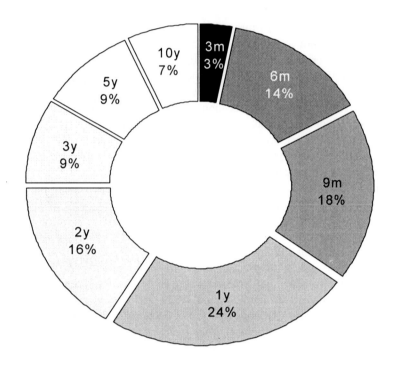

Note: up to 15 April 1996.
Source: Bulgarian National Bank, 1996.

Figure 2.3. Term structure of government securities

a Bulgarian acronym ZUNK).

As a consequence there followed issues of long-term BGL bonds with a nominal value of BGL 26.383 billion, an amortization term of 25 years with a 5-year grace period, and equal amortization disbursements. The bad debts incurred in foreign currency were covered with an issue of 25-year long-term bonds, denominated in US$, at US$ 1.808 billion nominal. They have a 5-year grace period and bear an interest of 6-month LIBOR for the same period. The main use of these ZUNK bonds was as a means of payment in the privatization deals or as collateral by the banks when loans were refinanced by the Bulgarian National Bank.

Although the ZUNK law targeted a balanced distribution of liabilities between the debtor enterprises, the banks and the budget, it did not produce the expected results, since the banks were burdened by new bad debts. The redistribution which followed resulted in a growing transfer of liabilities to the state budget. The transformation and redistribution of debt did not compensate for the lack of structural reform policies to do with the liquidation of the loss-making enterprises, but merely increased the government debt.

Table 2.5. The ZUNK market from January to October 1995

	October 1995	*January – October 1995*
Number of transactions	266	1992
Amount traded (BGL bn)	86.5	636.2
Sold to private investors and firms (BGL bn)	3.4	17.2
Average price of ZUNK (for BGL 1000 face value)	930.52	853.65
Average price of ZUNK (for US$ 100 face value)	102.6	n.a.

Source: Authors' interviews with several Bulgarian brokers, April 1996.

Initially, the ZUNK bonds were held and traded by eight Bulgarian banks. The deteriorating liquidity status of some of these banks, like Mineralbank and Economic Bank, led to schemes for bond conversion of their ZUNKs into government securities which could be resold more easily on the secondary market. A total of ZUNK bonds of US$ 824.3 million nominal value were withdrawn from the eight banks, leaving for the time being just one major holder of ZUNK bonds – Bulbank. The inter-bank market accounted for 97.3% of the trading volume in ZUNKs for the first ten months of 1995. The volume of trade to private investors was BGL 17.2 billion or 2.7% of the total (Table 2.5). 92.7% of the ZUNKs purchased by private investors have been allocated as portfolio instruments and the rest were used as payment in privatization deals. Similarly, 78% of the US$ 13.2 million of US$-denominated ZUNKs are held by investors and 22% have been spent on privatization deals.

Initially, the ZUNK bonds were traded on the interbank market at prices below par value, hence most of the banks who received ZUNKs under the government's debt settlement program incurred losses. With the aim of enhancing the bonds' liquidity, at the same time increasing investors' enthusiasm for privatization, the government introduced a premium of 40% on the value of ZUNK bonds used as a means of payment specifically related to privatization deals.

Table 2.6. BGL and US$-denominated ZUNK bonds

	BGL ZUNK bonds pur-chased	BGL ZUNK bonds used in privatization	US$ ZUNK bonds pur-chased	US$ ZUNK bonds used in privatization
1994	3.130 bn	1.523 bn	N/A.	N/A
01–08/1995	10.832 bn	1.134 bn	8.3 mn	1.063 mn
Total	*13.962 bn*	*2.657 bn*	*8.3 mn*	*1.063 mn*

Source: Authors' interviews with several Bulgarian brokers, April 1996.

The introduction of this premium, which increased the demand for ZUNKs, allowed the banks (as primary holders) to offer higher selling prices, which balanced past losses incurred by the sale of bonds with negligible profit margins. After the new regulation some banks even started offering ZUNKs at prices above face value. This encouraged the banks to trade them more actively. Until end of August 1995, ZUNK bonds with a total nominal value of BGL 2.657 billion and US$ 1 million have been used as instruments in privatization, redeeming government debt with the same value (Table 2.6).

EXTERNAL DEBT

The Restructuring of Bulgarian London Club Debt

In June 1994 Bulgaria and its international creditor banks settled on a debt-restructuring scheme involving about US$ 8.4 billion arrears, repayment of which was beyond the power of Bulgaria's financial system. The purpose of the settlement was a 48% reduction of the country's obligations to the London Club of creditors. US$ 6.4 billion of capital arrears and US$ 2.1 billion of interest arrears were the subject of negotiation and transformation. Three instruments were used to transform the capital arrears: debt-buy-back, discount bonds and par bonds. The interest arrears were partially written off (US$ 200 million) and the rest were either bought back or transformed into interest arrears bonds. Thus, the three types of bonds issued according to this agreement were: interest arrears bonds (IABs); discount bonds (DISCs); and front-loaded, interest-reduction bonds (FLIRBs). The main features of these bonds, summarized in Table 2.6, are described below.

The Main Features of Bulgarian Brady Bonds

IABs are bonds with a maturity of 17 years and semi-annual interest payment issued both as registered and bearer notes. They are the riskiest of all Bulgarian Bradies as they have no guarantee either of interest payments or of the principal.

DISCs have registered a 30-year bullet amortization issued at discount (or at discount to original face value of the sovereign loan). Their coupons are paid semi-annually and their interest has a floating rate pegged to the LIBOR. Bulgarian DISCs have rolling interest guarantees from 12 to 18 months (every 2 to 3 coupon payments) which cover the interest payments for this period. When the period ends and the coupon is paid, the collateral associated with that coupon rolls forward to cover the next period until maturity. Payment of interest is partially secured by US$-denominated AAA securities in an amount sufficient to cover 12 months' interest at an assumed rate of 7% per year. There are additional interest payments which would take effect if Bulgaria's GDP increases beyond a certain point. Their principal is collaterized by 30-year United States Treasury zero-coupon bonds and other full faith and credit obligations of the United States government.

FLIRBs are 18-year amortizing semi-annual bonds payable to the bearer. Initially, they are offered with a fixed below market coupon rate which is replaced by a LIBOR market rate after the seventh year until maturity. The 12-month rolling guarantees of the interest payments are available only during the first six years. There are no guarantees for the principal.

The Market for Bulgarian Brady Bonds

Several financial companies, such as Eurobrokers, Tullet & Tokyo, ING Capital, Chemical Bank, Deutsche Morgan Grenfell, SBC Warburg, Salomon Brothers, and others, are the prominent market makers on the Brady bonds market. Investors should contact these companies for daily quotations for the prices of Bulgarian Brady bonds. Because of the US$ 250,000 face value (see Table 2.6) Bulgarian Bradies are mostly held and traded by international investors. Due to their high risk premium and discounted price they are mostly used as portfolio diversification tools.

The current risk rating issued by Moody's is B3 for the Bulgarian foreign currency bonds and notes, Caa for foreign currency-denominated long-term bank deposits, and *not prime* for short-term obligations of issuers residing in Bulgaria. Moreover Moody's has assigned B3 ratings to approximately US$ 5 billion of Bulgaria's outstanding bond obligations. The reason behind these ratings were: (1) poor financial stability leading to a minimal guarantee of punctual, long-term repayments; (2) the credit rating of Caa for long-term dollar-denominated bank deposits suggests a probability of dividend payments with no guarantees for the future; (3) the increasing concern regarding the increase of foreign debt servicing against GDP, the rising share of debt servicing, and the growth of the share of foreign debt servicing in budget expenditure.

These factors as well as the relatively low level of foreign exchange reserves increase the probability of default on interest payments.

Bulgarian investors are represented by a few Bulgarian banks who offer high-interest-yielding US$ savings products based on returns from Brady bonds. The Bulgarian investments related to these instruments have for the past two years been estimated at US$ 100 million.

There are no official statistics for the Brady Bond trading volumes. Unofficial estimates for 1995 vary between US$ 500 and US$ 700 million per week. The major share of this volume belongs to the Latin American Brady Bonds and especially those issued by the three big debtors: Mexico, Brazil, and Argentina. Trade with Bulgarian Bradies amounts to 4.5% of this volume or US$ 22.5 and US$ 31.5 million weekly turnover. This ratio is higher than the percentage of Bulgarian external debt from the total debt of all Brady issuing countries. Therefore, the interest in Bulgarian Bradies as portfolio instruments is above the average.

Bulgarian Brady Bond's Prices and Price Influencing Factors

Up to mid-1996 the prices of Bulgarian Bradies have followed general market trends and fluctuations, because of the lack of close international monitoring of the economic situation in the country and the relatively small market capitalization share of Bulgaria Brady bonds from the Brady market: US$ 2.02 billion or 2% of the total Brady bond debt traded. The deterioration in the economic situation in Bulgaria during the second half of 1996 and especially suspicions of a Brady debt default have had a negative effect on the prices of the Bulgarian Bradies.

Quotations are made daily by different market makers. Recently there has been a tendency for an increased correlation between the prices quoted for other East European (Bulgarian, Polish and Russian) debt and Bulgarian Brady bonds (see Figure 2.4) as well as for separation of their price dynamics from those of the Latin American countries. The main price-influencing factors include:
- the risk estimate and the risk premium assigned to it;
- the price of the 30-year US zero coupon bonds which is serving as a

Table 2.7. Features of Bulgarian DISCs, FLIRBs and IABs

	DISC	FLIRB	IAB
Size of the issue	US$ 1.85 bn Tranche A: US$ 1.685 bn Tranche B: US$ 0.165 bn	US$ 1.658 bn Tranche A: US$ 1.489 bn Tranche B: US$ 0.169 bn	US$ 1.611 bn
Form	Registered notes	Bearer notes	Registered and bearer notes
Denomination	US$ 250,000	US$ 250,000	US$ 250,000
Date of issue/maturity	28 July 1994/28 July 2024	28 July 1994/28 July 2012	28 July 1994/28 July 2011
Interest	Tranche A: 6m LIBOR + 13/16% p.a. Tranche B: as above + 0.5% p.a.	Tranche A: Years 1 & 2: 2.0% p.a. Years 3 & 4: 2.25% p.a. Year 5: 2.5% p.a. Year 6: 2.75% p.a. Year 7: 3.0% p.a. Years 8 and 18: 6m LIBOR + 13/16% p.a. Tranche B: as above + 0.5% p.a.	6m LIBOR + 13/16%
Payment of the principal	disbursed in full upon maturity	8-year grace period; 21 equal semi-annual instalments, beginning 29 July 2002	7-year grace period; 21 growing semi-annual instalments, beginning on 31 July 2001; mandatory sinking schedule
Guarantees 1. On principal 2. On coupons	1. 30-year US Bond with 0% coupon 2. yearly renewable guarantee up to an interest rate of 7%	2. yearly renewable guarantee up to an interest rate of 3%	None

Source: Foreign Investment Agency (1996).

61

collateral for the DISCs (43% of the price) and for the FLIRBs (7% of the price);

- the general price development for all traded Brady instruments and particularly for those of their main market – Latin America;
- the opportunity to use Brady bonds for debt-equity swaps in the mass and cash privatization will probably both increase the demand for Bulgarian Bradies and change their price/return ratio.

Table 2.8 shows Bulgarian Brady bonds prices as of 31 October 1996.

Table 2.8. Daily spot prices for Bulgarian Brady bonds, as a percentage of their face value

	DISCs	*FLIRBs*	*IABs*
Bid price	50.313	31.750	43.500

Source: JP Morgan, Emerging Market Index Monitor, 31/10/1996.

There has been a trend towards a stable price development of Bulgarian Brady Bonds for the second half of 1995 when the Bulgarian economy seemed to have stabilized and the foreign exchange reserves had grown to US$ 1.4 billion. The biggest shock for the Brady market for 1995 was the Mexican crisis in the beginning of the year. This led to a withdrawal of investments and a sharp decline in the price of all Bradies. Bulgarian Bradies recorded their lowest prices at that time. However, by the end of 1995, prices have recovered and increased by 45% for the IABs, 33% for the DISCs, and 81% for the FLIRBs. Since the beginning of 1996, the recurrent problems in Bulgaria's financial and real sectors and the rapid depletion of the foreign reserves have led to an increased volatility in Bulgarian Brady bonds' prices and returns. The bonds' price fluctuations depend on the extent to which they are collateralized (see also Table 2.7). The price of the uncollateralized IABs, for example, is most likely to react to suspicions of default, while the price of those with the best guarantees, the DISCs, is likely to remain more or less stable.

Among the factors that influence the prices of Bulgarian Brady bonds are Bulgaria's relations with the IMF and the receipt of a Fund for Economic and Structural Adjustment loan from the World Bank in order to avoid a new moratorium on debt payments. Without significant financial assistance from the IMF, at the time of the current proposal for the introduction of a currency board in Bulgaria, it will be impossible for the country to sustain a 100% foreign reserve to local currency and at the same time meet all payment obligations for 1997.

Rates of Return, Risk Premia and Ratings of Bulgarian Brady Bonds

The international financial brokerage company JP Morgan, as one of the prominent market makers on the Brady bond market, has established an Emerging Markets Bond Index Plus (EMBI+) which tracks the yields on traded external debt instruments and includes:

1. external-currency-denominated Brady bonds;
2. the primary market for external debts and Eurobonds;
3. discounted country level instruments nominated in US$ (ZUNKs in the Bulgarian case).

In addition to listing the available instruments and serving as a benchmark for market trends, the EMBI+ provides an indicator for the rating of different emerging markets for forex debt and the terms of trade and returns on investment in Bradies. The index is based on the actual volume and prices of the broker-traded debt instruments as quoted by several market makers and takes into account only those issues with volumes above US$ 500 million.

Figure 2.4 below shows the development of the EMBI+ index of the Russian, Polish and Bulgarian Brady bonds. After the turbulent period in the middle of 1994 for the Bulgarian Bradies there has been an index growth of up to 160 over the period February 1995 – February 1996. Thereafter uncertainties regarding debt repayments have led to fairly marked oscillations with a downward trend.

The returns on Brady bonds are of two main types – long-term (on maturity) and short-term (on coupon interest and price).

The long-term returns are calculated as the ratio between the acquisition price and the interest rate to maturity. Due to Bulgaria's poor international credit rating, as mentioned above, such speculative debt instruments as Bradies may be traded only at a substantial discount from their nominal value. Hence the relationship of the current prices to the return at maturity which includes the principal plus interest is negatively correlated – the higher the price at which the Bradies are purchased, the lower the return on maturity.

The long-term return for IABs, for example, is 18.7% at the associated price level of 45.5% of their face value. The difference between these 18.7% and the 6.2% of AAA US Treasury bonds gives the risk premium, which in this case is 12.5%. There is a reciprocal relation between the risk premium and the Bradies' price – a fall in the risk premium is equivalent to an increase in Brady prices. The decrease of the risk premium by 3–5% since 1994, for example, has led to an increase in price. Usually, it is bonds with an overestimated credit risk and a large discount from the nominal which offer such opportunities.

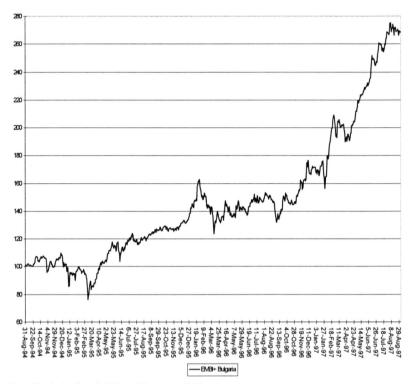

Note: The index base is 100 on 31 August 1994.
Source: JP Morgan (1997).

Figure 2.4. EMBI+ for Bulgarian Bradies

CONCLUSION

The current (short-term) returns (see Table 2.9) are based on the payments on
the interest coupons and the changes in the price of the Brady bonds. For
reasons already explained, the monthly current returns on the FLIRBs and the
IABs have been decreasing. The yield to date returns on the FLIRBs, however,
are almost twice as high as for the other two types of bond. During 1995
investors were interested mainly in the two former types of Bulgarian Brady
bonds. According to international brokers IABs have yielded a spread of 400
basis points (1 basis point = 0.01%) over the course of 1995. The total return
on IABs from the beginning of 1995 has been almost 33%. However, skilful
investors have managed to extract returns amounting to 41.33% on DISCs

using a shrewd combination of fund-raising and hedging techniques. The present instability in the Bulgarian economy, however, is likely to increase the risk of holding uncollateralized IABs and partially collateralized DISCs, and the negative tendency in their returns will continue.

Table 2.9. Returns on Bulgarian Brady bonds

	Total return			1-month return compo-nents end September/end October 1996			Return volatility for the period of (months)		
	% change over (months)			Price index	Return (%)				
	1	YTD	12		Price	Inter-est	1	3	12
Bulgaria average	-1.22	5.18	13.91	110.55	-2.36	1.17	16.08	20.42	24.24
DISCs	0.7	3.9	12.16	–	-0.25	1.2	11.04	14.64	19.14
FLIRBs	-1.67	9.88	20.91	–	-0.75	0.65	25.79	31.31	37.72
IABs	-2.97	3.98	11.99	–	-2	1.49	18.25	22.66	25.27

Source: JP Morgan, Emerging Markets Bond Index Monitor, October 1996.

During the first half of 1996 following an initial wave of active development in 1993–1994, marked by the establishment of a number of stock exchanges, stock trading companies, private banks and financial intermediaries, Bulgarian capital markets suffered badly from the most severe banking crisis since the beginning of transition. The investors' attention, both on secondary and primary market levels, was diverted from company stock and private initiatives to the more secure and rewarding government securities. Although this had a positive effect on the financing of government debt and the budget, this was at the expense of cash privatization and long-term capital investment.

Hopes for future activation of the capital markets hinge on the success of the mass and cash privatization processes as well as the privatization and restructuring of the ailing banking sector. The participation of large Bulgarian financial groups, such as the privatization funds and other holding companies, and, most of all, of foreign investors is expected to re-establish the credibility of the stock markets among middle and small investors and thus revitalize both the primary and secondary markets for enterprise and bank-related securities. This will probably balance the interest between the government and private investment, which will have a positive effect on the capital investments and the economy as a whole.

REFERENCES

Balabanov, T., D. Grozea-Helmenstein, T. Houbenova, B. Vladimirov, and A. Wörgötter (1996): *Investment Opportunities in Bulgaria*, Study commissioned by Bank Austria, Institute for Advanced Studies, Vienna.

Banker Weekly (1996), no. 38, September, p.11.

Business Central Europe (1995): *The Annual*, p. 37.

Foreign Investment Agency (1996): *Investor's Guide to Privatization with Debt Swaps in Bulgaria*, EBRD, London and Sofia.

Frankfurter Allgemeine Zeitung Informationsdienste (1996): *Osteuropa-Perspektiven Jahrbuch 1996/97*, vols. 1 & 2, *Frankfurter Allgemeine Zeitung*, Frankfurt/Main.

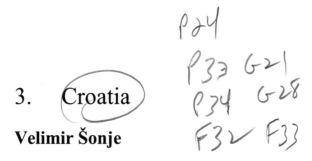

P 24

P 33 G 21

P 34 G 28

F 32 F 33

3. Croatia

Velimir Šonje

INTRODUCTION

In the past three years, Croatia has accomplished a most remarkable stabilization record. Since the end of 1993, the exchange rate has fluctuated within a
narrow band, and the end-year rate of consumer price inflation was -3% in
1994 and 3.7% in 1995. Although the unfavourable wartime and political
environment was an obstacle to growth and deeper capital market development,
economic activity has picked up since 1994 (GDP real growth was 1% in 1994
and 2% in 1995). The signing of the Dayton Agreement by neighbouring
Bosnia and Herzegovina, and the peaceful reintegration of Eastern Slavonia
(the only remaining occupied region at the Eastern border with Serbia) will
undoubtedly enhance the economic effects of stabilization and reforms carried
out in the period 1992–1995.

MONETARY POLICY

Under the Law on the National Bank of Croatia (NBC), the Central Bank is an
independent institution whose prime purpose is to foster a stable currency and
liquidity in domestic and international payments. There is no conflict of
interest between stability and growth embodied in its basic provisions, and
there is a clear collective preference towards stability as stated in the legislation.[1] In addition, the Governor is elected by the parliament for a period of six
years, two years longer than the election cycle. The independence of the
Central Bank is further strengthened by the council of the NBC. Members of

---

[1] Potential conflict arises, at least theoretically, between stability and domestic liquidity. However,
concern about liquidity in domestic payments has always been interpreted as a concern about the regular
functioning of the domestic payments system.

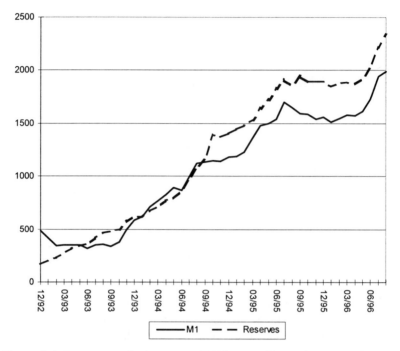

*Figure 3.1. International reserves and US$ equivalents of M1 in US$
millions*

the council are also elected for a six-year period,[2] and it is clearly stated that
the members should be 'independent experts'. Finally, long-term loans to the
government are forbidden in law. The law allows only short-term financing of
government expenditures, up to 5% of the budget in the relevant year. All these
loans have to be repaid within the fiscal year, and their purpose is to 'bridge'
a short-term discrepancy between public revenues and expenditures caused by
seasonal factors. These loans are usually extended monthly.

    Since 1992 interventions on the foreign exchange market have been the
main monetary policy instrument, for two reasons. First, the foreign exchange
reserves of the National Bank of former Yugoslavia were frozen by Belgrade,
and the NBC was founded without any international reserves in its portfolio.
The main monetary policy target in 1992 and 1993 was the accumulation of
international reserves, regardless of rapid exchange rate depreciation and high

---

[2] The exact dates of the election of individual members of the Council do not coincide with the election
date of the Governor.

inflation. Indeed, the international reserves of the NBC amounted to US$ 500 million before October 1993, when the stabilization program was announced. At the same time, the decline in real money supply during 1992 and 1993 was so sharp that NBC's international reserves at the end of October 1993 exceeded the US dollar equivalent of M1 by 32.7%. Only a minor part of the decrease in real money was due to a reduction in real GDP. The major part was caused by a sharp increase in money velocity driven by the currency substitution, common in all high inflation cases.[3] Hence, the announcement of an exchange-rate-based stabilization program took place at the moment when the money to reserves ratio reached a low level, providing a guarantee for the success of an exchange-rate-based program. Money demand recovered strongly immediately after the announcement, and monetary authorities were faced with a different set of options thereafter: either to expand the money supply, or to let the nominal exchange rate appreciate. The second reason for the accumulation of international reserves can be found in the post-stabilization period. Since mid-1993, and especially since the successful exchange rate stabilization and disinflation in late 1993, foreign exchange inflows into the country have been boosted, and NBC had to intervene by buying out foreign exchange in order to prevent a huge nominal appreciation of the exchange rate.[4]

One of the key factors in explaining such a sharp change in the behavior of the exchange rate is the change in the exchange rate regime. In the prestabilization period international reserves were accumulated on the basis of an administrative regulation which required commercial banks to sell 35% of their foreign exchange inflows to the NBC. New foreign exchange legislation that allowed free foreign exchange market and current account convertibility was adopted in October 1993 (it was the central part of the stabilization package), and Croatia adopted IMF's Article VIII in May 1995. Prior to October 1993, citizens could only sell hard currency to commercial banks, but starting from October 1993 hard currency has been freely traded, which explains how it was possible to achieve credibility within one month of the beginning of the program.

---

[3] M1 velocity reached its extreme value, 27 (annual level), in the end of October 1993.

[4] The strength of the inflows was due to reverse currency substitution. Private sector accumulated hard currency foreign exchange which was either held in cash or transferred to West European banks during the years of high inflation and wartime. Starting from the end of 1993, reversal of these flows put a strong pressure on domestic currency to appreciate. Indeed, the present level of the exchange rate vs. Deutsche mark, which is the referent rate in Croatia, is 19.9% stronger in nominal terms than the rate at the beginning of stabilization.

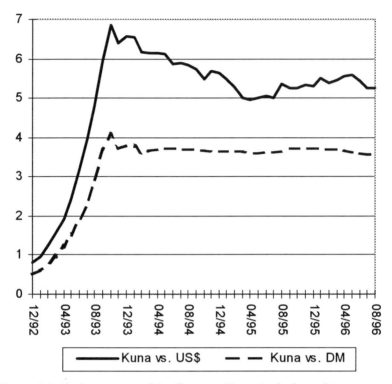

Figure 3.2. Exchange rate of the Croatian Kuna (end of month)

The accumulation of NBC's international reserves continued after stabilization, and the money supply continued to grow at a high rate, while at the same time prices and exchange rates remained stable. The velocity of M1 declined from 27 (annual level) at the beginning of stabilization, to 10 in mid-1996. In addition, NBC sterilized some of the effects of foreign exchange interventions. In late 1994 and 1995 NBC relied extensively on reserve requirements, since financial markets were not developed enough to support the required sterilization by open market operations. The rate of reserve requirements increased from 28.9% at the end of 1994 to the maximum of 41.4% at the end of 1995. In 1996, as financial markets developed, reserve requirements began to lose their central role. The rate of reserve requirements fell to 36.7% in August, but the NBC bill, a short-term financial instrument auctioned regularly by the NBC, started to play the central role. The share of the volume of the NBC bills outstanding in M1 increased from 2% at the end of 1995 to 8.8% at the end of August 1996. Consequently, a fundamental change took place in the structure

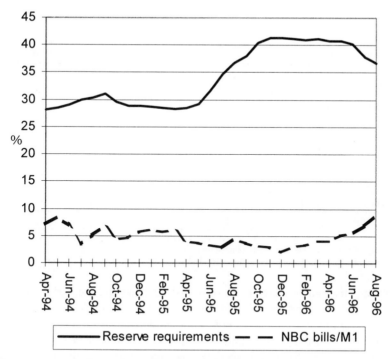

Figure 3.3. Rate of reserve requirements and the share of NBC bills in M1

of NBC's portfolio. The percentage of foreign assets within total assets increased from 0% at the end of 1991 to 94% at the end of 1995 and 97.3% at the end of August 1996.

The share of domestic assets dropped from 100% to 2.7%. Net credits to the government came down from 39% to 0% at the end of 1995 and -2.7% at the end of August 1996, mainly due to the transfer of government deposits from commercial banks to the NBC and also because of sound fiscal policy.[5] The level of international reserves reached US$ 2.3 billion by the end of August 1996 and this corresponds to 12.1% of GDP or three average monthly values of imports of both goods and services.

---

[5] Consolidated government sector recorded an overall surplus of 0.6% of GDP in 1994 and a 1% deficit in 1995.

Table 3.1. Structure of the NBC balance sheet (percentages)

	End Dec. 1991	End Dec. 1995	End Aug. 1996
Assets	100	100	100
Foreign assets	0	94.2	97.3
Domestic assets	100	5.8	2.7
Credits to government	39	3.7	2.6
Credits to banks	61	2.1	0.1
Liabilities	100	100	100
Cash in circulation	44	31.5	32.3
Required and excess reserves	39	32.7	38.2
Government deposits	0	3.7	5.3
Other liabilities*	17	32.1	24.2

Note: *Includes foreign liabilities (IMF's credits), restricted and frozen deposits, deposits of other domestic sectors, capital accounts and other items net.
Source: Author's calculations based on the NBC Bulletin and Main Statistical Indicators.

Monetary instruments have been reformed. General and earmarked quotas (selective refinancing facilities for agriculture and exports) have been the centerpieces of the old monetary policy regime, and they have been phased out during 1993 and replaced by indirect instruments of monetary management. Besides foreign exchange interventions, the lombard credit facility became the most important instrument (starting from 1994). Lombard credit is extended up to 50% of the NBC bills that commercial banks have in their portfolio. The lombard rate has been determined as a mark-up of 1.5% over interest rate on NBC bills, but from August 1996 it has been determined by the council of the NBC in the light of the prevailing market conditions. At present, the rate is set at 11%, which is 3% higher than the interest rate paid on NBC bills and approximately 1%–2% higher than the average interbank money market interest rate. In addition, there is a daily credit which ensures intra-day liquidity. Banks which are not able to cover their position at the interbank money market are forced to use intervention credit. This is a very expensive facility (the interest rate is 19%) that carries penalties for banks, since the bank and its clients have their accounts frozen for as long as the bank has to repay the intervention credit. If intra-month liquidity appears to be extremely volatile, NBC sometimes uses repurchase auctions of NBC bills and foreign exchange.

Table 3.2. End-period annual interest rates and financial ratios (percentages)

	1993	1994	1995	Aug. 1996
Money market interest rate	86.9	17.8	27.2	9.8
35-days NBC bills rate	63.1	12.0	25.5	9.5
Lending rate (kuna credits)*	59.0	15.4	22.3	20.8
Deposit rate (kuna deposits)*	27.4	5.0	6.1	5.5
Deposit rate (foreign currency deposits)*	n.a.	n.a.	4.6	4.2
Interest spread (kuna)*	31.6	10.4	16.2	15.3
Rate of remuneration	2.0	5.6	7.9	6.1
Total kuna deposits/M4	32.6	34.5	28.6	28.5
Total F.C. deposits/M4	53.7	50.2	57.5	58.9

Note: * Lending and deposit rates are weighted averages over all commercial banks, and the interest rate spread is simply the difference between them.
Source: Author's calculations, NBC monthly Bulletin, 1996.

NBC bills are the sterilization instrument developed in order to allow for open market operations, with 7-, 35- and 91-day maturities. This paper is auctioned weekly and its interest rate is market-determined. In times when money market interest rates were very high, the outstanding volume of NBC bills was small. The cost of sterilization implied by high money market interest rates was too high for the NBC, so it decided to rely on reserve requirements, which were remunerated at lower rates. When money market interest rates fell in 1996 (at the beginning of a credible bank rehabilitation process), the NBC bills market developed.

These developments bring interest rates into the forefront of our analysis. All the interest rates reported in Table 3.2 are market-determined (except the rate of remuneration which is set by the NBC). A tax on lending interest rates was imposed for two months in the spring of 1994, being subsequently abolished as policy-makers perceived it to be ineffective.

The end of 1993 data show extremely high interest rates, and a large interest spread because the expectations of market participants did not adjust immediately after exchange rate and price stabilization occurred in November 1993. Nominal interest rates decreased in 1994 thanks to the growing credibility of the program and also to price deflation (real lending interest rates in 1994 were strongly positive, amounting to more than 18%), and then increased again in 1995, mainly due to a rise in inflation (real interest rates rose only marginally compared with 1994). However, it is the interest rates spread that rose significantly in 1995. Šonje, Kraft and Dorsey (1996) found that this was due to very high and increasing overhead administrative expenses in banks, and costs of exchange rate volatility that were passed on to clients.[6] Finally, it should be noted that the share of foreign exchange deposits in total liquid deposits increased in 1995 due to stronger inflow of foreign exchange to domestic bank accounts. The public does not yet have full, long-term confidence in the economic policy, and, consequently, it keeps large parts of its portfolio in foreign currency, mainly in DEM.

Interest rates on domestic public debt instruments vary, depending on the type of instrument. Overall domestic debt is low, and it amounts to 18% of GDP. The main part of it are so-called 'counterparts to blocked foreign exchange deposits'. These foreign exchange deposits accumulated in Croatian banks while Croatia was a member of the ex-Yugoslav federation, and all foreign exchange inflows had to be sold at administrative exchange rates to the National Bank of Yugoslavia. After the break-up of the former state, claims on NBY became non-performing and the Croatian government declared them to be public debt, payable in 20 half-year instalments with 5% annual interest rate (the principal is indexed to the exchange rate). Three-year bonds with 12% and 8.5% annual interest rate were issued recently as a marketable refinancing instrument. In addition, Croatian external debt (after adjustment for the London and Paris Club agreements) amounts to 26% of GDP, so that the overall public indebtedness of about 34% of GDP is relatively low.

In conclusion, the nominal interest rates developments in the post-stabilization period can be classified in four phases. In the first phase, at the very beginning of stabilization, real and nominal interest rates reached high levels due to inertia in the expectations of market participants. In the second phase, during 1994, expectations adjusted and nominal interest rates declined. In the third phase (1995), nominal interest rates and interest spread increased again, mainly due to the lack of credibility of the reforms and the hostile wartime and political environment. Bank rehabilitation lagged behind other macroeconomic reforms, markets remained underdeveloped, and budget priorities were devoted to financing the liberation of occupied regions. The NBC had to rely on reserve requirements instead of open market operations in order to sterilize excess liquidity created by foreign exchange interventions. In the fourth phase (beginning in 1996), credible bank rehabilitation began, money market interest rates dropped (as well as the costs of sterilization), and open market operations

---

[6] Bole (1996) offered a similar explanation for Slovenia, emphasizing exchange rate volatility itself, while Šonje, Kraft and Dorsey (1996) stressed the role of the sudden exchange rate depreciation of the kuna that occurred in September 1995.

took the central role as a main tool of domestic monetary management. Hence, the sequence of phases has been determined largely by the speed of restructuring in the banking sector.

THE BANKING SECTOR

Although, already by 1989, Croatian banks were transformed into joint stock companies (mainly owned by enterprises), they continued to behave unprofitably, as reflected, for example, by lending to related parties. Moral hazard and adverse selection were fuelled by wartime difficulties, leading to a high proportion of non-performing assets in the banks' balance sheets.[7] These have been estimated at almost 50% of the total assets, and some informal estimates involving four 'problem' banks indicated up to 60%–80% of non-performing assets. Moreover, the Croatian financial sector is highly concentrated: the two largest banks (Privredna banka and Zagrebačka banka) comprise 50%–55% of both total assets and total capital.

However, the 1993 Banking Law introduced Western regulatory standards, for example: minimum capital (DEM 15 million for the full licence); capital adequacy ratios in accordance with BIS standards; limits on credit to related parties; limits on investment in buildings, land and equipment; and the obligation to hold an independent audit of accounts. Loan loss provisions became obligatory, and some additional prudential regulation measures have been imposed by the central bank. The most important one is the limit on the foreign exchange exposure which ensures sound banking business in times of strong capital inflows. A limit is set on currency mismatch at 30% of the bank's liable capital,[8] and banks are obliged to redeposit 53% of new short-term foreign exchange savings abroad.[9] The supervision of the banks is carried out by an independent department within the National Bank of Croatia, and foreign entrants into the banking markets are in no way discriminated against in favour of domestic ones.

The Law on Agency for Deposit Insurance and Bank Rehabilitation was

---

[7] This is in contrast to some other countries, such as Poland, where high inflation depreciated part of the nominal value of non-performing claims on enterprises. In Croatia this did not happen, as the indexation of loans became a widespread habit during a long high-inflation history starting in the early 1970s.

[8] Equity capital plus reserves up to 50% of the value of equity capital.

[9] This is a common measure in transitional economies experiencing capital inflows. In Slovenia, the measure is called 'forex minimum' and it amounts to 68% (Bole, 1996).

passed by Parliament in 1994 and the agency started operations in 1995. Two large state-owned banks are currently undergoing the rehabilitation procedure (Splitska banka, Riječka banka), and one bank (Slavonska banka) has already completed its rehabilitation. The commencement of the rehabilitation procedure has been announced for the last and the 'biggest' problem bank (Privredna banka). These four problem banks comprise 36.5% of the total liable capital of the banking system and 45.6% of the total assets.

The rehabilitation procedure requires changes in the management and the ownership of the bank. First, the NBC estimates the 'economic justification for the rehabilitation', which includes an estimation of potential losses and a proposal for the steps to be taken. The proposal is submitted to the government which takes further steps via the agency. Secondly, estimated non-performing loans are written off against capital. If capital adequacy ratio falls below the legal standard (8%), a bank is recapitalized by the government. Recapitalization occurs in the form of cash and bonds in order to improve both the solvency and the liquidity of the bank. The agency, which is an independent institution funded from the state budget, acquires non-performing assets against an ownership share in the bank. This share has to be privatized as the final step.

The procedure will significantly alter the ownership structure within the Croatian banking system. This will only happen, however, in the medium term. Nonetheless, significant improvements have already been achieved in the money market in the short term. Since cash-strapped banks generated interest rate inelastic demand for funds, the money market interest rate exceeded the average annual level of about 30% early in 1996. This type of demand vanished after the beginning of the reform process (due to initial liquidity injections), and the money market interest rate suddenly began to reflect supply and demand conditions more accurately. The interbank money market interest rate dropped to about 9% by August 1996.

Table 3.3. Ownership structure of the banking sector

	Share in total assets		Number of banks	
	1994	1995	1994	1995
State	62.3	58.9	19	19
Private	37.7	41.1	31	34

Source: Šonje, Kraft and Dorsey (1996).

In section one it was emphasized that the unfavourable structure of the banking system prior to its rehabilitation was reflected both in the level of the rate of reserve requirements and in interest rates. There is no straightforward connection between the two, because both were supply side-driven. On the one hand, since money was issued by interventions on the foreign exchange market and since the foreign liabilities of domestic banks expanded rapidly after stabilization (mainly due to inflows of foreign currency savings into domestic bank accounts of households), the Central Bank was understandably concerned about the rapid worsening of the banks' solvency and liquidity if credit was allowed to grow at too high a rate while important banks were still fragile. Reserve requirements were used as a prudential measure: instead of letting funds flow freely into loans of doubtful quality, the funds were used to improve the reserve position of the commercial banks.

On the other hand, competitive pressures were not strong enough to produce flexibility in interest rates. The wartime climate contributed to the rigidity of the banking structure. Foreign banks hesitated before entering the Croatian market, and numerous small, newly-established private banks were trading well below an efficient scale, and hence were unable to compete with large banks in retail banking. They mainly used capital as a source of funds, so that their capital adequacy and loans to deposits ratios were remarkably high. Indeed, the estimated capital adequacy ratio ranges from 65% in small private banks to 18% in the larger, older banks. Because of the suboptimal scale of their operations, small banks were not able to improve lending price competition, but acted as 'cream-skimmers' (Šonje, Kraft and Dorsey, 1996), taking good clients away from the older banks. That led to a kind of 'bad credit market equilibrium': high interest rates and large interest rate spreads reflected the fact that smaller private banks charged higher interest rates than larger and older state-owned banks.

Only an exogenous shock could force the system out of this stagnant underperformance. This shock could come either from strong foreign entrants and/or from credible bank rehabilitation and privatization.[10] Both actually occurred in the first half of 1996, leading to a sharp decline in money market interest rates and a milder decline in lending interest rates and spreads, giving cause for optimism for the future credit market development which will finally depend on the availability and the term structure of funds.

---

[10] EBRD made an important equity investment in a medium-sized Croatian bank (Varaždinska banka), and Zagrebačka banka, the second largest and at the same time private, bank, successfully sold 10% of its equity to US investors in the form of GDRs. Its shares are listed on the London and the Zagreb Stock Exchanges, and at present it is estimated that 20% of its equity is held by foreign portfolio investors. Austrian Raiffeisen bank has operated in Croatia since 1994. Until mid-1996 licences have been extended to Bank Austria and Hypobank from Austria, Banca di Risparmio di Trieste from Italy, while Société Générale from France have opened a branch in Croatia. Similar intentions have been voiced by other European, mainly German, banks. The share of the banks already present in the Croatian market is relatively small, but their presence is important at least in terms of contestability if not yet of effective competition.

It is interesting to look at the way in which the NBC took advantage of these developments. After the beginning of the rehabilitation, when interest rate inelastic demand for money market funds disappeared, the National Bank of Croatia started to reduce the rate of reserve requirements gradually. The required sterilization was achieved by open market operations, i.e. by auctions of NBC bills. The market demand for NBC bills picked up because all banks, especially those undergoing the rehabilitation procedure, wanted to build up their reserve position.[11] The other reason was a sharp drop in the money market interest rate, which swiftly reduced the profits available in the interbank market and increased the relative attractiveness of an open market instrument. This is a clear case of a good coordination between supply-side measures (bank restructuring) and monetary policy measures and instruments, the coordination which paved the way for the development of financial markets.

PRIVATIZATION

The legal framework for privatization in Croatia was set up in 1991.[12] It was changed later on, but its essence did not change significantly.

A large initial privatization deal was undertaken through management and employee buy-outs (MEBO) under the control of the State Agency for Privatization, which was later transformed into the Croatian Privatization Fund (CPF). Some 2,800 enterprises from all sectors took part in the process, while the largest infrastructural companies (oil, railways, telecom, etc.) were declared public companies, which meant entirely state-owned and not liable to privatization at the beginning of the process.

As a first step, the agency had to approve the estimated values of enterprises to be privatized (the value estimation was conducted by independent private auditors, although not necessarily foreign ones), and the management and employees were the privileged buyers in the first instance. They could buy up to DEM 20,000 in nominal terms per worker at a discount, and any additional amount without a discount. The rest of the estimated equity which was not bought out was transferred to three state funds: 2/3 to the CPF and 1/3 to two

---

[11] NBC bills are used as collateral for getting lombard credit from the NBC.

[12] It was called the Law on Transformation of Social Enterprises. The word privatization is absent in the title. This is because the starting point was different from that in other transitional countries, where equity capital was owned by the state. Former Yugoslavia established the so-called 'social ownership', often popularly labeled as 'no-one's ownership', and the purpose of the Law was to transform 'social ownership' partly into private and partly into state ownership.

state pension funds. Later it appeared that pension funds in general did not benefit from having these shares in their portfolio. The capital market environment was underdeveloped, pension funds' portfolio management divisions were understaffed, and the demand for minority stakes in the equity of individual enterprises held by funds was small because strategic investors acquired majority stakes during the buyout procedure, as did over-the-counter, secondary market trading.

CPF next developed later several new approaches to the additional privatization of the acquired portfolio. First, part of the portfolio was held in reserve against expected denationalization compensation owed in the case of a few old enterprises that had been nationalized after the Second World War. Secondly, a smaller part of the portfolio was freely distributed to those people who had suffered worst in the war. Thirdly, larger sums were used as swaps for public debt. Two techniques were used: a discretionary one that was intended to clear non-marketable public debt of the state health fund, and an open market one that was used for specific offers of shares that could be bought out by public debt instruments. While the first approach had been misconceived (because if claims on the state health fund were held by a state-owned company, then the transaction was just a clear-out within the state sector), the second approach proved to be rather successful. It helped to reduce the amount of public debt outstanding. Direct auctions conducted exclusively for buyers with public debt instruments reduced public debt to GDP ratio by 2%. It also helped to develop the secondary market for otherwise non-marketable public debt instruments (frozen foreign exchange savings – see section 2). Fourthly, CPF used direct offers with free access for foreigners (there are no limits for foreigners' participation in the secondary capital market).[13] Different techniques were applied. The most common one was a simple announcement of the offer, i.e. the company was auctioned off. The bidder could propose his own payment method, which could include payments in cash, on credit, or with public debt instruments, which had the additional positive impact of a reduction of public debt and the development of secondary market trading. This technique was used for controlling packages in larger enterprises. The second technique was employed for marginal stakes – offers at the Zagreb Stock Exchange (ZSE). These shares had to be paid immediately in cash. Not surprisingly, the

---

[13] Generally, foreign participation in Croatian enterprises is unrestricted. There are no obstacles to establishing an enterprise, enhancing the equity stake, repatriation of capital, and there are no tax discriminatory measures or any similar type of legislation. Foreign entrepreneurs enter the Croatian market either directly, by founding their own enterprises or joint ventures, or through the process of privatization. According to Rohatinski, Vojnic *et al.* (1996, p. 75), until the end of 1995 there has been DEM 460 million worth of direct foreign investment through the privatization process. Since the overall data are not reliable, it is hard to conclude if this has been more or less important than green field FDI.

technique proved to be the least successful one. From 1993 to mid-1996 the volume of trading at these auctions reached only 7% of total trading volume at ZSE. The largest transactions occured in 1993, and the market disappeared thereafter. For example, since 1994 the volume of trading at auctions for cash has reached only 6% of the volume of trading at auctions conducted exclusively for swaps with public debt instruments. The third technique was successfully applied in the case of Pliva, a large and successfull pharmaceutical company from Zagreb. The public offering was conducted by Zagrebačka banka and Union Bank of Switzerland, and the company was listed on the London Stock Exchange. Due to tremendous public interest the price rose far above the nominal value (simultaneously in London and in Zagreb), and the company has been successfully majority-privatized. The shares are freely traded both in Zagreb and in London at a high, and for the time being, also stable price (see section 4).

The overall results of the privatization process based on a sample of 2,557 enterprises that had completed the process by the end of December 1995 is presented in Table 3.4. When looking at the numbers of enterprises, the results are impressive. When looking at equity values, the results are less so although the majority of the equity capital is, in any case, controlled by private agents.

Table 3.4. Results of privatization 1995

	Share by number	*Share by equity*
Entirely privatized	44.8%	8.4%
Majority privatized	44.7%	55.3%
Controlled by the state funds	10.5%	36.3%

Source: Authors' calculations based on *Privatizacija,* no. 15, t.3, p.68.

However, the results should be judged in light of the fact that large infrastructural companies (which are major conglomerates that have not been downsized to their core activities), were not subject to privatization. According to estimates by Rohatinski *et al.* (1996, p. 33), 54% of the equity in the enterprise sector remained state-owned at the outset of 1996. However, these are nominal figures. The market value of the equity would probably give a very different picture because the state enterprise sector employs 32% of the total number of employees, but produces only 24.2% of total turnover.[14] Therefore, it is hardly surprising that this sector produces net losses. But interestingly enough, the

---

[14] The latest release of preliminary data for 1995 indicates that the relative importance of the state enterprise sector continues to diminish rapidly: the employment level fell to 23% and the share in total turnover to 18%.

average net wage in this sector was only 1.6% below the average wage in the economy. This indicates that this sector is still overemployed and is paying wages far above the value of the marginal product of labour. There is a clear pressure for a reallocation of factors of production away from this sector. The number of unemployed persons rose to 13–14% of the active population during wartime, and from the social and political point of view, it was not sustainable to speed up the reallocation of labor in times when there were no fast-growing sectors which could absorb the free labour. The size of the required reallocation is still a heavy burden for the economy which has started to grow only since 1994 and which operated in a wartime environment that was not supportive of the required supply-side restructuring.

The prospects for peace and growth have risen considerably since the signing of the Dayton Agreement in December 1995. The government feels that it can ease its control over the 'social pain of restructuring', i.e. over equity in the enterprise sector. But there are still a lot of political doubts and battles to be fought over the speed and scope of the process. The Law on Privatization was passed by Parliament in March 1996, but the process of privatization itself will not be affected dramatically by the new legislation. Although the law allows a wider distribution of shares, the privatization of large infrastructural companies is deferred, to be regulated by additional legislation. Obviously, the political consensus over privatization of these state-owned monopolies could not be reached, at least at this point of the privatization process.

In spite of this, the overall picture looks optimistic. Despite the war, the economy has undergone a profound restructuring process in the past few years. Although owning only 46% of total equity in the enterprise sector at the end of 1995, the private sector comprises 69% of total employment, 75.8% of total turnover and 80.3% of total profits before taxation (Rohatinski *et al.*, 1996).

EXCHANGES

Although Croatia has completed and implemented the body of legislation relating to capital markets,[15] the official markets remain thin. While money markets, including both the Kuna and the foreign exchange interbank market, work in a transparent way, equity and bond markets are still segmented.

The interbank Kuna money market works both as an OTC market and through a formalized institution called the Zagreb Money Market (ZMM). Overnight trading is mainly conducted through ZMM, while daily trading

---

[15] Securities Law, Law on Trading with Securities, Law on Investment Funds, Banking Law.

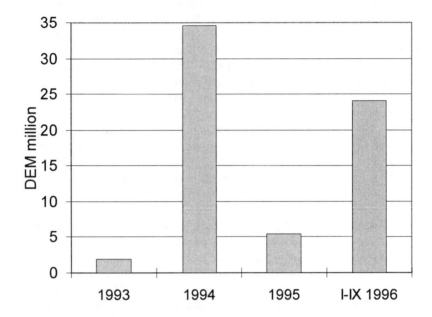

Figure 3.4. Average monthly trading volume on the Zagreb Stock Exchange

occurs mainly as OTC. The majority of Croatian banks are members of the on-line electronic money trading system, but on-line trading is used only occasionally because financial institutions are still adapting to its use. The interbank foreign exchange market is an on-line market, but interventions by the Central Bank are carried out by occasional direct foreign exchange auctions.

An important money market instrument in Croatia is the NBC bill – short-term paper issued by the Central Bank. This paper is auctioned every Wednesday on the primary market, and is freely traded on the secondary market created by commercial banks. The government started to issue T-bills at the end of July 1996 at auctions conducted by the Ministry of Finance (MF). The MF and the NBC coordinate auctions and liquidity projections, so that the NBC bills and T-bills do not compete on the market. In any case, potential buyers on the primary market are different. Although banks can participate in auctions for both instruments, the enterprise and household sectors agents' have direct access only to T-bills auctions, while they can participate in NBC bills trading only on the secondary market.

The Zagreb Stock Exchange (ZSE) is the most important official exchange in Croatia. There are also two important regional exchanges in Varaždin and Osijek. Stocks and bonds are traded on these markets. The number of listed companies in all exchanges together is about 40, and the trading volume is growing rapidly. While the average monthly volume of trading at ZSE in 1995 was below DEM 10 million, in the period from January to September 1996, the average monthly volume of trading has increased to about DEM 24 million mainly by the aforementioned companies, Pliva, Zagrebačka banka, and Podravka (food processing industry). Several types of government bonds are also traded, and investors recently showed particular interest in 3-year refinancing bonds with a 12% annual interest rate in the first issue and 8.5% in the second, issued by the Ministry of Finance.

The exchanges shared all the difficulties of the economy in general and capital markets in particular. However, since early 1996 a clear and strong upward trend has been evident in the number of traded instruments, volume of trading, and prices. In fact, market optimism is so plain that the rise in prices of the most traded securities from January to May ranges from approximately 100% for shares of Zagrebačka banka to 400% for Pliva shares. After a strong development in 1994, pessimistic expectations driven by wartime and regional security risk prevailed till the end of 1995, pushing the market prices down far below nominal values. Now the market shows clear signs of a well-founded optimism based on the development of the real sector.

SOURCES OF EXTERNAL FINANCE

According to the balance of payments statistics, in the 1993–1995 period US$ 252.3 million FDI entered Croatia. In relative terms, the official volume of FDI in 1995 amounts to 0.6% of GDP (the same ratio as for 1994). This figure is probably somewhat underestimated due to statistical deficiencies. According to the Ministry of Economic Affairs the number, based on committed rather than realized amounts, exceeds DEM 1 billion. The large discrepancy between BOP data and other data reflects expected instead of committed FDI.

The most important individual FDI projects occurred in the telecommunications and electronic industries (Ericsson, Siemens), breweries and the construction material industries. Investors hesitated to enter the tourism industry, although it has the best prospects in Croatia. It is expected that the change in the political and security situation in the region will speed up FDI largely due to investment in tourism. The most important foreign investors in Croatia come from Austria, Belgium, Germany, Sweden, Switzerland and USA. It is also expected that direct investment into the financial industry will play an important role from 1996 onwards.

Table 3.5. Foreign investments through the privatization process 1991–1995

Country	Invested capital (DEM million)	Structure in %
Austria	100.8	21.9
Belgium	40.4	8.8
Germany	38.0	8.3
Sweden	70.0	15.2
Switzerland	97.1	21.1
USA	37.4	8.1
Other	76.7	16.6
Total	*460.4*	*100.0*

Source: Rohatinski *et al.*, 1996, p. 75.

There is no doubt that the unfavorable wartime and political situation influenced the relatively low level of FDI in Croatia compared with the other transitional countries. There is also no doubt that FDI will speed up after good prospects for peace have been achieved. Indeed, BOP data for the first half of 1996 show the strong upsurge in FDI of 186% compared with the same period in 1995.

An upsurge in foreign aid is also expected, but it has not yet occurred because Croatia was cut off from EU aid programs, such as PHARE, during the war. The foreign aid consisted mainly of different forms of humanitarian aid that went to help people at large, but this type of aid is becoming less important. During the same period other forms of aid, such as US AID, and aid connected with international financial projects, mainly from the IMF and the World Bank, were still available to Croatia. However, Croatia became a full member of the Council of Europe in November 1996, so that inflows from EU funds can be expected from 1997 onwards.

At present, Croatia is strengthening its relations with international financial institutions, mainly with the IMF, the World Bank and the EBRD. Negotiations started in 1993, the first projects were realized in 1994, and the cooperation speeded up in 1995. As of 30 September 1996 EBRD has invested US$ 74.1 million and the World Bank US$ 53.1 million in Croatia (net outstanding amounts). However, the largest creditor is the IMF with US$ 209.5 million debt outstanding, due to a stand-by arrangement with the IMF effective from autumn 1994 till the end of 1995. The signing of an Extended Fund Facility arrangement extending from 1996 to 1998 is expected by the end of 1996.

1996 is a turning point for Croatia's relations with external financial sources. After the successful rescheduling of foreign debt with the Paris Club in 1995, an arrangement with the London Club has been concluded in spring 1996 and the burden of the past debt accumulated in the period of former Yugoslavia has been successfully rescheduled. As a result, debt was converted into tradable Croatian government bonds (the exchange date was the end of July) listed on the Luxembourg Stock Exchange.

The low overall foreign indebtness of the Croatian economy opens the way for running a BOP current account deficit that is needed in the period of post-war reconstruction of the economy. The expected and sustainable current account deficit to GDP ratio for 1996 and 1997 is about 5–6% (see Appendix 3A), and a large part of it will be financed by international financial institutions. The largest individual creditor in 1996 will be the World Bank with an amount of approximately US$ 300 million that comprises loans for road and post-war reconstruction, as well as public and financial sector adjustment loans.[16] The government is planning an Eurobond issue, but the amount and the conditions have not been yet settled. The Eurobond issue can be expected in early 1997, after obtaining a credit rating (the credit rating agencies are due to visit Croatia at the end of November 1996).

In addition, the private sector is expected to be an important channel for funds flowing into the Croatian economy. The private banking sector, which holds US$ 2 billion of reserves abroad, has built up international credibility and is capable of obtaining loans at interest rates far below those prevailing on the Croatian market. It is expected that some additional US$ 300–350 million will flow in during 1996, mainly in the form of loans syndicated by private banks.

CONCLUSION

The war severely affected Croatia's economic performance. Despite hardships, Croatia has managed to achieve remarkable success in macroeconomic stabilization and the development of the institutional framework for a market economy. By far the lowest inflation among all transitional economies has been achieved by the liberalization of the price system, the opening of the economy, fiscal discipline, and the full independence of the monetary authority. However, political uncertainty, banks burdened by non-performing loans in their portfolios, depressed expectations and high interest rates have prevented greater success in terms of a higher rate of real growth.

At the end of 1995 and in early 1996 the situation changed markedly. Political prospects for a lasting peace became firmly established. The bank

---

[16] *Source:* Budget law for 1996.

rehabilitation process started on a large scale which immediately lead to a decline in interest rates. Privatization was speeded up, foreign direct investments soared, and expectations became more optimistic, leading to a deepening of capital markets and a rise in asset prices.

Both theory and experience suggest that the simultaneous development of credit and equity markets is a basic precondition for sustainable growth in the long run (Kletzer and Roldos, 1996). On the one hand, there seem to be plenty of reasons for optimism, on the other, insufficient progress in the scope and speed of privatization of the large infrastructural monopolies appears to be the main obstacle to further progress. This is the chief problem that Croatia will have to resolve in the near future.

REFERENCES

Bole, V. (1996): *The Financial Sector and High Interest Rates: Lessons from Slovenia*, The Second Dubrovnik Conference on Transition Economies, Dubrovnik, 26–28 June.

Kletzer, K. and J. Roldos (1996): *The Role of Credit Markets in a Transition Economy With Incomplete Public Information*, IMF Working Paper 96/18, International Monetary Fund, Washington D.C.

Privatizacija (1996): various issues, Croatian Ministry of Privatization, Zagreb.

Rohatinski, Ž. *et al.* (1996): *Process of Privatization in Croatia*, Open Society Institute Croatia, Zagreb, and Central European University, Budapest.

Šonje, V., E. Kraft and T. Dorsey (1996): *Monetary and Exchange Policy, Capital Inflows and the Structure of the Banking System in Croatia*, The Second Dubrovnik Conference on Transition Economies, Dubrovnik, 26–28 June.

APPENDIX

Table 3.A. Balance of payments (US$ million) and related indicators 1993–1996

Balance of payments	1993	1994	1995	1996*
Current account balance	104.0	103.4	-1712	-1097.3
Goods	-762.5	-968.9	-2877.2	-2780.0
Services	631.9	737.5	612.7	832.7
Income	-141.3	-124.5	-93.3	-100.0
Transfers	376.0	459.3	645.8	950
Financial account	269.8	583.6	901.7	910.0
Direct & portfolio investment	74.3	97.6	80.5	150.0
Other investment	195.4	486.1	821.2	760.0
Central bank's reserves	-449.6	-788.8	-490.2	-454,8
Net errors and omissions	75.8	101.7	1300.5	642.1
Related indicators				
Real GDP growth	-3.7%	0.8%	1.7%	6.7%
Central bank's intl. reserves (eop)	616.4	1405.0	1895.2	2350.0
Current account/GDP	0.6%	0.6%	9.7%	5.7%
International debt/GDP**	15.6%	18.5%	20.9%	25.5%
Total debt service/exports***	10.8%	8.5%	10.1%	11.0%
Kuna/DEM (eop)	3.8	3.6	3.7	3.6
Real effective exchange rate ****	-27.4%	7.1%	0.5%	0.0%
CPI (eop)	1149.-7%	-3.0%	3.7%	3.3%
Annual growth rate of base money	996.3%	109.6%	43.1%	18.6%

Notes:
* Author's unofficial projection based upon data for the first six months.
** Jump in 1996 is due to the inclusion of part of the non-allocated debt of former SFRY which Croatia recognized by the agreement with the London Club. Ratio refers to end-of-year data.
*** Exports of both goods and services included. Principal and interest payments and arrears included.
**** End-year rate of change of the trade-weighted real effective exchange rate.
Source: NBC Bulletin, various numbers; author's calculations.

Table 3.B. Most active shares by turnover during January–September 1996

Company	Core Business	Turnover (HRK '000)	High (HRK)	Low (HRK)	Last (HRK)
PLIVA d.d. Zagreb	Pharm.	361,867	13500	1853	13150
Zagrebacka banka d.d. Zagreb ordinary shares	Bank	118,762	1010	140.81	1010
Podravka d.d. Koprivnica	Food Processing	59,150	275.00	70.24	275.00
Kras d.d. Zagreb	Confectionery	5,329	550.00	110.95	550.00
Laguna d.d. Porec	Tourism	3,963	915.00	369.76	915.00
Jadran Turist d.d. Rovinj	Tourism	2,857	300.00	100.00	300.00
Elka d.d. Zagreb	Cables	985	195.00	125.00	195.00
Elcon d.d. Zlatar Bistrica	Car parts production	953	141.03	140.64	140.73
Arenaturist d.d. Pula	Tourism	925	110.00	73.784	100.00
Riviera Holding d.d. Porec	Tourism	541	115.00	55.35	115.00
Suncani Holding d.d. Hvar	Tourism	495	50.00	32.50	45.00
Karlovacka pivovara d.d. Karlovac	Brewery	487	190.00	144.00	180.00
Croatia banka d.d. Zagreb	Bank	259	326.60	118.21	135.00
Aitoproizvod d.d.Karlovac	Agriculture	229	144.00	133.00	143.00
Zagrebacka banka d.d. Zagreb (E series of shares)	Bank	184	400.00	174.08	400.00
Istraturist d.d. Umag	Tourism	181	185.00	44.29	185.00
Other		528	–	–	–
Total		557,695			

G21 P33 F33
G28 P34
E52 L33

4. Czech Republic

Oldřich Rejnuš and Radek Schmied[1]

INTRODUCTION

The Czech Republic has gone through its major period of transition, which in fact started at the beginning of 1993. At that time, a new economic legal framework was introduced in the new Czech Republic. These laws were created in accordance with European Community practice and became the basis for the transition from the former centrally-planned economy to the conditions of a market economy.

MONETARY POLICY

Czech monetary policy is based on a two-level banking system, that is, the functions of the central bank are clearly defined and separated from those of other banks. The Czech National Bank is established under the Constitution of the Czech Republic as an independent state bank. Any interference in the bank activities is possible only by law. The Act governing the Czech National Bank was framed in accordance with similar legal acts of other developed European countries, as well as with the proposals of the European System of Central Banks and the European Central Bank.

The status of the Czech National Bank and its role in the economy is determined by the Act governing the Czech National Bank (Act No. 6/1993 Sb.). The main task of the Bank is to preserve the stability of the Czech currency. To meet this task, the Czech National Bank is legally entitled to determine monetary policy, to issue bank notes and coins, to control the circulation of money, the system of payments and the bank clearing procedures,

---

[1] The authors acknowledge the advice of Antonin Rusek, Department of Economics, Susquehanna University in Selingrove, Pennsylvania, USA, and Eric Hake, CEP visiting lecturer at Mendel University in Brno, Czech Republic.

to supervise banking activities and to guarantee the functioning and the effective development of the banking system in the Czech Republic. Furthermore the Czech National Bank is required to present a 'Report on Monetary Development' to Parliament at least twice a year and to provide information to the public on the subject every three months.

The supreme statutory body of the Czech National Bank is the Bank Council which determines both the monetary policy and the instruments for its implementation. The governor, vice–governors and also the other members of the Bank Council (consisting of seven members) are directly appointed or dismissed by the President of the Czech Republic, which is a proof of the independence of the Council from government control. Furthermore, membership of the Bank Council is incompatible with being a Member of Parliament or a government minister, and it is also incompatible with membership of any of the management and supervisory boards of other banks and/or commercial companies. The Act establishes the right of the governor to take part in government meetings with an advisory vote and guarantees the independence of the Czech National Bank from the government.

After most legal changes became effective on 1 January 1993, the monetary policy stance was relatively restrictive. Worries about the effects of the new tax system on the price level were the major reason for this policy. Price liberalization, the increased demand of commercial banks for foreign exchange and the effects of this demand on the CNB reserves, together with the expectations of a Czech–Slovak monetary split also played important roles in producing a restrictive monetary policy. At the beginning of the second quarter of 1993, it became possible to soften this rigid monetary policy, mainly because the monthly rate of inflation decreased below 1% in March and the foreign exchange reserves of the CNB began to grow steadily. This softening was reflected in particular steps taken by the CNB, for example, in an increase in the refinancing volume for commercial banks, followed by a lowering of the discount rate, the unification of required reserves, a decrease in the lombard interest rate, and a number of other measures. As a result, the aggregate money supply M2 increased and the interest rates in the interbank depository market started to decline steadily, which caused a gradual decline in the interest rates of commercial banks. This policy was pursued until the end of the year. Then, there was a relatively strong foreign capital inflow to the Czech economy, which forced the CNB to switch from refinancing loans to sterilizing the surplus liquidity.

The first half of 1994 was altogether more optimistic – there were positive trends in the relative stability of consumer prices, a low unemployment rate and also a moderate surplus in the current account and the state budget. Companies found themselves in better financial shape, and the positive economic outlook spurred investment. Accordingly, the CNB policy focused particularly on draining the surplus liquidity from the monetary market, caused by the strong inflow of foreign capital. To carry out this task, the CNB issued its own CNB bills and sold them to commercial banks. The state budget kept having high surpluses at that time, while interest rates in the money market were declining – even below the discount rate. Commercial banks were rapidly lowering the interest rates on credits from the originally high level of 1993. The growth of credit accelerated, but at the expense of an increasing percentage of risky loans.

In this situation the CNB tightened monetary policy by means of raising required reserves, which brought a slight increase in interest rates in the money market, which in turn halted the decline in interest rates on credit. The commercial banks were forced to be more cautious in their credit policy and to evaluate the risk. Anticipating the danger of increasing consumer prices (already apparent in the second quarter of 1994), in September the CNB raised both the discount and the lombard rates by 0.5%. However, it did not have an equivalent effect on the interest rates of commercial banks owing to more intense competition among them and their easier access to cheaper foreign credit sources. In spite of this, the CNB succeeded in slowing down inflation by the end of the year. In line with the continuous inflow of foreign capital into the economy it became obvious that the stability of the currency exchange rate had been encouraging a strong inflow of capital and the inevitable pressure for revaluation. However, the CNB did not alter its exchange rate policy during the whole of 1994 – mainly because of the expected setback in the current account. On the other hand, it did accelerate preparations for an extension of the convertibility of the currency and a further liberalization of the capital account in 1995.

In 1995, the foreign capital inflow increased further. Together with the growth in real wages, it induced a surge in aggregate domestic demand, which could not be met by the supply side. As a result of the different rates of growth in the supply and the demand sides, a relatively large deficit in the balance of trade emerged. The CNB restricted its policy in June in recognition of the fact that money creation had exceeded the limits of the monetary program. Without enforcing any regulations against the inflow of external capital and given the fixed exchange rate policy, the CNB policy focused on sterilizing the effects of the capital inflow (particularly on limiting liquidity in the banking sector). The Central Bank implemented the policy by means of various instruments, such as issues of CNB notes, repo operations, increases in reserve requirements and deposits of particular yields from privatization at the CNB.

Another crucial change was made on 1 October 1995, when the Czech Crown (CZK) became convertible for current transactions in accordance with IMF Article VIII. The impact of these measures is shown in Tables 4.1 and 4.2.

Table 4.1. Economic and financial indicators

	1993	1994	1995	1.Q. 1996
Consumer Price Index [%]	20.8	10.0	9.1	8.9
M 2 [%]	20.3	20.8	19.4	-0.3

Notes: Per cent against December previous years. Money supply M2 comprises: Cash, demand deposits, time deposits and foreign currency deposits.
Source: Czech National Bank, 1996.

Table 4.2. Average interbank depository offer rate (PRIBOR)

	1993	1994	1995	1.Q. 1996
7 days	10.74	8.46	10.87	11.18
3 months	13.15	9.14	10.95	10.86
6 months	13.95	9.26	10.96	10.79

Source: Bankovnictvi, 1996.

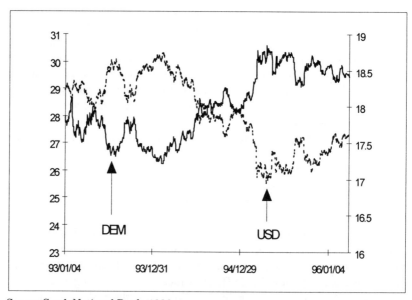

Source: Czech National Bank, 1996.

Figure 4.1. Exchange rate CZK/US$ and CZK/DEM

In response to the risk of rising inflation the CNB took further steps in the first quarter of 1996 while the currency continued to be tied to the DEM and US$, weighted with 65% and 35%, respectively. The CNB extended the fluctuation range of the currency from 0.5% to 7.5% on either side of the parity.

First reactions have so far shown an outflow of some speculative capital, which caused a decline in the unnecessarily high CNB foreign exchange reserves. This trend continued in the second quarter of 1996. The crucial problem was fighting mounting inflationary pressures in the first half of that year. For this reason CNB started to enforce restrictive measures in a more intensive way.

THE BANKING SECTOR

The banking system in the Czech Republic is a universal system similar to the German one. Under the Act governing the Czech National Bank, all commercial banks residing in the Czech Republic are subject to banking supervision by the CNB. This supervision concentrates on managing banks' liquidity and limiting the risks involved in banking activities (protecting the interests of depositors). The CNB is a coordinator of banking activities – through various rules and regulations which are mandatory on all banks. Any violation of the regulations can be sanctioned by the CNB. The sanctions used depend on the violation – ranging from a fine, to banning particular activities, limiting the license, and enforcing administration, right up to recalling the license. The supervisory function of the CNB also includes granting licenses to new banks and foreign bank branches, which is conducted in close cooperation with the Ministry of Finance.

Banking supervision exercises particular control over the solvency and liquidity of banks, because the whole Czech banking system has been developing under relatively risky conditions. Therefore, all banks in the Czech Republic are obliged to monitor and keep strictly to the four basic discretion rules enjoined by the recommendations of the Basle Committee for Banking Supervision. These are the ratios of liquidity, capital readjustments, credit activity and the conditions of open positions in the foreign currency markets. All banks are obliged to have their balances supervised by an independent auditor, in accordance with the Act governing banks.

Until the end of 1989 the Czechoslovak State Bank dominated the home banking sector, and it served not only as the central bank, but also provided the majority of deposit and credit services in the commercial sector. Besides the State Bank, there were two large institutions accepting deposits from the public and issuing credits to individuals. These were the Czech and the Slovak State Saving Bank, together with several other small specialized financial institutions.

The number of banks in the Czech Republic has been rapidly increasing since new legal conditions were introduced after 1989 (Table 4.3.).

Table 4.3. Number of commercial banks in the Czech Republic

Financial institution	Number
State-owned financial institution (Konsolidacni banka)	1
Commercial banks without foreign capital	14
Commercial banks with partial foreign capital	19
Commercial banks with 100% foreign capital	21
Total number of commercial banks	*54*

Source: CNB, 1996.

All banks in the Czech Republic, including the branches of foreign institutions, are subject to CNB banking supervision. To obtain a banking license, applicants must fulfil various conditions, among which the most important one is the minimum required capital stock that was increased from CZK 300 million in 1993 to CZK 500 million. Bank activities are guided by set rules, aimed at limiting the risks involved in banking operations. CNB banking supervision is carried out inside the banks themselves, as well as monitoring their economic situation externally through financial statements and other information provided by them.

There are two major problems shared by most Czech banks – the quality of the credit portfolio and an imbalance in the time structure of receivables and liabilities. Such problems originated in the process of transformation to a market economy, primarily through a lack of experienced and skilled bank management and also through inappropriate organizational structures. As a result, in 1993 the volume of 'classified credits', in other words, of credits which showed particular failures in payments, increased significantly. On the other hand, this increase was caused particularly by the requirements of CNB banking supervision, to satisfy which the banks started to evaluate the quality of issued credits systematically and in accordance with given standards. The banks also had to form special reserves for lower quality credits.

This trend continued in spite of the fact that several small banks went bankrupt in 1994, when the behaviour of banks clearly changed. The ownership structure started to change: the owners mobilized their activities to serve the needs of long-term development; in several cases management was replaced, reserve funds were reinforced at the expense of low dividend payouts; and there was also diversification of assets. The criteria for issuing credits were made stricter and policies for resolving difficult credit decisions were developed. In many cases, the commercial banks even went to the lengths of revaluating their entire business policies and strategies.

CNB banking supervision was underpinned by the Amendment of the Act on Banking of July 1994. Under this Amendment, the CNB is legally entitled to impose a wide range of sanctions, including the replacement of management and fines up to CZK 50 million, in instances of negligence in a bank's activities. Furthermore, the CNB administrator's executive power was broadened. Confidence in the banking system increased after an insurance scheme for the deposits of savers was introduced. This system ensures the payment of named deposits to their owners to the value of 80% of the deposit, to a maximum of CZK 100,000 for each depositor in each bank, in the event of the bank's affairs being wound up.

The development of the Czech banking sector in 1995 followed the trend of the previous years. It is possible to characterize it as relatively stable in spite of the fact that the poor quality of the credit portfolio has remained the major problem in the whole sector.

Table 4.4. Comparison of domestic banks, according to various criteria

Capital stock (CZK million)		Balance sum (CZK billion)		Net profit/loss (CZK million)	
Komercni banka	9502	Komercni banka	407.2	Komercni banka	5162.0
Ceska Sporitelna	7600.0	Ceska Sporitelna	367.8	Ceskoslovenska obchodni banka	3087.0
Konsolidacni banka	5950.0	Ceskoslovenska obchodni banka	201.7	Investicni a postovni banka	1127.0
Ceskoslovenska obchodni banka	5105.0	Investicni a postovni banka	201.4	Zivnostenska banka	406.5
Investicni a postovni banka	4031.0	Konsolidacni banka	123.3	Agrobanka	373.0
Agrobanka	3990.0	Agrobanka	69.5	Ceska Sporitelna	263.0
Zivnostenska banka	1360.4	Zivnostenska banka	31.9	Union banka	63.7
Pragobanka	1357.0	Banka Hana	19.2	Foresbank	19.1
Union banka	1340.0	Pragobanka	18.0	Prvni mestska banka	12.2
Universal banka	1100.0	Ekoagobanka	16.9	Ceskomoravska hypotecni banka	7.0

Source: MF Dnes, 1996.

Another positive development during 1995 was the growth in deposits, particularly in smaller banks, and increasing competition in the banking sector influenced primarily by foreign banks (to be precise, their branches) trading in the Czech Republic. This process produced moves to increase the capitalization of banks by means not only of new stock issues, but also of mergers between small financial institutions. The CNB has persisted throughout 1996 in its efforts to consolidate the domestic banking sector and to create the conditions that would allow the integration of Czech banks into international banking structures. At the end of the first quarter of 1996 the volume of classified credits at nominal value grew to CZK 352.5 billion, i.e. by 4.9%. This increase, which was reflected in the growth of its share from 34.9% to 35.4% in the total volume of credits granted, was effected by a more precise classification following from the results of audits carried out in individual banks. At the same time, the growth of credits losses slowed; their share grew by only 0.7% in the first quarter 1996. This, together with the continued creation of reserves and provisions amounting to CZK 109.0 billion as of 31 March 1996, i.e. 3.7% more than at the end of 1995, and with an improved collateralizing of classified credits, led to a drop in the volume of uncovered losses from credits. These stood at CZK 6.2 billion as of the end of the first quarter, i.e. 0.7% of the total volume of credits granted, or 0.2 point less than at the end of 1995. Following the failure of several small banks and one middle-sized one (Kreditní banka), there have been intensive negotiations held not only in the banking sector, but also in parliament. These negotiations are expected to bring about significant changes in the regulation of the banking sector.

PRIVATIZATION

The privatization process in the Czech Republic was launched in 1991. It started with the so-called 'small privatization'. Its aim was to form small and medium-sized entrepreneurial social groups by the privatization of small businesses (i.e. shops, services and local producers, restaurants, etc.). However, the major element in the economic reforms and the whole privatization process was what became known as the 'large-scale privatization'. It started in 1992 and continued in two waves until 1994, when the large-scale privatization formally ended.

The privatization methods adopted varied according to each sector. In trade and services the privatization was basically carried out following standard methods (i.e. direct sales, public sales and auctions) mainly within the framework of the small privatization. The voucher method was applied in the manufacturing and construction industries. In the agricultural sector the process was complicated by restitutions of property, movable assets, farm animals, and also by the low profitability of the whole industry. Therefore direct sales to restituees and tenants were preferred and instalment payments with long pay-off periods were used more frequently than in other sectors. Direct sales were also used in the health services sector. Employees working in privatized health service institutions were preferential buyers for the privatized units. The payment periods were extended in this sector and there was the additional bonus of cheaper credits provided by Ceska Sporitelna.

The results of the privatization of property from the beginning to the end of 1995 are summarized in Table 4.5.

Table 4.5. Results of privatization (CZK billion end of 1995)

	Shares privatized through the National Property Fund (FNM)	Restitutions, direct sales and auctions
Privatized property	474.63	111.37
Still state-owned property	230.12	32.71
Still not-book shares	1.69	–
Property total	706.44	144.08

Source: Hospodarske noviny, 1996.

The above description does not, however, mean that under the voucher method of privatization the citizens of the Czech Republic own the privatized businesses directly. First, it is necessary to state that more than half of all those involved in both privatization waves invested their voucher points through investment and mutual funds. As a next step, people received shares and units issued by the funds. Moreover, by now the major banks and funds have largely bought up the shares previously held by individuals. It is to be expected that in the framework of the so-called 'third wave of privatization' this buying-up of shares will have been completed by the end of 1996. As a result, the majority of all shares will be concentrated in the hands of mainly large, usually institutional, investors. This is the way by which the privatization process itself, and the following process of redistribution and centralization of capital, will probably be completed.

According to data from the Security Register (SCP), 546 investment funds were registered by the Ministry of Finance of the Czech Republic at the end of 1995. From the figures given above it should be clear that such a large number of fund-type organizations is quite unsustainable for the Czech Republic in the long term.

It is expected that a large number of investment funds will convert themselves into standard joint-stock companies, mainly of the holding type, during the first half of 1996. As a result of inadequate legislation, such conversion will help these funding companies to rid themselves of Ministry of

Finance supervision, as well as the legal barriers which would prevent them from controlling more than 20% of the shares in a particular company. This process is being accelerated in anticipation of new legislation which will make such 'transformations' more difficult. The new law should come into effect on 1 July 1996.

The knowledge and information concerning privatized businesses as well as accessible ways of moving securities from one organization to another played an important (and even essential) role during the privatization process.

In spite of the fact that special information bulletins were issued for particular auctions and both waves of voucher privatization, there were always groups of investors who were able to obtain better and more precise information. These groups of investors (particularly former management and/or investment funds) were then able to use their information to their advantage.

Furthermore, both waves of voucher privatizations had been preceded by intensive advertisement campaigns by investment funds and companies. This effort greatly influenced decisions made by mainly small investors to invest their vouchers. The Security Register (SCP) also played its part during privatization. Through the SCP it was (and it still is) possible to transfer securities between particular companies through intentionally distorted prices which make tax evasions possible. As a consequence it is necessary to admit that the Czech tax system still contains some shortcomings which may allow 'legal tax evasions'.

As far as the taxing of foreign economic nationals is concerned, the Czech Republic has signed agreements on the prevention of double taxation with most developed countries. On the other hand, these agreements are not entirely harmonized with the Czech tax system. For example, it is possible to reduce or even avoid paying tax by specific securities transactions between domestic and foreign investors. These facts become important in connection with the Czech Act on the Foreign Exchange Economy, according to which foreigners are allowed to buy foreign currency for the Czech currency and vice versa, and also to import and export either Czech or foreign currency in accordance with the, quite liberal, conditions of the Act.

EXCHANGES

The basic strategic decision taken by the former Czechoslovak federal government and the federal parliament was that there would be two competitive public markets from the very beginning: the Prague Stock Exchange and the RM-System over-the-counter market.

The Prague Stock Exchange began its regular operations on 6 April 1993.

Until then, there had been only a 'temporary secondary market' where only seven titles had been traded. The Prague Exchange works on the membership principle. At the beginning the exchange had 17 constituent members. This number has been increasing up to the present state of 104 members (figure from 2 February 1996).

The period of the Czech capital market development (June – September 1993) was initially marked by the consistent downward movement of prices. This way the initial, artificially inflated prices of securities were able to converge with the market price level. This quite lengthy process of downward price adjustment was due not only to thin trading during the summer season but also due to the fact that the Prague Stock Exchange was operating only once per week, and the RM-System was running just one so-called 'periodic auction' per month.

The second period of the capital markets development in the Czech Republic started around the end of September 1993. It was characterized by an exceptional enthusiasm for investments by larger parts of the public as well as of certain institutional (including foreign) investors. This development period lasted approximately half a year and ended at the beginning of March 1994. The official index of the Prague Stock Exchange PX 50 reached its historical maximum of 1244.7 points on 1 March 1994. At that time, the prices of particular stocks exceeded their September values by more than 1000%. Helped by the insufficient degree of capital market regulation, the second period became the basis for the third period of the development, which started with more than a year of persistent decline in both markets, interrupted by occasional increases.

To understand the causes of the rapid decline in stock prices during the third period, it is necessary to link considerations related to the behavior of investors to the analysis. During this period the banks began to raise their capital stocks, resulting in a reorientation of freely available funds to the primary market. After successful trades were made by investors who managed to buy newly issued stock in the first tenders for low prices and then to sell it, thereby achieving large profits, this type of investment became so popular that it began to drain the secondary market. Combined with the factor of increasing supply in the secondary market, this resulted in a significant decline in stock prices.

In the second part of this period, similar tenders were issued even by investors from the non-banking sector. This contributed to a further decline in stock prices and had a negative effect mainly on the banking sector as the banks had underwritten most of the new stock. Moreover, state or corporate and municipal bonds were being issued at the same time. These were considered to be fairly safe and profitable securities under the conditions of the government's successful monetary policy aimed at keeping inflation under control as well as cutting interest rates.

The position of the stock market worsened at that time owing to the below-expectation financial results for the year 1993 that were announced by a large number of companies at their general meetings. The main causes of the poor performance seemed obvious – the new management regulations valid from 1993, the splitting-up of privatized companies and the audit of problematic foreign assets allocated mainly in the former Soviet Union countries. The above-mentioned facts, together with exceptionally low profits, resulted in a scarcity of dividend announcements by Czech companies.

After the decline there was a short revival of trading especially in the shares of investment funds. These had often a 40% to 50% discount between their stock prices and the market value of their portfolios. During August and September 1994 the competitive Prague Stock Exchange and RM-System shortened the trading intervals. However, the thinly-traded market could not bear the stress for a long time. Moreover, many investors stopped trading shares in the morning auctions and started buying the shares in the form of additional orders. This way it was possible to keep the prices low during the morning trading due to insufficient demand and then to buy up the surplus stock through the terminal.

The second wave of privatizations reached its peak in March 1995, when the National Property Fund (FNM) released the stock of the companies privatized in that wave. The end of 1994 and first months of 1995 thus saw a remarkable inflow of capital. Some companies encouraged the inflow, buying out vouchers, particularly future shares, from individual voucher holders. Such conduct led to an even sharper fall in the Czech stock market, because the supply of shares was rising steadily owing to investors' fears of falling prices. Luckily, the remainder of the shares which had been rendered to physical persons at the beginning of March did not come on the market until three months after, i.e. in June (to avoid taxation). Combined with the general demand for cash before the summer break, this explains the final decline in prices of stock. At that time the PX 50, with an original value of 1,000 points on 5 April 1994 fell to its lowest recorded value of 387.2 points (on 29 June 1995).

The situation first stabilized and then improved during the second half of the year 1995. The index showed a considerable surge of stock prices which was accompanied by a rising trade volume. This development can be traced to the beginning of the process unofficially known as the 'third wave of voucher privatization'. It is the name given to the still-continuing struggle of banks and several other large institutional investors to acquire majority shares in investment funds as well as in selected industrial corporations and banks. Such redistribution is still the main factor in the present revival not only in the stock market, but also in the OTC capital market.

As a result of voucher privatization, 2,000 issues of securities (most of which are shares) are traded in the capital markets of the Czech Republic. At the end of March 1996, there were 1,723 issues of shares and units traded on the Prague Stock Exchange. Their market capitalization amounted to CZK 539.1 billion, while at the same time only 59 issues of bonds were traded, with a capitalized market value of CZK 108.1 billion.

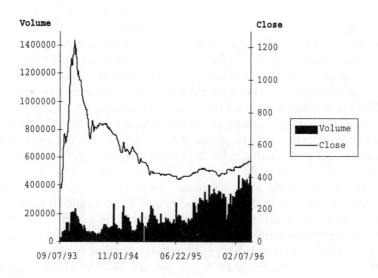

Source: Prague Stock Exchange, 1996.

Figure 4.2. Prague Stock Exchange Index PX50

From the facts stated above it may be seen that the number of security issues traded on the Prague Stock Exchange seems to be exceptional in comparison with other stock markets. On the other hand, most of the shares listed on the Prague Stock Exchange and in the RM-System are not traded at all. Most of these securities are in fact unmarketable. This has led to a concentration of ownership which is represented mainly by the above-mentioned merging of mutual funds into holding joint-stock companies and the merging of other companies including banks. There is another trend in which the majority shares in small joint-stock companies have been taken over by one or more large investors – and consequently many of these companies have disappeared from the market.

The Prague Stock Exchange is fully computerized, which means that all transactions between buyers and sellers are realized electronically. It is possible to trade securities in three independent ways. Firstly, there is the central market (Automatic Trading System, ATS), then there are direct trades, and finally block trades. The only price-setting market is the central market. Neither direct nor block trades affect the registered prices of stocks in any way – although the volume of these trades exceeds the volume traded on the central market several times over. Direct and block trades are also provided by the RM system, apart from the fact that the transfer of securities is mainly made directly through the Security Register (SCP) which is not a market maker nor designed for this purpose. To sum up, such – in fact hidden – direct trades are not conducive to fostering an important feature of any developed market – transparency.

The securities traded in the central market are spread among three markets. There are the main market and the secondary market which are considered to be the prestigious (elite) ones. The Stock Exchange Committee for Quotation decides whether to allow a certain security to enter the main and the secondary markets, taking into consideration the overall economic situation of the issuer and also the quality of the issued security. At the same time, the issuer is obliged to inform the Stock Exchange and the public about its economic performance and the actual financial conditions. The obligation is quarterly for issuers in the main market and half-yearly for those in the secondary market. The listing of selected stocks on the main or secondary market serves as a useful indicator of the soundness of a particular company. By the end of March 1996, there were 45 issues of stock and units and 23 issues of bonds placed in the main market and 42 issues of stock and units with only one issue of bonds in the secondary market. The rest of the securities are still traded only in the OTC market where there were 1,636 issues of stock and units and 35 issues of bonds on 31 March 1996.

In addition to the division described above, the securities are subdivided into three trading groups, according to liquidity:
- The first trading group includes the issues which are traded daily – firstly with the method of fixing followed by continuous trading at variable prices.
- The second trading group includes securities traded daily – using also the method of fixing first, but followed by additional orders at fixed price.
- The third trading group includes less liquid issues traded in the same way as the issues of the second group, but only twice a week.

The orders for purchase of securities in the central market are inserted into the system up till 10:00 a.m. The loading sequence is irrelevant. After 10:00 a.m.

no more orders are accepted. After that, the automatic system, working to accurate and fixed algorithms, calculates the market price and at the same time pairs up the buy-and-sell orders. All transactions are anonymous. The noon prices are announced at 11:00 a.m., including actual supply and demand overhangs. Between 11:30 a.m. and 2:00 p.m. additional orders are accepted. These orders are registered in the automatic system according to the loading sequence. The closing results of trading are announced at 4:00 p.m. each trading day. The difference between the follow-up price and the previous price must not exceed an allowed margin. The margin is dependent on the trading group in which the security is traded. This price also becomes the mid-price of the margin for the next day. The trades are usually settled within three days. Besides the anonymous trading in the central market there are also direct and block trades taking place. Direct trade is a concerted trade between two Stock Exchange members where the number of securities and the price must correspond on both sides. The minimum volume of such trades is at present fixed at CZK 200,000. The price at which the contract is concluded is considered irrelevant to the market price of the security and is neither limited nor tied to the actual market price.

Block trades are anonymous trades with blocks of securities – sets of one issue included in one order. At present, the minimum value of such a trade is CZK 500,000. The price of the security purchased in a block trade is not tied to the actual market price of the security and there are no margins limiting it. It is possible to set a minimum acceptable number of securities offered to sell or buy. The orders are filled in chronological order.

The Prague Stock Market founded two daughter companies: the Stock Exchange Security Register, which provides the settlement of trades effected in the Stock Exchange; and the Czech Capital Information Agency (CEKIA), which collects data, carries out analyses and provides information on the Czech capital market.

In addition, the Prague Stock Exchange has so far introduced 22 indexes. Since these indexes are price indexes, there is no dividend adjustment included in the calculations.

The official Prague Stock Exchange Index PX 50 was created according to the International Finance Corporation (IFC) Index Methodology. The index sample consists of 50 issues which are selected according to market capitalization, liquidity, and branch classification. Any issue can be selected to become one of the base issues of the index except the ones belonging to investment funds, and it does not matter which market (main or secondary) the security is placed in. The PXL documents the price development of stocks traded in the main and secondary markets. Its base is formed by all issues listed in these two prestige markets except those of investment funds. The global index PX GLOB

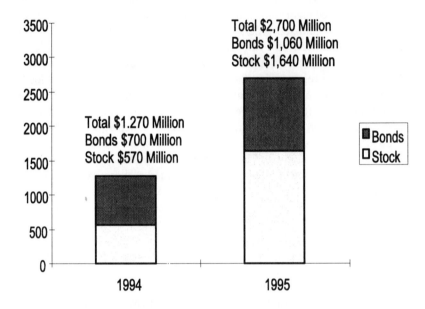

Source: PlanEcon Report, 1996.

Figure 4.3. Change in foreign portfolio investment between 1994 and 1995

includes all issues of stock (including investment funds) and units that were priced in the market. The branch indexes BI01–BI19 reflect the stock exchange branch classification. The index sample is constituted in the same way as the PX GLOB index sample.

Besides the indexes described above there are other indexes which are published in the press and which meet the specific requirements of various financial institutions. The RM-System publishes its own index, the PK-30. Moreover, an official index for bonds has not yet been created. There are indexes published by Ceska sporitelna and Patria Finance.

The Prague Stock Exchange intends to introduce trading with financial derivates in the near future. Derivate trading will be adopted in the Amendment to the Act on Securities which has come into force on 1 July 1996. The foundation of a futures exchange is expected in 1997. At present there are two Commodity Exchanges in the Czech Republic. These are the Agricultural Commodity Exchange in Brno and the Commodity Metal Exchange in Kladno. The trades conducted there have insignificant volume.

Table 4.6. Selected indicators of the Prague Stock Exchange

	1993	*1994*	*1995*	*1.Q 1996*
Number of members	62	71	101	104
Issues in the market	982	1055	1764	1782
Volume of trades (CZK)	9 bn	62 bn	195.4 bn	100.8 bn
Volume of trades (US$)	301 mn	2.3 bn	7.23 bn	3.72 bn
Market capitalization total, CZK	n.a.	403.1 bn	566.4 bn	647.2 bn
Market capitalization – shares and units, CZK	n.a.	353.1 bn	478.6 bn	539.1 bn
Market capitalization – bonds	n.a.	50 bn	87.8 bn	108.1 bn
P/E ratio Issues of Main and Secondary Market	n.a.	12.51	10.40	12.75
Number of market days	41	161	234	60
Average daily volume CZK	220 mn	385.3 mn	835 mn	1679.8 mn
Average daily volume US$	7.34 mn	14.29 mn	30.93 mn	62.01 mn

Source: Prague Stock Exchange, 1996.

SOURCES OF EXTERNAL FINANCE

Following the division of Czechoslovakia and the successful completion of the currency separation, an upsurge of confidence led to a remarkable inflow of foreign capital starting with the second half of 1993. The positive Moody's rating together with the opening of capital market institutions (both the Prague Stock Exchange and the RM-system) also contributed to the growing interest of foreign investors.

There were significant changes in the structure of capital inflow, particularly concerning the origin of the capital – in comparison with the early years of transformation the share of capital resources drawn from official financial institutions (IMF, European Union, the World Bank and G24) declined in favor of private capital. This change is associated with growing confidence on the part of foreign investors who started to divert their resources particularly into CNB bonds, moving from granting credits to portfolio investments. Such changes resulted in a decline in foreign direct investments.

A similar trend could also be seen in 1994, when the private capital already dominated the Czech capital market. Growth in foreign currency reserves led to a decision to settle a debt of US$ 1,110 million to the IMF in advance. As a result indebtedness to international financial institutions declined rapidly. Major sources of capital inflow were money loans drawn by domestic businesses and direct and portfolio investments. The structure of capital usage was continually changing, which could be seen particularly in the growth in volume of loans for investment. There were also significant changes in the structure of portfolio investments. Unlike previous periods, when the inflow of capital from this type of investment was provided only by means of issues of CNB bonds in international capital markets, the capital inflow from portfolio investments in 1994 was provided by private institutions. Besides this, portfolio investments denominated in CZK and traded in the domestic capital market slowly became dominant. This trend continued during the whole of 1995. The sources of capital inflow were still foreign direct investments. The growth in portfolio investments increased. At that time, syndicate loans from foreign bank consortiums were also realized, totalling US$ 425 million.

Table 4.7. The capital account in US$ million

Convertible currencies	1993	1994	1995	31.3. 1996
Capital account	2639.0	2445.4	7546.7	54.1
Direct investments	516.6	841.5	2526.1	298.6
– abroad	-51.2	-20,9	-32.4	-20.3
– in Czech republic	567.8	862.4	2558.5	318.9
Portfolio investments	1059.1	819.3	1615.1	-129
Long-term capital	528.4	859.5	3172.6	159.2
Short-term capital	534.9	-74.9	232.9	-274.7

Source: Czech National Bank, 1996.

The inflow of direct investments carried on through the first quarter of 1996. On the other hand, short-term capital (hot money) was draining out of the economy.

CONCLUSION

This chapter covers capital market developments in the Czech Republic during the years 1993–1996. Generally, it can be expected that the trends described here will continue throughout 1997, although changes to government policy are possible due to the failure of the government coalition to win a majority in the new Czech Parliament in the June 1996 elections. Such changes in government policy may influence the overall economic figures in some ways, but no significant change in basic economic strategy is to be expected.

Among the current main problems of the Czech economy, the negative current account must be given pride of place. During the first quarter of 1996 the deficit in the current account exceeded the surplus in the capital account for the first time ever. Together with the outflow of short-term speculative capital this resulted in a partial decline in foreign currency reserves. At present, the new government is expected to take specific measures which were considered premature by the former government. Carrying out and completing the recovery program in the Czech banking sector seems to be another crucial task in the near future.

Because the majority of Czech companies already belong to one or more major owners, the process of the concentration of ownership will probably come to an end soon. It may be assumed that the volume of transactions will be negatively affected by this process. On the other hand, shares are likely to be traded in larger volumes per transaction, i.e. the stock will be traded in larger blocks due to the merger of companies, and mutual and share funds. The reverse can be expected in the case of bond trading. The number and the volume of bonds traded in the market so far have been relatively low, although these securities will certainly play a very important role in the economy. Furthermore, both organizers of stock markets (Prague Stock Exchange and RM-system) will try to draw the majority of trades at present being executed directly through the Security Register into transparent public markets. This way the transparency of the capital market should benefit, particularly with respect to the availability of information.

REFERENCES

Bankovnictvi (1996), nos. 9, 16.
BCPP (1996): Vysledky obchodovani na BCPP 1. ctvrtletí 1996
BURZA (1996), no. 102/1996.
CzechInvest Information Factsheet (1996), no. 1, Czech Invest, Prague.
Czech National Bank (1993): *Zprava o vzniku*, Prague.
Czech National Bank (1993): *Vyrocni zprava*, Prague.
Czech National Bank (1994): *Vyrocni zprava*, Prague.
Czech National Bank (1994): *Zprava o menovém vyvoji v Ceske republice za prvni pololeti*, Prague.
Czech National Bank (1995): *Zprava o menovem vyvoji v Ceske republice za období leden - zari*, Prague
Czech National Bank (1996): *Zprava o menovem vyvoji v Ceske republice za prvni ctvrtleti*, Prague.
Hospodarské noviny (1996), nos. 60, 69, 97, 102.
MF Dnes (1996), no. 114.

PlanEcon Report (1996), nos. 5–6, PlanEcon, Washington, D.C.

Rejnuš, O. (1996): *Vybrane aspekty Ceskeho kapitalového trhu a perspektivy jeho dalsiho rozvoje*, Politicka ekonomie 1/1996, VSE Praha.

P33   G21
P34   G28
P24   G12
F32

5. Hungary

István Ábel

MACROECONOMIC DEVELOPMENTS AND ECONOMIC POLICY

As a result of harsh stabilization measures, the Hungarian current account and fiscal deficits have been reduced significantly in 1995. The volume of imports declined, exports increased, and the current account deficit of USD 3.9 billion in 1994 was reduced to USD 2.5 billion in 1995. As a percentage of GDP the current account deficit decreased from 9.5% in 1994 to 5.3% in 1995. The 4.2 percentage-point improvement in the current account in a single year is impressive even in an international context. The public sector deficit to GDP ratio also declined from 8.1% in 1994 to 6.5% in 1995. General public sector borrowing requirement remained at the 1994 nominal level as a result of a significant macroeconomic adjustment (Kopint-Datorg, 1996).

The improvement in the two balances has a common origin, commonly known as the Bokros' Package, named after the new finance minister who introduced the import surcharge and other measures of fiscal restraint at the same time as a 12% devaluation and the introduction of a crawling peg was declared in March 1995. The fiscal correction was reflected in the fast growth in revenues (27%) and the moderate increase in expenditures (8%). In the first year of the fiscal correction the impact came mainly on the revenue side through the increase of revenues from customs (67%) and corporate taxes (20%).

The moderate growth of output was due to the expansion of exports (8%), while the domestic market shrank. In 1995, industrial output increased by 4.8%, while industrial exports increased by 19.1% at the same time as domestic sales declined by 1.4%.

Monetary policy was rather restrictive as M2 increased by 17.4%, while CPI inflation reached 28.2%. Deducting foreign currency deposits from M2, the increase was only 8.1%, which indicates a 15.7% decline in real money balances. Monetary policy has been used effectively to contain the impact of capital inflows and the conversion into Forint of foreign exchange deposits in banks.

The nominal devaluation of the Forint against a basket of ECU and DEM amounted to 29% in 1995, and represented a minor real depreciation of the currency. The pre-announced crawling peg, introduced on 12 March 1995, calmed devaluation and inflationary expectations, but it had its shortcomings, too. Once it proved to be sustainable, the high domestic interest rates triggered a significant inflow of foreign currency, and its conversion to Forint would have resulted in an appreciation of the Forint, since the crawling peg obliged the central bank to buy foreign currency at the bottom of the intervention range. Such interventions, however, would have increased domestic liquidity and contributed to inflationary pressures. To handle the excess liquidity, the central bank has increased mandatory reserve requirements, which at the same time increased the costs of financial intermediation by banks. Sterilization incurred significant costs and also contributed to the preservation of the high interest premium, raising domestic interest rates above foreign rates. Sterilization in this case basically meant the accumulation of relatively low-yield foreign currency reserves when selling high-yield government bonds to the population to neutralize the inflow of foreign currency converted into Forints. The loss resulting from sterilization occurs directly in the central bank but it is eventually born by the budget, so it represents an additional fiscal burden.

The monetary policy instruments used in open market operations include repurchase agreements of government securities, short-term swaps, and outright buying and selling of government securities in secondary markets. The repo interest rate is the reference rate for the market. The central bank determines the repo interest rate and regularly reviews it in its operation. Availability is unlimited for reserve repos, while there are limits broken down by banks on the repo side. There is also an unlimited overnight repo facility carrying a penalty interest rate. There are overnight and one-week maturities for repos, while for reverse repos there is in addition to these maturities a one-month maturity. Central bank financing is also available for banks' liquidity purposes in the form of one-week and spot swaps. Interest rates posted by the central bank include in addition to repo and swap rates the rediscount rate used for discounting bills of exchange with less than 90-day maturities, interest rates paid on mandatory reserves, and the base rate. The base rate charged by the central bank on long-term refinancing loans is a floating rate during the term of the refinancing contract. The mandatory reserve requirement is 12%, and the base for the calculation is linked to components of the M3 money supply aggregate.

Central bank independence is enhanced by the fact that the governor is appointed by the president of the country for six years and that the bank reports to the House of Parliament.

THE BANKING SECTOR

At the end of 1995 there were 42 banks active in the banking system in Hungary. The number of large banks is 7, of which 2 are state owned, and 5 are private. Their combined market share is 70.8% (Table 5.1). The number of medium-sized banks is 12 with a market share of 19.6%. The 23 smaller banks represented 9.6% of the market.

Table 5.1. Market share of groups of banks

	Number of banks	Market share (Percentage)
Large banks	7	70.8
Private	5	50.7
State-owned	2	20.1
Medium-sized banks	12	19.6
Private	7	12.3
State-owned	5	7.3
Small banks	23	9.6
Private	14	6.4
State-owned	9	3.2

Note: According to total balance sheet 1995.
Source: National Bank of Hungary, Budapest, 1996.

Table 5.2. Total balance sheet by groups of banks in Hungary 1995

Groups of Banks	Private	State-owned	Total
Large	120.7	96.4	112.7
Medium-sized	153.4	123.3	140.6
Small	157.3	120.6	142.8
Total			119.8

Note: Percentage change, 1994=100.
Source: National Bank of Hungary, Budapest, 1996.

The aggregated balance sheet total of the banking system has increased by 19.8%, while the group of private banks has increased its balance sheet much faster (see Table 5.2). Large state-owned banks, however, have not been able to maintain their balance sheet total at the level of the previous year.

In a series of bank bail-outs (called loan, bank, and debtor conciliation) the state took over HUF 150 billion of bad debt from 17 banks and 69 savings cooperatives in the period 1990–1994. The number of default clients covered by the bail-out was 2,619. The procedure had three basic components: there was a limited capital increase by the state; the banks also got state funds (consolidation bonds) to replenish their risk reserves; and part of the bail-out was passed to the clients to help them in financial restructuring.

In those banks that have been bailed out in the bank conciliation process a significant internal restructuring continued in 1995. In several cases this was accompanied by staff reductions. While in previous years state intervention and crisis management dominated the market, in 1995 even the consolidated banks already had sufficient reserves to start a significant cleaning of the portfolio. Bad debt for the whole sector was 4.7% of aggregate balance sheet total in 1995 compared to 8.1% in 1994.

Profitability was restored and the aggregate profit of the banking system reached HUF 40 billion for the year 1995. The main effort of most banks was devoted to moving ahead in retail banking to enhance their funding capacity. Some joint venture banks continued to expand their regional network. Electronic banking is also gaining momentum.

Table 5.3. Ownership structure of banks in Hungary

	1994	1995
State ownership	66.8	43.2
– Direct state ownership	65.9	39.4
– Social insurance funds	0.9	3.8
Private	33.2	56.8
Total	100.0	100.0
Domestic	84.9	64.4
Foreign	15.1	35.6

Note: In percentage.

PRIVATIZATION

By the end of 1995, more than 70% of state-owned assets had been privatized, and the share of the private sector in GDP had increased to about 60–70%. Privatization is more and more dominated by market-oriented methods.

The 'first wave' of privatization was completed before the political changes targeted the development of private entrepreneurial concerns. The Company Act (No. VI of 1988), the Act on the Transformation of State-Owned Enterprises (No XIII of 1989), the Law on State-Owned Enterprises (SOE) (No. VI of 1977) and its modification of 1984, in addition to the above mentioned laws, made it possible that the SOEs were relatively independent: they were self-governed and could start their own privatization (known as 'spontaneous' privatization). To promote a controlled acceleration of privatization in every sector of the economy, the government established the State Privatization Agency (SPA) with a similar mandate as that of the Treuhandanstalt in Germany. (No. VII of 1990 Act on State Property Agency, No. VIII of 1990 Act on the Protection of State Assets, No. LXXIV of 1990 Act on Retail trade, Catering trade and Consumer services, No. XVI of 1990 on Concessions, further on Laws on Compensation Coupons to compensate people whose property was confiscated – by making possible their participation in the privatization process – also belonged to the 'first wave'.)

In 1992 a unified privatization law supported the start of the 'second wave' of privatization. The institutional body managing the process remained the SPA, but its specialization and focus on transactions was enhanced by the fact that the Hungarian State Holding Company (HSHC) was established by the government to manage the assets of the state that were to remain partially or totally under state ownership in the longer term (Law No. LIII of 1992). The State Property Agency (Law No. LIV of 1992), belonging to the state budget, was made responsible for the privatization of the remaining entrepreneurial assets of the state.

In addition to the organizational changes, it was obligatory to transform SOEs into corporations. This process is called 'commercialization' of SOEs. The Law No. XLIV of 1992 on Employee Share Ownership Program was also adopted at that time. This law created a legal basis for ESOP-type privatization of commercialized enterprises.

Following the second free Parliamentary elections of May 1994, the new government clearly began to evaluate the privatization experiences of the previous years and decided to put greater emphasis on those techniques which generated larger cash proceeds and more hard currency revenues from selling state assets. In order to reach these targets it was decided that the context – including the legal background – and the practice of privatization had to be reformulated.

The Act XXXIX of 1995 on the Sale of State-Owned Entrepreneurial Assets means the 'third wave' of privatization laws. The preparation of the New

Privatization Law suffered a long delay because of the conflicting interests of several pressure groups – political, professional, administrative, trade unions etc. (Some of the subjects of the debates were: who decides on the privatization of the strategically important companies, government or parliament? will the cash payment be prioritized in view of the limited purchasing power of domestic entrepreneurs? how do you guarantee control over possible abuses, corruption? how should the new organization be established? will the representatives of the trade unions be included on the board of directors (BOD)? how will the representatives of the parliamentary groups be involved?)

The Privatization Law was approved by Parliament on 9 May 1995 and came into force on 16 June 1995. Consequently, the debates preceding the new law slowed down the privatization process, even though it was possible to launch tenders on the basis of the former laws but focusing on the new priorities.

The new privatization law merged the two state agencies, the State Property Agency and the State Holding Company into one unit, the State Privatization and Holding Company (SPHC). The appendix to the law lists the companies and the size of the stake which will remain in long-term state ownership. Altogether 88 out of 1,857 companies will remain partly or wholly in permanent state ownership. Railways, the Hungarian Postal Services, Eximbank, and some other companies of strategic importance belong to this list.

On the basis of the new privatization Act the newly created institution set out a very ambitious program, namely, to change the, to-date, rather bleak general view of investors about Hungary. Evidently, the SPHC proved successful in its efforts, because proceeds in 1995 were much higher than expected. The total of privatization revenues in 1995 reached HUF 474 billion, about the same amount as in the whole of 1990–1994. Another remarkable difference in 1995 is that 95% of the revenues were in cash and 87% in hard currency. In earlier years special loan facilities (subsistence and start-up loans) and instalment payment schemes used by members of ESOP had a much greater role in privatization.

Out of the privatization revenues a total of HUF 250 billion was paid into the budget, as required by the budget laws 1995 and 1996, and HUF 92 billion were used for repayment of the public debt. Total expenditure connected with the sales amounted to 7% of revenues.

The most important events in privatization in 1995 in Hungary were the selling of some strategic companies. First among the transforming economies Hungary has started the large-scale privatization of public utilities. In December 1995 50% plus 1 share in all 6 gas distribution companies, an average stake of 47.8% in all 6 electricity supply companies, and 34–49% in

2 (out of 7) power-generating companies were sold to foreign strategic investors. Privatization of the country's integrated oil company (MOL) was begun successfully. Shares of MOL were sold to financial investors in Europe and the US.

Table 5.4. The privatization of MOL

1. A private placement of shares with financial investors combined with an introduction on foreign stock exchanges. A stake of 25% was offered to foreign investors. The shares will be listed on the Budapest Stock Exchange, on the Luxembourg Stock Exchange and will also be traded on the London SEAQ International market (Stock Exchange Automated Quotation). Total *foreign ownership* reached 30.15% with this issue.
2. Sales offer of shares to management and employees on preferential terms include 5.5% of shares. The actual *employee and management ownership* realized was 4.9%, as not everyone could utilize the offer at full capacity.
3. Domestic public offering of 3% of shares was sold either for cash or on a cash instalment basis. Small domestic investors had a choice of two options: either to buy the shares at a 10% discount of the issue price or on a cash instalment basis. In the case of a cash instalment purchase, 30% of the price is payable on subscription, the remaining 70% is payable not later than 15 November 1996, with the first instalment only permitted to be paid on 1 February 1996, at the earliest. Total *domestic private* and institutional ownership reached 5.3%.
4. As MOL is the national oil company, the government decided to retain 50% of shares in permanent *state ownership* plus one ordinary share and one share with preferencial rights later. The latter share provides the right of veto for the state in some important issues like liquidation of the company, or merger with another company. Thus the Hungarian state will continue to have a major influence on the company. The actual 58.7% state stake still leaves room for further issues. 1.1% of shares are owned by municipalities.

MOL is Hungary's national oil and gas industry company. Apart from OMV of Austria this is the only fully integrated oil and gas company in the region. In terms of sales MOL is the largest industrial company in Hungary. It deals with the exploration of natural gas and crude oil fields, field development and exploitation, the transport, distribution, storage and refining of crude oil, and the wholesale as well as the retail sale of oil products. The steps undertaken to privatize MOL are listed in Table 5.4.

The privatization of the *electricity sector* had several setbacks during 1995.

A fairly long dispute preceded the decision, concerning the size of the block of shares to be acquired by foreign investors. Finally, the government decided that most of the shares could be privatized, and no distinction will be made between domestic and foreign investors, although in the first round bids for only 48% of the shares were invited. The new owner, however, will also get the right of pre-emption to acquire the remaining stake and can exercise this right up to 31 December 1997.

The Hungarian Power Companies Ltd. (MVM) represents the controlling level in the existing business organization in this branch of the energy industry. MVM and the power plants as well as the distribution companies belonging to the group provide the electricity supply for the whole country. After privatization the power plants and the distribution companies will be separate from MVM. This method of privatization is expected to generate competition between the independent power plants. MVM will, however, retain its strategic planning and coordinating function for the industry as a whole. It will also reserve to itself the control of the formation of the tariffs, as specified by the Electrical Energy Act. The high-voltage basic network which connects the customer centres and ensures the international connections belongs to MVM.

The separation of power plants and the retail distribution network is achieved using a complex chain of share exchanges and capital reductions. Local governments also get a significant share in the privatized network in return for their own investments in developing the current network. The privatization procedure for the electricity sector is shown in Table 5.5.

The privatization of the *gas distribution companies* completes the reorganization of the energy sector in Hungary. The newly-established Hungarian Energy Office has issued licences and defined the rights and obligations of the gas distribution companies, as well as participating in the creation of the new price regulation system, which, with an indexed price mechanism, assures the long-term profitable operation of the gas distributing companies.

At present, there are six gas distribution companies in Hungary, and the pipelines operated by them encompass the entire country. The gas distribution companies operate as natural monopolies. In order to prevent the new owners from abusing their monopoly position the operations of these companies are controlled by the state and the principles for price calculation and price corrections are given by decree. One of the most important preconditions for privatization is the introduction of a gas price regime reflecting value ratios and bringing long-term profits.

During the privatization of the gas distribution companies tenders could be submitted for the purchase of all five companies. However, in order to prevent a monopoly situation, each applicant was restricted to shares in a maximum of two gas distribution companies. 50% plus one voting share (i.e. majority ownership) was for sale in each gas distribution company.

Table 5.5. Privatization of the electricity sector

1. Selling of minority shares of six power distributor companies and seven power plant companies of MVM through a tender to strategic investors.
2. Restructuring of electricity industry in such a manner that MVM receives about 49% of the shares of Paks Nuclear Power Plant (the largest supplier) and about 42% of the shares of OVIT (high–voltage network), from SPHC. In exchange for this MVM transfers 50% of its shares in electricity distribution companies.
3. The buyers winning the tender of MVM companies (step 1) may increase their holdings up to 25% plus one share at MVM.
4. Preferential sale of shares to employees of the companies and transfer of shares for the portfolio of the distribution companies.
5. Procurement of majority interest in the distribution companies and at certain power plant companies.
6. Public offering of shares in the distribution companies to domestic small investors as well as to Hungarian and foreign institutional investors.

MATAV, the Hungarian Telecommunication Company, was established in 1990, when it was separated from the Hungarian Post. It had been in exclusive state ownership until December 1993, when privatization began. This was the first privatization project involving telecommunications in Central and Eastern Europe. The first year of privatized MATAV – 1994 – was a year of creating a competitive telecom market in Hungary. MATAV faces competition from the local concessionary telephone companies and the rapidly developing GSM network. During the past three years, the technical development in the field of telecommunications has accelerated. In the first round of privatization MagyarCom, a consortium of Ameritech International and Deutsche Telekom, bought 30.29% of shares. EBRD and IFC also joined in by buying 2.97%. After the first round the state still retained 66.74% ownership in the company.

The new privatization strategy originally included a plan for introducing the shares on the Budapest and New York stock exchanges. Simultaneously, talks began with the strategic foreign owner, MagyarCom, on the purchase of an additional share package, which could give them a 65–70% stake in the company. With the transaction now completed MagyarCom has a 67% stake and APV Rt. retained a 24% plus one voting share stake. The remaining 9% is held by various institutions and MATAV.

It was also important that the privatization of the banking sector was resumed. The foreign owners of the Hungarian Foreign Trade Bank increased their stake to over 65%, and 20% of OTP (the national savings bank) were sold to foreign and 13% to domestic investors. In December 1995, 60% of the shares of Budapest Bank was sold to EBRD and General Electric Capital Services. Hungarian Credit Bank (MHB) was sold to ABN-Amro Bank in 1996.

The next steps in privatization include further offerings in MOL, Antenna Hungaria (telecom), and gas and electricity companies.

EXCHANGES

Regulatory Framework

The Securities Act (Law VI of 1990) laid down the basic rules of public share issues and determined the provisions for establishing the State Securities and Exchange Commission (SSEC) and the Budapest Stock Exchange (BSE). The Stock Exchange is organized as a self-governing body and the Charter of the BSE describes the conditions of membership, jurisdiction, termination, the organization of the BSE and the tasks and responsibilities of its bodies. The BSE has established separate rules for listing and trading securities, stock exchange transactions and trading, and the rules of the membership and settlements (Bíró, 1995).

The Charter and its modifications are passed by the general assembly of the BSE, while the other rules and amendments are established by the BSE council. The approval of the SSEC is required for any new regulations. The SSEC also monitors whether the activities of the BSE are in accordance with the statutory rules as well as whether they meet the requirements of investors' security. For this purpose the commissioners nominated by the Commission are entitled to monitor individual transactions and to attend the general assembly as well as the meetings of the BSE council and its committees. They also have the right to inspect the records.

The Securities Act delegates the right of approval of the share-issue prospectus before publication to the SSEC. The conditions of public issues differ for bonds and shares. In the case of bonds the issuer should have operated for at least one year, should entrust a broker with the tasks of the public issue and must also follow the guidelines for the content of the prospectus. In the case of share issues the issuer must be either a limited liability company (KFT) or a registered shares company (RT). The requirement for brokerage activities is a minimum capital of HUF 5 million.

The regulations related to foreigners

The basic rules for foreigners are included in the Act of Law XXIV of 1988 on Investments by Foreigners in Hungary. It guarantees that their investments enjoy full protection and safety. Foreigners are free to establish businesses or obtain equity in companies in Hungary with the following restrictions: When a foreign investor acquires bearer shares, such shares must be transformed into registered ones. The time for this in case of succession must be within a year from probate, in any other case within three months from the acquisition of the shares. Further restrictions apply for investment in financial institutions which are regulated by the Act of Credit Institutions. Foreign investors, however, also enjoy special benefits. Investments in case of withdrawal (capital reduction, liquidation, etc.) can be freely transferred abroad in the currency in which the investment was effected.

Foreigners may place their convertible Forint accounts with any domestic bank. Such deposits may be converted to a freely convertible currency. The balance of such accounts can be transferred abroad or inland. Foreigners investing in Hungary are liable to taxes according to the laws of their domicile, provided that there is an agreement on the elimination of double taxation between Hungary and the given country. Joint ventures may enjoy tax benefits of varying degrees, depending on the proportion of the foreign equity participation.

Conditions for admission to the BSE

For *shares* the admission criterion is that they have to be of public issue, which requires that the articles of association of the company are harmonized with the Hungarian legislation and the rules of the BSE. The minimum size of the equity is HUF 500 million for listed and HUF 100 million for traded shares. The operation of the firm must be transparent and the rights attached to the securities must be disclosed. SSEC has the final say on admission, assuming that the hearing and any request for additional information are complied with.

After the introduction of a share issue a market maker must be nominated for a period of 15 days. This market maker must maintain a bid and offer continuously each day to a minimum value of HUF 100,000. The bid and offer prices must be within a 10% range. Offers must be maintained until the daily total turnover reaches HUF 10 million or at least 0.5% of the nominal value of the shares introduced (Szendrei, 1995).

The issuer has to supply the BSE with a specified number of copies of the prospectus as well as the shares in duplicate. The prospectus contains general information about the company, the ownership structure, types of shares, previous bond issues (including those which have already matured), the scope of the activity and history of the organization, a summary of the financial data,

balance sheet, profit and loss accounts, ratios, forecasts and expectations. The
risks involved in the activity must also be presented. The prospectus also gives
information about the business plans based on appropriate forecasts. The
methods used in the planning must also be indicated.

The issuer is obliged to disclose information regularly by submitting an
annual report by 31 May each year to the BSE. This annual report is audited
by a stock exchange auditor. Other quarterly and half-yearly reports are also
required by the BSE. In addition, the exceptional information disclosure
obligation means that the issuer must, within one working day, state all
available information which may lead to a modification of the quotation price
of the paper due to the operation or financial performance of the company.
Such events include the change in rights attached to the paper, the ownership
structure, initiation of a bankruptcy or liquidation procedure, the loss of more
than 15% of share capital, undertaking a loan in excess of 50% of equity, a call
for an extraordinary general meeting, dates of dividend payments, etc. The
conditions for admission to the BSE are summarized in Table 5.6.

Table 5.6. Budapest Stock Exchange listing requirements

	Listed shares (A)	Traded shares (B)
Share series to be introduced	min. HUF 500 million on exchange prices	min. HUF 100 million on exchange prices
Public ownership proportion	either min. 25% and min. HUF 200 million or min. HUF 500 million	either min. 10% and min. HUF 50 million or HUF 200 million or min. 100 owners
No. of owners	min. 100 persons	min. 25 persons
Financial year	3 completed and audited years, last year with stock exchange auditor	one year audited by stock exchange auditor
Series	can only consist of registered shares	
The stock exchange obligation of trading	trading can only take place through the stock exchange via exchange members	
Commissions	can only be fulfilled through the stock exchange	can only be fulfilled through the stock exchange

Source: BSE Company Fact Book 1996, Bank & Tõzsde, 1996, p. 14.

Trading

The role of the BSE in channelling domestic and external funds to the private sector and the government is increasing. By the end of 1995 foreign investors invested more than USD 1 billion in listed securities which accounts for about one-tenth of the overall foreign capital invested in Hungary since 1990. The turnover exceeded HUF 250 billion (USD 2 billion) in 1995, when there were 166 securities listed, including 42 shares and 84 government bonds and treasury bills in addition to 36 investment funds and the compensation note (restitution coupons). The aggregate market capitalization is HUF 1220 (USD 8.8) billion.

Share prices have been volatile during the last five years. The market started in a bullish mood in 1990, which was followed by a long correction period lasting from the second half of 1991 to early 1993, when the BUX index bottomed out at 667. Then there was a positive trend until February 1994 when the BUX reached 2,255. Political uncertainties about the forthcoming elections brought another correction to the prices. The BUX declined over the rest of 1994 and bottomed out at the end of January 1995. Since then there has been an impressive increase and market capitalization reached USD 12.5 billion by July 1996.

The official share index (BUX) of the BSE closed at 3,561.88 points on 12 November 1996, 240% higher than at the beginning of 1995. Among world stock markets the BSE registered the second highest rise in prices (95% in USD terms) during the first six months of 1996. Since 1 February 1996, the BSE has introduced the Central European Stock Index (CESI). (See Appendix 1.)

Markets of the Budapest Stock Exchange

Equity market

The 42 traded companies represented a market capitalization of HUF 328 billion, providing 27% of the total market capitalization at the end of 1995. This represents an 80% increase over 1994. This increase was a result of the flotation of some of the largest Hungarian companies, such as MOL and OTP.

Most of the Hungarian shares traded on the BSE are also traded outside Hungary. There are ADR and GDR issues traded in the USA and other markets. London is the largest market for Hungarian equities where a number of shares are traded on the SEAQ International. There is also significant activity on the Stuttgart, Munich, and the Vienna Stock Exchanges in Hungarian shares.

Domestic investors were attracted to the shares with low-priced IPOs and privatizations like Pick (food), Primagas (gas), and Danubius (hotel). The trade in compensation notes and the offerings of shares against compensation notes are also important factors in increasing the activity of domestic retail investors. Compensation notes were distributed in the restitution process.

BSE, in comparison to other exchanges in Central Europe, is less privatization-oriented and more private-sector oriented, since only 24 companies of the 42 are privatized companies.

A domestic OTC market has also developed in some of the shares. Many OTC-traded shares are issued by large, well-established companies which have a good prospect for future growth, such as Hungarian Foreign Trade Bank, Budapest Bank, MATAV, etc.

Fixed income securities market

This is dominated by government securities which are mostly bought by financial institutions and investment funds rather than private investors. Most of the government debt securities are traded on the OTC market.

Investment Funds appeared on the market after 1991 when the appropriate legislation was passed. Investment funds have mainly private investors. Most funds invest in government securities and only a few in corporate bonds. The law requires that closed-end investment funds should be listed on the stock exchange. At the end of 1995 there were 36 funds listed on the BSE with a market value of HUF 43 billion.

Derivative markets

These have also developed since March 1995 when they were launched. The BSE trades the following five contracts: 3-month treasury bills; the BUX index; and futures in USD, DEM and ECU against the Forint.

Membership and Operation of the BSE

The BSE is the only stock exchange in Hungary. Only incorporated entities (brokers or dealers) are allowed to participate in securities intermediation. The minimum registered capital is HUF 10 million (USD 70,000) for brokers and HUF 50 million (USD 350,000) for dealers. These companies are banned from other activities so banks cannot participate directly as intermediaries on the securities market. However, banks may establish subsidiaries in this field. The BSE has 56 members at present.

Since March 1993 a Central Market Support System has been used where each member firm of the BSE has its own workstation on the floor through which they can enter public orders to the Public Order Book. The back office system provides the information for the participants on the market. In March

1994 an automatic trading system was introduced in which orders are automatically matched in the computer network. Trading hours are from 10:15 a.m. to 1:15 p.m.

Clearing and Settlement

Transactions are settled through the central settlement system. A Central Clearing House and Depository (KELER) provides the safe and timely settlement of the securities and derivatives transactions and also the storage of securities. For current transactions on the BSE a rolling settlement system is applied where every transaction is settled on the fifth day following the trading day. The money and security positions of every broker are netted multilaterally. A clearing fund was established to minimize the risk of failure for the buyer and a buying-in procedure is applied to reduce the risk of failure for a seller.

Outlook for the Budapest Stock Exchange

Total market capitalization increased by 40% and reached USD 9 billion in the first quarter of 1996. At the same time equity market capitalization doubled, now reaching USD 2.4 billion. There are several factors which look set to maintain future growth. The macroeconomic stabilization is continuing, and with a strong commitment to privatization the country's credit risk has improved. Standard and Poor's gave Hungary an investment grade in November 1996. A sufficient supply of new securities is also provided by new issues and the continuing privatization process. There will be operational improvements both on the BSE and KELER, and their international connections with other exchanges are expected to be developed further. Institutional changes under way include allowing banks to trade in government securities directly and increasing minimum capital requirements for brokerage companies, while large brokerage companies will get the investment banking license.

Modernization includes the immobilization of securities enforced by the amendment of the Securities Act. The elimination of the physical movement of securities and the introduction of the nominee concept will improve the administration. BSE will implement a two-tier clearing system to replace the present unstructured model. The settlement cycle will be reduced from five to two days, beginning in the government securities market.

The centralized automatic trading system has been replaced by a partially decentralized one, in which a number of BSE members conduct trading from their offices. This will eventually help to extend trading hours and increase the number of market participants

PRIVATIZATION AND THE BUDAPEST STOCK EXCHANGE

The first public offering of a state-owned company was IBUSZ Co. Ltd. on 21 June 1990. It generated a great deal of interest on the part of investors but later, because of management problems, proved to be a failure. The next major issue came much later, in December 1992, when the sale of Pick and Danubius Hotels proved to be a success story. In 1994 a special instalment payment opportunity, the Small Investors' Share Purchase Program, increased the variety of privatization techniques.

BSE lists the shares of 19 privatized and 21 private (not formerly state-owned) companies. In December 1994 the capitalization of privatized companies amounted to HUF 110 billion, 61% of total capitalization.

Shares of privatized companies are traded more often and the velocity of circulation is three times higher than those of other shares. The share prices of privatized companies have increased faster than those of other shares. After one year, the share price of privatized companies was on average 54% higher than the introductory price. By contrast, the shares of private companies increased by only 10% in the first year (Szakmáry 1995, p. 20). This outstanding performance is explained by the excellent growth prospects of the company and the wide ownership base which provides liquidity in trading.

The experience of the following privatized companies provides insights into the common characteristics of companies realizing the best performances on the BSE: Egis, Global, Globus, Graboplast, Pick, Primagas and Richter Gedeon. In the majority of cases a public issue was combined with a capital increase. For domestic investors payment with cash and compensation coupons was also possible. It also seems to be important that in most cases the domestic issue was combined with the sale of a significant percentage of shares abroad (Szakmáry 1995, p. 20).

SOURCES OF EXTERNAL FINANCE

In Central and Eastern Europe Hungary attracted the most foreign capital (almost half of all investment was made in Hungary). It is, however, argued that the attractiveness of Eastern Europe can only be increased if other countries in the region can also offer favorable opportunities.

Direct foreign investment in Hungary between 1989 and 1995 has reached US$ 12 billion. While earlier investments mainly flowed into the manufacturing sector, in 1995 only 14% of new investment was in this sector. More than half of the joint ventures were established both in 1994 and 1995 in the services sector, in particular in wholesale and retail trades, repair of vehicles and household goods. Real estate and renting has recently become one of the most attractive sectors for investments. Foreign investment in order of the number of ventures established are dominated by German, Chinese, and Austrian companies. However, in term of total investments in 1995, the leaders are the USA, followed by the Netherlands, Germany, Cyprus and Austria. In terms of total investments since 1992, Germany leads, and Austria, France, the Netherlands, Belgium and the USA follow.

REFERENCES

Bíró, V. (1995): *The legal regulation of the Hungarian securities market*, in: *Five Years of the Budapest Stock Exchange*, Bank & Tõzsde, June.
Budapest Stock Exchange (1996): *BSE Company Fact Book 1996*, Bank & Tõzsde.
Kopint-Datorg (1996): *Economic Trends in Eastern Europe*, vol. 5., no. 1.
National Bank of Hungary (1996): *The Hungarian banking system in 1995*, National Bank of Hungary, Budapest.
Rotyis, J. (1996): *Developments and prospects of the Budapest Stock Exchange*, mimeo.
Szakmáry, D. (1995): *Stock exchange and privatization*, in: *Five Years of the Budapest Stock Exchange,* Bank & Tõzsde, June.
Szendrei, C. (1995): *Conditions for admission to the stock exchange*, in: *Five Years of the Budapest Stock Exchange,* Bank & Tõzsde, June.

APPENDIX

Table 5.A. Main figures of the Budapest Stock Exchange

	21 June 1990	31 Dec. 1990	31 Dec. 1991	31 Dec. 1992	31 Dec. 1993	30 Dec. 1994	29 Dec. 1995	28 June 1996
Number of the BSE members	42	42	48	48	47	51	56	57
Brokerage firms, banks	23+19	21+21	31+17	41+7	46+1*	50+1	55+1	56+1
Number of securities admitted on the BSE	1	6	22	40	62	120	166	163
– stocks	1	6	20	23	28	40	42	41
– government bonds			1	4	16	25	34	37
–corporate bonds			1	1	1	3	3	2
– t-bills				10	10	31	50	50
– investment funds				1	6	20	36	32
– compensation vouchers				1	1	1	1	1
Securities admitted on the BSE on nominal value (US$ mn)	8.1	99.3	440.4	2261.5	4387.3	7736	8731.4	10414
– stocks	8.1	99.3	240.7	343	380.3	720.9	1517.7	1472.9
– government bonds			198.4	952.7	2353.5	3380.6	2999.6	3617.9
– corporate bonds			1.3	1.2	3	14.5	11.3	7.7
– t-bills				706.2	763.7	2318.2	2964.8	4210.2
– investment funds				20.2	89.4	215	308	257.5
– compensation vouchers				238.2	797.4	1086.8	930	847.5

Table 5.A. Main figures of the Budapest Stock Exchange (continued)

	1990	1991	1992	1993	1994	1995	Jan.–Jun. 1996	Total
Capitalization on the BSE (mn)	1.6	266.9	708.8	2404.4	4538.2	7984.5	8757	12504
– stocks	1.6	266.9	505.2	562.1	811.3	1639.7	2350.2	4160.1
– government bonds			202.3	980.1	2400.2	3549.6	3255.5	4016.5
– corporate bonds			1.3	1.2	3	16.3	12.5	8.5
– t-bills				647.9	734.9	2164.6	2698.2	3766.6
– investment funds				22.6	54.6	174.4	306.7	264.6
– compensation vouchers				190.5	534.3	440	133.9	288.1

Note: 21 June 1990 – 28 June 1996. * Commercial banks have been excluded from the stock exchange and have established separate brokerage firms.
Source: BSE Company Fact Book 1996, Bank & Tőzsde, 1996, p. 6.

Table 5.B. Turnover of the Budapest Stock Exchange

	1990	1991	1992	1993	1994	1995	Jan.–Jun. 1996	Total
Prompt turnover on market value (US$ mn, duplicated)	96.8	135	426	2018	1960	2022	2472	9130
– stocks	96.8	131	76.1	198	530	696.9	1271	3000
– government bonds		4	157	797	500	616.2	991	3065
– corporate bonds		0	0	0	0.1	0.4	3.9	4.3
– t-bills			191	924	754	647.7	148	2664
– investment funds			0.4	1.1	2.4	27.4	17.8	49
– compensation vouchers			2.7	97.2	174	33.2	40.5	347.6

127

Table 5.B. Turnover of the Budapest Stock Exchange (continued)

Number of transactions	4 962	14 509	8 565	23 749	73 784	71 240	70 884	267 693
Average daily number of transactions	27	58	34	94	293	286	576	171
Average daily turnover (US$ mn)	0.5	0.5	1.7	8	7.8	8.1	20.1	5.8
Turnover/transaction (US$ thousand)	19.5	9.3	49.8	85	26.6	28.4	34.9	34.1
Number of working days	181	252	252	252	252	249	123	1 561

	Apr.–Dec. 1995	Jan.–Jun. 1996	Total
Futures turnover on market value (US$ bn, simple)	81.1	43170	51280
3-month t-bill	47.2	148	195.2
BUX	4.2	51.2	55.4
DEM	11.2	35.6	46.8
USD	10.7	74.1	84.8
ECU	7.7	123	130.6

Note: June 1990 – June 1996.
Source: BSE Company Fact Book 1996, Bank & Tőzsde, 1996, p. 6.

ES 2

G21 P33

G28 P34

G12 L33

6. Macedonia

Gordana Bival and Vladimir Gligorov

INTRODUCTION

The Macedonian[1] economy is only now in 1996 emerging from years from a depression that has been deeper and more prolonged than in most transitional countries.[2] Four main reasons for its present condition can be singled out:

1. *Break-up costs*. Macedonia suffered a great deal from the break-up of the Socialist Federative Republic of Yugoslavia (that occurred in 1991) because it was highly integrated into the former Yugoslav market. Much of its trade, over 70%, was within this market.

2. *The isolation from its main markets*. After becoming independent, Macedonia found itself in a difficult international environment, especially with the UN-imposed sanctions on the FR Yugoslavia (Serbia and Montenegro) that occurred in May 1992 and effectively closed Macedonia's main market, as well as with the embargo imposed on Macedonia by Greece (early 1994). The borders with Bulgaria and Albania were open, but the inherited rail and road links, where they exist, are quite bad.

3. *Internal instability*. The new country had to solve significant internal political problems connected especially with the stabilization of democracy, respect for human (especially minority) rights, and the rule of law. Also, there was much legislative work to be done, starting with the drawing-up of a constitution and with the introduction of practically a whole new legal environment.

4. *Slow transformation*.[3] Because of the international and internal problems,

---

[1] For the time being this state is recognized by international organizations under the name of The Former Yugoslav Republic of Macedonia (FYRM or FYROM). According to the Macedonian Constitution the name of the country could be translated as The Republic of Macedonia.

[2] For some comparisons see EBRD (1995), ECE (1996), Gligorov (1994) and Gligorov (1995).

[3] An early study is Wyzen (1993).

the reforms were slow in materializing. The major reform package was introduced only in the first half of 1994 when an agreement with the World Bank became possible and it was accelerated in the first half of 1995 when the stand-by agreement with the IMF was signed. In 1996 a new three-year extended stand-by agreement with the IMF is expected to come into effect. In 1995 GSP (gross social product) shrank by 3% and was down to just over 52% of what it was in 1989. It has to be pointed out that the former Yugoslavia's definition is still in force, namely, the gross social product (GSP) does not include the so called 'non-profit' services such as: healthcare, education, defence and government. It is usually estimated that GDP is 10% higher than GSP under normal circumstances.[4] Industrial production decreased by 11% and was down to just over 42% of its 1989 level.[5] Employment was also lower by about 10%, bringing the number of employed persons to just over 80% of what it was in 1989. The unemployment rate stood at over 37% at the end of 1995. However, inflation (retail prices) was curbed to 16% for the year as a whole (producer prices to 5%) and to just 6% in December 1995, compared with December 1994 (producer prices 3%). The average real wage was down 4%. Exports went up by 11%, imports by 12%. The trade balance showed a deficit of US$ 217 million while the current account deficit was slightly over US$ 200 million. The general government deficit was just over 1% of GSP. Foreign currency reserves stood at over US$ 250 million (about two months of imports) while gross debt was US$ 1.4 billion. [6]

---

[4] However, recent GDP estimates in FR Yugoslavia, which uses the same GSP methodology, put the GDP at between 17 and 20% above the official GSP. The reason for such a large difference was not given. The probable reason is that the so-called productive sector, which is captured by GSP, shrank faster than the unproductive sector, which is added to the GDP, so that the difference has increased. Therefore, one could expect that the GDP in Macedonia is about 15% higher than its GSP. Both figures do not include the black market activity that, according to some estimates, adds more than one-third to the GDP.

[5] Although industry accounts for about 43% of the GSP, Macedonia could be described as an agricultural society. Actually agriculture contributes about 19% in GSP. Unlike many other countries under transformation, it has already 85% of the land in private hands and 90% of the agricultural production is private. The main problems this sector faces stem from the fact that the largest market for the country's agricultural products were the republics of the former Yugoslavia. Therefore, the main goal in the future should be to re-establish the former trade relationships.

[6] More information can be found in: Zavod za Statistika (1996a). Also see Narodna banka (1996).

MONETARY POLICY

The monetary policy of the Macedonian Central Bank is based on the nominal exchange rate anchor. Officially, there is a floating exchange rate regime, but the Macedonian Denar has been in effect fixed to the Deutsche Mark for more than two years now. This has led to a real appreciation of the Macedonian currency while inflation has been successfully reduced.

Table 6.1. Money supply (M1) growth and inflation (CPI) dynamics

Year	M1 target	M2 growth	Difference	Price target	CPI growth	Difference
	1	2	(2-1)	3	4	(4-3)
1992	755.1	704.5	-50.6	2,408.40	1,925.20	-483.2
1993	268.3	239.7	-28.6	434.2	229.6	-204.6
1994	80.7	83.2	2.5	70	55.4	-14.6
1995	23	19.3	-3.7	8	9.2	1.2
I–VI 1996	5.9	-5.4	-11.3	2.2	-1.9	-4.1

Source: Bišev *et al.* (1996), pp. 83–84.

The central bank's monetary policy has relied on three main instruments:
1. Discount rate adjustments.
2. Sterilization.
3. Reserve requirements.

The discount rate is used as an instrument to influence the banks' interest rates. There is a close relationship between the movements in the discount rate and the interbank interest rate. Both rates (in real terms), have been highly positive, but also highly negative. In the past two years the discount rate has been positive in real terms, while the interbank interest rate has been even more positive in real terms (exceeding 20% p.a.).

The sterilization requirement has been significant because of the considerable inflow of foreign currency that threatened the Central Bank's control over money supply. The Central Bank buys back its debt instruments and the cost is covered from the central budget.

Table 6.2. Discount and interest rates in Macedonia (by end of period)

	December 1995	June 1996
Discount rate	15%	10%
Loans	25–30%	19.9%–30%

Deposits
  sight
  time (maturity)
	2.3%–5%
	7%–27%
		2.4%–7%
		3.6%–27%

Interbank		25%

Source: National Bank of the Republic of Macedonia (1996).

The reserve requirement is an instrument of credit rationing. The rates of compulsory reserves as well as the minimum rate of liquidity have not changed much during the period under consideration. At the end of 1992, the rate on sight (demand) deposits was 15%, while that on time deposits (over 3 months) was 5.5%. They were lowered to 8% and 3.5% respectively in 1993 and have stayed at that level ever since. In the savings banks the rates are lower (4% and 1.5% for sight and time deposits, respectively). The minimum liquidity rate was 7% in December 1992, 4% in December 1993, 2.5% in December 1994 and since then remained at that level.

For this reason a move is under consideration to change from reliance on the exchange rate anchor to a policy of money-supply targeting. The Central Bank of Macedonia has concluded from the experience of the past two years of relative price stability that there exists a close relationship between M2 and price level movements.

Inflation slowed down significantly in 1995 as an outcome of the stabilization program that was worked out with the IMF and the World Bank in 1994. The four main instruments of this program are:
1. a fixed exchange rate (around 27 Macedonian Denars for 1 Deutsche Mark);[7]
2. fixed wages for state sector employees;
3. a reserve requirement for the banks which tightens the possibilities of credit expansion;
4. a reduction in the general budget deficit.

---

[7] The average exchange rate in 1995 was 37.7 Macedonian Denars (DEN)/US$. Macedonia declared monetary independence in April, 1992, when it introduced its own currency, the Macedonian Denar (MKD or DEN), initially on par with the former Yugoslav Dinar. In May, 1993, a new Denar, equivalent to 100 of the old units, was put into circulation. Denominations of coins are 0.50, 1, 2 and 5 Denars and of bills 10, 20, 50, 100 and 500 Denars. 'Internal convertibility' of the Denar is permitted, while the 'external convertibility' of the Denar, i.e. trading abroad, is expected in a few years after IMF conditions have been met.

These measures did not produce instant price stability because it took some time for the government to gain credibility. However, the inflation rate in the first quarter of 1996 is as low as 5% per year (3% for producer prices). Support for the disinflation process also came from fiscal policy: the government deficit has been cut very significantly, mainly through eliminating subsidies. This has allowed the central bank to lower its discount rate several times and thus to spur investments.[8] They are expected to grow by 10% (in real terms) in 1996.

PRODUCTION

The production figures for 1995 do not tell the whole story. In fact, Macedonia's industrial production started growing in the first half of 1995, only to slow down in the second half. However, the direction has changed again after the Greek embargo was removed in mid-October 1995. Indeed, in the first quarter of 1996 production was growing steadily. The government is targeting 2% growth for 1996 as a whole. Gross social product, on the other hand, may very well grow even faster (the government expects a 2.6% increase) because agriculture is growing (by 5% already in 1995). It is expected that services will grow, and some black market activities that were connected with sanctions-busting may, now that the sanctions have been suspended, be better recorded (see footnote 4). In addition, the ongoing privatization and restructuring should have positive effects on the future development of industrial production.

PRIVATIZATION

According to official proclamations the primary objective of the privatization process in Macedonia is to increase the efficiency of the economy through the conversion of companies with 'social capital' into companies with defined ownership.[9] That is why in Macedonia the main method is the privatization by

---

[8] The discount rate developments are as follows 1992: 250%; 1993: 295%; 1994: 33%; 1995: 15%; June 1996: 10%. Figures for 1992–1993 are year averages, others are recorded eop.

[9] In former Yugoslavia there where four types of company ownership: social, private, mixed (social and private), and cooperative. State-owned enterprises were for the most part public utilities. Social ownership was not considered to be state or public ownership, but the companies and other institutions were considered to be owned by the community or public at large. Essentially the people employed by the company are the nominal owners, but in fact they do not hold title to shares nor may they transfer their ownership, nor do they have much responsibility for the conduct of the business. In other words 'everybody but nobody' is the owner.

sale, or case-by-case method, rather than voucher privatization or some other non-cash system. However, as a sort of a substitute and also to make the process as fair as possible, employees are offered a generous discount scheme. Furthermore, at the beginning, when a company enters into the privatization process, it must automatically transfer 15% of its book value to the Macedonian Pension Fund.

Under the Law on Transformation of Companies with Social Capital,[10] also known as the Privatization Law, the institution responsible for the administration and the support of the process is the Agency of the Republic of Macedonia for Transformation of Companies with Social Capital (Macedonian Privatization Agency or, briefly, Agency). The Agency is an independent state institution. The management is appointed by the government, and the employees are paid from the national budget.

The Agency does not manage the companies in which it owns shares, except in the case of the new private owners failing to pay for their shares. That has happened so far in the case of about 100 companies. In these cases the Agency takes over the management of the companies until the shares are sold to new owners. Besides the Agency there is also a Government Privatization Commission which makes final decisions regarding the transformation of companies.[11]

Foreign investors have exactly the same status as domestic investors under the law, and there are no restrictions on the repatriation of profits. However, there have been no significant foreign investments so far. The cumulative value of foreign direct investments up to December 1995 was about US$ 50 million which were mostly invested in small and medium-sized companies. In Macedonia there is a 30% corporate profit tax.

Several methods or models of privatization are available depending on the size of the company. Small and medium-sized companies are allowed to propose their own models, whereas large ones must select a model in consultation with the Agency.

For small companies the following models are possible:

---

[10] See: Official Gazette of the Republic of Macedonia No. 38/93. Other important laws connected with the privatization process are the Foreign Investment Law (Official Gazette of the Republic of Macedonia No. 31/93), the Concession Law (Official Gazette of the Republic of Macedonia No. 42/93), and the Securities Law (Official Gazette of the Republic of Macedonia No. 5/93).

[11] An important supporting institution that was very much involved at the beginning of the privatization process is the Uprava za Javni Prihodi (Public Revenue Office). It controls the privatization undertaken on the basis of former laws, verifying whether the procedure was in accordance with the then existing laws. In the meantime a number of auditing firms, management consulting firms, valuation firms, etc., which are also engaged in the privatization process, have been established.

- Employee buy-out (EBO).
- Sale of a part of the company (in the form of quotas or stakes).[12]

Medium-sized companies may be privatized according to the following models:

- Sale of the company or a part of it.
- Buy-out of the company.
- Leveraged management buy-out/management buy-in (LBO).
- Issuing of shares for additional investment.
- Debt/equity conversion (D/E swap).

Large companies may be privatized using the same models as medium-sized ones. The only difference is that the down-payment for a leveraged MBO/MBI is only 10% rather than 20% and that the additional capital investment required is 15% instead of 30%.[13] In addition to these models, there are three more possibilities for transformation. They may be applied to all companies irrespective of their size:

- Leasing.
- Sale of assets of the company.
- Transformation of companies under the bankruptcy procedure.

Mutual funds, investment funds, as well as other financial intermediaries have not so far been introduced in Macedonia, owing to the fact that there is still no legal basis for them to be established (and to operate).

Until 10 December 1994, the privatization process was largely autonomous and decentralized. Starting from that day, small and medium-sized companies with 100% of social capital had to be privatized. Another important date was 28 June 1995 (two years after the Privatization Law was enacted). Starting from that date the privatization of all companies with mixed capital which had not yet been initiated had to be decided upon by the Agency. The deadline for large companies with social capital to initiate their privatization was 10 December 1995 (two years after the detailed methodology for valuation was decided upon). All values used in the privatization process (appraisals, share prices, etc.) must be stated in Deutsche Marks (DEM). Payments, however,

---

[12] Refers to the part of the company which can be sold by a public call for bids announced by the Agency (after which an auction can be organized).

[13] The Agency also plays a much more active role in the privatization of large companies compared to small or medium-sized ones. A special body, the Transformation Board, has been established to prepare the privatization of large companies. Half of the voting power in this Board is vested in the Agency and the other half in the company.

may be made in local currency, frozen foreign currency or foreign currency.[14]

At the beginning 1,200 companies were earmarked for privatization. This figure was later revised to 1,216, 113 out of them being large, 273 medium-sized, and 830 small, with a combined total of almost 230,000 employees.[15] These companies represented over half of the total assets of the Macedonian economy and employed roughly half of all workers. The book value of the total companies to be privatized was 83.2 billion Macedonian Denars, or about DEM 3.3 billion as of 31 December 1994 (this date could be considered as the actual beginning of the privatization process).

The Agency expected to meet its commitment to the World Bank to privatize 791 firms by 15 January 1996. In fact, up to 31 March 1996, a total of 717 companies have been privatized, employing 95,344 workers (41.7% of the planned figure). These companies represent a book value of about DEM 1.45 million (44.0% of the planned figure). The developments are satisfactory so far. As of October 1996 866 firms have been privatized, employing 133,603 people and representing a book value of about DEM 2.3 million.

The figures in Table 6.3 suggest the conclusion that the trade sector seems to have the most relatively positive changes in the process of transformation, an outcome which does not differ much from those achieved by other post-communist countries in the early periods of transformation.

The process was initially slow, but it picked up and is now proceeding surprisingly quickly. In the period January–June 1996 the private sector already employed about 150,000 people (47% of the total) and was responsible for 65% of total economic activity.

---

[14] At the moment there is about US$ 1 billion worth of foreign currency savings frozen in the Macedonian banks since the declaration of independence. That money consists of Macedonian citizens' savings in foreign currency that were deposited in the Macedonian banks prior to 1992. Frozen foreign currency can be used for a number of specified purposes, privatization being one of them.

[15] In accordance with the Privatization Law at least two conditions out of three should be met for a company to be classified as small, medium, or large. A 'small' company has no more than 50 employees, its total annual revenues are less than 8,000 average monthly salaries, and the book value of its operating assets is not higher than 6,000 average monthly salaries. A 'medium-sized' company has no more than 250 employees, its total annual revenues are less than 40,000 average monthly salaries, and the book value of its operating assets is not higher than 30,000 average monthly salaries. Companies exceeding these limits are categorized as 'large'. Companies in public utilities, public works, large infrastructure systems, natural monopolies, social services, agriculture, land, forestry, and other natural resources management are excluded from privatization in this phase. Also excluded are some mixed and already private companies with foreign partners. Banks and other financial institutions are to be transformed according to another law, part of a wider financial sector reform.

Table 6.3. Privatization process by sectors

At the beginning of the privatization process			
Sector	*Percentage of Companies*	*Percentage of Employees*	*Percentage of Book Value*
Manufacturing	33.1	65.2	65.3
Construction	9.6	14.6	7
Trade	31.7	9.1	15
Transport and communications	5.2	5.3	4
Financial intermediation	9.9	1.9	1.6
Handicrafts	4.8	1.3	0.6
Hotels and restaurants	5.7	2.6	6.5
Total	*100*	*100*	*100*
Privatized by 31 March 1996			
Sector	*Percentage of Companies*	*Percentage of Employees*	*Percentage of Book Value*
Manufacturing	27.8	55.3	55.4
Construction	10.5	20.8	7.7
Trade	39	14.8	25.1
Transport and communications	4.3	3.4	2.4
Financial intermediation	9.8	2.5	4.7
Handicrafts	5.1	1.7	1.1
Hotels and restaurants	3.5	1.4	3.6
Total	*100*	*100*	*100*

Source: Agency of the Republic of Macedonia for Transformation of Enterprises with Social Capital (1996); authors' calculations.

The expectation is now that privatization will be completed by the end of 1997, including the companies and cooperatives running agricultural land (about 250 of them should be transformed), as well as the transfer of the state-owned capital in companies.[16] In general, it could be concluded that, although the

---

[16] According to: The Law on Transformation of the Enterprises and Cooperatives Running Agricultural Land, Official Gazette of the Republic of Macedonia, No. 19/96 and The Law on State Capital in Enterprises, Official Gazette of the Republic of Macedonia, No. 37/96.

Macedonian privatization process got its share of blame for corruption and injustice, there is now no longer any opposition to privatization in principle.[17]

RESTRUCTURING

In accordance with the strategy to introduce a market economy, privatization and restructuring are considered as the most efficient means to implement structural reforms. In principle, the new private owners should initiate the restructuring of the companies themselves. However, a number of large companies have required restructuring before being privatized. The 25 largest loss-making, socially-owned companies are, both economically and politically, very sensitive. In 1993 they generated losses equivalent to 13% of the GSP, or more than 80% of the total losses of the business sector. Loans to these companies made up about 60% of the total bad debts in the banking system. The 60,000 workers employed in these companies at the end of 1994 represented over 10% of the national labor force.

In January 1995 to halt the further deterioration of these 25 largest loss-making companies, the Government enacted a Law on Restructuring of Some of the Companies Showing Losses,[18] also called the Special Restructuring Program (SRP). The principal elements of the SRP were the creation of a new structure to provide a system of governance focused on the reduction of costs, the closing of non-viable units, and the permanent reduction in the size of their workforces. The objective was to force the companies to be self-financing during the life of the program, and the program incorporated a requirement that each of the companies should be in the process of privatization by 31 December 1995, when the Law expired.

The Special Restructuring Program required the mandatory conversion of certain categories of debt (primarily obligations due to banks and government agencies) into equity. Each of the companies in the program has now issued the required shares, with the result that, so far, 123 companies have effectively been privatized by this step alone. The expressed intention of the government and the Bank Rehabilitation Agency is to sell the SRP shares which they hold as soon as possible. Those companies which retain a significant proportion of social capital are going through the normal process set out by the Privatization Agency, and are expected to have their privatization plans approved, as

---

[17] A restitution or denationalization law has not yet been enacted but is expected during 1996. In the meantime the Privatization Law deals with the problem.

[18] See: Official Gazette of the Republic of Macedonia, No. 2/95.

Table 6.4. Macedonian current account 1990–1995

	1990	*1991*	*1992*	*1993*	*1994*	*1995*
Exports of goods	1113	1150	1199	1055	1086	1,204
Imports of goods	1,531	1,375	1,206	1227	1527	1424
Services: inflow	79	50	61	122	265	185
Services: outflow	154	56	103	133	200	385
Net transfers	84	-24	30	147	184	233
Errors and omissions	444	424	87	33	189	10

Note: In USD million.
Source: National Bank of the Republic of Macedonia (1996).

mentioned before, by the end of 1997. Of the loss-making companies 23 out of 25 are actively participating in the Special Restructuring Program, although the electric utility company and the railway company are relatively passive participants.

In reality, this restructuring program often meant liquidation. Though it was feared that this would not be easy to do, the restructuring, i.e. closing-down, is proceeding rather smoothly. In most cases the firms were liquidated, and most of the employees put on the dole. Again, this went on without serious social conflicts, mainly because there was nothing to be gained from protests, rather than because there were any elaborate social plans or safety nets. This process has led to a significant de-industrialization with mainly small and medium-size firms surviving, and the services sector increasing its share in economic activity.[19]

FOREIGN TRADE AND FOREIGN ASSISTANCE

Trade was very much affected by the UN sanctions imposed on the FR Yugoslavia in 1992 and by the Greek embargo on trade with Macedonia imposed at the beginning of 1994. Nevertheless, the Macedonian economy remained fairly open, with exports and imports of goods and services amounting to about 75% of its GSP (exports plus imports amounted to about US$ 2.65 billion in 1995 while GSP was around US$ 3.5 billion, or

---

[19] This provoked increases in the unemployment rate as well as in the emigration (ethnic Albanians choose European countries mostly, Macedonians traditionally go to Canada and Australia). For data on migration see: Zavod za statistika (1996b).

approximately US$ 1,800 per capita).

The main trading partners were the EU countries (over 30% of trade), Bulgaria, FR Yugoslavia, and Russia. Exports are expected to grow quite significantly in 1996, with the Greek embargo being lifted and the sanctions against Yugoslavia suspended.

The IMF's first contribution was in the form of an STF (systemic transformation facility) loan in 1994 to support the reform package. In 1995, a stand-by arrangement was concluded that has been working quite smoothly, indicating that the IMF is satisfied with the fulfilment of the usual conditions. By mid-1996 Macedonia has received from the IMF a total of US$ 75 million plus a total of US$ 260 million from the World Bank project funding and structural adjustment loans.

The STF loan is to be extended to a three-year stand-by agreement in 1996. An agreement with the Paris Club (government creditors) was worked out in mid-1995, and the negotiations with the London Club (commercial creditors) are progressing. Macedonia is expected to take over 5.4% of former Yugoslavia's US$ 4.4 billion debt, or US$ 5.7 billion with the interest on principal and arrears. The arrears have accrued because repayment of the debt was due to start in 1994 according to the agreement reached in 1988 with the former Yugoslav government. Macedonia's debt to the London Club amounts to US$ 280 million to be paid over a 15-year period. Payments start on 1 January 1998. For the first four years only interest will be paid (3.5% for the first two years and 3.75% for the next two). The repayment of the principal starts in 2002.

With the normalization of relations with Greece, Macedonia could establish better relations with the EU and start participating in its programs (e.g. PHARE). It has been in the process of working out a cooperation agreement signed in June 1996. This agreement is less than an association agreement, but it is supposed to evolve in the direction of the latter.

THE BANKING SYSTEM

At the moment the Macedonian financial system consists of the central bank ('Narodna banka na Republika Makedonija'), commercial banks and savings 'houses',[20] as well as insurance companies, and a stock exchange. The

---

[20] Under the Law on Banks and Saving Institutions (see Official Gazette of the Republic of Macedonia No. 31/93–705) savings houses (savings banks) are defined as: post-office savings houses (post-office savings banks) and savings houses (savings banks). They are legal entities and financial organizations which trade with the framework and practice prescribed by the central bank. Their main operations are

commercial banking sector consists of 4 traditional banks, 17 private banks, and 22 savings institutions. Interbank payments, including payments between banks and the central bank, and all commercial financial transactions, are settled through the Payments Operations Service, formerly known as the Public Accountancy Office.

Although the central bank is independent of the government, it is the latter which sets the country's major economic objectives, such as inflation and growth targets as part of the next year's economic program.[21] The central bank, however, is free to undertake monetary measures and to determine which instruments are necessary to achieve these goals. The parliament appoints the members of the central bank's board. The President of the Republic proposes a candidate as governor of the central bank, but parliament confirms the actual appointment.

The government is pursuing a strategy of bank rehabilitation, restructuring and privatization, which is presently underway and has started to produce significant results as described below.

By far the largest of the traditional banks is Stopanska Banka, Skopje, which had an extended branch network across the entire country. It had held about 65% of all assets and liabilities in the commercial banking system up to June 1995. To create greater competition in the banking sector, five independent banks (actually its branches in different Macedonian cities) were created from the Stopanska banka. Mainly as a result of this splitting-off, its market share has subsequently fallen to about 45%. Komercijalna Banka (a private bank which was until 1990 a part of Stopanska banka) and Makedonska Banka (formerly Ljubljanska Banka from the former Federal Republic of Slovenia), Skopje, are the other two main traditional banks.

The traditional banks, which are joint-stock companies, for the most part still majority-owned by the largest loss-making, social-capital companies, suffer from the consequences of the unsound financial practices of the former system. Accordingly, the Bank Rehabilitation Agency (BRA) was set up early in 1994. The BRA[22] is taking over the non-performing Denar loans and managing the

---

holding savings deposits of individuals and charitable organizations and granting loans to individuals. Post-office savings banks and savings banks cannot be set up by foreigners and may not operate under the name 'bank'. Or briefly: the savings institutions are restricted to operations with private individuals and households, and they cannot lend directly to legal entities (i.e. businesses).

[21] For further details see: Agency of the Republic of Macedonia for Transformation of Enterprises with Social Capital (1996), Section 8.

[22] According to The Law on Restructuring and Rehabilitation of a Portion of the Banks, published in the Official Gazette of the Republic of Macedonia No. 14/95.

foreign credit liabilities of the traditional banks, as well as providing oversight of bonds issued by the government.

Stopanska banka's bad debts were the first to be taken over by the BRA, which attempted to dispose of them in the domestic financial markets. The next step in the transformation of this bank will be taken with its privatization, while, unlike most of the other banks, it is still 'socially' owned, i.e. it is owned by its main debtors and by the state. Furthermore, in the near future the government plans to recapitalize the banks by exchanging their debts for treasury bills (albeit with a very low interest rate), and to privatize several other banks (e.g. Ohridska banka, Ohrid).

Many of the commercial banks have correspondent relationships with banks in other countries, but local banks still need to improve their worldwide communications. Although here are no legal restrictions on foreign ownership, so far no West European, North American or Asian bank has established a direct presence in Macedonia, except for very small equity participation by Austrian, Slovenian, and Bulgarian interests. Also, Stolichny Bank from Moscow has a branch in Skopje.[23]

The traditional financial system is still rather weak by Western standards, but it compares favorably with other Eastern countries in transition. The use of cheques and credit cards is not yet widespread, and a large portion of small-scale financial transactions take place in cash outside the formal market. Because of the high inflation of recent years, first the former Yugoslav Dinar and then the Denar lost worth as stores of value. Businesses may freely negotiate foreign currencies with licensed commercial banks. Individuals may convert foreign currency cash at licensed banks or at licensed exchange offices.[24]

The freezing of foreign currency deposits (about US$ 1 billion) also contributed notably to the erosion of confidence in the financial system. After independence all then existing foreign currency accounts held by individuals were put into suspense. The new government assumed these liabilities, but has been unable to service them, and they remain essentially frozen. It has taken a number of measures to try to alleviate this situation. Since 1993 it has

---

[23] Since May, 1993, some 15 new commercial banks have been licensed, but several have not survived or not been relicensed. The rules for establishing a new bank, besides the usual licensing procedures, include having a minimum capital equivalent of DEM 3 million, and of DEM 9 million if foreign transactions are to be conducted.

[24] Exchange rates are freely negotiated. The central bank announces daily guideline rates based on data from commercial banks, amounts of currency bought and sold on the local foreign currency market, and information from international currency markets. Rates are adjusted daily and may vary among institutions. The posted central bank rates are used for statistical and accounting purposes.

permitted these deposits to be used in limited amounts for certain purposes, such as emergency or essential needs: medical expenses, deaths, marriages, educational expenses abroad, etc.[25] It is still unclear when or if private persons will ever receive foreign currency cash for their deposits. However, a secondary market exists in which frozen currency deposits are traded.

All these factors encouraged private household and business preference for foreign currency as a store of value. At present the Deutsche Mark circulates widely and openly plays the part of a parallel currency. Many transactions involving households and small businesses take place in cash, whereas medium-sized and large businesses for the most part operate within the established financial system.

THE STOCK EXCHANGE

In 1996 for the first time in its history Macedonia founded a stock exchange. In fact, in March 1995 the Securities & Exchange Commission had approved rules for setting the criteria and other conditions for the Exchange and its members. The founders of this stock exchange were 11 banks, 2 insurance companies and 4 savings houses which held the inaugural shareholding assembly of the Macedonian Stock Exchange (hereafter MSE) on 13 September 1995. It was established as a joint-stock company and operates as a non-profit organization. According to its Founding Act its main objectives are primarily to provide an efficient capital market in support of the liberalization of the countries' economy, and to provide the government with the means of covering financial deficits by market instruments. The trading instruments are shares as well as government and corporate bonds. As basic functions of the MSE the following are to be quoted: listing securities, trading securities, determining the market price of securities, settlement of transactions, public announcement of pertinent and reliable information relating to companies, and trading on the stock exchange.

The managing bodies of the MSE are the Shareholder Assembly, the Managing Board (having five Committees), and the Supervisory Board. The MSE consists of the three major departments and is financed by membership fees, listing fees and transaction fees, as regulated by the Managing Board.

A member of the MSE must be a legal entity with its headquarters in Macedonia, and initially only financial institutions (banks, insurance

---

[25] Later it was permitted to use the deposits to acquire assets from the state, such as privatized apartments, shares in privatized enterprises, business real estate, as well as to pay customs duties, etc.

companies, post-savings houses and savings houses) can apply for membership. Within the first year of operation all members must form a separately capitalized subsidiary whose sole activity should be trading in securities.[26] The initial capital required is DEM 150,000, and the member must always maintain a minimum liquidity margin requirement of DEM 30,000.

The first official trading day was 28 March 1996. The listed companies trade in two tiers, and the unlisted ones (mostly companies offered for privatization) trade in a third tier.[27] The statistics show that in the first three

Table 6.5. The first three months of trading on the Macedonian Stock Exchange

Member	Type	Trading Value* in DEN	% of total
Investbanka a.d., Skopje	Bank	9114269	82.2
Radobank a.d., Skopje	Bank	1185386	10.7
Balkanska banka a.d., Skopje	Bank	259070	2.3
Stopanska banka a.d., Skopje	Bank	223600	2
Tabak a.d., Skopje	Insurance	219000	2
Feršped štedilnica a.d., Skopje	Savings house	47200	0.4
Izvozno–kreditna banka a.d., Skopje	Bank	23600	0.2
Almako banka a.d., Skopje	Bank	12889	0.1
Winner Broker a.d., Skopje	Insurance Comp.	5312	0
Total**		11090326	100

Notes:
* Both buying and selling.
** Securities of ten further Companies were listed but were not traded.
Source: Makedonska berza (1996).

---

[26] All members are automatically members of a Guarantee Fund of the MSE.

[27] For a listing in the first tier the free float in the securities for which is sought must be at least 25% (15% in the second tier), with a minimum of 250 shareholders (100 in the second market). A new applicant must have an expected initial market capitalization for all securities to be listed of at least DEM 20 million (DEM 9 million in the second tier). For purposes of a listing in the first tier, an adequate trading record will normally be at least three financial years (two years in the second tier). There are possible exceptions for both floors. The Trading Status is referred to all securities but to those listed in the previous two tiers. There are no requirements for the third tier other than that a company

months (28 March to 30 June) 26 trading sessions took place.[28] On the official markets 7 securities were listed, of which 1 was a government bond, 2 were derivatives from this government bond, and 5 were ordinary or preferred shares of two banks. About 15 securities are listed in the third tier. Only 10 securities were actually traded, the total trading volume was 1998 shares and one bond, with a total value of around DEN 5.5 million. The share of second-tier trading reached 81.36% in total turnover compared to 16.84% in third-tier trading, and a mere 1.8% in first-tier trading.

The largest part of the whole quarterly trade occurred in March itself (DEN 1.13 million or 20.5% of the whole trade) and in April (DEN 4.03 million or 73.3%) while in the following months of May and June turnover/trading activity was extremely low.

Most active trading occurred in Investbanka with over 82.2% of all transactions during the first three months of the MSE existence (Table 6.5), followed by Radobanka with a share of 10.7%. On the other hand, all the other listed companies were much less active or did not trade at all.

For the time being trading on the Macedonian Stock Exchange is still thin and not very attractive to investors, because the choice of investible securities is still rather poor. It is to be expected that it will start to play a more active role once the economy starts picking up and after the shares acquired through privatization start to be traded. However, as in most economies in transition, it is not to be expected that the stock exchange is going to play all that significant a role in the Macedonian economy in the near future.

CONCLUSION

There is no question that the uncertain environment in some neighboring Balkan countries gives potential investors in Macedonia cause for concern. This country has made major strides in stabilizing and restructuring its economy. Nevertheless, complaints are still voiced with respect to many areas.

Macedonia is adjusting its political and legal systems, and is still developing structures, procedures, and methods for conducting private business. Financial institutions are in the process of being restructured, banks are now being inspected regularly, there are strict requirements for opening and operating new banks, and interest rates have been falling. For the first time in

---

must submit the latest financial report.

[28] For further details see: Makedonska berza (1996).

history a Macedonian Stock Exchange has been founded, which has started trading in 1996. But there are still certain segments of the population who need to be convinced of the benefits of the new system, which takes time to show broad results.

Short-term prospects have improved. The year 1996 should record a growing GSP and industrial production for the first time in almost a decade (GSP started declining in 1987 and industrial production in 1988).[29] Economic growth is likely to continue over the next couple of years, but in the longer term it will depend on the effects of the privatization and reconstruction measures that have been taken, on the soundness of the financial sector, and on developments in the neighboring countries. There are significant infrastructure projects under way that should improve Macedonia's road and rail communications with Bulgaria and Albania (the connections with Yugoslavia and Greece are already adequate).

As a small economy, Macedonia's growth will be constrained on the one hand by its openness,[30] and by external political factors arising from its immediate surroundings, on the other. On top of this, the swift rehabilitation and adaptation to Western styles of the whole financial system should be assigned the highest priority in the transition of the Macedonian economy and society.

REFERENCES

Agency of the Republic of Macedonia for Transformation of Enterprises with Social Capital (1996): *Doing Business in Macedonia – A Guide for Investors*, Deloitte Touche Tohmatsu and USAID, Skopje.

Bišev, G., T. Nenovski, and M. Petkovski (1996): *Finansiski pazar i institucii (Financial Market and Institutions)*, unpublished paper, September, University of Skopje.

Bogoev, K., N. Uzunov (1996): *Perspectives of the Republic of Macedonia,* Balkan Forum, vol. 4, pp. 63–112.

EBRD (1995): *Transition Report 1995*, European Bank for Reconstruction and Development, London.

ECE (1996): *Economic Survey of Europe in 1995–1996,* European Commission for Europe, New York and Geneva.

Gligorov, V. (1994): *Why Do Countries Break Up?*, Acta Universitatis Uppsaliensis: Uppsala.

---

[29] See ECE (1996), Tables B1 and B2.

[30] For some strategic considerations see: Bogoev and Uzunov (1996).

Gligorov, V. (1995): *Fears and Passions: The Prospects for Former Yugoslavia,* Balkan Forum, vol. 3, pp. 167–190.

Kraft, E. (1995): *Stabilising Inflation in Slovenia, Croatia and Macedonia: How Independence Has Affected Macroeconomic Policy Outcomes,* Europe–Asia Studies, vol. 47, pp. 469–492.

Makedonska berza (1996): *Bilten – prvite tri meseci na berzata (Bulletin – The first three months on the Stock Exchange),* no. 1, Makedonska berza na dolgoročni hartiji od vrednost (Macedonian Stock Exchange), Skopje.

Narodna banka (1996): *Godišen izveštaj (Annual Report),* Narodna banka na Republika Makedonija (Macedonian Central Bank), Skopje.

National Bank of the Republic of Macedonia (1996): *Bulletin II/1996,* Skopje.

Official Gazette of the Republic of Macedonia, No. 5/93, Skopje.

Official Gazette of the Republic of Macedonia, No. 31/93, Skopje.

Official Gazette of the Republic of Macedonia, No. 31/93–705, Skopje.

Official Gazette of the Republic of Macedonia, No. 38/93, Skopje.

Official Gazette of the Republic of Macedonia, No. 42/93, Skopje.

Official Gazette of the Republic of Macedonia, No. 2/95, Skopje.

Official Gazette of the Republic of Macedonia, No. 14/95, Skopje.

Official Gazette of the Republic of Macedonia, No. 19/96, Skopje.

Official Gazette of the Republic of Macedonia, No. 37/96, Skopje.

Wyzen, M. L. (1993): *Monetary Independence and Macroeconomic Stabilization in Macedonia,* Communist Economies and Economic Transformation, vol. 5, pp. 351–368.

Zavod za statistika (1996a): *Mesečen statistčen izveštaj (Monthly Statistical Report),* vol. 6, Zavod za statistika, Skopje.

Zavod za statistika (1996b): *Otseleni i doseleni lica bo Republika Makedonija bo 1995 godina (Immigrated and Emigrated Persons in the Republic of Macedonia in 1995),* Zavod za statistika, Skopje.

G24 P33
G28 P34
G12 E52 L33

7. Poland

Ryszard Kokoszczyński[1]

INTRODUCTION

Some financial markets in Poland have evolved autonomously, while others have been established as an integral part of the transformation program. In the most general terms the beginning of the money market was the natural outcome of introducing a two-tier banking structure in the first half of 1989. Some new banks were established in this time as a spin-off from the previous monobank system and had a well-developed credit portfolio, but with no deposit base to finance it in a reasonable way; on the other hand, savings banks had a dominant share of the deposit market with no experience in the area of commercial loans. An interbank deposit market was therefore a natural way to balance this asymmetry, though in later years most banks attempted to develop into universal banks and the volume of the interbank deposit market stabilized on a level, making it a secondary segment of the money market [cf. Kokoszczyński (1994)].

Another segment of the money market, i.e. short-term domestic sovereign debt, had come into existence as a device for controlling the liquidity of the banking system. In 1990, both the budget situation and the balance-of-payments developments were different from what had been envisaged. A budget surplus and the favorable position of the trade balance brought a measure of liquidity in a situation when the stabilization program required a restrictive control over money supply growth. The central bank faced at the same time some reluctance on the part of the government to issue treasury securities while maintaining a budget surplus. The first instrument in this segment of the money market was then an own bill of the National Bank of Poland, which had a maturity of 30 days and was sold from July 1990 at weekly auctions as a zero-coupon security. The treasury started to issue t-bills only in

---

[1] The opinions expressed here are those of the author and do not necessarily represent the position of the NBP.

May 1991 but they soon dominated this market.

The equity market has been established in a very different way. The privatization of state-owned enterprises formed one of the most important parts of the Polish systemic transformation. Creating an equity market was perceived as an important part of a framework for privatization. This market then – in some opposition to those described earlier – had been created by introducing first legal regulations, establishing a regulatory authority (Securities Commission modelled along the US SEC example, being a relatively autonomous part of the executive arm of the government, with members from various ministries and the central bank, and chairman proposed jointly by the Minister of Finance and the Governor of the NBP and nominated by the Prime Minister with the consent of the relevant parliamentary committee) and the Warsaw Stock Exchange. In 1991 this 'blueprint' was in place and this is usually thought of as the beginning of the Polish capital market. Equity is still the instrument which dominates this market, though its functions extend far beyond facilitating the privatization processes.

As it can easily be seen from this brief description of the different backgrounds of the various segments of the Polish financial markets, there is a wide range of factors determining their current state and their future prospects. These issues are presented in the following sections of this chapter, though the focus is rather on the current situation and the prospects for the near future.

MONETARY POLICY

The basis for a modern monetary policy has been created in Poland by the pre–1990 reforms of the banking system. The Banking Law and the Act on the National Bank of Poland, introduced at the very beginning of 1989, and the changes in the central bank law after 1992 have created the basis for central bank independence, which extends far beyond the legal aspects.

The National Bank of Poland (NBP) is legally responsible for 'the strengthening of the domestic currency'. This is currently understood for practical purposes as a responsibility rather for bringing inflation to a 'civilized' level than for maintaining price stability. That is due in a major part to the historical background. These legal changes were introduced in the period of systemic change at the beginning of the 1990s. One important feature of this period was hyperinflation, so the stabilization of the Polish economy was an important precondition for a successful transformation. The control of inflation, being a final goal of the NBP, is facilitated by the control of the money supply growth as an intermediate target of monetary policy. At the very beginning of the 1990s – when financial markets were virtually non–existent – money supply growth was controlled by reserve requirements, various conditions for central bank refinancing and credit ceilings for state–owned banks. These instruments were substituted later by interest rates for various refinancing instruments and finally, when the money market reached a satisfactory level of development, open market operations were established as a major instrument for implementing monetary policy targets [cf. Kokoszczyński and Kondratowicz (1993)].

At the same time interest rate policy had been designed with another goal in mind. The level of monetization of the Polish economy (i.e. money/GDP ratio) was always low. An increase in the savings ratio, especially household savings in domestic currency, has been considered a decisive factor in bringing inflation down. Real positive interest rates have been thought an indispensable instrument in this respect.

With the development of the money market, the central bank's interest rate policy has two distinct channels of transmitting its direct impact to the financial sector and to the economy. Central bank's refinancing rates,[2] e.g. the lombard rate and the (re)discount rate, are perceived as a kind of official position of the central bank on future inflation. Their direct impact, mostly because of certain legal considerations, consists in the fact that they influence the interest rates commercial banks offer for households' term deposits. The interest rates, which the central bank maintains in its money market interventions (mostly one-day repo rate), by contrast, influence more strongly the asset side of commercial banks' balance sheet. This has another dimension – a major part of the Polish domestic public debt is in the form of short-term t-bills. Thus monetary policy faces a budget pressure directed at maintaining the lowest possible level of money market interest rates.

In 1995 money market developments were heavily influenced by foreign investors. To grasp this requires a broader understanding of the Polish exchange rate policy. In the initial period of transformation the exchange rate played the role of a nominal anchor. The Polish zloty, after a period of large and frequent devaluations in the last months of 1989, was fixed against the most popular foreign currency, the US dollar, at the level of 0.95 PLN.[3] The inflation differential between Poland and her major trading partners was not declining as fast as envisaged, and that was the reason for introducing the

---

[2] These rates are often called 'headline rates', and this is the name used further in the text.

[3] There was a so-called denomination of Polish zloty introduced in 1995; one new Polish zloty (PLN) is equal to 10,000 old Polish zloty (PLZ). To make comparisons easier, the new zloty is used throughout the whole text, including the parts describing the period before denomination.

crawling-peg regime in October 1991. The major features of this regime are, first, to define the value of the zloty in terms of a five-currencies basket (US$ 45%, DEM 35%, GBP 10%, FRF 5%, CHF 5%) and secondly, to devalue the zloty rate by a constant amount per each working day; the monthly rate of devaluation equaled 1% per month during 1996. This rate is, of course, one of the major parameters in monetary policy and is chosen in such a way as to maintain the role of a nominal anchor (the annual rate of devaluation has been always lower than the assumed change in the PPI, cf. Figure 7.1) and to stimulate favorably domestic exports by cutting part of this inflation differential, mentioned earlier. This regime had to be incremented by a few discretionary devaluations in the years before 1994, while balance-of-payments developments did not always maintain foreign exchange reserves at an adequate level (cf. Ebrill *et al.*, 1994).

This situation changed dramatically in 1995 for a number of reasons. A precondition was the liberalization of the Polish forex regulations. As far back as 1993 the government introduced free access for foreign investors to the treasury securities market. The foreign demand was not high at that time. Nevertheless, when Poland finally settled her relations with her foreign creditors in 1994 (the Paris Club settlement had been reached much earlier, but it was the London Club deal which was important for the international markets' perception of Poland) her risk premium as perceived by foreign investors decreased substantially. This, coupled with the steady growth in the Polish economy, caused the Polish balance of payments to turn strongly positive, which caused Poland's country risk to further decrease significantly in 1995. This brought some short-term capital inflows, which went mostly into the t-bill market. Both a positive interest rate differential and appreciation expectations, fueled by the rapid growth of the forex reserves, contributed to a substantial downward pressure on money market interest rates. This necessitated a large-scale sterilization if the control over the money supply growth was to be maintained. Of course, sterilization is not a sustainable policy, so the Polish authorities brought in further changes in the exchange rate regime by introducing a so-called 'crawling band'. The zloty value is still defined in terms of the five-currencies basket, but there is a 14% band around this so-called parity rate, in which the zloty is free to float. There were some revaluations in the parity rate introduced in 1995 and further reduction in the rate of crawl to control these speculative movements of foreign capital into the t-bills market. Some kind of equilibrium, however, was finally reached only in the second quarter of 1996. Declining interest rates (on a par with declining inflation) and volatility caused by the central bank's intervention in the interbank forex market cut the interest rate differential in such a way that some months of 1996 even saw a small net outflow of short-term capital. However,

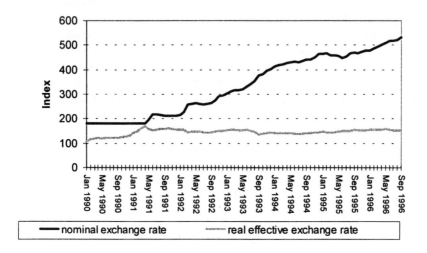

Figure 7.1. The US$-Zloty exchange rate

the share of foreign investors in the public debt has been always low.

In the meantime, the liberalization of the Polish forex regulation proceeded. First, Poland formally adopted article VIII of the IMF in May 1995,[4] and secondly, in the first half of 1996, on the eve of Poland's accession to the OECD, there was a wide liberalization of capital account transactions (Polish residents are practically free to invest in real estate and equity, and Polish enterprises may invest in foreign t-bills and publicly-traded bonds issued in OECD countries; cross-border trade loans with maturity over one year may be also freely granted, and the same is true of debt securities, though here there will be some quantitative limits for the next few years).

To recapitulate, here are the most salient features of the Polish monetary policy in 1996:

- Inflation as a final goal, money supply growth as an intermediate target, and reserve money as an operational target.
- A wide integration of the domestic money market with the foreign capital flows, i.e. close interrelations between interest rate policy and exchange rate policy.

---

[4] The most important obligation coming from this is that 'no member shall, without the approval of the Fund, impose restrictions on the making of payments and transfers for current international transactions' (IMF Articles of Agreement, Article VIII, section 2 (a)).

- Open market operations as a major tool, reserve requirements and headline rates as secondary ones.

THE BANKING SECTOR

The Polish banking system in its present form was established in 1989 through the introduction of a two-tier banking structure. The Banking Law went through numerous minor changes and amendments between 1989 and the present. Major legal developments influencing commercial banking in Poland were introduced mostly in the beginning of the 1990s, when the central bank issued highly prudential regulations based on the Banking Law.

The current regulatory framework consists of the following regulations:

- Licensing requirements: minimum number of founders, legal form of a joint-stock company as the dominant one, minimum capital requirement of 5 million ECU, professional experience required of incoming management, 3-year business plan, proven competence in potential owners, and provisions regulating the trade in large blocks of shares in existing banks' stock.
- Accounting standards (international standards were introduced first in 1991 for the banking sector only, then under the Accounting Law were extended into all sectors of the economy from 1995) and disclosure rules.
- Prudential regulations: capital adequacy ratio, concentration limits (the limit to all loans for a single borrower is 15% of capital and for a single loan 10%), limits for capital investment (bonds plus equity must not exceed 25% of bank's capital, although the Governor of the Central Bank may increase this limit to 50%) and for forex open positions (single currency − 15% of capital, maximum limit for all foreign currencies − 40%), asset classification schemes and provisioning rules being among the most important ones.
- Rules against money laundering (introduced initially by central bank regulation and later implemented by parliamentary law).
- Deposit insurance regulations (implemented mostly by the Bank Guarantee Fund established in February 1995).

This framework is the result of gradual developments which took place between 1989 and 1996 with some important landmarks worth mentioning here. The legal changes introduced in 1989 made their full impact on the Polish banking system only in 1990. There were more than 40 new licences issued in 1990, and the central bank issued its first recommendation prepared by the newly

established banking supervision department.[5] Their final and legally binding
form is contained within the amendments to the banking law and central bank
regulations issued on this basis in 1992 and 1993. They have introduced the
current framework for the capital adequacy ratio, defining bank's own funds,
risk weights for various categories of assets and minimum levels of the ratio
itself (generally 8%, but 15% for newly established banks during the first year
of their activities and 12% during their second year). The most important part
of this regulation is obviously the definition of the bank's own funds. In Poland
this is very similar both to the Basle Committee standards and the European
Union regulation as far as own gross funds are concerned. They are, however,
to be corrected for lacking the provisions, cumulated loss and investment in
other financial institutions to establish the amount of the bank's capital.
Because of earlier regulations giving banks a grace period for reaching a ratio
equal to 8%, this would be no difficult task for banks within the framework of
the initial loan classification scheme. It was based only on the promptness of
loan repayments. Regulatory changes in 1992 introduced the stability and
creditworthiness of a bank's customer as a secondary criterion to be taken into
account. This, on average, reduced the quality of banks' loan portfolios.

Table 7.1. Polish banks by ownership structure

	1988	1989	1990	1991	1992	1993	1994	1995
Total	5	17	43	89	103	104	82	83
Fully state-owned	2	11	11	2	2	2	2	2
Commercialized[a]	1	1	1	9	9	8	6	6
Private	0	3	27	34	77	77	64	63
Foreign[b]	0	0	1	8	11	11	12	18
Cooperative	1662	1662	1662	1662	1662	1650	1600	1550

Notes:
a. Joint-stock companies with stock fully owned by the treasury.
b. Banks incorporated in Poland with dominant foreign ownership.

At the same time, Polish banks began to feel the impact of the recession at the
beginning of the 1990s and of the Comecon trade breakdown in 1991. Both
regulatory changes and the adverse macroeconomic framework resulted in a
large increase in the proportion of non-performing loans in banks' portfolios.
To counteract this the government introduced a special restructuring program

[5] Banking supervision in Poland is a relatively autonomous part of the central bank. There is currently
some discussion about establishing a separate government agency responsible for banking supervision,
but the matter now rests with Parliament.

for state-owned banks[6] and the central bank employed its own resources to restructure and/or liquidate private banks.[7] This twofold approach was justified by the, then, valid legal nature of the deposit insurance system. Savings deposits in all banks existing before February 1989 (which meant virtually state-owned banks) were fully insured by the treasury; there was, however, no legal framework covering deposit insurance for private banks.

Such a restructuring program is widely perceived as an effective solution to a banking crisis in a transitional economy. Making banks deal with the difficult parts of their portfolios neutralized the problem of moral hazard to a large extent – being given responsibility for purging bank portfolios the bank staff understood much better the need for new rules governing credit. At the same time weaker banks had to go: they were merged, taken over or liquidated. Most of these processes were undertaken and controlled by the central bank.

These developments reached their peak in 1993 and 1994. This was, fortunately for commercial banks, a period of intensive growth in the treasury securities market. Polish banks were able to invest in virtually risk-free assets when restructuring their bad loans and learning new rules for credit policy.

Table 7.2. Market share of major bank groups in assets, loans and deposits

	State banks	Private banks	Foreign banks	Private and foreign
Assets[a]	72.6%	23.2%	4.2%	27.4%
Assets[b]	71.3%	23.4%	5.3%	28.7%
Loans 1995[a]	70.8%	24.3%	5.0%	29.2%
Loans[b]	68.1%	26.0%	5.9%	31.9%
Deposits[a]	76.0%	21.2%	2.8%	24.0%
Deposits[b]	75.1%	21.8%	3.1%	24.9%

Notes:
a. 31 December 1995.
b. 30 June 1996.

These regulatory developments were one of the major factors determining the rate of growth in the volume and structure of commercial bank assets. A rapid

---

[6] This program is extensively described in the literature, cf. e.g. Kawalec *et al.* (1994).

[7] Total amount of funds engaged in approximately 30 banks (loans, bonds and equity) up to the end of 1994 was less than 0.25% of GDP.

growth in credit in the economy was not evident before 1995, though GDP had been growing since 1992.

To summarize, the regulatory framework in the Polish banking system is already quite compatible with the Basle Committee recommendations and European Union directives. This process took a few years and only from 1995 on we may describe the Polish banking sector as entering another, more advanced, stage of development.

PRIVATIZATION

Privatization in Poland is, as in most transitional economies, one of the pivotal elements of the country's systemic transformation. Therefore, it is being undertaken on a wide scale and utilizes a whole array of different procedures. The initial legal framework for the privatization process was introduced in July 1990 with the Act on the Privatization of State-Owned Enterprises. Another important part of the changes in ownership was the mass privatization program – its legal basis, the Act on the National Investment Funds and Their Privatization, was approved by Parliament in May 1993.

The most spectacular method of privatization is the so-called capital privatization. It starts as the transformation of a state-owned enterprise into a joint-stock company with 100% of shares being owned initially by the treasury. The next stage of the privatization is either offering the stock to the public or a negotiated sale. This approach has been applied mostly to large and medium-sized enterprises in relatively good financial shape.

Another approach – known as 'privatization through liquidation' – has been applied mainly in the case of medium-sized and small enterprises. This approach has been implemented in three forms:

1. Asset sale, which usually has the form of a public tender.
2. Employee buy-out, where a newly established company leases the assets of the state-owned enterprise from the treasury; the majority of shareholders have to be former employees of the state-owned enterprise, which is then liquidated.
3. Establishment of a new joint venture with external investors, to which the enterprise to be liquidated contributes assets, liabilities, etc., as an in-kind contribution to the share capital of the new company.

At the very beginning of the transformation process there were discussions in practically all the transitional economies about mass privatization, which was being thought of as a way for all citizens to share in the benefits of the past economic development of the countries. The usual solution to this problem was to draw upon the so-called 'coupon' (or voucher) privatization method, in which the entire adult population is entitled to coupons which may later be exchanged for shares in the former state-owned companies rather than to some well-defined part of the state-owned assets. Polish economists had pioneered this concept back in the 1980s, but its implementation in Poland came rather late. In part this was through attempting to introduce the mass privatization program within a tight legal framework following the existing regulation of the Polish capital market. However, the program itself was 'politicized' by quite a number of pressure groups, for whom delays formed a tool for politically motivated leverage in other areas. Finally, the program went into the implementation stage only in 1995 with vouchers being distributed – for a nominal fee of 20 PLN – from November 1995 onwards.

The program currently includes 512 companies (approximately 10% of the country's economic assets). These were transformed into joint-stock companies with 60% of their shares being distributed among 15 specially-established National Investment Funds (NIFs), 25% of the shares still belonging to the state, and 15% being transferred free to the employees of the privatized companies.

The basic idea behind mass privatization in Poland was not only to privatize the companies taking part in the program but also to improve their corporate governance. This is the major reason for having the NIFs managed by externally-hired consortia. These were selected by tender and formed by the larger Polish and foreign banks, investment companies, and consulting firms. Their initial task is to prepare and implement restructuring processes in the companies owned by the NIFs. The final goal is to prepare as many companies as possible for the public issuing and trading of their shares.

It is definitely too early to make any kind of economic assessment of this program; notwithstanding this, we would like to stress that the number of people buying the mpp vouchers has already reached 23 million (that is, 82% of all those entitled to buy them).

The NIFs are one group of institutional investors active in Poland's capital market. The others are not so numerous – there are currently three mutual funds (the Polish Pioneer and two joint ventures by West European financial institutions and large Polish banks: BGZ and PKO SA) and two or three others are to get licences in the near future. There are some regional and foreign investment funds, but their activities are fairly limited due to their relative small volume. The major domestic players are still commercial banks.

Foreign investors can take part in all privatization schemes. They may even buy mass privatization vouchers in the secondary market. Taxation is also

Country Profiles

defined on a uniform basis, i.e. corporate income tax has a flat rate of 40%.[8] Moreover, there are various, generally available, tax deductions related mainly to exports and real-assets investment.

Profits from the sale of securities by private persons are tax-exempt till the end of 1996; there is as yet no formal decision on this rule in 1997. The profits of legal persons from the sale of securities are tax-exempt if these securities have been acquired through the stock exchange. There is a general withholding tax of 20% on dividends and royalty payments. However, Poland is a party to more than 50 treaties on double-taxation avoidance.

There are no restrictions on the repatriation of profits (in any form) and capital by foreign investors. The only condition is the audit of the financial statements of the company as a basis of such a transfer.

THE WARSAW STOCK EXCHANGE

As mentioned in the introduction, the Polish equity market has been established *via* special legal and economic blueprints prepared by the government. This assumed from the very beginning the existence of only one stock exchange, the Warsaw Stock Exchange (WSE), though legally speaking it is possible to establish other ones as well.[9] The Law on the Public Trading of Securities, approved by Parliament in March 1991, constitutes the legal basis for the WSE activities. It is organized as a joint-stock company with approximately 50 shareholders (banks and brokerage houses) with the state treasury still having a majority stake. The annual shareholder meeting elects the Supervisory Council of the WSE, which is, on the one hand, a typical supervisory board of a joint-stock company,[10] and, on the other hand, a decision-making body in the

---

[8] There is a draft law currently in the parliament which prescribes a decrease in the corporate income tax of two percentage points in 1997; that is part of a government program to cut taxes by the same amount in every year till 2000. However, there is some discussion within the ruling coalition regarding the timetable for this program.

[9] The Law on Public Trading of Securities introduced a special licensing procedure for establishing a stock exchange, where the licensing authority is the Prime Minister acting on the formal motion of the Securities Commission. Another condition is that the stock exchange may only be established as a joint-stock company with only banks, brokerage houses, and the state treasury being eligible to buy shares in this company.

[10] Polish commercial code provides for a management structure in joint-stock companies similar to the German one, i.e. there is an executive board (*Vorstand*) responsible for managing the company's business, and a supervisory board (*Aufsichtsrat*) formally representing the owners and overseeing the board on their behalf.

area of detailed regulations concerning trading and approving those issues to be traded on the stock exchange.

There are both equity and bonds traded at the Warsaw Stock Exchange. There is also the potential for trading the pre-emptive rights in a company listed already on the WSE. The WSE offers, in practice, two markets for equity trading; the first, called the 'basic market', is for larger companies, with a greater number of shareholders and with a relatively long track record. The parallel market, by contrast, is mostly for smaller companies. The WSE began its activities in April 1991 with five companies listed. By mid-1996 there were more than 60 companies listed on the basic market and another 15 on the parallel market. Trading is conducted with prices being fixed once a day, but recently the WSE has introduced continuous trading, initially for the five most liquid companies, with the group being increased by five every 2–3 weeks (in November 1996 this group consists of 15 companies: 5 banks: BIG, BPH, BRE, BSK, and WBK; 6 large conglomerates based on former foreign trade companies, i.e. Animex, Budimex, Elektrim, Rolimpex, Stalexport, and Universal; two tyre companies: Dębica and Stomil; Górażdże, cement makers, and Okocim, brewery). Mass privatization vouchers are traded in the same way.

The brokerage houses of commercial banks play the major role in trading on the WSE. However, there is a substantial number of brokerage houses controlled by other agents (*inter alia* the Pioneer mutual fund, and foreign investment companies). Commercial banks and mutual funds are also the largest domestic investors; there are however approximately 800,000 individual investment accounts mostly dating back to the peak period of 1993–1994. There is also a substantial foreign investment in equity listed on the WSE. According to some cautious estimates it may be (around mid-1996) in the range 20–30% of aggregate market capitalization.[11]

The performance of the WSE (cf. Figure 7.2) was always heavily influenced by two – largely independent – groups of domestic factors: the macroeconomic framework as mirrored by the yields on bank deposits, and the fundamentals of the listed companies. Notwithstanding this, there is a lot of interest in charting among some individual investors. The market is relatively limited, with aggregate capitalization fluctuating around 5–6% of GDP, and it lacks large institutional investors.

The WSE began its existence as a vehicle for the privatization of state-owned enterprises. It was only in 1994 that the WSE began to play a genuine role of a stock exchange, i.e. it became a substantial source of capital for private companies.

---

[11] This estimate is based on the disclosures required by the law from any investors acquiring more than 5% of the total stock of any public company.

Another group of securities traded at the WSE are treasury bonds: 2- and 5-year fixed-rate securities and 1-, 3- and 10-year floating notes. There are currently 13 issues of them, but their turnover (large package deals included) is only about 1/3 to 1/4 of the turnover in the equity market. The prospects for this market are quite promising, while government plans are to increase the range of maturities of t-bonds.

Figure 7.2. Warsaw Stock Exchange Index and main market turnover

The corporate bonds market, by contrast, is in a very early stage of development. There is practically no futures and options market in existence now, though the Warsaw Commodity Exchange is considering introducing futures for 13-week t-bills early in 1997. The major forex market is an interbank market.

SOURCES OF EXTERNAL FINANCE[12]

At the very beginning of the 1990s the major source of external capital for Poland were international financial institutions. Both the Polish record in foreign debt service and the macroeconomic and political uncertainties justified the reluctance of foreign investors to come to Poland. But even the credits granted by the World Bank, the EBRD and similar institutions were not – measured against the gross inflow basis – a large item in the Polish balance of payments. They were much more important from another viewpoint, *viz* that of establishing new procedures, strict requirements for disbursement, and the similar features they brought with them.

Annual foreign direct investment exceeded US$ 0.5 billion only in 1993, and over US$ 1 billion in 1995. This is still mostly thanks to large privatization transactions, though some major greenfield projects have been implemented in Poland during the last 2–3 years.

However, with the Polish sovereign debt having an investment grade rating in 1995, and Polish economic growth remaining high, the latest forecasts predict an FDI net inflow exceeding US$ 2.5 billion in 1996 and growing even more in 1997.

REFERENCES

Ebrill, L. *et al*. (1994): *Poland: The Path to a Market Economy*, Occasional Paper 113, International Monetary Fund, Washington, D.C.

Kawalec, S. *et al* (1994): *Dealing with Bad Debts – the Case of Poland*, in: G. Caprio, D. Folkerts-Landau, T.D. Lane (eds), *Building Sound Finance in Emerging Market Economies*, International Monetary Fund and the World Bank, Washington, D.C.

Kokoszczyński, R. (1994): *Money and capital market reforms in Poland*, in: J.P. Bonin, I.P. Szekely (eds), *The Development and Reform of Financial Systems in Central and Eastern Europe*, Edward Elgar, Aldershot.

Kokoszczyński, R. and Kondratowicz, A. (1993): *Banking, credit, and monetary policy*, in: H. Kierzkowski, M. Okólski, S. Wellisz (eds), *Stabilization and Structural Adjustment in Poland*, Routledge, London.

---

[12] All data quoted here, if not described otherwise, are from the balance-of-payments statistics of the National Bank of Poland. The Polish Agency for Foreign Investment compiles data based not on payment flow, but on all kind of investments. They include reinvested profits, in-kind contributions, etc., so the PAIZ's figures are usually much larger (2–3 times).

APPENDIX

List of members of the Warsaw Stock Exchange:

Brokerage arms of commercial banks (not separate legal persons):
PKO SA, Bank Slaski (BSK), Bank Gdanski, Bank Staropolski, Bank Przemysłowo-Handlowy (BPH), Bank Zachodni, Polski Bank Rozwoju (PBR), Kredyt Bank, PKO BP, Bank Rozwoju Eksportu (BRE), WBK, Bank Gospodarki Komunalnej (BGK), Powszechny Bank Gospodarczy (PBG), Bank Depozytowo-Kredytowy (BDK), BGZ, PBK, Bank Handlowy, Pomorski Bank Kredytowy (PBKS), Pierwszy Komercyjny (PKBL), PBI, BOS.

Brokerage houses:
WDEM, DDEM, Creditanstalt Securities, DEML, Istalexport, Elimar, MDEM, Citibrokerage, Amerbrokers, CS First Boston, Pioneer-PDEM, Raiffeisen C&I, Penetrator, DEM BIG, IB Austria Securities, ING Barings Securities, Robert Jardine.

G21 P33 L33
G28 P34
E52 P24

8. Romania

Ion Drăgulin and Daniela Grozea-Helmenstein

INTRODUCTION

The transformation process within the Romanian economy – aimed at the full adoption of market mechanisms – was faced with various adverse circumstances and inadequate policy synchronization. It has been accompanied by major macroeconomic disequilibria: output collapse, inflation, and external deficits. In retrospect, the authorities had first to resume growth, then control inflation and, finally, restore external equilibrium.

Since 1993 Romania has achieved an average annual growth rate of 4.1%, a cumulated expansion of GDP of 17.4%, together with progress in macroeconomic stabilization. From the end of 1993, monetary policies have controlled inflation more effectively, while a tighter fiscal policy has also contributed to bringing inflation down. On the microeconomic level, restructuring and privatization have been proceeding rather slowly in the early years of transition, accelerating however during 1996. At the same time, in the external sector, things have not improved as was hoped. The inter-bank forex market has been performing unconvincingly and only very recently has autonomous financing (without making use of exceptional financing from IMF and IBRD) of the current account of the balance of payments become a reality.

MONETARY POLICY

Designing and implementing monetary policy is the core responsibility of the National Bank of Romania (NBR). Legally and institutionally, the NBR enjoys a high degree of independence (from the government), basically consistent with the Maastricht Treaty provisions. This independence may, however, be challenged by a clause in the NBR's Statute, which states that NBR policy should be conducted within the framework of the economic policy of the government. At times, the effective independence of the NBR has been affected by pressures from government and parliament in some key policy areas, such as exchange rate and refinancing policies.

The analytical framework of the monetary policy consists of final, intermediary, and operational objectives, as well as the policy instruments (Table 8.1). Maintaining the stability of the national currency, Romanian Leu (ROL), is the legally required final objective of monetary policy. The current intermediate objectives – effectively assumed by mid-1993 – are quantitative targets for broad money and positive real interest rates. In terms of operational targets, the NBR has used banks' reserves and the average refinancing interest rate. At present, the monetary policy instruments in operation are refinancing credits and interest rates, and the mechanism of minimum reserve requirements. Starting from 1 July, 1996, the NBR has introduced a forex liquidity ratio requirement (the weighted average between the forex assets and the liquidity level corresponding to each category of assets), closely connected with the reserve requirements, which is aimed at discouraging the expansion of forex loans.

A better coordination of policies, including a more appropriate mix of base money control and interest rate policy, has resulted in a disinflationary trend in 1994 and 1995, associated with the remonetization of the economy. Interest rate policy, actively employed from the end of 1993 onwards, was intended to restore public confidence in the ROL and to pave the way for sound growth. The NBR average nominal interest rates, which started moving upward rapidly in the last quarter of 1993, reached a peak in January 1994 (136.3% p.a.), and then decreased gradually, to 47.2% at the end of 1995 and to 35.5% at the end of August 1996 (Figure 8.1). Market interest rates, deregulated since 1991, followed closely the pattern of those of the NBR. They also displayed an increasing trend since October 1993, reaching 106.5% p.a. (on average) in May 1994. At the end of August 1996, their average was 55.4% (Figure 8.2). In the last couple of years, market deposit rates have been positive in real terms. In 1995, they ranged (as monthly nominal averages) between 31% and 44.3% p.a. In August 1996 the rate was 38.7% p.a., against a CPI inflation forecast of 45–48% for the year. Foreign exchange deposit rates are broadly in line with those prevailing on the euromarkets.

The conduct of monetary policy in 1996 has been particularly difficult. First, because a significant quantity of resources (directed credits) has been required by parliament or government (for example, at the end of September 1996, 54% of total NBR refinancing consisted of such directed loans). Secondly, the government (or parliament) imposed the refinancing interest rate for these loans. Thirdly, in order to avoid a systemic risk, the NBR assisted two failing banks (37% of total refinancing in September). Finally, the expansionary fiscal policy, requiring a revised budget deficit 34% higher than the original figure, puts huge pressure on domestic banks to finance the deficit

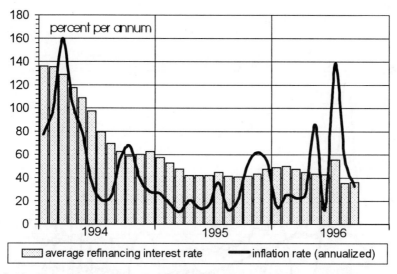

Source: National Commission for Statistics (1996), National Bank of Romania (1996).

Figure 8.1. Refinancing interest rate and inflation rate

(more than 90% of the budget deficit is financed by the commercial banks through t-bills purchase) with a clear reflection in the NBR refinancing pattern. In a nutshell, it can be said that in 1996 the inflation target (20% initially, and 30% since mid-year) has been missed or, from a different perspective, that inflation has been the price paid for attaining the desired growth rate.

Currently, the problems confronting monetary policy are: the high financial needs of agriculture involving large structural loans from the NBR (an evergreen challenge!); expansionary fiscal policy (with the associated large budget deficits); and the solvency and liquidity crises of two commercial banks. To these problems can be added the impact of the inter-enterprise arrears, which are recognized, more and more, as a structural phenomenon, rather than a monetary one (Dăianu, 1994, Clifton and Mohsin, 1993). Since December 1991, when the parliament imposed a law requesting the NBR to clear the arrears, the pressures to monetize the net arrears have decreased significantly, as it became evident that monetizing the arrears does not have the long-lasting effect of reducing inter-enterprise arrears but, on the contrary, increases inflationary pressures. The impact of gross arrears in terms of GDP also declined, from about 85% in 1991 to 23% in 1995.

During the first half of 1996, the NBR succeeded in controlling monetary

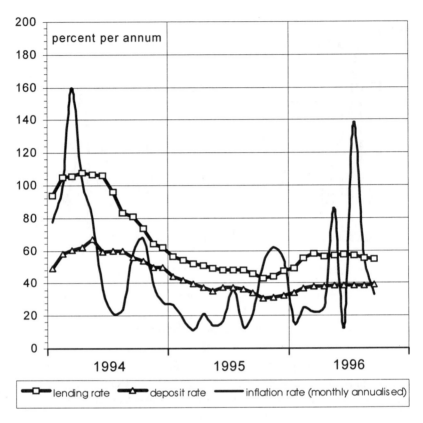

Source: National Commission for Statistics (1996), National Bank of Romania (1996).

Figure 8.2. Interest rates applied by banks

developments, in line with the initial targets, and as agreed with IMF
(December 1995 Stand-by Agreement). After six months, base money had
grown by 8.1%, fully consistent with the annual target. However, in the third
quarter that indicator went up to 12.5%, reflecting a loosening of the control
over the money supply (average refinancing growing by 16.6%). The
deterioration of monetary conditions in the third quarter of 1996 against 1994
and 1995 is reflected by a decreasing demand for money, while the growth of
both money and credit aggregates contributed to an upward trend in inflation.
The velocity of money has therefore gradually reduced its downward profile,
while household savings stopped growing in real terms (Table 8.1).

Table 8.1. Monetary indicators 1996

Percentage change	March	June	July	August	Sept.
Broad money	5.9	17.1	23.5	27.1	31.9
Base money	-1.5	8.7	15.4	18.7	22.3
Refinancing credits	2.0	21.7	31.9	38.4	41.9
Credit to non-government	10.0	21.0	27.9	30.9	34.8
Household savings	17.6	34.7	38.8	41.9	44.7
Inflation rate (%)	4.9	13.7	22.4	27.0	30.1

Note: December 1995=100.
Source: National Bank of Romania, 1996.

Throughout the entire reform process a tremendous challenge has been the exchange rate policy. Since 1992 a full retention forex regime has been operating, and starting August 1994 a fully-fledged direct dealing inter-bank market has been implemented, which has, however, suffered from repeated crises. The main reasons behind this have been the structural disequilibrium of the economy and the weak price elasticity of imports. In particular, energy imports figure largely in Romanian imports (25% in 1995), and their prices are still controlled. The exchange rate policy has reflected the conflicts of interests between the growth priority and the current account challenges. As a result, a stable exchange rate has rarely, and then only for short periods, characterized the forex market. The consequences have been market segmentation (very poor inter-bank forex transactions with most taking place between the commercial banks and their clients), non-market clearance, and premiums on parallel forex markets. In 1994, the operation of the inter-bank forex market was satisfactory, and the current account deficit was smaller (1.4% of GDP). In the subsequent period, even if the ROL depreciated in real terms (by 13.6% in 1995 and further in 1996 – Figure 8.3), the performance of the forex market remained problematic, while the current account worsened significantly in 1995 (3.6% of GDP) and is forecast to reach about the same level in 1996.

The operation of the forex market deteriorated sharply in November 1995, and continued in this way throughout 1996. The factors behind this were associated with the large energy imports effected in the winter months, weak trade balance developments, below-target foreign financing, low international reserves, pro-depreciation expectations, and failure to observe market rules on the part of banks. As a result, market segmentation widened, the turnover inter- and intra-banking diminished, a lack of liquidity prevailed, and the 'grey' market re-emerged.

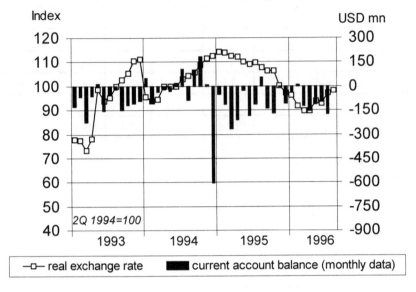

Source: National Bank of Romania (1996).

Figure 8.3. Real exchange rate and current account balance

In an attempt to address these problems, the NBR reduced the number of banks licensed to operate as dealers to four, which were, supposedly, observing the regulatory framework more scrupulously and were refraining from speculative operations. The measure alleviated the problems only temporarily. In June supplementary measures were undertaken, including the introduction of the foreign exchange liquidity ratio, and the enlarged scope for manoeuvre for brokers (end-of-day open position of US$ 100,000, from earlier US$ 10,000).

There is an internal and limited current account convertibility for the ROL. Authorities have not yet officially accepted the IMF Article VIII regarding the current account convertibility of the national currency, but they have stated their intention to do so by the end of 1997. Capital transfers require prior authorization from the NBR. International reserves (consisting of gold and forex in the NBR and the commercial banks) remained relatively low throughout these years, equivalent to 2–3 months of imports. In October 1996, official forex reserves (at the NBR) reached US$ 1,040 million, or approximately 1.5 months of 1995 imports. The guidelines of the policy in this field – not yet officially assumed – focuses on encouraging capital investment, direct purchases from the forex market, and foreign borrowing.

THE BANKING SECTOR

The banking sector in Romania has been reshaped in 1991, when two basic laws were passed to cover the banking activity and the status of the NBR. The law distinguishes between the Central Bank and commercial banks. However, a new (mid-June, 1996) law for Casa de Economii si Consemnatiuni classifies it as a savings bank. Commercial banks can be licensed for most general banking transactions but they cannot operate on the capital markets. Foreign investors can hold up to 100% of a Romanian bank. Equal treatment is accorded by law to all banks, irrespective of the structure of capital. At present there are 26 banks, plus 9 branches of foreign banks. The market is quite concentrated, with five banks holding (at the end of 1995) 72% of total deposits and 74% of total assets. Short-termism is still a feature of the banks' credit policy.

The supervisory function is performed by the NBR. Basically, the prudential regulations in force are fully consistent with the European standards (Table 8.2). This tough regulatory framework prevents the over-expansion of banks and lays the foundations for a sound banking system. Banks have to comply with a standard (8%) capital-adequacy ratio (the ratio of the total risk-weighted assets to the capital base), a difficult task given both the inherited and the newly-created problems within the banking system. Every six months, banks classify their loan portfolio and the interest due (from 'standard' to 'loss') and make risk provisions accordingly. Since 1995, the fiscal deductibility of general reserves for credit risk and for risk provisions has been applicable. Foreign exchange exposure (as open positions) is limited to 10% of banks' own funds.

Banks maintain mandatory reserves with the monetary authority as a share of the domestic currency and forex deposit base. Since 1 July 1996, reserve requirements against forex deposits depend on each bank's actual forex liquidity ratio: the higher that ratio, the lower the reserve rate. But both mechanisms are intended as monetary policy tools, i.e. to limit the expansion of credit in ROL and forex. Supervision is undertaken through both on-site and off-site examinations. In general, the financial position of banks gradually improved. However, some of the five banks reported losses for the financial year 1995. This number does not include two the most troubled banks, 'Dacia Felix' and 'Credit Bank', which presumably recorded important losses. For major infringements of prudential regulations (both banks heavily exceeded the exposure limits towards individual debtors, with no proper collateral) the NBR has placed both banks (in 1995 and 1996 respectively) under a special supervisory procedure. By mid-year, it had brought the two banks to the court. So far, the prosecutor has not decided whether to restructure or liquidate them.

Table 8.2. Prudential rules

Capital adequacy
       Risk-weighted assets ratio of 8%
Large exposures
       Loans to a single borrower may not exceed 20% of the bank's own
       funds
Insider lending
       Loans to all insiders may not exceed 20% of the bank's own funds
Foreign currency exposure
       Total open forex position may not exceed 10% of the bank's own funds
Investments in non-banking companies
       Individual investments may not exceed 20% of the capital of the non-
       banking company
Ownership of banks by non-banks
       Central bank's needed for shareholdings above 5% of the bank's capital
       and for their subsequent increases
Loan classification
General and specific reserves

In dealing with the two troubled banks, the NBR – as supervisory authority – opted to minimize the risk incurred to depositors/creditors and to the banking system. In the case of 'Dacia Felix', the NBR covered most of the household withdrawals. By the end of December 1995, the two banks held, collectively, 9.7% of the deposits in the banking system and 13.7% of household deposits. By the end of September 1996, the two indicators stood at 2.5% and, 3.2%, respectively. Since the problems of the two banks are of a solvency nature (while the liquidity crises have only been the above-the-water part of the iceberg), these banks have very limited chances for survival.

However, owing to staffing difficulties in the relevant department and the lack of unitary book-keeping procedures, the effectiveness of prudential regulations has been questionable. The NBR intends to introduce new accounting procedures based on international accountancy standards, in 1997. To further improve the banks' stability and efficiency, the authorities (the NBR and the government) are currently examining a number of initiatives, among which privatization appears to be a matter of priority. In 1996 one bank (Banca de Dezvoltare) will be privatized and the procedures for privatizing a second one (not yet nominated) will be initiated. A law on deposit insurance has been passed by Parliament in autumn 1996. The scheme covers household deposits, in Lei and forex, amounting to ROL 10 million per depositor.

In retrospect, the reform process in the banking sector has not been made sufficiently clear. Dual regulations on deposit insurance – one already effective for CEC (the Savings Bank), and the other for the remainder of the banks – the recapitalization process (with no requirements for restructuring) and bad-debts clearance (again with no major responsibilities for the banks) support this conclusion. Authorities have also to clarify the statute of Banca Agricolă (Agro Bank), which gradually seems to change itself into a de facto government financing agency for the agricultural sector.

PRIVATIZATION

One of the key elements in economic reform in Romania is the privatization process. The privatization methods adopted by the Romanian government since 1990 share some common features with those undertaken in other Central and Eastern European countries – the use of vouchers – while also including specific characteristics, such as: the initial implementation of a tradable vouchers privatization system, its subsequent abandonment, and the introduction of a nominal voucher privatization system; the creation of ownership funds and the allocation of assets among these funds. In Romania, privatization tried to allocate fairly state-owned assets to all eligible Romanians, creating a broadly-based ownership and avoiding the concentration of ownership in privately-run funds.

The legal and institutional framework was initiated in 1990 and provided for the privatization of the state-owned companies in several stages:
1. The conversion of state-owned companies into commercial companies[1] (about 6,300 or 53% of the total assets of the former state-owned companies, as of 1990) and règies autonomes (about 400, corresponding to 47% of the total).
2. The establishment of a State Ownership Fund (SOF) and five regionally distributed Private Ownership Funds (POFs) to be responsible for the privatization of the companies.
3. The distribution of vouchers, the so-called certificates of ownership (COs), free of charge, to about 15.5 million Romanian residents over 18 years at 31 December 1991, equivalent to 30% of the state-owned companies' equity under the administration of the POFs).
4. The sale of 70% of the state-owned companies' equity to Romanian and foreign investors by the SOF.

Several privatization programs were subsequently implemented, such as:

The *early privatization program,* comprising 0.5% of the total number of

---

[1] This process has been labelled 'commercialization'.

companies included on the privatization list. Of these, 22 companies have been sold to Romanian and foreign individuals and firms for a total of ROL 9.7 billion (US$ 3.1 million). The program was finalized in 1993.

The *sale of assets* was the method used by the companies owning assets that could be operated independently. Initiated by the management of the companies concerned, the sales could be carried out by the company itself, through public auctions or sealed bids, with the starting price set by the company. In those cases where the assets have already been leased or contracted out, the lessee or contractee were preferred, followed by the employees or retired employees. Special credit arrangements from the company have been possible for these cases.[2] The proceeds of the sale remained in the company and could be used only for investment purposes. A total of 7,842 assets from more than 500 commercial companies have been identified for sale, and by July 1994 about 3,100 assets have been sold.

In the period between its establishment in December 1992 and 1 October, 1995 (the date when SOF started implementing the Law on the acceleration of privatization), the SOF has privatized 1,329 commercial companies (accounting for about 25% of the companies assigned to them) with more than 520,000 employees. Most of the deals have been concluded through the *MEBO* method that allowed the management and the employees to swap their vouchers for shares in the companies. Other privatization methods that were also widely used were: public offers, direct negotiations, open auctions or auctions with preselected participants. 34% of the privatized companies were engaged in agriculture and the food processing industry.

The *public share offering* was launched in November 1994 with just three companies. In March and April 1995, the POFs sold (partially or completely) by public offer the 30% equity share under their administration in about 100 companies.[3] The companies privatized through public offer can be listed for quotation on the Stock Exchange.

The *mass privatization* was initiated early in 1992 by distributing 15.4 million certificate of ownership (COs) booklets. However, during the subsequent years for most Romanians the COs remained only empty paper. The main problems with this program were:

• strong favoritism shown to insiders (management and employees close to management) who bought COs on the open market (at discounted prices) and used them to purchase shares in the company undergoing MEBO privatization, thus gaining control of the company;

---

[2] Frydman, Rapaczynski and Earle (1993).

[3] Coopers & Lybrand (1995).

- limited cash down-payment, since the largest share of companies were privatized through MEBO and highly subsidized loans (at below market interest rates) from the state were available;
- the value of a CO was up to ten times higher for a person able to use it in a MEBO privatization than for an ordinary citizen;
- lack of the necessary information for the ordinary citizen to make rational CO allocation decisions;
- although, theoretically, CO holders were shareholders in the POFs, in practice they had no influence on the POFs' management, nor did they receive dividends;
- lack of corporate governance in the POFs;
- no private investment funds were allowed to engage in the mass privatization.

These disadvantages were aggravated by a lack of domestic savings, limited foreign investment, bureaucratic obstacles and resistence to privatization on the part of some companies' management. As a result, in the period 1992–1995 the progress achieved in privatization remained modest.

To cope with these problems, a new law on speeding-up the privatization process was passed in July, 1995. According to this law, *mass privatization* was to be reactivated, starting August 1995 through the distribution of new coupons to about 17.8 million eligible Romanian residents, and accelerated during the next months so that the whole process was planned to be completed by the end of April, 1996. The, presumably, most profitable 3,905 companies (according to the 1994 balance sheets) in the portfolio of POFs selected for mass privatization were divided into two groups: for one group 60% of their assets and for a second group 49% of their assets were included in the mass privatization. The 3,905 companies accounted for 25% of Romania's industrial capacity and about 56% of the total remaining number of state-owned companies representing the main branches of the Romanian economy (see Figure 8.4). They were selected out of 5,201 commercial companies not yet privatized as of 19 June, 1995. However, among them, 911 companies or 23.3% were unprofitable (as of December 1994) since they registered losses amounting to a cumulated ROL 500 billion (US$ 300 million). For some of these companies the losses (supposedly a matter of unfavorable circumstances such as financial blockage or bad management) accounted for about 15% of their registered capital. To create a break-even situation (even though artificial) these losses were deducted from their registered capital.

The choices Romanian citizens faced were: to swap their COs (distributed in 1992, valued at Lei 25,000 or about US$ 12.5) and coupons (valued at Lei 975,000 or US$ 487.5 or four monthly wages) for shares in the companies on the privatization list; to trade them for shares in the companies they worked for

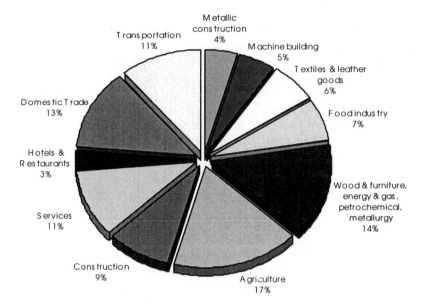

Source: Ministry for Reforms and Privatization (1996).

Figure 8.4. Companies in the mass privatization program by branches

(also when that company was not on the privatization list); or to invest them in one of the five POFs which were supposed to become investment funds. In the end, 90.8% of all coupons offered had been subscribed. Of the Romanian public taking part in this process 88.6% registered directly with the companies offered for privatization and 11.4% registered with the Private Investment Funds that have been transformed (in November 1996) into investment companies. The 40% or 51% equity share left in these companies was to be sold to local and foreign investors.

At the end of the mass privatization process the shares were allotted to the subscribing citizens in a dematerialized form. They were issued in share accounts, each citizen receiving a shareholder certificate specifying information for shareholder identification, as well as the number of shares and the nominal value of a share. However, as mass privatization brought a diffuse ownership structure, the newly opened OTC market is expected to assist the privatized companies in achieving the ownership concentration necessary to foster a responsible attitude towards the company.

The remaining 40% quota in companies that falls outside the scope of mass privatization was to be sold by SOF through *cash auctions* (about 300 companies) and IPOs (50 companies). As a result of these first auctions carried out during the first half of 1966, 5–40% of the shares have been sold for 270 companies, accounting for 74% of the commercial companies listed for auction. The average selling price represented 214.6% of the starting value.

In 400 other companies a share of 51% (instead of 40%) has been offered for privatization. These companies are active in trade, food and textile industry, tourism, metallurgy, transportation and chemical industry. The proceeds obtained from the sale for cash privatization together with some PHARE funds will be used by SOF for restructuring, so that the problem companies may become profitable and privatized. The remaining 60% of proceeds will be used by the privatized company for covering its debts and investments.

Until September 1996 the accumulated total of companies privatized since the end of 1992 reached about 2,500. However, insiders continue to play a decisive role, since more than half of the firms have been sold to the employees on reasonably favorable terms (paying 20% of the price as principal, and the rest in instalments over a 10-year period, with 5–10% p.a. interest). The amount of power given to the present management and employees and the lack of new finance in the absence of outside investors reduces, however, the restructuring potential of these newly privatized companies.

Of the proceeds obtained from the sale for cash privatization together with PHARE funds 40% will be used by SOF for restructuring, so that the 'problem' companies can improve their financial situation in preparation of privatization. The remaining 60% of the proceeds will be used by the privatized companies for covering debts and for investments. A post-privatization fund having at its disposal ECU 40 million from the EBRD and PHARE will provide additional funds for the privatized companies.

THE CAPITAL MARKET

The capital market in Romania is still in the formative stage. With a time-lag of five years since restructuring began in the Romanian banking sector, compared with the opening of stock exchanges in some other transitional economies, the Bucharest Stock Exchange became operational on 20 November 1995. During 1994–1995, the legal framework[4] was passed providing for:

[4] The Romanian capital market is regulated by the following legal acts:
Government Ordinance no. 18/1993 on the regulation of the securities markets and the organization of intermediary institutions; Government Ordinance no. 24/1993 on the establishment and operation of open-end investment funds and of investment companies as financial intermediation institutions; Government Decision no. 788/1993 regulating public offers for securities; Government Decision no.

- strict regulation through the stock exchange law and the whole set of regulations issued by the National Securities Commission (who also have the supervisory function) making the regulatory framework comparable with that of mature capital markets;
- measures to secure investor protection. As in the United States or Japan, in Romania banking activity is separated from the capital market activity, that is, banks are not allowed to engage as intermediaries or to act on their own account on the capital market. The legal framework provides also for transparency and punishes insider trading.

There was also a time-lag between the emergence of the primary market (shares or other securities issues) and the organization of a formal secondary market for securities transactions. Already in 1990 the legal framework allowed commercial companies to issue shares and bonds. Some commercial companies issued shares which however did not contribute to creating more than a modest primary market. With the COs issued in 1992 as a result of the mass privatization process and their subsequent exchange for shares in commercial companies, the share supply on the secondary informal market was significant. Starting in April 1995, this informal market became very active, thanks to the privatization of more than 100 companies and to the activity of local business newspapers which started publishing advertisements on transactions with shares belonging to commercial companies. In the beginning, these advertisements belonged to private individuals; starting in September 1995, however, securities companies also joined this market. Three categories of companies could be found on this secondary informal market:

1. Companies privatized during the first stage of privatization with good financial results in the post-privatization period, such as: Industrialexport and Ursus SA.
2. Private banks, considered attractive by investors, such as: Bankcoop and Ion Ţiriac Bank.
3. Commercial companies privatized in 1995 by the Private Ownership Funds through public offer.

In 1995, prior to and after BSE becoming operative this market was attractive to investors, with share prices exhibiting a clear upward trend. Furthermore, the market was selective as mainly shares belonging to the companies with high performance were traded on this market, a kind of 'Romanian blue chips'.

The Bucharest Stock Exchange opened with just six companies listed in November 1995: Sanevit (the only totally privately-owned company), Artrom, Carne Arad, UAMT, Comelf, and IAIFO. Mobila Alfa joined the Stock

---

788/1993 regulating licensing of brokers and financial intermediaries; Law no. 52/1994 on securities and stock exchanges (no. 52/1994).

Exchange at the end of November 1995, Apsa and Astra in December 1995, Azomureş in January 1996, Foraj Sonde in February 1996, and Condor and Neptun at the end of March 1996. Thus during the middle of 1996, 13 companies were listed on the Stock Exchange. Their number increased to 17 by the end of 1996, of which only 13 were effectively trading. All listed companies entered the basic category of the exchange as they did not qualify for the upper level (first tier).

During the first year of operation the market capitalization, turnover, and the number of shares traded remained low (Figure 8.5). After recording a peak in May 1996 with a level of US$ 670 million, the capitalization of BSE took a downward turn with a low of US$ 336 million in September 1996. Total turnover volume peaked at US$ 1.52 million in March 1996, up from US$ 218,000 in November 1995 and slipped to just US$ 116,000 in September 1996. The rise in monthly turnover before March 1996 was mainly due to newcomers and the increasing interest of investors. In the same month the number of shares traded (238,000) and the number of transactions (2,600) also peaked.

In April 1996, eight of the 13 stocks that were traded on BSE were suspended from trading due to the companies' failure to comply with the Exchange's disclosure requirements. This reduced the total trading turnover in April to only a quarter of that registered in March. Coupled with a new evaluation methodology issued by the National Securities Commission that almost halved the value of investment funds' assets, the turmoil on the Romanian financial market increased and confidence plummeted among investors. Consequently, on 18 April the average turnover dropped to its lowest value ever with a negligible US$ 67.

At the same time the market was characterized by illiquidity (the reduced volume of transactions was determined by the low supply of stocks and funds) and heavy dependence on the fate of two stocks. In the first months of operation the shares of Sanevit (the one-use syringe maker), although with an unrealistic price/earnings (P/E) ratio of 68.12 calculated according to 1995 financial results, made up the largest share of the bourse turnover. In January 1996, it lost out to Azomureş, a producer of chemical products. In March 1996, these two stocks accounted for 90% of the total turnover on the BSE. Thanks to its good financial results, Azomureş (P/E ratio of 5.42) stayed in the limelight in the period January–June 1996 with a share of 80–90% in total turnover while occasionally Foraj Sonde (with a P/E ratio of 5.53) became more frequently traded.

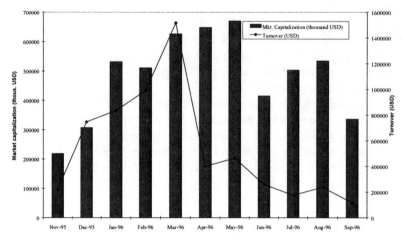

Source: Bucharest Stock Exchange, Institute for Advanced Studies, 1996.

Figure 8.5. Market capitalization and turnover on the Bucharest Stock Exchange

Compared with the informal market, BSE was under the bear sign. The share prices registered a continuous downward path, especially after the general suspension of trading in April 1996, unable to arise the interest of investors. By the end of the first nine months of BSE's operation 11 of the 13 listed companies recorded losses (Table 8.3). The biggest loser was Sanevit, its shares registering a 84% loss in their value, followed by Artrom (-66.7%).

Table 8.3. Share price dynamics on the Bucharest Stock Exchange

Listed shares	27.12.1995* (ROL)	03.10.1996 (ROL)	Percentage change
Sanevit	64,500	10,300	-84.0
Artrom	6,600	2,200	-66.7
Carne	8,800	3,400	-61.4
Comelf	7,700	3,200	-58.4
IAIFO	6,500	2,750	-57.7
Foraj	11,000	5,300	-51.8
UAMT	13,600	7,200	-47.1
Azomureş	19,000	10,200	-46.3

Listed shares	27.12.1995* (ROL)	03.10.1996 (ROL)	Percentage change
Apsa	13,200	7,800	-40.9
Neptun	5,100	3,950	-22.5
Mobila	11,000	8,500	-22.7
Astra Vagoane	3,600	3,900	8.3
Condor	3,750	4,500	20

Note: For Azomureş (16.01.96), Foraj (13.02.96), Condor, and Neptun (28.03.96) the closing value of the first trading day was taken as base for comparison.
Source: Bucharest Stock Exchange, own calculations, 1997.

During its first year of operation BSE remained mainly at the experimental stage. The main problems faced by the Stock Exchange are its limited attractiveness both for potential investors who prefer other investment forms, or the informal market, and also for potential listed companies. Successful private companies that could join the exchange remain, however, outside or prefer to seek listing abroad (Elvila International is listed in London) where the pool of investors is larger. Turnover is expected to stay relatively thin until new, more attractive, companies join the bourse. Companies that have just been privatized during the mass privatization program are expected to join during the following months. Bourse officials expect about 40 companies including more private companies and banks to be listed during the first months of 1997.

Starting at the end of October 1996, the Romanian financial market received a new stimulus from an over-the-counter market in privatization stocks (RASDAQ, designed on the model of NASDAQ). RASDAQ may develop in parallel with the Bucharest Stock Exchange, securing its companies' entrance to the secondary market or may become a competitor for the exchange, which thanks to its flexibility and lower entrance requirements, may prove to be more attractive to companies seeking listings on an exchange. Indeed, during its first two months of operation up to the end of 1996, RASDAQ managed to attract more than 1,500 companies (mostly newly privatized).

SOURCES OF EXTERNAL FINANCE

Financing the current account deficit has become a key challenge for the Romanian authorities. Due to the structure of the real sector which depends heavily on imports and to the need to reshape the industry with the focus on technology upgrading, the task is difficult. A major solution to the problem of balance of payments constraints is to attract foreign investors. However,

Romania has not succeeded in convincing external investors and, from this point of view, it compares rather poorly in per capita terms with other transitional economies. Foreign direct investment (subscribed capital), reached by October 1996 about US$ 2 billion, with a peak of flows in 1994 (US$ 650 million). Over the period 1991–1995 the flows of foreign investment, as paid-up capital, represented only 4.5% of imports (Figure 8.6). A modest but sustained confidence on the part of foreign investors in the broad Romanian political and economic climate would explain this development.

The legal framework for foreign investment in Romania has been quite liberal. The Foreign Investment Law of 1991, amended in 1993, offers a broad array of opportunities. Except for the insurance industry where a partnership with a domestic company is required, foreign investors can set up companies, as general partnerships, limited liability, or joint-stock companies in all economic sectors without a Romanian partner. The last two legal forms have been the ones generally preferred. Romanian legislation protect foreign investment from nationalization, confiscation, expropriation or any similar measures. Investors may repatriate profits fully as well as the proceeds from selling shares, loans or those from the liquidation of the investment. A 10% dividend tax is applicable. Foreign companies registered in Romania (along with the local ones) can either retain their foreign exchange proceeds or sell them on the inter-bank forex market.

The current account deficit varied in size in recent years. As a share of GDP, it peaked at 8.8% in 1992 and plummeted to 1.4% in 1994. The ability of the Romanian authorities to finance external deficits has gradually improved. In 1990, for instance, the sources of financing consisted almost exclusively of short-term borrowing and in a steep reduction of the forex reserves of the NBR. Starting in 1995 Romania (through the central bank) succeeded in tapping private capital markets. In 1996, the NBR borrowed US$ 1.4 billion on the euromarkets, after obtaining investment credit ratings from the major rating agencies.[5]

At the end of 1989 Romania's foreign debt was practically negligible. However, in subsequent years it grew by US$ 1–1.2 billion a year. By the end of 1995, the country's medium- and long-term debt amounted to US$ 5.9 billion, or 18.8% of GDP, and short-term debt totalled US$ 0.8 billion. At the end of July 1996, these two indicators stood at US$ 6.3 billion and, US$ 1.1 billion, respectively.

---

[5] IBCA – BB-; Japan Credit Rating Agency – BB+; Moody's Investors Service – Ba3; Standard & Poor's – BB-.

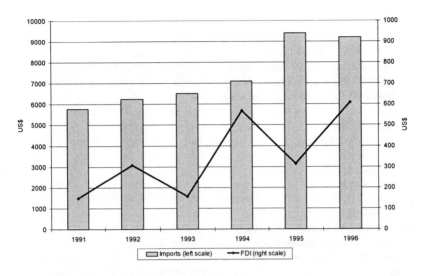

Source: Romanian Development Agency (1996).

Figure 8.6. Imports versus foreign direct investment

Most debt indicators reflect a reasonably good position (see Table 8.4), but, if the current debt growth rate is maintained for much longer, the country's indebtedness may rapidly reach a relatively high level. A strategy which should focus on attracting foreign direct investment is badly needed to counteract the current pattern of debt flows. Consistent policies, aimed at curbing inflation and budget deficits, at restructuring and privatizing enterprises, and at further liberalizing markets, remain a pivotal requirement.

Table 8.4. External sector (eop)

	1990	*1991*	*1992*	*1993*	*1994*	*1995*
Total external debt (US$ bn)	1.1	2.1	3.2	4.2	5.1	6.7
Medium- and long-term external debt (US$ bn)	0.2	1.1	2.5	3.4	4.6	5.9
Medium- and long-term external debt/GDP (%)	3	7.4	16.6	16.1	18.3	18.8
Foreign reserves in months of imports	1	1	2	2	3	2

Note: Excluding gold and SDR.
Source: National Bank of Romania (1996).

REFERENCES

Clifton E. and K. Mohsin (1993): *Enterprise Arrears in Transforming Economies. The Case of Romania*, IMF Staff Papers, vol. 40, no. 3, September 1993.

Daianu D. (1994): *Inter-Enterprise Arrears in a Post-Communist Economy*, IMF Working Papers, No. 54, Washington, D.C.

Frydman R., A. Rapaczynski and J.S. Earle (1993): *The Privatization Process in Eastern Europe*.

Grozea-Helmenstein, D., C. Helmenstein and A. Wörgötter (1997): *Investment Opportunities in Romania*, study commissioned by Bank Austria, Institute for Advanced Studies, Vienna.

Guvernul Romaniei (*The Government of Romania*) (1995): *Trei Ani de Guvernare (Three Years of Governing)*, Government Printing Office: Bucharest.

National Bank of Romania (1993a): *Annual Report*, Bucharest.

National Bank of Romania (1993b): *Quarterly Bulletin*, Bucharest.

National Bank of Romania (1994a): *Annual Report*, Bucharest.

National Bank of Romania (1994b): *Quarterly Bulletin*, various issues, Bucharest.

National Bank of Romania (1995a): *Annual Report*, various issues, Bucharest.

National Bank of Romania (1995b): *Quarterly Bulletin*, various issues, Bucharest.

Popa, I. (1996): *Lansarea Pietei de Capital în Romania. Impactul asupra Dezvoltării Sectorului Privat (The Launching of the Capital Market in Romania. The Impact upon the Development of the Private Sector)*, mimeo, Bucharest.

Romanian Development Agency (1995): *Romania, Yes! An Investment Guide*, RDA and Coopers & Lybrand: Bucharest.

ANNEX

Table 8.A. Selected macroeconomic indicators 1990–1996

	1990	1991	1992	1993	1994	1995	1996
Gross Domestic Product (in Lei bn)	858	2,204	6,029	20,036	49,773	72,136	108,391
Annual change (%)	-5.6	-12.9	-8.8	1.5	3.9	7.1	3.9
GDP Deflator (%)	113.6	295.1	300.0	327.7	239.0	135.3	144.6
Consumption share in GDP (%)	79.2	75.9	77.0	76.0	77.3	81.3	83.7
Public consumption share in GDP (%)	13.3	15.2	14.3	12.3	13.8	13.7	11.6
Investment share in GDP (%)	19.8	14.4	19.2	17.9	20.3	21.4	23.1
Industrial output (%) [1]	76.3	77.2	78.1	101.3	103.3	109.4	109.9

	1990	*1991*	*1992*	*1993*	*1994*	*1995*	*1996*
Industrial producer prices (%) [1) 2)]	126.9	320.1	284.8	265.0	240.5	135.1	149.9
Labour productivity per employee (%) [1)]	89.2	85.0	86.6	109.0	114.8	113.7	111.1
Number of employees (thousand)	3,702	3,409	3,093	2,900	2,717	2,400	2,228
Trade balance							
Exports fob (US$ mn)	5,775	4,266	4,364	4,892	6,151	7,910	8,085
Imports fob (US$ mn)	9,202	5,372	5,784	6,020	6,562	9,487	10,555
Balance (US$ mn)	-3,427	-1,106	-1,420	-1,128	-411	-1,577	-2,470
Coverage of imports through exports (%)	62.8	79.4	75.4	81.3	93.7	83.4	76.6
Balance of current account (US$ mn)	-3,337	-1,012	-1,564	-1,174	-428	-1,774	-2,571
Net real earnings (%) [1)]	105.2	81.7	87.0	83.3	100.4	112.6	109.5
Consumer price index							
Average annual level [2)]	105.1	270.2	310.4	356.1	236.7	132.3	138.8
End of period level	137.7	322.8	299.2	395.5	161.7	127.8	156.9
State budget deficit in % of GDP	+0.3	-1.9	-4.4	-2.6	-4.2	-4.1	-4.9
Exchange rate							
Annual average (ROL/US$)	22.4	76.4	308.0	760.1	1,655	2,033	3,082
End of period (ROL/US$)	34.7	189.0	460.0	1,276	1,767	2,578	4,035
Unemployment rate (%)	–	3.0	8.2	10.4	10.9	9.5	6.6

Notes:
1) Annual index;
2) Average level of current year compared to the average level of previous year;
Source: National Commission for Statistics, Ministry of Finance, National Bank of Romania, 1996.

184 - 213

G12
G21 P33
G28 P34
E52 L33

9. Slovak Republic

Jarko Fidrmuc, Viliam Páleník and Ladislav Unčovský

INTRODUCTION

Slovakia is one of the smallest nations in Central and Eastern Europe. The Slovak economy has been affected by three major developments: (i) its isolation from its West European neighbors following World War II; (ii) its transition to a market economy that started in 1990 when the country was still a part of Czechoslovakia; and (iii) the creation of a national state in January 1993. Before 1990, the Czechoslovak government undertook no serious reforms. There was hardly any private ownership, and the banking and insurance sector and foreign trade were under strong state control. Stock exchanges were created only in the process of transition. Nevertheless, the economic situation was better than in other post-communist countries (no large external debt and a relatively small monetary overhang).

The reforms in Czechoslovakia were substantially more successful than in other post-communist countries. The Slovak Republic succeeded in liberalizing and stabilizing the economy. Inflation (7% in 1995) was virtually the lowest in Eastern Europe, while GDP growth (7.4%) was among the highest in the region. Slovakia privatized a significant share of state property and the capital market has already been liberalized. The country is expected to become a member of the OECD in 1997 and aims at joining EU. However, political tensions in Slovakia are an unfortunate counterweight to its economic success and endanger the country's acceptance by foreign observers and investors.

MONETARY POLICY

Prior to the economic reforms, Czechoslovakia followed a relatively sound monetary policy that avoided (hidden) inflation and a monetary overhang like those in some other transitional economies. However, the monetary policy of the State Bank of Czechoslovakia (SBCS) relied heavily on administrative regulation, mainly to do with price development and exchange rates. Therefore, price liberalization was one of the first tasks of the reform policy in Czechoslovakia. Simultaneously, limited convertibility was introduced after three devaluations of the Czechoslovak Koruna (CSK) from 16.29 CSK/US$ in January 1990 to 28.0 CSK/US$ on 1 January 1991.[1] In 1991, price liberalization, exchange rate devaluation and other factors resulted in a price increase of 61.2% in the Slovak part of the former federation. Nevertheless, the SBCS has succeeded in avoiding persistently high inflation rates in later years. In 1992, inflation dropped to only 10.1% in Slovakia.

The National Bank of Slovakia (NBS) emerged at the end of 1992 from the former SBCS. In the first year of independence, Slovak monetary policy has suffered from a lack of credibility leading to sharp losses of foreign reserves. This situation improved in the second half of 1993 when the governor of the NBS was approved by parliament and the NBS defended its independence. Interestingly, this new institutional arrangement is mirrored in the development of foreign exchange reserves (see also *Foreign financial assistance* and Table 9.8). The NBS is responsible for monetary policy, issues banknotes and coins, directs financial flows, coordinates capital exchanges with other banks and maintains the internal and external stability of the domestic currency.

The main target of the NBS is to maintain stable exchange rates. Although the IMF recommended a flexible exchange rate system, the NBS continued a policy of fixed exchange rates after the split of the federation. Despite a 10% devaluation of the SKK in June 1993, in retrospect the fixed exchange rate policy was successful. In October 1995, Slovakia introduced full convertibility.

The Slovak Koruna is pegged to a basket of foreign currencies. The weights of each currency have been changed several times since convertibility was established. The initial weighting scheme[2] was as follows: US$ 49.07%, DEM 36.15%, ATS 8.07%, CHF 3.79% and FRF 2.92%. Since May 1993, there have been different currency baskets for the Czech and Slovak currencies. The Czech National Bank (CNB) replaced the aforementioned basket of five currencies with a more simple pegging to the DEM and the US$ with a weight of 65% and the US$ (35%) in the basket. The NBS followed the CNB in July 1994 and

---

[1] Between 1991 and 1993, the exchange rate remained stable.

[2] This currency basket corresponded to the weight of the currencies in the Slovak foreign trade (trade with other Eastern European countries was settled in US$). The later changes of the currency basket were prompted by the increasing importance of trade with the EU as well as the increasing orientation of other East European countries (including the Czech Republic) towards the West European currencies.

replaced the currency basket with DEM (60%) and US$ (40%). Therefore, the exchange rate to the Czech Koruna is nearly stable despite the fluctuation of the DEM *vis-à-vis* the US$ exchange rate. The Czech Republic is still the most important single trade partner of Slovakia (see Fidrmuc and Fidrmuc, 1997). Therefore, the exchange rate of the SKK is likely to follow the development of the Czech currency.

Since 1993, the exchange rate has been allowed to move within a rather narrow fluctuation band of ±1.5%. Following the developments in the Czech Republic, the fluctuation bands were extended to ±3% in January 1996 and finally to ±5% in July 1996. The extension of the fluctuation band of the Czech and the Slovak exchange rates should lower the inflationary pressure resulting from the inflow of short-term capital.

As in other reform economies, the Slovak currency is below its purchasing power parity. In 1994, the purchasing power parity was according to the OECD (1996) 12.0 SKK/US$, while the nominal exchange rate stood at 32.05 SKK/US$. The marked difference between the purchasing power parity and the nominal exchange rate allowed for a stable exchange rate despite higher inflation rates (7% in 1995) than in the main trading partners (with the exception of other transitional economies).[3] Nevertheless, the stabilization of price dynamics is a medium-term goal of the NBS. As far as the intermediate targets of monetary policy are concerned, like the German Bundesbank NBS adopted (see Kominkova and Nemec, 1995, pp. 7–9) monitoring monetary aggregates. NBS chooses M2 growth according to expected inflation and GDP growth. Furthermore, NBS adjusts discount and lombard rates, minimum reserve requirements and credit limits in response to macroeconomic development.

An important tool of NBS's monetary policy, associated with prudential banking regulations, are minimal reserve requirements which in 1995 were as follows:
- 3% on time deposits.
- 9% on demand deposits.
- 1% on building saving deposits (since 1 April 1995).

In the past three years NBS has assumed lower real growth rates of GDP for its monetary programs than the Slovak Ministry of Finance for fiscal planning purposes. The NBS estimates were also lower than the realized figures. This strengthened the anti-inflationary effects of the monetary policy of the NBS.

At the beginning of transition, the discount rate (9.5% in 1993) and interest

---

[3] Currently, a devaluation of the Czech currency is being discussed. Insofar as the Czech Republic is the most important trade partner of Slovakia, such a step could trigger a similar policy action in Slovakia.

rates were low in comparison with the inflation rate (23.2% in 1993), as a result of the anti-inflationary policy maintained by the central bank, the low demand for credits and inherited credits with low interest rates. In 1994, the discount rate was set at 12.5% while short-term and medium-term rates were above the inflation rate (13.5%). The discount rate was lowered to 11% in March 1995, to 9.75% in October 1995, and finally to 8.8% in January 1996. In 1994, the lombard rate was set at 1 percentage point above the interest rate achieved on auction refinancing loans. In March 1996, the lombard rate was fixed at 13.1% and at 15% since August 1996.

Average interest rates declined following the stabilization of the price level and the movement of the discount rate during the period. The relatively low level of the interest rate on long-term credits is caused by a high share of loans to large-scale investment projects and housing development projects prior to transition. Such loans yielded interest rates of only about 1% annually,[4] while long-term credits originating already from the transition period yielded average interest rates of above 15% in 1995 (NBS, 1996, pp. 33). The bias in the medium- and short-term credits caused by bad debts was negligible in 1995, although it lowered the medium-term interest rates even below the short-term ones.

THE BANKING SECTOR

The process of creating an efficient capital market can be best seen by looking at the development of its commercial banking sector. A well-functioning banking sector is a necessary condition for successful transformation. Subsequently, we consider both the institutional and operational aspects of its development.

In the Slovak Republic, the legislative framework for the new organizational structure and the development of the banking sector was initiated in the period of early economic reforms 1990–1992. In this period, the central bank (SBCS or NBS after the division of Czechoslovakia) and several banks in state ownership were created. This list includes Slovenska sporitelna (originally Slovenska statna sporitelna), fully owned by the Fund of National Property (FNP), Vseobecna uverova banka (covering the former commercial activities of the SBCS) with the FNP as the dominant shareholder (48%), and Investicna a Rozvojova banka (also originating from the Statna Banka

---

[4] Since a significant part of these credits is overdue (see *The banking sector*), we refer to these credits as bad debts.

Ceskoslovenska), with the FNP owning 36%. This framework was developed progressively: The state banks were privatized, new banks were established, and, last but not least, foreign banks entered the market (a detailed list of the relevant legislation is provided in the Appendix).

Since the beginning the newly created norms and regulations followed legislation in the EU. The adoption of the decree on the protection of deposits was the final step in the completion of the most important stage, that of building the organizational and legal framework for the banking sector in Slovakia. By the end of December 1995, there were 24 domestic banks (resident legal entities), 9 branches of foreign banks and 12 representative offices of foreign banks in the Slovak Republic. In addition, there are two banks that are in process of entering the banking sector in Slovakia.

As the controlling body in the Slovak banking system, the NBS issues bank licences and sets the general terms and conditions for accepting deposits, granting loans, and other banking transactions. These decisions are taken in agreement with the Ministry of Finance of the Slovak Republic, which is responsible for overseeing the commercial activities of banks. The National Bank of Slovakia granted a universal banking licence to 20 out of the total of 24 commercial banks. The remaining four are holders of a specialized banking license for specific activities and 16 banks have full permission to conduct operations in the field of foreign exchange.

Most of the Slovak banks are joint-stock companies (22 banks) and only two are state financial institutions. Most of these banks have their headquarters in Bratislava (20), two are based in Banska Bystrica, and the remaining two are located in Zilina and Kosice. Considering the relatively small size of the Slovak economy, one may regard the size of the banking sector as quite adequate.

Although the domestic banking sector is still to a significant degree regulated by the state, at the same time it enjoys international connections through foreign investments. The same applies to branches of foreign banks. By 31 December 1995, the volume of subscribed capital in the banking sector (excluding the National Bank of Slovakia) totalled SKK 21.49 billion. The weighted share of foreign capital participation was 30.84% and was allocated to 14 domestic commercial banks. Of the total volume of foreign capital in the Slovak banking sector, Austria still accounted for the largest part (43.3%), followed by the Czech Republic (14%), Germany (13.6%), USA (11.0%), France (5.6%), UK (5.2%), Russia (4.9%), and Italy (2.5%).

Furthermore, another decree by the NBS regulated the evaluation of the receivables and off-balance-sheet liabilities of banks according to the risk contained and the creation of resources to cover such risks. This decree unified the classification of bank receivables and tightened the criteria for the calculation of estimated uncovered losses on receivables, which lowered the capital actually available for the computation of capital adequacy ratios. The minimum ratio of capital adequacy (the proportion of modified total capital to risk-weighted assets) which had been set at 8% for 1995 (or 7.25% for banks established before 1992), was kept by all commercial banks with the exception of one bank that is undergoing transformation in its credit portfolios under state participation, and one state financial institution. Other important criteria for the proper functioning of banks in Slovakia are limits to credit and foreign currency exposure.

Since the start of independence in the Slovak Republic in 1993, total assets of commercial banks increased nominally by 60%. At the beginning of 1993, for all banks, total assets reached SKK 371 billion and at the end of 1995 SKK 598 billion. This impressive increase can be attributed to the rapidly growing transaction volume in the banking sector.

In this category, as in other quantitative categories in Slovakia, Vseobecna Uverova Banka accounts for the largest share, SKK 170 billion, followed by Slovenska Sporitelna with SKK 160 billion, and Investicna a Rozvojova Banka with SKK 50 billion. Since these banks are restructured state banks from before the year 1990, they are in the primary position in the market. By contrast, Polnobanka and Tatra banka (both created in 1990 as the first private banks) are of smaller size, their assets exceeding SKK 20 billion. Istrobanka and Priemyselna banka with asset values of SKK 10 billion also belong to this group. Two guarantee and consolidation banks and another two building savings banks found themselves in a unique position. The branches of foreign banks (including six Czech banks) make up the last group. The leading institution in this group is the branch of Ceskoslovenska obchodna banka (Czech Republic) with a long tradition in the Slovak market. With asset values of over SKK 40 billion, this bank comes after the first three Slovak banks. In 1995 the branch of the Dutch ING Bank doubled its assets to SKK 10 billion.

Despite the overall profitability, in some cases considerable losses on loans were registered. This seems to be a result of an unusual high ratio of bad debts in the portfolios of some of the largest banks. And even though in 1995 the banking industry experienced a significant rise in its lending activities, the volume of outstanding credits still grew at a lower rate than the volume of deposits.

Unfortunate experiences in the approving of credits contributed to the diversification and the change in the structure of the main profit-yielding assets. Banks directed their attention to interbank asset transactions and securities which are considered to be more liquid but less risky and, furthermore, turned out to be quite profitable. Since 1993, the balance on the profit-yielding assets has increased by SKK 100 billion. Of this increase, 23.2%

was in loans, 25.6% in interbank asset transactions and as much as 51.2% in securities.

The history of bad debts originated in the pre-reform period when many banks offered large, long-term, low-interest rate loans to insolvent and unprofitable enterprises in the energy and armaments industries, and in housing. According to the NBS, a total of SKK 125 billion of all outstanding loans to state enterprises from before 1989 (40% of total credit volume) were identified as bad debts whose repayment is seriously in doubt. Of this amount, about SKK 90 billion (30% of total credit volume) will not be repaid at all. In 1995, commercial banks and the NBS concentrated on the restructuring of the portfolios of the largest Slovak banks.[5]

PRIVATIZATION

The privatization in the Slovak Republic was realized in the context of the CSFR and on the basis of generalized legislation. Before 1989 the state- and the cooperatively-owned sectors were overwhelmingly dominant.

After 1989 the privatization took two forms – the so-called 'small-scale' and 'large-scale' (including voucher privatization) privatizations. The small-scale privatization took the form of auctions on the basis of privatization projects. It included mainly shops, restaurants, hotels, etc. The inventory and equipment of these business units were privatized. The contractual relationship with the owners of the buildings in which the privatized concerns were situated was settled by leasing.

Large-scale privatization consists of the transfer of state property to the FNP and then to private citizens on the basis of privatization projects. In the Slovak Republic it was realized by the Act of the National Council of the Slovak Republic No. 92/1991 'On conditions of transfer of state property to other persons' (the so-called Act of Large Privatization). Two methods of privatiza- tion were proposed: direct sales of whole entities or parts of them, and the voucher method as the main method of privatization in the CSFR.

Voucher privatization was realized in five waves. In the Slovak Republic 2,592,500 people were registered (out of total of 8,451,000 in the CSFR). The value of a voucher was 1,000 points for a registration fee of CSK 1,000.

For the first wave of the voucher privatization, 165 privatization investment funds were registered in Slovakia (out of 429 in the CSFR). The owners of

---

[5] See NBS Ordinance No. 3 of 3 March 1995, which is a part of this process and demonstrates these problems in more detail.

investment vouchers transferred 1.81 billion points (6.14 billion), i.e. 69.82% of all points allocated to Slovakia. The FNP of the Slovak Republic offered 487 joint-stock companies with 90,111,742 shares, the Federal Fund 61 companies with 2,857,121 shares (in total 1,491 companies and 299,393,282 shares). The corresponding capital was 90.11 billion CSK in the Slovak Republic (CSK 299.39 billion in the CSFR). In the first wave of voucher privatization, 79.8 million shares were sold to Slovak investors, while 7.1 million shares (8.1% of all shares available in Slovakia and 7.2% in CSFR) remained in state hands.

The voucher privatization was the main method of privatization for the second wave of privatization. However, the Act No. 190/1995, changing and amending the former legislation, replaced the voucher privatization by the so-called 'bond' method. The bond of the FNP is a registered security with a nominal value of SKK 10,000. It authorizes the owner to receive this principal and the accumulated interest after five years. The interest depends on the discount rate of the National Bank of the Slovak Republic for the particular years. During 2001 the Fund of national property will pay the nominal value of the bond and the corresponding yields.

Every citizen of the Slovak Republic who is registered for the second wave of the voucher privatization became an owner of the FNP bond at 1 January 1996. The owner of the bond has the right to choose whether to wait until the expiration date and then to present it for payment, or to use the bond before its maturity in one of the following ways:

1. Acquisition of bonds by legal entities or individuals for the settlement of debts against the FNP or the Slovak Fund of Ground (SPF). Acquisition of bonds may be realized as (a) direct sale, (b) sale on the base of public auction, or (c) anonymous sale. The minimum purchase price has been set at SKK 7,500 per bond and is subject to inspection by the RM-S.
2. Investment in companies for the purpose of settling their debts with the FNP or SPF. The investment increases the equity of the company.
3. Acquisition of apartments in private property by agreement with the proprietors.
4. Supplementary pension insurance and supplementary health insurance. The insurance companies must be registered as authorized.
5. Transfer to authorized banks, earmarked for restructuring.
6. Secondary transfers among authorized persons acquired bonds from original owners. Authorized banks, insurance companies and owners of apartment houses are allowed to sell bonds to debtors of FNP or SPF and to authorized banks.
7. Acquisition of parts of property from the FNP by these means:
   - direct sale from the original acquirers, realized by the representatives of FNP;

- sale of stocks offered by FNP to authorized banks, insurance companies and owners of apartment houses in the form of direct sale;
- purchase of stocks offered by the FNM through an authorized person.

The market for bonds among persons authorized to acquire the bonds before their maturity is organized by the FNP. The RM-System Slovakia on the base of an agreement with the FNP secures the technical services for transfers of bonds through the Center of Voucher Privatization and the network of its own trading offices. The bonds can be traded directly by the authorized persons or through authorized security dealers. The FNP makes agreements through its district representatives.

The practice of using bonds is still in its infancy. Furthermore, a group of deputies of the Slovak National Council appealed to the Constitutional Court to have the above mentioned Act repealed.

The companies that were scheduled for privatization in the second wave of voucher privatization were transferred directly to their new owners. By 31 March 1996 of the 715 proposed privatization projects for the second wave of privatization 603 companies were scheduled with a volume of SKK 136 billion. From the point of view of the chosen methods of privatization, 36,7% of the value of the state property was privatized by standard methods, 2.2%, by transfer without payment, and 61.6% by investment in stock companies. The so-called standard methods include direct sales (85% privatized property) and public bidding (15% of privatized value).

At present, the management buy-outs (MBO) are the main form of the privatization, i.e. a privatization by the former management of state-owned firms. On average, only 10%–15% of the value is paid on the date of purchase. The rest is paid according to a schedule of payments covering several years. This sum can be reduced up to 50% by reinvestment in the privatized company. An agreement by the buyer with the FNP states the aims and results of the purchase. In case of non-fulfilment of the agreement, the FNP can withdraw the privatization contract.

THE CAPITAL MARKET

The Slovak capital market was created and is developing in tandem with the transformation of directive economic system to a market economy. The first steps towards the establishment of a capital market in the Slovak republic were already undertaken within the Czechoslovak federation in 1990. However, the trading on the Slovak capital market started only at the beginning of 1993. The most important institutions of the Slovak capital market are:

- The Bratislava Stock Exchange;

- Off-exchange market RM-System Slovakia;
- Securities Centre;
- State Supervisory Office of the Capital Market;
- Securities traders;
- Brokers;
- Investment companies;
- Investment funds.

These institutions are working within current legislation, and together with issuers and shareholders make up the Slovak capital market.

Transitional countries are facing the need to create a new legislative framework for the capital market resulting from forty years of the total absence of a capital market. In Slovakia the following pieces of legislation were introduced:

- Securities Act No. 600/1992 Zb.
- Stock exchange Act No. 214/1992.
- Bonds Act No. 530/1992.
- Investment Companies and Investment Funds Act No. 248/1992.
- Commercial Code No. 513/1991.
- Foreign Exchange Act No. 528/1992.

However, these laws are going through continuous development (see list of all related legislation in the Appendix). The greatest number of amendments are related to the already-mentioned Securities Act and the Act on Investment Companies and Investment Funds. The amendments to the Securities Act arose from the obligatory dematerialization of the main types of securities. Moreover, the protection of small stockholders was established and later modified on the basis of experiences during the early years and the obligation to announce direct trades was made mandatory to improve the transparency of the Slovak capital market.

On the basis of the experience of the first wave of the voucher privatization as well as their role in the capital market, the Act on Investment Companies and Investment Funds was revised. The stipulations for membership of the board of directors and supervisory boards of investment companies and funds were adjusted so as to avoid possible conflicts of interest. The position of portfolio investors was changed by the obligatory diversification of the risk of collective investment (that is, they cannot own more than 10% of the shares of one issue), as well as the prohibition of membership of investors' collectives in the directing bodies of joint-stock companies.

Bratislava Stock Exchange

The Bratislava Stock Exchange is a joint-stock company, which was created on

15 March 1991. Physical trading started on 6 April 1993. The legislative base of the Bratislava Stock Exchange is provided by the Act on Bratislava Stock Exchange no. 214/1992.

The Bratislava Stock Exchange is owned by banks, investment and broker companies. Its rules and principles are based on the experiences of internationally renowned exchanges. The exchange is based on a membership principle: Trading is allowed only to persons whose membership is approved by the stock exchange chamber. The law grants membership to the Slovak National Bank and the National Property Fund. At the end of 1993, the exchange had 21 members and at the end of 1995 46 members (see Appendix). Under the rules of the Bratislava Stock Exchange, members have to be legal entities and have to fulfil the following conditions:

1. The member must be registered in a court trade register in the Slovak Republic.
2. The member must have security trading registered as an object of its business activity.
3. The member must be the holder of a trading permission of the Ministry of Finance of the Slovak Republic.
4. The member must keep an account with the Slovak Bank Clearing Center or with any other Bratislava Stock Exchange member that has such an account with the Slovak Bank Clearing Center and who will mediate clearing of the financial matters of trades.
5. The member must fulfil all obligations and liabilities resulting from the Bratislava Stock Exchange rules and regulations as well as obligations and liabilities resulting from the legal requirement of the Slovak Republic generally in force.

Equity trading
The Bratislava Stock Exchange is the place where the demand for and the supply of stocks are matched, and which is gradually being supplemented by a system for the support of reliable and fair trading, which includes:
- the electronic exchange trading system, working on a T+3 settlement basis;
- the connection to the Securities Center and the Bank Clearing Center;
- the Guarantee Fund;
- the Stock Exchange Arbitration Court.

An important boost to the activity on the Bratislava Stock Exchange was given by the start of trading of about 600 shares that originated from the first wave of voucher privatization. Trading is made possible by the Securities Center, which is the only legal institution providing an electronic system for showing clearly the issuer and the ownership of all registered stocks.

On 1 July 1993 trading started with all types of listed shares, and from 15

July 1993 also with registered shares from the first wave of voucher privatization which were issued by companies in the Slovak Republic. After the initial 14-day trading period, trading began on a weekly basis, i.e. on Tuesdays with listed securities and on Wednesdays with registered securities. The Bratislava Stock Exchange started to trade on a daily basis on 11 October 1993. The trading system of the exchange underwent a couple of changes that enhanced its safety and transparency. On 22 November 1993 a new electronic system of exchange trading was approved. This is computer-monitored on the basis of demand and supply from each Bratislava Stock Exchange member individually. This means that the trade is performed directly between the representatives of individual members without the traditional mediation by dealers.

The electronic system of exchange trading allows trading in two basic subsystems :

• In the subsystem of continuous trading, exclusively used for listed securities where orders are continuously processed.
• In the subsystem of batch trading which deals exclusively with unlisted types of securities where buy and sell orders are processed on a fixed-price basis.

The next important step was undertaken on 1 January 1995, when the Bratislava Stock Exchange entered into the interbank clearing center as a third party. This decision of the Bank Committee of the National Bank of Slovakia enabled complex settlement of the stock exchange trades at the Bratislava Stock Exchange. As a result the Bratislava Stock Exchange has become the principal coordinator of the whole process of trade settlements.

A guarantee fund ensures that sellers of securities are compensated financially if the other party should be unable to meet its financial obligations in time. All Bratislava Stock Exchange members take part in the guarantee fund through their initial contribution of SKK 200,000 and a variable amount representing 5% of the average daily trading volume realized by the member on the Bratislava Stock Exchange floor in the previous month.

The safety system for the clearing of exchange trades reduced the risk to a minimum. Of the total of 28,755 trades realized at the Bratislava Stock Exchange only 50 have been suspended. In 48 cases of the suspended trades discrepancies were removed immediately and clearing of these trades was performed in T+3 terms. In the remaining two cases, the trades have been settled in T+4 terms. It was never necessary to draw upon money from the guarantee fund.

The Stock Exchange Arbitration Court was founded by the Stock Exchange Chamber on 10 November 1995. Its main task is to resolve lawsuits which arise from exchange trading. The court is independent. Proceedings can be filed at the Stock Exchange Arbitration Court on condition that both sides freely demonstrate a willingness to resolve the particular case before it. This willingness has to be confirmed by an arbitration agreement, which is signed by both parties.

Listed securities

The Bratislava Stock Exchange consists of three market segments: the senior market with listed stock; the junior market with listed stock; and the market with unlisted (registered) stock. Only publicly tradable securities are listed on the Bratislava Stock Exchange, and only the issuer or a mandatory member of Bratislava Stock Exchange can ask for the listing of a particular issue. The minimum conditions for listing an issue can be found in Table 9.1.

All securities, with the exception of government bonds, are first listed in the junior market of the Bratislava Stock Exchange. An issue can be transferred from the junior market to the senior market after a trading period of a minimum of 6 months in the junior market.

Issuer's obligations, as set out by the Listing Rules, mostly pertain to the disclosure of information. They require a prospectus for each issue, a business performance report, financial statements, an annual business performance report, records from shareholder meetings, information about any amendments of the articles of association and about any amendments to the entry in the trade register. The obligation on the exchange is to ensure that this information is accessible to all investors.

Table 9.1. Minimum listing conditions on the Bratislava Stock Exchange

	Senior Market	Junior Market
The amount of share capital		
(in SKK million)	500	100
(in US$ million)	16.7	3.3
Volume of the issue (subject to application for listing in nominal value)		
(in SKK million)	100	100
(in US$ million)	3.3	3.3
The period of business activities (in years)	3	1
Financial years to be covered by the prospectus	3	1
Audit of annual financial statements (in years)	1	no

Source: Bratislava Stock Exchange, 1996.

Any publicly tradable security issued in compliance with the generally binding regulations can be registered and traded on the market with unlisted securities. When required, the exchange can ask the issuer for some information about the actions of the issuer and about any changes in the issuing and trading terms of the registered issue.

The number of listed securities has been rising rapidly since the beginning of exchange operations in 1992. In 1992 only two bonds were listed on the Bratislava Stock Exchange (Table 9.2) but already in 1995 44 securities were being traded. The junior market is expanding due to newly listed stocks. Most of these are gradually moving to the senior market. In cases when issuers did not satisfy the listing conditions, the issue was not accepted on the junior market, was not moved to the senior market, or was even removed.

Table 9.2. Securities listed on the Bratislava Stock Exchange

Senior market												
Year	Shares			Government bonds			Bank bonds			Corporate bonds			Total
	[+]	[-]	[=]	[+]	[-]	[=]	[+]	[-]	[=]	[+]	[-]	[=]	bal.
1992	0	0	0	0	0	0	0	0	0	0	0	0	+0
1993	0	0	0	3	0	3	0	0	0	0	0	0	+3
1994	0	0	0	3	0	3	0	0	0	0	0	0	+3
1995	11	0	11	11	2	9	4	2	2	7	2	5	+27
Total			11			15			2			5	33
Junior market												
Year	Shares			Bank bonds			Corporate bonds			Participation certificates			Total
1992	0	0	0	2	0	2	0	0	0	0	0	0	+2
1993	9	0	9	0	0	0	1	0	1	2	0	2	+12
1994	8	0	8	2	1	1	3	0	3	0	2	-2	+10
1995	1	10	-9	0	3	-3	3	4	-1	2	2	0	-13
Total			8			0			3			0	11

Market of registered securities												
Year	Shares			Municipal bonds			Bank & corporate bonds			Participation certificates			Total
1992	0	0	0	0	0	0	0	0	0	0	0	0	+0
1993	510	9	501	3	0	3	0	0	0	0	0	0	+501
1994	5	4	1	3	0	3	1	0	1	2	0	2	+8
1995	288	0	288	11	2	9	16	2	14	0	0	0	+313
Total			790			15			15			2	822

Source: Bratislava Stock Exchange, 1996.

The market for registered securities experienced its most important changes in 1993 and in 1995. In 1993, 501 shares which had emerged from the first wave of voucher privatization were registered, followed by another 313 in 1995. A strong surge in the number of registrations was caused by the amendment to the Act on Securities, which introduced the requirement that all publicly traded securities should be registered and traded on the Bratislava Stock Exchange.

Table 9.3. Trading volumes on the Bratislava Stock Exchange

Year	Anonymous trades in SKK bn	Direct trades in SKK bn	Total volume in SKK bn	GDP in SKK bn	%
1993	0.04	0.13	0.17	369.90	0.04
1994	0.83	5.45	6.28	441.30	1.42
1995	0.47	39.60	40.07	518.00	7.74
1996 1–2.Q.	5.91	44.03	49.95	280	17.84
1996 1–3.Q.	11.53	68.73	80.27	n.a	n.a.

Source: Bratislava Stock Exchange, 1996.

Trading volume

The volume of trades closed on the Bratislava Stock Exchange is growing dynamically (Table 9.3). In 1993, the turnover of the Bratislava Stock Exchange accounted for only 0.04% of Slovak GDP. In 1995, its share increased to almost 8% and in the first half of 1996 it reached 18%. A major part of the turnover is attributed to the direct trades including some privatization deals.

The scale of anonymous trades was influenced by the first revival of the Slovak capital market in 1994 as well as by the second one in 1996, while 1995 was characterized by a muted trading activity.

SAX index

The aggregate development of stock prices is measured by the SAX index. This index is collectively managed by the Bratislava Stock Exchange and the Creditanstalt Securities as the official index of the Bratislava Stock Exchange. The index is based on a weighted algorithm known as the 'Paasche formula' with a base date of 14 September 1993. The SAX index value is calculated on a daily basis. As a performance index, the SAX index is adjusted for dividend disbursements. The index includes the eight most intensively traded issues (see Table 9.4). Since 12 May 1995, the number of constituents has been twelve. The second column of Table 9.4 shows the original weights of the SAX index before the first change in its composition (22 December 1994), the third column those after the change on 12 May 1995, while the last one shows the current values.

Table 9.4. SAX index component stocks

Constituent stock	Weight in the index in %		
	22 December 1994	12 May 1995	28 June 1996
Nafta	12	19	16
Slovnaft	46	30	27
Ozeta	2	1	1
Biotika	3	2	2
Vseobecna uverova banka	10	13	13
Vychodoslovenske zeleziarne	16	17	23
Investicna a rozvojova banka	3	3	3
Slovenska poistovna	8	7	6
Chirana PREMA	–	2	2
Slovenske lodenice	–	2	2
Povazske strojarne	–	2	3
Plastika Nitra	–	2	2
Total	*100*	*100*	*100*

Source: Bratislava Stock Exchange, 1996.

The SAX index represents the aggregate price development on the Bratislava Stock Exchange, as the 12 constituent stocks account for around 70% of the aggregate market capitalization. The development of the SAX index (Table 9.5) shows a revival in the Slovak capital market in 1994 and 1996. During the first revival of the Slovak capital market in 1994, the difference between the highest and the lowest value of the SAX index was much higher (approx. 300 points) than during the second revival in 1996 (approx. 70 points). This is mostly the result of a gradual decrease in the high volatility of the Slovak capital market, a sign of market maturity.

Table 9.5. Development of the SAX Index

	1993	1994	1995	1–2.Q. 1996
Closing Value	109.58	214.27	153.82	217.61
High Value	114.39	405.49	216.25	219.87
Low Value	100.00	109.58	147.08	150.40

Source: Bratislava Stock Exchange, 1996.

Unified average prices
With the aim of improving the transparency of the Slovak capital market, the Bratislava Stock Exchange and the RM-S Slovakia (see Páleník, 1999) have offered unified average prices since 22 September 1995. The computation algorithm calculates the prices of anonymous trades recorded on both markets with the unified average price being determined as their weighted average.

In relation to this, the price spreads of both market organizers also have been unified in the range of ±15%. The mid-range is given by the unified average price. The price is reported by both market organizers in daily price lists, while each uses its usual methodology. The unified average prices of the Bratislava Stock Exchange and RM-S computation was performed for the first time on the fourth Monday in December 1995.

The information service provided by the Bratislava Stock Exchange is indispensable to foreign investors. The stock exchange has relations with the International Federation of Stock Exchanges (FIBV), the Federation of European Stock Exchanges (FESE) and the Federation of Euro-Asian Stock Exchanges (FEAS). Among the Bratislava Stock Exchange clients are the information agencies Finsat, Reuters, Telerate, Telekurs as well as foreign daily newspapers like the *Financial Times*. The Bratislava Stock Exchange regularly offers daily and weekly price lists to selected economic newspapers. It also prepares monthly, semiannual and annual statistics.

Securities traders
On the Slovak capital market brokers and their agents are allowed to work subject to their satisfying the conditions required by the Securities Act no.

600/1992. A broker must be legally recognized and have permission from the Ministry of Finances of the Slovak Republic. This permission requires proof of professional, technical, financial and ethical suitability. The scope of permitted activity usually consists of securities trading, the issuing of securities on behalf of companies, the safe keeping of securities, repaying securities or their rents for the issuer, and advisory services related to securities.

In mid-1996 there were 108 brokers. The most important of these are the members of the Bratislava Stock Exchange (see Appendix) or special customers of the RM-System Slovakia. Brokers always carry out their professional trading activities through a physical representative, who has permission from the Ministry of Finances. The traders have to fulfill the following criteria: experience in trading with securities, successful professional examination, qualification for legal actions, and an unblemished record. A trader on the public market can act through an agent who likewise has to meet the requirements of legal status and honesty.

Investors
Collective investment has had a great impact on the development of a capital market. In Slovakia, with no collective investment before 1989, the first wave of the voucher privatization contributed significantly to the introduction of investment funds because a large number of participants in the voucher privatization committed their investment vouchers to investment privatization funds. Following the voucher privatization, the investment privatization funds have been transformed into standard investment funds and have issued their securities, which are also traded. Some investment companies set up standard forms of collective investment and created new open and closed investment funds. A proportion of potential savings is invested in these funds.

In mid-1996 there were 64 investment companies and 146 investment funds. These institutional investors had the opportunity to invest in around 1,200 publicly traded securities from 867 companies.

The commercial banks also play an important role in the Slovak capital market. They belong to the largest investors as well as important issuers (mostly bank bonds). Foreign investors have entered the Slovak capital market through commercial banks and broker companies.

Futures and Options Exchanges

Option and future trades have a short but interesting history in Slovakia. The Bratislava Options Exchange started as the first exchange for futures and options trading in the post-socialist countries. The largest shareholder of the exchange was the Swedish company Option Market Systems International.

Other shareholders were various individuals and institutions not participating in the capital market. The Bratislava Options Exchange was created on 1 September 1992. Permission was granted by the Ministry of Finance on 8 October 1992. Opening on 2 October 1993, the floor of the Bratislava Options Exchange was a trading place for options and futures contracts with a maturity of six month for the stocks of ten companies The size of one contract was ten stocks. The spectrum of derivatives was gradually transformed: the maturity of options and futures contracts was lowered from six months to two. The series were listed every month and contracts could be made for stocks of five joint-stock companies. By 2 July 1993, one-day futures trades as standard futures with non-standard life were introduced on the Bratislava Options Exchange. On 12 October 1995, the Bratislava Options Exchange stopped trading with one-day futures, the next day starting the trade with American call options with low strike prices for the stock of 77 joint-stock companies with six-month maturity. This new product provided the opportunity to acquire market exposure without requiring any registration through the Securities Center. On 13 November 1995, the floor of the Bratislava Options Exchange ceased trading because its license for organizing a derivatives market was not renewed following a change in the law. Table 9.6 shows that the activity of the Bratislava Options Exchange was rising dynamically. In 1994, the turnover accounted for 0.45% of GDP.

In 1995 the Bratislava Options Exchange began a project with the Central European Clearing House and Exchange (CECE) in cooperation with the Austrian Options and Futures Exchange (ÖTOB). The RM-S Slovakia took over the project after the Bratislava Options Exchange was closed. The goal of this project is to render an automated net of West and East European markets for options and futures trading. The RM-S Slovakia is currently engaged in improving the conditions for the inflow of foreign capital and is to resume trading with derivatives in Slovakia.

Table 9.6. Total trading volume on the Bratislava Options Exchange

Year	Options (SKK bn)	Futures (SKK bn)	1-day futures (SKK bn)	Total volume (SKK bn)	GDP (SKK bn)	Share in %
1993	0.006	0.001	0.026	0.032	369.9	0.01
1994	0.291	0.002	1.700	1.993	441.3	0.45
1995	0	0.000	1.114	1.114	518.0	0.22
Total	*0.297*	*0.002*	*2.840*	*3.139*		

Source: Bratislava Options Exchange, 1996.

In 1996, no options and futures trades were organized in Slovakia. A working group of experts from the Bratislava Stock Exchange is mapping out the needs of the exchange members for derivative trading and is working towards the creation of a new trading system, tailored to options and futures trading.

Money Market

The standard interest rate plays an important role in creating and valuing an investment portfolio. The National Bank of Slovakia sets the daily fixing rates for the interbank market. In order to improve the transparency of the interest rates, the interbank market requires them to be standardized. Accordingly, the NBS has introduced the Bratislava inter-bank offering rate (BRIBOR) for 1-month and 3-month interbank deposits in July, and for 2-month deposits in October 1996. The BRIBOR represents an important source of information for the NBS about the actual situation on the money market, necessary for the open market operations of the NBS. For commercial banks, BRIBOR constitutes a survey of interest rates on the interbank deposit market.

Perspectives on the Slovak capital market

The rise in the importance of the Slovak capital market can be seen in Table 9.7, which shows the development of the ratios of trade volumes on the organized markets to Slovak GDP. The last column demonstrates the dynamics of this market. In 1993, all capital trades made in the organized markets accounted for less than 0.1% of GDP, but this value reached almost 22% in 1996. In the past few years the number of investment companies, funds, commercial banks, securities traders and brokers has risen, but thanks to voucher privatization the volume of publicly traded issues of securities has also increased significantly.

Table 9.7. Trade volume as a percentage of GDP

Year	Bratislava Stock Exchange	RM System Slovakia	Bratislava Options Exchange	Total
1993	0.04	0.01	0.01	0.1
1994	1.42	0.45	0.45	2.3
1995	7.74	3.48	0.22	11.4
1996*	17.84	3.96	NA	21.8

Note: * January till June 1996.
Source: Bratislava Stock Exchange, 1996.

SOURCES OF EXTERNAL FINANCE

Foreign Financial Assistance

Like other transitional economies, Slovakia used credits from abroad and financial assistance from international institutions in order to improve its low level of foreign exchange reserves and to provide financing for the restructuring of the economy. Although the macroeconomic indicators of the economy were good relative to other transitional economies, the newly independent country had to gain access to the international capital market. For this, good relations with international institutions were of crucial importance (see Fidrmuc and Fidrmuc, 1997).

Czechoslovakia was a founding member of the IMF. Its membership was renewed in September 1990. The Slovak Republic has been a member of the IMF since January 1993.[6] However, Slovakia did not succeed in preparing a stand-by agreement with the IMF until July 1994. Nevertheless, Slovakia received a Systemic Transformation Facility (STF) loan (US$ 90 million in 1993 followed by US$ 24.41 million in November 1994). In July 1994, the IMF approved a stand-by loan of US$ 183.41 million. Of this amount, only two tranches (US$ 46.78 million) were drawn in the second half of 1994. In January 1995, in response to the strong growth of the foreign exchange reserves the Slovak government decided not to draw any further tranches from the stand-by loan.

In 1994, the World Bank (WB) approved an Economic Recovery Loan (US$ 80 million). In 1995, the Slovak government and the NBS began negotiations concerning a Financial and Enterprise Structural Adjustment Loan for the restructuring of enterprises and the banking sector.

In addition, the European Investment Bank approved the Apex Global Loan (ECU 28 million) in 1993 and extended this loan in 1995 (ECU 50 million). The loan should finance up to 50% of selected projects in the field of environmental protection, tourism, and energy efficiency improvement. The EXIM Bank of Japan approved a Two-Step Loan (JPY 4.29 billion) aimed at small and medium-sized private businesses and joint ventures. Slovakia received further foreign financial assistance from the European Bank for Reconstruction and Development, the European Union (PHARE Program), and other institutions.

Between 1993 and 1995, the gross national debt of the Slovak Republic

---

[6] The liabilities of Czechoslovakia to the IMF were split between the Czech Republic and Slovakia in the ratio 2.29:1.

increased from US$ 2.98 billion in January 1993 to US$ 5.8 billion in December 1995 (see Table 9.8). However, the increase of gross debt in 1995 was influenced by a change in methodology[7] concerning liabilities to the Czech Republic with effect from October 1995. The gross debt is still modest, that is, gross debt per capita was only US$ 1,099 in December 1995. As in the Czech Republic (see Rejnuš and Schmied, 1999), short-term capital inflows gained in importance during 1995. Short-term liabilities accounted for 29% of gross debt in December 1995.

The official debt of the Slovak government and the NBS increased from US$ 1.6 billion in January 1993 to US$ 2.0 billion in December 1995. During 1995, the official debt of the government and NBS decreased by US$ 0.3 billion mainly due to the repayment of IMF loans. However, the Slovak government approved significant credit guarantees between 1993 and 1996.

Table 9.8. External finance and foreign debt in Slovakia

	Unit	1993	1994	1995
Net direct investment	SKK bn	4.13	5.43	3.98
Slovak direct investment abroad	SKK bn	-1.88	-0.45	-0.23
Direct investment in Slovakia	SKK bn	6.01	5.88	4.22
Net portfolio investment	SKK bn	-8.10	8.70	7.32
Slovak portfolio investment abroad	SKK bn	n.a.	n.a.	5.10
Portfolio investment in Slovakia	SKK bn	n.a.	n.a.	2.12
Credits received	SKK bn	4.92	10.25	9.63
Disbursement	SKK bn	19.99	25.71	23.41
Repayments	SKK bn	-15.07	-15.47	-21.60
Credit extended	SKK bn	7.66	5.83	2.04
Disbursement	SKK bn	-0.68	-0.67	-2.33
Repayments	SKK bn	8.44	6.50	4.32
Official debt of the government and NBS	US$ bn	2.0	2.3	2.0
Total gross debt	US$ bn	3.7	4.3	5.8
Total gross debt per capita	US$	695	808	1099
Foreign exchange reserves (including gold)	US$ mn	0.45	1.75	3.42
Exchange rate	SKK/US$	30.790	32.039	29.735

Source: National Bank of Slovakia, 1994, 1995, 1996.

---

[7] According to NBS (1996, p. 40), the total gross debt of Slovakia increased by US$ 0.4 million only due to the methodology change in October 1995.

Credits from abroad and the surplus in the current account[8] of the balance of payments resulted in a significant increase in foreign exchange reserves between 1993 and 1995. The foreign exchange reserves (without gold stock) of the State Bank of Czechoslovakia (SBCS) were as low as US$ 1.1 billion on 31 December 1992. This amount reflected a sharp fall of SBCS's foreign exchange reserves (US$ 2.1 billion in June 1992) even before the division of Czechoslovakia. The total reserves of the NBS were only US$ 0.7 billion on 1 January 1993. The first half of 1993 was characterized by a further decline in the foreign reserves of NBS to US$ 0.3 billion in June 1993. After the devaluation in June 1993, foreign exchange reserves recovered and reached US$ 1.7 billion in December 1994 and US$ 3.4 billion at the end of 1995 (see Table 9.8).

Foreign Direct Investment

The volume of foreign direct investment (FDI) in Slovakia has so far been modest. Slovakia enjoyed only about one quarter of total foreign investments in Czechoslovakia before the division of the federation, although the economic weight of the Slovak part represented about one-third of the CSFR. However, the region of the capital Bratislava and neighboring West Slovakia received foreign investment at a level comparable with foreign investment in Central Bohemia and Prague (see Fidrmuc *et al.*, 1994). On the other hand, Slovakia exhibits large regional differences in its industrial structure, the quality of its infrastructure and the level of wages, resulting in a very low FDI level in the Eastern regions of Slovakia. Therefore, low FDI figures are due both to the small size of the country and a bias in perception on the part of international investors.

Compared with other Central European countries, the incentives to invest in Slovakia are low wage levels together with a geographical proximity to potential markets in the EU. Wages in US dollar terms in Slovakia (US$ 278 monthly at the end of 1995) were lower than in the Czech Republic (388), Hungary (347), or Poland (314). The relatively stable macroeconomic situation and low foreign debt are providing a good framework for foreign investors in Slovakia. However, this is partly offset by the absence of an infrastructure, an undefined economic policy towards foreign investors and political uncertainty. As a result the approach of international investors faced with this mixture of investment incentives and the countervailing factors could be best described as

---

[8] However, the current account was again in deficit in 1996. Makuch and Nemec (1996) estimate a current account deficit of US$ 737 representing about 8% of GDP in 1996.

'wait-and-see', that is to say, many potential investors enter the Slovak market without to-date committing significant amounts of funds.

According to the balance of payments statistics (Table 9.8), the net inflow of FDI amounted to SKK 4.1 billion (US$ 134 million) in 1993. After a slight increase to SKK 5.4 billion (US$ 169 million) in 1994, FDI inflow again declined to SKK 4.0 billion (US$ 134 million) in 1995. On the other hand, net portfolio investment increased to SKK 8.7 billion (US$ 272 million) in 1994 and SKK 7.3 billion (US$ 246 million) in 1995. The portfolio investment is influenced mainly by trading with shares of enterprises privatized by the voucher method between the Czech Republic and Slovakia.

According to the Slovak Statistical Office (data on the base of the business register),[9] the stock of FDI increased from US$ 231.2 million in 1992 to US$ 366.2 million in 1993, US$ 551.7 million in 1994, and US$ 732.9 million in 1995. Czech investments accounted for US$ 40.0 million (11% of total FDI) after the split of the federation in 1993 and its investment increased to US$ 119.6 million (18%) in 1995. Austria and Germany are the largest investors accounting for 21% (US$ 157.7 million) and 18% (US$ 128.8 million) of total FDI, respectively. The next main investor nation is the USA with 11% (US$ 84.2 million). Among other countries, only the UK, the Netherlands, and France enjoy investments exceeding 5% of total FDI.

In general, the Slovak Republic adopted the same legislation framework concerning FDI as the Czech Republic (see Rejnuš and Schmied, 1999). Already during 1990, the 'Law on Enterprises with Foreign Participation' of January 1989 had been liberalized by two amendments. The new Commercial Code liberalized foreign direct investments in 1992. The Commercial Code created equal conditions for the entrepreneurial activities of domestic and foreign entities. Foreign investors are allowed to acquire a share in a company in excess of 50% and are free to establish new enterprises. With the introduction of limited convertibility at the beginning of 1991, all restrictions on the repatriation of profits and capital have been removed. Repatriation of capital gains is also permitted. In addition, Slovakia has introduced investment incentives aimed at a better regional distribution of FDI and greater participation by foreign investors in the Slovak banking sector. However, only the latter aim was accomplished by these incentives.

Foreign investors have been allowed to organize investment privatization funds and in this manner to take part in the voucher privatization. They prefer joint ventures to greenfield investment and the acquisition of Slovak firms. There are no legal restrictions on foreign investors participating in public sales

[9] Growth of FDI does not correspond to balance of payments statistics due to different definitions and exchange rate movements.

of state property (except for the so-called 'small-scale privatization' that was completed in 1992), but Slovak authorities lay greater stress on privatizations aimed at Slovak owners. In 1995, the Slovak parliament approved the Act on Strategic Enterprises that ensures the right of the Slovak Republic to have a say in the direction of about 30 so-called 'strategic enterprises'. In turn, this policy reduces the participation of foreign investors in these enterprises.

CONCLUSION

Slovakia is one of the smallest countries in Central and Eastern Europe, becoming independent after the division of Czechoslovakia on 1 January 1993. As a newly independent nation, Slovakia was less well-known to international investors. Furthermore, political tensions in Slovakia have offset its economic success and delayed the country's acceptance by foreign observers and investors. On the other hand, Slovakia has shown considerable progress in many economic indicators since 1993.

Privatization in the Slovak Republic was successful in creating a private sector. In 1995, nearly 65% of Slovak GDP was generated by the private sector, which employed over 55% of the Slovak labor force. The privatization in the Slovak Republic began within the legal and economic framework of the CSFR in the so-called small-scale and the large-scale privatization (including voucher privatization). After the division of Czechoslovakia, the Slovak authorities stressed the so-called 'standard' methods of privatization (mainly management buy-outs) and introduced the so-called 'bond privatization' to replace the second wave of the voucher privatization.

Privatization was a necessary condition for the development of the Slovak capital market which has experienced considerable legislative and institutional changes as well as a quantitative expansion. Another indispensable factor for a prosperous capital market is the reorganization of the banking sector. Reforms began with the establishment of the National Bank of Slovakia and several state-owned banks. Later the latter banks were privatized while new, also foreign, banks entered the market. As the banking sector diversified, more effort was evident on the part of the government and the NBS to improve the sector structure with prudential banking regulations. It was considered a matter of urgency to revitalize the loan portfolios of the largest Slovak banks since bad debts slow down economic growth. At present banks continue to increase their size, extend their services, improve their efficiency and strengthen their viability under market economy principles.

REFERENCES

Fidrmuc, J. and J. Fidrmuc (1997): *Slovakia*, in: Cooper, R. and J. Gacs (eds): *Trade Growth in Transition Economies: Export Impediments for Central and Eastern Europe*, Edward Elgar, Cheltenham and Lyme, NH.

Fidrmuc, J., J. Foltin, P. Huber, M. Jarosova, J. Kohutova, I. Kosir, R. Kovac, P. Ochotnicky, S. Szerdahelyiova, and A. Wörgötter (1994): *The Slovak Republic − After One Year of Independence*, study commissioned by Bank Austria, Institute for Advanced Studies, Vienna.

Kominkova, Z. and M. Nemec (1995): *Money Supply in the Slovak Republic*, Institute of Monetary and Financial Studies, National Bank of Slovakia, Bratislava.

Makuch J. and M. Nemec (1996): *Monetary Policy in Slovakia: Strategy, Instruments and Transmission Mechanism*, report presented at the conference 'Monetary Policy in Transition', Vienna.

National Bank of Slovakia (1994): *Annual Report 1993*, National Bank of Slovakia, Bratislava.

National Bank of Slovakia (1995): *Annual Report 1994*, National Bank of Slovakia, Bratislava.

National Bank of Slovakia (1996): *Annual Report 1995*, National Bank of Slovakia, Bratislava.

OECD (1996): *Short-Term Economic Indicators*, Transition Economies No. 1/1996, Center for Cooperation with the Economies in Transition, OECD, Paris.

Páleník, V. (1999): *RM-System Slovakia*, this volume.

Rejnuš, O. and R. Schmied (1999): *Czech Republic*, this volume.

APPENDIX

Instruments of Monetary Policy of the National Bank of Slovakia

Interest rate policy

Table 9.A. Instruments of interest rate policy

Since 1 January 1995
Discount rate: 12%
Lombard rate: 1% above the current interest rate for auction refinance loans
Penalty rate on stand-by loans: three times the discount rate: 36%
Penalty rate for exceeding the technical deficit of the state budget performance
(twice the discount rate): 24%
Since 10 February 1995
Penalty rate for exceeding the technical deficit of the state budget performance: 18%
Since 7 March 1995
Discount rate: 11%
Lombard rate: 13.1%
Penalty rate on stand-by loans: three times the discount rate: 33%
Since 6 October 1995
Discount rate: 9.75%
Penalty rate on stand-by loans: three times the discount rate: 29.25%

Credit limits

Credit limits are imposed on banks whose lending exceeds SKK 20 billion.

System of refinancing

The refinancing of commercial banks takes one of the following forms:

- Auction refinance loan (monthly) at auction interest rates (not drawn).
- Redistribution loans:
  1. Traditional – at a rate of 9.5%.
  2. Soft loan – at a rate of 7.5%.
- Lombard loans, loans associated with the pledge of securities at the lombard interest rate (not drawn).
- Rediscounting of bills – bills of exchange are rediscounted at the discount rate, a form of refinancing which includes bills discounted for export promotion and ones rediscounted in support of agriculture.

Exchange-rate and foreign policy exchange

Table 9.B. The currency basket of the SKK as of 14 July 1994

Currency	US$	DEM
Weight	40%	60&
Exchange rate SKK	31.209	20.227

Note: Absolute definition of the currency basket: 1 IDX = 0.01287 US$ + 0.029663 DEM
Source: National Bank of Slovakia, 1995.

The turnover of foreign exchange transactions (according to the payment items specified in groups 1 to 6 in convertible currencies) reached a level of SKK 441.8 billion in the period of January – November 1995. The average monthly turnover of foreign exchange transactions amounted to SKK 40.2 billion, representing an increase of 35.8% compared with the same period in the previous year. The currency structure of the turnover of foreign exchange transaction was stable in the period under consideration, and corresponded to the structure of the currency basket to which the exchange ratio of the Slovak crown is pegged. The leading currencies (DEM and US$) had a dominant share in this turnover (39.2% and 36.3% respectively). The other European currencies, with a strong correlation to DEM, accounted for 22.5%. Together with DEM, these currencies represented 61.7% of the total turnover. The share of non-continental currencies including GBP was substantially lower (2%) which together with US$ accounted for 38.8% of the turnover. The exchange rates of the Slovak Crown against fully convertible currencies upon foreign exchange fixing are influenced by the rate of IDX/SKK which represents the effect of demand and supply on the activities of commercial banks. The IDD/SKK rate may move within the fluctuation band of 1.5%.

Investment Legislation

The legislation of the Slovak Republic with respect to the banking sector is tied to the legislation of the Czech and Slovak Federative Republic. In the past few years, this legislation has been completed and further improved. The most important acts and decrees (including their amendments) are as follows:
Act No.566/1992 Zb. 'The National Bank of Slovakia.'
Act of the National Council of the Slovak Republic published in Collection of Laws
No.566/1992 Zb. of 18th November 1992, article 113, pp. 3322–3329 as amended
by:
Act of the NC No. 26/1993 Z.z.
Act of the NC No. 159/1993 Z.z.
Act of the NC No. 249/1994 Z.z

Act of the NC No. 374/1994 Z.z.

Act of the NC No. 202/1995 Z.z.

Act No. 62/1996 Z.z. 'Banks.'

Act of the Federal Assembly of the Czech and Slovak Federative Republic published in Collection of Laws No. 62/1992, article 22, pp. 494–509, as full wording of the Banking Act No. 21/1992 of 20th December 1991, as amended by:

Act No. 264/1992 of 28th April 1992 Zb.

Act No. 249/1994 of 19th August 1994 Z.z.

Act No. 374/1994 of 22nd December 1994 Z.z.

Act No. 58/1995 of 7th March 1995 Z.z.

Act No. 223/1995 of 14th September 1995 Z.z.

Act of 31st January 1996 Z.z.

Act No. 118/1996 Zb. 'Protection of deposits.'

Act of the National Council of the Slovak Republic published in Collection of Laws No. 118/1996, article 43, pp. 918–924.

Act No. 214/1992 Zb. 'Securities auction.'

Act of the Federal Assembly of the Czech and Slovak Federative Republic published in Collection of Laws No. 214/1992 of 21st April 1992, article 42, pp. 1098–1104.

Act No. 530/1990 Zb. 'Bonds.'

Act of the Federal Assembly of the Czech and Slovak Federative Republic published in Collection of Laws No. 530/1990 of 26th November 1990, article 87, pp. 1978–1982 as amended by Act of No.600/1992 Zb. 'Securities.'

Act No. 600/1992 Zb. 'Securities.'

Act of Federal Assembly of the Czech and Slovak Federative Republic published in Collection of Laws No. 530/1990 of 2nd December 1992, article 122, pp. 3691–3640, as amended by:

Act No. 88/1994 of 23th March 1994 Z.z.

Act No. 246/1994 of 25th August 1994 Z.z.

Act No. 249/1994 of 19th August 1994 Z.z.

Act No. 171/1995 of 13th July 1995 Z.z.

Act No. 194/1995 of 7th September 1995 Z.z.

Act No. 248/1992 Zb. 'Investment organizations and investment funds.'

Act of the Federal Assembly of the Czech and Slovak Federative Republic published in Collection of Laws No. 248/1992 of 28th April 1992, article 51, pp. 1313–1321, as amended:

Act No. 91/1994 of 23th March 1994 Z.z.

Act No. 191/1995 of 7th September 1995 Z.z.

Act No. 202/1995 Zb. 'Foreign exchange act.'

Act of the Federal Assembly of the Czech and Slovak Federative Republic published in Collection of Laws No. 202/1995, article 69, pp. 1690–1700.

Act No. 513/1991 Zb. 'Commercial law.'

Act No. 191/1950 Zb. 'Banking and checking note act.'

Bratislava Stock Exchange Full Members as of 31 December 1995

Banks	Brokers
Agrobanka, a.s., filialka Banska Bystrica (Agricultural Bank)	Eastbrokers, a.s.
Banka Hana, a.s., organizacna zlozka Nitra ('Hana' Bank)	Economic Brokers Manager, a.s.
Ceska sporitelna, a.s. (Czech Insurance Bank)	Creditanstalt Securities, a.s.
Ceskoslovenska obchodna banka, a.s. (Czechoslovak Commercial Bank)	Hardvardska burzova spolocnost, a.s. (Harvard Exchange Company)
Devin banka, a.s. ('Devin' Bank)	ING Baring Securities, a.s.
Investicni a Postovni banka, a.s. (Investment and Postal Bank)	LIMITA, a.s.
Investicna a rozvojova banka, a.s. (Investment and Development Bank)	Prva slovenska brokerska spolocnost, s.r.o.
Interbanka, a.s.	Prvni investicni, a.s. (First Investment)
Istrobanka, a.s.	Sevisbrokers, a.s.
Komercni banka, a.s. (Komercial Bank)	Siveco Brokers, a.s.
Ludova banka, a,s. (People's Bank)	Slavia Capital, a.s.
Polnobanka, a.s. (Agricultural Bank)	
Postova banka, a.s. (Postal Bank)	*Temporary Members*
Priemyselna banka, a.s. (Industrial Bank)	Aval Kapital, a.s.
Prva komunalna banka, a.s. (First Communal Bank)	Contact Brokers, a,s.
Prvni investicni, a.s. (The First Investment)	Conto-Invest, a.s.
Slovenska kreditna banka, a.s. (Slovak Credit Bank)	Danubia Invest, a.s.
Slovenska sporitelna, a.s. (Slovak Saving Bank)	Financial, a.s.
Tatra banka, a.s. ('Tatra' bank)	IB Austria Securities, a.s.
Vseobecna uverova banka, a.s. (General Credit Bank)	Invest Brokers, a.s.
	J & T Securities II, a.s.
Other members	Palco Brokers, a.s.
Fond narodneho majetku Slovenskej republiky (National Property Fund)	Prva paroplavebna, a.s.
Narodna banka Slovenska (National Bank of Slovakia)	R.C.A., a.s.
	Schultz & Ostrovsky, a.s.

G21 E52
G28 P33
G28
L33 P34
G12

10. Slovenia

Gordana Bival and Vlado Dimovski

INTRODUCTION

In the past five years the Slovene economy underwent a major transition towards a market-oriented economy. Such a transition has affected many areas of life and many activities and is probably most strongly reflected in the capital market. This paper attempts a brief overview of the major changes and achievements of the Slovene economy. Focusing on the changes in the capital market, we investigate the roles of monetary policy and the privatization process, as well as those of exchanges and of external financial assistance, which have contributed to a major transformation of the economy and society.

MONETARY POLICY

The Bank of Slovenia is the central state bank. Its establishment is based on the legislative framework issued on 25 June 1991. The Bank of Slovenia was reorganized in accordance with the requirements of the Law on Banks and Savings Banks and the Law on the Bank of Slovenia. It assumed effective control of the implementation of full monetary authority on 8 October 1991, (following a three-month moratorium on the implementation of the legislation to do with independence). The Slovene parliament adopted a resolution introducing a new Slovenian currency. On 7 October 1991 the creation of the Slovene Tolar (hereafter Tolar or SIT) was announced, and the currency conversion from Yugoslav Dinar to Tolar was implemented in a very short period from 9–11 October 1991. The status of the Bank of Slovenia as the central bank was ratified by article 152 of the Constitution of the Republic of Slovenia, according to which the central bank was recognized as an autonomous institution independent in its decision-making and in the implementation of monetary policy. The central bank is directly responsible to the Parliament of Slovenia.[1]

By law, the main task of the Bank of Slovenia is to maintain the stability of the national currency. In order to implement this task, the Bank of Slovenia targets the quantity of money, thus ensuring the liquidity of banks and savings banks, as well as that of cross-border payments. Other major tasks of the Bank of Slovenia include:

1. the monitoring of banks and savings banks;
2. the issuing of banknotes and coins;
3. the regulation of deposit insurance;
4. the performance of various operations on behalf of the state treasury.

The Bank of Slovenia has additional responsibilities set forth in the Law on Banks and Savings Banks, the Law on Foreign Exchange, the Law on Foreign Credit Transactions and the Law on Pre-rehabilitation, Rehabilitation, Bankruptcy and Liquidation of Banks and Savings Banks.[2]

On 1 September 1995, Slovenia changed its IMF status from 'temporary regime' to full convertibility for international transactions, based on IMF Statute Article XIV. In reality, as this regime was already in place in 1992, the change in status did not bring any substantial modifications for international transactions (Saje, 1995).

The Bank of Slovenia distinguishes between goals, intermediate targets, and instruments (Lavrač and Stanovnik, 1995). The primary objective of the Bank of Slovenia is price stability, the intermediate target of the monetary policy is the money supply (M1), and the most important indicator of monetary policy is the base money supply, with monthly targets based on a money demand function and the money multiplier. The money supply is determined exogenously by the Bank of Slovenia, whereas the exchange rate and interest rates are determined endogenously (such an approach is consistent with a

---

[1] Bank of Slovenia (1995) and (1996a).

[2] At present two laws are in force: The Law on Pre-rehabilitation, Rehabilitation, Bankruptcy and Liquidation of Banks and Savings banks (Official Gazette of the Republic of Slovenia No. 1/91), and, briefly, The Law on its Modifications (Official Gazette of the Republic of Slovenia No. 46/93). Pre-rehabilitation measures in the following cases: non-liquidity of a bank or savings bank; bank's excess of individual multipliers; bank's failure; potential losses arising from risky investments; failure of a bank or savings bank to fulfill other prescribed terms and conditions relating to operation or monetary policy measures. The assessment of economic justification of the bank's rehabilitation primarily focus on the identification of: the amount of loss and potential losses; the amount to be disbursed in the event of the bank's bankruptcy; the approximate amount of funds required for rehabilitation; the offers by other banks to take over the bank subject to rehabilitation, the terms and conditions of take over, and the effects of the takeover on their financial standing; the willingness of other entities to buy up such bank; the effect of the bank rehabilitation on the national economy.

Country Profiles

Table 10.1. Bills issued by Bank of Slovenia

	SIT million		
	Tolar Bills	Foreign Currency Bills	TOTAL
31 December 1992	2443	38317	40760
31 December 1993	2827	47558	50385
31 December 1994	12447	87321	99768
31 December 1995	6623	120049	126672
30 September 1996	12190	139422	151612

Source: *Monthly Bulletin*, Bank of Slovenia, October 1996.

flexible exchange-rate regime). Within this basic framework of monetary policy the Bank of Slovenia has adapted its array of instruments to the current conditions in the foreign exchange markets with the intention of preventing unforeseen changes in the level of the real effective Tolar exchange rate, thus maintaining the competitiveness of Slovenian exports.[3]

With regard to interest rate policy the Bank of Slovenia is taking various steps to lower them gradually given the decreasing inflation rate and developments on domestic and foreign markets. Despite the fact that interest rates and the exchange rate are determined endogenously, the central bank attempts to influence developments in both rates but only within given money supply targets.

However, by using monetary instruments and other measures, the Bank of Slovenia can directly influence the interest rates on the interbank money market and, indirectly, the levels of interest rates charged by commercial banks.[4]

---

[3] The annual inflation rate decreased from 247.1% in 1991 to 18.3% in 1994, and to 8.5% in 1995. The latest available rate for the first nine months of 1996 was 9.7%. The money supply increased in 1995 in real terms by 22.5% compared to the year 1994 which was primarily due to an increased demand for money. This increase was based on lower inflationary expectations and the increased volume of money transactions. The credit multiplier, representing the ratio between money and base money (bank reserves, currency, and non-banking sector deposits) decreased from an average of 1.99 in 1994 to 1.86 in 1995. This decrease can be attributed to the increase in the ratio of bank reserves to deposits, and to a lesser degree to the change in the ratio of money circulation and non-banks' deposits at the central bank to bank deposits. (The latest available data as of October 1996 (monthly average) for the base money is SIT 111 billion, M1 SIT 208 billion, M2 SIT 741 billion, and M3 1,087 billion.)

[4] The Bank of Slovenia introduced nominal interest rates at the end of 1994 that were expressed in annual percentages without separating the rates into the revaluation part and the real part. Due to very high inflation at the beginning of the 1990s, annual interest rates have since then incorporated a 'real'

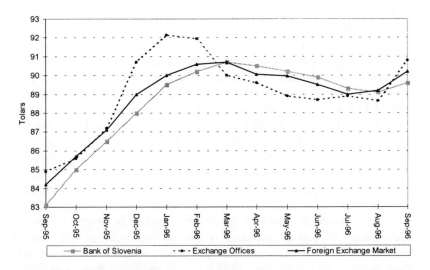

Source: Bank of Slovenia (1996b).

Figure 10.1. Exchange rates SIT/DEM in Slovenia

In its efforts to lower interests rates, the Bank of Slovenia has also adopted the practice of stipulating that banks with above average interest rates have to hold a part of their required reserves on special accounts as liquidity reserves. At the same time, this measure has lowered banks' deposit rates, thereby curbing excess liquidity, and has indirectly led to a reduction in lending rates.[5] The treasury policy also contributes to the reduction of interest rates; liquidity surpluses which exceed 30 billion Tolars are deposited at banks which are not creditors on the interbank market and which pay no higher interest on deposits than the average effective deposit rate (Kranjec 1995).

The Bank of Slovenia has adopted the system of a managed floating of the exchange rate. Thus the exchange rate is market-determined, basically reflecting supply and demand on the foreign exchange market. Owing to

---

interest rate plus a revaluation element which has made all borrowings expensive. The Bank of Slovenia and the Ministry of Finance are trying to bring interest rates down to a level acceptable to companies.

[5] In December 1995 the discount rate of the Bank of Slovenia was 10% and the lombard rate 11% . Banks' interest rates, by contrast, were: with the maturity of 31 days 6.2%; for time deposits, with the maturity of 1 year 9.4%, and for short-term loans 12.5%. Altogether, there was a major decrease in the discount rate and consequently of the lombard rate in April 1995 from 16% to 10% and from 17% to 11%, respectively.

increases in the net foreign exchange assets of the monetary system, one of the tasks of the Bank of Slovenia in influencing the exchange rate has been to ensure the sterilization of the monetary effects of foreign exchange transactions with the appropriate choice of monetary instruments. The period of efficient sterilization has coincided with an active exchange rate policy, the aim of which is to prevent an uncontrolled rise in the real effective exchange. The Bank of Slovenia tries to maintain an unchanged real exchange rate in the long-run in order to protect the export sector. Thus, the central bank has had to absorb the excess of foreign exchange supply. Instead of a monetization of the increase of the central bank's foreign reserves through buying the excess foreign exchange, it has chosen to sterilize the excess of foreign exchange by issuing short-term paper bills. Their total volume was as presented in Table 10.1.

By these means the Bank of Slovenia eliminated the pressure from the excess supply of foreign exchange on the foreign exchange rate without incurring negative effects on money supply. However, to avoid excessive costs in sterilization, the central bank ceased intervening in the foreign exchange market. In Slovenia there are actually three major foreign exchange markets with separately-determined exchange rates as presented in Figure 10.1. Although they legally should be independent, they do influence one another: first, the Bank of Slovenia exchange rate; secondly, the so-called foreign exchange market rate in Slovenia (between companies and between companies and banks); and finally, the exchange rate used by licensed foreign exchange offices.[6]

The annual averages[7] for Bank of Slovenia Tolars/DEM were as follows: 52.1280 (1992), 68.4290 (1993), 79.3740 (1994), and 82.6606 (1995). While the relationship between the above-mentioned foreign exchange markets in these years appears to be similar to the presented monthly dynamics.

Nevertheless, the Bank of Slovenia uses various instruments for the conduct of its monetary policy (Borak, 1995). These are:
- required reserves;
- government deposits;
- foreign exchange minimum reserves;

---

[6] The Bank of Slovenia exchange rate is a politically fixed variable, which means that the Bank of Slovenia has the authority to create and implement financial policies independent of the Government. The SIT floating exchange rate is calculated as an average of exchange rates used in all Slovene international business transactions within 60 days. The Bank of Slovenia influences the SIT exchange rate by the redemption of foreign exchange and by the selling of Tolar bills. The SIT rate also depends on the foreign exchange market situation in Slovenia.

[7] Both annual and monthly exchange rates are averages weighted with respective turnovers.

Table 10.2. The top five Slovenian banks by total assets* as of 30 June 1996

Rank	Bank	Assets in SIT million	Market Share in %
1	Nova Ljubljanska Banka	472,716	27.9
2	SKB Banka Ljubljana	194,021	11.5
3	Nova Kreditna Banka Maribor	187,536	11.1
4	Splošna Banka Koper	90,960	5.4
5	Abanka Ljubljana	83,297	4.9
	Total Top 5	1,028,530	60.8

Note: * Unaudited, unconsolidated.
Source: Kapital (1996).

- the Bank of Slovenia bills;
- Lombard loans;
- short-term loans;
- liquidity loans;
- repurchase agreements;
- intervention in the foreign exchange market (i.e. purchase of foreign exchange from banks undergoing the rehabilitation process, purchase of foreign exchange – the right to repurchase, purchase of foreign exchange – the obligation to repurchase, sales of foreign exchange).[8]

The system of required reserves is in force at all banks and savings banks and has been one of the most effective monetary policy instruments since April 1992. A reliable amendment was adopted at the end of 1994 which cancels the required reserves on deposits exceeding one year, reduces the rate of the required reserves on three-month to one-year deposits, and increases the rate on deposits from one to three months in order to stimulate real investment.

In 1995, the required reserve was calculated for all Tolar deposits, received loans and securities issued at a rate which varies according to maturity as

[8] Furthermore in 1994, the Bank of Slovenia introduced a number of legislative Acts which are in line with international standards. They cover the following: accounting standards and financial statements; methods of calculation of capital and capital adequacy; criteria for the classification of balance sheet and off-balance-sheet items; levels of provisioning for potential losses; the level of exposure to a single borrower; capital investments and fixed assets reducing the capital. The above prudential legislation was adopted with the aim of ensuring safer bank operations which would be more in line with the basic principles of liquidity, solvency and profitability.

mentioned previously.[9]

The actual level of reserves exceeded necessary reserves in all months: balances on giro accounts (deposit accounts) , cash in vaults, and balances on special accounts grew by an average of 5.1 % thanks to the usual favorable liquidity position and because of the requirement that all banks have to hold a part of their reserves on a special daily account. The share of required reserves held by the banks and savings banks on special accounts is around 50%, and the remaining part is held in giro accounts and as cash in vaults. This measure allows the Bank of Slovenia to influence positively the liquidity risk exposure of those banks that pay above the average deposit interest rates, and to bring about a decrease in the banks' deposit and lending rates. The results are: a less volatile stock of required and liquidity reserves for making payments, and the reduction of liquidity risks due to an increased or unexpected outflow from the banks' giro accounts.[10]

THE BANKING SECTOR

The regulatory framework for the banks and savings banks and the Bank of Slovenia is based on the Law on Banks and Savings Banks and the Law on the Bank of Slovenia. Currently, a new Banking Law is under preparation that is based on the European Union directives for banking and will soon replace the two aforementioned laws.

Banks and savings banks[11] are supervised by the Bank of Slovenia. There

---

[9] Deposits used to calculate the required reserves increased throughout the year by a monthly rate of 2.3% or in nominal terms from Tolars 441.5 billion to Tolars 577.9 billion. Due to the changes in the rates of required reserves the structure of deposits also change in favor of long-term deposits. The calculated reserves of banks and savings institutions amounted to Tolars 37.7 billion in August 1995. (Bank reserves continued to grow steadily, and they amounted to Tolars 42.9 billion in October 1996).

[10] The Slovenian pay milieu is characterized by a dualism in cashless payments; legal persons are required to hold giro accounts at the Agency for Payments while natural persons hold current accounts at commercial banks.

[11] In accordance with the Law on Banks and Savings Banks (Official Gazette of the Republic of Slovenia No. 1/91. No.38/92 and No. 46/93.) the Bank can conduct the following banking transactions: 1. acceptance of all types of money deposits of legal entities and natural persons; 2. granting and obtaining of loans; 3. conducting of payment transactions; 4. purchase of checks and bills of exchange; 5. transactions with foreign means of payment; 6. issuance of securities and credit cards; 7. purchase, sale and management of securities of domestic and foreign issuers; 8. acceptance and issuance of collateral and guarantees and assumption of other obligations for its clients that can be fulfilled in money; 9. purchase and redemption of claims; and 10. custody of securities and other valuables. By contrast, a Savings Bank is an independent financial organization offering the facility of safe depositing

Table 10.3. Summary balance sheet structure of the banking sector

Assets	in %
Cash	3.2
Interbank credits	24.4
Credits	24.6
Securities	27.3
Non–profitable assets	12.5
Other categories	8
Liabilities	
Interbank liabilities	21
Obligations towards non–banking sector	57.1
Capital	3
Reserves and reservations	11.3
Other categories	7.6

Note: Data as of December 31, 1995.
Source: Štiblar (1995).

are currently 28 operating banks in Slovenia (plus two banks incorporated under the Constitutional Law in 1994). The rehabilitation process in two major banks is coming to a close. Only two banks have nationwide branch networks (SKB Banka, Abanka), others are more or less regional banks, but as seen in Table 10.2 Nova Ljubljanska Banka is ranked first on the Slovenian market.[12] In addition, there are 9 savings banks and over 70 savings and loans associations (services). But their market share in assets is very small (only 1.8% of the total in 1995).

As of 31 December 1995 the three main banks in Slovenia had a 52% share of the market, the five main banks a 62% share, and the seven main banks as much as a 72% share. In general, given that Slovenia is a small market, the present number of banks is considered to be too high. Undoubtedly the growth in competition between banks has improved the range and the quality of banking services, but a number of banks are small regional players and mergers and acquisitions are expected to take place in the next 3–4 years, so that the

---

of savings. The Savings Banks hereunder include: 1. Postal Savings Bank, 2. Savings Bank, and 3. Savings and Loan Service.

[12] It is a leading bank in Slovenia judged by other criteria also. As of 31 March 1996 it had 23% of total customer deposits, 21% of total customer loans, and 25% of total international payment transactions.

number of banks will eventually be reduced to five or six.

Regarding the question of ownership in Slovenian banks it may be noted that all banks in Slovenia are organized as joint-stock companies. In most banks shareholders are local companies or private individuals, though two banks are state-owned and undergoing rehabilitation. Foreign investors are shareholders in six banks.[13]

The central bank carries out supervision by auditing the banks' annual financial reports. This task is performed by authorized (usually internationally recognized) auditing companies. Based on the reports that banks and savings banks are obliged to submit, the Bank of Slovenia performs:

1. off-site supervision (i.e. quarterly classification of credit portfolios, semi-annual supervision of capital adequacy, the extent of capital investments and fixed assets; the extent of credits to bank management and owners, plus the audited banks' annual financial reports);
2. on-site supervision of the banks and savings banks, ensuring the reliability of banks' and savings banks' reports and the quality of their accounting systems, testing the quality of the credit portfolios, judging the diversification of credit risk, checking the capital adequacy calculation, assessing the banks' management's ability to cope with operational risks, evaluating the internal control systems and their findings, the electronic data processing, and the register of shareholders;
3. diagnostic supervision based on agreement between the Commission of the European External Relations and the Slovene Government.

In cases of irregularities the Bank of Slovenia acts in accordance with the Law on Banks and Savings Banks and the Law on the Bank of Slovenia, and in the case of major problems in operations according to the law on Pre-rehabilitation, Rehabilitation, Bankruptcy and Liquidation of Banks and Savings Banks. Banks facing major problems may become bankrupt and go into liquidation, which has not happened so far.

In 1995, reserve requirements were calculated for all Tolar deposits, received loans and securities issued at a rate which varied according to maturity: 12% for sight (demand) deposits up to 30 days, 6% for deposits from 31 days to 3 months, 2% for deposits from 3 to 6 months and 1% for deposits over one year. In addition, banks are required to keep a foreign exchange minimum in liquid foreign currency investment abroad. The system requires each bank to determine the amount of its exchange minimum on a monthly basis with regard to its foreign payment operations (35% of average monthly foreign payments over the past three months) and its liabilities from foreign

---

[13] In four of these banks foreigners have 100% stakes: Bank Austria d.d. Ljubljana; Banka Creditanstalt d.d. (Austria), Banka Société Générale d.d., and Ljudska banka d.d. (Volksbank, Austria).

currency deposits of households (sight deposits 100%, time deposits up to three months 75%, time deposits over three months and up to one year 35%, and time deposits over one year 5%). Besides the foreign exchange minimum, banks also have a net foreign exchange position which is the difference between a bank's foreign exchange holdings and its short-term liabilities abroad. This must exceed 75% of the foreign exchange minimum.

At the end of 1993 more rigorous standards for the calculation of capital and capital adequacy were introduced. This, in turn, made the process of reaching the required level of capital even more difficult for the banks. The standards had to be achieved by the end of September 1995. Following the change of the Law on Banks and Savings Banks in July 1993, the minimum adequacy ratio was changed from 6.25% to 8% which follows the European Directive and is in line with BIS standards.[14]

The structure of the commercial banks of Slovenia is summarized in the balance sheet of the banking sector (Table 10.3).

The central bank classifies assets into five categories using the likelihood of repayment as the criteria of classification. The categories range from A where there is no default risk, to E with 365 days payment overdue. Given this classification, banks are required to set a specific provision against the identified potential loss: 10% in class B, 25% for those in class C, 50% for those in class D, and 100% for those in class E.

PRIVATIZATION

In December 1990 two government institutions were established with the purpose of supervising, structuring and assisting the privatization process in Slovenia: the Agency for Restructuring and Privatization of the Republic of Slovenia (hereafter the Agency for Privatization) and the Development Fund of the Republic of Slovenia (hereafter the Development Fund). The procedures of ownership transformation also involve other state institutions such as the Pension Fund, the Compensation Fund, and the Social Accounting Service. The Agency for Privatization has a monitoring and control function. It sets guidelines and approves privatization programs. The Development Fund is involved in selling socially-owned companies and financial restructuring, followed by privatization of its own portfolio.[15]

---

[14] The capital adequacy ratio is measured as the ratio of capital to risk-weighted assets.

[15] Bival and Wörgötter (1995).

The centerpiece of the legislation regulating privatization in Slovenia is the Law on Ownership Transformation of Companies adopted in November 1992. The other important privatization legislation dealing with privatization includes the Restitution Law, the Law on Cooperatives, the Law on Agricultural Land, the Company Law, the Law on Commercial Public Services, the Bankruptcy Law, the Law on the Securities Market, the Law on Investments Funds, and the Law on Auditing. [16]

There have been three main groups of companies to be privatized. The first and the largest group are fully or partly socially-owned companies (social capital stock without a defined owner) which are the subject of the Privatization Law.[17] The negotiating partner in this case is the company's management, which is also responsible for the preparation of the ownership transformation program to be approved by the Agency for Privatization.

The second group are those companies providing special public services (railways, telecommunications, airports, etc.). The status of these companies is regulated by the Law on Public Service Companies. They are exempted from the provisions of the Privatization Law and will remain, at least in the short term, in majority state ownership. Banks, insurance companies, enterprises engaged in gambling and companies subjected to bankruptcy procedure are also exempt from this Privatization Law.

---

[16] The new Company Law adopted in 1993 is based primarily on German (continental) law. This Law allows the establishment of three types of partnership (limited, general and silent) organized according to the general provisions of continental law. For corporate structures, the German model for limited partnership by shares is used. It is possible to establish a joint-stock company and a limited liability company as well as economic interest groups. For accounting and disclosure purposes, companies are divided by size in three groups: small, medium and large. According to the law, at least two of three conditions have to be fulfilled for each group: small company: less than 50 employees, annual turnover less than SIT 200 million (US$ 1.6 million), average value of assets less than SIT 100 million (US$ 0.8 million); medium-sized company: less than 250 employees, annual turnover less than SIT 800 million (US$ 6.4 million) and average value of assets less than SIT 400 million (US$ 3.2 million); large company: more than 250 employees; annual turnover and the average value of assets are the same as for medium-sized companies. Under this definition, all banks and insurance companies as well as all interconnected companies (such as trusts, subsidiaries, affiliated companies) are considered large companies. The US$ amounts are calculated here on the basis of the central bank average rate of September, 1994.

[17] In former Yugoslavia, there were four types of company ownership: social, private, mixed (social and private) and cooperative. The 'social' companies were considered to be owned not by the state but by the community at large. Owing to worker self-management of firms, the legal term 'owner' was undefined for many firms when Slovenia entered transition (as was the case in other former Yugoslavian countries). Indeed, the owners of firms were unknown. Therefore, privatization in Slovenia necessitated transferring firms with 'unknown owners' into the hands of some legal entities that could take over the rights and duties of owners. In the Slovene debate this is referred to as transferring property to a 'known owner', irrespective of whether this is a private individual or a government agency, and is considered a central part of the privatization process.

The third group of companies in Slovenia are those in the portfolio of the Development Fund, which holds a controlling stake in 90 companies. After undertaking necessary restructuring measures such as the implementation of corporate governance, the reduction of employment, and the rescheduling of debts, the Development Fund has a mandate to privatize its portfolio as quickly as possible. From the standpoint of the foreign investor, the main advantage of acquiring a company presently owned by the Development Fund is the freedom to start immediate negotiations; there is no need to participate in transformation programs as required by the Privatization Law (Gospodarski Vestnik, 1995).

Another group are bankrupt companies or companies in the process of liquidation. Foreign investors may buy a company from this group at auction without any responsibility for its employees (whose employment with the company is terminated on the first day of the bankruptcy or liquidation procedure) and without any liabilities. The buyer is free to decide on the legal form in which the company is to operate in the future.

The Privatization Law imposes some restrictions on the immediate resale of shares acquired through free distribution or with a discount. The privatization legislation therefore regulates both commercial privatization and the initial 'free' allocation of shares.

The initiative to start the privatization of a company must come from its management and its employees. After the transformation program is prepared it has to be adopted by the governing body of the company. Once the transformation program has been approved by the Agency for Privatization, the company can begin its implementation.[18]

As noted before, the transformation of company ownership under the new legislation means the transfer of social capital to known owners. The shares are issued on the basis of the book value of the company which is undergoing the transformation as derived from the opening balance.

Transfer of company ownership is performed by a combination of free distribution and commercial privatization methods:

1. The free transfer of 40% of ordinary shares to the financial institutions as follows: 10% to the Compensation Fund,[19] 10% to the Pension Fund and

---

[18] For the final implementation of the Law on the Ownership Transformation of Companies, the Investment Companies Act was also adopted in January 1994 and set the legal basis for the formation of authorized investment companies.

[19] The Compensation/Restitution Fund is a fund established to pay off the owners who received back their property after it was nationalized following the Second World War, but are willing to sell it now.

20% to the Development Fund.[20]

2. Internal distribution: up to 20% of shares distributed in exchange for ownership certificates to employees, former employees, and relatives of employees. These shares cannot be transferred for two years.

3. The internal buyout of shares is limited to 40% of the shares of the social capital. This attractive scheme enables employees and others to acquire an ownership stake gradually (at a 50% discount), paying in annual instalments for four years. Before an internal buyout can take place, a free transfer of 40% of shares to financial institutions, as well as internal distribution of shares, should have been carried out (see points 1 and 2).

4. Sale of the shares (i.e. already existing shares representing social capital and newly issued shares) should be carried out either in the form of a public offering of shares, public auction or (restricted) public tender.[21]

5. Sale of all assets of the company, combined with liquidation, is contracted by the Development Fund, which also takes over all liabilities which are subsequently to be repaid from the proceeds of the assets sale.

6. Ownership transfer by raising additional private equity (including foreign): this is possible only if new shares are issued for more than 10% of the existing equity.

7. Transfer of shares to the Fund for Development.

Companies are free to choose the method, or combination of methods, that suits them best according to circumstances, but the overall transformation program has to be approved by the Agency for Privatization.

When the social capital of a company is sold as a whole or partially to domestic or foreign investors, this is carried out on the basis of open competition by the collection of offers, or by the sale of shares at a public auction. The company determines the price of shares based on the estimated value of the company, revalued according to the change in the consumer price index to the day of the public notice, sale or public auction. Citizens of Slovenia hold pre-purchasing rights under the same conditions.

---

[20] The Development Fund later sells this portfolio to special investment funds that will pay for the shares with ownership certificates collected from Slovene citizens. Actually, citizens have been granted ownership certificates according to the age of the nominal value ranging between DEM 4,000 and DEM 6,000.

[21] Guidelines for these particular techniques have been worked out by the Agency for Privatization. The seller of the shares representing the existing social capital stock is the Development Fund, which signs the share purchase contracts and receives the proceeds from the sale.

Table 10.4. The Ljubljana Stock Exchange listing requirements

Shares		
	Tier A*	Tier B
Years of operation	4	2
Audited financial report	✓	✓
Share capital	DEM 15 mn	DEM 7.5 mn
Size of class of securities to be listed	1	2
% of publicly distributed share capital **	25%	10%
Number of shareholders	300 and over	150 and over
Bonds		
	Tier A	Tier B
Years of operation	4	2
Fair & true	Audited Financial Report	Audited Financial Report
Total value of bonds issued	DEM 7.5 mn	DEM 3.75 mn
% of publicly distributed bonds **	25%	10%
Number of holders	300 and over	150 and over

Notes:
* For shares issued by banks the same criteria are applied with the only exception: Tier A requires a full operating licence issued by the Bank of Slovenia.
** Excluding holders exceeding 10% of the total issues and excluding directors and officers of the issuer.
Source: Ljubljanska Borza (1992).

The holder of ownership certificates may use them for the purchase of shares of a company that is being transformed with a public sale of shares, but only to a limit of 60% of the total value of the company. The surplus value of the purchase money is transferred by the company in the form of cash or ordinary shares to the different funds as described above.

When the sale of a company is concluded as a sale of all that company's assets, the sale contract is made by the trust to which the company transfers the entire social capital of the company. The proceeds from the purchase belong to the trust. The company ceases to exist from the day that is specified in the sales contract, and is expunged from the court register. All the liabilities of the company are taken over by the trust.

In the first half of 1993 special ownership certificate accounts were opened, one for each citizen (regardless of age) of Slovenia, with the nominal value depending on the age of the citizen. The total nominal value of the certificates represented 40% of the book value of the social equity on 31 December 1992. Certificates can be used by employees to participate in the internal distribution within the companies in which they are employed or to purchase shares of companies offered for public sale or shares of Special Investment Funds. The certificates are not transferable and can be used only for the purchase of social equity.

By the end of 1995 more than 90% of companies eligible for privatization had prepared and submitted their privatization programs, with the remaining 10% representing the companies that for various reasons could not prepare them. Altogether, before the end of November 1995, out of 1,467 companies with social capital the Agency for Privatization had approved 938 privatization programs, of which 400 have completed the privatization process. These companies are now operating as privately-owned companies. The typical ownership structure of a privatized company is that 40% of the equity is owned by the Pension Fund, the Compensation Fund, and the Specialized Investment Funds (which bought 20% of the shares on the auctions organized by and from the Fund for Development), 40% owned by employees, and 20% by small investors.

Corporate income tax is calculated and collected for the business year.[22] Payment of corporate income tax is regulated by the Corporate Income Tax Act which was passed on 22 December 1993. Taxable entities are all those legally established and registered in Slovenia and whose activities are profit-making, as well as all resident and non-resident individuals performing economic activities on permanent basis.

Taxpayers operating businesses in free zones do not pay taxes for the first five years of activities on that part of the profit realized by the export of goods and services. Afterwards they pay the usual taxes. Exempt from corporate income tax are: Bank of Slovenia, companies performing public services, charities, investment funds and management companies, public institutions, associations, public and private funds, humanitarian, religious, and 'green' organizations.

The tax base is the profit the company generates in a business year. The corporate income tax is 25%. The tax base is reduced in the case of profits received from abroad, if those profits have been subject to foreign corporate taxes (elimination of double taxation), and by interest or dividends from

---

[22] Ministry of Economic Relations and Development (1996).

securities issued by the Republic of Slovenia, municipalities or public companies founded by the Republic of Slovenia or its municipalities.

Taxable profits are calculated by deducting expenses from revenues. Tax deductible expenses are only those which are considered essential to or a consequence of carrying on the business. Interest payments on loans are deductible, but only to the amount of the average annual bank interest rate, determined by the central bank. Other deductions are as follows:

1. For workers in their first employment (in the first 12 months of employment the tax base is covered by 30% of the wages), and for workers previously unemployed (for at least 6 months).
2. Tax allowances amounting to 20% of invested financial resources in tangible assets and long-term intangible assets that must not exceed the amount of the tax base.
3. Investment reserves in tangible assets and long-term portfolio investments in Slovenia may be deducted up to 10% of the tax base.

The Foreign Investments Law guarantees to the foreign investors the free transfer of profit. Based on the rule of avoiding double-taxation foreign investors also have the right to free repatriation of invested capital, including in the case of liquidation, compressing settlement[23] or bankruptcy. Transfer of profits and repatriation of capital is carried out through the purchase of foreign currency in one of the Slovene commercial banks, according to the Law on Banks and Savings Banks.

EXCHANGES

The regulatory framework for securities exchanges in Slovenia is determined by the Securities Market Law[24] and the Law on Investment Funds and Management Companies. Responsibilities related to the trade in securities are carried out by the governmental Securities Market Agency[25] which acts as an independent organization. The Securities Market Law governs the securities exchange, market participants, any public offer, the role of the Agency and the

---

[23] Compressing settlement is a procedure in which debtors agree to debt-to-equity swaps or to write off part of their claims.

[24] On 24 January 1994 a new Slovene Securities Market Act was adopted which entered into force on 14 March 1994 and is still in force.

[25] This Agency is similar to the Securities Exchange Commision (SEC). It is financed through the state budget, and through its own activities (training and exams for brokers and similar activities).

other elements of the securities market.

The Stock Exchange in Ljubljana was founded in 1924 and was active until 1941. After almost fifty years it resumed business on 29 March 1990.[26] The LSE is a legal entity, funded out of membership fees (initial and annual) and commission fees charged on the volume of trading. It is a self-governing and self-regulating organization. It serves as a transfer center for transactions in securities and for other instruments, forms the link between the demand and supply of securities, and provides information to the investing public about daily stock prices and other important data referring to trading on the LSE.[27]

On 8 December 1993 the LSE introduced electronic trading on BIS – complex Stock Exchange Information System three times a week (floor trading still continued on Tuesdays and Thursdays). Floor Trading was finally discontinued on 14 December 1995.[28]

After a short trial period, in October 1995 another module of the complex stock exchange information system came into operation in support of electronic foreign exchange trading. Electronic trading in foreign exchange is new to foreign exchange traders in Slovenia and is based on a system of automated trading. The module offers its users (banks) an overview of the ranking of the Slovenian Tolar in comparison to other currencies in the foreign exchange list of the Bank of Slovenia and calculates cross-rates for some important currencies. This overview is based on actual bank orders for sales or purchases.

---

[26] Historically, the Ljubljana Stock, Commodities and Foreign Exchange was established in 1924. Among securities listed on the exchange, government bonds and corporate debentures dominated. Currency and commodity transactions accounted for all the foreign exchange transactions in 1928, amounting to US$ 20 million. This Stock Exchange was closed in 1941 during World War II and was abolished in 1953. In 1989, two of former Yugoslavia's federal laws (Securities Act and Capital Market Act) were adopted and provided the necessary legal basis for the re-establishment and re-opening of the Slovenian capital market. On 26 December 1989 the Ljubljanska borza (Ljubljana Stock Exchange or LSE) was officially established, and on 29 March 1990 its first trading session took place, involving 14 stockbrokers who traded 11 securities. To comply with the Securities Market Law, the LSE adopted many different rules and procedures: the LSE Articles of Association, Rules of Procedures, Rules of Electronic Trading, Listing and Membership Rules, as well as other Stock exchange usages. Precious metals, such as gold, silver, platinum, as well as golden coins are traded here.

[27] Veselinovič (1995); Veselinovič and Gabrijelčič (1995).

[28] When it organized its last floor trading session, LSE ended the six-year tradition of open outcry trading sessions and moved to completely electronic trading on a daily basis. The decision to abolish floor trading resulted from a low turnover on days of floor trading compared to a much higher turnover on days of electronic trading, as well as from the efforts of the LSE to achieve greater transparency in the market and lower operational costs at the same time. Electronic trading on BIS takes place every day on the basis of continuous automated trading: a trade is concluded when an ask order matches a bid order, priority being given to orders entered earlier. Trading is subject to surveillance by the LSE and the Securities Market Agency.

By trading on the electronic system, the information on exchange rates is more transparent, although it is available to market participants only and is not published externally. BIS, the complex stock exchange information system, now offers access to four trading modules that are interlinked: securities market, foreign exchange market, money market and derivatives market. By being able to observe the current situation on the four markets on a single screen, users of the system can monitor and manage their portfolios much more easily.[29]

The LSE consists of three markets:

1. Listed securities, tier 1 (A and B listing).
2. Listed securities, tier 2 (C listing).[30]
3. Unlisted securities.

All companies seeking to have their securities listed must fulfil certain conditions which are extensive for tier 1, whereas only formal conditions for sales through the unlisted securities market apply. The listing requirements for the official listing sections A and B (See Table 10.4) are comprised in the Listing and Membership Rules that were adopted in 1994 and are stricter in terms of the size of the capital, number of shareholders, and the size of the issue as well as requiring an annual audited financial report. New listings are subject to the approval of the LSE Admission Board, consisting of independent financial and legal experts and LSE employees.

Securities listed on the LSE can be traded on either the market A or market B, depending on listing requirements that are met after a company files an application for listing with the Admission Board. After a company has been

---

[29] Reuters Real time Information System enables its users to get on-line information on trading on official markets A and B and the unofficial off-the-exchange open market C during LSE trading hours; every day from 9:30 to 13:00. SBI, the Slovenian Stock Index, which is calculated continuously, is also available on the same screens.

[30] Trading on the LSE off-the-exchange open market began in January, 1995. In the same month Central Securities Clearing Corporation (hereafter KDD) was established. From November 1995, when the first dematerialized shares were actually included in the KDD central register, until 1 October of this year, there have been 175 issuers included in the register. The KDD now performs securities and cash settlement of all trades concluded on the organized market of the LSE (the transfer of clearing from LSE to KDD was made on 3 June 1996). In July 1996, the KDD finalized the on-line access system into the issuers share book and is about to complete a dial-in service which will enable transfers in the share book database. The KDD is continuing in its efforts to include more institutional investors in its membership base. At the moment, KDD has 49 members (45 of the latter are also members of the LSE) and of these, 31 are brokerage houses, 15 are banks, 2 management funds plus the Development Fund. On 19 June 1996, KDD opened a public information window. Its principal purpose is for the convenience of individual investors and it also makes information available to the public regarding the operations and procedures of the Central Securities Clearing Corporation as well as a list of KDD members.

listed on the LSE, it has the duty of continuous disclosure to the Stock Exchange and the public of any event or change in its operations that may be important to the company and/or its investors. Only those shares and bonds which are freely transferable, paid in full, and approved by the Admission Board, can be listed on the official markets A or B. A company applying for listing on either market must submit its application together with documentation proving that both legal and listing requirements have been met, and a form of prospectus which contains the necessary information to enable an investor to make an informed investment decision. Decisions on whether or not to list a company are taken by the LSE Admission Board, which consists of four independent legal and financial experts and one LSE representative. The listing procedure usually takes two months.[31]

Figure 10.2 shows that the LSE has grown considerably during the past six years. The total equity turnover also rose. In 1991 it amounted to only DEM 0.5 million, while in October 1996 the total equity turnover proved to be DEM 492.3 million.[32] The relative structure of the LSE turnover in securities in 1995 was as follows: 49.3% (shares) 24.6% (short-term securities) and 26.0% (bonds). On the other hand, the total number of listed equities increased from 1 in March 1990 to 24 in October 1996.

The relatively small number of new listings resulted from the slowness of the privatization process, the absence of regulation concerning foreign investments,[33] takeovers and dematerialization processes,[34] and from eligible

---

[31] Companies listed on the official market A or B are supposed to: 1) submit audited financial statements 30 days after auditing has been concluded together with comments and changes that were announced in the prospectus to the LSE; 2) publish the most important information from audited financial statements in one of the daily newspapers; 3) prepare a biennial financial report not later than three months after the half year has ended and submit it to the Stock Exchange; 4) publish the most important information from the biennial financial report in a daily newspaper. Furthermore, a company listed on this stock exchange has to inform the LSE and the public of any change in its operations that could affect the price of its shares. The information refers particularly to: 1) changes in performing main activities of the company; 2) planned crucial changes in the financial and accounting policy of the company; 3) shareholders meetings (date, agenda, decisions); 4) crucial (substantial) changes in management staff and management policy; 5) changes in ownership structure; 6) new issues of securities; 7) decisions on dividends; 8) inability to perform payment of liabilities that arise from bonds and debentures; and 9) amount of approved capital and related issue of shares.

[32] Such a positive development showed data for bonds as well. In 1991 the total bonds turnover was DEM 93.0 million (government: DEM 84.6 million), and in October 1996 the total bonds turnover was DEM 105.4 million (government: DEM 73.9 million).

[33] According to a recent interpretation given by the Ministry of Economic Relations and Development, foreign investors can buy Slovenian securities in the secondary market. For that purpose they must obtain an identification number from KDD if it involves a passive portfolio investment. Their local broker, who is also a member of KDD, assists in this process. Should the investment be a foreign direct

companies being unaware of the advantages of being listed on the stock exchange, listing requirements and procedures as presented above.

The Law also regulates the organization and membership of the stock exchange. Membership of the stock exchange is restricted to domestic legal entities, in which a foreign individual or institution may have a maximum stake of 24%. In reality, foreign brokers can only become authorized participants on the securities market if they have founded a branch or joint-venture company in Slovenia. The exception are the banks, since they can become 100% owners with the approval of the Bank of Slovenia.

The LSE is a corporate body with its share capital distributed among shareholders/members of the LSE. Ownership of the corporation is restricted to its members on the basis of equal share, while in the case of new members, if no shares are available, the stock exchange can issue the required number of shares out of approved capital. Trading in publicly offered securities may only be conducted by stockbroking companies, banks, and the central bank acting as an agent of the Republic of Slovenia. The Securities Market Law also regulates the public issue of shares of all companies whose capital exceeds SIT 7 million and the procedure for that public offering.

On 9 October 1995 on the initiative of the LSE the Derivatives Exchange was established by 13 banks and brokerage firms, which began trading on 28 March 1996. This is a separate legal entity that together with the Ljubljana Commodity Exchange[35] forms two markets on which derivatives (options, futures), currencies (since October 1995) and goods (grain: maize and barley) are traded.

The future potential of exchange markets in Slovenia can be summarized as:

---

investment or a joint venture, then this identification number is obtained from the Agency for Privatization or the Development Fund. Nevertheless, foreign portfolio investment could so far be described as insignificant. As reported by the Bank of Slovenia foreign portfolio investment for the year 1994 were only US$ 198 million which is about 19% of all the investments in Slovenia (beside foreign direct investments and joint ventures). For the time being there is still no strict legislative framework for portfolio investments, but there are currently three laws in various stage of parliamentary procedure that would also affect the foreign institutional investor. This legislation is expected to be in force by the beginning of 1997.

[34] The first dematerialized privatization shares (company: Kolinska) was listed and traded on 8 January 1996. Actually, according the Ljubljanska Borza (1996) issuers of publicly offered securities have to issue dematerialised securities (i.e. only electronically available securities). The same is required for banks and insurance companies regardless of whether or not their shares have been publicly offered. In compliance with the Law on privatization and the Decree on dematerialization, dematerialization is mandatory for all companies going public and privatization companies that have over 50 shareholders.

[35] This Exchange reopened after 53 years on 21 January 1994.

- further development of the off-exchange markets and several new listings on the official market;
- a complete dematerialization of the securities market;
- further development and implementation of the BIS in trading in securities;
- a general internationalization of the Slovene financial market.

SOURCES OF EXTERNAL FINANCE

Foreign investments are regulated by two basic Laws: the Law on Commercial Companies and the Foreign Investments Law.[36] Foreign investments in any form enjoy full national acceptance, so that the companies with foreign capital participation registered in Slovenia are treated in the same way as domestic companies.

As may be seen from Table 10.5 all sectors are open to foreign investors except companies in the military equipment field, rail and air transportation, communications and telecommunications, and insurance. Companies with foreign capital have the same rights and obligations as Slovene companies in terms of import, export, customs, taxation, etc. with some additional benefits and privileges: import of equipment, constituting a foreign investor's contribution, is not subject to customs duties if the investment contract is signed for a minimum period of five years and if the foreign investor's shareholding is at least 20% of the company.

According to the Foreign Investment Law certain rights are guaranteed to the investor that cannot be limited by any other law or regulation: to participate in the management of joint venture companies, to share in the profits in proportion to the investment, to participate proportionally in the proceeds from liquidation, to transfer their share of profits outside Slovenia and to repatriate their share upon disinvestment.

Foreign direct investment started to grow after the legislation was adopted in 1989. At that time it amounted to only US$ 114 million but rose to US$ 1,253 million in 1994 which, however, still represents less than 1% of GDP. Similarly, the ratio of foreign assets to total assets in Slovenia was only 1.6%

---

[36] In Slovenia, as well as in the other republics of former Yugoslavia, foreign direct investments were possible (but severely restricted) in various forms up to 1967; after this, legislation on FDIs was gradually liberalized and the importance of FDIs rose. In December 1988, the Federal Yugoslav Government implemented a new Foreign Investment Law which introduced a fundamental liberalization of the FDI legal framework and its harmonization with international standards.

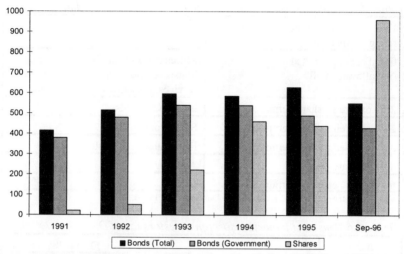

Source: Bank of Slovenia (1996c).

Figure 10.2. The Ljubljana Stock Exchange Market Capitalization

in 1993 for the whole economy, and 2.2% taking only manufacturing into account (Rojec 1995).

The characteristics of FDI projects in Slovenia so far are that the large majority:
1. are small;
2. are concentrated in a few sectors, such as the paper and pulp industry and car industry;
3. originate from a limited number of countries (as seen from Table 10.6).

Foreign direct investment is hence more important because of its positive externalities (management style, internationalization and integration into the world market, and technology) than because of its quantitative impact.

Slovenia received international funds primarily through international financial assistance (Table 10.7), amounting to US$ 582 million at the end of 1995 and through special programs (i.e. PHARE and US Aid) primarily for the restructuring of the banking and the real sector and for harmonization with European Union standards.

The total foreign debt of Slovenia outstanding at the end of 1995 was US$ 2.9 billion out of which more than 95% was long-term debt. The Slovenian international monetary reserves exceeded total foreign debt by 15.9%. In 1995 the volume of new foreign loan agreements continued to increase due primarily to the reduced country risk. A total of US$ 1.1 billion of new loans was

Table 10.5. Openness of the selected sectors for foreign investment

Upper limit for permitted share of foreign ownership	Sector(s)
0% of share permitted (not allowed at all)	Military equipment field, rail and air transport, telecommunications and post services, insurance and reinsurance
20% of foreign share permitted	Investment funds
24% of foreign share permitted	Stockbroking
33% of foreign share permitted	Publishing, broadcasting
49% of share permitted	Auditing
up to 100% of share permitted	Others

Source: Ministry of Economic Relations and Development (1996).

Table 10.6. The most important foreign investors (as of December 1995)

Country	Investors*	FDI in US$ million
Austria	Brigl & Bergmeister, OMV, Henkel, Bank Austria, Creditanstalt	245
Germany	Reemstma, Pfleiderer, Siemens	181
Italy	Saffa Group	101
France	Renault	94
Croatia	Nuclear Power Plant, Krško	72

Note: * Listed here according their share within respective country of origin.
Source: Ministry of Economic Relations and Development (1996); authors' calculations.

Table 10.7. Foreign financial assistance by international financial institutions

	Long–term debt in US$ million	
Financial institution	31 December 1995	30 September 1996
IBRD	165	153
EBRD	127	160
EIB	235	262
IFC	33	22
EUROFIMA	22	19
Total	582	616

Source: Bank of Slovenia (1996c).

contracted, thus representing a 19.6% increase from the previous year. The increase stems mainly from debt incurred by the private sector, while new loans contracted or guaranteed by the government decreased by 28.9% compared to the year before. The term structure also changed in favor of longer-term sources.

The Bank of Slovenia usually acts as an agent for all operations such as the US$ 33.5 million loan from IBRD for the restructuring of the banking and entrepreneurial sector in 1994 and the US$ 100 million loan from a foreign commercial bank syndicate, granted in 1993, that was used to finance the federal budget deficit.

CONCLUSION

The Slovene economy has undergone major changes in the previous five years which reflect its irreversible transformation into a market economy. The most dramatic changes appeared in the capital market area, as follows:

1. The establishment of an independent monetary authority.
2. The introduction of a flexible exchange rate system.
3. The reform of the banking sector with more rigorous performance standards and increased competition.
4. The establishment of a taxation system harmonized with the EU.
5. The liberalization of financial and capital flows.
6. the establishment of an organized stock exchange market.

Nevertheless, Slovenia remains so far the most successful economy in transition. The GDP per capita was US$ 9,352 in 1995, and the GDP real growth rate was 4.5% in the same year. A 4% increase in real GDP in 1996 is expected, and a 5% growth in 1997. By the end of July 1996, Slovenia had US$ 3,759 million foreign currency reserves and total foreign debt of US$ 3,652 million.[37] The main reasons for such optimistic forecasts could include:

*   improved economic performance (lower inflation, lower interest rate);
*   foreign trade and investment prospects (growth in exports of 7% is forecast, and 11% growth in investment);
*   transformation and fine-tuning of the economic system (the rehabilitation of the banking sector, and the completion of the privatization process of companies);
*   the development of business strategies in companies related to the process of adapting to EU standards and criteria.[38]

---

[37] Institute of Macroeconomic Analysis and Development (1996).

[38] Slovenia applied for full membership of the European Union, after signing on 10 June 1996 a long-delayed association agreement with the EU, the first step to EU membership. In addition, in March 1996 Slovenia signed an administrative agreement with the OECD, the final step before joining.

REFERENCES

Bank of Slovenia (1995): *Annual Report 1994*, Ljubljana.

Bank of Slovenia (1996a): *Annual Report 1995*, Ljubljana.

Bank of Slovenia (1996b): *Monthly Bulletin September*, Ljubljana.

Bank of Slovenia (1996c): *Monthly Bulletin October*, Ljubljana.

Bival, G. and A. Wörgötter (1995): *The Republic of Slovenia*, study commissioned by Bank Austria, Institute for Advanced Studies, Vienna.

Borak, N. (1995): *Financial Institutions and the Financial Market*, Banking Newsletter, The Bank Association of Slovenia, Ljubljana.

Gospodarski Vestnik (1995): *Legal Framework for Business in Slovenia*, Ljubljana.

Institute of Macroeconomic Analysis and Development (1996): *Slovenian Economic Mirror*, Vol. II, No. 8–9, August–September.

Kranjec, M. (1995): *Quantitative Features of the Slovenian payment system*, Banking Newsletter, The Bank Association of Slovenia, Ljubljana.

Lavrač, V. and P. Stanovnik (1995): *Monetary Policy under Flexible Exchange Rate in Slovenia*, Banking Newsletter, The Bank Association of Slovenia, Ljubljana.

Ljubljanska borza (1992) *(Ljubljana Stock Exchange)*: *Listing Rules*, mimeo, Ljubljana.

Ljubljanska borza (1996) *(Ljubljana Stock Exchange)*: *Annual Report 1995*, Ljubljana.

Ministry of Economic Relations and Development (1996): *Slovenia: A Place to Invest*, Investment Promotion Office, Ljubljana.

Official Gazette of the Republic of Slovenia No. 1/91, Ljubljana.

Official Gazette of the Republic of Slovenia No. 38/92, Ljubljana.

Official Gazette of the Republic of Slovenia No. 46/93, Ljubljana.

Rojec, M. (1995): *Neposredne tuje investicije, Zunanjeekonomska strategija Slovenije (Foreign Direct Investment, Slovene Foreign Economic Strategy)*, Center za mednarodno sodelovanje in razvoj, Ljubljana.

Saje, J. (1995): *Monetary Policy and Banks in 1994 and First Half of 1995*, Banking Newsletter, The Bank Association of Slovenia, Ljubljana.

Štiblar, F. (1995): *Development of Slovene Banking Sector*, Banking Newsletter, The Bank Association of Slovenia, Ljubljana.

Veselinovič, D. (1995): *Borzni priročnik (The Stock Exchange Guide)*, Gospodarski Vestnik, Ljubljana.

Veselinovič, D. and L. Gabrijelčič (1995): *Ljubljana Stock Exchange in 1994 and 1995*, Banking Newsletter, The Bank Association of Slovenia, Ljubljana.

11. FR Yugoslavia

Vladimir Gligorov

G24 P33
G28 P34
L33 P24

INTRODUCTION

The economic development of FR Yugoslavia (Serbia and Montenegro) following the break-up of former Yugoslavia (1991) can be characterized as almost catastrophic. Gross social product (GSP) at the end of 1996 was less then 50% of that in 1989.[1] Industrial production was less than 40%. Registered unemployment was close to 30%. Inflation was more than 90% (average 1996 over average 1995). Trade deficit was over US$ 2 billion (more than 15% of GSP) in 1996. More importantly, the country is still not accepted as a full member of the international community and has done little to transform its economy from a socialist to a market one and from a war economy to a peaceful one. Indeed, one can characterize the current government's strategy as that of sidestepping the transformation. How this came to be the case will not be discussed extensively here.[2] The chapter will deal with the current macroeconomic situation and specifically with the role of the banking sector.

A broad characterization of the current, early 1997, situation can be seen as follows. Expectations of speedy improvement following the suspension (in December 1995) of UN imposed sanctions (in May 1992) have been disappointed.[3] The government has been reluctant to undertake the necessary

---

[1] Yugoslavia still uses GSP rather than GDP (gross domestic product). The former does not include some 'non-productive' activities, i.e. health, education, some services, etc. GDP is about 10% larger than GSP in normal circumstances. Recent GDP estimates (see *Ekonomska politika* 21 October 1996, pp. 12–13) based on official statistics point to a larger difference between these two measures (close to 20%). This may be the result of some black-market activities being included in the GDP estimate or of some inaccuracies as is alleged by some critics.

[2] For more on this subject see Gligorov (1994, 1995).

[3] The sanctions were removed in October 1996.

reforms and that has led to a steady rise in tensions amidst worsening economic conditions. The country is facing the following economic policy dilemma: hyperinflation or transformational recession or both. Worst hit is, and will continue to be, the banking sector because of the huge accumulated debts and because of the outdated institutional and legal environment in which it works. The situation has been aggravated by the deepening political crisis that has erupted in the aftermath of the federal and local elections held on 17 November. The attempt by the government to annul the opposition victories in the local elections in some major cities of Serbia (including the capital Belgrade) has brought people and especially students out in the streets. The demonstrations have lasted for more than two months. In addition, the government has been facing growing international political and economic isolation. This is certain to aggravate the already deep economic and financial crisis that the country has been going through. Some kind of a political resolution can be expected in 1997 because Serbia is facing parliamentary and presidential elections that have to be held some time this year.

SOCIAL, STATE OR PRIVATE BANKS?

Commercial banking was introduced in the, then, Yugoslavia in the mid-1960s. The banks were originally state-owned. In the mid-1970s, the *de facto* state ownership was transformed into the so-called social ownership. The latter essentially meant that the banks were taken over by their customers, i.e. by the bank's debtors. In 1989, banks were transformed into joint-stock companies. This was reconfirmed by the new Law on Banking from 1993 in the, by then, new Federal Republic of Yugoslavia (Serbia and Montenegro). The 1989 law as well as the 1993 law liberalized the banking and the whole financial sector in the sense that it became possible to establish banks and other financial institutions with private, social or foreign capital.[4]

The outcome of liberalization was that the number of the banks increased significantly, while the number of the other financial institutions (mainly savings and loans organizations) increased dramatically. However, the banking sector suffered from huge scandals that involved a number of newly created private banks with significant government connections that collapsed during the hyperinflation that raged in the country in 1993. Essentially what happened was that the already existing banks suffered a huge credibility loss when the foreign currency savings of individuals were frozen at the end of 1991. This

---

[4] On the legal changes and their consequences see *Yugoslav Survey*, 3, 1993, pp. 57–68.

development created an opportunity for the new and private banks to offer attractive terms for the new foreign currency savings. As people in Yugoslavia save mainly in German marks, a great deal of hard currency went into these private banks. Two of those banks collapsed (Yugoskandic and Dafiment Bank) in 1993 and a lot of people lost a lot of money.[5]

After these setbacks, banking business reverted mostly to the old banks. These are registered as joint-stock companies, but are in fact state-owned. The decisive say in their decisions is enjoyed by the government and the debtors, i.e. the large state- or socially-owned, loss-making firms. Thus, in spite of a long history of bank reform in Yugoslavia (old and new), the banking sector is quite outdated and in need of significant transformation and restructuring.

The same can be said of the central bank, the National Bank of Yugoslavia. Though it was nominally made independent in the 1989 bank reform, it has remained an instrument of the government. In addition, due to (i) decentralization (there are now the Federal Central Bank and the Central Banks of Serbia and of Montenegro), (ii) insufficient control of the money supply, and (iii) the significant role of the banks operating abroad (e.g. in Cyprus), the central bank is just an instrument of government and not a very important one at that.

RATIONING INFLATION

The Yugoslav economy is highly unstable. It went through a short-lived hyperinflation period in the fall of 1989 and through a much more severe one again in 1993. The latter was one of the worst ever recorded. It ended after a stabilization program, known as Avramovic's Program, was introduced on 24 January 1994. However, this stability did not last for too long. Already at the end of 1994 inflation was back and continued to rise throughout most of 1995. At the moment, there are again significant hyperinflationary risks.

In 1995, inflation was over 70%, 126% in December (over December 1994). In the first half of 1996, it was running at more than 100% per year, though it has slowed somewhat in the second half. The government has tried to contain it by introducing price controls, but that only leads to eventual outbursts of higher inflation. The fixed exchange rate, reintroduced in November 1995 after the Yugoslav Dinar was devalued from 1 Dinar for 1 German mark to 3.3 Dinars for 1 German mark, influences the slowdown of inflation only to the extent that the currency market (essentially a colored and black market) believes that the central bank will resist requests to print money for this or that

---

[5] See Dinkic (1995) on the whole affair.

special interest. In spring 1996, the central bank resisted the request to grant so-called selective credits with low interest rates for agriculture and for export subsidies. As a result, the Dinar stabilized and inflation calmed down somewhat. However, starting from May 1996, the monetary policy was relaxed (central bank's discount rate was lowered significantly, from just over 100% to just over 70% on a yearly basis). As a result, the July monthly inflation rate was 6.6%. Together with the rise in inflation, there was some improvement in output. This exemplifies the well-known characteristic of the Yugoslav economy: prices and production react with a very short time-lag to changes in monetary policy (the lag can be as short as one month).[6]

This characteristic, together with the lack of reforms in the financial system, left the Yugoslav economy constantly facing the crucial macroeconomic dilemma – inflation or recession? Indeed, it brings closer the even more difficult dilemma – transformational recession or hyperinflation? The latter dilemma was brought out clearly in spring 1996's confrontation between the government and the central bank. The central bank (headed at the time by Dragoslav Avramovic, the highly popular author of the above-mentioned stabilization program) was resisting the relaxation of monetary policy, hoping that the credit squeeze, which the economy was starting to experience, would put pressure on the government to look for credits abroad and, in order to get them, to adopt the necessary reforms. Indeed, the, then, governor of the central bank put out a program, called Avramovic's Program 2, as a platform for negotiations with the IMF and the World Bank. The government responded by removing the governor of the central bank and by relaxing monetary policy.

The Yugoslav experience with inflation and hyperinflation is typical of an economy with a repressed banking and financial system that aims to ration price increases and the growth of production. Two main aspects have to be noted here.

First, because of the short time-lag between money, price and output movements, the government is capable of using both monetary and non-monetary mechanisms to target the development of the inflation level. The instrument used are so-called selective credits and price controls, i.e. rationing. What the government does is to approve the giving of credits by the central bank for special purposes at a lower discount rate. This increases the money supply and, hence, prices. Then the government introduces selective price controls to keep prices from increasing even further. Over a period of time, a variety of selective credits with different interest rates will be issued and a maze of price controls will be created. The government then has a choice of partial

---

[6] On this see Petrovic and Vujosevic (1995).

liberalization and of introduction of comprehensive price controls. From time to time, it relies on both, but this is only to enable it to revert more easily to its usual policy of selective favoritism.

Secondly, with this policy of 'inflation rationing', the government is capable of extending the period between rising inflation and the eruption of hyperinflation. Both in the case of the 1989 hyperinflation and in that of 1993, the period of rising inflation preceding the actual outburst of hyperinflation was fairly long, though once the developments got out of hand the collapse came very quickly. This ability to rely on inflation for such a long time is an interesting phenomenon. The expectations that support this kind of process are yet to be more precisely identified. Intuitively speaking, however, the population seems to have adapted to the circumstances quite thoroughly and relies on reasonable expectations of the level of inflation that the government is targeting and of the level of 'inflation tax' it is willing to pay. This insight is supported by the fact that, regardless of the inflation level in a given year, the share of budgetary revenues is practically constant.

CHANGING FORTUNES

Whatever the more specific mechanisms of 'inflation rationing' turn out to be, the role of the banks and of the financial markets is without doubt crucial. The development of the banking system has been under a lot of scrutiny in the press and in the scholarly publications.[7] This was prompted by a series of scandals involving the banks. Some of these scandals related to banks that used basically pyramid (or Ponzi) schemes. Others had to do with political favoritism. Finally, the likely scandal, if it ever erupts, will have to do with the Yugoslav banks' operations abroad, especially in Cyprus.

There are over 100 banks in Yugoslavia. Most of them are fairly small. In fact, the banking sector is quite concentrated with four or five banks controlling much of the market. Nominally, all of the banks are owned by their shareholders. However, in most cases, and especially in the case of the largest banks, the shareholders are the socially- or state-owned companies. Some banks are in mixed ownership. In some of those, usually small ones, the majority of the shares are privately owned.

The most important *de facto* state-owned banks are Beogradska Banka, Invest Banka, Jugobanka, Vojvodjanska Banka and the Montenegro Banka. Of

---

[7] See Dinkic (1995).

these, by far the most important is Beogradska Banka. Slobodan Milosevic, the current president of Serbia and the strong man of Yugoslavia, served as a president of this bank in late 1970s and early 1980s. The bank used to have offices in the major financial centres of the world and still has branches or owns banks in Cyprus, London, Vienna, Moscow and in other places. It has been the main instrument of the government's international financial operations that had to be conducted through rather obscure and probably illegal operations during the time Yugoslavia was under tight international sanctions.

The most important private bank is Karic Banka. It is described as a bank in mixed ownership, but is in fact a family business with significant government connections and with significant foreign capital participation (about 40%). It is mainly involved in foreign trade, investment and in foreign currency transfers for private citizens and companies. It is the only significant private bank to have survived the banking scandals of 1993 and 1994 and to have actually expanded.

The banks entered a fresh crisis in Spring 1995. The whole banking sector faced insolvency. As part of the package of new measures, so-called Program 2 of Mr Avramovic, the then governor of the central bank, their situation was alleviated. Their reserve requirements were lowered, their bad debts were rescheduled, the central bank started issuing short-term bonds to control liquidity through open market operations, the interest rates were partly freed, and the supervision by the central bank was tightened. Eventually, interest rates were liberalized too. As a result of these measures, the state of the banking sector improved significantly. By the end of 1995, most of the banks reported profits (though the banking system as a whole reported losses of about US$ 100 million, still significantly less than the year before) and this favorable situation extended into early 1996.

The improvement in the banking sector proved to be only temporary. In the second half of 1996 interest rates were lowered, and in September the government raised the reserve money requirement significantly. These measures led to banks making losses and eventually to the failure of a number of them, initially some small and essentially insignificant ones, but by the end of 1996 and beginning of 1997 at least two significant, medium-sized banks, were declared illiquid and were facing bankruptcy proceedings. This situation can only get worse because the overall financial situation in the economy is worsening.[8]

The banks are burdened with the huge amount of bad debts that in most cases are owed by those who own the banks (the banks are mostly owned by

---

[8] On that see Madzar (1996).

enterprises who are also the main customers of these same banks). This ownership structure is responsible for the specific macroeconomic conse-quences discussed above. Banks serve as the main channel for 'inflation rationing'. In essence, they extend credits as a form of subsidy. They lend to their owners at interest rates that are negative in real terms. They, of course, also borrow at negative real interest rates (from the central bank and from the public). Thus, savings are predictably low, while loans are predictably high. Because of that, from time to time their bad debts have to be taken over by the central bank or be wiped out through hyperinflation. As long as the banks are capable of preserving some balanced level of negative real interest rate, they are able to keep the rise in the inflation rate under control. Once it becomes obvious that this is no longer possible, hyperinflation is used to clean up the balance sheets. Therefore, no improvement in the profitability of the banks can ever be more than temporary.

This also explains, at least partly, the short time-lag between the changes in the monetary policy, prices and the output growth. As soon as money supply is tightened, there are no credit subsidies and the production is adjusted accord-ingly because there are no alternative sources of finance. Firms cannot revert to lower prices to boost their sales, because their prices are already too low to cover costs without subsidy. Thus, they reduce their output to minimize losses. Once this uncertainty about the monetary policy is resolved, production can immediately increase.

This system could work for decades in former Yugoslavia because the country had no difficulty in borrowing money abroad and could also rely on the foreign currency savings of its citizens. Thus, investments were generally financed from foreign credits, while the banks made money on their foreign currency deposits. However, this funding source disappeared when the foreign currency deposits were frozen, i.e. confiscated. In addition, with the introduc-tion of international sanctions, foreign credits and investment became unavailable. As a consequence, the whole banking system has simply gone broke. It makes some money on transfers and payments services which it renders to its mainly territorially limited customers. Otherwise, it will have to go through a thorough program of restructuring.

The structural problems the banking sector faces can be seen from Table 11.1. The picture given by Table 11.1 is one of a seriously overextended banking system. It is short of capital and long on big loans exposure. It also has a lot of money tied up in equity investments. The banking system needs to be re-capitalised and to be cleaned of bad loans and investments. This process of restructuring will take some time and will certainly be very costly.

One of the main problems that the Yugoslav banks face is that of the so-called 'old foreign' currency savings. Yugoslav banks have accepted foreign

Table 11.1. Indicators of bank performance

	Sept. 1995	Dec. 1995	Mar. 1996
Capital adequacy (8% min)	15.12	8.12	8.65
Equity share (20% min)	13.89	7.90	8.21
Deposits (50% max)	24.79	31.62	30.47
Short term loans/deposits (100% min)	156.26	160.36	161.11
Forex deposits/loans (95%-105%)	93.93	96.05	95.85
Share of big loans (80% max)	255.89	545.56	502.24
Share of direct investments in firms (15% max)	7.54	7.74	8.45
Share of direct investments in banks (51% max)	9.87	8.95	9.11
Equity investments (20% max)	52.44	59.69	58.36

Source: Yugoslav Banking Assocation, 1996.

currency deposits since the mid-1960s. Most people held their savings in foreign currency. With the break-up of Yugoslavia those accounts were frozen. They appear on the balance sheets of the Yugoslav banks, but, more importantly, they impede the banks in their attempts to attract new foreign currency savings. The amount of money that was frozen is quite significant. It probably comes to more than US$ 4 billion. At the moment, only very small amounts of money can be withdrawn from these accounts (DEM 1000 per year per account holder). This debt will also have to be rescheduled or solved in some other way if the banks are to start to regain their credibility. However, this is not an easy matter. If interest is added to the stock of frozen savings, this may prove to be a very significant debt indeed. On the other hand, if this situation persists, it may prove to be a devastatingly long-term constraint on the whole banking system.

The role of the central bank has fluctuated in importance. It the 1990 reform, the central bank was given a degree of independence when it became responsible to Parliament and not to the government. The Federal Parliament also appointed the governor of the central bank. This system was retained after the new Yugoslavia came into being. However, the bank did not show any practical independence as it continued to play a major role in the policy of high inflation, and hyperinflation followed in 1992 and 1993. Its independence was somewhat reasserted in the stabilization year of 1994, but came under attack in the second half of the same year. In the second half of 1995, the central bank was given new powers when it became responsible for the supervision of the payments system and of the commercial banks. In that period it tried to eliminate the use of selective credits and also to liberalize interest rates. It also tried to shore up the foreign currency reserves which were falling to a fairly critical level. They stood reportedly at about US$ 300 million at the end of 1995 and also at the end of 1996. This policy was abandoned in the spring 1996. The bank reverted to the policy of selective credits and of ignoring the foreign currency reserves, which are in any case not under its control, being kept in bank or even private accounts abroad. Thus, the central bank's independence was short-lived and largely theoretical.

CONCLUSION

The Yugoslav banking system is completely outdated. It has arrived in this predicament because the government decided that it wanted to sidestep the transformation and to increase the role of the government. Thus, banks were left with the huge foreign debt burden, with the burden of the frozen foreign currency savings and with mounting bad debts that they could not do anything about, because the debtors are at the same time the owners of the major banks. In addition, the banking sector lost almost all of its credibility in a series of scandals that have yet to be resolved. At the moment, it is difficult to tell when the banking reform is to come. Whenever it does come, it will take a lot of time and it will be very costly.

PART II

Selected Topics

12. The Role of Central Bank Independence for Seigniorage: A Study of Transitional Economies

Eduard Hochreiter, Riccardo Rovelli and Georg Winckler[1]

INTRODUCTION

Central banking in the Economies in Transition of Eastern Europe (EITs) is exposed to conflicting pressures. On the one hand, there are pressures to speed up the integration with the European Union, and to adopt as soon as possible those 'rules of the game' that would facilitate this integration – e.g. EITs are required to strengthen the stability of the Union's monetary systems, to avoid the inflationary financing of budget deficits, and to implement financial reforms to support an efficient financial system. On the other hand, the financial needs of the government and the corporate sectors are huge. In addition, it is difficult to discriminate between 'good' and 'bad' demands for new credit and to dispose of the bad old debts, i.e. the non-performing loans inherited from the past.[2] If both the domestic capital market and the banking sector (as well as the tax system) are only nascent, central banks may be exposed to strong pressures to 'soften' the budget constraints of various sectors.[3] The inflation tax is a likely candidate for such softening.

Central banks thus find themselves in a delicate position. They have to design monetary policies which stabilize the macro economy and they have to

---

[1] This is an extended version of an article published in the European Economic Review (Hochreiter, Rovelli, Winckler, 1996).

[2] See Begg and Portes (1992) and Perotti (1995).

[3] See, e.g. Calvo and Coricelli (1992).

contribute to the phasing-in of the new financial system (which sometimes is in part a spin-off from the old 'monobank' system).[4] Yet, at the same time, they are asked to smooth the transition between the old and new rules of the lending game. In the EITs, despite the adoption of new central bank laws during the past few years, central banks have positioned themselves in quite different ways. As a result, inflation rates have also varied substantially. In this paper we examine the behavior of central banks of the Czech Republic, Hungary and Romania using Germany and Austria as benchmarks, by referring to a more comprehensive and wide-ranging set of statistics, rather than just comparing inflation (or monetary growth) rates. Thus we shall examine in detail the process of generation and distribution of seigniorage by the central banks defined above.

The chapter focuses on two issues:

1. To what extent have central banks effectively 'softened' the budget constraints of the government and of the banking sector, by creating and distributing an additional amount of seigniorage?
2. Is the amount of seigniorage created by central banks in the EITs significantly different from that of the 'virtuous' economies in the European Union and, if so, which steps should be recommended to facilitate the integration of the EITs in the EU in this respect?

We shall seek answers to these questions for the Czech Republic, Hungary and Romania. Our choice of countries has been motivated by easy access to the relevant data.[5] Our EU benchmarks are Austria and Germany. We focus on these two as they both are models of monetary stability and, at the same time, have strong geographical and historical links to the EITs under scrutiny.

The choice of focusing on seigniorage and its distribution is based on the consideration that above an acceptable threshold of about 1% of GDP, seigniorage provides a comprehensive measure of excessive fiscal financing by the central bank (or at least of financial underdevelopment or repression), as it includes the revenue both from the inflation tax and from monetary restrictions (such as reserve requirements and other compulsory deposits with the central bank). In particular, large amounts of seigniorage appropriated by the governments would indicate the amount by which the budget deficit would increase if government expenditures and taxes remained unchanged, but monetary stabilization were pursued.

---

[4] See Carlin and Mayer (1992).

[5] For the same reason, we have confined our analysis to one single year, 1993. We are planning to extend our analysis to other EITs.

The chapter is organized as follows. In the next section we discuss the definition and some measurement issues which arise in relation to the concept of 'central bank seigniorage', and describe the data sources. In the third section we present and discuss the empirical results. In the fourth section we discuss the results in relation to the legal provisions concerning the financing of government deficits and central bank independence. The fifth section contains a brief conclusion.

MEASURING SEIGNIORAGE

Definitions

The term seigniorage is not unambiguously defined. As Drazen (1985) sums up, three definitions have traditionally been used in the literature: seigniorage as
1. *inflation* tax, i.e. $\pi\, h$, with π as the inflation rate, and h as real balances (real high-powered money); with $h = H/p$ and H being nominal high-powered money;
2. *opportunity cost of holding money*, i.e. ih, with i as the nominal interest rate;
3. *revenues actually collected by printing money,* i.e. the monetary growth rate μ multiplied by real high-powered money, yielding $\mu h = \Delta H/p$.

To these three definitions, Drazen adds an encompassing one:
4. *total revenues associated with money creation*, i.e. $\mu h + (r-n)a$, with μ being the nominal growth rate of high-powered money, $r-n$ the difference between the real rate of interest and the population growth rate, and a the real stock of interest-earning government assets (with $a \leq h$).

As Drazen (1985) points out, definitions (1) to (3) arise as special cases of (4). For instance, if one assumes constant velocity and perfect foresight ($i=\mu$) and also that $n = r$, then (2), (3) and (4) coincide. In high inflation countries most seigniorage accrues as inflation tax, hence, definition (1) approaches definition (2). In this case measuring seigniorage according to definition (1) appears to be the only practicable alternative, *inter alia*, because of the difficulties in finding an appropriate nominal interest rate.

Recently, attention has focused on the status of central banks as institutions which are independent of (or at least legally separated from) the government. In this context the amount of seigniorage that is being generated becomes logically independent of the question of 'who is entitled to benefit?' from seigniorage. That is, the distribution (or the appropriation) of seigniorage is independent (at least, up to a certain extent) of the process of its creation (Klein and Neumann (1990) and Fry (1993)). As a consequence one may question if the more traditional definitions of seigniorage fully capture the extent to which governments benefit from their priviledged relation with the central bank. In this vein, expanding on Drazen's own definition (reported above as (3)), Rovelli (1994) distinguishes between *central bank seigniorage* (defined as the opportunity cost of the monetary base, i.e. as in (2) above) and *government seigniorage* (which could be more precisely defined as 'overall government benefits from money creation'), that is, the amount of debt on which the government either pays no interest or an interest rate below market rates, because of its special relationship with the central bank. Empirically the latter turns out to be equal to the former (to the extent to which seigniorage is appropriated by the government) plus the net increase in central bank claims towards the government, that is (measuring government seigniorage as a ratio to GNP):

$$\frac{\alpha i H}{Y} + \frac{\left| \Delta B^c - g B^c_{-1} \right|}{Y} \tag{12.1}$$

where α is the proportion of central bank seigniorage appropriated by the government, iH/Y is central bank seigniorage as a ratio to GNP, and the term in square brackets measures *excess monetization*, that is the increase in government net liabilities with the central bank, ΔB^c, above the amount which would be required to keep their ratio constant relative to GDP, after taking into account the growth rate of GDP, g.[6]

In this paper, however, we use the more traditional concept of central bank seigniorage using alternatively, where appropriate, the opportunity cost or the inflation tax definitions. In particular, we shall enquire to what extent (central bank) seigniorage is appropriated by the government, retained by the central bank, or distributed to other sectors of the economy. At this juncture, it may be useful to clarify through which channel this might take place. To this end, we make three observations:

1. Seigniorage may be appropriated by the government through any combination of:
    * an interest rate subsidy or refund on government liabilities with the central bank;
    * a transfer of central bank pre-tax profits;
    * central bank dividend payments;

---

[6] Note that the Maastricht Treaty strictly prohibits direct credit from the central bank to the government as well as privileged access. However, the concept of excess monetization as defined above is of particular importance for EITs, whose central bank legislation (and practice) is not yet in line with Maastricht requirements.

- central bank tax payments;
- a transfer of central bank residual (post-tax and post-dividend) profits.[7]

2. Interest rate subsidies may be used by the central bank to transfer seigniorage to other institutions, e.g. to bail out financial institutions in distress.

3. A central bank may want to or be legally required to keep (some part of central bank) seigniorage for itself. In simple terms, this fraction may be either 'consumed' (i.e. by increasing the costs of running the central bank), or 'invested' (by accumulating own capital and reserves of various kinds). In the latter case, an intertemporal problem arises. Since central banks usually retain part of their seigniorage to increase reserves, today's accumulation of reserves out of retained profits will further increase tomorrow's profits beyond the opportunity cost of holding money. However, reserve accumulation may be necessary for the central bank to provide a buffer to cope with the vicissitudes of financial markets.[8] This poses the practical problem of distinguishing reserve accumulation aimed at increasing future seigniorage from reserve accumulation as a tool of risk management.

To sort out this measurement problem, we shall use as a benchmark (admittedly, with a considerable degree of arbitrariness) the strict rules laid down for the German central bank. In Germany, accumulation of reserves is permitted only up to 10% of the currency in circulation.[9] Therefore, we shall consider (for the other countries) any accumulation of reserves beyond 10% of currency as motivated by the desire to earn more central bank profits in the future, and we shall consider that amount (in addition to the traditionally measured monetary base) as part of central banks' seigniorage-earning liabilities.

Finally, we must also consider that in some instances central banks pay interest on that part of the monetary base which is held in compliance with minimum reserve requirements. Hence these payments must be deducted from the computation of seigniorage.

---

[7] See Rovelli (1994) and references therein for examples of these arrangements.

[8] E.g. the Austrian National Bank Act (Art. 69) stipulates that the Bank transfers the exchange profits (i.e. the difference between the book value and the buying price of forex holdings) to a reserve fund to cover forex risks, irrespective of the business results.

[9] The precise rule is: The legal reserve is restricted to 5% of banknotes in circulation, other reserves to the Bundesbank's capital, the pension fund to full funding, all totalling in practice around 10% of currency in circulation. In Austria a similar rule refers to the General Reserve Fund. Other reserve funds may be created in addition.

Analysis of Central Banks' Balance Sheets

As shown in the above, the seigniorage-generating liabilities of the monetary authority may be defined as including the following items:

$$H + H' + EK \tag{12.2}$$

where $H + H'$ is the monetary base, defined as: $H + H' = Cu + R$. This reflects the fact that the monetary base may be held either as currency *(Cu)*, or as (remunerated or non-remunerated)deposits *(R)* of domestic residents (generally, these will be bank reserves), and that most of it is a liability of the central bank *(H)*, but, to a lesser extent, it may also include liabilities of other monetary authorities *(H ')*.[10] Central bank reserves accumulated beyond 10% of currency are indicated by *EK*.

Other items in the balance sheet of the monetary authority are, on the liability side, capital plus reserves up to 10% of currency *(K)*, loans from the IMF *(IMF)* and other foreign liabilities *(F$_L$)*. On the asset side, we find gold *(G)*, convertible foreign assets, denominated in domestic currency *(F$_A$)*, claims on government *(B^c)*, claims on banks *(L^c)*, claims on other agencies *(A^c)*, net non-convertible assets *(N)*[11] and other net assets *(OA)*. Thus, the following identity holds (note that, for balance, *OA* on the asset side must be defined inclusive of *H '*):

$$H + H' + EK = G + (F_A - F_L - IMF) + B^c + L^c + A^c + OA + N - K \tag{12.3}$$

Using the opportunity cost concept, and in accordance with the previous discussion, we may define the amount of seigniorage of the central bank as:

$$CBS\ (net) \equiv i_M(H + H' + EK) - i_R R \tag{12.4}$$

where i_M is the relevant opportunity cost measure, a money market rate, to be identified below. Variable i_R represents the rate of interest on deposits. This rate, as is the case in Austria, may be zero for legal or policy reasons.

In most western countries, the seigniorage-generating liabilities of the monetary authorities are about 10–15% of GDP. Assuming also that, in low

---

[10] Both in Austria and in Germany, coins are issued outside the central bank. Also, before 1 July 1995, some liabilities of the Austrian Treasury could be held by banks towards the fulfillment of reserve requirements.

[11] Non-convertible assets may be important in EITs.

inflation economies, nominal interest rates are rarely expected to be higher than 10% , it is evident that central bank seigniorage should not be expected to be much higher than 1% of GDP. Hence we shall use this value as a rough benchmark in determining whether or not monetary policy is used as a 'budget softening' tool. Of course, if the ratio of the monetary base to GDP is high, e.g. due to extensive reserve requirements or to the absence of modern payments techniques, the 1% benchmark may be exceeded, even if the inflation rate and the nominal rates of interest are low. In this case a high level of CBS may be an indicator of financial underdevelopment or of financial repression, rather than of monetary abuse by the central bank. (Note that CBS is also boosted by a high EK, i.e. accumulating reserves beyond the 10% rule.)

The final question is how, given the amount of CBS, we measure the distribution of seigniorage to the various sectors of the economy. The amount of seigniorage accruing to each sector is measured by the difference between the opportunity cost of seigniorage and the rate charged on the liabilities of that sector to the central bank, plus the difference between the interest received by that sector on its claims towards the central bank, less the opportunity cost, i.e:

$$(i_M - i_{LX})L_X + (i_{AX} - i_M)A_X \qquad (12.5)$$

where L_X and A_X are the liabilities of and claims of sector X on the CB.

If the sum of the two differences is negative, then the sector is 'subsidising' the central bank. In addition, and in particular for the government sector, one has to compute non-interest payments received from the central bank, such as taxes, dividends, and other transfers.

Our empirical results on measuring central bank seigniorage and its distribution are presented in the following section.

RESULTS

Data

Our analysis is based on data from domestic sources (central bank reports and, for Romania, communications courtesy of the central bank), concerning particularly the balance sheets and profit and loss accounts of the central banks, for the year 1993.[12] We use annual averages of data with the highest available frequency (daily for Austria and Germany, monthly for the Czech Republic and

---

[12] The Czech National Bank was established on 1 January 1993.

Table 12.1. Central banks: liabilities and assets, 1993 (ratio to GDP, percentage points)

	Austria	Czech Rep.	Germany	Hungary	Romania
Liabilities					
Cu	6.42	6.02	6.68	10.59	3.66
R: banks	2.75	5.34	2.5	14.98	3.62
R: publ. sector	0.01	4.49	0.23	4.86	2.63
R: others	0	2.21	0.73	0.44	0.00
H'	1.5	0.00	0.45	0	0
EK	3.85	1.03	0.54	2.39	1.73
K	0.65	0.60	0.65	1.23	0.09
F_L	0.01	2.95	0.78	46.27	5.42
IMF	0	3.70	0.00	5.43	2.53
Total	15.18	26.35	12.57	86.18	19.68
Assets					
G	1.74	0.42	0.44	0.11	2.74
F_A	7.04	8.20	3.36	17.86	3.03
B^C	0.08	5.68	0.46	59.37	8.1
L^C	3.6	8.57	7.31	8.88	4.9
A^C	0	0.35	0.01	0.00	0
N	0	2.51	0.00	0.00	0
OA	2.73	0.62	0.98	-0.03	0.89
Total	*15.18*	*26.35*	*12.57*	*86.18*	*19.68*

Note: See *Analysis of central banks' balance sheets* for explanation of symbols.

Romania and quarterly for Hungary).

For each country, the data are in domestic currency, with foreign currency assets or liabilities evaluated at average exchange rates. Nonconvertible assets and liabilities were not considered for calculating seigniorage. The basic balance sheet data are reported in Table 12.1.

For the purpose of measuring central bank seigniorage, it is crucial to identify the interest rate reflecting the opportunity cost of holding central bank liabilities. In our opinion a domestic short-term rate constitutes such a measure,

Table 12.2. Seigniorage earning liabilities and imputed central bank seigniorage (1993)

	Austria	Czech Rep.	Germany	Hungary	Romania
π	3.6	20.8	4.1	22.5	256.1
i_M	7.2	9.6	7.5	14.9	—
Ratios to GDP:					
H+H´+EK	14.53	19.09	11.14	33.25	11.64
i_RR	0.03	0.72	0.05	0.76	0.3
CBS	1.02	1.11	0.79	4.20	29.4

Note: See text. CBS (imputed) = i_M (H+H´+EK) - i_RR
For Romania, π is used in place of the interest rate.

since money is a short-term asset for the economy. We chose (yearly averages of) the money market rate for Austria, the Czech Republic, Germany and Hungary. For the two EITs, it could be questioned whether this is the correct measure: in 1993 this interest rate was below the current inflation rate in both countries. However, for the purpose of this paper we decided to stick to the money market rate since, despite the apparent evidence of negative (short-term) real rates, the money markets are well established and seem to be functioning on the basis of those rates. If one were to use the inflation rate as the relevant opportunity cost, the corresponding measures of central bank seigniorage would be more than doubled for the Czech Republic, and would be increased by 50% for Hungary (Table 12.2). For Romania, on the other hand, we felt there was no alternative but to use the inflation rate, as the money market in 1993 was still relatively undeveloped and the rate of inflation much higher than quoted interest rates.

For the purpose of measuring the distribution of seigniorage through interest rate subsidies, interest rates on different groups of assets (and liabilities) were measured on the basis of actual interest received (and paid) (see Table 12.3).

Generation of Seigniorage

Table 12.2 shows the computation of central bank seigniorage for each of the five countries in 1993. Note that interest payments by the central banks are quite low in Austria and Germany: this, in particular, reflects the fact that reserve requirements are not remunerated. In Austria, almost all interest payments attributed to the central bank originate from government liabilities eligible for reserve requirements and held outside the central bank. In the other countries,

Selected Topics

Table 12.3. Appropriation of central bank seigniorage (ratio to GDP, %)

	Austria	Czech Rep.	Germany	Hungary	Romania
Government	0.53	-0.24	0.61	6.26	21.94
– interest rate subsidies	0.06	-0.24	0.02	5.98	20.68
– transfers & payments	0.47	0.01	0.59	0.29	1.25
Financial institutions	0.04	0.11	0.04	0.20	10.04
Foreign institutions	-0.03	0.38	-0.02	-1.95	-12.20
Retained seigniorage	0.18	0.53	0.02	0.07	0.34
Operating costs & exp.	0.12	0.10	0.09	0.15	0.14
Foregone seigniorage	0.17	0.25	0.09	0.34	9.05
– on gold	0.13	0.04	0.03	0.02	7.00
– on other assets	0.04	0.21	0.06	0.33	2.06
Other receipts	0	-0.03	0.00	-0.34	0.00
Measurement error	0.02	0.00	-0.03	-0.54	0.09
TOTAL CBS	*1.02*	*1.11*	*0.79*	*4.20*	*29.39*

Notes: See section *Analysis of central banks' balance sheets* of text for details on calculations. See *Appropriation of central bank seigniorage* for comments. Data refer to 1993.

especially in Hungary and Romania, the high level of interest payments by the central banks to depositors indicates that there is still an important banking department within the national banks of the former socialist countries. This distinction is illustrated by the composition of the liabilities of the balance sheets as well (here deposits of residents are the dominating items, whereas in the EU countries it is currency). In Romania, however, no interest has to be paid on deposits from the public sector.

As Table 12.2 shows, central bank seigniorage in Romania is about 30 times higher, in relation to GDP, than our assumed benchmark value, whereas for Hungary it is about four times higher. The Czech Republic, on the other hand, is quite in line with Austria and Germany.[13] Comparing the two high

---

[13] Gros and Vandille's (1995) results differ significantly, because they measure flow seigniorage. As far as seigniorage, defined and measured as inflation tax is concerned, they obtain similar results for Romania (25.87% of GDP for 1992).

seigniorage countries, we notice that in Romania, despite a relatively low monetary base to GDP ratio (less than 12%), high seigniorage is the result of an extremely high inflation tax rate (255%); in Hungary the opportunity cost is much lower (less than 15%) but the stock of seigniorage-generating assets is much higher (one-third of GNP), due to high reserve requirements and to the low velocity of circulation both of bank deposits and currency. The Austrian CBS exceeds the German one due to higher excess reserves (EK). If one leaves out the Austrian EK in calculating CBS, CBSs for the two countries reach the same levels in terms of GDP (0.8%).

Appropriation of Central Bank Seigniorage

In this section we ask who benefits from the creation of central bank seigniorage. All relevant data are presented in Table 12.3 (as ratios to GDP) and will be discussed below. Note that our calculations have been made on the basis of aggregate balance sheet data and of an opportunity cost concept which only can be regarded as approximate (this is especially true for Romania, where we used the inflation rate). For this reason our numerical evaluations are only indicative.

First, we examine the expenses of running the central bank, calculated to be in the range between 0.09 and 0.15% of GDP, with a minimum in Germany and a maximum in Hungary. However, in Hungary central bank assets amount to a rather high 86% of GDP. Their management presumably requires considerable resources.[14] Thus we cannot conclude that, in this respect, the Hungarian data are out of line with the others.

Second, *seigniorage retained* for the purpose of accumulating reserves is relatively high in the Czech Republic (0.53% of GDP) and Romania (0.34%), while it is low in Germany and Hungary, with Austria in an intermediate position. Taking into account both capital and reserves (K) and excess reserves (EK) measured according to the German rule, we see that both in the Czech Republic and Romania (as well as in Germany) these liabilities are relatively low (less than 2% of GDP), so that it appears quite justified to retain seigniorage for the purpose of building up reserves. Moreover, the Czech National Bank has been accumulating reserves as a shield against doubtful loans, and especially to write off the claims on Slovakia.

---

[14] Note that we are unable to distinguish between costs and expenses attributable to the banking rather than to the issue department of the central banks. Also note that the Hungarian National Bank fulfills additional tasks such as managing the accounts of government agencies and organizations (e.g. hospitals and universities) and a large part of the (official) foreign debt of Hungary.

Third, *foregone seigniorage* (that is, interest 'wasted' by holding zero or low yielding assets) appears high in Romania (7% of GDP, due to gold reserves valued at 2.74% of GDP). However, we should note that gold is a good inflation hedge in high inflation countries. Since for Romania the assumed opportunity cost is indeed the inflation rate, it is thus legitimate to assume that there is no foregone seigniorage on gold, and that the corresponding seigniorage is retained by the central bank.[15]

Next, we evaluate the distribution of central bank seigniorage to the other sectors. As we remarked in the section 'Analysis of Central Banks' Balance Sheets', if the central bank charges less than the money market rate for its claims, it distributes seigniorage to its debtors. This is tantamount to a subsidy. Hence, being entitled to be a debtor of the central bank at a subsidized interest rate is of special relevance to our study. Moreover, central banks may (or are required to) transfer seigniorage to governments by means of various other institutional arrangements, as discussed in (1).

Seigniorage distributed to the *government* is about 0.5% of GDP in Austria and Germany. As claims on the government are quite modest in both countries, seigniorage accrues almost entirely from transfers, e.g. the distribution of central bank profits, not from interest rate subsidies. In contrast, claims on the government amount to 60% of GDP in Hungary. Interest rate subsidies on these claims are approximately 6% of GDP. In Romania government debt with the central bank is only 8% of GDP but, due to the high inflation tax, the opportunity cost is much higher. Hence the total subsidy is about 20% of GDP. The case of the Czech Republic is of interest for a different reason. There, it would appear that the Czech National Bank is subsidized by the government, and not vice versa. However, this result reflects the fact that the central bank has aimed at transforming the direct credit to government, granted on the occasion of the devaluation of the Czechoslovak crown in 1990, into securities and that the rate on securities is naturally higher than the money market rate.

In 1993 interest rate subsidies to the *banking sector* were of minor importance in all countries, with the exception of Romania, where the inflation tax appropriated by banks through their claims on the central bank amounted to 10% of GDP.

---

[15] An equivalent correction could be made for the other central banks, but the numerical changes would be negligible. Also note that for Germany we have considered only gold reserves which are still attributable to the Bundesbank. German gold reserves at EMI (20%) are considered part of its foreign assets.

As regards the *foreign sector*,[16] all central banks, with one exception, obtain a subsidy (or a profit beyond the opportunity cost) on their net foreign position. In Austria and Germany the interest rate on foreign assets was, on average for 1993, higher than the money market rate, whereas in Hungary[17] and Romania net foreign liabilities were charged with a rate lower than the opportunity cost. For Romania the subsidy amounts to more than 12% of GDP. The exception was once more the Czech Republic, where the central bank's foreign liabilities were associated with an interest rate higher than the market rate, despite the fact that about half of them are loans granted by the IMF (being charged with an interest rate of about 1–2 times the interest rate on SDR deposits).[18] In addition, the interest rate on foreign assets was lower than the money market rate. Both facts resulted in a subsidy of about 0.38% of GDP from the Czech National Bank to foreign institutions.

Summing up, in Hungary and Romania the government seems to be the recipient of the lion's share of central bank seigniorage (and even more so in Hungary, thanks to the interest rate subsidy which accrues from foreign institutions). Moreover, in Romania both the central bank (through its gold reserves) and the domestic financial institutions also benefit considerably from the inflation tax. Austria, the Czech Republic and Germany instead clearly belong to a group of low-seigniorage central banks, with the Czech National Bank receiving a modest interest rate profit (beyond the opportunity cost) *from* the government, and paying subsidy *to* foreign institutions.

THE ROLE OF CENTRAL BANK INDEPENDENCE FOR SEIGNIORAGE

As has been shown in the previous sections, seigniorage collection can be an important source of revenue for the government. Modern central bank

---

[16] Strictly speaking, gains or losses on the net foreign position should be accounted to the banking rather than to the issuing department of the central bank, as they bear no relation to the monetary base. However, gains obtained on this position may be redistributed as subsidies to other sectors (as seems to be the case in Romania), together with seigniorage earned from seigniorage-earning liabilities (as defined in section 2.2.). Hence it is useful to take them into account in this context.

[17] Note that the Hungarian National Bank manages a significant part of the commercial banks' foreign exchange reserves and pays market interest rates on them.

[18] Calculations concerning the IMF are done in accordance with the IMF rules.

legislation as exemplified in the draft statutes of the ECB,[19] the Bundesbank Act or the Austrian National Bank Act[20] attempts to limit the generation of seigniorage by employing specific legal stipulations:
1. The prime objective of the central bank is to maintain price stability.
2. The central bank is prohibited from extending direct credit to the government (and government-controlled public entities). More generally, privileged access of the public sector to financial institutions is also banned.
3. In order to facilitate the adherence to (1) and (2), the central bank needs to be legally and politically independent of the government.
The aim of those stipulations is to establish a structure of rules and incentives which makes monetary abuse by the government impossible, i.e. the stipulations of the central bank law must not be overridden by other laws, e.g. the annual budget law. One way to look at this issue is to compare legislated central bank independence with actual practice, restricting the analysis to issues (prime task, provision regarding the extension of direct credit to the government) related to the generation and distribution of seigniorage.

From this viewpoint, the legal provisions in all three reform countries under consideration identify price stability as the prime objective of the central bank (see Table 12.4). Yet, the outcome is very different. It can be argued that inflation rates in reform countries in the range of 10–20% for some years after the implementation of the reform are consistent with stability-oriented monetary policy (this is, e.g. the case in the Czech Republic), because of sizeable price rises in the non-traded sector and further price level effects due to continued liberalization. However, this cannot be said for 3-digit inflation rates over several years, such as in Romania. Hence, we may conclude that the legal constraint on the rate of inflation has not been binding in some countries.

As has been analysed elsewhere (e.g. Hochreiter (1995) or Siklos (1994)), the new central banks of the countries under review have been given a high degree of legal and political independence. For the purpose of this study it is the degree of political independence that is of particular relevance.[21] In this context,

---

[19] Protocol on the Statute of the European System of Central Banks and of the European Central Bank.

[20] For a brief comparison between the Bundesbank, the Swiss National Bank and the Oesterreichische Nationalbank Acts see Hochreiter (1990).

[21] Note that political independence can be defined in different ways: It could refer to the process of *defining* the goal of monetary policy (e.g. a specific inflation target) or only to the process of *pursuing* that goal (i.e. to avoid deviations caused by political pressures). Furthermore, if the central bank wishes to influence the real economy and this can only be accomplished through the generation of 'inflation surprises', then the question of who defines the goal of monetary policy

not only the appointment procedures have to be considered (and which, in any case, do not deviate from the established practice in market economies where the central bank is independent) but in particular the reasons for dismissing the governor. In contrast to Czech legislation or that of the benchmark countries where the governor can only be removed if he commits a criminal offence or suffers from a terminal illness, the Hungarian central bank law is rather vague in this regard (e.g. unworthiness of office), while the Romanian central bank act does not specify reasons for dismissal at all (dismissal by parliament on recommendation of the prime minister). These formulations of the law may allow the government to exert pressure on the governor to pursue a more compliant, expansionary monetary policy, to devalue the currency or to extend (subsidized) credit to the government and/or loss-making (state) enterprises. In at least one case a central bank governor in one of these countries has resigned under pressure from the government. Note that these arguments can be brought in line with Cukierman's conclusion that more politically unstable countries collect a higher level of seigniorage (cf. Cukierman (1992, pp. 76)).

Interestingly, in many of the new central bank laws, there are quite strict limitations on the extension of direct credit to the government (and other public entities). In the case of Hungary, these limitations are even stricter than in Germany (before 1994) and in Austria (before mid-1995). Romania more recently has moved closer by limiting the access of the government to the central bank to 10% of the total approved budget (outlays). Nonetheless, this provision still has to be classified as rather weak. Moreover, and this is in marked difference to other reform countries, the Romanian National Bank extends (subsidized) credit to the banks, presumably to aid (loss-making) enterprises. This type of activity is yet another manifestation of the delayed process of reform in Romania.

The decisive point, however, is that the limitation to extend direct credit to the government has been respected in the Czech Republic, whereas the even stricter provisions in Hungary have been overridden by the budget law in every single year since the new law came into force in 1992.[22] As a result, while the 1993 (reported) consolidated government deficit in Hungary amounted to more than 7% of GDP, seigniorage appropriated to the government in that year came to 6.3% of GDP. Hence, almost all of the government deficit has been financed

---

is secondary. If, however, the idea is to increase the inflation tax (raise more seigniorage) to help in financing the public budget, then the question of who defines the goal of monetary policy becomes relevant.

[22] See Hochreiter (1995).

through seigniorage. It is likely that a similar statement could be made for Romania.

Seigniorage is also generated through reserve requirements. In this context we note that, while still higher than in Austria and Germany, the average level of reserve requirements in Hungary and Romania has been declining, up to 1993, from the very high levels of 1990–91. However, in Hungary bank reserves with the central bank were still, in 1993, an outstanding 15% of GDP. We must note, however, that a significant reduction in reserve requirements can only be phased in as the payments system becomes more efficient: until the latter operates with high volumes of float, reserve requirements must also be high, to provide the central bank with a buffer against risks in the system.[23]

In summing up we may conclude that there is, in Hungary and Romania, a sizeable gulf between legal and actual central bank independence and that this gulf is reflected in high inflation and actual (budget) legislation which overrides the – in most cases – rather strict provisions to severely limit direct credit to the government.

CONCLUSION AND RECOMMENDATIONS

In this paper we have analysed the process of the creation of central bank seigniorage (CBS) and its distribution among the macro sectors in three EITs for 1993, using Austria and Germany as reference countries. Our main findings (based on the opportunity cost approach and, for Romania, on the inflation tax approach) and recommendations may be summarized as follows:

1. CBS was 30 times higher than our benchmark value (defined as 1% GDP) in Romania, and 4 times higher in Hungary. This was due mostly to the high inflation rate in Romania,[24] and to the high ratio of central bank assets to GDP in Hungary. Austria, the Czech Republic and Germany were around the benchmark value.
2. High gold reserves (2.74% of GDP) helped Romania to raise a substantial amount of seigniorage.
3. CBS appropriated to the government was about 0.5% of GDP in Austria and

---

[23] The central bank earns seigniorage on reserve requirements, at the expense of the banking system, if the requirements are remunerated below the opportunity cost. However, it may 'refund' (part of) the cost to the banks, by supplying interest free float. See, e.g. Deutsche Bundesbank. Monthly Report, 1990, p.21.

[24] Since then inflation in Romania has steadily declined and, at the end of 1995, stood at around 25% p.a.

Germany, 6% in Hungary, and 20% in Romania. In Hungary and Romania, the bulk of CBS was in fact appropriated to the government. As a result, a large share of the government deficit has been financed by seigniorage. By contrast, the government appeared to receive no benefits from the central bank in the Czech Republic.

4. In Romania, the central bank received a subsidy on its net foreign liabilities equal to 12% of GDP. At the same time it distributed a subsidy of about 10% of GDP to domestic banks.

5. In principle, limitations on the extension of direct credit to the government by the central bank appear stricter in Hungary than in Germany. In practice these limitations can be overridden by the budget law. This has in fact happened in Hungary in every single year from 1992 to date. Prohibition or strict limitation of these overriding possibilities is the single most important reform we would advocate to enforce effective central bank independence.

6. Another recommendation concerns the reasons for the dismissal of central bank governors. In the central bank laws of Hungary and Romania these reasons are either specified too vaguely or simply unspecified. We suggest that the reasons for dismissal of the governor should instead be precisely determined, and related only to criminal offences or grave incapacity or illness.

7. Reserve requirements are a significant source of seigniorage creation in both Hungary and Romania. However, we recognize that reduction of the requirements can only proceed as long as the efficiency of the payments system is also improving, and as indirect instruments of monetary policy have been further developed.

REFERENCES

Begg, D. and R. Portes (1992): *Enterprise debt and economic transformation: Financial restructuring in Central and Eastern Europe*, in Colin Mayer and Xavier Vives (eds): *Capital markets and financial transformation*, Cambridge University Press, Cambridge.

Calvo, G. and F. Coricelli (1992): *Stabilizing a previously centrally planned economy: Poland 1990*, Economic Policy, 14, pp. 176–226.

Carlin, W. and C. Mayer (1992): *Restructuring enterprises in Eastern Europe*, Economic Policy, 15, pp. 311–346.

Caprio, G., D. Folkerts-Landau and T.D. Lane (1994): *Building Sound Finance in Emerging Market Economies*, International Monetary Fund and The World Bank, Washington D.C.

Cukierman, A. (1992): *Central Bank Strategy, Credibility, and Independence: History and Evidence*, MIT Press, Cambridge, MA.

Drazen, A. (1985): *A general measure of inflation tax revenues*, Economics Letters, 17, pp. 327–330.

Fry, M.J. (1993): *The Fiscal abuse of central banks*, IMF Working Paper, No. 93/58, July.

Gros, D. and G. Vandille (1995): *Seigniorage and the Inflation Tax in Economies in Transition*, CEPS, mimeo.

Hochreiter, E. (1990): *The Austrian National Bank Act – What does it say about Monetary Policy?*, Konjunkturpolitik, 36, pp. 245–256.

Hochreiter, E. (1995): *Central Banking in Economics in Transition*, in T.D. Willett, R.C.K. Burdekin, R.J. Sweeney and C. Wihlborg (eds): *Establishing Monetary Stability in Emerging Market Economies*, Westview Press, Boulder, CO., pp. 127–144.

Hochreiter, E., R. Rovelli and G. Winckler (1996): *Central banks and seigniorage: A study of three economies in transition*, European Economic Review, 40, pp. 629–643.

Klein, M. and M. Neumann (1990): *Seigniorage: What is it and who gets it?* Weltwirtschaftliches Archiv, pp. 205–221.

Perotti, E.C. (1995): *Inertia and arrears in transition economies*, mimeo.

Rovelli, R. (1994): *Reserve requirements, seigniorage and the financing of the government in an Economic and Monetary Union*, European Economy, Notes and reports, No. 1., pp. 11–55.

Siklos, P. (1994): *Central Bank Independence in Central Europe: A Preliminary Investigation of Hungary, Poland, The Czech and Slovak Republics*, in J.P. Bonin and I. Szekely (eds): *The Development and Reform of Financial Systems in Central and Eastern Europe*, Edward Elgar, Aldershot, pp. 71–98.

Winckler, G. and S. Butschek (1995): *Central Bank Seigniorage: A Comparative Study*, University of Vienna, mimeo.

Table 12.4. Central bank legislation relevant to the generation of seigniorage

Country	Price stability				Prohibition of fiscal financing		Overrides by budget law	Reserve requirements	
	legislated	target set by	target 1993 (1994)	inflation in % 1993 (1994)	legislated	exemptions		legislated	% (1993)
Austria	yes	Bank	fixed DEM-peg	3.6 (3.0)	yes	until mid-1995	no	yes	6, 7 and 9%
Germany	yes	Bank	M3	4.1 (3.0)	yes	no	no	yes	from 2–12.5%
Czech Republic	yes	Bank	fixed exchange rate	20.9 (10.0)	yes	5% of budget in previous year	no	yes	4 and 12%
Hungary	yes	Bank and Government	adjustable peg	22.5 (18.8)	yes	3% of budget revenue	yes	yes	14%
Romania	yes	Bank in cooperation with other state institutions	money supply	256.1 (136.8)	weak	10% of total approved budget	no but extensive refinancing of the banking system	yes	10% reduced to 5% after November 1993

Sources: National Bank Acts, BIS, IMF, national publications, Hochreiter (1995).

L33 L12
P31 G33

13. Collusive Trade Credit and Stabilization Policies

Enrico Perotti

INTRODUCTION

In the first stages of financial reform in a post-socialist economy, the tools available to the authorities in the absence of a strong regulatory and contractual framework are very blunt, consisting mostly of control over monetary and credit aggregates. However, financial discipline cannot be established by the central bank, as a successful stabilization depends on inducing firms to substitute internal finance for bank credit to fund operations. The necessary adjustment requires a process of restructuring which involves wage restraint, increases in productivity, changes in output composition, and layoffs. This process is clearly painful to a firm's insiders, and is likely to be resisted. When the monetary authorities attempt to force restructuring through a tight credit policy, there is a risk that enterprises will respond collusively, resisting by inertia any adjustment and building up unenforceable trade claims which soon become overdue. The political pressure caused by the sheer volume of bank and trade arrears is likely to result in an expansion of outside money by the authorities.

This chapter has the aim of illustrating the potential for a collusive creation of financial arrears, arising from the temptation even for potentially profitable firms to collude against a centralized imposition of credit discipline (Perotti, 1994 and 1998). The reason is that in the presence of a large number of value-subtractors, a tight initial credit stance will subtract more liquidity than the corporate sector may generate by internal restructuring. Lack of liquidity forces firms with no alternative sales outlet to accept trade credit from their traditional buyers. Easily available trade credit in turn encourages collusive resistance to restructuring, by ensuring the supply of inputs to illiquid firms.

There are serious potential costs associated with a high volume of arrears. First, there are significant imbalances across sectors and enterprises: thus the likely failure of direct enforcement of credit will result in illiquidity and financial rationing for viable enterprises, redistributing liquidity from the better to the worse firms (Ickes and Ryterman, 1993; Rostowski, 1993).[1]

Secondly, involuntary or collusive trade credit to non-creditworthy enterprises leads to a shortage of information on the true financial position of individual firms, challenging the development of independent financial intermediaries and hindering privatization.

Finally, the easy availability of collusive trade credit allows enterprises to finance unprofitable production, reducing the pressure (in the short term) to restructure operations.

The formal analysis underlying our approach is developed in Perotti (1998), and is summarized in a later section of this proposal. It is based on the notion that collective attitudes on the part of business managers reflect their rational expectations about the likely response by other state-owned business managers to a reduction in bank credit. These attitudes/expectations are crucial in determining their behavior and, ultimately, the whole of the microeconomic response to stabilization policy. (For evidence related to the Bulgarian state sector, see Kotzeva and Perotti (1995)).

The analysis shows that a main cause of the collective collusive incentives is the indiscriminate nature of *ex post* reflationary bail-outs. More generally, it is the confusion between the credit channels and the social safety net which causes political pressure for that relief, and pushes potentially reformable firms into becoming entangled with hopeless ones, in an attempt to delay or deflect the impact of restructuring. This results in a confusion between the subsidy and credit channels, and weakens the proper view of credit as unenforceable.

The ultimate challenge raised by this paper is to examine the possibility of a strategic credit policy aimed at discouraging collusion even in the context of such scanty information about the potential profitability of given enterprises.

THE ANALYTICAL APPROACH

No formal model can describe the economic behavior of enterprises and financial institutions in an economy in transition, unless it explicitly accounts for the many peculiar features of these economies. We describe here the analysis in Perotti (1998) which is based on a set of realistic microeconomic assumptions about the structure of the economy.

---

[1] For this reason it is impossible to compare the extent of trade credit in Eastern Europe with its levels in the West, where enforcement of credit terms and liquidation law is more reliable. Although receivables in arrears are common in the West, this is due to an established practice of paying trade credit with some delay to reduce working capital.

The first is the recognition of an inflexible trading structure (see also Dăianu, 1994). Because of the highly monopolistic structure of production under central planning, Eastern European firms have trading relations with few other firms, for which they may be also monopsonistic buyers. Thus the trading opportunities of enterprises, absent substantial restructuring of their productive and marketing structure, are closely linked to only a few other state-owned firms.

The second is the unreliability of contractual obligations, in the current situation of incomplete legislation and uncertain enforcement. In these circumstances, even creditworthy firms may not be relied upon to repay on time, and only direct pressure or a concern for reputation may elicit repayment.

A third element is that a significant proportion of enterprises are value-subtracting and have no chance of becoming productive. As a result, the aggregate response to a tight credit policy will be weakened as they drag their feet,[2] since their payment arrears could cause a chain reaction of insolvencies which will create pressure for financial relief and destroy incentives.

A fourth element is uncertainty over the government's determination to sacrifice loss of output in order to achieve macroeconomic stabilization.

Under relative favorable conditions, a tighter monetary policy will result in greater adjustment. Figure 13.1, which maps the percentage of enterprises adjusting as a function of the initial credit policy, shows that as credit is reduced there is some creation of illiquid trade credit, but adjustment does rise with tighter credit and achieves its maximum when credit is minimized. However, when initial conditions are sufficiently unfavorable in terms of enterprise-adjustment costs or initial credibility, even a modest degree of uncertainty may be sufficient to justify a collective effort to delay adjustment, relying on the limited ability of policymakers to face a massive failure in the enterprise sector without providing relief. In such a context, an excessively tight contraction of credit may actually reduce the extent of restructuring, inducing even potentially profitable firms to delay adjustment or to extend trade credit to non-creditworthy buyers. In other words, adjustment response in a weak economy following tight monetary policy may follow a 'Laffer' curve because of political considerations about policy sustainability. Figure 13.2 illustrates the interrelated effects at work.

At first, as credit is reduced, a few firms (namely, those with minimal adjustment costs) will restructure to avoid any risk of illiquidity. But the enterprise sector overall is unable to compensate fully for the loss of liquidity

---

[2] This attitude is likely to be shared by an enterprise in which insiders have an interest in overstating its present difficulties or understating its economic potential, in order to delay privatization or obtain ownership at minimal cost.

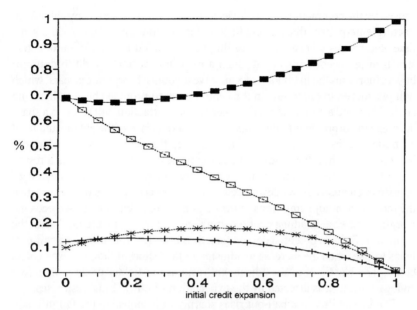

Figure 13.1. Adjustment under a credible program

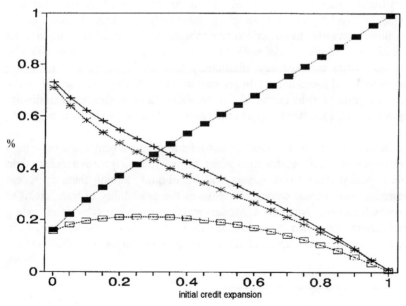

Figure 13.2. Adjustment under a program with low credibility

caused by the contraction of credit, because of the presence of many value-sub-tracting enterprises; thus, as credit is reduced, illiquidity rises. At the same time, enterprises whose buyers are illiquid are forced by the rigid productive structure to accept trade credit. Such a diffusion of trade credit to doubtful buyers increases the likelihood of a massive amount of corporate arrears, which will put increasing pressure on the central bank to provide cheap refinancing credit.[3] Beyond a certain level, a further credit contraction will result in a sharp decrease in corporate liquidity and a corresponding rise in the anticipated level of trade credits. As these become overdue, the probability of a bail-out increases, which in turn adds to the attractiveness of trade credit. As a result, the return to the option of 'no restructure' increases, and the degree of adjustment actually slows down because of tighter credit. This will occur when the ratio of non-adjusting firms to the degree of credit contraction exceeds the marginal increase in adjustment resulting from tighter bank credit; that is, the number of firms in potential default (and thus also the probability of a bail-out) tends to rise when the increase in adjustment falls short of the decrease in bank credit. The elasticity of the adjustment response to tighter credit is therefore endogenous, as it is affected by the expectation of other firms' responses.

The probability of a bail-out rises sharply in response to the fall in credit when the degree of adjustment decreases as credit is contracted; the result is a very rapid collapse in the degree of adjustment once credit falls below a certain threshold. As Figure 13.3 indicates, ultimately, the crucial factor is the credibility accorded to the government to withstand political pressure to resist reflation ('credibility' is defined here as the clearly perceived determination by the authorities to resist any inflationary bail-out in the face of mounting insolvency and social unrest). In general, lower credibility (measured by a low A in the graph) results in less adjustment; below a minimum initial credibility the authorities can afford only a limited degree of tightening to avoid triggering a collective inertial response.

In conclusion, in the face of considerable adjustment costs or a high proportion of unsalvageable enterprises, firms will anticipate that under a tight credit policy other firms' buyers will be illiquid, forcing them to accept (unenforceable) trade credit. This ensures the availability of trade credit to firms which resist adjustment. Moreover, it increases the value of extending trade credit even when the borrowing firm is known to be unable to service it, as it is expected that a longer chain of trade arrears will force a collective bail-out.

---

[3] The view that the credibility of stabilization programs in Eastern Europe suffered as a consequence of a tight credit policy was advanced in Calvo and Coricelli (1992), who focus on its credit crunch effects.

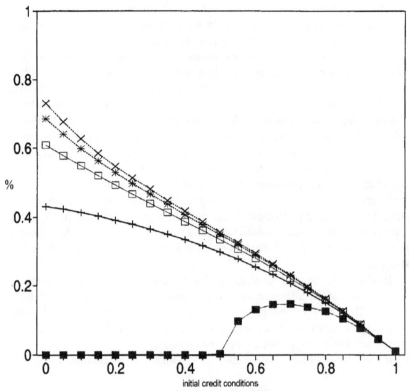

Figure 13.3. Adjustment as a function of credibility

DETERMINANTS OF COLLUSION

The cause of this perverse reversion in the degree of adjustment is the externality across firms' strategies through the possibility of a collective, indiscriminate bail-out. This collusive outcome may easily result from self-fulfilling expectations; because of this externality entering firms' restructuring decision-making, there are multiple equilibria. In particular, there are trivial collusive equilibria in which no firm is expected to adjust for any level of credit; then the degree of adjustment is always zero. Given that firms expect that the pressure on the monetary authorities to relieve them through concessionary credit will be irresistible if all enterprises extend trade credit, reasonable equilibrium behavior will be that none will restructure. However, the phenomenon does not require explicit collusion or self-fulfilling beliefs: it is sufficient for all firms to recognize the limited ability of the enterprise sector as a whole to compensate internally for a contraction in liquidity, which quite rationally leads to corresponding, inertia-encouraging attitudes.

It can be demonstrated that expectations about the percentage of firms which will choose to adjust are based rationally on the assumption that a firm will be willing to restructure only as long as it considers that the improved probability of survival is not outweighed by the adjustment costs borne by its insiders. Thus, under normal market conditions (namely a small proportion of value-subtracting firms and a central bank with an established reputation) more enterprises are induced to adjust as credit is progressively tightened. The higher the percentage of unprofitable, unsalvageable firms, the lower will be the expected adjustment response. Moreover, as the extent of restructuring affects the return to postpone restructuring for better firms as well, their impact is more than proportional to their actual number. In other words, marginal firms which could have adjusted would recognize the systemic effect of this subset of firms on the collective expectations of a bail-out, and will choose not to restructure.

In summary, the analysis suggests that the collusive outcome depends on:
- the ability of the corporate sector to generate liquidity by internal restructur-ing. This ability (and propensity) depends on whether the individual enterprise can adjust at a tolerable cost to its insiders. This is crucial, given the self-governing nature of most enterprises;
- the availability of alternative markets to which to redirect output away from illiquid clients;
- the number of value-subtractor enterprises for which restructuring is impossible. These have a direct effect on the level of internal financial compensation undertaken by enterprises to balance a reduction in bank credit;
- the degree of established credibility for monetary discipline awarded to the monetary authorities; while even the least possibility of a bail-out generates an externality effect (and thus reduces adjustment), the effect of lower credibility on the degree of adjustment is quite large;
- the lack of discrimination between firms in the bail-out process, which encourages potentially reformable firms to postpone the internal costs of restructuring;
- the historical reliance of Eastern European governments on the financial system as an instrument for the redistribution of resources and the subsidization of production.

This analysis of the causes of involuntary arrears and rational collusive arrears has serious implications for economic policy. The next section aims to identify the elements of a discriminative credit policy which would counteract such inertial behavior.

POLICY IMPLICATIONS

The conclusion from the graphical analysis is that, in the face of considerable adjustment costs and a high percentage of unsalvageable enterprises, firms will anticipate that under a tight credit policy other firms' buyers will be illiquid, forcing them to accept (unenforceable) trade credit. This ensures availability of trade credit to firms which resist adjustment. Ultimately, a massive chain of trade arrears may force a collective bail-out.

This raises the question of which institutional features might account for the varying importance of the inter-firm debt phenomenon in different countries. The evidence suggests that in countries which have succeeded in controlling inflation – Hungary, Czechoslovakia, and Poland – trade arrears did not display such explosive growth (Calvo and Coricelli, 1993; see also Balcerowicz and Gelb, 1994). Thus a reasonable conjecture is that stronger monetary credibility discourages the creation of arrears. In addition, the relative success in stabilization and adjustment within certain economies may at least in part reflect their proximity to Western markets, a more recent memory of market mechanisms, and more generally a more limited proportion of enterprises which have no chance of restructuring to adapt to a market economy at world prices. These advantages may have the indirect benefit of discouraging the inertia and implicit collusive behavior which undermines microeconomic adjustment. By contrast, in those economies in a vulnerable political and economic situation, and afflicted by considerable collusive instincts, monetary credibility may be best achieved by means of a steady progress in the tightening of credit conditions, rather than by the initial credit squeeze. However, the analysis so far has assumed a passive, indiscriminative bail-out policy, and a *de facto* confusion of the subsidy and credit channels. The ultimate goal is to examine the possible form of a credit policy which might discourage collusion even in the context of scarce information about the prospective profitability of individual enterprises. A discriminative credit and transfer policy may disentangle those enterprises able to be restructured from those with no future, thus creating the foundations for a credit market which rewards adjustment and discourages collusive strategies and inertial behavior.

The graphical analysis surveyed does offer a few guidelines to reduce the temptation to collude. This section analyses the possible policy choices under the assumption that a tight monetary policy, indispensable for stabilization and the construction of an inside money circuit with intermediation of savings, is likely to result in an excessive degree of illiquidity; this would create collective incentives to resist restructuring and gamble on an *ex post* reflation. Given the political and economic environment, these considerations may *a fortiori* have a bearing for the CIS countries. Graphically, this implies that the preferred monetary option lies on the left hand side of a Laffer curve (namely, the interval where a further reduction in total credit would reduce microeconomic adjustment).

The question is then how to direct a limited amount of credit in order to maximize restructuring, without unduly increasing the chance of a collapse in output which may by itself force a bail-out.

The first principle is to separate the credit and subsidy channels; the confusion between the two instruments is one of the connecting links between potentially reformable and unreformable firms. Such linkages nurture collusion, as reformable and unreformable firms will identify the opportunities to be lumped together, and will enjoy the resulting political clout.

The second principle is to channel limited funds to the recognized value-subtractors, thus delinking them from the creation of trade credit. These funds must be aimed at allowing these firms to remain solvent while they progressively reduce their scale of operations. An essential ingredient is that other firms must perceive these liquidity transfers as conditional on a whittling-down of productive activity.[4]

Separation of the Credit and Transfer Circuits

A general conclusion is that it will be necessary to untangle the destinies of different enterprises, in order to eliminate the externality effect of other firms' behavior on an individual firm's decisions. In particular, it is imperative to reduce the opportunism of firms which are perfectly capable of restructuring so as to be able to rely on internal finance, but are tempted to gamble on indiscriminate bail-outs. The ultimate goal is to allow the authorities to distinguish between strategic, collusive illiquidity and actual insolvency, and thus to take discriminatory action to counteract any expectation of unconditional, collective bail-outs.

A policy of conditional subsidies, rather than cheap credits, to the worse firms will reduce the proportion of firms which choose to resist restructuring. There are two reasons for this to be successful. The first is that a subsidy does not require repayment; this makes it possible to distinguish *ex ante* between

---

[4] Any extension of trade credit to these firms by other enterprises should either not be allowed, or repayment on new credits may be made subordinate to tax and other arrears.

binding credit and a pure transfer of financial resources, and thus to restrict the enforcement of credit terms only to those enterprises which may be able to fulfil them; in contrast, the extension of credit to firms with no such capability is indefensible. Moreover, such a financial transfer provides liquidity without adding to insolvency and without detracting from the restructuring, since these firms could simply not adjust. On the opposite side, credit which cannot be repaid has an indirect effect on the total number of insolvent firms: it introduces a perverse external influence on firms which are potentially able to restructure, but prefer to take refuge in collective insolvency.

On the other hand, notwithstanding the indirectly beneficial effect which giving subsidies to the unreformable firms has in disciplining other firms (as insolvency is now separated from illiquidity), their direct effect on the receiving firm is clearly one of disincentive.[5]

The terms of such transfers must, therefore, include explicit terms and conditions governing any future outlay, and some form of *ex post* sanction for failure to meet such conditions. First, they should be directed through state or foreign-sponsored institutions directly involved in supervising the welfare aspects of the downsizing and restructuring process of value-subtractors, and which are not involved in industrial policy. Secondly, these transfers must be clearly designed to be sharply reduced over time. Thirdly, they may in part at least be linked with privatization and a decrease in state-financed operations. Fourthly, any future extension of working capital subsidies may be linked to a progressive scaling down of operations; firms which reduce inventories more than the average, for instance, may be rewarded with higher transfers. Although the credit expansion required for these transfers will be reflected in higher current inflation, it would be conducive to lower inflation tomorrow if it succeeded in scaling down the value-subtracting sector without causing an illiquidity crisis. Finally, smaller firms should largely be ignored since their relative flexibility carries greater potential for adjustment, and their liquidation may in fact nurture the transfer of productive assets to the private sector.

The Retreat of the State From Directed Credit

The analysis in the appendix concludes that while bank- and trade-financed

---

[5] A possible rationale for a policy of directed state loans to hopeless firms may be that in theory it grants the state the ability to demand repayment and, upon insolvency, declare bankruptcy and replace management, when other forms of direct control may fail (for a related argument, see Legros and Mitchell (1993)). However, such a policy is unrealistic and thus lacks credibility, both for the limited bargaining power and managerial capacity of the state and the limited enforceability of bankruptcy laws in the region.

firms have similar incentives to gamble on a bail-out, firms which must rely on trade credit are more likely to be cash-constrained, and have thus more incentives to restructure. In addition to this direct effect, directed state credit programs have a history of developing beyond the size originally intended. In a situation of financial repression and highly negative interest rates, it is likely that massive effort will be directed at rent-seeking and political lobbying for access to credit. Evidence from various countries in the region suggests that a few large enterprises and sectors capture most of the state-directed credit. Thus it must be recognized that, in the presence of a large directed state credit program, the distribution of state credit is likely to become concentrated, and permanently commandeered by large value-subtractors or large enterprises in sectors concentrated vertically or geographically.

The implication is that state credit programs can hardly avoid maintaining a policy of renewed financing to its borrowers, thus becoming *de facto* subsidy transfer channels.

An aggravating effect is that politically it becomes impossible to refuse credit to any one sector while extending financing to another. In fact, the ability of the state to enforce credit terms is probably much weaker than for other institutions, particularly private banks, which have no welfare obligations and thus can be more ruthless in enforcing partial liquidation or bankruptcy. This is consistent with the idea of privatization as a tool to toughen commitment by the state not to intervene *ex post* to bail out unprofitable ventures.

Exceptions to this principle may be made for specific lending programs whose purpose is to increase incentives for restructuring or sensitivity to financial constraints, such as in the case of the financing of demergers or buy-outs. Evidence gathered on enterprise behavior in the region suggests that credit terms are perceived to be stringently binding for smaller firms. Thus directed credit should be aimed to induce large, unprofitable firms to reduce the scale of operations.

More practically, for the larger enterprises it is more feasible to adopt outright transfer programs conditional on downsizing than to control directed credit schemes which have the potential to affect incentives for improper credit and financial irresponsibility.

CONCLUSION

The analysis has shown that the risk of an *ex post* bail-out increases when the liquidity subtracted is only partially compensated by a limited adjustment by the enterprise sector; the result is an endogenous increase in the number of enterprises choosing to rely on trade credit. A tighter credit policy is self-defeating if the probability of a future reflation increases significantly. However, the main cause of a limited, collusive adjustment response for potentially profitable firms remains the expected lack of discrimination between firms in the clearing process. The credibility of an initial credit restriction is greater, the stronger the commitment to discriminate *ex post* between firms.

This suggests that any future form of financial relief must be made explicitly contingent on restructuring and downsizing programs which are likely to be costly for insiders. This may induce firms to self-select on the basis of their potential for adjustment, as the insiders in the better enterprises would have greater incentives to avoid painful and unnecessary downsizing.

This suggestion is quite consistent with the modern view of credit, which envisages creditors as exercising effective constraints on the action of enterprises through the threat of a loss of control over assets, either partial (liquidation) or total (bankruptcy, lay-off of management). It is also consistent with the notion that control is valuable in itself, and that its benefits arise from an opportunistic use of assets. Thus, if the maximization of the scale of assets under control is a natural objective for Western managers, it is even more true for Eastern European managers, who are less constrained by owners or supervisory boards and whose compensation is even less related to profits.

REFERENCES

Balcerowicz, L. and A. Gelb (1994): *Macropolicies in Transition to a Market Economy; A Three-Year Perspective*, Proceedings of the World Bank Annual Conference on Development Economics.

Calvo, G. and F. Coricelli (1992): *Stabilizing a Previously Centrally Planned Economy: Poland 1990*, Economic Policy, vol. 13, pp. 175–208, 213–226.

Calvo, G. and F. Coricelli (1993): *Credit Market Imperfections and Output Response in Previously Centrally Planned Economies*, mimeo, International Monetary Fund: Washington, D.C.

Clifford, E. and M. Kahn (1993): *Enterprise Arrears in Transforming Economies: The Case of Romania*, International Monetary Fund Staff Papers, vol. 40, no. 3, pp. 680–696.

Coricelli, F. and G. Milesi-Ferretti (1993): *On the Credibility of 'Big-Bang' Programs: A Note on Wage Claims and Soft Budget Constraints in Economies in Transition*, European Economic Review, vol. 37, pp. 387–395.

Dăianu, D. (1994): *Inter-Enterprise Arrears in a Post-Command Economy: Thoughts from a Romanian Perspective*, International Monetary Fund Working Paper WP 94/54, Washington, D.C.

Fan, Q. and M. Schaffer (1993): *Government Financial Transfers and Enterprise Adjustment in Russia*, CEP working paper, no. 394, London School of Economics.

Ickes, B. and R. Ryterman (1993): *Roadblock to Economic Reform: Inter-Enterprise Debt and the Transition to Markets*, Post-Soviet Affairs, vol. 9, pp. 231–252.

Kotzeva, M. and E. Perotti (1995): *Exogenous and Opportunistic Financial Arrears: Evidence from a Survey of Bulgarian State Managers*, mimeo, Central European University, Prague.

Legros, P. and J. Mitchell (1993): *Bankruptcy as a Control Device in Economies in Transition*, mimeo, Cornell University.

Mitchell, J. (1993): *Creditor Passivity and Bankruptcy: Implications for Economic Reform*, in: C. Mayer and X. Vives (eds): *Capital Markets and Financial Intermediation*, Cambridge University Press: Cambridge, New York, and Melbourne.

Perotti, E. (1993): *Bank Lending in Transition Economies*, Journal of Banking and Finance, no. 17, pp. 1021–32.

Perotti, E. (1994): *A Taxonomy of Post-Socialist Financial Systems: Decentralized Enforcement and the Creation of Inside Money*, Economics of Transition, vol. 2, pp. 71–81.

Perotti, E. (1998): *Inertial Credit and Opportunistic Arrears in Transition*, European Economic Review, vol. 42, pp. 1703–1725.

Roland, G. and T. Verdier (1994): *Privatization in Eastern Europe: Irreversibility and Critical Mass Effects*, Journal of Public Economics, vol. 54, pp. 161–183.

Rostowski, J. (1993): *The Inter-Enterprise Debt Explosion in the former Soviet Union: Causes, Consequences, Cures*, CEP Discussion paper no. 142, London School of Economics.

283- 300

G2I P34
G28

14. Banks in the Czech Republic: Current State and Prospects

Petr Zahradník

THE TRANSITION OF THE CZECH BANKING SECTOR

The first step in the transformation of the Czech banking sector was taken on the basis of principles adopted even before November 1989. The monobank structure of Czech banking had already been dismantled on 1 January 1990. The former State Bank of Czechoslovakia (SBČS), which both defined monetary policy and provided commercial banking under the conditions of a centrally-planned economy, was restructured to become an independent central bank. The functions of commercial banking began to be carried out by the existing commercial banks, until then visibly subordinate to the SBČS (*Česká státní spořitelna, Československá obchodní banka, Živnostenská banka* in the Czech Republic, and Slovak State Savings Bank in Slovakia), as well as by the newly-established successors to the SBČS in the commercial sphere (*Komerční banka* in the Czech Republic, and *Všeobecná úverová banka* in Slovakia) supplemented by *Investiční banka*, already an established bank at that time, which took over some activities of the former SBČS.

This initial structure has determined the still-incomplete transition of the former Czechoslovak (and current Czech) banking sector. However, the range of products offered as well as the level of competition have already improved significantly in comparison with its previous underdeveloped state. Four of the most important banks (*Komerční banka, Česká spořitelna, Investiční a Poštovní banka, Československá obchodní banka*) have undergone partial privatization and currently the state has only a minor stake in their ownership. Efforts to reform the banking sector have focused on improving the balance sheets of the banks – those both with inherited non-performing loans issued before 1990 and 'newly created' non-performing loans resulting from activities since 1990. Many banks, especially the larger ones, have made significant progress in building up loan provisions to levels comparable with international standards.

THE CURRENT STATE OF THE CZECH BANKING SECTOR

It is possible to divide the Czech banking sector into the following broad groupings according to their position and influence in the bank market:
1. Larger banks, most of them existing before 1990.
2. Newly-created domestic banks, most of which are small or medium-sized.
3. Foreign banks, which can be formed as branches in association with domestic ones, or a legal Czech concern with 100% foreign capital participation.
4. Specialized banks.
In addition, there are currently six banks going into liquidation.

An alternative view of the Czech banking sector, which partially corrects the previous view, can be made on the basis of foreign participation in banks operating on Czech territory. This participation varies from zero to 100%. According to this view, the Czech banking system comprises Czech banks, banks with minor foreign capital participation, and banks with major foreign capital participation (incl. branches of foreign banks). In the middle of October 1996, after *První slezská banka* and *Kreditní banka* lost their licences, there were effectively 53 banks in the Czech market. Of these 13 have no foreign capital participation (including three specialized banks *Česká exportní banka*–Czech Export Bank, *Českomoravská záruční a rozvojová banka*–Czech-Moravian Guarantee and Development Bank, and *Českomoravská hypoteční banka*–Czech-Moravian Mortgage Bank), a foreign partner has minor participation in 16 of them (including the five largest banks, where the foreign partner´s share is very low, and six building savings banks), and in 24 banks a foreign partner has more than 50% capital participation (including *Bankovní dům SKALA* and *Živnostenská banka*) with a number of them having 100% capital participation by a foreign bank (of those foreign banks operating on the Czech territory, 10 are branches of foreign banks and 12 are registered as Czech legal entities with 100% capital participation by a foreign partner). On 23 May 1996, the Czech National Bank (CNB) granted two new licences to operate in the Czech market to *Westdeutsche Landesbank* and *Midland Bank*.

The Largest Czech Banks

As Tables 14.1–14.4 show, the five largest banks maintain their privileged position across the whole spectrum of the banking sector. This ascendancy is clear enough in the case of the structure of total assets and credits, but absolutely glaring in the case of deposits. The shares of deposits increased considerably after 1994, when some smaller banks (first *Banka Bohemia* followed by *AB Banka, Kreditní a prùmyslová banka, Česká banka, První slezská banka*, and *Kreditní banka*) went into bankruptcy.

Table 14.1. Market shares of the largest Czech banks
(%, 31 December 1995)

	Total assets	Deposits	Credits
Komerční banka	22	25	25.9
Česká spořitelna	19.9	31	13.6
Československá obchodní banka	10.9	9.3	9.2
Investiční a Poštovní banka	10.9	11.2	13.7
Agrobanka	3.8	5.2	4.9

Source: Patria Finance, 1996.

Table 14.2. Market shares of the largest Czech banks
(billion CZK, 31 December 1995)

	Total assets	Deposits	Credits
Komerční banka	407.2	237.7	227.2
Česká spořitelna	367.8	295	119.3
Československá obchodní banka	201.6	88.1	80.8
Investiční a Poštovní banka	201.4	106.7	120.1
Agrobanka	69.5	49.5	43
(Konsolidační banka)	*123.3*	*73.8*	*73.1*

Source: Patria Finance, 1996.

Table 14.3. Concentration in the Czech banking industry by market shares
(%, 31 December 1995)

	Total assets	Deposits	Credits
Total of the five largest banks	67.5	81.7	67.3
Other banks	32.5	18.3	32.7
Total	100	1 00.0	100

Source: Patria Finance, 1996.

The clients' confidence in the health of a bank is measurable and expressed most objectively by market share in the sphere of deposits, where the five largest banks hold more than 80% of total deposits. Considering that some – especially foreign – banks offer private banking services for well-placed clients and those with large balances, space in the deposit market is very limited for small and medium-sized banks; in other words, the preference by depositors for large banks is obvious.

Table 14.4. Concentration in the Czech banking industry by assets and liabilities (billion CZK, 31 December 1995)

	Total assets	Deposits	Credits
Total of the five largest banks	1,247.5	777	590.4
Other banks	600.7	173.6	286.8
Total banks	1,848.2	950.6	877.2

Source: Patria Finance, 1996.

Small and Medium-sized Banks

Small and medium-sized banks were established after 1990. Their subsequent development showed that although the need for expansion in the banking sector was enormous, the services offered by most of the small and medium-sized banks were almost identical and competition among them especially fierce. Only first-class management and a reasonable degree of specialization in, at least, a partial product allow the banks to survive and develop some prospects.

Although the banks had an indisputable advantage in having no risky credits hanging over from the past, the huge upsurge in new entrepreneurial activities also brought with it many risky projects of doubtful quality. In the face of intensified competition and the enormous boom in banking credit operations, small and medium-sized banks endeavored to secure a firmer place in the banking market through a disproportionate and unhealthy credit expansion. Compared to the larger or the foreign banks operating in the Czech Republic, their ratio of credits to total assets has been the highest in the banking sector, despite a natural decrease in the past years (in 1991 more than 85%, in 1992 81%, and in 1993 72%).

Specialized Banking Institutions

Specialized state banking institutions

Konsolidační banka (Consolidation Bank, KOB) is a specialized state banking institution established in 1990 to help consolidation in the banking sector, taking over existing short-term, non-performing loans from *Komerční banka, Investiční banka* a *Československá obchodní banka*. In 1992 KOB purchased another package of underperforming loans from Komerční banka and Investiční banka. Management of these claims at more favorable interest rates and their restructuring was the main activity of the bank until 1994.

However, the new management of the bank has contributed substantially to its present, more active, role. Management of the so-called 'old block' of claims currently represents only one of the activities undertaken by the bank. Within the framework of the realization of government industrial projects, the bank is now focused on other credit activities. The ratio of new and old credits is currently 1:5.

Recently, KOB has been engaged in the recovery of Czech banking in a different way. In close cooperation with the Czech National Bank, KOB took over the management of Ekoagrobanka, a medium-sized bank which has been in deep financial trouble. Currently, along with the adaptation of the recovery program, the final phase of the search for a strategic partner for Ekoagrobanka is in progress. A series of restructuring and revitalization programs for large Czech companies is another very important activity of the bank. Finally, KOB is engaged in the financing of long-term projects within infrastructure and utilities and for environmental protection.

Despite some criticisms about the excessive and ill-advised influence of KOB as an extended arm of the state, especially on the structure of industry, and possibly also affecting underperforming companies, we can observe not only the dramatic transformation in the quality of the bank itself, but also its positive influence on some companies under its management.

Česká exportní banka (Czech Export Bank, ČEB) is a specialized state banking institution with specific objectives in export promotion and financing. It offers export financing with state support. The Czech government has granted the bank an explicit guarantee to repay any obligations resulting from borrowing on the capital and money markets for the purpose of providing financing on preferential terms. The preferential terms are related especially to the interest rate and the length of credit. The state guarantee enables the bank to enjoy optimum conditions for fund-raising, in principle at the same rating as received by the Czech Republic or the Czech National Bank.

To be granted preferential terms by ČEB, exporters must fulfill the following conditions:
1. Exports of goods must be provided under standard conditions.
2. A minimum 60% of the value of exports must be of Czech origin.
3. Export credits must be insured by EGAP (Export Guarantee and Insurance Company).
4. A minimum 15% of the contract value must be paid by the importer in cash, either in advance or upon delivery.
5. The goods must be exported on a medium-/long-term credit basis (at least 2 years, maximum 10 years).
6. The exporter must be resident or a legally recognized concern within the Czech Republic.

By 1999 ČEB plans to extend credits amounting to approximately CZK 20 billion a year with a proportional increase in fund-raising on international capital and money markets, especially for funds of medium and long-term maturities. It is evident that the position of ČEB will reflect state requirements for the support of exports. We expect a stronger emphasis on the quality of credit operations and the preparation of a strategy focused on the intentions of the state concerning the sectoral and territorial structure of exports of the Czech Republic.

Specialized private banking institutions

In accordance with the Law on Banking, among 52 effectively operating banks there are also 6 building savings banks (*AR s.s.*, *Českomoravská s.s.*, *ČS-ST*, *Hypo s.s.*, *Všeobecná s.s.*, *Wüstenrot*). The strongest position among them belongs to *Českomoravská* (45% share on the relevant market). The other building savings banks have the following shares: *AR* (17%), *ČS-ST* (16%), *Všeobecná* (12%), *Wüstenrot* (8%), *Hypo* (2%). In addition, the CNB granted to 5 banks licences to provide mortgage products and services (*Českomoravská hypoteční banka, Bayerische Vereinsbank, Česká spořitelna, Komerční banka, HYPO-BANK CZ*).

Rating

Recent activity by the international rating agencies has been focused not only on the evaluation of particular banks (and evaluations concerned with some particular operations of theirs) but also of the Czech banking sector as a whole.

Standard & Poor´s long-term evaluation 'A' (investment part of the rating chart, or the area recommendable for investments, to put it another way) for the Czech banking sector means the best possible evaluation (the same as for the Czech National Bank or the Czech Republic as a whole). In other words, it is impossible to have a better evaluation, unless that of the Czech Republic is improved. Among the countries of Central and Eastern Europe, Czech banking was evaluated as the best. The others received positions in the speculative part of the rating chart, for example Hungary has 'BB+', Poland and Slovakia 'BB'.

However, the evaluation contains the following negative findings:
1. Insufficient control and internal audit.
2. Lack of objective information about the financial position of the banks.
3. Inadequate experience in risk analysis.
4. Unsuitable arrangement for taxation of unprofitable credits.

It is a moot point whether the positive attitude of S&P reflects confidence in state support for the major Czech banks in the case of difficulties. Regarding the very strong connections between the banking and industrial sectors, the rating agencies presuppose that the central bank and the state will help in a case where banks have problems which might erode confidence in the banking sector, or cause a negative 'domino effect' in the industrial sphere.

It shows that the central bank and the state use selective policy measures depending on the possible scale of the domino effect. The fact that the largest banks are, in case of need, almost certainly underwritten by the state or the central bank raises the rating of those banks as well as of the banking sector as a whole.

Moody's evaluation of particular banks was the subject of the second of the renowned rating agencies. Its results are given in the Table 14.5.

Table 14.5. Moody's ratings of Czech banks

Bank	Long-term evaluation	Short-term evaluation	Financial strength
Česká spořitelna	Baa2	Prime – 2	D
Komerční banka	Baa2	Prime – 2	D+
ČSOB	Baa2	Prime – 2	D+
IPB	Baa2	Prime – 2	D
Agrobanka	Ba1	Not Prime	E+

Source: Patria Finance, 1996.

These evaluations of the financial strength of banks are intended to provide investors with a measure of a bank's 'intrinsic safety and soundness'. Accordingly, the ratings exclude most external credit risks and support. The financial strength rating is a globally comparable indicator covering different countries and currencies. The need to use the financial strength indicator is based on the fact that the traditional bank rating, which is often influenced by external factors, has frequently diverged from a 'pure financial strength'. That occurs most frequently in two circumstances:

1. In those countries with guaranteed state support, some low bank ratings may be raised on the basis that they are too important to the economy to be allowed to fail, and as a result ratings diverge substantially from what they would be if the banks were rated solely on their own merits.
2. In countries with low rating ceilings for the economic area as a whole, high and very favorable bank ratings may be deflated by this ceiling. (A particular evaluation cannot be better than that of the economic area as a whole. In this case external risks overshadow considerations of 'pure financial strength'.)

The situation with the ratings of the major Czech banks shows that the first factor especially plays a very topical role, because one could anticipate that the largest banks are, for many reasons (including social and political ones), 'too large to fail' and therefore guaranteed by the state or the central bank.

The third of the renowned rating agencies, IBCA, focused on limited rating activities with the results described in Table 14.6.

Table 14.6. IBCA ratings of Czech banks

Bank	Long-term	Short-term	Individual
Česká spořitelna	BBB+	A2	C/D
Komerční banka	A-	A2	C
Živnostenská banka	–	–	B/C

Source: Patria Finance, 1996.

THE DEVELOPMENT OF DEPOSITS

In the Czech Republic, deposits traditionally represent the most important part of the financial assets of a household. Despite the fact that privatization and the reform of the financial sector has given a significant boost to other types of financial assets, deposits have remained the first choice of private savers.

During the transformation period, the development of deposits and other monetary aggregates has reacted sensitively to the confidence of the Czech population in the domestic currency. Analysing the period of the independent Czech Republic, certain changes were visible especially in the time just before and just after the division of Czechoslovakia. At that time, the most liquid elements of the money supply were reacting the most sensitively. In 1992, 88.9% of the total money assets of the population were kept in local currency, with term deposits predominating. Since that time, a limited growth of deposits in foreign currency has occurred (as a consequence of the decline in confidence in the domestic currency and also the expectation of currency depreciation, as well as increased opportunities to work abroad, together with a boom in the tourist industry). In 1992, deposits in the domestic currency increased by 11.1% (term deposits by 14.5%, sight deposits by 3.5%) while those in foreign currencies increased by almost 100%. These factors, accompanied by the accelerating propensity to consume, led to a substantial decrease in the rate of savings. Total sight deposits by households and companies, along with cash, decreased by a substantial CZK 41 billion in the first quarter of 1993. Time deposits of household savings increased by CZK 10 billion in the same period. After this period of sensitive and volatile development, the tension was markedly relieved and followed by development without important deviations.

Within the structure of deposits, a privileged position is held by a small group of banks led by *Česká spořitelna*. Despite the leading position of that bank in the area of deposits, we can observe a declining share by *Česká spořitelna* in the total market for deposits, due especially to the decision by the enterprise sector to place its deposits with the other banks.

Table 14.7. Average interest rates from primary deposits compared with the rate of inflation (in %)

	1990	1991	1992	1993	1994	1995
Interest rate	3.2	9.1	8.3	7.6	6.9	7
Rate of inflation	9.9	56.9	11.1	20.8	10	9.1

Source: Patria Finance, 1996.

From the point of view of the total money supply, the growth of M2 has tended to accelerate compared with cash and sight deposits. The rapid growth of M2 has recently been influenced especially by term and savings deposits, and also by commercial ones. Simultaneously, the share of household savings deposits in the domestic currency has been declining steadily. Therefore, sight deposits represent in absolute terms the most slowly developing part of the money supply, and in relative terms a shrinking proportion of the total money supply as well as of M1.

Table 14.8. Structure of the money aggregate M2 (in %, end of period)

	1992	1993	1994	1995
Currency in circulation	9.9	8.3	9.5	10
Sight deposits	41.3	41.6	39	33.5
Term deposits	39.5	42.1	44.5	48
Deposits in foreign currency	9.3	8	7	8.5

Source: Czech National Bank, Patria Finance, 1996.

Households in the Czech Republic prefer bank deposits (short-term sight deposits, because a growing number of personal income and expenditure arrangements are made through the corresponding accounts, and also long-term savings deposits) to the other forms of money investment in different financial instruments.

Household Deposits

Household deposits represent the most important source of capital creation and the decisive part of the structure of the money aggregate M2. However, during the transition period their share of the total money supply as measured by M2 has been declining (the share of household deposits amounted to 52.5% in 1990, while in 1995 it was 44%). Household deposits have increased absolutely and are undoubtedly preferred by the Czech population. On the other hand, there is an unambiguous decline in the percentage of household deposits within total deposits in the banking sector. It is related both to sight deposits and time deposits (in 1990, the share of household deposits in total deposits was 59.1%, in 1995 it was 49%).

During the transition period the population has proven very sensitive and rational in its reactions and behavior. The expectations of price liberalization at the turn of 1990 and 1991 increased the propensity of population to consume, which at the beginning led to a decrease in dynamism in the savings accounts market and for a time even to an absolute decline in deposits.

If, in the period before transformation, the main motive for saving was the expectation of the future consumption of consumer durables, and only a fraction of savings was directed towards the creation of general financial reserves, the ratio is now quite the opposite. We conclude that creating financial reserves seems to be a stronger motive than acquiring future consumer durables.

In the past a deviation in household deposits represented a very important factor which influenced the development of the total money supply. Also in the past, expectations and estimates about the likely behavior of households were relatively reliable, including regularly-repeated, seasonal patterns. The share of household deposits in the total money supply was high. Unexpected deviations were almost excluded. The public used to accumulate more than 80% of its reserves in the form of banking deposits, almost 100% of them in *Česká spořitelna*. The current pattern of savings is substantially different. It is characterized by irregular development and a generally declining share in the money supply. In the long term, there will be a growing number of term and savings deposits.

Deposits in building savings banks have had a very dynamic development but their volume is so far fairly marginal. We can expect a steady and stable growth in these kinds of household financial reserves.

Commercial Deposits

The declining proportion of household deposits to total deposits has gradually been balanced by the growing proportion of commercial deposits. In the first period of transformation, this was not the case, because the main factor in the growing demand for transaction money was the creation of a completely new economic structure with a number of small and private economic units. In subsequent years, this was accompanied by factors associated with the recovery of economic growth in 1993 and 1994, which led to an increase in commercial deposits as well as to some changes in their structure. The gradual consolidation of the private sector has led to a higher visibility in the share of term deposits (from about 7% in 1990 to more than 30% in 1996).

CREDIT DYNAMICS

The growth of the total credit issue has been determined especially by the growth of credits to the private sector. Credits to individuals have been gradually declining.

Table 14.9. Total volume and development of credits in the banking sector (in billion CZK)

	1992	1993	1994	1995
Denominated in domestic currency	567.8	672.9	776.5	825.7
Denominated in foreign currency	16.9	28.6	45.7	104.3
Total	584.7	701.5	822.2	930

Source: Patria Finance, 1996.

Since 1991, the time structure of credits has gradually changed. In the first transformation phase, there was a decline in short-term credits, a visible increase in the share of medium-term credits, and a modest decline in long-term credits. However, currently, there is a marked improvement in the role of short-term credits. This is partially based on limitations in the long-term resources of banks, and especially on the banks' effort to minimize the risks associated with the rise of non-performing loans.

In comparison with previous years, the dynamics of non-performing loans has substantially declined. At the end of the first quarter of 1996, the value of non-performing loans amounted to CZK 318 billion. In a year-on-year comparison, the value of non-performing loans has increased by about CZK 25 billion (8.5%), while in 1994 non-performing loans compared to the previous year reached CZK 140 billion (92%).

From a total volume of credits of CZK 930 billion, the share of non-performing loans amounts to about 35% of the total portfolio. At the end of 1994, the share was 38.6% (CZK 327 billion), and after a slight increase in mid-1995 to record levels, we have observed a gradual decline in the share of risky credits.

The figures do not, however, distinguish between the weights of particular classified non-performing loans based on the degree of risk involved. The important decline in non-performing loans in the first phase of this year is connected with the following factors:

1. AB Banka, Česká banka, and Kreditní a prùmyslová banka were excluded from the observed data.
2. Several banks wrote off the most risky and loss-making credits from their provisions.

The introduction of the external convertibility of the Czech koruna and interest differential have accelerated the inflow of foreign credits into the Czech economy. In the first half of 1995, foreign credits even became the most important source of foreign capital inflow. The balance of foreign credits passed the CZK 100 billion level at the end of 1995 and their average interest rate was lower than 9%. At the same time, recent developments show a decline in the share of long-term credits (over five years) in favor of short-term ones. The most important borrowers of syndicated foreign loans are major banks (almost all the large banks, plus Živnostenská banka) as well as non-financial companies (ČEZ, SPT Telecom).

While the foreign debts of the private sector represented less than one-quarter of total Czech long-term foreign obligations at the beginning of 1993, their current share amounts to more than one-half.

THE PROSPECTS FOR THE CZECH BANKING SECTOR

Creation of Non-performing Loans

It is possible to distinguish two phases in the emergence of non-performing loans. The first appeared at the time of restructuring from the former SBČS and represented not only credits which were granted under the previous economic system for ineffective projects, but also credits to industries without prospects, facing closure or the restructuring of a number of companies due to the economic transformation, and especially long-term credits with a mainly social motive and at very low interest rates. Universally, they were inherited credits.

The second phase of the emergence of non-performing loans was related to the newly-established banks or those expanding markedly after 1990. This phase is entirely the responsibility of the management of new or inexperienced banks, which were simply not prepared for operation under the new conditions. The total number of projects financed from banking credits has multiplied several times. It is possible to discern some of very poor quality. In addition, some of the newly established banks were created to finance doubtful projects primarily belonging to their own shareholders. The range of such credits, which exceeded the limits of caution, has led to a worsening in quality of the credit portfolio in the banking sector as a whole.

A more consistent attitude on the part of the central bank and the strengthening of the financial positions of a number of banks could prevent new credit being extended to unsound concerns, and encourage the development of long-term credit and the broadening of the service offered by the banks to particular types of clients (e.g. widening credit relations with small and medium-sized companies, or offering investment banking services to larger companies).

Adequacy of Reserves

For the period 1994–1995 the massive creation of provisions for classified non-performing and risky credits and credit losses was typical. There were very important differences between the attitudes of large and small banks to the central bank's provision policy as well as in the consequences of this policy.

The obligation to create provisions applies to all banks without exception. The larger banks have taken their duties seriously from the very beginning, creating some provision at the time the problem started to be relevant. In the course of time, they have now increased the volume of provisions to a level which is acceptable according to the international auditors' statements.

On the other hand, in a number of cases the smaller banks minimized or ignored completely the need to create provisions. The increase in provisions has been slow and lengthy. In some cases, the profit created has been distributed to pay dividends rather than to strengthen the creation of provisions.

In the current turmoil in the small banks sector insufficient provision and low capital adequacy are probably the main factors that could lead to some changes in the banking sector as a whole. The inability to create a sufficient volume of provisions according to the central bank's criteria, as well as the undercapitalization of a number of small banks and excessively risky exposure to one client, could lead to some important changes in the Czech banking sector in the coming period. Accordingly, we can expect a spectacular wave of mergers among the small banks themselves (a failed small bank with another, successful small bank), between a small bank and a large bank, or, in some cases, even with the participation of a foreign partner. The last version is, however, only likely in the case of a bank with long-term prospects.

Privatization Prospects

So far the state still controls – as in the other Central European transitional economies – important equity stakes in the Czech banks. It is a very relevant, but so far not quite clearly answered, question: how will these stakes be dealt with in the future? Will the state adopt the same attitude to all privatized banks, or will the banks be privatized differently? Will the simple replacement of state ownership by private ownership be preferred, or does privatization come with some additional features? Among the other expectations we can mention, for example, the improvement in the international prestige of a bank (which can be attributed especially to privatization through a portfolio investor), or the quality of management and the adoption of new banking technology and know-how (which can be attributed especially to the participation of a strategic direct investor). It is evident that each of the Czech banks to be privatized has currently somewhat different requirements and expectations from privatization.

There are further questions to be answered – for example, whether the investor should be domestic or foreign. The current situation shows that both the banks themselves and the National Property Fund and the government prefer foreign investors.

Privatization is not the only way for foreign partners to participate and invest in the Czech banking sector. Some medium-sized and small banks with a strong performance can also be very attractive to foreign investors. After the privatization and consolidation process is completed, Czech banking as a whole will become a very attractive sector.

Last but not least, cutting into the notorious vicious circle among the large banks (often state-owned), investment companies established by these banks, and industrial companies which are owned by the investment companies and frequently deeply indebted to the large banks, is among the problems expected to result from privatization. (In total, the 15 largest investment funds, frequently owned by the large banks, control more than 30% of all publicly traded securities in the Czech market.) The influence wielded by the Czech banks over the management of Czech companies is enormous and the instances of collusive relationships are close to Japanese or Korean levels.

Foreign observers most of all do not appreciate the interdependence of the banking, financial and industrial sectors. Making comparisons with the other transitional economies, they even describe the development of banking and its influence on Czech industry as misguided. Particularly from a dynamic perspective, the excessive influence of the banking and financial sectors upon the industrial sector in the Czech Republic may turn out harmful. Observers usually stress that Czech investment funds, which control about 70% of Czech industry, are owned by domestic banks. According to them, this, in combination with insufficient capital market regulation, could lead to the stagnation of Czech industry.

Some of the banks are now in trouble. A tougher approach on the part of the CNB might lead to a situation in which a few of these will be liquidated. Others will probably be taken over by larger or healthier banks, while the rest of those involved will probably be granted refinance credits or other life-support systems by the Czech National Bank, or will use some schemes organized by another bank and supported by the central bank.

This process will probably determine the future pattern of the Czech banking sector. It will probably lead to the elimination of weak and uncompetitive small banks, greater stress on specialization in a limited number of products, and the consolidation of the dominant position of the leading banks. These will probably prefer to keep their universal character and follow the German model of the organization of the banking structures. On the other hand, some banks will prefer to specialize in their traditional market segments (*Česká spořitelna* as a dominant body in attracting national savings, *Československá obchodní banka* as a specialist in foreign trade financing and private banking).

INTERNATIONAL EXPOSURE AND COMPETITIVENESS

Market Capitalization

Czech banks are among the most prominent in Central and Eastern Europe. Along with, especially, their Polish counterparts, they have the highest values of market capitalization in the region and are not far behind, for example, the two largest Austrian banks.

Table 14.10. Banks by market capitalization

Bank	Market capitalization
Czech Republic	
Komerční banka	1062.3
Česká spořitelna	439.4
Investiční a Poštovní banka	252.5
Živnostenská banka	149.5
Poland	
Bank Slaski	557.9
Bank Przemyslovo-Handlowy	360.9
Bank Rozwoju Eksportu	252.6
Polski Bank Rozwoju	135
Bank Inic Gospod	101.8
Slovakia	
Všeobecná úverová banka	136.4
Austria	
Bank Austria	4661
Creditanstalt-Bankverein	2208

Note: The largest banks in Central Eastern Europe and Austria, US$ million, January 1996.
Source: Patria Finance, *The Wall Street Journal Europe, 1996.*

Total Assets

However, comparing their total assets in a world or European ranking, the scale of the largest Czech banks is fairly negligible, not only by comparison with large European countries, but also to small, open economies (Belgium, The Netherlands, Switzerland). Only Austria has no representative in a survey of banks with total assets over US$ 75 billion.

Table 14.11. Banks by total assets

Bank	Total assets	World rank
Czech Republic		
Komerční banka	14.7	
Česká spořitelna	13.3	
Investiční a Poštovní banka	7.3	
Československá obchodní banka	7.3	
Agrobanka	2.5	
Germany		
Deutsche Bank	365.7	9
Dresdner Bank	257.5	25
Westdeutsche Landesbank	242.7	31
Commerzbank	218.9	34
Bayerische Vereinsbank	203.1	37
Bayerische Landesbank	178.2	39
Bayerische Hypo-Bank	174.4	41
Kreditanstalt für Wiederaufbau	163.1	45
France		
Crédit Lyonnais	328.3	11
Crédit Agricole	328.1	12
Société Générale	277.9	21
Banque Nationale de Paris	271.5	22
Cie. Financière de Paribas	242.5	32
CENCEP	188.1	38
The Netherlands		
ABN Amro Holdings	290.7	20
Rabobank	155	49
Internationale Nederlanden	125.3	60
Switzerland		
Union Bank of Switzerland	249.5	27
Crédit Suisse	177	40
Swiss Bank Corp.	161.3	47

Bank	Total assets	World rank
Belgium		
Generale Bank	126.9	58
Crédit Communal de Belgique	100	72
Kredietbank	83.6	91
Banque Bruxelles Lambert	81.3	93
Italy		
San Paolo Bank	154.7	51
Cariplo	108.5	67
Banca Nazionale del Lavoro	99.3	73
Banca di Roma	94.2	78
Banca Commerciale Italiana	93.4	79
Monte dei Paschi di Siena	88.3	84

Note: Selected large banks in Europe by country, US$ billion, December 1995.
Source: Patria Finance, *The Wall Street Journal Europe, The Banker, 1996.*

Association with the European Union

Banking services, along with the other areas covered by the Europe Agreement, may enjoy advantages stemming from the asymmetric arrangement of this Agreement. For a period of 10 years, the Agreement allows the Czech banks relatively easy access to the territory of the European Union. However, in practice Czech banks have so far taken advantage of this only to a very limited extent. On the other hand, a bank operating in the territory of the European Union (as well as any other banking institution) can operate in the Czech Republic only under a licence granted by the Czech National Bank. A number of prominent banks took advantage of this at the very beginning of the transformation, while the later tightening of the licence policy limited the access of foreign banks to the Czech Republic.

There are several thousand standards set by the European Union (irrespective of sector). The main aim of the application of the Europe Agreement is to collect a file of the most important standards, without which it is almost impossible to imagine the preparatory phase to full membership of the European Union. It means that priorities mentioned in the Europe Agreement represent the preferred subject of interest for the following three or four years (taking into account a 10-year period of association as well as the basic block of the most topical measures for 1995 and 1996). A scenario and a timetable combining the most crucial issues of the process of association for particular sectors is given in the White Paper on the Preparation of the Associated

Countries of Central and Eastern Europe for Integration into the Internal Market of the European Union of June 1995. The other standards not included in the Europe Agreement follow a longer time frame.

Despite the fact that the banking sector is not explicitly mentioned in the text of the Europe Agreement, its implementation has had a very significant impact on the institutions within the banking sector in the Czech Republic. The Czech Republic is committed to converge with banking laws in European Union countries. The Agreement also obliges the monetary authorities to implement prudential, non-discriminatory regulations towards banks after an interim period. Among the areas specified in the Agreement are the following:
1. Harmonization of legislation.
2. Monetary policy and the liberalization of the foreign-exchange regime.
3. Conditions for entrepreneurial activities in the banking sector and international financial services.
4. Information and technical cooperation (information exchange, statistics, accounting and standardization, and a temporary principle – loans and technical assistance from the institutions of the European Union).

It can be seen that these priorities represent (compared with the comprehensive block of EU standards) rather an incongruous mixture of economic policy, legislation, and standardization measures with a partially outdated form of one-track cooperation.

A riskier alternative on the Czech side would be to start from any enumeration of regulations adopted on the level of the European Union. None of them is self-contained. We quickly meet another connected principle and the risk of taking some measure out of context is extremely high. An important truth is to be remembered: the process of adjustment of the Czech banking to European Union standards has two dimensions:
1. Standardization and legislative adjustment.
2. Competitiveness.

To meet both these conditions, the most important banking regulations set a minimum initial capital of 5 million ECU for credit institutions (Czech standards define a much higher minimum of CZK 500 million, or ECU 14.5 million), the solvency ratio directive sets a capital standard of 8% of risk-weighted assets, and the large exposures directive limits the exposure of a bank to a single client to a maximum of 25% of its own funds.

301 - 17

G-21 P34
G-28

15. Establishing and Cooperating With Promotional Banks in Central and Eastern Europe

Norbert Irsch and Heike Wiegand

INTRODUCTION

Kreditanstalt für Wiederaufbau (KfW) was founded in 1948 for the purpose of administering the counterpart funds of the Marshall Plan Aid (European Recovery Program) to finance the most urgent reconstruction projects of the German economy. More than forty years later, KfW is faced once more with the similar task of financing reconstruction in the Eastern part of Germany. In its capacity as Germany's central public credit institution, KfW extends loans to promote the German economy and to finance projects worthy of promotion outside Germany.

KfW is a Promotional Bank both for the national economy and for other economies. Finance outside Germany is channelled mainly in the form of supply-tied export credits and within the context of German development cooperation. Since the start of the decade the German Federal Government has actively assisted also the countries of Central and Eastern Europe (CEE) in introducing democratic and market economy structures. In order to make the most effective use of the limited budgetary funds available for this task, KfW was entrusted with providing assistance to CEE countries in the phase of transition to a market economy, through loans, grants and advisory services as well as in the financing of specific programs and the supervision of their implementation. In this field KfW can also draw on the experience it gathered from its activities in Eastern Germany, for instance in connection with the privatization of state-owned enterprises.

KfW will enhance the coordination of these advisory measures and integrate them in one comprehensive approach. At the same time KfW helps ensure that the funds are used for their precise purpose and provides the Federal Republic of Germany with a promotional profile of its own by focusing on the main areas

301

of advice. One central issue is promoting the creation of market-economy-orientated banking, stock trading and insurance. Within this one major activity consists in supporting these countries in the setting-up and further development of promotional banks; here KfW can share more than forty years of experience as a promotional institution. As the promotional bank for the German Economy, KfW provides direct support in individual cases if it is asked to do so.

In order to give a concrete example of KFW's consultation practices, the basic concept of a promotional bank is introduced below, followed by a discussion of experiences in the respective countries.

BASIC CONCEPT

Economies in Transition to a Market Economy

The transition to a market economy poses extremely difficult problems for the CEE countries. The development of diversified company-scale structure in these countries is a precondition for gradually improving economic efficiency and the supply to the public. The constraints emerging in the process cannot be overcome by capital transfer alone. But national promotional banks can be a sound instrument for easing the process.

In particular, as long as the system and involvement of institutions that characterize modern market economies have not yet developed fully, promotional banks are an appropriate instrument for directing capital into economically important areas. They can also facilitate the mobilization of domestic savings. Helping to set up promotional banks aims to awaken endogenous potential and helps economies to help themselves.

Funding Needs of Small and Medium-Sized Businesses

The investment activity of small and medium-sized enterprises (SMEs) is the key for them to assert themselves in the marketplace, to revive competition and to create the employment and income that go with their growth. What is needed first is a significant number of people who wish to be independent, who wish to use business opportunities, and who are prepared to put in the effort and take risks. In many cases the capital needed for the first steps towards setting up an independent business is relatively low, but it usually exceeds the equity available, particularly when the possibilities for long-term preparation and amassing capital savings have been limited. In addition, the need for capital quickly increases in the course of the consolidation and expansion of a business, while for many young firms the lack of collateral hampers financing.

The rhythm of investment and the funding possibilities open to SMEs are different from those of larger enterprises. Because of the technical requirements and the limited divisibility of capital goods, small enterprises do not invest continuously or in regular amounts. Rather, they concentrate their investment activities in short intervals, and then these often reach amounts corresponding to their total annual turnover. This is often accompanied by considerable surges in capacity which must subsequently be followed by a corresponding turnover. The business risks of such investment leaps are therefore very high. So it is all the more important to limit the risks from the funding side. Specifically, this means distributing the funding costs over time, in accordance with the useful life of the acquired equipment, to keep repayments during the difficult start-up years as low as possible, to solve problems when collateral is not available, and to enable a definitive calculation of the overall financing costs. Even in the developed market economies the commercial banking system fails to fully satisfy these requirements for the appropriate financing of small, new businesses in the start-up and expansion phase.

The disadvantages which SMEs suffer in the competition for investment finance because of their size are many and varied:

- Generally speaking, it is either impossible or very difficult for small and medium-sized firms to raise equity capital, whereas large companies can do so by going public.
- When borrowing long-term funds from commercial and savings banks small and medium-sized firms must expect to be classified as a higher risk than large firms.
- Small and medium-sized firms lack the negotiating strength which a big borrower has. It is relatively expensive for the commercial banks to handle smaller loan applications.
- Institutions or groups of institutions that specialize in lending to SMEs often cannot offer long-term finance from their resources owing to a limited funding basis or statutory regulations.

For these reasons most Western countries have special institutions for SMEs, with a mandate for promoting SMEs through loan programs, as well as equity investment firms and guarantee banks, as self-help facilities of the industry. These institutions are either supported or maintained by the state.

All state influence on the economic activity of private businesses raises the question to what extent this distorts market signals and ultimately leads to a less-than-optimal allocation of resources, but there is obviously no easy way to measure success *ex post*. The actual development of a national economy or a sector hinges on many factors and cannot be attributed to individual economic policy measures alone.

What is important for assessing a small and medium-sized firm policy is, first, to analyse the problem thoroughly, to fine-tune the instruments with a view to defining constraints and objectives, and to conduct a continuing, critical evaluation.

Secondly, the quality of small and medium-sized firm policy also depends on the practical shape of the promotional programs and promotional institutions. The support should not act against market developments but with the market, enhancing growth. The instruments should use existing institutional structures and financing channels (banks) and, thus employ methods allowing an efficacious division of tasks.

The success of promotional programs has also been studied repeatedly in Germany by independent research institutes. One result is that young and small businesses that receive promotion display on average higher stability and grow faster than unpromoted ones. On the one hand, this is because projects and companies are appraised by banking criteria, which forces a firm to plan its project and business in a rational fashion, and, on the other, because the financing is tailored to the specific needs of the project.

Aspects of and Instruments for the Development of the SME-sector – the Role of the Promotional Bank

The entrepreneurial spirit, i.e. the willingness to set up an independent small business, is readily available in most populations. This even applies to countries with a modest entrepreneurial tradition. Thus, the existing context should already form an adequate breeding-ground for the seeds of a market economy. Small enterprises in the field of consumer-related services and the handicrafts are the fastest to develop. Medium-sized and larger market-oriented enterprises are also urgently needed for the development of a diversified company size structure, especially in the manufacturing sector. This development, however, needs much more time because the planning and implementation of the corresponding investments are more complex and risky.

The small and medium-sized business will evolve predominantly from new structures, with parts of them also emerging from takeovers of state-owned enterprises or parts of enterprises. Privatization can be the way to start operating in bigger business units from the word go. The crucial point however, is not so much the transfer of ownership itself, but the need for subsequent investments without which the affected enterprises cannot operate efficiently and competitively.

The task of the state is to establish the framework of the economic and legal system for the development of the market economy, to supervise and enforce compliance with the rules, and to ensure a functioning administration. In addition, the state is responsible for the measures required to achieve overall economic stability. The establishment of a two-tier banking system and the creation of an efficient commercial banking sector are crucial. These are necessary preconditions for the process of building up small and medium-sized companies to develop successfully.

But this process also needs direct support. Promotional banks that mainly offer help to the SME-sector but also cater for other economically urgent investments are an effective instrument. In the initial stage they can also take the place of the, still often inadequately, developed banking sector. They can take part in its initial development and then withdraw later from some of their original involvement. It must be noted that in some countries deficits can cause paralysis and the obstruction of possible economic-policy action. The urge for independence and for taking risks in the marketplace can be used as a starting point to break open the vicious circle.

In KfW's view promotional banks are not instruments to be used against the market. On the contrary, they should help market mechanisms advance more quickly and with less friction. They can help build up the necessary institutional framework and combine national and international efforts to awaken endogenous potential. They are not designed primarily to distribute subsidies or collect international aid. Their financial assistance should be easily available and comprehensive and involve as little red tape as possible (e.g. through the on-lending mechanism). The promotional bank has to ensure that uniform lending criteria are applied in all parts of the country. These criteria should remain constant over a longer period and be formulated so as to allow the applicant to reach a reliable judgement about whether he will receive promotional funds. The funding of promotional programs should be sufficient to make them available over a longer period of time.

The establishment of a SME-sector is a very complex task. National promotional banks are not the only institutions required, but they are among the ones to be set up first and also the most important. Guarantee banks should be mentioned secondly; they should be designed as the self-help facilities of the banking industry with state support. Equity capital investment firms are very important, but will not be all that quick to make a general impression. The same applies to institutions such as technology parks. These are factors that are important for differentiating the branch structure and therefore for medium-term planning. Because the available funds and personnel resources are limited, priority should be given to individual measures, but without losing sight of the overall concept that embraces all the factors relevant to the development of a strong SME-sector. Without doubt, a very important initial step is the complex of measures for training and advice. Promotional banks, guarantee banks and equity capital investment firms complement each other in their financing functions. Promotional banks should also support basic training and advisory services; however, these services are generally provided by other specialized institutions.

The constituent principles of the promotional bank

A promotional bank should be devised in such a way as to carry out three major functions. The first is financial support to the target groups (or target areas). These are, first and foremost, small and medium-sized enterprises in almost all the countries of Eastern Europe. The creation of a broad, strong competitive sector of small and medium-sized enterprises is crucial for the success of the transformation process, since these enterprises, because of their strong market-orientation and proximity to their customers, their high flexibility and unbureaucratic organization, can adapt more easily to structural upheavals. Besides supporting small and medium-sized enterprises, the tasks of a promotional bank can also include the restructuring, modernization and privatization of industry, the development of infrastructure, the support of housing construction or the promotion of innovation. The priorities in these areas must be established in coordination with the makers of economic policy and in answer to the specific problems of each country.

The methods, working procedures and instruments with which the promotional bank performs its major functions should be chosen and conceived in such a way that two further functions can also be carried out at the same time. These are:

1. the promotion and development of the commercial banking system;
2. the support of the creation and development of a strong national capital market.

In order to enable a promotional bank to fulfil these functions satisfactorily, the following characteristics should be taken into account for its structure and activities:

1. The main function of a promotional bank is to support economic development, orientated towards the general economy, but in particular to promote small and medium-sized enterprises. The maximization of profits, as in the private sector, will usually conflict with this development function. Thus, the promotional bank cannot be an institution striving for maximum profit. For this reason it needs shareholders who are not primarily interested in profits. This is why the shareholders should be mainly the state or state institutions.
2. The promotional bank must have an excellent standing in the capital market. Therefore, it must be endowed with sufficient start-up capital. The institution must frame its lending conditions in such a way that sufficient funds are generated so that its equity can grow in an appropriate relation to

its overall functions. Moreover, the state should secure the payment obligations of the promotional bank with a (general) guarantee over and above the equity capital liability provided by the state. This general state guarantee and adequate equity capital should allow the institution to fund its business at favorable terms and to pass on these funding advantages to the target groups (such as small and medium-sized enterprises) in the form of favorable loan conditions.

3. In order to perform its development function the promotional bank needs an autonomous promotion potential that enables it to act independently of the state and to support the target groups with favorable financing without recourse to budget funds. Such an autonomous structural promotional potential should basically be created by
   • exempting the institution from taxation;
   • generally waiving dividend payouts to the shareholders.
   The latter allows profits to be used to strengthen the reserves of the institution (equity) and, thus, to expand the promotional activity.

4. While the promotional bank is majority-owned by the state and its tasks include general support to economic policy, it is very important for it to be autonomous in its decisions and to act independently of the state. All the bank's internal decisions should be taken professionally and purely according to sound banking criteria. The state may not intervene in the internal decision-making processes of the institution. This professionalism and independence should protect the institution from abuse by the dominant shareholders but also from undesirable bureaucratic pressures. In order to ensure efficiency, flexibility and professionalism the position of the board of management must be strengthened accordingly in relation to the supervisory bodies. In addition, it is recommended that representatives of important interest groups as well (such as business and banking associations) which are not shareholders should be included on the supervisory board.

5. Equipped with an autonomous potential for promotion (tax exemption, waiver of dividend payouts), the institution could become a dangerous competitor for commercial and saving banks and could hinder the development of the commercial banking system. In order to avoid distortions in competition, the promotional bank must act in a subsidiary way, that is, it must become active only in those areas in which the commercial banks offer little or no finance. To ensure this subsidiarity (additionality), it should work together with the commercial banks using a sensible division of tasks and generally channel its loans to the investors through the commercial banking system. Direct loans should be restricted to exceptional cases and specific areas – at least, that is, after the first

development phase of an institution. The principle of on-lending through commercial banks thereby ensures the subsidiarity of the promotional bank's activity, but beyond this it also has considerable cost benefits for all parties involved. In assessing the creditworthiness of the investors the commercial banks can use their insider know-how and their often longstanding customer relationships. Thus the promotional bank will not be forced to set up a countrywide network of branch offices.

The channelling of the promotional loans usually allows the commercial banks in transitional countries to enter the field of long-term investment financing for the first time. The promotional bank chooses the commercial banks that are suitable for channelling according to objective quantitative and qualitative criteria, and contributes towards transferring the relevant know-how to the commercial banks. In general terms, the exercise of promotional activity in this way also supports the positive development of the commercial banking system.

6. The promotional bank should try as early as possible to reimburse itself in the local capital market. A crucial precondition for this – as already mentioned – is an adequate standing, based on sufficient equity capital and the general state guarantee. Thus equipped, the promotional bank can first tap the local capital market, and over the medium to long term also the international capital market by issuing securities. This way its funding contributes to the establishment of a strong national capital market that will be of interest to the investors.

7. In principle, the promotional bank may offer various financing services (participations, guarantees, loans). In order to achieve the broadest possible effect quickly – which is necessary particularly in the support of small and medium-sized enterprises – it is recommended to the bank first and foremost to extend loans. Participations and guarantees are also important financing instruments, but they should be extended by specialized institutions. At any rate, the accumulation of risks from allocating different financing instruments to a single project is to be avoided.

8. The promotional bank must calculate its credit conditions in such a way that it can cover its costs, form the necessary risk provisions and allow its equity capital to expand in an adequate relation to the business volume. Compared with the terms of commercial banks, all the promotional bank does here is pass on to the target groups the financing advantages created by its autonomous promotion potential. The main promotional impact of the loans granted should lie in the long-term maturity of the funds offered and, possibly, in the readiness to assume higher risks (to a limited degree) than the commercial banks.

The refinancing function of the promotional bank

The task of the promotional bank, structured according to the above principles, is to finance eligible enterprises and projects and to raise the necessary medium and long-term capital. Refinancing from domestic savings was, and partly still is, seriously hampered in an economic environment like that of the CEE countries.

The low savings ratio, the lack of an institutional framework and, in particular, high inflation do not permit the formation of a capital market. The most important funding source of a country, domestic savings, cannot be mobilized except with great difficulty. Savings are invested for short periods, if at all. Like the central bank, the interbank market's transactions are of a short-term nature. This way, investments from domestic funds can be financed only over the short term or from equity. Both are inadequate in structure and volume. With some exceptions, what is financed are mainly high-profit commercial transactions or investment projects with extremely short repayment periods.

Consequently, the main long-term funding source for the bank should be the foreign capital markets. But since it has no access to the international capital market because of the country risk, the promotional bank must rely on funding from multilateral and bilateral donors.

As inflation diminishes and overall conditions become more stable, the bank can gradually attract capital from the emerging national and international markets. To accomplish this, the bank must, in addition to its own strength and independence from direct political influence, have equity capital and, in particular, a creditworthiness reflecting the performance of the state. The state must endow the bank with its own creditworthiness, which usually requires a corresponding guarantee declaration. With this the promotional bank can become a nucleus for the national capital market.

In both cases – drawing upon both foreign and domestic funding sources as far as possible – the promotional bank uses its link to the state to raise urgently needed funds and, in this way, from the viewpoint of the commercial banks as well, performs a refinancing function that may not be achievable otherwise. The above-mentioned arguments concerning the division of functions and acceptance hence gain additional support.

The risk function of the promotional bank

In an economy in transition the promotional bank must initially bear a relatively large part of the risks that arise from the lending business. This applies to loans channelled by banks as well as to those extended directly. The essential limiting conditions that the institution faces can be listed as follows:

- The system of commercial banks through which the lending business is

largely to be conducted is still being set up. Initially risks can be selected and assumed only to a limited extent, and only on a step-by-step basis.
• Risk-hedging instruments (including guarantee banks), together with the pertinent ownership legislation and procedures exist only in a rudimentary form. The corresponding legal system does not yet function adequately.

The upheaval situation does not allow for the evaluation of credit risks and collateral in figures of national or business economics. The markets for assessing collateral do not yet exist.

This makes it very difficult for SMEs to finance urgently-needed investments. An adequate investment process can hardly get started. As long as overall conditions, legal instruments and market partners (banks, loan guarantee associations, equity capital investment firms, and others) that are available in stable market economies, enabling a satisfactory risk assessment and a risk distribution to a number of competent parties, do not exist, the promotional bank must itself bear an increased proportion of the risk for the period of transition. And, if necessary, it should contribute constructively to setting up structures that allow decentralized risk assumption in the medium term. Also, the bank should be equipped appropriately by its owners for this task. Various solutions are conceivable and should be made specific with a view to entering the real world. This can include the depletion of capital mentioned before, as well as internal risk funds guaranteed by the government. Irrespective of the path taken, in each individual case the necessary close cooperation between the promotional bank and the state will be able to make an important contribution through the commercial banks. In the course of economic stabilization the state will be able to withdraw its co-responsibility here as well and leave this task to the market.

Theses for the creation of a national promotional bank

Altogether, a promotional bank conceived this way represents an institution that performs development tasks motivated by economic policy with commercially-orientated flexibility and efficiency. In selecting the projects and structuring the programs, banking professionalism is decisive. The system of on-lending loans through commercial banks[1] makes it possible to minimize the

---

[1] This means that the application for a loan is to be filed with a credit institution of the applicant's choice. The credit institution then passes on the application to the promotional bank together with their own comments. Thus, the promotional bank does not enter into any direct relationship with the ultimate borrower. A direct relationship exists only between the ultimate borrower and the on-lending bank.

This procedure has the following advantage: The local bank knows the applicant far better than the promotional bank does. A credit institution that has assumed the function of a company's house bank has often entertained long-standing business relations with that company and knows its specific situation very well.

costs associated with the granting of state support to target groups. Backed by its adequate start-up capital and the state guarantee, the institution can perform its functions using its autonomous promotion potential without resorting to the state budget. This strengthens its independence from the state majority shareholder.

From the financial and macroeconomic perspective, providing the start-up capital and creating the autonomous promotion potential are to be interpreted not so much as the waiver of earnings but rather as an investment by the state. It is an investment because these inputs will provide a financial return for the state after a relatively short time. The activity of the institution creates new tax sources and expands existing ones, so that the additional tax revenue thus induced very soon more than makes up for the initial costs, the earnings waived by exempting the institution from taxation and from dividend payouts. It must also be remembered that the government will usually find it much easier to deny requests for subsidies by interest groups when financial support is being offered through a promotional bank.

EXPERIENCES MADE IN THE FIELD OF FINANCIAL ASSISTANCE

Content of Advisory Assistance

KfW's advisory activities in the phase prior to the establishment of a promotional bank consist in developing a concept for the bank's functions and activities and drawing up draft versions of the foundation documents (law, statutes, etc.). Here it is essential to take into consideration the specific national environment and problems. Advisory services rendered after the founding of a bank or to already existing promotional banks focus on building up the bank's infrastructure, in particular the organizational structure and processing procedures within the promotional loan department, developing an efficient on-lending mechanism and designing specific promotional programs. The banks are to be enabled to develop and implement their own promotional programs to combat the economic problems of their countries.

In designing programs KfW's advisory assistance focuses on programs

---

The promotional bank is a central credit institution that does not need any local branch offices and does not compete with commercial banks. Therefore, two aspects are important in the cooperation with commercial banks: Subsidiarity – the promotional bank extends loans where other credit institutions are not in a position to provide the necessary funds; work sharing – the promotional bank uses the commercial bank's know-how and information.

promoting small and medium-sized enterprises, since these play a leading role in establishing a properly functioning economy. In addition, KfW supports the development of programs for environmental protection, in particular energy-saving in residential buildings, and programs for improving communal infrastructure.

To help realize the promotional programs developed with KfW's assistance, KfW also provides credit lines for start-up finance. In this way the advisory services will not be a pointless exercise with no lasting effect, for the want of concrete opportunities to put them into practice. In providing credit lines KfW takes account of the intention of the German government to foster a market economy and democracy in Central and Eastern Europe.

In its advisory services to promotional banks in almost all of the countries concerned KfW cooperates closely with German embassies, and in particular the KfW coordination offices housed there, which ensure that the various advisory projects in the countries in transition are consistent. This cooperation ensures a rapid and smooth exchange of information, thus rendering the advisory measures more efficient and better targeted. KfW also cooperates with the European Union, in particular the EU delegations in the partner countries, when projects have similar objectives. It is often the joining of forces of all those concerned that makes projects successful.

The Advisory Projects in CEE in Detail[2]

Bulgaria: State Investment and Development Bank of Bulgaria (SIDB)

In autumn 1993 the Bulgarian government asked the German government for support in establishing a similar institution to KfW, in particular for the promotion of small and medium-sized enterprises. In 1994 the concept for the bank was discussed and a first draft foundation law prepared. Several government changes led to considerable delays.

Since the formation of a new government in February 1995 backed by a sound majority in parliament, the draft law, statutes, and a business plan have been finalized relatively quickly. In August 1995 the SIDB project was discussed for the first time by the Bulgarian Council of Ministers. The Council of Ministers approved the draft law at the beginning of 1996 after slight modifications. It is expected that the draft law will be passed by parliament after clarifying where the equity capital will come from.

Part-financing of SIDB's equity from EU PHARE is being discussed. KfW has suggested taking the next steps towards establishing SIDB actually during

---

[2] The examples are limited to those countries that are the subject of this book.

the parliamentary debate on the draft law. KfW's support in this phase will concentrate on building up a promotional loan department.

Croatia: Croatian Loan Corporation for Reconstruction (HKBO, HBOR)

Even before the foundation of HKBO (Hrvatska kreditna banka za obnovu) in 1992, KfW had started to advise the Croatian government on the strategic orientation of HKBO. KfW has always advocated a structure of HKBO which adheres to banking principles and excludes political influence on individual loan decisions.

Further elements of consultancy included the improvement of the organizational structure and processing arrangements, reorganizing the accountancy system and establishing a risk-management and liquidity planning system. Furthermore, an SME program has been planned.

The SME program of HKBO was finalized in 1995; the program was started in mid-1995 and met with strong demand in Croatia. It is being refinanced from HKBO's own funds. It was planned to sign a loan agreement between KfW and HKBO for refinancing this program in 1995; this was, however, postponed by the German government until further notice for foreign policy considerations.

KfW has continued to assist HKBO in building up the organizational areas mentioned above. In particular, the processing of lending arrangements was improved with KfW's assistance. Furthermore, KfW has participated in working out the law governing HKBO, which was passed by the Croatian parliament late in 1995. The name of the bank was then changed to the Croatian Bank for Reconstruction and Development (Hrvatska kreditna banka za obnovu i razvoj, HBOR).

Czech Republic: Czech-Moravian Guarantee and Development Bank (CMZRB)

CMZRB, founded as a guarantee bank in 1992, approached KfW in the actual year of its foundation. It intended to enlarge its field of operations and to embark on lending activity by financing environmental protection projects. KfW has designed a corresponding advisory scheme which has been under implementation since 1994.

CMZRB was also assisted in developing a loan program for promoting investments in environmental protection. As a result of a change in political priorities CMZRB decided to postpone the implementation of the environmental loan program in favor of a program for modernizing the housing stock of the Czech Republic. KfW also supports CMZRB in developing this program, since the creation of additional promotional programs is an opportunity for CMZRB to apply the set of instruments already developed in practice and to extend the range of the bank's products.

Hungary: Hungarian Investment and Development Bank (MBFB)

KfW was contacted in early 1992 by MBF, the predecessor of MBFB (Magyar Befektesi Es Fejleztesi Bank RT.). MBF was an investment company whose function was to restructure and privatize the state enterprises in which it held shares. In mid-1993 MBF was given a banking licence and transformed into a bank whose main functions were within the domain of economic policy. Contact has intensified since. Finally KfW was asked by MBFB to lend its support in developing an SME program.

Under a project financed by the German Ministry of Finance MBFB was advised on elaborating the documentation for this SME program. Alongside the advisory services KfW negotiated with MBFB an agreement for DEM 50 million to refinance the SME program of MBFB. This agreement was signed in August 1995. The program was launched in early 1996. Under a currency swap between MBFB and the Hungarian National Bank SME program loans can be extended in Forint without sub-borrowers having to bear any exchange risks. In addition, the interest rates are subsidized by the Hungarian government.

In a joint declaration of the Hungarian and the German governments the German federal government agreed to cover loans to a total volume of DEM 500 million for projects in Hungary. KfW will assist in developing such projects and lend the necessary funds. Besides the SME program, there is an energy-saving program, which was more or less finalized by the end of 1995. This program will serve to finance modernization works on buildings constructed from large concrete panels. Since tenants usually have relatively low incomes, the Hungarian government considers an interest subsidy indispensable. The level of interest reduction to be financed from the Hungarian state budget and possibly from supplementary EU PHARE funds could, however, not be agreed on by the end of last year; therefore the program cannot be launched yet. It is also planned to develop, together with MBFB, a communal loan program as part of the DEM 500 million package from the federal government.

Poland

Poland founded its development bank, Polski Bank Rozwoju (PBR) in 1990. Thanks to widespread international support this bank was built up rapidly. Contacts between PBR and KfW were established very early, in the first half of 1991. It was agreed to cooperate by assisting PBR in developing its operations, setting up a KfW credit line, and creating a German-Polish Association for Economic Promotion. This model of cooperation is based on the dual concept for the promotion of the German-Polish border region developed by KfW in cooperation with the German Ministry for Economics and built on a study elaborated for the government of the Land Brandenburg entitled 'concept for the promotion of the Oder region'.

Cooperation with PBR. KfW has conducted a number of training programs for PBR staff since 1992. PBR wanted to benefit from KfW's experience in promotional lending. There was, however, no custom-made consultancy package for developing PBR's promotional lending business. Then, a credit line for SME promotion was negotiated. In connection with the restructuring of the Polish banking sector PBR is now to be taken over by Pekao Bank. We expect PBR to adopt a purely commercial orientation after this takeover. Should the bank, however, continue promotional lending, our offer to support PBR by targeted advice and refinancing credit lines will still be valid.

German-Polish Association for Economic Promotion (AEP). The AEP was founded in March 1994 in Gorzow/Poland after the German-Polish government commission had given its consent. Its task is to promote economic relations between Poland and Germany and, in particular, to attract investors to the border region. KfW, as the mandatory for the German side, together with PBR charged by the Polish side prepared the foundation of the AEP in organizational and conceptional terms. On the German side, the federal government and the four federal Länder, Berlin, Brandenburg, Mecklenburg-Western Pomerania, and Saxony support the AEP financially. On the Polish side, the Polish government contributes an equal amount to finance the AEP's expenses.

The AEP with a staff of more than 30 has meanwhile become a recognized institution in the German-Polish border region. KfW organized the financial support of the Federal Government and the four federal Länder to the AEP and examined the use of the funds at the association's domicile once more in 1995. KfW will be charged with the same task again in 1996. The federal and the Länder governments are considering continuing their financial support to the AEP until 1999.

Guarantee Institution for Western Poland. The German-Polish government commission for regional and local border cooperation recommended to the AEP during its meeting an examination of whether suitable guarantee instruments could be created which would improve the chances for small and medium-sized enterprises in the border region to borrow funds. At the request of the AEP KfW has submitted proposals for a guarantee institution in Western Poland and has carried out large-scale preparatory work for structuring the content of the project. The German government has consented to finance the advisory services provided for this project.

Romania

After initial contacts with Romanian government institutions in spring 1995, KfW presented its blueprint for a project for the establishment of a promotional bank in Romania. The project was approved by a Romanian government commission in November 1995. In December a Romanian-German work group was formed to prepare the conceptual and legal steps leading to the foundation of the bank. The work group has already adopted the basic concept presented by KfW and has started to discuss KfW's draft foundation law. Alongside the discussion of the draft law it will have to be decided whether it will be necessary to set up a new institution in Romania, or whether there is an existing institution suitable for conversion into a promotional bank.

Slovak Republic: Slovak Loan Corporation (SLC)

Preparations for founding a Slovak promotional bank were started in late 1994. KfW assisted in these preparations by drawing up draft law, statutes, and a business plan for the Slovak Loan Corporation. Furthermore, different options for establishing such an institution were evaluated, in particular the advantages and drawbacks of a newly-founded institution as compared to a conversion.

In the year under review the Slovak government has not yet adopted any of these alternatives. A decision is expected in 1996.

CONCLUSION

Since 1991 KfW has advised the countries in transition in Central and Eastern Europe on establishing and consolidating promotional and development banks. In its advisory services KfW has pursued the objective of building up financially solid promotional institutions operating according to sound banking principles, which will be able to develop and implement their own promotional programs. Such banks facilitate the efficient implementation of national or international promotional measures.

Setting up promotional banks makes an important contribution to the development of banking systems and capital markets. As a rule, local commercial banks and savings banks become involved in lending-on the loans. They assume the major role in credit assessment and always take on part of the risk relating to the ultimate borrower. Potential on-lending banks are all commercial banks considered competent, efficient, and financially sound. Generally it is only this on-lending function that gives commercial banks access to long-term investment finance and makes it possible for them to develop the necessary financial know-how. Furthermore, competition is intensified among commercial banks which have the opportunity to refinance themselves from the promotional bank.

The general function of promotional banks in the CEE countries is to support the transformation of the economic system. This is achieved by promotional banks financing investments in priority sectors of the economy and generating positive spill-overs for the development of banking systems and national capital markets. In this connection small and medium-sized enterprises play a crucial role: since the beginning of the reform process they have been a driving force for economic renewal, and their contribution to the creation of new competitive jobs can hardly be overestimated.

Insufficient long-term finance for investment is a severe problem facing almost all SMEs in Central and Eastern Europe. A qualified promotional institution providing suitable long-term finance can promote this target group effectively and region-wide. Comparable tasks arise in connection with the restructuring and privatization of state-owned enterprises and the renewal or development of communal infrastructures.

Another function of promotional institutions is to channel funds from state budgets or international financial institutions such as the World Bank or the European Bank for Reconstruction and Development (EBRD) to investors. Here the promotional bank has the task of appraising the commercial viability of the projects and enterprises to be financed and, thus, to guarantee that only commercially sound projects are realized. KfW had fulfilled a comparable function in post-war Germany.

The guiding model for our advisory assistance is KfW's promotion of the domestic economy. It is, however, essential to be flexible enough to adjust to particular national circumstances. These include not only the economic environment, but also the political situation, the legal system, and, last but not least, the basic cultural make-up of the partner country. It is thus not surprising that the promotional institutions set up so far sometimes show marked differences from each other and from KfW.

16. Privatization: A Comparative Experiment – Poland, the Czech Republic and Hungary

Lina Takla

'In the transition, privatization is a process whereby assets whose real owners are not known and whose real value is uncertain are sold to people who do not have the money to buy them.'

Janusz Lewandowski, twice Polish Minister of Privatization

'...it is the economy as a whole, not a particular state-owned firm or firms that calls for transformation. In other words, however efficient or inefficient, financially healthy or unhealthy individual businesses may appear, it is not them, but the whole economy, which requires a change.'

Vaclav Klaus, 1993

INTRODUCTION

Privatization is the mechanism which redefines property rights and should thus in transitional economies bring about '*de novo* the basic institutions of a market financial system including corporate governance of managers, equity ownership, stock exchanges and a number of financial intermediaries' (Lipton and Sachs, 1990). We can distinguish between 'small' and 'large' privatization. 'Large' privatization mainly involves industrial enterprises and utilities, while 'small' privatization generally relates to smaller units in services or retail. The former Czech and Slovak Federal Republic[1] (CSFR) led

---

[1] On 1 January 1993, the Federal Republic of Czechoslovakia was separated into two constituent parts: Czech Republic and Slovakia. There were economic difficulties associated with this division, some were connected with the privatization process; the continuation of voucher privatization and solving the repercussions of the fact that the first wave of privatization took place at a Federal level, with cross-

the way with voucher privatizations for large firms in 1991, based on (virtually) free distribution of shares to the population at large. Hungary's privatization path is also unique. Unlike Poland and the Czech Republic, Hungary explicitly opted from 1990 to sell its productive assets instead of giving them away. Because of balance of payment difficulties, Hungary also chose to sell assets to the highest bidder, typically foreigners. In Poland, despite an early intention to rely on the free distribution of assets, the most important element behind private sector growth has been what is termed in the Polish context 'organic' privatization. Gomulka (1993)[2] defines this as a form of privatization from below where new businesses are established by both domestic and foreign investors, sometimes as a result of asset privatization (Gomulka and Jasinski, 1994). All three privatization paths have achieved a rapid change in the share of output nominally in state hands although the resulting distribution of firms by size in the private sector is very different. This provides us with the opportunity to evaluate the link from ownership change to the establishment of corporate governance and financial market institutions.

The first section of this paper reviews the main issues involved in privatization, examining its preconditions, outcomes and aims. We survey the theoretical and policy debates which have surrounded the drafting and subsequent implementation of privatization programs. Section two describes the three privatization processes, while section three considers and evaluates the alternative privatization methods in the context of the country-specific experiences of Poland, Hungary and the Czech Republic. Next, we draw out the main conclusions and introduce the issues for the subsequent section.

THE ISSUES

The concept of privatization is deceptively uncomplicated: a simple transfer of property from state hands into private hands (Vickers and Yarrow, 1988), in the West relying on the public sale of assets e.g. the experience of countries such as the UK where 'there were only 24 major privatizations in the first decade of the conservative administration, 1979–89' (Estrin, 1991). In practice, privatization debates have flared and the implementation of privatization has turned out to be a complex procedure. In this section, we first survey the definitions of privatization and present the privatization debate to date.

---

republican investments.

[2] Gomulka 'Poland: Glass Half Full', in Portes R. (1993).

Preconditions

Differences in privatization policies and in the differential outcomes of privatization policies across Poland, Hungary and the Czech Republic can be explained by each country's initial economic situation, differences in their economic progress thus far and contrasting political developments (Estrin, 1994). Central European countries were broadly similar in their industrial structure prior to reform, but varied in initial macroeconomic conditions, economic performance during transition and the degree of political stability and continuity.

At the outset of reform, the major part of GDP in the Czech Republic was provided by state firms. Poland and Hungary were exceptional by Eastern European standards because their private sectors accounted for about 18% and 30% of output respectively in 1989. In Poland's case this can be explained by a high proportion of private sector agriculture activity. The share of the state sector in the economy reflected these differences in management and employee autonomy at the enterprise level. It ranged from nearly 100% in the Czech Republic to just about 65% in Poland (see Table 16.1).

Table 16.1. The share of the state sector in the Czech Republic, Hungary and Poland

	Percent of output	Percent of employment
Czechoslovakia (Czech Republic) *1986*	97	n.a.
Hungary *1984*	81.7	69.9
Poland *1985*	65.2	71.5

Source: Milanovic (1989), Tables 1.4 and 1.7.

Central planning was to a varying extent the dominant method of enterprise management in all three countries covered in this chapter. At the extreme, in the case of former Czechoslovakia, the enterprise had very little financial or decision-making autonomy (see Ellman, 1990). Developments towards greater decentralization of control at the enterprise level occurred at a differential pace, with Hungary and Poland leading the way. Enterprise councils sprang up in both countries, but autonomy was much restricted and largely based on the result of bargaining processes between firms and various state (and party) bodies (see Kornai, 1992 for the case of Hungary).

Table 16.2. Ownership and legal form structure of industrial companies at the onset of reform

Type of Ownership	CSFR 1989	Hungary 1989	Poland 1990
Foreign owned firms/joint ventures	55	658	1,645
State-owned firms	3,619	1,983	8,453
Economic Association (Hungarian data)			
Association		299	
Limited Liability Company		3,782	
Corporation		237	
Liquidation started but not completed (Polish data)			
Article 19 of the 1981 SOE Law			18
Article 37 of the 1990 Privatization Law			31
Joint-stock companies	117		38
Other state	22	484	
Cooperatives	520	4,840	
Small private businesses		240,000	33,239
Total state	4,333	11,625	8,453

Note: The number of joint ventures in Hungary is that of both industrial and non-industrial units.
Source: Czech Statistical Office enterprise data, *Hungarian Yearbook of Economic Statistics 1990*, OECD 1993, OECD, 1996.

Table 16.2 shows first the differences in the size of the task facing each of the countries in terms of the number of state-owned firms needing transformation. It also shows that even in 1990, Hungary had already built contracts with the West and had begun to diversify. Links with foreign entities had also began to be established in Poland in 1990.

Unlike Hungary and Poland, the CSFR could not build on substantive earlier reforms and had to perform complete transformation almost overnight. The whole debate about gradualism versus 'big-bang' reforms (see earlier section) arose from a comparison of the merits of Hungarian reforms against Czech and Polish style macro-stabilization programs.[3] In the Czech Republic, centralization persisted as the dominant influence up until 1989. Reforms in the 1980s had thus been less comprehensive than those of Poland and Hungary.

---

[3] Bruno (1993) and Balcerowicz and Gelb (1994) provide a full and comprehensive comparative discussion of the stabilization policies adopted by East and Central European countries.

Hungarian 'reforms' started after the restoration of communism in 1956, when the government became more open. Reforms were partial as the government sought to avoid any serious threat to the Communist Party. However, Hungary's reforms in the 1980s were 'the most far reaching in the socialist world, with the possible exception of China' (Hare and Revesz, 1992).

The Czech Republic only began significantly granting enterprises greater decision-making power in 1990. Prior to 1990 Czechoslovakia's market structure was less decentralized and competitive than that of Poland and Hungary because planning persisted for a longer time (see Estrin and Takla, 1993). Business plans were very detailed, setting out the physical quantities that each firm was to produce and the inputs and financial resources which were to be made available to it (see Ellman, 1987). From March 1980, the socialist government applied a succession of cosmetic reforms, merging firms horizontally (Koncern) or vertically (Kombinat).[4] These reforms did not affect decision-making at the enterprise level. Tentative steps toward the decentralization of decision-making were taken in the late 1980s because of the impact of Gorbachev on Czechoslovakia.[5]

These experiments involved major decentralization, with firms' economic and technical decisions being made by their own managements. Ministries were to be confined to investment projects affecting the industrial sector as a whole, and faced constraints. They were supposed to avoid distributing profits from successful firms to less successful ones, for example. A Law on State Enterprises was passed in 1988, but was not supposed to come into effect until 1991. It legislated for reductions in subsidies and the possibility of liquidation for the first time.

In Hungary enterprises became increasingly independent in the early 1980s and significant property rights were granted to managers and workers in 1985–86. In 1985 self-governing enterprises (enterprise councils) were introduced, and in 1987 the operation of commercial banks was separated from the National Bank. As Hare and Revesz (1992) point out, 'Hungary was the first country in East and Central Europe to allow new private or cooperative businesses (and various types of business association) to be established (without the need for high ministerial permission), to lease out shops restaurants and

---

[4] This was a result of a 'Set of Measures to Improve the system of Planned Management of the National Economy After 1980', introduced in March 1980.

[5] In 1987, there was a scheme for 'the Comprehensive Restructuring of the Economic Mechanism'; 37 principles of restructuring were laid out in January 1987 and adopted in December 1987. Experiments began in 1987 with 22 enterprises which constituted almost 8 per cent of the output of the centrally-controlled economy, mostly in the export-oriented consumer goods branches. In January 1988, a further 38 enterprises – or more than 19 per cent of output – were placed under the new system.

other establishments to their managers, and to accept that such activity be legal and taxed rather than illegal as was the case elsewhere.' Over 200,000 new small private small businesses had been formed by the end of the 1980s (see Table 16.2). This small business sector was allowed to function 'with little political interference and little attempt to regulate incomes or prices'. Nevertheless, the enterprise sector remained to a great extent regulated by the central authorities; for example Kornai and Matits (1987) study in great detail the range of special taxes and subsidies which were devised to protect 'weak' firms by transferring profits from profitable firms to less profitable ones (see also Kornai, 1986).

In Poland, a notable number of enterprises were, in effect, run by Workers' Councils. Even before the fall of socialism, Workers' Councils had attained a decision-making position that included the right to appoint the senior management and to approve the annual business plans (Aoki 1994). Until the reforms of the 1980s, state-owned enterprises were controlled 'by the upper tiers of the command hierarchy'. Nevertheless the rules of control were not clearly defined. 'This left room for discretion on the part of various administrative bodies involved in the management of the economy on many levels' (M. Iwanek, 1992). Reforms in the early 1980s virtually replaced outside intervention in the management of state firms with a new control structure, and set out legal rules for the governance of enterprises. Enterprise control was divided up between three newly-defined and distinct parties: the Founding Organ (usually a ministry representing the state), the Workers' Council representing employees, and the Enterprise Manager. Sharing control often led to conflicts over decision-making. From 1981, the Law on State Enterprises of 25 September allowed the closing down and selling off of insolvent enterprises to private buyers as one entity, or broken up (Article 19). Insolvent enterprises could also be made bankrupt (Article 24 of the 1981 Law) on the basis of the bankruptcy procedures described in the Decree 24-10-1934 of the President of the Polish Republic. 'Article 19 liquidation differs from bankruptcy procedures primarily because it can only be applied if there are 'grounds for stating' that liquidation net revenues are sufficient to satisfy all creditors claims' (Nuti, 1996). Table 16.2 reveals that, by 1990, the liquidation of only 18 enterprises had been initiated and none completed. 'Other, economically viable firms were being sold or leased, also as a whole or in parts, to private buyers and consortia of buyers, with priority granted to new companies formed with employee participation; this was allowed by the 1990 Privatization Law, Article 37 (enterprise assets could also be contributed to a new company without preference for employees)' (Nuti, 1996).

Hungarian industrial structure was less concentrated than that of the Czech Republic. Only 0.1% of Czech output was provided by firms with less than 200

employees (Zemplinerova, 1994 Table 16.2). In contrast, by 1990, it is
estimated that small firms – which were legalized in 1981 – accounted for
about 10% of industrial output in Hungary. This small business sector's activity
benefited from the reduction in political interference. In addition, Hungary had,
by 1990, liberalized imports, extended export licences to companies and
significantly reformed the structure of prices. Poland had also liberalized some
prices prior to its 1990 reform package. It started significant legal reform in
1985 when the 1934 Commercial Code was reinstated. This was followed by
the 1988 Law on Economic Activity, which was introduced by the Rakowski
government.

Table 16.3. Initial macroeconomic conditions

	Hungary	Poland	Czecho-slovakia
Population (in million 1989)	10.6	37.9	10.1
Real GDP 1990[a]			
in US$ million	102	297	220
United States = 100	1.7	5.0	3.7
GNP growth (average rate in % at constant prices)			
1970s	4.5	3.5	4.6
1980s	0.5	-0.07	1.4
Administered prices (% of total)	15%	100%[b]	100%
Inflation rate (1989, in %)	11.6	351.1	1.4
Unemployment rate (1990, in %)	1.7	6.1	1.7
State ownership	90%	70%	Economy-wide
Money (M1)/GDP, 1990	0.4	0.9[c]	0.7
Export to CMEA			
in % of total exports	43	41[d]	60
in % of GDP	16	14	25

Notes:
a Source OECD (unofficial data).
b Excluding food prices.
c (M2)/GDP 1989.
d 1989 figure.
Source: Estrin (1994) and National Statistics Yearbooks.

Table 16.3 reviews the position of all three countries before the introduction of economic reform programs. On the microeconomic front, as stated earlier, Hungary's system was more liberal. As can be seen in Table 16.3, only 15% of prices were government-administered, while in Poland and former Czechoslovakia all industrial prices were administered. In addition, in contrast to 100% state ownership in former Czechoslovakia, 90% of Hungarian assets and 70% of Polish assets were state-owned in 1989.

In terms of size according to population, Poland was, and still is, far larger than both the other countries and thus the size of the economic and especially political task of reform weighed much heavier. All three countries had relatively low GDP levels, ranging from US$ 297 billion (Poland), US$ 200 billion (former Czechoslovakia) and US$ 102 billion (Hungary) and, although GNP growth averaged above 3% in the 1970s, that rate of growth dropped significantly in the 1980s (negative for Poland). This was due, in part, to inefficient economic management under central planning (see Ellman, 1990). In addition, although former Czechoslovakia had the highest export ratio as a percentage of GDP in 1989 (25%), most of these exports were destined for former CMEA markets (60%). Only 43% of Hungary's and 41% of Poland's exports were destined to CMEA markets at the end of the 1980s.

In the Czech Republic, although firms had been under tight state control until 1989, macroeconomic stability was maintained throughout most of the communist period (see Tables 16.3 and 16.4). Czechoslovakia inherited a system which was characterized by fiscal conservatism, which was reflected in restrictive macroeconomic policies. Important contrasts between the three countries are highlighted in their inflation and current account records prior to reform (see Table 16.3). Inflation had never emerged as a serious problem in the Czech Republic – 1.4% in 1989 and averaging less than 2% from 1980 to 1989 (OECD 1991), with hidden inflation estimated at 2.5% per annum over the same period. In 1989, Hungarian inflation stood at 11.6% and Poland was heading towards hyperinflation (351.1). Poland therefore had a bigger macroeconomic problem to contend with and its reform program relied heavily on price stabilization measures.

Previous policies left the new Czechoslovak regime in 1990 facing neither the external debt nor the monetary overhang (indicated by M1/GDP) of Poland and Hungary (see Table 16.3). Polish M1/GDP ratio was perhaps twice the OECD average (Estrin, 1994). According to Table16.4, in 1990 external debt as a percentage of GDP was 65% in Hungary and 80% in Poland, while it stood at only 19% in Czechoslovakia. The CSFR also weathered the deterioration in terms of trade and external financing difficulties of the 1980s better than other countries in the region. External debt service obligations and external debt[6] in convertible currencies remained in the 1980s well below those of Hungary and Poland.

Table 16.4. Debt cross-country comparisons 1989

	External debt as % of GDP	External debt as % of exports of goods and services	Debt service as % of exports of goods and services
CSFR	14.9	108.7	18.8
Hungary	58.8	475.8	44.5
Poland	71.3	239.8	40.6
Portugal	45	115.7	17.5

Source: OECD 1991.

As Table 16.4 demonstrates, the CSFR was about on a par with Portugal and in a substantially different position from Poland or Hungary. In 1988, the hard currency debt service ratio was 76% for Poland, 54% for Hungary and 16% for CSFR. Czechoslovakia attained a net-creditor position in transactions in transferable roubles, in particular *vis-à-vis* the USSR and Poland. It experienced annual surpluses in non-convertible currencies, averaging US$ 336 million between 1985 and 1989.

The difference in debt situations pre-reform further emphasizes the different methods which were incorporated into the privatization schemes of all three countries. The decision of whether to distribute assets freely was easier for Czechoslovakia than it was for Poland and Hungary. This has meant that subsequently the Czech Republic could afford not to rely on the direct sale of its assets in order to finance its budget deficit. Czech foreign direct investment policy – which did not offer special incentives to foreign investors and which relied on a low wage policy – could be sustained as there was no foreign reserves requirements urgency and no threat of a foreign debt crisis. The Czech Republic paid back its IMF standby loans well ahead of its allotted time period.

To sum up, whatever the divergence in past performance, all three Central European countries faced similar problems at the outset of change: how to initiate competition and how to change the ownership structure of the economy, while preserving macroeconomic stability. Currently all three countries have experienced a lengthy transition period – at least five years. Hungary can be

---

[6] Domestic debt was even more insignificant. The government budget was close to balance; net government debt in 1989 stood at less than 1% of GDP.

considered to have started economic reforms in 1988, Poland in 1990 and former Czechoslovakia in 1991.

This background has in part shaped privatization debates and conduct in all three countries. For example, the issue of insider control was not a major stumbling block in the Czech Republic. In Poland, where the decentralization of decision-making at the enterprise level started in 1981, employees had to be incorporated into privatization legislation as they held effective control over enterprise assets. In Hungary, managers and/or employees guided– at least at the beginning of the process – the conduct of many privatization initiatives regardless of actual government legislation and debates. Preconditions were, however, not the only factor that shaped individual privatization packages. Academic and political debates about the aims of privatization were also crucial in shaping adopted policies.

The Aims of Privatization Policy

'At root, the transformation from socialist central planning to a market economy entails a radical adjustment in the balance of power between the state and civic society in favour of the latter. In this light privatization is arguably the most important, and probably the most complex element of the transformation process. This is because privatization, broadly defined as transfer of state-owned assets to private ownership, alongside the creation and fostering *de novo* private businesses is about the (re)-distribution of property (wealth) and the means of generating wealth. Hence, ultimately, it is about the longer-term distribution of economic and political power. Decisions related to privatization impinge on almost every aspect of the transformation process. They profoundly affect the future shape of the country's economy and its performance both on the domestic and international markets. In the CEE context, privatization involves a huge upheaval at every stage of society: changes in regional patterns of economic activity, in the labor market, and at the same time, as a new class of entrepreneurs, property owners and shareholders emerges, some social groups will almost inevitably find themselves excluded or marginalised. Policy misjudgements or mismanagement could have grave consequences for social cohesion, threaten the consensus for reform as a whole and seriously undermine the country's political stability. Privatization thus brings a myriad of interest groups to the fore and into confrontation with each other' (Canning and Hare, 1996).

Before embarking on our own analysis and categorization of the aims of privatization, we have to make clear that our approach schematizes the 'objectives' of policy-makers as if there existed a rational 'designer' to establish them. These normative objectives are probably good approximations to what governments arrive at when devising an overall privatization policy. On the other hand, one could analyse the objectives of various players (or, rather interest groups) in specific privatization cases in a descriptive/positive way (see Antal (1996), Canning and Hare (1996)). In a specific privatization case, the broader goals described in what follows (ensuring equity, depoliticizing the economy) are only secondary and probably only form part of a wider framework.

There is quite a wealth of literature about the objectives of privatization, listing all the relative benefits of one method of privatization against another in attaining these objectives, and sometimes also taking into account political and institutional feasibility constraints. Estrin (1991), Tirole (1991), Blanchard and Layard (1990) and Lipton and Sachs (1990) are amongst the many early papers that survey the important issues in privatization. Bolton and Roland (1992), Dewatripond and Roland (1993), Schmidt and Schnitzer (1993) and Schleifer and Vishny (1994) have encapsulated the both political and the efficiency objectives of privatization into stylised models. In all three countries, privatization advisors and analysts agreed that the aims of the privatization of state property were multi-dimensional. For example, voucher privatization was viewed as a way to circumvent the stock-flow problem involved in the selling-off of assets to domestic buyers (see Roland, 1990). The arguments for voucher privatization are best summarized in Nuti (1994) as intentions to:

1. *ensure equity*:   as industrial assets are assumed to have belonged to the population at large under the previous system, privatization methods that insured some form of fair initial distribution of wealth were advocated by certain reforming governments (Czechoslovakia in 1990–1991, President Walesa in his September 1993 campaign). It was held that all adult citizens have equal claims on state assets, and that capitalism should start with an egalitarian distribution of this wealth. Equity considerations not only focus on the population at large; they also have been used to bolster the position of certain groups in society. In Poland, for example, Lavigne (1994) states that 'equity considerations have been dominant in allowing the most extensive workers' preferential share in the assets of privatising companies.'

2. *depoliticize the economy*:   the major difference between Western European governments grappling with the privatization dilemma and former socialist countries is that in the latter countries the share of the state sector in the economy at the start of transition far exceeded the western average, which ranged from 1.3% of total output in the United States in 1983 to 16.5% in France in 1982 (Milanovic, 1989). Reformers in all three countries concluded that their previous economic system meant that the behavior of the state as owner would always lead to active interference in

enterprise activities and thus obstruct competition. The speed of privatization has been linked to the need for the rapid de-politicization of the economy (Vishny and Schleifer 1988, Lipton and Sachs 1990). The new ownership structure should be installed as soon as possible in order to minimize 'the probability of degeneration in the sense of devolution to state ownership, assuming this would represent a step backward rather than forward' (Earle and Estrin, 1995).

The formation of new post-communist states is challengingly described in Batt (1996). Post-communist states are viewed as opting for a model of statehood built upon the Napoleonic tradition 'particularly for the purpose of implementing economic transformation. Too often, this has been seen in terms of 'rolling back the state', reducing its powers and the scope of its intervention in the economy, in line with trends towards liberalization, deregulation and privatization in Western economies'. But, the task of economic reform is one where the state cannot take a back seat. It has to implement 'capitalism from above' (Offe, 1991) and what is needed is not the disappearance of the state or a less powerful one, but a state which 'plays different roles and does so more effectively' (Nelson, 1989).

Another (economic) criterion for examining the degree of de-politiciza-tion attained is the extent to which state subsidies to industry were run down. Table 16.5 shows that the ratio of subsidies to GDP fell by 43% in the first year of reform on Poland, by 28% in Hungary and by 52% in Czechoslovakia.

In the first year of reforms subsidies decreased dramatically (see Table 16.5). Czechoslovakia administered the harshest cut (by 52%). The level of subsidies as a percentage of GDP was highest in the Czech Republic and in 1995 subsidies represented only 5% of GDP compared with 25% in 1989. Both Hungary and Poland started off with lower subsidy to GDP levels in 1989 (12.9% and 12.1% respectively) and decreased less rapidly to reach 3.3% and 4.4% of GDP in 1992.

3. *stop the appropriation of state assets by insiders*: this aim is a political objective where privatization is a sufficient end-result in itself. It is not the economic effect of privatization that matters, but the fact that, by turning property into mainly outsider private hands, you remove it from the control of its former Communist management. This was a major motivation in the Czech Republic and is demonstrated in its choice of voucher privatization with coupon sales to the population at large at a nominal price. Other political motivations mentioned in the literature (see Estrin 1991, Roland 1993) include the fact that privatization should help prevent a reversion to the old system and ensure that reforms are virtually irreversible.

Table 16.5. Subsidies outcome in Poland, Hungary and the Czech Republic in the first years of transition

	Poland	Hungary	Czecho-slovakia
Percentage change in the Subsidies/GDP, first year of reform	-43	-28	-52
Subsidy fiscal expenditure as % of GDP			
1989	12.9	12.1	25.0
1990	7.3	9.8	16.2
1991	4.6	7.1	7.7
1992	3.3	4.4	5.0

Source: Balcerowicz and Gelb (1994).

Political support for a reformist government may be extended and consolidated by the egalitarian pursuit of some forms of mass privatization. The population at large can thus acquire a stake in the economy and so in the success of the reform process. In the case of Hungary and Poland, different groups within the population had already assigned themselves a stake in the enterprise sector (managers / employees) and their interests clashed with other groups. Privatization policy had therefore to contend with different interest groups, and political support from these separate interest groups was as important as that from the population at large, as these groups were already entrenched in the corporate sector and could hijack the whole micro-restructuring process if their objectives and claims were sidelined. As pointed out by Batt (1996), 'in the more homogeneous national states such as Poland and Hungary, economic reforms were accompanied by a diffusion of political power to regional and sectoral lobbies, who proved able to stymie reforms when they threatened their interests.'

4. *to increase government revenues*:   the financial aim of privatization is prevalent in western economies where it was viewed as a means of raising government revenue. The governments in Eastern Europe could opt for measures based on the sale of assets for reasons such as financing their foreign debt or increasing costs of unemployment and other social benefits as restructuring begins. This financial aim has only been actively aspired to by Hungary, where the government initially decided to sell rather than give away property.

5. *to harden budget constraints*:   firms under the old planning system are assumed to have operated under soft-budget constraints (see Kornai, 1982; Hare, 1994). They were heavily subsidized by the centre through the pricing

system, the willingness of governments to cover company losses and the investment allocation mechanism (see Keren, 1992). Soft-budget constraints meant that demand for inputs such as labor had a 'tendency to grow without limits' (Kornai, 1982) given that financial constraints on managers were virtually non-existent.

Budget constraints will however harden with the move from planning to market through price liberalization, as well as through the decision by the government to privatize firms and cut subsidies and thus sever the direct link between the government's budget and the enterprise sector.

It is even more widely argued that public ownership favors intervention. Arguments that link the effect of private ownership with the hardening of budget constraints are mostly based on empirical findings that study the limits of market socialism and assert that introducing competitive markets is not a sufficient condition for imposing hard-budget constraints (see Kornai, 1986 and 1992, Nuti, 1988).

6. *to raise efficiency and speed up the physical and financial restructuring of enterprises:*[7]   the main objective of mass privatization in the Czech Republic was purely the transfer of property out of state hands. In the words of Vaclav Klaus (1993), 'We consider it unnecessary to design techniques and legislation with respect to the objective of selecting perfect owners. An objective like this is far beyond the capacity of post-communist governments and first (initial) owners may not be the final ones ... it is the economy as a whole, not a particular state-owned firm or firms that calls for transformation. In other words, however efficient or inefficient, financially healthy or unhealthy individual businesses may appear, it is not them, but the whole economy, which requires a change'.

Nevertheless, privatization – whichever form it takes – is assumed to lead to increased efficiency through better resource allocation, a hardening of budget constraints and the exercise of effective control over enterprise management. Poor enterprise performance in the last ten years of the socialist system in former Czechoslovakia offers support for the idea that developments in corporate governance should lead to output and welfare gains (see Brada, 1989; Crane, 1991).

Theoretical and empirical studies of planned economies find that managerial incentives were geared towards meeting output targets (see Ellman, 1989). If expenditures on labor, capital or material inputs exceeded set levels, the relevant state organs were inclined to underwrite them. Managerial incentives will change once new ownership and corporate governance

---

[7] We visit this topic in depth in the next section.

structures are developed and once the economy is liberalized.

Various papers have attempted to formalize the privatization / restructuring link (Earle and Estrin, 1994, 1995, 1996; Vishny and Schleifer, 1994; Aghion and Carlin, 1994; Takla, 1995). Underlying the various theoretical approaches in the literature is an exploration of whether different privatization strategies (voucher privatization, direct sale to an outside buyer or transfer to an insider – manager or employee) result in a different efficiency/restructuring outcome or a different tempo in reaching efficiency and/or restructuring outcomes. The literature compares the merits of each form of ownership and provides inconclusive evidence on the ownership/restructuring link. Suffice to say that the micro-restructuring debate usually focuses on shortcomings at the firm level and the ability of the new owners to influence restructuring at the firm level via active managerial involvement, access to capital and financing and specialized knowledge.

Some theoretical models of privatization explicitly model the privatization/ efficiency/incentives link (see Aghion and Blanchard, 1993; Schmidt and Schnitzer, 1993; and Hare and Estrin, 1994). For example, Aghion and Blanchard's (1993) model builds a relationship between fast restructuring, privatization and (technical) efficiency where the impact of structural change is studied through labor market developments. A rise in unemployment is viewed as an increase in restructuring. Such a rise is associated with lower 'labor hoarding', a higher rate of privatization and decreases with a higher rate of growth in the *de novo* private sector. The *de novo* private sector is assumed to absorb workers made redundant because of restructuring measures. On the other hand, Schmidt and Schnitzer (1993) provide a different approach to linking privatization with efficiency. They formally model the privatization process using standard contract theory and develop a simple theoretic framework which analyses systematically the impact of different corporate governance structures on management incentives, the efficiency of restructuring, and the social costs of the adjustment process. They find managers of a firm will work harder and restructure more efficiently in privately-owned firms than in government-controlled ones, since they know firms are less likely to go bankrupt under government control. The government will try to rescue the firm in order to avoid the social costs of liquidation. In their model, 'privatization is a commitment device of the government not to subsidise unsuccessful firms'.

The change in management incentive structure is thus the key to linking privatization with increases in productivity. The problem of creating effective corporate governance has been raised by many observers (Aoki, 1994; Dittus and Prowse, 1994; Berglof, 1994; Baer and Gray, 1994; Mitchell, 1994; and Phelps *et al.*, 1993). If privatization leads to control by a private non-bank entity, then managerial incentives will be checked through the stock exchange and the market for corporate control. A private owner is more likely than a state owner to design managerial reward schedules in order to fulfil its profit-maximization objective.

The key point is that the nature and speed of privatization leads to different ownership configurations, which in turn lead to a range of incentives to restructure. For example, through its choice of mass privatization, the Czech Republic had privatized around half of its large enterprises by mid-1993, with the other half being privatized subsequently in 1994. Although the intention might not have been fast restructuring, privatization in this case is postulated as likely to lead to restructuring because the new external environment is more likely to enforce a bankruptcy threat on enterprises. Private enterprises will notionally be monitored through the market for corporate control via the stock exchange, through lending arrangements with the new private commercial banks or equity stake holdings by these same banks. Active involvement of funds as owners will increase the importance placed on the profit motive.

Privatization of large firms has been sluggish in Poland (see next section) with the privatization process being slower than initially planned and followed a multi-track course which 'all ... involved some form, often significant, of employee ownership' (Nuti, 1996). Theoretical predictions of employee ownership are described in Nuti (1996), Earle and Estrin (1995) and Uvalic (1991). A non-controlling interest is viewed positively as encouraging productivity, inducing better labor relations and promoting economic democracy. On the negative side, when employees have control over an enterprise, they may:

1. keep employment levels higher than is compatible with profit maximization;
2. raise gross earnings above the market wage rate irrespective of the positive profit constraint;
3. have a tendency towards lower self-financed investment, with lower access external finance and no access to external equity relative to a profit-maximizing firm (see Kamshad, 1995).

In Hungary the sale of firms to foreign investors has been most emphasized, although is not the dominant form of ownership. Such privatization is deemed to generate 'deeper restructuring and lead to significant performance improvement' (EBRD, 1995). Estrin, Hughes and Todd (1996) survey the theoretical incentives of foreign direct investment (FDI) and provide case studies of the effect of such investments on specific companies. The 'restructuring' outcome in such cases depends on the capital backing of investors and the potential injection of capital for investment purposes, as well as the introduction of new technologies, marketing and management practices.

In this section we have schematized the objectives of policy-makers faced with the dilemma of how to privatize the economy. In practice, 'attitudes to and understanding of the issues underlying the privatization of state-owned (SOEs) in transitional economies have evolved and changed since 1990, bringing concomitant changes in the focus of privatization policy and continuous modification in the strategy, pace and methods adopted' (Canning and Hare, 1996). The transition environment has been one 'where the rules of the game have been altered by the players while playing the game'. Some of these changes were pragmatic and others could be attributed to the influence of various interest groups (political / economic and social). In the words of Batt (1996), 'The challenge facing the builders of new states in post-communist Europe is thus an enormously complex one, involving a delicate balancing act between the demands of economic transformation, which seem to require a strong state in the sense of an authoritative and effective centre, and demand for managing multi-national societies which seem to point towards a more pluralistic and devolved state structure. There are no ready models to prescribe the appropriate institutional framework. Each state will have to hammer out its own eclectic formula in an extended and open-ended process of negotiation and compromise.'

Description of Privatization

In this section we chart the evolution of privatization in our three focus countries. The main privatization methods are listed in Table 16.6, which highlights the point that all three countries have followed privatization strategies which have encompassed a mix of different methods. It is only the emphasis on methods which has varied. This emphasis reflects government concern about management and employee control of enterprises, budget revenue considerations and the perceived speed of privatization, as well as the effective control of the state over the privatization process.

Table 16.6 charts privatization plans as perceived in 1991 and contrasts them with actual outcomes. In 1991 all three countries aimed to privatize the major part of their industrial assets within the following five years. By mid-1994, the share of the private sector in GDP was above 50% in all of them. This rise in recorded private sector shares can initially be attributed to an increase in trade and services activities, but later to other sectors also (Balcerowicz and Gelb, 1994).

The extent to which this private sector growth can be directly attributable to the privatization of state enterprises will be examined later. Table 16.6 also reveals that the Czech Republic and Poland both assigned the task of privatizing the economy to a newly created state organ the 'Privatization

Table 16.6. Privatization plans in the Czech Republic, Hungary and Poland in mid-1991 compared to privatization outcomes

	Czech Republic	Hungary	Poland
Period to privatize *1991 plan*	over 5 years	in 5 years	in 3 years
1994 outcome Private sector share in GDP Private sector share in total employment	over 60% in 1994 over 60%	over 60% around 50%	55% 60% (end 1993)
Privatization institutions	Ministry of Privatization National Property Fund	State Property Agency State Asset Management Company	Ministry of Privatization
Privatization method *planned*	Mass privatization through the issue of vouchers used to purchase shares or entrusted to investment funds in the period, 1990	Mass privatization through the distribution of shares on subsidized credit from 1992; sale primarily through the stock exchange also auction and tender 1990	Mass privatization through the issue of certificates in investment funds set up by the state
1994 outcome	Voucher privatization mixed with other methods 1992–94	'Spontaneous' 1990–91; case by case on the capital market 1993–95; direct sale to foreign investors 1990–96	'Liquidation' 1990–95 Mass privatization 1996

Source: EBRD 1994, Estrin 1991, Lavigne 1994.

335

Ministry'. The Czech Republic created an additional state body, the National Property Fund – where the shares of enterprises 'to be privatized' were stored. The NPF also received the income from privatization sales. It was further intended that the NPF should manage the state's stake in enterprises in the interim period, before their shareholdings are turned over to a private entity. The Hungarian privatization strategy separated the two roles of the NPF and assigned each role to a distinct agency the State Privatization Agency and the State Asset Management Company (or State Holding Company (SHC)). We will compare further the functioning of these institutions and their involvement in the enterprise sector and in the choice of privatization method.

The state had to take two important considerations into account when implementing its privatization program. First, it had to decide about the mechanics of privatization (property to be allocated, timetable, choice of enterprise, choice of industries, and type of privatization). Secondly, when opting for a privatization strategy, the state had to address the outcome of privatization on the allocation of power between the different economic actors at the onset of privatization (the state and its various ministries, the managers and the employees, the investment funds and the banks).

The initial plans of both Poland and the Czech Republic favored privatization based on give-away schemes. The equitable aim of mass privatization was prevalent in all three programs. In Poland, Lech Walesa's electoral campaign was based on returning to the people the property they had worked for, thus enriching them. In the Czech Republic the aim was to place property in the population's hands. In Hungary, privatization was understood as 'compensation for four decades of economic injustice' (Nuti, 1994).

In practice, in all three countries, mass privatization has been used in conjunction with other schemes, namely restitution. In the Czech Republic, 3% of property was set aside for restitution; in Hungary former owners have been given vouchers instead of physical assets. Mass privatization was further politicized in Hungary, as vouchers were also used to compensate victims of political persecution.

In Central Europe at the onset of reform, capital markets were underdeveloped and the levels of savings were such as to render the population powerless to purchase the majority of state assets. In addition, even if purchase of the assets were possible, mass privatization only requires simple valuation techniques and minimal financial and physical restructuring prior to auction.

The direct sale of state property requires more complex individual valuations of property. Other forms of privatization, such as the 'spontaneous' form, which was prevalent in Hungary, could also be termed as 'fast'. However, spontaneous privatization violates the objective of equitable privatization as the former *nomenklatura*, the managers or the employees of the enterprise, are seen to be appropriating state property. This creates resentment because of perceived inequality. This is especially true if the ownership of enterprises is regarded as being *de facto* in managers' and employees' hands.

Privatization methods come in four basic guises: direct sales, give-away schemes, liquidation, and employee or management buy-outs. The first three variants have typically relied on centralized governmental control, while management and employee buy-outs have tended to be decentralized and sometimes labelled as 'spontaneous'.

Although not an aim in itself, employee ownership has been introduced in Poland and in Hungary. In the Czech Republic, on the other hand, it has played a relatively minor role (see Earle and Estrin, 1995, Table 1). Employee ownership was either a consequence of political compromise or it just transpired by default. In Poland, and to a lesser extent in Hungary, the previous regimes had experimented with different forms of self-management.

Privatization methods, as perceived in the earliest plans, all encompassed a mass privatization element. This element was emphasized in the Czech and Polish case and less so in the Hungarian. Privatization outcomes in all three countries exhibit a mixture of methods. We next provide a step-by-step description of the evolution of privatization in each country.

Poland: the emergence of employee ownership
Poland was amongst the first countries to announce (September 1989) and to launch 'large-scale privatization' . The first privatization law 'the Law on Privatization' was passed on 13 July 1990. Initially the most favoured method by policy makers had been that of 'capital privatization'. However, in the words of Nuti (1996) this method 'proved to be slower, costlier and harder than anticipated'. A mass privatization scheme was devised to resolve the problem of lack of liquid savings (pulverized by high inflation) and the problem of asset valuation. It is also the country that has experienced the most delay in implementing its mass privatization program due to technical and political delays, while the *de novo* private sector rapidly flourished alongside the old state sector.

Since 1989–90, successive Polish governments have debated the above-mentioned issues related to mass privatization. The dilemma of the debate prior to the drafting of the Act on the Privatization of State-Owned Enterprises of 1990 concerned the issue of whether to sell shares or distribute them free of charge. The implementation of the mass privatization program was to wait until 1996. In the intervening period Polish privatization has emerged as one characterized by the following traits:

1. The early target of privatizing 50% of state enterprises by 1992 was not reached, even when the target was moved on to the end of 1995, it was still

not achieved. By the end of 1995, 54% of the initial 8,453 enterprises were still in state hands; the rest were in the process of being privatized. Completed privatizations represented only a fifth of that initial total.

2. This has meant that, although mass privatization was slow, other methods were introduced to overcome unexpected difficulties as they arose. Regardless of difficulties with capital and mass privatizations, privatization according to Article 19 of the 1981 Law and Article 39 of the 1990 Law proceeded fairly quickly. Although these two methods, already briefly described, reflected radically different conditions of the firm, they had in common the so-called 'liquidation' of state enterprises; they were taken off the Registry of state enterprises by the Tribunal.

3 New, additional channels emerged after 1993, (Law of 3 February 1993 on 'Financial Restructuring of State Enterprises and Banks'), where 'at the initiative of either creditor or debtor in case of actual or prospective inability to pay' privatization can take the form of a debt-equity swap.

4 All the Polish variations of privatization involved some form – often significant – of employee ownership. For example, employees of enterprises privatized following capital privatization were initially offered 20% of capital equity at half-price and subject to a one-year wage bill maximum. This rule later became a free 10% share and was subsequently raised to 15%. In the case of mass privatization and commercialization, 15% of the capital was set aside for employees. Article 37 liquidation was the most common channel for management-employee buy-outs (MEBOs) taking the form of a lease purchase agreement. By the end of 1995, 788 enterprises followed this route – i.e. 68.6% of directly privatized enterprises.

In our description of Polish privatization we will concentrate on three aspects of privatization, mass privatization, commercialization and employee ownership as a collateral of liquidation. Privatization, to date, has been voluntary and has adopted a multi-track approach. The most popular privatization methods used in Poland include capital privatization (i.e. commercialization), privatization through liquidation for large enterprises using the 1990 Privatization Act or the Law on State-Owned Enterprises 1981, and branch privatization. The role of the government is evident both in the preparation of privatization projects and in the ownership of commercialized companies. Privatization projects were decided through 'direct negotiations between the government and state enterprise managers'. As a consequence, of the 200 enterprises first chosen for voucher privatization, 50 sought to pull out and 32 succeeded in doing so. The reason behind the success of some applications was that the enterprises were negotiating sales or joint ventures with foreign buyers (Nuti, 1994).

Details of actual outcomes of privatization are presented in Table 16.7.

Despite delays in the implementation of mass privatization, Poland's private sector activity has risen. This is due in part to a move in practice towards other privatization methods. Unlike the Czech Republic, the growth in the share of the private sector in Poland's GDP has not been driven by the mass transfer of ownership rights from the state to the private sector.

Table 16.7. Summary of the progress of privatization (cumulative number of enterprises eop)

	1990	1991	1992	1993	1994	1995
Total no. of state-owned enterprises	8,453	8,228	7,245	5,924	4,955	4,563
Total Liquidations						
started		989	1,576	1,999	2,287	2,507
completed		201	561	893	1,248	1,405
Article 19 of the SOE Law						
started		540	857	1,082	1,845	1,358
completed		10	86	1,886	303	396
Article 37 of the Privatization Law						
started		449	715	917	1,402	1,149
completed		182	475	707	945	1,054
Companies converted to joint-stock companies	38	260	480	527	723	958
Capital privatization of which:	6	27	51	99	134	160
public offerings	5	11	12	15	19	22
trade sales	1	16	39	81	110	132
mixed methods	0	0	0	3	5	6
Total privatizations						
started	936	1,276	2,107	2,625	3,144	3,625
completed		228	612	992	1,382	1,610

Note: Percentage change 1990–1995: 48%

The dominant factor behind the rise of the private sector from 28.6% of GDP in 1989 to 50% in 1993 has been the growth of a *de novo* private sector, the commercialization of the former cooperative sector and the leasing of small businesses (see Gomulka and Jasinski, 1994). The quickest and most popular method of privatizing the economy has thus been *organic* privatization (Gomulka, 1993). Organic privatization is defined as the establishment of new private businesses by both Polish and foreign investors and the growth of existing private companies.

This growth of private sector activity has happened in parallel with the privatization of old state enterprises. By 1993, 2,265 enterprises qualified to take part in the privatization process, around 13% of which were to be privatized by direct sale, 7.4% by mass privatization and 79% by liquidation.

Only 38.7% of the total number of firms were privatized. There were no privatizations though mass privatization. By 1995, the picture had not radically changed, although the number of enterprises marked for liquidation started to drop. The number of SOEs fell by 48%.

As can be seen from Table 16.7, liquidation was dominant as the major method of privatization up until 1995. The pace of capital privatization, on the other hand, has been closely linked to political developments: privatization by direct sale and floatation practically came to a standstill throughout most of 1992, but gathered pace again before the elections in September 1993. In contrast to Czech developments, in Poland, although it debated voucher privatization extensively, by mid-1994 – four years after the first Privatization Law (June 1990) was passed – not one single enterprise has been privatized through mass privatization.

The mass privatization process – a delayed experiment. Large-scale privatization was to use four initial methods (Gdansk surveys, 1990–94 and Belka *et al.*, 1994) restitution, liquidation, commercialization (restructuring) and preparatory restructuring. One of the methods of privatization which results from the commercialization of enterprises is mass privatization, which would involve three distribution methods: the issue of shares and their sale; the issue of investment certificates to the National Investment Funds; and auction tenders. The final division of property rights was so framed as to allocate 10–20% of assets to employees, the rest to be divided up between domestic investors, foreign investors and the state.

Five consecutive Privatization Ministers relaunched the debate, holding as they did conflicting views about the extent and method of mass privatization and its relative importance. The problem of setting up funds – whether they should be managed by the state or the private sector – the role of foreign capital, the role of managers and intermediaries and shareholders, the appointment of new management teams, the rules for the selection of enterprises and the share of coupon privatization are all facets of the political and technical difficulties faced by a succession of Polish governments from 1990 to 1993.

Investment funds were set up by the government as in Poland (the Law on National Investment Funds and their Privatization, 30 April 1993). The government granted the National Investment Funds the ownership of assets. The debate about funds, their portfolio, their role in enterprise restructuring and the choice of fund-managers was part of government policy.

This caused a further delay in mass privatization. The selection of funds, given the agreed criteria, was deferred during the May 1993 political crisis. The new government of 1995 went ahead only in 1996 with the first wave of privatization having established a new funds' selection committee. Although the new government has reduced the emphasis on voucher privatization, it has retained the mass privatization plan as a sign of its commitment to market transition. After long deliberation, the government decided that it would establish around 24 funds, with government-selected foreign management bodies.

The mass privatization plan can be described as follows; companies were paired with teams of domestic and foreign management experts in NIFs, and the NIFs provide them with restructuring capital. NIF shares were then issued, for a nominal fee, and a year later listed on the stock exchange. Share value will depend on the performance of companies on the stock exchange and management incentives would be in the form of cash dividends or equity under their ten-year contract.

The government gave the go-ahead to the mass privatization program in late November 1994 and 60% of the shares of 512 commercialized companies have since been turned over to 15 NIFs. Each fund holds 33% of the shares of each company allocated to it. Another 27% is spread among the remaining funds, 15% retained by employees and the rest will remain in state hands. Employees will be allowed to sell their shares to each other or to the investment funds.

The government issued mass privatization participation certificates available to all adult Polish citizens officially resident in Poland. Participation certificates are bearer certificates and it is possible to trade them on the Warsaw Stock Exchange as well as outside it. To avoid price differentials in different parts of the country, the Ministry of Privatization launched a media campaign to inform bearers of the prices.

The certificates issues were followed by the issue of shares in investment funds purchasable in exchange for the participation certificates, but only on the Warsaw Stock Exchange. The funds' shares are exactly the same as those of other quoted companies. Regulations to facilitate over-the-counter trading in mass privatization certificates and other unlisted securities are in force. There are nineteen Polish, foreign and mixed consortia competing for management contracts which will be negotiated and awarded by the investment funds' supervisory boards. Their task would be to restructure and then privatize the companies under their management.

Privatization techniques have thus evolved and been adapted to circumvent the slow pace of mass privatization and other policy constraints. The political sphere has been characterized by a high turnover of governing parties and ministers. This has made the conduct of a consistent privatization policy difficult, as each successive government has tended to reverse or alter previous legislation. Regardless of this, state-owned enterprises have shrunk in number and by percentage in the period 1990–1995.

Employee ownership – a de facto outcome.   Another concern of Polish
policy-makers and legislators has been the power of trade unions and workers
councils at the enterprise level. The downfall of the Communist Party in Poland
led to firms being managed by a 'triumvirate' of management, workers'
councils and trade unions (usually Solidarity). Polish reforms in the 1980s were
in the direction of self-management. As the Communist party lost its hold over
the enterprise sector, managers, workers councils and trade unions took control
of firms. Gomulka and Jasinski (1994) claim that Solidarity Union controlled
the workers councils and they in turn controlled the managers. Consequently,
negotiations with employees were an integral part of the preparatory phases of
mass privatization. The 1990 Privatization Act, which resulted from heated
discussions between politicians and economic advisors, was complex in
structure.

Given the precarious political power of successive governments, mass
privatization legislation has been plagued by amendments resulting from
political compromises under pressure from coalition partners or minority
parties in Parliament, as well as other constraints. The final version of the Law
(April 1993) is an illustration of this. The amendments to the rejected 1992
proposed legislation allow enterprises to withdraw from the schemes, place
constraints on the managers of the National Investment Funds (NIFs), and limit
voucher eligibility to pensioners and civil servants in the first round of
privatization.

Management and employee buy-outs (MEBOs), described as 'liquidation'[8]
privatization, has been the most popular means of privatization, with over
1,300 buy-outs by the middle of 1993 (Gomulka and Jasinski, 1994). The
number of small and medium-sized companies privatized via liquidation rose
phenomenally between 1990 and 1993 and actually represented 90% of total
privatizations in 1993. This predominance continued into 1995 where the share
of total privatizations was 79% of all started and 90% of all completed
privatizations. There are two main differences between liquidation according
to Article 19 of the 1981 Enterprise Law and liquidation according to Article
37 of the 1990 Privatization Law. First, the economic state of the enterprise –
a point expanded upon earlier. To illustrate – by the end of 1995, out of the
total of enterprises privatized under Article 37, 18.8% were sold quickly and
were probably vulnerable enterprises which would have disappeared under
Article 19 liquidation; 5.6% were turned over to new companies, 68.6% were

---

[8] To re-emphasize the point, the term 'liquidation' in the Polish context covers viable enterprises and
not insolvent ones.

leased and the remainder transferred according to a mixture of the above methods (Nuti, 1996). Secondly, Article 37 liquidations had a higher rate of completion than Article 19 procedures (see Table 16.7). This channel of privatization was the one that led most often to employee ownership through leasing contracts. Typically, the MEBOs were management-led, taking the form of 'a lease purchase agreement, or rather a lease with an option to purchase, by a company established by at least 50% of employees; ownership would be transferred after cumulative rentals matched by the stipulated capital value and interest' (Nuti, 1996).

Table 16.8. Distribution of shares by end 1995

	Total	Liquidation
Total number of firms actually privatized	1,610	2,507
% of total state-owned enterprises	35%	55%
Total number of firms set aside for privatization	3,625	1,450
% of total state-owned enterprises	79%	32%

Source: OECD 1996.

It is also interesting to note the sectors where employees have opted to chose liquidation as their preferred method of privatization (see Figure 16.1). They are, in general, sectors which do not require a great deal of restructuring and are more favorable to employee ownership and participation (trade, construction and services).

A further interesting point is that firms that opted for liquidation were on average smaller than the average for total firms set aside for privatization (see Figure 16.2).

Commercialization. The commercialization of 958 Polish companies took place between 1990 and 1995. These companies are awaiting privatization; 350 are expected to be privatized via the mass privatization program and the rest should be sold by tender. According to the law, companies may only retain the 'joint-stock' Ministry of Privatization ownership form for two years. About 30 companies have already remained in this legal status for longer than this. Needless to say, the state is left with a significant number of enterprises. In mid-1994 the number of SOEs was 5,298, with around 12.5% of these enterprises employing more than 500 workers. A program of mass commercialization has taken place and around 5,000 enterprises have been newly corporatized. A new board of directors has been appointed for these companies to replace the old representatives of state organizations.

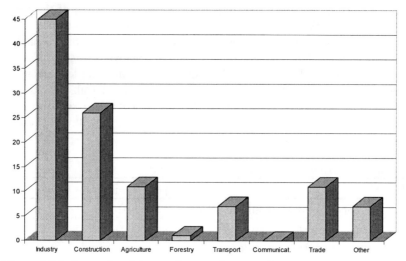

Figure 16.1. Sector breakdown of ownership transformation type as a percentage of total

Commercialization of self-managed enterprises has meant ensuring a 10% employee ownership stake.

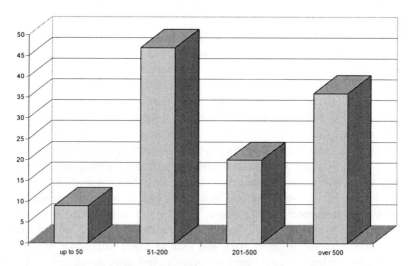

Figure 16.2. Size breakdown by ownership transformation type as a percentage of total

Table 16.9. Employment distribution of Polish state enterprises, 30 June 1994

Employment	Number of Firms	Number of Firms (%)	% of sales
Up to 100	2,648	50.3	4.5
100–300	1,403	26.7	10.9
301–500	555	10.6	11.6
501–700	232	4.4	7.2
over 700	420	8.0	65.8
Total	5,258	100.0	100

By the middle of 1994 the number of SOEs was 5,258. These companies had as yet neither changed their ownership nor their legal form. These companies account for 50% of industrial production and 60% of Polish industrial exports. They are however heterogeneous in size. Table 16.9 shows that the majority of firms in the state sector (77%) have less than 300 employees. However these firms only account for 15.4% of sales, while firms with over 700 employees account for just over 65% of sales.

In addition, Table 16.10 shows that firms transformed into joint-stock companies were on average large (over 500 employees) regardless of the way they were incorporated. Commercialization could result from Articles 5 or 6 of the 1990 Privatization Law or from Article 7 of the Law on National Investment Funds. A single 'Law on the Commercialization of State Enterprises', involving their generalized transformation into joint-stock companies, regardless of their privatization prospects, has had a difficult course and by the middle of 1996 is still not in force: approved by Parliament, hit by a Presidential veto overturned (Nuti, 1996). In addition, motivation for enterprises to agree to being corporatized has fluctuated over time. It was first suggested that some of the firms that chose to be incorporated did so to avoid special taxes on SOEs such as the *popiwek* and the *dividenda*.

Direct sales. The majority of Polish sales were by tender, with preference given to a 'strategic investor', often a foreign one. In 1993, of the 99 firms privatized through capital privatization, 32 were sold to domestic buyers and 44 to foreigners. The deals were complex, since political and environmental objectives had to be met. This means that contracts have included commitments with respect to employment, wages and investment. Sales revenues from privatization (Table 16.11) have been modest and there is still debate about the selling price, foreign direct investment and the establishment of effective corporate governance.

Table 16.10. Employment distribution of Polish joint stock companies, end
1995

Employment	Number of Firms	Article 5	Article 6	Article 7
Up to 50	1	0	0	1
51–200	42	16	0	26
201–500	184	77	19	88
over 500	731	294	211	226
Total	958	387	230	341

However, even if the number of enterprises sold to foreigners was relatively
small, they have displayed an increasing importance in terms of revenue
generation. In 1995, two-thirds of privatization revenue came from foreign
buyers (OECD, 1996).

Table 16.11. Sales revenues from privatization

	1991	1992	1993	1994	1995
Income from privatization (trillion zlotys)	1.7	5.2	8.0	16.0	26.4
Capital privatization	1.6	3.2	4.4	8.5	17.1
Leasing and sales of liquidated assets	...	1.6	2.8	3.2	4.1
Bank privatizations	0	0.4	0.8	4.3	5.2

Source: Dynamika Prywatyzacji, Ministry of Ownership Changes, Warsaw, various issues 1993–96.

In conclusion, MEBOs have emerged as an important vehicle for ownership
transformation in Poland. However, various academic and non-academic
observers are increasingly viewing this phenomenon as transitory,[9] although
highly pragmatic, given the circumstances. As Nuti (1996) concludes, 'the
current direct privatization track in general and MEBOs in particular are now
regarded in Poland as a 'dead end'. More promising developments in current
privatization policies in Poland are represented by generalized commercialization, debt for equity swaps, linking privatization with pension fund reform,
raising funds for the state budget (. . .) – rather than the further development
of MEBOs and other forms of employee ownership' (Nuti, 1996).

---

[9] See Nuti(1996) for a survey of both issues and opinions regarding this matter.

Czech Republic – mass privatization and the emergence of funds

The process of Czech privatization has been amply surveyed (see Singer and Svejnar, 1994; Takla, 1994; Coffee, 1994; Mejstrik *et al.*, 1994). The techniques and decisions most identified with Czech privatization are:

1. the use of vouchers to effect a rapid disposition of state property;
2. the free entry permitted to privately-formed Investment Privatization Funds (IPFs);
3. the use of such IPFs as a corporate governance solution to dispersed ownership.[10]

Kenway and Chlumsky (1995) identify 'three salient facts' about Czech privatization, namely: Firstly, funds have emerged from the voucher privatization as holding the majority of shares sold by voucher: 73 per cent in the first wave (1992) and 64% in the second wave (1994). Secondly, although there are hundreds of them, the largest few funds have an enormous weight; thus the funds founded by the top six investment companies acquired over 40 per cent of the vouchers in the first wave and 24 per cent in the second. Thirdly, a single fund could hold up to 20 per cent of a firm's equity while funds founded by the same investment company could jointly hold up to a maximum of 40 per cent. The Czech Republic is the only one of our three cases where mass privatization has been effectively adopted. The voucher scheme was intended to ensure the rapid transfer of state-owned property to the private sector and to offer Czech citizens a stake in the reforms. Funds were privately set up by domestic and foreign banks to act as possible intermediaries for citizens' investments.

Czech privatization is thus an often-quoted 'successful' example of mass privatization, 'understood as offering the free or very heavily subsidised transfer of a large proportion of state assets to the whole population' (Nuti, 1994). Voucher privatization[11] is a component of 'large-scale privatization' aimed at manufacturing, banking and insurance organizations which often have a domestic monopolistic character and invariably operate on a large scale.

The option of a privatization method also determines the state's interest in managing ownership changes. In both Poland and the Czech Republic mass privatization has been heavily managed by the government. The emphasis on mass privatization has differed across the three countries and, although in the Czech case voucher privatization was a high profile activity, it is important to

---

[10] Coffee, 1994.

[11] *Note:* No fixed equity was set aside for the voucher program. However, all equity not sold to a buyer had to be privatized through the voucher program. Moreover, 3% of equity automatically went to the restitution fund.

note that it was only one component of a multi-track approach to privatization.

The Czech Republic has benefited from a stable government and broad political support. This has allowed the government substantial leverage in the conduct of its privatization policy. Once discrepancies between parties were resolved in Parliament, the government was able to pursue its policy without recourse to further substantial political compromises. The involvement of the government in Czech privatization is central to 'large privatization'. The state took an active role in the privatization of enterprises by managing the process through its approval of privatization projects. The inherited coalitions and hierarchies between the government and state enterprises are largely still in place. Branch ministries were sometimes at odds with the privatization ministries in their evaluation of projects, and have often supported existing management.

Excluded from the impact of the Large-Scale Privatization Act 27 February 1991[12] are properties to be restored to former owners by special legislation, and all Church property confiscated after 25 February 1948 [Restitution Act 22 February 1991]. The corporatization of SOEs was a precondition for their inclusion in the voucher privatization program. Corporatization entailed the transfer of 100% of the share capital of enterprises to National Property Funds (NPFs).

There were three such funds: one for the Czech republic, one for the Slovak republic, one for the federation. While the organization and activity of the Federal National Property Fund was determined by the Act, it left the republican legislatures to determine the legal relations and activity of the Republican National Property Funds. The federal and republican governments had a set time to issue guidelines for ministries and local government, which were called upon to submit lists for governmental approval of enterprises which should be privatized.

A multi-track approach.   By the end of 1995 most enterprises had been privatized. 'Large-scale privatization' employed a broad range of privatization methods, in addition to voucher privatization. The nature of the enterprise involved and the 'time factor' were the decisive influences when deciding the method. Table 16.12 charts the distribution of privatization methods by the end

---

[12] The Federal Ministry of Finance classified firms at the inception of the program as follows. **Category A** consisted of public utilities and other regulated SOEs which were not to be privatized in the near future. This included at the federal level 30% of state-owned companies in sectors such as defence and some public utilities. **Category B** covered state-owned medium to large heavy and light industry firms. These firms took part in the large-scale privatization process. **Category C** covers property which took part in the small-privatization or 'municipalization' process (restaurants, local services, flat rentals, etc.).

of 1993 for joint-stock companies for the Czech Republic at the end of the first wave, and shows a breakdown by privatization method used; 61.4% of all shares of joint-stock companies privatized up until the end of 1993 were in the form of coupons.

Heavy reliance on the voucher method was chosen by the enterprise management in four types of firm; those which were financially 'troubled' and too large for alternative methods; those in which workers saw privatization as a form of worker buyout as they could chose to place their points in their own firm; those where managers favored the voucher method as a way of maintaining control; and those where management could not find an alternative to the voucher scheme (e.g. they could not find a foreign partner) (see Takla, 1994 for further details).

Table 16.12. Distribution of shares by 31 December 1993

Approved privatization method	Number of units	Value of property
Method	Percent of total	Percent of total
Public auctions	6.8	0.7
Public tenders	6.7	2.2
Direct sales	22.3	5.3
Sold or transferred as shares of joint-stock companies	23.6	86.5
Free transfers	30.8	3.4
Restitution	8.1	0.8
Restitution with buy-in	1.7	1.1
Total	100 (number: 7,553)	100 (871.6 bn Kcs)

Source: Pistor and Turkowitz 1994.

Most enterprises used corporatization as a first step in their privatization project. Through their projects enterprises were also able to divide up their shares between different privatization methods, including standard options such as direct sale, public auction or more unusual measures such as vouchers. Table 16.12 charts the progress of large-scale privatization up to the end of 1993. It shows that 23.6% of companies were sold or transferred as shares of joint-stock companies, direct sales accounted for 22.3% and free transfer for 30.8%. In the privatization of shares of joint-stock companies nearly 52% of shares were privatized through vouchers and 31.5% of shares remained in the hands of the NPF (see Table 13, Kotrba, 1994). Table 16.14 charts the progress up until the end of 1994 and reveals that most units were sold through direct sale to an outside investor. However, Table 16.13 shows that the percentage nominal stock value of property sold using direct sales is only 7%, while entities privatized via vouchers represented around 51% of the nominal stock value.

Table 16.13. Privatization of stocks

	December 1994 *Percent nominal stock value*
Secondary markets	3.7
Voucher privatization	50.7
Direct sale	7.0
Free transfers to municipalities, pension funds, banks or savings banks	7.2
Restitution or restitution investment fund	3.2
Stock held by the NPF long-term	9.8
Stock held by the NPF temporarily	18.4

Source: The Privatization Newsletter of the Czech Republic, February 1995.

Mass privatization. The 'Large-Scale Privatization Act' came into force on 1 April 1991. In the context of the voucher scheme, shares were to be acquired by voucher holders (individuals or investment funds) through a complex bidding process. A basic privatization project (submitted by the enterprise management) included a statement of the proposal disposition of shares: the proportion available through voucher privatization, the proportion for direct sale, etc. The government decided centrally on the allocation of property for mass privatization. It was the enterprises' responsibility to submit their projects and the outsiders' prerogative to present their own competing projects.

Table 16.14. Approved privatization projects in the Czech Republic in the two waves

	December 1994 % number of units
Public auction	10.3%
Public tender	5.8%
Direct sale	51.7%
Commercialization	9.6%
Free transfers to municipalities, pension funds, banks or savings banks	22.6%

Source: The Privatization Newsletter of the Czech Republic, December 1994.

The winning project was chiefly decided upon by Privatization Ministry officials. The project specified the proportion of shares allocated to voucher privatization. Although drafted by the enterprise, a privatization project was the responsibility of the 'founder'. The founder selected the project it deemed to be most suitable and recommended it for approval. The winning privatization project was generally chosen by a team consisting of officials from the Ministry for Privatization and those of the relevant founder ministry in whose jurisdiction the particular enterprise initially found itself. Exceptions to this rule were instances where the selected project recommended sale of some or part of the property to a private owner, or of any sale to a foreign investor. In these cases, it was the national government which made the final decision. This principle also applied to the sale of enterprises with a large number of employees (over 3,000 workers). The founder also had to submit to the ministry those projects it did not recommend. Projects which recommended the break-up of enterprises were approved. Most competing projects proposed the break-up of the existing SOE. This could be viewed as a positive development if it created small and medium-sized enterprises. On the other hand, some projects have sought to divide indivisible property.

A considerable number of SOEs were set aside to be privatized through the sale of shares within the framework of the voucher scheme. Most enterprises used corporatization as the first step in their privatization project. Through their projects enterprises were also able to divide up their shares between different privatization methods, including standards options such as direct sale, public auction or more unusual measures such as vouchers.

Foreign buyers were also allowed to collaborate with Czech firms in the formulation of the basic project. If the enterprise was too slow, it could be given a time limit by the Supervisory State Agency, described in the Act as the 'founder' (usually a ministry responsible for a particular sector of industry). Not surprisingly, management was reluctant to deliver the necessary information for outside parties to develop their own competing projects and withholding information was made illegal by the amendment to the law on 'large scale privatization', passed in February 1992. This legislation also blocked up a loophole which had allowed existing management to sign long-term rental agreements. Such agreements would *de facto* predetermine the fate of the property before privatization. Management and worker ownership was thus not explicitly encouraged in the Czech case, although management took part in the privatization process as it was in charge of submitting basic plans for privatization.[13] Privatization of large enterprises has rarely involved

---

[13] See Coffee (1994), Mladek (1993) and Buchtikova and Capek (1992) for an account of management privatization proposals.

leveraged buy-outs. Management buy-outs were only common in 'small-scale privatization', because managers took long-term leases in 1990, so 'a buy-out was a logical solution to avoid a gridlock' (ECE, 1993, p. 3–12).

Table 16.15. State-led restructuring as part of the privatization program

Industry	Number of enterprises prior to the approval of privatization projects	Number of enterprises after the approval of privatization projects	% increase in number of firms
Ferrous metallurgy	20	51	155.00
Non-ferrous metallurgy	16	50	212.50
Chemicals and rubber	57	131	129.82
Machinery	303	676	123.10
Electronics	74	212	186.49
Building materials	119	280	135.29
Wood-processing	81	230	183.95
Metal products	18	41	127.78
Paper and cellulose	22	84	281.82
Glass, china and ceramics	55	159	189.09
Textiles	94	409	335.11
Apparel	23	72	213.04
Leather	19	72	278.95
Printing and publishing	31	50	61.29
Food-processing	198	683	244.95
Others	49	93	89.80
Total	1179	3293	179.30

Source: Zemplinerova (1994).

Prior to initiating the process of 'large-scale privatization', enterprises were divided up into three broad categories. The first category contained enterprises included in the first wave of privatization, characterized by the perceived relative ease and speed of their privatization. The second category was second-wave enterprises, dominated by large engineering, chemical and metallurgical companies. Also included in the second wave were key branches of the power sectors, as well as public utilities and infrastructure. Finally, the third category contained businesses to be kept in state hands for at least another five years: for example, railways and airports. These shares were to be formally held by the National Property Fund, although rights are entrusted to other state bodies (for example, ministries).

'Large-scale privatization' was a two-stage program (preparation and implementation), with the second stage having started in 1992. Privatization was compulsory and in the first wave 1,700 enterprises in the Czech Lands, 700 firms in Slovakia and one 'federally-owned' firm had until the end of 1991 to submit business plans to their 'founder' sponsoring ministries.

Adult citizens over 18 years of age were allowed to buy a 14-page book of vouchers entitling them to 1,000 shares in at most 10 listed privatized enterprises for about US$ 30.[14] They had the alternative of turning the vouchers over to mutual funds which would then bid for shares. The vouchers came with a 30-page instruction book. Most of the eligible population, about 8.5 million adults, purchased these books. Vouchers were not transferable, though they could be transferred to heirs. They could not be used as a security for a loan. The obvious problem with this scheme lay in the fact that voucher holders would need information to appraise the enterprises on offer. Property to be privatized was separated into joint-stock companies; a list of enterprises involved in voucher privatization was published along with basic data on the share of stock offered for voucher sale. Balance sheet information was also printed in daily newspapers. Individual investors could place their vouchers with the funds in return for certificates. The issue of how many funds to set up, and whether funds were to be active or passive investors was removed from government responsibility. The private voucher holders could decide independently whether to bid for shares by themselves or to place their shares with investment funds.

The exact number of bidding rounds within each wave was not predetermined. Rather it was anticipated that the process would end when a 'decisive share of the property would be sold and further continuation would not lead to the sale of the remainder' (Skalicky, 1992). Bidding for shares was to proceed as follows. First, shares of all enterprises were offered at the same 'nominal' value, expressed in investment points per share. In the first wave, this price was set at 100 investment points per three shares. As the bidding process proceeded, the demand of shares by investors was supposed to reveal the 'true' value of the firm. Bidders knew the calling price of a share of an

---

[14] In the first quarter of 1992 the average monthly wage was US$ 135.9, the average weekly salary was thus about US$ 34 (Ham, Svejnar and Terrell, 1993).

enterprise (in terms of points) and bid accordingly. If the supply of shares exceeded the demand, shares were exchanged for points. When demand exceeded supply by 25%, shares were first allocated to the bidding individuals and the remainder rationed amongst bidding IPFs. If excess demand was over 25%, points were not converted into shares and the price of shares was raised by the government before a new round of bidding; the process continued until excess demand was below 25%.

Once initiated, the first wave of voucher privatization proceeded relatively fast (see Svejnar and Singer, 1993 for details). Although progress was slower than expected. Investors received their shares from the first wave of privatization in the Summer of 1993. Their decision to purchase was taken 12–15 months earlier, and on the basis of 1991 balance sheets. Around 93% of total share supply in the first round of privatization was sold and 99% of all disposable voucher points were used. In the first round, bids were mainly orientated to high value companies. Ninety-two per cent of disposable points were bid, indicating a high participation rate. Only about 30% of the shares bid for were sold. The success rate plummeted in the third round, as the price of shares was set too low at the start of the round. Only 24.5% of shares ordered in this round were sold.

Table 16.16. Importance of vouchers and other privatization methods in the first privatization wave

	Percentage of shares privatized					
	Total	*0*	*0[b]*	*0–25[a]*	*0–25[b]*	*26–50[a]*
Vouchers	988	0	0	14	1	108
Direct sale domestic	988	898	91	24	2	28
Direct sale foreign	989	947	96	12	1	14
NPF temporary	978	658	67	217	22	83
NPF permanent	988	960	97	23	2	5
	Total	*26–50[b]*	*51–75[a]*	*51–75[b]*	*> 75[a]*	*> 75[b]*
Vouchers	988	11	177	18	689	70
Direct sale domestic	988	3	35	4	3	0
Direct sale foreign	989	1	15	2	1	0
NPF temporary	978	8	17	2	3	0
NPF permanent	988	1	0	0	0	0

Notes: [a] number of firms, [b] % of total number.
Source: Database published by the Centre for Voucher Privatization 1994.

In the first wave of Czech privatization, property valued at US$ 23 billion was put up for sale, US$ 7 billion of which through vouchers. Only 7.2% of shares remained unsold and 277.8 million shares were sold to private investors. Of 1,471 companies, 291 were fully sold. The unsold shares are temporarily being held by the National Property Fund, which will dispose of them mainly by arranging direct sale through an intermediary.

As a by-product of voucher privatization, a large number of Investment Privatization Funds were established voluntarily, with most funds sponsored by commercial banks and several banks sponsoring more than one. The relationship between funds and banks is as follows; banks have established a 'management company' which runs the fund. Evidence suggests that the top three sponsoring banks, through management contracts with funds, have acquired around 40% of all points in the first round of privatization.[15] Voucher privatization was dominated by funds in the first (63.4% of shares sold to funds against 36.6% to individuals) and second waves of privatization (51.4% of shares sold to funds against 36.6% to individuals). All the major banks as well as numerous other institutions and individuals set up Investment Privatization Funds (IPF). Voucher book holders could allocate part or all of their points to one or several of the 437 privately formed IPFs, or bid directly for the shares. Funds could not hold more than 20% of shares in any individual company. Many of the funds are affiliated to a single founder. 'Investicni Banka, for example created twelve different funds in the first wave.' (Pistor and Turkowitz, 1994). Five of the top seven fund groups were founded by banks.

The role of the state.   The Ministry of Trade and Industry, the Consolidation Bank (responsible for bad debts), and the National Property Fund (NPF), and in the medium-term, the Privatization Ministry, are likely to remain in control of government management of industry and enterprises.

By the end of the second round of voucher privatization 48% of Czech enterprises which existed in 1989 were privatized. The number of enterprises remaining in the state sector was estimated at no more than 500 as early as the end of 1995 (Pistor and Turkowitz, 1994). These enterprises were ones held by their 'founding' ministries, with the Ministry of Trade and Industry holding the bulk of enterprises. By the end of March 1994, it held 316 firms in thirteen 3-digit industries, employing 2.1% of the total workforce. These firms were on average medium-sized (337 employees) with the largest firm, a uranium mining company, employing 7,000 workers.

---

[15] See Mejstrick *et al.* (1994).

Table 16.17. First wave results – the importance of funds

	Points	Shares Obtained	Number of shares obtained as percentage of points	Percentage of total shares in first wave
Ceska Sporitelna	950,432,200	21,376,611	2.25	7.69
Investicni Banka Group	724,123,600	13,594,068	1.88	4.89
Harvard Group	638,548,000	15,225,108	2.38	5.48
Vsebocna Uverova	500,587,700	11,985,444	2.39	4.31
Komercni Banka	465,530,300	11,931,808	2.56	4.30
Ceska Pojistovna	334,040,900	7,623,311	2.28	2.74
Slovenska IB	333,045,400	10,986,751	3.30	3.95
Total top 7 fund groups	3,946,308,100	92,723,101	2.35	33.38
Total in first wave	8,541,000,000	277,800,000	3.25	100
Top 7 funds as percentage of total	46.20	33.38		

The state also retained 20% of the value of property privatized through vouchers (Brom and Orenstein, 1994) via the National Property Fund. The NPF emerged as the single largest shareholder after the first wave of privatization. At the end of the first wave of voucher privatization the NPF still held a stake of 10% or more in more than 50% of voucher privatized companies. The NPF also kept a golden share option in 37 companies in the first wave. Forty approved privatization plans in the second wave stipulated that golden shares should be used.

The NPF has had some success in divesting itself of property. Pistor and Turkowitz (1994) estimate that between the end of the first wave of voucher privatization and the end of 1993, the NPF 'reduced its ownership stake to under 64% in 64 firms'. The state also holds some property indirectly through the NPF. The NPF owns between 34% and 45% of the main banks involved in founding the bank-backed investment funds.

The distribution of NPF holdings is as follows: 22% of NPF holdings is on average below 25% of total shareholding, 8% between 26% and 50%, 2% between 50% and 75% and there is no shareholding above 75%. Of the firms to remain in permanent NPF hands none of the shareholding is above 50%. On average more than 75% of shareholding is voucher-controlled. By contrast only 4% of firms have foreign ownership of over 50% and only 7% of domestic direct sales hold more than 50% of a company.

Table 16.18. Structure of NPF ownership after the first wave of privatization at the end of 1993

	Percentage of shares privatized									
	Total	0	0^b	$0-25^a$	$0-25^b$	$26-50^a$	$26-50^b$	$51-75^a$	$51-75^b$	over 75^a	over 75^b
NPF temporary	978	658	67	217	22	83	8	17	2	3	0
NPF permanent	988	960	97	23	2	5	1	0	0	0	0

Notes: [a] number of firms, [b] % of total number.
Source: Database published by the Centre for Voucher Privatization 1994.

The role of the above-mentioned state institutions should be diluted by the end of the century. The Privatization Ministry as expected was dissolved. The NPF is intending to decrease its involvement in the management of industry. The Czech National Property Fund (NPF) plans to speed up the sell-off of state-owned companies under its control. During the last two quarters of 1994, the NPF plans to offer Kcs 50 billion worth of small and medium-sized companies for direct sale to domestic and foreign investors.

Hungary – systematic sale of assets: a gradualist approach
Hungarian politics have been distinguished by a sequence of coalition governments and the approach to privatization has been mainly decentralized (Canning and Hare, 1994). Mass privatization was not an option that was seriously considered in Hungary. It depended first on domestic direct sales to managers and, less important, to workers, and secondly, on foreign direct sales. In 1990, the former government inherited assets valued at 2,000 billion Forints, around half of which have since been sold. The Hungarian government has tried to monitor the privatization process by pursuing a World Bank provision which stipulates that: 'the whole property of a company at sales of more than 50% and the property value of the business part at sales below 50% are regarded as property involved in privatization.'

Progress with privatization can be examined in two separate time periods – 1990–94 and 1995 (policies are described below). Between 1992 and 1993 the private sector's estimated contribution rose from 25% of GDP to 65%. The Ministry of Industry and Trade (MIT) provides a lower percentage (60%) for the end of 1995 which contrasts with UN-ECE 70% estimate for the end of 1994. The MIT also provides data on the contribution of the private sector to different parts of the economy (Canning and Hare, 1996). They estimate that 90% of trade, 75–80% of construction, 75% of textiles (25% foreign capital), 60% of the paper industry (50% foreign capital), and 55% of printing is in private hands. Table 16.19 illustrates the early development in the SPA's holding of state assets by the end of 1993. SPA holdings decreased in book value by 76% between 1989 and January 1994. The SPA has succeeded in selling 100% of 438 firms and part of 186 firms. Most of the decrease in the SPA holdings is due to the bankruptcy or liquidation of firms (439 companies). The SPA also transferred 236 firms to other state agencies.

Table 16.19. Distribution of shares by the end of 1993

	Number	%
Transfer to other state bodies	236	13
SPA-owned	534	29
Liquidated / Bankrupt enterprises	439	24
100% sale	438	24
Partial sale	186	10
Total number of enterprises accounted for	1833	100
Total number of enterprises transferred to the SPA in 1989	1876	
Percent of firms accounted for in 1994	97.7	

1992–94 can also be characterized as a period in which the sale of small and medium-sized firms was relatively high (230 in 1993, 240 in 1994 compared with only 119 in 1995). 1995 was characterized by a dramatic increase in revenue-generating privatizations. Table 16.20 illustrates the path of the evolution of privatization in Hungary through data charting privatization revenues by ownership transformation type. Total cash revenues from privatization have risen steadily. The SPA's revenues peaked in 1992. The share of foreign exchange in revenues was high up until 1992 for the SPA. In 1993 it fell to 59% of total cash revenues, but the SHC's share in total cash revenues was very high in 1993 at almost 96%. The overall figure of 84% of total joint cash revenues is unique when compared with Polish and Czech results.

Table 16.21 illustrates the marked differences between the two periods. In 1995, in book value terms HUF 481 billion were transferred to private owners, 20% more than in the previous five years put together. Between 1991 and 1995, vouchers with a nominal value of HUF 70 billion were used as payment for shares (34%) or assets sold via tender or auction (64%) (Canning and Hare, 1996).

Table 16.20. Revenues from privatization SPA/SHC separate accounts 1990–1994 Q3

	1990	*1991*	*1992*	*1993*	*09/1994*
SPA cash revenues total in HUF billion	0.67	30.37	62.23	43.2	16.49
of which foreign exchange (%)	*79.1*	*81.00*	*65.85*	*59.03*	*27.53*
SHC cash revenues total in HUF billion			3.50	91.40	9.90
of which foreign exchange (%)				*95.62*	*55.56*
Total for both agencies in HUF billion	0.67	30.37	65.73	134.60	26.39
of which foreign exchange (%)	*79.1*	*81.00*	*65.85*	83.88	38.04

Source: SPA and SHC.

Table 16.21. Revenues from privatization SPA/SHC joint accounts 1990–1995 (HUF billion)

	1990	*1991*	*1992*	*1993*	*1994*	*1995*	*1991–1995*
Cash							
Hard currency	0.53	24.61	40.98	110.67	10.95	412.05	599.79
HUF	0.14	5.74	24.92	22.96	35.41	39.52	128.69
Privatization loans							
Hard currency	0	0	0	0	16.84	0	16.84
HUF		1.01	9.07	21.72	29.27	3.92	64.99
Compensation vouchers	0	0	2.26	14.56	64.2	18.48	99.5
Total	*0.67*	*31.36*	*77.23*	*169.91*	*156.67*	*473.97*	*909.81*

A study of the Hungarian experience between 1990 and 1992 (Hamar, 1993) shows that in Hungary foreign investment in the form both of direct and portfolio assisted the Hungarian balance of payment position and helped moderate the burdens of debt servicing. Hungary has thus been an attractive destination for foreign direct investment (FDI); total inflows by the end of 1995 amounted to US$ 13 billion or almost half the total inflow into Central and Eastern Europe; around US$ 5 billion were for privatization purposes and US$ 8 billion for greenfield projects. Foreign joint-ventures in Hungary cannot be determined; according to Ministry of Industry and Trade sources, they account for around 25% of privately-owned assets and produce 70% of Hungary's export income.

The politicization and evolution of the process. Hungarian managers enjoyed increased autonomy from the beginning of the 1980s and had certain control over access to capital, both domestic and foreign. This meant that employees' management rights over the enterprise had to be converted into ownership entitlements, if a privatization scheme was to be successfully implemented. In the first round of privatization, managers were encouraged to acquire an ownership stake in their company at a low price. Privatization in Hungary should be traced back to debates about enterprise reforms starting in 1968. Political and academic debate in Hungary between 1968 and 1989 centred on four issues: institutional ownership of assets, cross-ownership of state assets through corporatization, individual small entrepreneurship, and self-management. Influential legislation of that period includes: the 1984 Enterprise Act that introduced workers' councils into most SOEs (70%) (see Stark, 1994). These enterprises were granted the right to take decisions about 'restructuring, mergers and de-mergers' and setting up joint ventures. Although technically employees were intended to play a major role in decision-making, managers retained the majority of control (Frydman and Rapaczynski, 1993). This feature was emphasized in 1987 when managers discovered a loophole in the legislation that allowed them to found 'subsidiary companies with up to 10% of enterprise capital or assets in kind' (Canning and Hare, 1994).

The Company Act of 1988 legalized this development. It enshrined the right of the enterprise council to create a new business entity and to exchange enterprise assets for a share in the newly-founded joint-stock or limited liability company. The organizational restructuring of companies started after the implementation of the 1988 Company Law. Enterprise management powers were extended with the intention of increasing the independence of state firms without changing the underlying ownership structure. Managers had the right to restructure the whole or part of companies into a limited liability or joint-stock company. Managers used this opportunity to siphon off enterprise assets. This resulted in a complex network of interlocking firm ownership with both private and state interests. This has allowed managers to break up enterprises into numerous semi-independent corporations where the parent company acts as a holding company.

The 1989 Law on the Transformation of Economic Organisations and Business Associations was also aimed at curbing management control of ownership reforms. It allowed the corporatization of the whole of a company not just in part, and was extended to cover all enterprises and not only those run by workers' councils. It was hoped that this new legislation would reverse the trend towards managers running down the mother company's assets and creating an empty shell. The 1989 Transformation Law was intended to clarify confused property rights and to create a new corporation which inherited both the assets and the liabilities of the old one. However, the new transformed firm could purchase the 20% of shares in the old firm at a high discount (up to 90%). Enterprise insiders were thus allowed to abuse the system further by buying up assets at a greatly discounted price. The state thus lost control over a majority of assets, and public outcry resulted as managers were perceived as appropriating state assets for their own personal benefit.

The privatization policy which was initially conceived by Hungary's first post-socialist government in May 1990 and it was characterized by the following features described by Canning and Hare (1996):

1. An emphasis on economic efficiency gains aimed at reducing subsidies, increasing revenues and thus easing the budget deficit.
2. An emphasis on commercial privatization through the sale of assets rather than free distribution.
3. An emphasis on involving larger investors and attracting foreign ones.
4. An emphasis on gradual privatization, the target set being 50% of total enterprises (by value) by 1994.
5. An emphasis on transparency in a decentralized framework where privatization could be initiated by the State Property Agency (SPA), the enterprises themselves and potential investors.

The newly-elected Antall government created the State Property Agency (SPA) and a privatization strategy was devised. The SPA was made the formal owner of 2,300 enterprises. Under the new framework, the insiders of self-managed enterprises still retained the right to initiate the transformation of an enterprise, but the SPA could veto the proposal. The process of privatization was thus highly decentralized until the formation of the SPA. However, these stated aims and the instruments to achieve them began to evolve from as early as July 1990, when the SPA was made accountable to the government rather than to Parliament. From this point on, the privatization process became increasingly politicized. Enterprise Councils were abolished and all enterprises were earmarked to be corporatized, with ownership rights transferred to the SPA. This amounted to virtual 'renationalisation' and the goal of decentralization was abandoned. The need to accelerate the privatization process was also perceived as early as 1991, when the government began mentioning its political aim of 'creating and fostering a property owning middle class' (Canning and Hare, 1996). The emphasis on maximizing budget revenues was also relaxed and schemes were initiated to encourage wider share ownership. It was only in July 1992 that the government passed a law on privatization to replace the 'Temporary Asset Guidelines', in force since 1989, by a new Privatization Act (Act LIV, 1992) . In October 1992 a new state body involved in privatization was established, the State Holding Company or State Asset Management Company. Around half the assets in value terms earmarked for privatization were transformed to the SHC. Companies deemed of strategic importance, natural monopolies and 'companies whose privatization would be an exceptionally long and complicated process' (Kopint-Datorg, 1992) were transferred to this new institution. The Hungarian government's stated aim and main concern was that privatization and the management of state assets was not an issue. The problem now facing these bodies is setting up guidelines for the management of state assets and how to exercise ownership control over the interim period when assets remain in state hands. The Hungarian State Holding Company was conceived to fulfil this role.

Favorable loan schemes were initiated, such as Existence (E) loans to enable individuals to participate in the privatization process (especially small privatization) in mainly the retail and catering sectors. Other methods of privatization also sprang up in Hungary after 1992 (Karsai, 1993), amongst them: Employee Share Ownership Programs (ESOPs). Allowing the combining of ESOPs with other techniques such as leasing and granting low interest borrowing incentives has resulted in a proliferation of ESOPs. Privatization by leasing is another method which has been adopted since spring 1992 to counter the delays in privatization and the fall in foreign direct investment. Initially only 5–10% of a company's shares were set aside for purchase by employees at preferential rates. Employee share ownership was subsequently given a higher priority and backed by preferential loans. The terms attached to E-loans were eased in 1993, and the use of such loans was extended to cover ESOP schemes. In addition, leasing schemes (zero interest loans with repayment by instalments) and MEBOs and Management Buy-Ins were established and expanded. This trend culminated in 1992 with the announcement of a privatization plan based on credit vouchers, available to all adult citizens with the avowed aim of 'creating the widest possible range of domestic owners' (Canning and Hare, 1994). Hare and Canning (1994) state that 5% of the value of socially owned capital – estimated at 2,000 billion Forints – was to be distributed to employees in various forms (ESOPs, MEBOs) through the voucher privatization process.

The Hungarian government has in general shown a clear preference for cash sales over mass privatization. The concept of mass privatization was only formulated at a late stage in ownership transformation and was encapsulated in the Small Investors' Share Program, which was developed with the help of Schroeder Wagg (UK). This project was approved in April 1993. The law allowed all citizens to purchase vouchers to a maximal value of 1,000 Forints for a fee of 1% of the total value. Over 70 enterprises, with an estimated book value of 120 billion Forints are included in the first wave of privatization. Privatization was to begin at the beginning of April 1994 and was expected to involve around 1.2 million people. The decision to promote domestic investors was accompanied by a resolution to phase out the tax relief available to foreign investors from January 1994.

In conclusion, one can described the first phase of Hungarian privatization

1990–94 as one in which there was a shift away from decentralization towards centralization and away from economic goals toward political ones. A budget crisis and IMF standby agreement stringency led to a U-turn in privatization policy from 1994. The new Hungarian left coalition government which came into power in May 1994 decided to phase out the Small Investors Share Program which provided Hungarians with preferential loans for buying at public offerings, before it was ever fully implemented. The E-loans scheme which also provided investors with state-subsidized loans for buying stock in state assets were scrapped. The new government's position on privatization can be summarized as one calling for an acceleration of privatization, favoring sales rather than give-away schemes, increasing the decentralization of the process by encouraging the involvement of independent consultancy companies and a diminished role for governmental agencies in the management of enterprises. The new government thus decided to speed up the privatization process and complete the sale of remaining state assets within the next two to three years. Part of the new government's privatization strategy was to give multinational investors priority in the privatization of large state companies and banks. The main reason behind new developments in the privatization strategy of Hungary is that the new government was strapped for cash and an investigation of privatization deals terminated from April to mid-June 1994 shows that only 3% of assets were sold in cash.

Developments from the end of 1994. The privatization bill proposed that the SPA be scrapped and that a new privatization organization, the State Privatization and Asset Management Company should be established on the basis of the State Holding Company. The Assets of the Treasury Asset Management Organization were also transferred to the new state institution. The State Privatization and Asset Management Company operate as a one-member state shareholding company and the company law was amended so that the owner of such a company should have unlimited liability – i.e. the state automatically underwrites the activities of the new organization.

Invitation of tenders should remain the primary method of privatization and if such a method should be unsuccessful, preferential privatization methods such as purchase by employees and/or management will be applied. Management and employees could put up 10% of the purchase price and buy the rest of the 51% stake in instalments over five years. On completion of payment the remaining 49% would be handed over. One of the most debated issues was the terms for employee acquisition. In the versions of the bill presented to Parliament, employees as well as management would be able to bid for the control of 300–400 small to medium-sized companies.

The government plans to start the privatization of electricity and gas companies with a book value of 500 billion Forints in the first half of 1995. Of 159 major companies owned by the state with assets of a book value of 1,500 billion Forints, the state aims to retain a stake of 200 billion Forints for the long term.

The state. In Hungary state management of ownership change has focused on the sales price of assets. Case study evidence (Antal 1996) reveals that in certain instances disputes between different government bodies can delay the process of privatization and tenders have fallen through because of SPA's exceedingly high price expectations. It should be noted that the high price expectation could be a tactical ploy by the SPA; an open tender is not necessarily driven by the desire to secure a large amount of cash. Instead, the tender may serve the purpose of showing to the public that the privatization process is transparent, whereas in fact there may be a preselected buyer to whom the SPA wants to sell the shares.

Although most of the property remained notionally in state hands, the state lost all control of the transformation process. It could not document the new interlocking ownership arrangement and lost the record of its own holdings. These developments were behind the establishment of the SPA, which was devised to monitor and supervise ownership changes and to curb management excesses. The SPA was ineffectual at providing a clear and comprehensive record of ownership structure. The State Privatization Agency (SPA) was created to manage this so-called 'spontaneous' privatization. The SPA was to ensure that sales were conducted at fair prices and that assets were not undervalued.

The SPA's centralization effort failed because it was checked by bureaucratic obstacles, asset valuation delays, and a failure by the government to pass a piece of legislation that updates the 'Temporary Property Policy Guidelines' (1990), and Hungarian privatization was left with a case-by-case approach devoid of a general strategy.

SPA's problems in controlling the privatization process are illustrated by the outcome of its two Active Privatization Programs of 1990 and 1991. The first program (September 1990) planned to sell a selection of 20 enterprises. Because of unrealistically high price expectations, a year later only three had been sold and the program was abandoned. The second program aimed specifically at solving the problem of empty shells and twelve cases were picked for a pilot study. Again, the program was dropped; this time because closer examination of shell companies revealed a web of legal and financial complications.

Therefore, from 1991 onwards the SPA decided to continue to rely on spontaneous privatization stating that it aimed to make 'the process of spontaneous privatization smoother and better organized' (Voszka, 1991). This task was termed 'self-privatization' and consultancy firms were invited to value the enterprises taking part in this scheme. In conclusion, the legal environment only provided a guiding framework for SPA activities and actual privatization results were shaped by the outcome of bargaining between the various parties involved.

Table 16.22. Incidence of state ownership in Hungary December 1992

State ownership stake (in %)	Number of firms as a % of large firms
100	16.6
99.9– 75	6.7
74.9–50	3
49.9–25	3.6
24.9–.01	4.3
Total	*34.2*

Source: Hungarian Tax Database.

Hungarian tax data from 1992 estimated that the state in one form or another owned a third of enterprises capitalized at more than Ft 10 million. The breakdown of firm categories in Hungarian statistics 'systematically under-reports state holdings'. Firms listed as 'domestic legal persons' could be owned by state-owned companies.

The minimum percentage of shares owned needed to block important decision at the enterprise level is 25%. According to the 1992 tax data in Table 16.22, the state is a minority shareholder in 4.3% of large enterprises. Its ownership prerogative in these enterprises is very limited. Table 16.22 illustrates the point that state ownership is broad and diluted. It also shows that most direct state ownership is in the form of majority stakeholding, although indirect stake holdings are very common. 'Temporary' stakeholdings may pose a problem for the state bodies which are left holding them. National Property Funds and Privatization Agencies were themselves set up as temporary agencies.

Between 1990 and 1993, the SPA sold off only around 10% of its assets. A large number of these sales occurred in the run-up to the 1994 national elections. Equity granted to the SHC was intended to remain in state hands indefinitely, The SHC up until its demise held shares in 169 firms and was the sole shareholder in 129 firms. Its holdings in the remaining 40 companies ranged between 50% and 95%. The value of its portfolio was concentrated in energy, manufacturing and financial services.

Table 16.23. The role of the state: State Property Agency (SPA)

1989
2,000 medium – large-sized enterprises in the economy
1,876 of these firms transferred to the SPA

January 1994
SPA as
  sole owner of 534 commercialized companies
  majority owner in 38 companies
  minority stake in 158 companies
  designated owner of 100 companies

Total SPA involvement at the beginning of 1994:
820 companies or 44.2% of total firms transferred to the SPA in 1989

Managers.   Nevertheless, the SPA did not managed to usurp the control rights of managers. This is because the task of doing so was huge and led to technical processing difficulties. This has meant that, in practice, the SPA has only been involved in settling controversial cases and in the case of new transformations under the 1988 law the SPA only supervises transactions valued at over US$ 400,000. In addition, the SPA has not been successful in transferring back into state hands all property that was moved into shell organizations. A loophole in the law excluded companies already created on the basis of the 1988 Act outside SPA jurisdiction.

Ownership structure changes of companies held by the State Holding Company and the SPA up until 1994 are represented in Table 16.24. At the time of transformation 92% of companies held by the State Holding Company and 84% of companies in SPA hands were state-owned and 43% of state-holding in the SHC was of a permanent nature. The SHC's state ownership dropped by ten percentage points to 82%. This drop can be explained by a rise of local government holding from 2% to 4%, a rise from 4% to 6% in domestic private ownership and a hike to 8% foreign investor holdings from 0%. The share of state ownership in SPA holdings fell from 84% state to 55% by the end of September 1994. This fall is mostly explained by sales to domestic investors who now account for 29% of SPA property of which 7.4% has gone to employees. Sales to foreign investors have also picked up rising from 5% to 12%.

Table 16.24 Changes in ownership structure

	Upon transformation	%	End September 1994	%
	SHC	SPA	SHC	SPA
State ownership	92	84	82	55
of which permanent	*43*		*43*	
Local government	2	5	4	5
Domestic	6	7	8	29
of which employees		*0.30*		*7.40*
Foreign investors	0	5	6	12
Total	100	100	100	100

Source: Privinfo, November 1994.

In conclusion, although Hungary's privatization was slow to start with, it accelerated in 1995. Hungary is a unique case of reliance on the sale of assets rather than their free distribution and attracting substantial foreign investment. However, with respect to the depoliticization of former state enterprises and the disappearance of the state from the enterprise sphere, Hungary has largely failed to deliver in the 1990–94 period. Only since the beginning of 1995 have political problems begun to be resolved; state organs responsible for the process were merged and external debt constraints spurred the selling-off of major utilities for foreign exchange. As in previous cases, when the profitable assets are sold, fewer attractive firms will remain and the prospect of their privatization will lead back to the discussion about method, speed, and restructuring costs. The issue of who will bear the financial and social costs of restructuring will return to the forefront of the political debate. Responsibility for the new privatization agency in Hungary has now been shifted to the MIT; this could indicate a 'more hands on approach to restructuring' (Canning and Hare, 1996).

CONCLUSION

Privatization in practice has entailed a number of controversial and complex decisions at every stage of the operation. Delays in decision-making can be summarized as stemming from protracted policy debates and institutional and technical problems (see Nuti, 1994) regarding:
1. the inclusion of foreign capital;
2. the politically and economically inevitable mix of privatization methods

and the interaction of mass privatization with the other methods (restitution, direct sale to domestic and foreign buyers, allocation of shares to employees, management buyouts, etc.);

3. the regulation of the process and the rapid establishment of a legal institutional framework to consolidate the transfer of ownership;
4. the inception of capital markets.

The evaluation of the comparative experiences will be done in part in the light of some of the objectives proposed in Section 1. To recap – these normative objectives are: to ensure equity; to depoliticize the economy; to stop the appropriation of assets by insiders; to increase government revenues; to harden budget constraints; and, finally, to raise efficiency and to speed-up restructuring. All three privatization programs scrutinized in this chapter have faced the dilemma of deciding between some of these sometimes divergent objectives. There may be, for example, contradictions between the best restructuring outcome and equitable schemes based on restitution or vouchers. The new owners might not have the required level of knowledge or capital backing to undertake the restructuring required.

From our descriptions we can draw out the following conclusions. First, given that the starting position was that of the near-total state ownership of industrial assets, we find that ownership, in all three cases, was successfully transferred out of state hands, albeit at a differing pace and using very different methods. Secondly, if speed is a reflection of depoliticization, even in the Czech case, the actual speed of privatization did not correspond with the projected timetable and unforeseen obstacles have tended to slow down the process. The implementation of privatization schemes in the three countries surveyed reveals that the state remains an important player in the privatization process in the form of residual owner. New private enterprises share their markets with old state enterprises, privatized firms, joint ventures and, increasingly, with foreign competitors. Thirdly, our examination of the nature of the state apparatus still running the remaining SOEs, reveals that in all three cases it has been very hard for these bodies to step back. It is difficult for the Czech NPF to give up control of the banking sector and to privatize banks fully without first resolving the bad debt problem. The Hungarian government did not easily part with its control over major utilities.

The role of government in privatization cannot be ignored. Mass privatization in both the Czech Republic and Poland was very much a top-down policy. Its meaning and conduct has, however, differed greatly between the two countries. In the Czech Republic, it was administered quickly and found to be an easy solution to transfer property out of state hands. It led to the predominance of investment funds, a large number of individual minority shareholders, the quick introduction of a stock market and the predominance of a state body, the NPF. In Poland, it was a slow process and was until recently overshadowed by privatization through liquidation and subsequent employee ownership and the quick proliferation of *de novo* private firms. Hungary, on the other hand, put little emphasis on mass give-away schemes and preferred to sell its assets to foreign buyers. The participation of foreign investors has differed from country to country. Nevertheless, a small number of large sales to foreign buyers has contributed to maintaining a balanced budget even in the case of the Czech Republic. Receipts from the National Property Fund covered the budget deficit in 1993. Foreign direct investment in all three countries represented a high percentage of the total for all of Eastern Europe (76.5%); the share of Hungary being the highest (36%) (Hughes, 1994).

Mixed ownership is therefore a common feature of ownership patterns in all three countries and new state institutions have sprung up to fill the role of managing state interests in the enterprise sector. This renders the separation between state and private ownership difficult. All three governments have attempted to create new systems of management of state property. These efforts have revolved around changing the legal structure of state enterprises (commercialization or corporatization), altering the governing structure of enterprises, designating a body to manage state interests and, finally, altering the legal and regulatory framework under which state enterprises operate. The stake of the Czech, Hungarian and Polish government in industrial enterprises is of two kinds: enterprises that have been classified as 'of national importance' and those that have been difficult to sell or auction away. The first category of firms has been intentionally kept in state hands, while the second could be described as 'residual' holdings (Pistor and Turkowitz, 1994) that the state intends to be rid of. There has been a tendency for state shares to move between classifications and between different state owners (between Treasury-owned and non-Treasury-owned, between different state bodies and ministries, and between different privatization agencies). In addition, what is strategic at one point in time (utilities in Hungary in 1995) can be come less so when the cash-generation requirement starts to bind because of a budgetary crisis.

Privatization debates in Central and Eastern Europe have thus in practice been highly politicized and long-drawn-out. The preparation of schemes on the political level has involved protracted discussions about objectives, welfare, and allocation of power in the industrial and financial sectors. Some of the problems encountered during the process of privatization could have been avoided, if a number of implementation issues had been discussed beforehand. Many of these problems might have been attributed to the fact that privatization has been proceeding in parallel with the evolution of various market economy institutions. Governments have had to build up the relevant institutions and legislation while undertaking the transfer of property. It would have been very difficult for them to announce their privatization plan with all its relevant contingency clauses and its implementation timetable, and at the same time stick to their schedule. Other problems faced when implementing privatization were caused by the conflict between objectives and interest. And finally, in reality, many problems arose because of the inherently political (and politicized) nature of the privatization process. Governments have generally enacted privatization policies which have at times been inconsistent with their overall policy. This has led to a series of amendments to privatization legislation, delays in the implementation of schemes and paralysis in state enterprises. Some of the delays encountered were inevitable, given the complexity and magnitude of the task. In practice, government policy has been interactive with changing conditions and unforeseen hiccups. Although some of these problems were predictable, it is unlikely that these new governments would have been able to cover all eventualities. In general, their response to unanticipated problems has been *ad hoc* and improvised. Other delays in implementation have occurred either because of technical problems with the mechanisms of privatization, or legal loopholes which have had to be plugged quickly, or, finally, because of political problems which have necessitated the amendment or reversal of programs.

17. RM-System Slovakia

Viliam Páleník

INTRODUCTION

Like the capital markets of other post-socialist countries, the Slovak capital market, was recreated during the last couple of years. A central element of this market is the existence of the RM-System.

The intention of this contribution is to offer information about the activities of RM-S, which can be useful for potential investors, who seek better information about the organization of the capital market in the country in which they are interested investing in. This work may also inspire experts from countries building off-exchange organized markets, and for institution-builders from countries that feel the need for capital market modification or enlargement.

THE RELEVANCE OF THE RM-SYSTEM

About a hundred investment companies and funds, 33 banks and a permanently increasing number of stock traders are participating in the Slovak capital market (see RM-S, 1994, 1995, 1996). In addition, there are at least 2 million private small stockholders who represent about 40% of all citizens of Slovakia. For the trading activities of these groups, two organized marketplaces are available in Slovakia: Bratislava Stock Exchange and the RM-System with about 700 stocks.

The RM-S is a nationwide system of workstations created for the voucher privatization in the former Czechoslovakia (see Figure 17.1). The name RM-System is derived from the description 'Registracne Miesto' meaning place of registration during the voucher privatization. The individual trading desks are connected through a nationwide web with the main server of the RM-S. The huge number of trading desks requires extraordinary handling capacities of this system. The non-membership philosophy of this market allows everybody to trade by entering RM-S directly or indirectly through banks, brokers, investment companies or funds. By mid-1996, 60 of these companies were directly connected to the RM-S computer network so they could trade from their office computers. Moreover, 140 other customers (70 specialized companies and 70 individuals) are using on line services. Hundred of thousands of small clients enter the market directly through more than 70 marketplaces spread evenly throughout the whole country.

The most important method of trading on RM-S is that of continuous auction, which is organized every working day for five hours. During this auction, stocks of different types and issues are traded non-stop.

THE CREATION AND DEVELOPMENT OF RM-S

During the first quarter of 1993, the first wave of voucher privatization was finished. The voucher privatization was accomplished in a couple of rounds and the result was a large group of stockholders. The company PVT provided a nationwide web of computers and took care of the technical side of voucher privatization. In parallel with the ongoing privatization, a task force was preparing the project of a secondary market for shares, addressing legislative, technical, and organizational issues. Since there was no experience with a stock market available in Czechoslovakia, foreign expertise needed to be creatively applied to the specific conditions of Czechoslovakia, and the RM-S emerged as an original product of the Bratislava and the Prague PVT. After the division of Czechoslovakia, two RM systems (one in each country) were created. At the beginning of 1993, the RM-S Slovakia was created as a 100% daughter company of the PVT. On 19 March 1993, the RM-S received the license from the Ministry of Finance to organize a public stock market.[1]

Periodic Auction Technique

On May 3, 1993, the RM-S became active by launching the first round of periodic auction. The periodic auction was the basic function of RM-S during its first stages. Each round of periodic auction consists of the following phases:
1. Definition and publication of a feasible price range and the closing time for the acceptance of orders for the respective auction round.
2. Acceptance of sell and buy orders.
3. Verification of validity and pre-trade validation of orders.
4. Inclusion and evaluation of orders.

---

[1] Under the new legislation the RM-S was granted a license by the Ministry of Finance of the Slovak Republic to organize a stock market on 11 December 1995.

THE NETWORK OF THE RM-SYSTEM SLOVAKIA STOCK MARKET

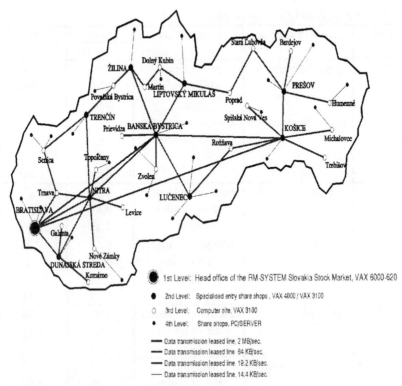

1st Level: Head office of the RM-SYSTEM Slovakia Stock Market, VAX 6000-620

2nd Level: Specialised entry share shops , VAX 4000 / VAX 3100

3rd Level: Computer site, VAX 3100

4th Level: Share shops, PC/SERVER

Data transmission leased line, 2 MB/sec.

Data transmission leased line, 64 KB/sec.

Data transmission leased line, 19.2 KB/sec.

Data transmission leased line, 14.4 KB/sec.

Source: Economic Institute SAV, 1996.

Figure 17.1. Regional Structure of RM-System Slovakia

5. Publication of the results of the auction round, in particular purchase prices.
6. Implementation of the results of the auction round.

The length of individual rounds (consisting of these six phases) was getting shorter in the course of time. The last periodic auction took place in July 1995.

In 1993, following the first wave of voucher privatization, seven rounds of periodic auction took place, and 207,000 shares were traded (see Table 17.1) with a total value of SKK 40 million (US$ 1.44 million). At this time, the supply was larger than the demand as the financially weaker part of the population sold their shares, while the institutional investors and potential buyers were not yet well-established. As a result, the average traded price of shares amounted to only SKK 209 (the nominal price in the voucher privatization was SKK 1000) in 1993. However, there was as yet no continuous auction, and the periodic auction was in its initial phase of development.

Table 17.1. Results of trading at RM-S

Year	Kind of auction	Kind of trade	Volume of trade	
			SKK bn	US$ mn
1993	periodic auction	anonymous trades	0.04	1.39
		direct trades	0.00	0.05
		total	0.04	1.44
	continuous auction	anonymous trades	–	–
		direct trades	–	–
		total	–	–
	total 1993		0.04	1.44
1994	periodic auction	anonymous trades	0.71	23.59
		direct trades	0.87	29.14
		total	1.58	52.73
	continuous auction	anonymous trades	0.38	12.52
		direct trades	0.01	0.43
		total	0.39	12.95
	total 1994		1.97	65.68
1995	periodic auction	anonymous trades	0.05	1.58
		direct trades	0.05	1.76
		total	0.10	3.34
	continuous auction	anonymous trades	1.39	46.19
		direct trades	2.28	76.01
		registered direct trades	14.29	476.19
		total	17.96	598.39
	total 1995		18.06	601.73
1993–1995	periodic auction	anonymous trades	0.80	26.55
		direct trades	0.93	30.95
		total	1.73	57.50
	continuous auction	anonymous trades	1.76	58.70
		direct trades	2.29	76.45
		registered direct trades	14.29	476.19
		total	18.34	611.34
	total 1993–1995		20.07	668.84

Source: RM-S, 1996.

In 1994, 26 auctions took place. Their liquidity was rising step by step. In addition to the shares of companies privatized in the voucher privatization, the shares of investment funds included in the voucher privatization were issued in 1994. This, together with an inflow of foreign portfolio capital, improved the liquidity of the Slovak market considerably. To give an example, in January and February 1994 for the first time demand exceeded supply. From this time on, the market showed all the typical characteristics of a bullish market. The maximum was reached in March 1994, when demand was 3.4 times higher than supply, which prompted a sharp rise in prices. At the beginning of April, supply again became higher than demand and the market settled down. Taken together, the accumulated turnover of the periodic auctions amounted to SKK 1,580 million (US$ 53 million) with an average price of SKK 602 per share. At this time, the continuous auction began to be established and in 1995 periodic auctions were terminated.

Periodic auctions played an important role in the development of the Slovak capital market. During the time of developing a market with thin liquidity, it allowed supply and demand to be concentrated and a fair price to be rendered. Simultaneously, this was the time of building and testing the on-line connections between the individual market participants, thereby ensuring a successful start to the continuous auction (see Páleník *et al.*, 1995a).

Continuous Auction Technique

The continuous auction technique, by contrast with the periodic auction technique, does not collect supply and demand over a period (e.g. a week), but instead matches sell and buy orders immediately – that is, it trades in real time. The history of the continuous auction started on 3 March 1994, when the first one was conducted, and for the first time, trading was carried out on-line. The continuous auction technique had a very dynamic development. In March 1994, the RM-S performed one continuous auction per week. Market participants, however, requested a gradual increase in the number of trading days. Finally, a continuous auction on every working day was introduced in October 1994. Between March and November 1994, the turnover had risen 20 times. In one year, a total of 130 trading days, a trading volume of one million shares was turned over (in 1994). This corresponds to an accumulated turnover of 1,970 million SKK (US$ 66 million). However, the periodic auction was the dominant technique. The most important element of liquidity was provided by the investment privatization funds, with 40% of the turnover at the RM-S.

1995 was the pivotal year for the continuous auction technique when its trading volume was several times higher than the corresponding value of the periodic auctions. The continuous auction had 246 trading days, which means almost all working days in 1995. Altogether, 32 million shares were traded at an average price of SKK 556. This corresponds to a total turnover of SKK 17,950 million (US$ 598 million) with 8% originating from anonymous trade, 13% from direct trade, and 79% from registered direct trades. These registered direct trades with shares appeared with the new legislation, under which share trading has to be conducted either on an organized market, or has to be registered on an organized market. A significant share of direct trades are the result of privatization.

Trading on the RM-S market is quite dynamic. Share trading on RM-S as a percentage of GDP amounted to only 0.01% in 1993, in 1994 to almost 0.5%, and in 1995 already to 3.5%. In the first half of 1996, the share was 4%. This marked increase in turnover, together with the reduction in trading time from 6 weeks to a couple of seconds, demonstrates the development of the RM-S market.

INDICES OF RM-S

A part of RM-S services to investors is the calculation of indices. For the periodic auction sessions, the TREND-OTC index was created. TREND, a Slovak economic weekly magazine, used to compute this index, using the results of trading in each round of the periodic auction in the years 1993 to 1995. All shares with at least one trade were used as component shares for the index. The index was constructed as a harmonic average of price relatives with daily chaining. This index played an important role in the early stages of the capital market development since it documented the market trend in an aggregate form.

The development of the continuous auction on the RM-S required the construction of an official index for this market as an indicator of price dynamics and as a benchmark for portfolio performance. This index was constructed by the Economic Institute of the Slovak Academy of Sciences (see Páleník *et al.*, 1995b). The structure of this index was based on the analysis of various stock market indices abroad as well as the existing Slovak ones (SEVIS, SIX, TREND 40, SAX, OTC). It turned out that in some of them the largest companies exert an overly large impact on their dynamics. Furthermore, an index should mirror the sectoral structure of the economy appropriately, and special attention should be paid to the price dynamics of investment funds.

In constructing the official RM-S index, the Economic Institute SAV opted for a Paasche price index which relates the actual price to basic ones of shares weighted by the market capitalization of the issue. The index has a value of 1000 at the base date (31 December 1994). The index is composed of a fixed sample of companies that is updated twice a year.

At the time the index was constructed, a total of 690 stocks were listed on the RM-S. To determine the index sample, 440 were dismissed since these were rarely traded. From the remaining 250, the component stocks were chosen according to the following criteria:

* representation of their sector, meaning that sectors are equally represented according to their relative importance in the structure of RM-S;
* high trading frequency and trade volume;
* the size of the issue and the market capitalization of the company;
* company's fundamentals.

Using these criteria, 100 company issues were chosen for the broad-based RM-S 100 that is intended to represent the market as a whole. On 1 January 1995, these 100 issues represented 58 % of the nominal capitalization at RM-S and 66 % of its market capitalization. In addition, there are two structural indices:

* RM-S INDUSTRIAL index which is composed of the 30 most important companies in the industrial sector.
* RM-S FOND index, representing the price development of the 22 most frequently traded funds.

As the index was only ready for implementation in September 1995, its daily values between January 1995 and September 1995 were calculated backwards. Starting from 1 October 1995, the index has been calculated in real time.

The RM-S 100 started with a value of 1000 in 1995 (see Figure 17.2). In the first quarter of 1996 the RM-S 100 rose to a high in February 1995 at 1035 points and dropped to its yearly low at 815 points at the end of June 1995. After a quiet second half of 1995, it closed the year at 856 points. The difference between the maximal and minimal value of the index is 22 % of its base value.

The RM-S INDUSTRIAL developed in line with the RM-S 100. In the first quarter of 1995, the two indices moved in parallel, but the RM-S INDUSTRIAL was slightly higher than the RM-S 100 (about 20–30 points difference).

In the first half of 1995, the RM-S FOND index also behaved similarly to the RM-S 100. However, both indexes experienced significantly different developments in the second half of 1995. This cannot be explained by the abilities of the funds' management, but rather by investors worrying about the new legislation of the capital market with respect to the collective investment in Slovakia (see Fidrmuc, Páleník, and Unčovský, 1999).

The RM-S indexes are published as a part of the systematic information services provided by the RM-S. The indices of the RM-S market mirror market movements, serve as the primary source of information about the development of share prices, and as a criterion for the performance of portfolios.

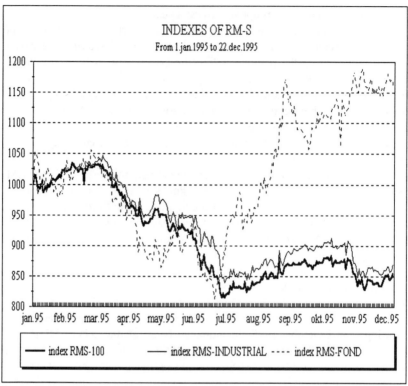

Source: Economic Institute SAV, 1996.

Figure 17.2. RM-S Indices

TRADING SAFETY AND OTHER SERVICES OF RM-S

From the legislative point of view, the RM-S is an off-exchange, organized market subject to licensing by the Ministry of Finance of the Slovak Republic and to the RM-S trading rules. These rules include a spectrum of possible kinds of orders for purchase or sale of shares and the computer algorithms for realizing the trades. The basic principle of the computer algorithms is to make the largest possible number of trades.

In addition, the RM-S provides pre-deal validation, in which the RM-S verifies whether the selling person owns the shares he is selling. This is confirmed through the Center of Securities which provides central electronic evidence of all securities. The RM-S suspends the shares from sale for the time of the transaction in order to prevent any manipulation. Furthermore, the RM-S verifies whether the person buying the shares has the appropriate amount of money for the trade. This amount is reserved as with the shares. The RM-S moves the suspended stock from the seller's account to the account of the buyer and the suspended money from the buyer's account to the seller's account. In a case where no matching orders are present in the time of the order, the reserved shares and money are released so that they are once again at the owners' disposal. This pre-deal validation allows the organizing of anonymous dealing in a fully open system.

Transactions at RM-S are based on anonymous bids and anonymous offers (the so-called anonymous trades), when buyers and sellers do not know each other. Trades of this type are most effectively made through continuous auctions, when after each new order issued a new auction price is made, using bid and offer prices. However, trades can only be realized within a feasible price range, based on the results of the trades of the last day, in order to prevent sudden price jumps that may originate from the use of insider information.

The application of computer technology and techniques as well as high-performance servers allows on-line trading. This allows remote ordering which is regarded as the most modern way of constituting a marketplace for share trading. The duration of transactions can be modified according to the intensity of trading or the net load. However, even under the worst conditions the trade lasts up to a maximum of half a minute. A share can change its owner many times during a day. The RM-S has reached the technical and organizational level of advanced markets in other countries.

Apart from anonymous trades, direct trades are also allowed. In this case, the RM-S will secure the transaction to two previously known people for a previously known price of previously known stock. The RM-S also transfers the money and the shares.

The RM-S offers complex services to issuers related to public issues. Furthermore, it provides the automatic processing and handing of dividends on shares and yields on bonds. In addition, the RM-S organizes the trading of the bonds of the Fund of National Property (FNP) that replaced the second wave of voucher privatization in Slovakia. These FNP bonds are owned by some million Slovak citizens (see Pálenik, Fidrmuc and Unčovský, 1999). The Centre of Securities uses the nationwide net of the RM-S to perform some of its tasks.

The RM-S also offers fundamental information about the issuers and the outcomes of trading on the secondary stock market. This information is available in printed form (current information from newspapers, historical facts from the periodical Fact Book), but also on electronic media. Owing to the participation of the general public in RM-S trading, an important means of spreading information is the teletext. The prices of the 200 most-traded shares are available on the teletext of the Slovak Television in real time (between 10:00 and 15:00 on every working day). Complete data are also available in the Internet.

Information in data form can be acquired on a diskette, a CD, or by modem from a dedicated computer within RM-S. The RM-S operates its own Bulletin Board System (BBS) with basic data (offices, list of all stocks, a tariff list, daily statistics, indexes, etc.). Moreover, the complete daily, weekly and monthly data can be subscribed. The RM-S also provides information according to the special needs of customers.

CONCLUSION

The RM-S Slovakia that started operation in March 1993 is the administrator of a public stock market. In according with global trends, the RM-S puts stress on the application of modern techniques, including global computer networks and accurate trading algorithms. To further enhance the value of its product, the RM-S provides various related services, including information dissemination and issuer support.

From the beginning, the RM-S has striven to have all professional traders connected on-line. Moreover, this opportunity is offered to private investors, and all participants can trade from the offices of the RM-S, which are available in all regions in Slovakia.

REFERENCES

RMS (1994): *The Factbook 1993*, RM-S: Bratislava.
RMS (1995): *The Factbook 1994*, RM-S: Bratislava.
RMS (1996) *The Factbook 1995, First Part*, RM-S: Bratislava.
Fidrmuc, J., V. Páleník and L. Unčovský (1999): *Slovakia*, this volume.
Páleník, V. *et al.* (1995a): *Economic Policy Analysis of the Slovak Republic in the Sphere of Financial Market Development*, EMPA, Bratislava.
Páleník, V. *et al.* (1995b): *Indexes of Continuous Auction of RM-S* (in Slovak), mimeo, Economic Institute SAV, Bratislava.

(C. and E. Europe) P34

G12

18. Managing Central European Financial Risks – With a Case Study on the CECE Index Family

Günther Schiendl

INTRODUCTION

Increasingly international investors are directing their portfolio investments into the Central and Eastern European financial markets. This influx of foreign money accelerates the development of their financial markets and intensifies the need to adapt to market structures. International investors and dealers/brokers are aware of the profit potential in these markets, but frequently they are put off by the uncertainty about legal frameworks, higher transaction costs or settlement problems – all of which however are in the process of being clarified and/or solved. Moreover the capital markets in Central and Eastern Europe are at different stages in their development. Common to all, however, is the very dynamic development of the institutional framework. The stock and currency markets are attracting most of the interest today; as inflation rates come down, the long-term bond markets will become more attractive.

At the beginning of 1996, the distribution of banks, dealers/brokers, mutual and investment funds present and/or active locally in the Central and Eastern European equity markets was as follows:

Table 18.1. Number of banks and brokers

Market	Local brokers	International brokers	Austrian banks
Czech Rep.	7	5	2
Hungary	7	7	4
Poland	9	10	2
Slovakia	9	1	1
Slovenia	n.a.	n.a.	1
Total	32	23	10

Source: World Equity Directory, 1996.

Table 18.2. Number and volume of mutual funds

Target Region	Number and volume of funds
'Eastern Europe'	11 Open-End Funds, 5 Funds under Austrian Fund Management
'Emerging Europe'	14 Closed-End Funds, volume US$ 880 million
'Global Emerging Markets'	73 Closed-end Funds with a total (known) volume of US$ 6.493 million

THE DEMAND BY GLOBAL INVESTORS AND TRADERS

The financial markets of these economies in transition enter the world markets – and thus competition for the money of global investors – at a time where electronic trading and remote membership have become the dominant trading regime. Physical trading places *per se* have lost their importance, since trading is done on the screen in electronic networks.

The competition between trading networks and financial intermediaries is about providing exposure and hedging facilities (the competition between exchanges) and payment streams of all kinds related to these exposures (the competition between banks and dealers/brokers), and the cost of such provisions (the competition between exchanges and banks, dealers/brokers, etc). Competition is, therefore, about the accessibility, availability and efficiency of exposure and hedging provision.

As the international market players learn more about emerging markets and gain transaction experience, their appetite for more advanced and sophisticated structures is growing and their trading strategies are becoming more demanding on their counterparties and local market structures. To begin with, investors want exposure, that is, entering new markets via shares, share options, share index options, share futures or share swaps may make less of a difference, as long as the desired exposure and investment or trading aim is met (or sufficiently approximated) within the required time horizon. Such a situation is only temporarily acceptable; it is acceptable when returns in the respective markets are as high as 50% or 100% per year. Transaction costs and available instruments clearly matter less in such an environment. As the markets mature, and as these returns are less guaranteed and achievable, more subtle and controlled exposures and instruments for actively managing risks are demanded.

The availability of risk management instruments, transactional efficiency, market integrity and easy clearing and settlement are required by international investors and traders. Providing hedge funds, mutual funds, pension funds, banks, insurance companies and dealers/brokers with such solutions is a highly competitive – but also a highly rewarding – business. Competition between the various intermediary agents in the financial markets is, therefore, on the exposure/instrument and transactional efficiency side.

SERVICES OF AN EXCHANGE: EXPOSURE MANAGE-MENT, HEDGING TOOLS AND CLEARING

Part of the service of an exchange in this situation is in providing the building blocks for exposure management and hedging tools. By careful instrument design ('What to trade?') and market structure design ('How to trade?') an exchange can become the (non-physical = electronic) marketplace for those exposure- or risk-building blocks that are traded by most of the different market participants, especially those intermediaries that are providing others with more sophisticated financial structures.

For the investor and end-user, the availability, scope and variety of financial instruments offered will be broader and the available liquidity in the instruments offered over-the-counter higher, with such building blocks easily available and easy to integrate seamlessly into the operations and strategies of the intermediaries.

The efficiency of the prices quoted for the more sophisticated or specialized financial instruments by the intermediaries will be highest, when hedging back these instruments is cheapest; usually that is in a standardized exchange market where liquidity in the building block-instruments is highest.

MARKET RESEARCH

International market research carried out at the beginning of the development of the CECE Product Line – ÖTOB's line of Central and Eastern European products – with interviewing market players in the UK, US, Germany, Switzerland, the Netherlands, Austria and the local markets showed that there is a high demand for risk management and trading instruments for Central and Eastern European financial risks. Interest is concentrating on the equity side and major clients are US$-based. A typical route of investment in Central and Eastern Europe is, for example, an American hedge fund, giving an order to his London broker, who executes the trade. Another typical example is a London-based dealer/broker providing his clients with OTC-structured products and trying to hedge his risks. Many market players also stated that there were no efficient derivative products available or directly accessible to them at the local markets and that cross-border equity trading in Eastern Europe was possible only with limitations. Because of that, many dealers/brokers have difficulties structuring the financial products or exposures required by some of their more aggressive or sophisticated customers. What was needed, therefore, was a family of indices for the Central and Eastern European equity markets.

ÖTOB's family of equity indices for the Central and Eastern European equity markets – the CECE index family – has been designed in close cooperation with active market participants, to ensure relevant indices that meet their needs and interests as closely as possible. A network of local and international dealers/brokers, fund managers, exchange and regulation specialists, analysts and sales people have contributed valuable inputs.

This situation seems to be the natural case for derivatives: giving the market players the exposure and hedging vehicles they want, but without the associated settlement problems. This can typically be achieved through equity index derivative products that are cash-settled, i.e. no stocks have to be traded or moved (physically) and exposure changes are transmitted via cash payments. The currency for the cash settlement can be either the local currency or an international standard currency. The latter has the major advantage of attracting participants from other markets and thus helps to increase the liquidity pool. The US$ is one such currency for the Central and Eastern European markets on the one hand, and on the other it is the base currency for most international market participants. Thus on the basis of the US$, a higher number of market players is likely to access and trade on such a common trading platform, thereby integrating these markets into the world financial markets. So what can ultimately be created is an international market in standardized exposure building blocks.

That was proposed by ÖTOB with the CECE product line: as more and more international money continues to flow into these markets, a central market trading and clearing place on a US$-basis for all Central and Eastern European financial risks was a highly attractive alternative to them and seen as one being able to attract sufficient liquidity.

By design, such a trading platform should focus on the strategies and aims of the international investor. Efforts should be directed into designing an operational trading and clearing platform rather than into accommodating national interests.

The linkage with the underlying local markets is by the member banks making markets in the derivatives instruments. They will hedge part of their exposure in the local cash markets. (Another part of their exposure will be taken up by funds or private buyers of their warrants based on the same CECE indices.) Additionally, there is already substantial international, non-local trading in the Central and Eastern European stocks that can be used for that purpose.

Thus, non-local trading of derivatives based on shares from the Visegrad countries does not really pose a problem,[1] since many international dealers/brokers already operate on a cross-country basis and there is multimarket trading in the major Central and Eastern European shares.[2] ÖTOB's CECE indices comprise many of these stocks. Because of telecomunication, remote membership and local offices, which many of these dealers/brokers use in the major financial centres and in these local markets, a pan-Eastern European derivatives trading platform has real chances for success, because that structure is a logical equivalent to the trading organizations of many major international dealers/brokers.

Table 18.3. Foreign trading places for Central and Eastern European shares

Trading Place	Czech stocks	Hungarian stocks	Polish stocks	Slovak stocks
Munich	21	20	–	4
Berlin	21	4	1	–
Vienna	–	12	–	–
London (LSE, SEAQ Int'l)	1	7	1	

Note: This does not necessarily mean exchange trading, since there are some brokers that buy and sell these stocks over the counter.
Sources: Bavarian Stock Exchange, Berlin Stock Exchange, Vienna Stock Exchange, London Stock Exchange, Reuters, 1996.

A pan-Central European derivatives trading platform is probably more attractive, if it succeeds in setting a standard of easy trading and product clearance and accessibility of relevant information. Information accessibility is through the CECE index family, trading is through cash-settled, US$-based derivatives, and clearing via Cedel uses a worldwide platform with which most international market participants are familiar.

---

[1] Of course, however, short-sale restrictions and difficulties with stock lending pose problems.

[2] Figures on the trading volume of these stocks in the respective markets have not been available. There are only guesses by market participants.

INSTRUMENTS FOR CENTRAL AND EAST EUROPEAN STOCK MARKET RISKS

Derivative equity index products were seen as the logic ones to start ÖTOB's international trading platform for Central and Eastern European risks. Left open however was the question: on which underlyings (meaning: equity indices, because individual share options were seen as too prone to manipulation) to base this Central and Eastern European equity derivatives product line.

Standard-setting is preference-setting. Standard-setting in this sense has higher chances of success, if these standards are what people naturally accept. The development of a pan-Central and Eastern European share index family provided the opportunity to develop a certain standard focused on a specific target.

Table 18.4. Prominent emerging markets index families

IFC – International Finance Corporation Indexes
BEMI – Barings Emerging Markets Indexes
MSCI – Morgan Stanley Capital International Indexes

Benchmarks create confidence in markets and at the same time increase the need for market information. It takes time to obtain the relevant data to monitor and compare the markets in Central and Eastern Europe with each other and with other world markets from the point of view of an international investor – even though many indices are already available.

There are up to ten indices per market, many of them calculated by the exchanges, major newspapers, banks or brokers. Most – but not all – of them are part of index families. The most important of these are those of MSCI (Morgan Stanley Capital International), IFC (International Finance Corporation) and Barings Emerging Markets Indices. Additionally, there are indices covering all emerging markets (including Asian and Latin American markets).

However, emerging markets and emerging markets indices tend to be focused on Latin America. The field for consistent indices for the equity markets of the Eastern European transitional economies is not yet covered with constantly calculated/weighted indices serving specific *trading* interests. The available regional indices were not regarded by the international market participants as suitable underlyings for derivative instruments (Rademan, 1996). As investors' trading strategies are becoming more sophisticated, highly accurate information on a real-time basis becomes increasingly necessary. This situation provided the rationale for ÖTOB developing an own index family dedicated to the trading aspect.

Table 18.5. Local equity indices for Central and Eastern European markets

Czech Republic	Poland
All Market Index	BEMI Poland
BARRA Vola-X Czech R.	BARRA Vola-X Poland
CEBW 60 Central European Business Weekly	IFC Poland Index
CNB INDEX	MSCI Poland
CZECH SPORIT S	WIG INDEX
CZECH SPORIT G	WIG-20
HN Wood Index	WIRR
Main Market Index	
PX50 INDEX	*Slovakia*
ZB-Index Zivnostenska Banka	CAX Creditanstalt Akciovy Index
	SEVIS Index 100
Hungary	Trend-Index
BARRA Vola-X Hungary	
BET	*Slovenia*
BSE	SBI Stock Index
BUX	
IFC Hungary Index	

Note: As available via Reuters.

CASE STUDY: THE CECE INDEX FAMILY

The CECE Indices are consistently weighted and calculated tradeable benchmark indices for the Central and East European stock markets. A family of homogeneously constructed and calculated indices makes market comparison easier, thus raising interest in the markets and making investors more interested in trading. ÖTOB developed its CECE index family in close cooperation with international market participants to create the underlying indices for derivatives and to channel and concentrate market interest in the CECE index stocks.

The CECE index family reflects the movement of the Central and Eastern

European blue chip stocks. It comprises the Czech Traded Index (CTX), the Hungarian Traded Index (HTX), the Polish Traded Index (PTX), the Slovak Traded Index (STX) and the CECE benchmark index, which is made up all the stocks in the individual indices. The construction principles are uniform for all CECE indices and the CECE index, so that performance analysis between these markets and with world equity markets can easily be accomplished.

ÖTOB's indices are specifically designed for the foreign investor and trader with the aim of serving as underlying instruments for derivatives. Great emphasis is, therefore, placed on the tradeability of each index component share and on the replicability of the CECE indices – and thus on building the best possible basis for derivatives trading. ÖTOB calls this principle 'traded indices', 'traded' meaning that the index portfolio and all its constituent shares can be traded with sufficient liquidity.

All CECE indices are capitalization-weighted price indices, calculated on a local currency and a US$ basis. As capitalization-weighted price indices the CECE indices can easily be replicated, so that such index-based portfolios develop in accordance with the respective index.

Eligible Stocks: Share Type

Only ordinary shares of joint-stock companies domiciled in the respective country and listed on the official stock exchange are eligible for entry on the indices. This excludes investment funds or similar investment vehicles incorporated as joint-stock companies. In general, only shares listed in the premier market segments of the relevant stock exchange are eligible for ÖTOB's Central European share index universe, because this ensures the highest standards in the quality of information available on the respective index component shares and the best research coverage by a number of local and international dealers/brokers available.

Eligible Stocks: Other Criteria

Only major blue chip shares with sufficient market capitalization, enough liquidity and price availability and which are relevant and attractive to international market participants are to be included in the CECE index family, provided that their inclusion is not contrary to the intentions and objectives of the index family or irrelevant to the economic sector.

The number of stocks for each national index should be large enough to include all relevant stocks, but it should be confined to the major, actively-traded, blue-chip stocks. Additional aspects arising from the idiosyncrasies of these stock markets have been taken into account, resulting from the float factor and the representation factor as additional input to the index structures.

Specific Construction Feature 1: Free Float Factor

In the respective indices, the individual stocks are weighted according to their market capitalization. If the free float of a stock is equal to or less than 50%, the stock is weighted in the index at half its market capitalization. The float-adjusted market capitalization of a particular stock is then calculated as the number of shares listed as deliverable on the respective stock exchange times the float factor (0.5) times the stock price.

Specific Construction Feature 2: Representation Factor

Given that Central and Eastern European stock markets are still narrow, some stocks have such a high capitalization that they would distort the representativeness of the index itself. It could happen that on a normal capitalization basis the two largest stocks together make up a weight of over 40% of the index. In the interest of a more balanced index structure the weighting of such stocks is reduced by a factor of 0.5, which we call the representation factor. The representation factor of 0.5 can also be applied to smooth the sector structure of the indices in the case of one sector being overweight. The decision about the application of the representation factor is made by the CECE index committee. It will also examine quarterly the float and representation factors for all stocks in the CECE indices. The aim of the representation factor is to bring the (sector) composition of the indices closer to the market participants' interests and portfolio structures on the one hand, and to make it relevant to the economic structure of the respective economies on the other.

Relevance of the CECE Index Family

The CECE index family covers 70% of the market capitalization and 56% of the total trading volume of the Czech, Hungarian, Polish and Slovak equity markets. This 'CECE universe of premier Central and Eastern European stocks' comprises a broad range of shares which are highly attractive to international and domestic investors and traders. Table 18.7 gives an overview on the relevance of and key data on the CECE indices.

Table 18.6. The CECE index family

The **CECE index**, which is as a US$-based, replicable benchmark index for the whole region Emerging Europe is weighted by the capitalization of the national traded indices. The CECE index comprises all shares in the four national traded indices CTX, HTX, PTX and STX. It is designed as a replicable and tradeable benchmark index. Made up of 41 blue chip stocks from four countries, the CECE index currently represents 69% of the market capitalization and 56% of the trading volume of all exchange-traded stocks in the Czech Republic, Hungary, Poland and Slovakia. The CECE index constitutes an important step in the development of performance measurement in Central and Eastern Europe. Because the CECE index is made up of the national traded indices and constructed according to the same principles as a capitalization-weighted index, changes in the composition of each national index affect the CECE directly.

The **Czech Traded Index – CTX** consists of 10 Czech blue chip stocks, which together account for 59% of the total market capitalization and 47% of the total trading volume of all Czech tier-1 shares. The **Hungarian Traded Index – HTX** comprises 10 Hungarian blue chip stocks. The stocks in the HTX – a lot of them are traded as GDRs – make up 89% of the total market capitalization and 86% of the total trading volume of all Hungarian shares. The **Polish Traded Index – PTX** consists of 14 Polish blue chip stocks, which together account for 59% of the total market capitalization and 43% of the total trading volume of all Polish shares. The **Slovak Traded Index – STX** consists of 7 Slovak blue chip stocks. They account for 70% of the total market capitalization and 50% of the total trading volume of all Slovak shares.

Note: Data as of 1997. For the actual index composition see the Reuters pages OETOB16–OETOB20 or the Internet at www.wbag.at.

Table 18.7. Key data on the CECE indices

Index	Total market capitalization (cap.)	Total market cap. of index stocks	Index cap.*	Cap. index stocks/total market cap.	Volume index stocks/total market
CTX	19.4	8.43	2.88	43.45%	53.14%
HTX	5.27	4.23	3.36	80.27%	88.62%
PTX	8.35	4.38	2.23	52.46%	43.61%
STX	5.7	1.31	0.79	22.98%	36.17%
CECE	38.72	18.35	9.26	51.35%	46.00%

Notes: Values in US$ billion, December 1996, volume figures based on 1996. 'Index capitalization' is the total capitalization of all stocks in the index, calculated with the float and representation factors.
* as of April 4, 1997.

REFERENCES

Rademan, C. (1996): 'Just how good are emerging markets indexes?', *Institutional Investor*, June, pp. 82–87.

World Equity Directory (1996): *Emerging Markets: Brokers and Funds*, IFR, London.

G12 P34 (C, Europe)

19. The Extent of Efficiency in Central European Equity Markets[*]

Randall K. Filer and Jan Hanousek

INTRODUCTION

Perhaps one of the most controversial issues in modern economics is the level of efficiency in capital markets. Dozens of papers each year address some aspect of this debate. In general three forms of market efficiency are discussed. Each asserts that it is impossible to make predictable excess returns beyond the level justified by a security's riskiness on the basis of a particular information set. The difference between them lies in the information sets that prices are claimed to reflect.

1. A market is *weakly efficient* if prices fully reflect all information contained in historic price series. Such efficiency implies that stocks follow a random walk and that, therefore, it is impossible to earn excess returns by using information in the pattern of stock prices, a technique known as technical analysis.
2. A market is *semi-strongly efficient* if security prices fully reflect all publicly available information that might influence the value of a given company. This form of efficiency implies that a fundamental analysis of a firm's situation and the economy in general will not enable an investor to earn excess returns.
3. Finally, a market is *strongly efficient* if all information that is known to *any* investor, including insiders, is reflected in security prices. This implies that there is no way any market participant can be sure of making excess returns.

---

[*] This research was supported by the National Science Foundation of the United States (grant number SPR–9712336), the PHARE/ACE Research Program of the European Union (grant number P95–2063–R) and the National Council for Soviet and East European Research (grant number 811–15).

Although there is a great deal of controversy as to whether securities markets exhibit each of these forms of efficiency, a consensus seems to be emerging that while temporary pricing anomalies may exist, in the end 'one has to be impressed with the substantial volume of evidence suggesting that stock prices display a remarkable degree of efficiency' (Malkiel, 1996 p. 222).

A number of studies in recent years have investigated the efficiency of emerging equity markets, primarily in Asia and Latin America. Among these are Claessens, Dasgupta and Glan (1995), Cornelius (1993), Harvey (1995), Urrutia (1995), Zychowicz, Binbasioglu and Kazancioglu (1995), Agbeyegbe (1994), Agrawal and Tandon (1994), Ajayi and Meyhdian (1994), Annuar, Ariff and Shamsher (1994), Ayada and Pyun (1994), and Stengos and Panas (1992). Although the results of these studies can best be characterized as mixed, they find a surprising amount of evidence that emerging markets are approximately as efficient as those in developed countries such as the U.S. Claessens, Dasgupta and Glan, for example, find that 'stock price behavior in the twenty stock markets represented in the International Finance Corporation's Emerging Markets Data Base displays few of the anomalies found for industrial economies,'[1] while Urrutia concludes that investors in Latin American markets would 'not be able to detect patterns in stock prices and develop trading strategies that would allow them to earn abnormal returns'. In general, the strongest evidence against efficiency in emerging markets is the presence of autocorrelation in returns, a phenomenon that some have suggested is an 'indicator of economic growth rather than evidence against the efficient market hypothesis'.[2]

The past decade has seen one of the most extraordinary changes in economic systems ever recorded. Commonly called the transition, the shift from command to market economies in Central and Eastern Europe including the Former Soviet Union has radically altered the lives of nearly 10% of the world's population. A major component of this transition has been the rapid privatization of former state assets. By the end of 1997 between two-thirds and three-quarters of economic output in the Visegrad countries (Poland, the Czech Republic, Slovakia and Hungary) was produced in the private sector, an increase from virtually nothing in 1989.

A natural question is the extent to which the equity markets of Central Europe have achieved a degree of efficiency comparable with markets in developed countries or emerging markets with much longer histories. Efficient markets may play an important role in the success of the transition. There are

---

[1] Claessens, Dasgupta and Glan (1995), p. 150.

[2] Urrutia, (1995) p. 308.

obvious advantages to efficient markets, especially of the strong form. The transitional economies need large amounts of capital for restructuring. Banks are weak and undercapitalized and will have, therefore, limited ability to finance investment activity. Many firms are not yet profitable enough to finance necessary restructuring through retained earnings. This situation suggests that there must be a great deal of reliance on equity finance. Investors who have confidence that markets cannot be manipulated by insiders will be more willing to invest in such markets, thereby lowering the cost of capital. Similarly, especially in countries such as the Czech Republic where large-scale distribution of shares has played a major role in privatization, public support for the transition is likely to be a function of public perception of the fairness of the market in which they must dispose of their shares when they want cash. Thus, a finding of significant deviations from efficiency would be troubling for the transition process.

There are, however, other reasons why efficient markets may actually hamper the transition to a market economy in Central Europe. One of the biggest problems in the region is the need for effective mechanisms of corporate control. This may be especially important in countries such as the Czech Republic where voucher privatization has created a large number of dispersed owners. Without mechanisms for corporate control, privatization may fail because insiders from the former regime can strip firms of their valuable assets or otherwise hamper evolution to a market economy. Left unchecked, insiders in a firm (workers and managers) will tend to operate the firm for their private benefit, ignoring the owners' interests. Thus, such firms may pay excessive wages and salaries, sell assets to managers at below market prices, or sign 'sweetheart deals' with insiders or their relatives for materials and services at above-market prices[3]. Dispersed individual owners, each having only a small stake in the firm, cannot effectively monitor and control such practices. Large holders such as mutual funds, on the other hand, have both the power and the incentive to oversee managers. Thus, the evolution of mutual funds that can exercise corporate control is a particularly important aspect in the design of Czech privatization and is a component in many countries' privatization plans.

Mutual funds can only exist, however, if they charge their shareholders a fee

---

[3] Another problem comes from the fact that the government retains a significant stake in many 'privatized' firms. Without countervailing large stakeholders, the shares retained by the governments (typically in the privatization agencies or national property funds) become a controlling interest that may be used to direct the firm's activities in the interest of the government rather than the firm's owners. There are several instances in the Czech Republic where the Fund for National Property has used its influence to force supposedly private firms to invest in potentially failing firms at above market prices in order to enable the government to avoid having to rescue these firms from the public purse.

to cover operating costs. If markets are strongly efficient, so that the return available from funds is no greater than that available through individual investing, there is no reason for an individual investor to join a fund. This would necessitate paying a management fee for no added return. Even though investors as a whole would be better off with effective corporate control, there is a classic 'prisoners' dilemma' problem with each individual investor seeing that he or she would be better off outside the fund, no matter what other investors opted to do. Thus, few investors could be expected to join funds. This behavior implies that the more efficient the capital market, the more important it is for alternative institutions of effective corporate governance to develop in transitional economies.

Thus, the issue of the extent to which equity markets in Central Europe are or are not classically efficient is of more than intellectual interest since these markets may play a critical role in the future development of the region. This essay first discusses the extent to which the structure and operation of Central European equity markets approximates the conditions required for efficiency. It then reports the results of the some initial tests of various forms of market efficiency and suggests future approaches for evaluating other types of efficiency. Finally, it concludes with a discussion of the extent of efficiency in the artificial closed equity market created by the Czech voucher privatization process. The efficiency of this artificial market is of more than theoretical interest since other countries such as Romania, Bulgaria and Ukraine are in the process of implementing similar privatization mechanisms.

INSTITUTIONAL MARKET STRUCTURE

For markets to be efficient, it is widely assumed that they must possess certain fundamental characteristics. In particular:
1. there must be a reasonably large number of profit-seeking investors who actively participate in the market;
2. information must be freely available to all participants at approximately the same time.[4]

In short, markets are likely to exhibit a reasonable degree of efficiency if there is active trading, disclosure of relevant information, and prohibitions on taking advantage of inside information. To what extent do Central European equity markets exhibit these characteristics?

---

[4] Note that this can be achieved either if there is no inside information (an unlikely occurrence) or if trading on the basis of inside information is effectively prohibited.

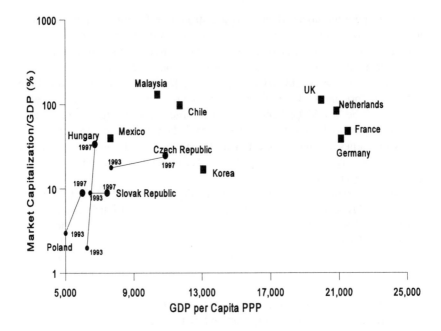

Figure 19.1. Capitalization of equity markets/GDP

Table 19.1 gives an indication of the extent of and degree of liquidity in Central European markets at the end of 1997 compared with other emerging markets and markets in Western Europe. Figure 19.1 presents one aspect of market extent, the ratio of market capitalization to GDP for selected countries for 1997 as well as for the Central European markets for the five years from 1993 to 1997. What the table does not show is the path that the Central European markets took to reach their current level of development. Because of the free distribution of vouchers, market capitalization in the Czech Republic reached 0.35% of GDP by 1995 when the other countries in the region had capitalizations of less than 10% of GDP. The slower process of privatization by direct sales adopted in Hungary and Poland resulted in a slower development of markets although Hungary had caught up with the Czech Republic by 1997.[5] On the other hand, the Czech Republic may have paid a price for this rapid development. At the end of 1995 over 1,600 companies were traded on the

---

[5] Slovakia represents an intermediate case, paralleling the Czech use of vouchers prior to the splitting of the former Czechoslovakia on 1 January 1993, buy relying on direct sales (often to politically connected insiders) since then.

Table 19.1 Extent and liquidity of equity markets (1997)

	Central Europe				Asia					
	Czech Rep.	Hungary	Poland	Slovakia	Malaysia	Korea	Taiwan	Indonesia	Thailand	Pakistan
Number of traded firms	276	49	143	872	708	776	404	282	431	781
Market cap. (US$ million)	12786	14975	12135	1826	93608	41881	287813	29105	23538	10966
Market cap./GDP	0.25	0.34	0.09	0.09	1.31	0.17	0.79	0.26	0.23	0.19
Turnover (US$ million)	7055	7684	7977	2165	147036	170237	1297474	41650	23119	11476
Turnover/ market cap.	0.55	0.51	0.66	1.19	1.57	4.06	4.51	1.43	0.98	1.05

	Latin America					Other Europe				
	Argentina	Brazil	Chile	Mexico	Venezuela	Greece	Portugal	Turkey	France	Germany
Number of traded firms	136	536	295	198	91	230	148	257	683	700
Market cap. (US$ millions)	59252	255478	72046	156595	14581	34164	38954	61090	674368	825233
Market cap./GDP	0.2	0.33	0.98	0.4	0.17	0.29	0.4	0.32	0.48	0.39
Turnover (US$ million)	25702	203260	7445	52646	3858	21146	20932	59105	405523	1029152
Turnover/ market cap.	0.43	0.8	0.1	0.34	0.26	0.62	0.54	0.97	0.6	1.25

Czech equity market as opposed to 42 in Hungary and 65 in Poland. Clearly this was more firms than were liquid enough for trading to establish reliable prices[6] and by 1997 major delistings on the Prague Stock Exchange had reduced the number of traded firms to a more reasonable 276 with minimal impact on market capitalization.

The Czech and Hungarian ratios of market capitalization to GDP are similar to that in many Western European countries and significantly higher than in southern members of the European Union.[7] On the other hand, they lag behind many 'Asian tiger' economies as well as Chile in Latin America where the shift to private, fully-funded pensions has created an equity boom. It is interesting to speculate whether this difference in market capitalization per dollar of current GDP represents only a speculative bubble in the Asian markets or an appropriate valuation of future growth rates in these largely unregulated and low-tax economies compared to the slow-growth environment of the European Union. Assuming that a similar share of GDP is produced by traded firms in each country,[8] the implication is that Central Europe has perhaps been too successful in achieving its desire to resemble the EU. The market may be judging, therefore, that its growth rate is more likely to resemble the stagnant European environment than the dynamic Asian one.

In addition to achieving a similar market capitalization as Latin American and Western European countries, the leading Visegrad markets in the Czech Republic and Hungary exhibited a similar level of trading activity as these more established markets. They lag considerably behind East Asia, however, where capitalization and turnover exploded in recent years during the regional bubble. It appears that by 1997 the most advanced Central European equity markets had managed to achieve the first precondition for market efficiency, the existence of an active market with many participants. It remains to be seen whether these markets are more efficient than the lagging Polish and Slovak markets.

Before addressing this issue we turn to a discussion of the second important condition for market efficiency, the prompt and public disclosure of relevant information. There is a great deal of debate in the academic literature regarding

---

[6] The number of traded companies in the Czech Republic in 1995 was greater than in any developed economy except Japan, the UK and the USA.

[7] Comparable figures were 17% in Austria, 28% in Germany, 39% in France and Denmark and 45% in Belgium. Among southern EU members market capitalization was 20% of GDP in Portugal, 21% in Greece and Italy, and 37% in Spain. The U.S. is exceptional in the value of its equity markets, with total market capitalization exceeding GDP, a feature it shares with only the United Kingdom and the Netherlands among developed economies.

[8] Something we have tried, but so far have been unable, to verify.

whether mandatory disclosure requirements are needed in order to overcome the incentives for firms to be overly restrictive in releasing information for strategic competitive reasons (see Dye, 1990 and Demski and Feltham, 1994) or whether firms have sufficient incentives to provide the optimal amount of disclosure voluntarily so that regulations would be, at best, irrelevant and, at worst, interfere with optimal contracting and impose costly burdens on financial markets (see Bentsen, 1973, Leftwich, 1980, and Phillips and Zecher, 1981). There have been sharp divisions among the Visegrad countries over which side of this debate has guided their policies. In Poland, disclosure requirements are derived from an order of the Council of Ministers (cabinet) and apply to all publicly-traded shares in similar manner to that in the U.S. In the Czech Republic and Hungary, on the other hand, legally required disclosure has been minimal. Instead, the stock exchanges have issued requirements for firms desiring to be listed for trading in the main market.[9]

In each country there is also a so-called 'free' or 'parallel' market where firms may trade without meeting the disclosure requirements for listed firms. Recently the Czech Republic created a securities commission with the power to extend disclosure requirements to all firms. In addition, the stock exchange in the Czech Republic created a formal secondary market (with slightly less restrictive disclosure requirements, mainly in that firms must file half-yearly reports rather than quarterly ones) and over time eliminate trading in the free market with no disclosure requirements in an attempt to persuade firms to shift to the primary or secondary markets.[10] By mid-1996 75% of market capitalization and 71% of trading volume in the Czech Republic were in stocks where extensive disclosure requirements applied. The coverage of these requirements is indicated in the appendix, which reproduces selected sections of the December 1995 'Requirements for Admission of a Security to Trading at the Prague Stock Exchange.' Requirements for listing in Hungary and Slovakia and for all firms in Poland are similar. Thus, for listed firms at least, disclosure rules seem to be as extensive as those in the U.S. (and probably more comprehensive than in most of Western Europe). They would appear to be sufficient to promote market efficiency provided that these rules are enforced.

In Central Europe, however, we must always ask if rules as written are followed in practice. There is at least some evidence that regulations that appear

---

[9] Interestingly, regulations were issued by the Stock Exchange Chamber in the Czech Republic and the Stock Exchange Council in Hungary, and may carry some hidden prima facie weight because they were issued by the 'S.E.C'. a set of initials that may register in investors' subconscious. We have no indication regarding whether the choice of names yielding these initials was deliberate. Recently the Czech Republic introduced a formal Securities Commission with regulatory powers.

[10] In a series of steps in 1997 and 1998, the vast majority of firms were delisted from the PSE.

to offer sufficient requirements for timely disclosure are not adhered to. In particular, firms assembling blocks of shares for the purpose of taking control of a firm have, reportedly, decided that shares bought by wholly-owned subsidiaries do not count towards the requirement that intentions must be announced once a certain number of shares have been purchased, on the grounds that these shares are owned by independent legal entities.

It is also clear that no market can be strongly efficient without effective prohibitions on insider trading. Once again, the Visegrad countries have adopted rules against insider trading that mirror those in more developed markets, although once again these often rely more on the stock exchange than national law enforcement agencies for the application of sanctions. The regulations of the Prague Stock Exchange, for example, state that:

> Any person who, due to his/her job, profession, position, and/or function, is authorized to acquire a confidential information on economic and/or financial position of an issuer and/or other facts important for the development of either the financial market and/or prices of securities is neither allowed to conclude trades in these securities nor to exploit his/her information for his/her own benefit or benefits of other persons until this information becomes generally public.

The sanctions that can be imposed, however, are limited. Maximum fines by the exchange are about US$ 1,500 while the maximum penalty from the Securities Commission is only about US$ 15,000. The most serious sanction involves a prohibition against future trading on the exchange. Once again, the face value of the sanctions would be greater if they were codified in criminal law and applied by the public authorities. Here again Poland has far more stringent rules than the other countries, with the law providing for between six months' and five years' imprisonment for anyone 'who uses insider information while trading in securities,' where insider information is defined as any 'information which has not been made public but which after publication could substantially influence the value or the price of a security.'

In summary, the extent of the Czech and Hungarian stock markets seems to be the most conducive to market efficiency, but the institutional structure of the Polish market contains more extensive disclosure requirements and prohibitions against insider trading. It is clear, however, that there are numerous reasons why these markets may fall short of efficiency, implying that no conclusion can be reached regarding which, if any, approximate to the degree of efficiency found in the West without empirical tests. In the only published work on efficiency in Visegrad stock markets to date, Gorden and Rittenberg (1995) show that limit trading rules (which suspend trading when a share price rises or falls by a given amount in a single session) create positive serial correlation in daily returns among Polish stocks, with the mean price change on days following coming near the upper limit of plus 10% being 3.32% as opposed to a 0.43% change on other days. This is not a surprising result and is likely to be the case in all the markets in the area since they all have similar limit-move rules. This type of serial correlation does not, however, necessarily represent market inefficiency, since it may not be possible to earn excess returns by following a trading strategy based on buying stocks that hit the upper movement limit. Suppose that all such stocks simply opened at a significantly higher price the following day so that buy orders entered at the end of day 1 were executed *after* the full move on day 2. Obviously, in this case serial correlation in daily returns would not enable an investor to earn excess returns.

TESTS OF WEAK-FORM EFFICIENCY

As discussed above, weak-form efficiency implies that stock prices should follow a random walk. One common way of testing whether this is the case is by examining variance ratios (Lo and MacKinlay, 1988). This test is based on the fact that, if the natural logarithm of a time series is a pure random walk, then the variance of its q-differences will increase in direct proportion to the length of the difference q. The variance ratio is defined as:

$$VR(q) = \frac{\sigma^2(q)}{\sigma^2(1)} \qquad (19.1)$$

where $\sigma^2(q)$ is $1/q$ times the variance of the q-differences and $\sigma^2(1)$ is the variance of the first differences.[11] Standard normal test statistics are provided by Liu and He (1991) under both homoskedasticity and heteroskedasticity.[12]

Table 19.2 presents the results of variance ratio testing of the hypothesis that securities prices follow a random walk in each of the Visegrad countries. In each case the test was performed on monthly returns of the main index for each

---

[11] Formulae for calculating $\sigma^2(q)$ and $\sigma^2(1)$ were taken from Lo and MacKinlay (1988) and are not reproduced here. Note that since these are the differences in log prices the test is one of whether returns (not prices) are predictable or follow a random walk.

[12] Again the reader is referred to the original source for the exact form of the test statistics. Both produce a z-score that is distributed $N(0,1)$.

Table 19.2. Variance-ratio tests of random walk hypothesis. Monthly
returns variance ratio

Number of Lags	Czech Republic	Hungary	Poland	Slovakia
$q=3$	1.14 (0.71) 0.31)	1.07 (0.41) (0.15)	1.29 (1.65) (0.49)	1.15 (0.74) (0.32)
$q=6$	1.18 (0.54) (0.24)	1.11 (0.37) (0.13)	1.58 (1.97)* (0.54)	1.13 (0.40) (0.19)
$q=9$	1.51 (1.22) (0.52)	1.19 (0.50) (0.16)	1.73 (1.93) (0.51)	1.22 (0.52) (0.24)
$q=12$	1.80 (1.62) (0.65)	1.29 (0.65) (0.19)	1.73 (1.64) (0.43)	1.36 (0.73) (0.33)
max z {3..12} max z' {3..12}	(1.62) (0.65)	(0.65) (0.19)	(1.98) (0.60)	(0.90) (0.36)

Notes: *Indicates that variance ratio is significantly different from 1 at the 5% confidence level, thereby implying a rejection of the random walk hypothesis.
z assuming homoskedasticity.
z' robust to heteroskedasticity.

country[13] from the date the index was first calculated to December 1998.[14] As can be seen in Table 19.2, in only one case can we reject the random walk hypothesis if we consider each lag length independently although some test statistics come close to significance given the small number of observations. Technically, rejection of a variance ratio equal to one for *any* lag length is sufficient to reject the random walk hypothesis. However, given that multiple tests are being performed, the appropriate significance level is not given by reference to the standard normal tables (see Chow and Denning, 1993). Thus, the final row in Table 19.2 reports the maximum z score across all lag lengths examined as well as an indication of statistical significance using appropriate Studentized Maximum Modulus (SMM) confidence intervals (see Stolin and

---

[13] The PX-50 for the Czech Republic, BUX for Hungary, WIG for Poland and SAX for Slovakia.

[14] We report results for $q = 3$, 6, 9 and 12. We have also performed the test for the intervening lag periods with no change in the pattern of results. Complete results are available from the authors on request.

Table 19.3. Variance-ratio tests of random walk hypothesis. Weekly returns variance ratio

Number of Lags	Czech Republic	Hungary	Poland	Slovakia
q=4	1.31 (2.65)* (0.75)	1.59 (5.57)* (1.22)	1.30 (2.81)* (0.83)	1.87 (7.38)** (0.84)
q=8	1.57 (3.05)** (0.83)	1.91 (5.42)** (1.03)	1.49 (2.94)* (0.73)	1.55 (2.96)* (0.36)
q=13	1.52 (2.13) (0.53)	1.87 (3.93)** (1.03)	1.83 (3.71)** (0.79)	1.23 (0.94) (0.13)
q=26	1.39 (1.10) (0.22)	1.87 (2.68)** (0.42)	2.26 (3.89)** (0.65)	0.86 (-0.40) (-0.06)
max z {3..26} max z' {3..26}	(3.15) (0.87)	(5.82)** (1.22)	(3.96) (0.83)	(8.47)** (0.98)

Notes: * Indicates that variance ratio is significantly different from 1 at the 5% confidence level, thereby implying a rejection of the random walk hypothesis.
z assuming homoskedasticity.
z' robust to heteroskedasticity.

Ury, 1979). Although we are rarely able to reject the random walk hypothesis, in most cases the actual variance ratios are greater than one. We must ask, therefore, if the results found are due to positive autocorrelation in returns or heteroskedasticity where, if we model the returns in any of the Central European markets as a mean value plus a random 'error' term, the magnitude of the random term is growing over time. This would not be a surprising finding in a world where markets are developing rapidly. Both volume and frequency of trading has been increasing in each of the markets under study, with all markets moving from trading one or two days a week with a single price fixing per day to daily trading with continuous pricing. It is to be expected that the more fully-functioning markets might exhibit more price movement per unit of time. In addition, there have been frequent, non-regular 'interventions' into the equity markets in the region by the local agencies charged with privatizing former state enterprises, typically in the form of selling blocks of shares in these enterprises on the secondary market as a part of the privatization process. These features suggest that heteroskedasticity may be characteristic of returns in Central European markets. When heteroskedasticity is allowed, in no country do we even come close to rejecting the hypothesis that variance ratios are equal to 1, which suggests that returns in Central European equity markets follow a random walk.

Although the literature testing for random walks often uses monthly data, as we did in Table 19.2, there is generally a longer time period over which to test the hypothesis than is available in Central Europe where we have at most six years of data. Table 19.3 reports the results of repeating the analysis using weekly returns for differences in q of one month, two months, three months and six months. With the larger sample size and shorter time period, the results follow a consistent pattern. If we do not allow for heteroskedasticity, weak form efficiency is rejected for every country for at least some lag lengths and for Hungary and Slovakia even when the joint nature of the test across lag lengths is considered. Once heteroskedasticity is taken into account, however, we are once again unable to reject the hypothesis of weak form efficiency for any country in the region.

One potential problem with variance ratio tests of the random walk hypothesis is that they rely on an assumption of normality in the random component of returns. Table 19.4 presents the first four moments of the distribution of returns for each Central European market. Since the distribution of returns consisting of a constant term plus a normally distributed random component will also be normal, rejection of normality for the distribution of returns indicates that variance ratio tests may be inappropriate for this data. As can be seen in Table 19.4, the assumption of normality in returns is rejected for every country. A general pattern of positive skewness and kurtosis indicates that returns are more flattened to the right and more highly peaked than would be the case if they were normally distributed. An alternative, distribution-free test for the independence of successive returns relies on the number of runs (Levene, 1952), where a run is defined as a sequence of consecutive changes in returns in the same direction. We report the results of such a test in Table 19.5. In general there are fewer runs in returns than would be expected if returns followed a random walk (e.g. were not predictable based on prior returns), indicating some persistence in returns. However, only in the case of monthly returns in the Czech Republic and weekly returns in Slovakia is this difference statistically significant at the 5% level. Thus, once again, the preliminary evidence is that equity markets in Central Europe are close to being weak-form efficient. Our results for monthly returns are similar to those reported for emerging markets in Latin America (Urrutia, 1995) and Turkey (Zychowicz *et al.*, 1995). Interestingly, we also find Central European equity markets weak-form efficient using weekly data, an hypothesis rejected by Zychowicz *et al.* for Turkey.

Table 19.4. Distribution of returns in Central European equity markets

	Czech Republic PX-50		Hungary BUX		Poland WIG		Slovakia SAX	
	Weekly Returns	Monthly Returns	Weekly Returns	Monthly Returns	Weekly Returns	Monthly Returns	Weekly Returns	Monthly Returns
Mean	-0.39	0.91	0.7	3.89	1.07	5.32	-0.52	1.12
Standard deviation	3.14	12.1	4.5	13.2	7.38	20.6	3.48	20
Skewness	-0.26*	2.11**	-0.48**	0.77**	0.41**	1.88**	-0.48**	5.22**
Kurtosis	2.88**	8.25**	6.87**	4.45**	2.81**	7.34**	5.50**	34.0**
Number of observations	241	63	309	71	311	71	244	63
Period of observation	9/93–12/98	1/94–12/98	1/93–12/98		1/93–12/98		9/93–12/98	1/94–12/98

Notes: * (**) Significantly different from 0 at the 5% (1%) confidence level. Standard error of skewness computed as $[6/N]^{1/2}$ and of kurtosis as $[24/N]^{1/2}$ where N is the number of observations.

405

Table 19.5. Runs tests of weak form efficiency

	Czech Republic		Hungary		Poland		Slovakia	
	Weekly returns	Monthly returns	Weekly returns	Monthly returns	Weekly returns	Monthly returns	Weekly returns	Monthly returns
Number of runs**	156	35	217	45	202	49	144	40
Expected number of runs	160.3	41.7	205.7	47	207	47	162.3	41.7
Standard error of expected runs	6.52	3.29	7.39	3.51	7.41	3.51	6.56	3.29
Number of observations	241	63	309	71	311	71	244	63
Z–score	-0.66	-2.02*	1.53	-0.57	-0.67	0.57	-2.79*	-0.51

Notes:
- Significantly different from 0 at 5% confidence level. The expected number of runs was calculated as $[2N-1]/3$ where N equals the number of observations. The standard error of expected runs was calculated as $[(16N-29)/90]^{1/2}$.
** There is an issue regarding how to calculate the number of runs for the Prague and Budapest Stock Exchanges. There are periods during which these exchanges did not trade for a week or more due to holidays. Since we are focusing on weekly returns we must decide whether to ignore the 'dark' weeks or to apportion the total return among them. We have done the latter in calculating the level of return but excluded constructed weeks in determining whether a run occurred. Thus, a total return of 3% over three weeks was reduced to 1% per week but only considered as one week in calculating the number of runs so as not to create an artificial pattern by the equality of the created weekly returns.

TESTS OF SEMI-STRONG-FORM AND STRONG-FORM MARKET EFFICIENCY

Semi-strong efficiency requires that no public information should be useful in predicting the future course of stock prices.[15] In other work (Hanousek and Filer, 1998) we have found that for every country in the region at least some economic variables are able to predict future returns on the main stock market index.[16] In three out of the four countries (all except Poland) changes in industrial production were related to subsequent stock market returns while in the largest markets (the Czech Republic and Hungary) changes in the money supply and rate of inflation also seemed to predict future equity returns. In Poland, only trade balances and foreign capital inflow seemed to matter. While there is some evidence that the Polish market has become more efficient over time, the larger Czech market actually has become less efficient. In the first part of the period we studied economic factors had no ability to predict future market returns while in the later period there were strong relationships. Overall, it appears that trading strategies based on public information might enable investors in Central Europe to earn excess returns, although we have not investigated whether these returns would be large enough to justify the transactions costs involved.

Other tests of semi-strong efficiency are possible for all of the markets under study but have not been carried out yet. By the summer of 1999 many of the securities involved in the first wave of Czech voucher privatization will have been traded for up to 72 months (312 weeks), with trading for firms in the second wave having taken place for over 216 weeks. The exchanges in Budapest and Warsaw have been in operation for an even longer period (since 1990 and 1991 respectively). Thus, there will soon be sufficient observations to calculate betas for all publicly-traded firms,[17] enabling the investigation of

---

[15] Note that the overall state of the economy will affect stock prices. Obviously there is strong correlation between monetary and fiscal policy and market value. This relationship is, however, contemporaneous, so that a change in money supply in a given period is immediately reflected in stock prices in that period.

[16] In no case did we find a causal relationship going the other way such that equity prices predicted macroeconomic variables. Thus it is clear that these markets are not efficient enough to rationally anticipate future policies or economic developments. This finding is not surprising given the number and magnitude of the external shocks markets in these countries have faced as they have evolved towards a market economy over the past five years.

[17] Low liquidity for some issues means that analysis of daily returns may be problematic in the Central European context. Estimation of betas will have to adjust for biases introduced by the failure of some securities to trade in a given interval. Techniques for such adjustments are well

whether returns are related to factors such as capitalization or price/earnings ratios after accounting for conventional measures of risk. Similarly, trading anomalies such as day-of-the-week effects should begin to be visible in series of this length if they are characteristic of these markets.[18]

Tests of strong-form market efficiency are more problematic. By definition, it is impossible for the researcher to observe inside information. Examining the pattern of price movements, Němeček (1998) found evidence that informed trading may actually be less common in the Czech market than in more developed markets such as the U.S. Tests of strong-form efficiency have, however, typically relied on comparing the performance of investors who might be supposed to have inside information with that of other investors. The most widespread form of such a study asks whether professionally managed mutual funds are able to outperform random investment strategies. Of course, this leaves open the question of whether such funds actually have access to inside information rather than simply having an incentive to hire the best analysts of public information.

Unfortunately, the limited number of mutual funds in most Central European countries will make such traditional tests impossible for countries other than the Czech Republic, where the special situation created by voucher privatization makes such tests practical. In fact, one of the most significant features of Czech voucher privatization was the role of mutual funds, known as Investment Privatization Funds (IPFs). Before the bidding process started, each voucher holder had the option of assigning all or part of his points to one or more of these funds. About three-quarters of citizens eligible to participate in voucher privatization did so, with approximately 72% of voucher points being placed with one of 264 IPFs, while 28% were retained by individuals. There was substantial concentration among the IPFs, with over 56% of their points controlled by the largest 13 funds. Behavior in the second wave was similar, with about the same fraction of those eligible participating but somewhat fewer (63.5%) points being assigned to one of the 354 investment funds.

In terms of tests of strong-form efficiency, one additional aspect of the structure of these funds is important. They were created and operated by a wide variety of entities including foreign banks and investment firms, local banks, and individuals. Given the concentration of banking in the Czech Republic and the interlocking relationship created by prior lending patterns, it is logical to assume that funds managed by local banks would have greater access to inside

----

established (see, for example, Bartholdy and Riding (1994)).

[18] End-of-the-year effects will obviously be more problematic to detect with only five or six years of observations.

information than those managed by outsiders. Thus, a finding of no difference in the performance of these two types of funds would be suggestive of strong-form efficiency.

THE EFFICIENCY OF CZECH VOUCHER PRIVATIZATION

Although it is still very early in the their development, the results discussed above at least suggest that the emerging equity markets in Central Europe may exhibit greater efficiency that is commonly supposed. The implication is that efficiency can emerge quickly in new markets. Perhaps the best test of the speed at which a *de novo* market can reach reasonable levels of efficiency is the artificial bidding market involved in the Czech voucher privatization process. The first wave of voucher privatization took place in five bidding rounds while the second had six rounds. Prices in the first round were the same for all stocks (since the number of shares issued was determined by a firm's book value). In each successive round prices were adjusted up or down as a function of the excess demand for or supply of the stock in the previous round.[19]

The efficiency of this artificial market is best assessed by observing the outcomes of the later rounds in each wave. If this artificial market was strongly efficient, we would expect to find that by the end of the voucher process neither professional investors nor individuals would be able, on average, to perform better than a random purchasing strategy. While they did not do quite as well as professionally-managed funds, individuals averaged 97% of the value purchased per point[20] by investment funds in the final two rounds of wave 1 and the final three rounds of wave 2. Even a random purchase of shares[21] achieved results equal to 91% of the value per point of shares purchased by funds in the final two rounds of wave 1 and 93% of the professionals' performance in the final three rounds of wave 2. This suggests that if this artificial market were not

---

[19] See Svejnar and Singer (1994) and Hlavsa (1996).

[20] We calculate market values as the traded price on the Prague Stock Exchange several weeks after shares opened for trading, since initial prices were determined by the final voucher price, which may not be reflective of true value. Results are insensitive to the exact time at which values are determined, and hold even several months later when many new investors have entered the market and much new information has become available.

[21] We constructed random portfolios on the basis of allocating a fixed number of points in proportion to the price-weighted shares available in each round and assuming that the portfolio bought those shares that were actually sold in that round and retained for future rounds the points bid on shares that were not sold in a given round.

strongly efficient, it was not far from it.

A unique feature of the voucher process was the collection of a uniform set of information for every firm that was made available to bidders in either published or electronic form. Thus, it is easy to control for publicly available information. We do so in Filer and Hanousek (1998) and find that public information is an important predictor of future market prices only in early rounds of the bidding process. After two or three price adjustments using excess demand as a signal of how far and in what direction to move the price, public information added nothing to the ability to predict future prices beyond what was reflected in the current price for all but the smallest firms. Even more powerful evidence of the efficiency of this process comes from analysis of the role of private information. Assuming that mutual fund managers seek at least partially to own more valuable portfolios (they may also have other goals) suggests that if prices do not fully reflect all information available to these funds there should be a positive correlation between their demand for shares in a company and the eventual price of that company's stock, conditional on the current voucher price. We find that the relationship between mutual fund demand and eventual price is quite strong for the first bidding round but has been totally eliminated by the end of the process, suggesting that the voucher price has fully incorporated all private information. Also interesting for our purposes is the finding that the demand for a firm by individuals was strongly influenced by demand for that firm by investment funds in previous rounds (something that was widely published) even after controlling for price and other public information.[22] This suggests that, despite the findings reported above, individuals may have believed that the market was not efficient and that funds had additional non-public information.

SUMMARY AND CONCLUSION

The new equity markets of Central Europe present a decidedly mixed picture with respect to their efficiency. The markets are very different in their size and structure. There is a widespread belief that they can be manipulated by insiders who certainly have ample incentive to attempt to appropriate assets in the privatization process. Yet, despite all this, the markets in these countries are similar in that, to the extent it is possible to test conventional types of efficiency with the limited data available to date, they do not appear less efficient than far more developed equity markets. If these preliminary results hold as more sophisticated tests become possible, it will provide strong evidence of the power of markets to achieve proper pricing even in the most difficult of circumstances.

---

[22] See the analysis by Ma and King (1996) and Hanousek and Kroch (1998).

REFERENCES

Agbeyegbe, T. (1994): 'Some Stylized Facts about the Jamaica Stock Market', *Social and Economic Studies*, vol. 43, pp. 143–56.

Agrawal, A. and K. Tandon (1994): 'Anomalies or Illusions – Evidence from Stock Markets in 18 Countries', *Journal of International Money and Finance*, vol. 13, pp. 83–106.

Ajayi, R. and S. Meyhdian (1994): 'Tests of Investors' Reactions to Major Surprises: The Case of Emerging Markets', *Journal of International Financial Markets, Institutions, and Money*, vol. 4, pp. 115–128.

Annuar, M., M. Ariff, and M. Shamsher (1994): 'Is Kuala Lumpur's Emerging Share Market Efficient?', *Journal of International Financial Markets, Institutions, and Money*, vol. 4, pp. 89–100.

Ayada, O. and C. Pyun (1994): 'An Application of Variance Ratio Test to the Korean Securities Market', *Journal of Banking and Finance*, vol. 18, pp. 643–658.

Bartholdy, J. and A. Riding (1994): 'Thin Trading and the Estimation of Betas: The Efficacy of Alternative Techniques', *Journal of Financial Research*, vol. 17, pp. 241–254.

Bentsen, G. (1973): 'Required Disclosure and the Stock Market: An Evaluation of the Securities Exchange Act of 1934', *American Economic Review*, vol. 63, pp. 132–155.

Chow, K. V. and K. C. Denning (1993): 'A Simple Multiple Variance Ratio Test', *Journal of Econometrics*, vol. 58, pp. 385–401.

Claessens, S., S. Dasgupta and J. Glan (1995): 'Return Behavior in Emerging Stock Markets', *The World Bank Economic Review*, vol. 9, pp. 131–151.

Cornelius, P. K. (1993): 'A Note on the Informational Efficiency of Emerging Stock Markets', *Weltwirtschaftliches Archiv*, vol. 129, pp. 820–828.

Demski, J. S. and G. A. Feltham (1994): 'Market Response to Financial Reports', *Journal of Accounting and Economics*, vol. 17, pp. 3–40.

Dye, R. A. (1990): 'Mandatory vs. Voluntary Disclosures: The Cases of Financial and Real Externalities', *Accounting Review*, vol. 65, pp. 1–24.

Filer, R. K. and J. Hanousek (1998): 'Efficiency of Price Setting Based on a Simple Excess Demand Rule: The Natural Experiment of Czech Voucher Privatization', CERGE-EI No. 121, Working Paper, Prague.

Gordon, B. and L. Rittenberg (1995): 'The Warsaw Stock Exchange: A Test of Market Efficiency', *Comparative Economic Studies*, vol. 37, pp. 1–27.

Hanousek, J. and R. K. Filer (1998): 'The Relationship Between Economic Factors and Equity Markets in Central Europe', CERGE-EI Working Paper No. 119, Prague.

Hanousek, J. and E. Kroch (1998): 'The Two Waves of Voucher Privatization of the Czech Republic. A Model of Learning in Sequential Bidding', *Applied Economics*, vol. 30, pp. 133–143.

Harvey, C. R. (1995) 'Predictable Risk and Returns in Emerging Markets', *Review of Financial Studies*, vol. 8, pp. 773–816.

Hlavsa, A. (1996): 'Determining Share Prices in Voucher Privatization', unpublished MA thesis (in Czech) Charles University Faculty of Mathematics and Physics: Prague.

Leftwich, R. (1980): 'Market Failure Fallacies and Accounting Information', *Journal of Accounting and Economics*, vol. 2, p. 193–211.

Levene, H. (1952): 'On the Power Function of Tests of Randomness Based on Runs Up and Down', *Annals of Mathematical Statistics*, vol. 23, p. 34–56.

Liu, C. Y. and J. He (1991): 'A Variance-Ratio Test of Random Walks in Foreign Exchange Rates', *Journal of Finance*, vol. 46, p. 773–85.

Lo, A. and C. MacKinlay (1988): 'Stock Market Prices Do Not Follow Random Walks', *Review of Financial Studies*, vol. 1, pp. 41–66.

Ma, C.-Y. and A. E. King (1996): *A Game Theory Model of Voucher Privatization*, Soochow University, Department of Accounting, Taipei.

Malkiel, B. G. (1996): *A Random Walk Down Wall Street* (6th Edn), W. W. Norton, New York.

Němeček, L. (1998): 'Liquidity and Information-Based Trading on the Order Driven Capital Market: the Case of Prague Stock Exchange', CERGE-EI Working Paper No. 117, Prague.

Phillips, S. and J. R. Zecher. (1981): *The SEC and the Public Interest: An Economic Perspective*. MIT Press, Cambridge (MA).

Stengos, T. and E. Panas (1992): 'Testing the Efficiency of the Athens Stock Exchange: Some Results from the Banking Sector', *Empirical Economics*, vol. 17, pp. 239–252.

Stolin, M. R. And H. K. Ury. (1979): 'Tables of Studentized Maximum Modulus Distribution and an Application to Multiple Comparisons Among Means', *Technometrics*, vol. 21, pp. 87–93.

Svejnar, J. and M. Singer (1994): 'Using Vouchers to Privatize and Economy: The Czech and Slovak Case', *Economics of Transition*, vol. 2, pp. 43–70.

Urrutia, J. L. (1995): 'Tests of Random Walk and Market Efficient for Latin American Emerging Equity Markets', *Journal of Financial Research*, vol. 18, pp. 299–309.

Zychowicz, E. J., M. Binbasioglu and N. Kazancioglu (1995): 'The Behavior of Prices on the Istanbul Stock Exchange', *Journal of International Financial Markets, Institutions and Money*, vol. 5, pp. 61–71.

APPENDIX

Disclosure Requirements of the Prague Stock Exchange[23]

A prospectus for registration must include:
a) Introductory provisions:
    i)   legal basis for issuing the security,
    ii)   a copy of the decision made by relevant Ministry on granting permission to issue the security or to trade it publicly,

---

[23] Sections applicable to stocks only. Omission of non-applicable material has resulted in renumbering for consistency. Reflects the rules as of 1996. There have been multiple changes since then, all in the direction of even greater disclosure.

iii)   purpose of the issue,

iv)   other relevant information important to investors (e. g. how the issuer discloses information on his business activities and position),

v)   a disclaimer by the Stock Exchange stating that by having admitted the security to its Main Market it assumes no liabilities attached to such securities.

b)   Characteristics and conditions of the securities issue:

   i)   type, form and sample of the security,

   ii)   ISIN,

   iii)   total value of the issue and nominal value of the security,

   iv)   price at issue or anticipated price,

   v)   business names of stock traders who either were or are arranging for the issue,

   vi)   date, place and way of releasing the issue (public offer, through a commission agent or within the framework of a firm overtake),

   vii)   type of subscription (free/open, preferential/with priorities, combination),

   viii)   place of payment,

   ix)   description of all rights associated with the security ownership (preemption and exchange rights inclusive),

   x)   method, deadlines and place of payment of the yields on the security and/or its repayment,

   xi)   method of keeping records on status and movements of the security, provided the issue has only been made as registered (in book-entry form),

   xii)   shares structure (individual shares or bulk certificates),

   xiii)   development in the share price for the last three years or from the time when the shares were introduced to other public markets (this also applies to both convertible and option bonds),

   xiv)   periods for holding General Meetings of Shareholders of joint stock companies,

   xv)   a list of changes in all the facts subject to recording in the Commercial Register which have taken place since the last entry,

   xvi)   the way of disclosing the facts important for claiming holder's rights to the securities,

   xiii)   method of taxation applicable to the yields on a given security.

c)   Basic details about the issuer:

   i)   company business name, its legal status (form), principal office address, company ID (IEO) number, date of its commencement and/or termination of its business activities or termination of its existence, if officially determined,

   ii)   basic organizational structure, including subsidiary companies, issuer's capital anticipation in businesses of other Czech or foreign entities, capital participation of Czech and foreign entities in the issuer's business,

   iii)   for a joint-stock company also the names of all their shareholders holding more than 10% of its shares; if known to the issuer,

   iv)   issuer's standing within the group of persons (entities) mutually linked by the property (each property interest exceeding 10% must be indicated).

   v)   company statement on existence of any whatsoever resolution of the General Meeting or right of company statutory body to make decision on floating an issue of stocks and/or on any whatsoever rights relating to the company registered capital (e. g. exchange bonds).

d) Information about issuer's business activities:
   i)   profile of business activities,
   ii)   standing (position) in both domestic and foreign markets,
   iii) strategy for the economic activity, trade policies, main goals of its investment and innovation policies, overall business prospects for at least a one-year period,
   iv)   investments made by the issuer in the last three years, including those made by his legal predecessor,
   v)   business activities broken down by market type, share in turnover by individual market, sales organization,
   vi)   patents and licenses both own and contracted as well as contracts concluded with other persons and having crucial importance to the issuer's business,
   vii) disputes both in the court (of law) and commercial if the disputed value exceeds 5% of the issuer's trading (employed) capital.
e) Issuer's financial position:
   i)   quarterly business (financial) results in a consolidated form (if produced), supported by balance sheet and profit/loss statement covering period from the last annual closing statement of accounts verified by the auditor,
   ii)   annual statements of accounts for the last three years verified by auditor(s) in a consolidated form (if produced); should the issuer have been existing in its current legal form for less than 3 years, he should submit either the same for his legal predecessor or reports covering period from the company emergence,
   iii) auditor's statements covering period of the last three years,
   iv)   details about securities already issued including: type, total value of the issue, number (volume) and nominal (par) value, the amount of dividends paid per share for the last three trading years or from the company foundation, ratio of 'dividends paid' to 'post-tax profit' in percentage,
   v)   bank and other loans received and payables with indication of their maturity, broken down as follows: short-term, long-term, non-performing credits (I. e. loans with payment overdue), type and extent of default in payment (insolvency),
   vi)   registered capital: structure by individual type of shares, share holding capital structure by type of shares, registered capital pending payment (not paid up yet), the option and exchange rights the registered capital of the company is subject to,
   vii) reserve funds
   viii) amount of dividends and all changes in the registered capital for the last three years (dividend paid per share),
   ix)   any and all rights of lien/mortgage tied to the company assets if exceeding 5% of the company registered capital (state their total book value),
   x)   characteristics of all impacts arising from long-term contractual relationship which may affect company business results,
   xi)   all company liabilities existing to the application date and implying from the guarantees issued.
f) Issuer's administration and management bodies:
   i)   statutory bodies,
   ii)   supervisory bodies,

iii)   management bodies – managers (directors): name of individual, position (function), education, qualification, professional competence/fitness, data proving an 'unblemished personal record' and/or the length of sentence imposed for any property-related criminal act committed, information about their business activities outside the company scope of business and about their jobs, membership in bodies of other companies, share of these members in the company registered capital,

g) Closing provisions:
   i)   names of persons who prepared the prospectus, including the date on which this was produced,
   ii)   statement by persons responsible for the information stated in the prospectus confirming that this is complete, true and accurate,
   iii) declaration of the issuer that he is assuming full responsibility for the correctness of the prospectus and signature of the issuer's statutory body,
   iv)   statement by bank on verification of the prospectus, including its business name, principal office address. and signatures of authorized persons.

Once a security is listed on the main market, the issuer is obliged to submit to the Exchange:

a) quarterly income development indicators to the extent of a complete balance sheet and profit and loss statement – within 8 weeks from end of a given quarter,

b) a copy of semi-annual business report encompassing a complete balance sheet and profit/loss statement together with the company comments – within 3 months from end of the respective 6-month period,

c) as many copies of annual report as there are Exchange members – without reasonable delay, after holding the Annual General Meeting of Shareholders,

d) a copy of closing statements of accounts to the extent of a complete balance sheet and profit and loss statement, including an enclosure with the cash flow statement as its integral part – immediately after these have been verified by the auditor but no later than 6 months from end of the respective year,

e) in the course of the year, also the information about income development, including comments on the company financial position, in accordance with the requirements of the Exchange Chamber.

In addition, the issuer of the security admitted to trading in the Exchange Main Market is obliged to submit to the Exchange without delay the following:

a) records taken of both regular and extraordinary General Meetings held by issuer's company,

b) any changes in the Articles of Incorporation, by-laws (the Statutes), or Articles of Foundation (Association or Deed of Foundation) of the issuer,

c) changes in entries kept on the issuer in the Commercial Register.

The issuer of a security admitted to trading in the Exchange Main Market is also obliged, without delay, to publish and notify the Exchange of any changes in his financial position as well as other facts which may directly or indirectly invoke a change in the price of the security or adversely affect the issuer's ability to comply with the obligations arising from the issue of this security. The issuer is not allowed to inform any other person about such changes and facts until these have been notified by him to the Exchange.

Among the specific items qualified as such changes and other facts are:

a) Changes in the terms of issue and trading in the security admitted to trading in the Exchange Main Market,
b) Changes in the issuer's statutory, supervisory and management bodies,
c) Changes in structure and size of the issuer's decisive (majority) shareholders, if known to him,
d) Any new issue of securities,
e) Any and each change in issuer's assets or net trading (employed) capital values by 10% or more,
f) Receipt or cancellation of important allotments and subsidies,
g) Any disputes before the court of law or trade disputes if disputed subject value exceeds 5% of issuer's trading (employed) capital,
h) Any decisions on a consolidation, merger, split, abolition and other important organizational changes as well,
i) Suspension or restrictions to issuer's activities on the basis of an official authorization (order),
j) Declaration in bankruptcy or approval of settlement proceedings,
k) Acceptance or cancellation of important commercial orders,
l) Market-sharing standing,
m) Acquisition or disposal of significant patents or inventions,
n) Shares in exports and imports,
o) Changes in trading policy,
p) Changes in production structure.

(Roland) P34

20. Modeling Polish Stock Returns   G12

Martin Scheicher[1]

INTRODUCTION

For our study of the Warsaw Stock Exchange (WSE) we have a dual motivation: first by focusing on the WSE our aim is to add evidence from an emerging market to the literature on the econometric modeling of financial time series. This literature is surveyed in detail by Pagan (1996), see also Campbell *et al.* (1996). Most studies focus on large and liquid markets such as US equity markets or the foreign exchange market. However, the financial markets in the transitional economies of Central and Eastern Europe have been studied by a small number of authors only: Erb, Harvey and Viskanta (1996) analyse returns and volatility for 135 markets, including Albania, Bulgaria, the Czech Republic, Hungary, Poland and Russia. Chobanov *et al.* (1996) estimate the distribution of the Bulgarian Lev/US$ rate. Emerson *et al.* (1996) propose a state space model to study the evolving market efficiency for Bulgarian bank stocks. Meszanos (1996) also studies the validity of the EMH on the Bratislava Stock Exchange. In our paper we compare directly returns from the Warsaw Stock Exchange with a sample from the Frankfurt Stock Exchange, which we have chosen as proxy for a 'grown-up' stock market. The analysis is performed by studying the statistical properties of returns and by evaluating the fit of two time-series models. This side-by-side comparison allows us to document the differences between a major equity market and an emerging one.

Secondly, we attempt an option-pricing perspective in the choice of models for stock returns. The reason is that the Vienna Exchange lists contracts on a stock index and – in the future – also on a selected number of individual stocks from the Warsaw Stock Exchange. Our paper rejects the assumptions of the benchmark Black and Scholes (1973) option-pricing model (OPM) (for a survey of the empirical issues regarding option pricing see Bates, 1996). We then

---

[1] We are grateful to Marcus Klug of Creditanstalt Investmentbank (CA IB) for providing detailed information on the Warsaw stock market.

evaluate two alternatives for the generating process of returns. These are the popular Generalized Autoregressive Conditional Heteroscedasticity (GARCH) model and the Poisson Jump process. The former model is widely used in empirical finance, the latter is less frequently studied.[2] The choice falls on these two models because they allow the pricing of options. This means that both specifications can be taken as the assumed stochastic process for the underlying asset. In the option pricing literature these two specifications thus serve as alternatives to the Geometric Brownian Motion assumed in the Black and Scholes (1973) OPM. GARCH is the basis for an OPM in Duan (1995), whereas jump processes have been used by Merton (1976). By studying the returns of the underlying asset we can thus decide which of the two option-pricing models is more plausible.

The rest of this chapter is organized as follows: the following section gives a few details about the WSE and describes our sample. The third section collects the statistical properties. On that basis the fourth section contains the estimation and testing of our models, and the fifth section offers a brief conclusion.

SAMPLE

The Warsaw Stock Exchange opened in April 1991. It currently lists 66 companies. For major stocks there is continuous trading throughout the four-hour trading period, whereas for smaller stocks only one price is set. Settlement is in t+3 days. In contrast to the Czech Republic Poland allows trading in stocks only on the floor of the exchange. Additionally there are detailed rules about the publication of price-sensitive information. All these characteristics have improved price transparency and liquidity on WSE and brought it close to Western standards. For a large investor the transaction costs are estimated to be 0.5%. Currently around 50 brokers are active on the exchange.

Our sample comprises Zloty closing quotes of the following stocks: BSK, BRE and WBK. All these are banks and among the companies with the largest market capitalization. In December 1996 BSK had a capitalization of US$ 965 million and BRE and WBK were valued around US$ 450 million. All companies have large free floats and belong to the segment of the most active stocks on the exchange. To represent the market portfolio we use the Warsaw General Index (WGI). This is a value-weighted index containing all 66 stocks. It has a free-float factor as an additional weighting. Currently banks account for 30% of the stocks in the index. In order to evaluate the behavior of returns from

---

[2] See the survey by Palm (1996).

the WSE the DAX index from the Frankfurt Stock Exchange (FSE) is taken as the benchmark.

Figure 20.1 plots the values of the WGI stock index from the start of trading in 1991 until August 1996. In the beginning we observe little movement, then in 1993 a huge rise took place from 1,000 points to 20,716 points at the peak in March 1994. This rise was mostly supported by the mass privatization program of the Polish government. However, the increase was followed by a sharp consolidation in the market, which almost halved the value of the market. In the early 'history' of the WSE there was no regular daily trading in the exchange, but only on selected days during the week. Trading started with only one weekly session, but was gradually extended. We have chosen August 1994 as a starting point for our study because the initial learning period seems to have ended around this time. So for all five series our sample comprises two years of daily observations from 12 August 1994 to 13 August 1996. The first half of our sample is dominated by the consequences of the crash in Mexican financial markets in December 1994. This event caused a fall in all emerging markets. In Eastern Europe Hungary and the Czech Republic saw the biggest consolidations. Poland experienced a relatively mild reaction, mainly in the form of reduced activity with little movement up or down. This period ended in

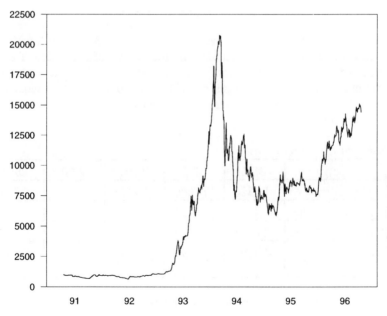

Figure 20.1. The Warsaw General Index

January 1996 when a major change in the asset allocation of global investors took place. The reason was that the large stock exchanges in the US and in Europe had already shown strong growth. So investors increasingly turned to emerging markets to achieve higher returns. Here in particular Poland was attractive as shares were cheap with healthy growth prospects. This produced a strong rise in share prices throughout the last year. In December 1996 the daily average of total traded volume was US\$ 27.6 million. The market capitalization was measured at US\$ 8.1 billion. One year earlier the exchange only had a capitalization of US\$ 4.07 billion.

STATISTICAL PROPERTIES OF RETURNS

As Campbell, Lo and MacKinlay (1996) document in the second chaper of their book, the standard hypothesis for the behavior of stock prices is the martingale, i.e. the logarithm of prices contains a single unit root. To test this hypothesis we performed an Augmented Dickey Fuller (ADF) test as given in equation (1). The null hypothesis here is nonstationarity,

$$\Delta \log(p_t) = \alpha + \beta \log(p_{t-1}) + \delta_1 \Delta \log(p_{t-1}) + \delta_2 \Delta Log(p_{t-2})$$
$$+ \delta_3 \Delta \log(p_{t-3}) + \delta_4 \Delta \log(p_{t-4}) + u_t .$$

(20.1)

Results, given in Table 20.1, show the *t*-statistic of ß and the MacKinnon critical values for the rejection of a unit root at 1%, 5% and 10%: The null hypothesis is never rejected. This means that a unit root is found in all series. This result supports the martingale model for stock prices. One consequence is that the first differences of returns should be uncorrelated if there is indeed only a single unit root.

Table 20.1. Unit root tests

	BSK	BRE	WBK	WGI	DAX
ADF statistic	-1.5826	-0.7606	-0.4375	-1.4529	-0.7500
1% Critical value	-3.4453	-3.4453	-3.4453	-3.4453	-3.4453
5% Critical value	-2.8674	-2.8674	-2.8674	-2.8674	-2.8674
10% Critical value	-2.5699	-2.5699	-2.5699	-2.5699	-2.5699

Figures 20.2 and 20.3 plot the compound returns for WGI and DAX which have been computed as

$$r_t = \log(p_t) - \log(p_{t-1}).$$ (20.2)

For the stochastic process of stock prices Black and Scholes (1973) assume a lognormal distribution. This implies that compound returns should be i.i.d. drawn from a multivariate normal:

$$r_t \sim N(\mu, \sigma^2).$$ (20.3)

Table 20.2 gives annualized mean and standard deviation, minimum and maximum return, skewness and kurtosis for the compound returns of our five series. Here several points should be noticed. First we can observe that the WSE is much more volatile than the FSE as the standard deviation of the WGI is three times the value of the DAX. It means that the range of returns is larger on the WSE than in Frankfurt. This is visible in the plot of returns: in our sample the largest returns were 7 and -8% in the WGI and only +/- 3% in the DAX.

Second we find non-normality in the form of pronounced leptokurtosis. In contrast to the DAX series there is no significant skewness in WSE returns. The leptokurtosis is similar in both stock market indices. So the tails of Polish and German returns alike contain more probability mass than the normal allocates. This is known as the stylized fact of *fat tails*. On the WSE the leptokurtosis is higher in individual stocks than in the index. To visualize the (unconditional) distribution the nonparametric density functions of DAX and WGI as estimated with an Epanechnikov kernel are given in Figures 20.4 and 20.5.[3]

Table 20.2. Statistical properties of returns

	BSK	BRE	WBK	WGI	DAX
Mean p.a. in %	4.975	35.25	14.62	2.70	7.85
St. Dev. p.a. in %	54.40	50.25	62.97	35.58	13.29
Maximal r_t in %	10.26	9.531	24.78	7.80	3.22
Minimal r_t in %	-10.53	-10.53	-14.73	-8.53	-3.35
Skewness	-0.064 (0.54)	-0.1054 (0.33)	0.2544 (0.00)	0.0864 (0.44)	-0.312 (0.00)
Kurtosis	2.4896 (0.00)	2.8020 (0.00)	3.5095 (0.00)	1.591 (0.00)	1.416 (0.00)
SIC of normal	1019.68	1062.00	931.92	1237.26	1746.87

Note: p-value in brackets.

---

[3] See Silverman (1986) for a description.

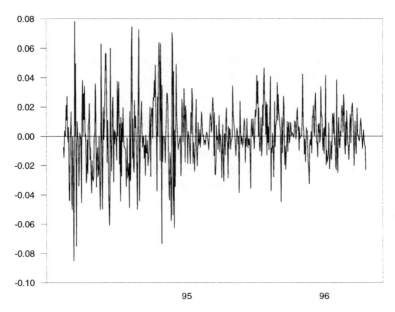

Figure 20.2. Returns of the WGI

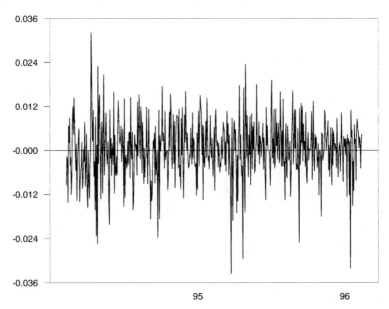

Figure 20.3. Returns of the DAX

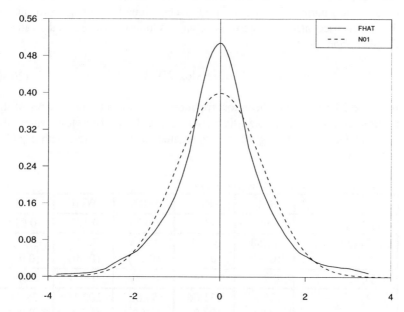

Figure 20.4. Normalized estimated unconditional distribution of the WGI

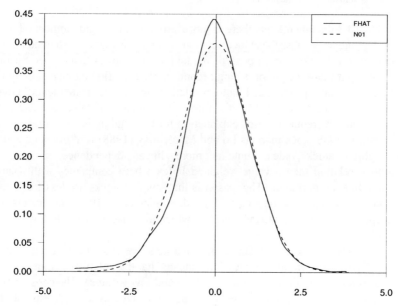

Figure 20.5. Normalized estimated unconditional distribution of the DAX

The last line of Table 20.2 contains the Schwarz Information Criterion (SIC) of the stationary normal. This will be used as a benchmark for the performance of the models used later on. The SIC is defined as follows, where L is the value of the likelihood function:

$$SIC = L - 0.5 \cdot \log(N) \cdot k. \tag{20.4}$$

In Table 20.3 we study the autocorrelations of the levels and squares of the returns and the Q(12) statistic. This is the Ljung-Box test where the autocorrelations up to lag 12 are aggregated to obtain a test with a $\chi^2(12)$ distribution.

Table 20.3. Autocorrelations of returns

	BSK	BRE	WBK	WGI	DAX
$\rho(1)$ of r_t	0.058	-0.037	0.125	0.182	-0.012
Q(12) of r_t	19.58	33.25	19.83	26.33	22.13
	(0.07)	(0.00)	(0.07)	(0.00)	(0.03)
$\rho(1)$ of r_t^2	0.219	0.29	0.129	0.304	0.060
Q(12) of r_t^2	123.82	151.06	53.62	202.15	28.51
	(0.00)	(0.00)	(0.00)	(0.00)	(0.00)

Note: Q-statistics show the *p*-value in brackets.

Table 20.3 documents that there is more structure in second moments than in first moments because the autocorrelation at lag one is higher in squared returns than in levels. For the purpose of modeling this implies that a specification should put more weight on fitting second rather than first moments. Only the WGI contains pronounced autocorrelation in the first moments. Given transaction costs of 0.5% this linear dependence is also economically significant. A frequently used explanation for this finding is the '*thin-trading*' effect. For US stock markets Lo and MacKinlay (1988) find that an equally-weighted stock index contains more linear dependence, i.e. higher autocorrelation than a value-weighted index where companies with a large capitalization dominate. The reason is that smaller stocks are less frequently traded and this is aggregated in the index. Scheicher (1996) documents this property for the Vienna stock market, which also has a relatively low market capitalization.

Across both German and Polish markets we find the stylized fact of *volatility clustering* in all series. This means that the volatility is time-varying and so returns go through periods of high and low variance. The consequence is that the squared returns, which can be interpreted as a rough estimate for volatility are significantly autocorrelated, as shown by the significant Q(12) statistics for all five squared series. This 'volatile volatility' also produces the excess kurtosis which we have found above. Bollerslev *et al.* (1994) show that a series where the variance is not constant but time-dependent generates leptokurtosis. To illustrate the behavior of the volatility we show plots of the 20-day annualized standard deviation of DAX and WGI in Figures 20.6 and 20.7. A structural break on the WSE around June 1995 is visible, as the volatility is much lower since then. However despite this recent fall, the WSE is still more volatile than the FSE, as the peak in the DAX is 23% versus 65.9% in the WGI. We can also observe that the growth period in the Polish stock market in 1996 was not accompanied by a rise in volatility.

The finding that returns have low autocorrelations, a time-varying volatility and fat tails has already been documented by Mandelbrot (1963) and Fama (1965). It means that the benchmark model of Geometric Brownian motion which is assumed in the Black-Scholes OPM is invalid. The evidence for fat-tailed returns is also supported by the distribution of returns which is implied by option prices. As Bates (1996) argues the 'smile' effect in implicit volatilities indicates leptokurtosis in returns. In the next section we evaluate two different approaches for modeling the statistical properties: GARCH and the Poisson Jump process.

MODELING RETURNS

GARCH

The ARCH model has been introduced by Engle (1982) and generalized by Bollerslev (1986). Bollerslev (1987) proposed the extension given below where the conditional normal is replaced by the conditional Student's *t* in order to generate more excess kurtosis.

$$r_t = b_0 + b_1 r_{t-1} + u_t \tag{20.5}$$

$$u_t = \varepsilon_t \sqrt{h_t}, \quad \text{with } \varepsilon_t \sim t_n(0,1) \tag{20.6}$$

$$h_t = a_0 + a_1 u_{t-1}^2 + a_2 h_{t-1}. \tag{20.7}$$

Here fat tails in the unconditional distribution of returns are generated by the time-varying conditional volatility h_t and by the Student's *t* distribution. There the additional parameter (degrees of freedom) allows more kurtosis than under

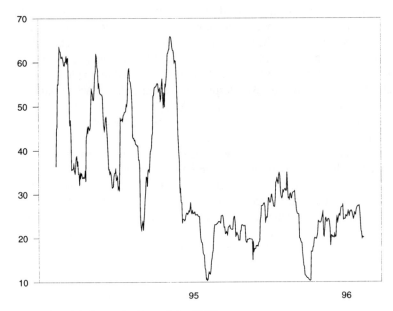

Figure 20.6. 20-day volatility of the WGI

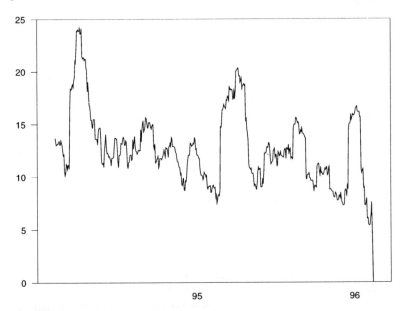

Figure 20.7. 20-day volatility of the DAX

the Gaussian. The Student's t converges to the normal for n going to infinity. The conditional density for GARCH-t is:

$$f(u_t \mid I_{t-1}) = \Gamma\left(\frac{n}{2}\right)^{-1}\left[\left(\frac{n}{2} - 1\right)h_t\right]^{\frac{n}{2}}(u_t + h_t)^{-1-\frac{n}{2}}$$

$$\cdot \exp\left[\left(1 - \frac{n}{2}\right)h_t(u_t + h_t)^{-1}\right].$$

(20.8)

Parameters are estimated by numerical optimization of the log likelihood function L:

$$L = \sum_{t=1}^{T} \log\left(f(u_t \mid I_{t-1})\right).$$

(20.9)

The standard errors are taken from the asymptotic estimate of the covariance matrix. We show the estimation results of the GARCH-t model in Table 20.4. In all series the heteroscedasticity is pronounced, as most coefficients in the variance equation are significant. Additionally the degrees of freedom of the Student's t distribution are low. This means that the time-varying variance alone does not cause all the leptokurtosis documented in the third section of this chapter.

Table 20.4a. GARCH-t with AR(1)

	BSK	BRE	WBK	WGI	DAX
b_0*100	0.0648	0.0677	0.1141	0.0371	0.0540
	(0.31)	(0.35)	(0.37)	(0.60)	(0.11)
b_1	0.0545	-0.0231	0.0587	0.2438	-0.0323
	(0.16)	(0.57)	(0.15)	(0.00)	(0.46)
a_0*1000	0.05198	0.0429	0.0034	0.0017	0.0379
	(0.48)	(0.26)	(0.17)	(0.03)	(0.00)
a_1	0.7648	0.8046	0.8643	0.7781	0.9004
	(0.00)	(0.00)	(0.00)	(0.00)	(0.00)
a_2	1.4273	0.5127	0.1351	0.2061	0.0442
	(0.00)	(0.18)	(0.00)	(0.00)	(0.08)
n	2.1212	2.3178	3.8979	6.234	6.8747
	(0.00)	(0.00)	(0.00)	(0.00)	(0.00)
SIC	1446.83	1465.42	1289.74	1601.32	2048.22

Note: p-value in brackets.

This again underlines the need for using Student's t instead of the Gaussian as the Likelihood Generating Function. Comparing the SIC of the stationary normal given in Table 20.2 with the values for the GARCH-t of Table 20.4 a strong improvement is visible. So a variety of evidence rejects the assumption of Gaussian returns in favor of GARCH.

Table 20.4b. Integrated GARCH-t

	BSK	BRE	WBK	WGI	DAX
a_0*1000	0.0186	0.0355	0.0339	0.0159	0.0002
	(0.02)	(0.03)	(0.11)	(0.02)	(0.86)
a_1	0.8036	0.8006	0.8642	0.7791	0.9803
	(0.00)	(0.00)	(0.00)	(0.00)	(0.00)
LRT: IGARCH	0.5336	0.4025	0.9864	0.7229	0.2594

Note: p-value in brackets and in last line.

Table 20.4c. Properties of standardized residuals

	BSK	BRE	WBK	WGI	DAX
Skewness	0.02	-0.5851	1.7261	0.0659	-0.6199
	(0.83)	(0.00)	(0.00)	(0.53)	(0.00)
Kurtosis	7.34	5.1781	18.1531	1.0195	1.783
	(0.00)	(0.00)	(0.00)	(0.00)	(0.00)
$Q(12)$ of $u_t/\sqrt{h_t}$	12.66	12.70	5.41	7.92	19.02
	(0.39)	(0.39)	(0.94)	(0.79)	(0.08)
$Q(12)$ of $(u_t/\sqrt{h_t})^2$	4.56	5.84	1.09	15.42	7.78
	(0.97)	(0.92)	(0.99)	(0.21)	(0.80)

Note: p-value in brackets.

The coefficients a_1 and a_2 for BSK and BRE in Table 20.4 violate the stationarity condition as the sum is larger than one. This means that the unconditional variance does not exist and that shocks do not decay. Thus we re-estimate the model with the restriction $a_1 + a_2 = 1$. This is the Integrated GARCH (IGARCH) model where the conditional variance contains a unit root and is thus non-stationary. The p-values of a Likelihood Ratio test and the estimates for a_0 and a_1 are given in the second segment of Table 20.4. We find that the restriction is valid in all four cases. Thus returns are indeed not stationary. The plots of the annualized GARCH volatility for DAX and WGI are shown in Figures 20.8 and 20.9. The GARCH volatility on the WSE reached values of 100% p.a. in the first half of our sample. In the second half of our sample the peak in volatility was at around 50%. This contrasts with a maximum of less than 20% p.a. in Frankfurt. Thus we confirm the findings from the

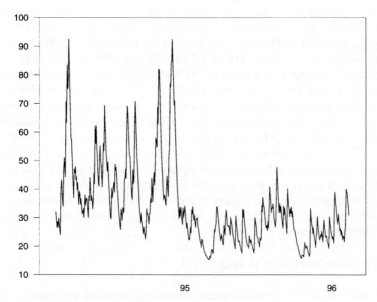

Figure 20.8. GARCH volatility of the WGI

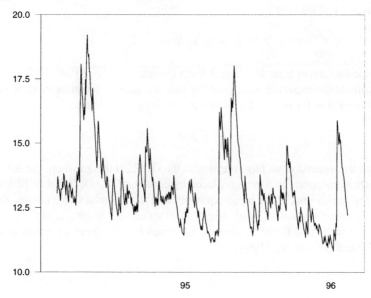

Figure 20.9. GARCH volatility of the DAX

rolling standard deviation in Figures 20.6 and 20.7.

To investigate the lower volatility since summer 1995 in more detail, we have attempted a re-estimation of the Integrated GARCH processes. However convergence of the BHHH algorithm failed as this subsample only has a length of about 270 observations. We also had problems with the non-negativity constraints. Therefore, we turn now to tests for the goodness of fit of the GARCH-t model. The last segment of Table 20.4 gives skewness and kurtosis of the standardized residuals. These series are all not normally distributed, which provides additional support for our use of the Conditional Student's distribution. If the model has a good fit, we expect the standardized residuals to be i.i.d. So the last lines of Table 20.4 gives the Q(12) test for autocorrelation in the standardized residuals and their squares. We see that there are no signs of significant autocorrelation. Thus the GARCH model is able to generate all the volatility clustering. The good fit of the GARCH approach to financial time series is documented in the survey by Bollerslev *et al.* (1992), see also Bauer *et al.* (1994) for Germany.

Extensions of the GARCH Model

For GARCH the literature offers many extensions. To model a univariate risk-return trade-off the GARCH-in-mean model has been introduced by Engle, Lilien and Robins (1987):

$$r_t = b_0 + b_1 h_t + u_t. \tag{20.10}$$

This model derives from the Capital Asset Pricing Model (CAPM). It allows us to estimate the expected returns or the risk premium π_t on an asset such as a stock market index or a widely diversified portfolio of stocks:

$$\pi_t = b_0 + b_1 h_t. \tag{20.11}$$

To test this extension we have reestimate the GARCH model where the AR(1) process in equation (20.5) was replaced by equation (20.11). In Table 20.5 we give the coefficients of the mean equation[4] and their p-values. We can see that the risk-return relation is not significant in either market. In context of GARCH-in-mean with conditional Student's t this result has also been documented by Baillie and DeGennaro (1990).

---

[4] Variance estimates are similar to Table 20.4.

Table 20.5. GARCH-in-mean

	BSK	BRE	WBK	WGI	DAX
b_0*1000	0.7071	-0.2514	3.002	0.8191	-1.458
	(0.34)	(0.79)	(0.14)	(0.49)	(0.38)
b_1	-0.032	0.7193	-1.5214	-1.4352	30.34
	(0.83)	(0.28)	(0.24)	(0.57)	(0.22)

Note: p-value in brackets.

A frequently used alternative specification for the conditional volatility process is Exponential GARCH (EGARCH), proposed by Nelson (1991). This model lifts the non-negativity constraint by using logs and it also allows for asymmetric behavior in the conditional variance in the form of the leverage effect. This posits that a negative shock leads to proportionally higher variance than a positive shock. The EGARCH-*t* specification is given below:

$$r_t = b_0 + b_1 r_{t-1} + u_t \qquad (20.12)$$

$$u_t = \varepsilon_t \sqrt{h_t}, \quad \text{with } \varepsilon_t \sim t_n (0,1) \qquad (20.13)$$

$$\log(h_t) = a_0 + a_1 \log(h_{t-1}) + a_2 \left[\frac{|u_{t-1}|}{h_{t-1}} - \sqrt{\frac{2}{\pi}} + a_3 \frac{u_{t-1}}{h_{t-1}} \right]. \qquad (20.14)$$

Here the parameter a_3 can generate the leverage effect as in contrast to the simple GARCH(1,1) the sign of yesterday's shock comes into the model. Estimation[5] results for EGARCH-t are given in Table 20.6. We see that in both markets there is no leverage effect. Comparing the SIC of GARCH and EGARCH we find that the additional parameters of the more complex model do not add explanatory value. Thus the simple GARCH model seems to have a good fit in both markets.

In general however there is wide evidence for the existence of the leverage effect, e.g. in Glosten *et al.* (1993) for the US or Sola and Timmerman (1994) for the UK equity market. The absence of the leverage effect in the DAX series may be related to our choice of sample, as Dankenbring and Missong (1995) document an asymmetry in volatility for a different sample of German equity returns.

---

[5] The maximum likelihood remains unchanged.

Table 20.6. EGARCH-t with AR(1)

	BSK	BRE	WBK	WGI	DAX
b_0*100	0.083	0.07061	0.0966	0.0385	0.036
	(0.22)	(0.22)	(0.46)	(0.59)	(0.27)
b_1	0.0629	-0.0005	0.0669	0.2539	-0.0408
	(0.10)	(0.98)	(0.08)	(0.00)	(0.36)
a_0	2.1805	0.291	-0.119	-0.4368	-0.5592
	(0.49)	(0.98)	(0.28)	(0.02)	(0.07)
a_1	0.9582	0.5849	0.9789	0.9419	0.9419
	(0.00)	(0.00)	(0.00)	(0.00)	(0.00)
a_2	3.2744	2.9070	0.1990	0.3449	0.0471
	(0.39)	(0.87)	(0.00)	(0.00)	(0.30)
a_3	0.0502	-0.0443	-0.1741	-0.0100	-2.3631
	(0.63)	(0.73)	(0.2984)	(0.93)	(0.31)
n	2.01	2.016	3.8438	6.4537	8.72
	(0.00)	(0.00)	(0.00)	(0.00)	(0.00)
SIC	1443.01	1446.39	1284.81	1600.50	2046.38

Note: p-value in brackets.

Jump-diffusion Processes

This specification has been used in the derivatives-pricing literature since Merton (1976) as a possible model for stock returns. The disadvantage was that there was no maximum likelihood estimation available and earlier authors used the cumulants approach which does not provide standard errors. However Ball and Torous (1985) derived the maximum likelihood function. This model has also been studied by Jorion (1989), Kim *et al.* (1994) or Bruand (1996). Below we give our specification[6] of the process:

$$r_t = m_b + v_b z + \sum_{i=1}^{n_t} Y_i,$$
(20.15)

where: z is a standard Normal white noise process;
n_t is a Poisson counting variable with 1 as the mean number of jumps;

---

[6] In contrast to Ball and Torous both means are allowed to be non-zero.

Y is the jump size with $Y \sim N(m_j, v_j)$.

The log likelihood function of the Poisson Jump process is:

$$L = -Tl - \frac{T}{2}\ln(2\pi)$$

$$+ \sum_{t=1}^{T} \ln\left[\sum_{j=0}^{\infty} \frac{l^j}{j!} \frac{1}{\sqrt{v_b + jv_j}} \exp\left(\frac{-(r_t - m_b - jm_j)^2}{2(v_b + jv_j)}\right)\right].$$ (20.16)

Here m_b, v_b and m_j, v_j are the moments of the Brownian and the Poisson processes respectively. For positive l we obtain fat tails and for non-zero m_j the distribution is skewed. Thus this model offers an alternative to GARCH for generating the non-normality found in the third section. The jump-diffusion process can be interpreted as a mixture distribution with two regimes. The mixture distribution is used in Empirical Finance in different versions, see chapter 22 of Hamilton (1994) for an introduction. In our specification the diffusion part of the process models returns as drawn from a Gaussian distribution. However in times of uncertainty, e.g. when new information arrives, discontinuities can appear. Their arrival into the market is modeled with a Poisson distribution. In the Merton option pricing model the latter component is assumed to be idiosyncratic, i.e. firm-specific and diversifiable. The large number of extreme price moves on the WSE which we noted earlier gives additional support for using the Jump process. Ball and Torous (1983) propose replacing the Poisson density with the Bernoulli function. However, as the latter is only a restriction of the former model we do not evaluate this alternative.

To perform Maximum Likelihood estimation of the process Ball and Torous (1985) propose to truncate the infinite sum in (20.16) at n = 10 and in common with Jorion (1989) or Bruand (1996) we follow this practice. We show the estimation results in Table 20.7. The first observation is that the intensity of jumps is relatively similar for both markets as the coefficient l is close to 0.4. However we see again that the WSE is very volatile because the variance of jumps in the WGI is more than 10 times the estimate in Frankfurt. The mean of jumps is not significant. This is in accordance with the intuition as there is only little skewness in returns. Because of the assumption of a Gaussian distribution for the jumps we can conclude that positive and negative jumps have the same probability.

Table 20.7. Poisson jump process

	BSK	BRE	WBK	WGI	DAX
m_b*1000	0.6834	0.3484	-0.1567	-0.2637	1.010
	(0.44)	(0.62)	(0.92)	(0.84)	(0.09)
m_j*1000	-0.5166	1.425	0.2295	0.5330	-1.0433
	(0.84)	(0.38)	(0.93)	(0.80)	(0.31)
v_b*1000	0.0862	0.0826	0.3642	0.1411	0.0354
	(0.00)	(0.00)	(0.00)	(0.00)	(0.00)
v_j*1000	1.507	1.246	1.8493	0.5390	0.049
	(0.00)	(0.00)	(0.00)	(0.00)	(0.00)
l	0.4659	0.4694	0.4394	0.4442	0.4167
	(0.00)	(0.00)	(0.00)	(0.00)	(0.00)
LRT	445.97	334.98	297.24	190.45	119.30
	(0.00)	(0.00)	(0.00)	(0.00)	(0.00)
SIC	1179.89	1211.44	1029.79	1317.91	1810.13

Notes: p-value in brackets; likelihood ratio test (LRT) for H_0: $m_j = v_j = l = 0$, i.e. no jumps.

The fact that jumps appear also in the index has important consequences for option pricing. The reason is that the model of Merton (1976) requires that jump risk can be diversified. However, as the WGI series also contains jumps, this assumption is rejected for the WSE. Kim *et al.* (1994) also discuss this drawback to the Jump OPM. Finally we can note that the jump component is highly significant as documented by the Likelihood Ratio test for H_0: $m_j = v_j = l = 0$. This test, given in the last line of Table 20.6 rejects the Null in all five series and so jumps play an important role in the generating process of returns. This can be confirmed by comparing the SIC values. As with the LRT the clear improvement relative to the Normal is evident.

Overall, when we compare the fit of GARCH-t and the jump process by means of the SIC we see that the model with time-varying moments clearly dominates the static one by a wide margin. This finding has also been noted by Kim and Kon (1994) for US stock returns.

CONCLUSIONS

With regard to our dual motivation we can draw two sets of conclusions: first we have seen that the Polish stock market which we have chosen as an example for an emerging market has very similar properties compared to a major market in an industrial country, the Frankfurt stock exchange. Thus for the Polish market, the initial learning period from 1991 to 1994 seems to have been sufficient. In this context the study by Harrison (1996) is also interesting. With a similar methodology the paper also evaluates 'emerging' markets, namely the British and Dutch markets in the eighteenth century. The conclusion is very similar to ours, including also the relatively higher level of volatility compared with today's values on large markets.

Secondly, for option pricing we have seen that the Black-Scholes world of returns drawn from a Normal distribution with constant returns is clearly inappropriate. In our evaluation of two alternative models we found that the GARCH approach is clearly superior to the assumption of a Poisson jump process. Thus to price options the methodology of Duan (1995) seems a better choice than the procedure used by Merton (1976). An additional reason is that by contrast with the assumptions of the Merton model jump risk is not diversified.

REFERENCES

Baillie, R.T. and R.P. DeGennaro (1990): 'Stock Returns and Volatility', *Journal of Financial and Quantitative Analysis*, pp. 203–214.

Ball, C. and W. Torous (1983): 'A Simplified Jump Process for Common Stock Returns', *Journal of Financial and Quantitative Analysis*, pp. 53–65.

Ball, C. and W. Torous (1985): 'On Jumps in Common Stock Prices and Their Impact on Call Option Pricing', Journal of Finance, pp. 155–173.

Bates, D. (1996): *Testing Option Pricing Models*, in G.S. Maddala and C.R. Rao (eds): *Handbook of Statistics*, vol. 14, pp. 567–612.

Bauer, R., F. Nieuwland and W. Verschoor (1994): 'German Stock Market Dynamics', *Empirical Economics*, pp. 397–418.

Black, F. and W. Scholes (1973): 'The Pricing of Options and Corporate Liabilities', *Journal of Political Economy*, pp. 637–659.

Bollerslev, T. (1986): 'Generalized Autoregressive Conditional Heteroscedasticity', *Journal of Econometrics*, pp. 307–327.

Bollerslev, T. (1987): 'A Conditionally Heteroscedastic Model for Speculative Prices and Rates of Return', *Review of Economics and Statistics*, pp. 542–547.

Bollerslev, T., R. Chou and K. Kroner (1992): 'ARCH Modeling in Finance', *Journal of Econometrics*, pp. 5–59.

Bollerslev, T., R. Engle and D. Nelson (1994): *ARCH Models*, in R. Engle and D. McFadden (eds): *Handbook of Econometrics*, vol. 2, pp. 2961–3038, Elsevier: Amsterdam.

Bruand, M. (1996): 'The Jump-diffusion Process in Swiss Stock Returns and its Impact on Option Valuation', *Finanzmarkt und Portfoliomanagement*, pp. 75–98.

Campbell, J., A. Lo and C. MacKinlay (1996): *The Econometrics of Financial Markets*, Princeton University Press.

Chobanov, G., P. Mateev, S. Mittnik and S. Rachev (1996): *Modeling the Distribution of Highly Volatile Exchange-rate Time Series*, Working Paper no. 90, Institute for Statistics and Econometrics, University of Kiel.

Dankenbring, H. and M. Missong (1995): *GARCH-Effekte auf dem deutschen Aktienmarkt*, Working Paper no. 85, Institute for Statistics and Econometrics, University of Kiel.

Duan, J. (1995): 'The GARCH Option Pricing Model', *Mathematical Finance*, pp. 13–32.

Emerson, R., S. Hall and A. Zelweska-Mitura (1996): *Evolving Market Efficiency with an Application to Some Bulgarian Shares*, mimeo.

Engle, R. (1982): 'Autoregressive Conditional Heteroscedasticity with Estimates of the Variance of U.K. Inflation', *Econometrica*, pp. 987–1008.

Engle, R., D. Lilien and R. Robins (1987): 'Estimating Time Varying Risk Premia in the Term Structure: The ARCH-M Model', Econometrica, pp. 391–407

Erb, C., C. Harvey and T. Viskanta (1996): *Expected Returns and Volatility in 135 countries*, mimeo.

Fama, E. (1965): 'The Behavior of Stock Market Prices', *Journal of Business*, pp. 34–105.

Glosten, L., R. Jagannathan and D. Runkle (1993): 'On the Relation between Expected Value and Volatility', *Journal of Finance*, pp. 1779–1801.

Hamilton, J. (1994): *Time Series Analysis*, Princeton University Press.

Harrison, P. (1996): *Are All Financial Time Series Alike: Evidence from the 18[Th] Century Stock Markets*, mimeo.

Jorion, P. (1989): 'On Jump Processes in Foreign Exchange and Stock Markets', *Review of Financial Studies*, pp. 427–445.

Kim, D. and S. Kon (1994): 'Alternative Models for the Conditional Heteroscedasticity of Stock Returns', *Journal of Business*, pp. 563–598.

Kim, M., Y. Oh and R. Brooks (1994): 'Are Jumps in Stock Returns Diversifiable: Evidence and Implications for Option Pricing', *Journal of Financial and Quantitative Analysis*, pp. 609–631.

Lo, A. and A. MacKinlay (1988): 'Stock Market Prices Do Not Follow Random Walks – Evidence From a Simple Specification Test', *Review of Financial Studies*, pp. 41–66.

Mandelbrot, B. (1963): 'The Variation of Certain Speculative Prices', *Journal of Business*, pp. 394–419.

Merton, R. (1976): 'Option Pricing When Underlying Stock Returns are Discontinuous', *Journal of Financial Economics*, pp. 125–144.

Meszanos, D. (1996): *On Efficiency and Anomalies of the Slovak Capital Market*, paper presented at the Institute for Advanced Studies, Finance Workshop.

Nelson, D. (1991): 'Conditional Heteroscedasticity in Asset Returns: A New Approach', *Econometrica*, pp. 347–370.

Pagan, A. (1996): 'The Econometrics of Financial Markets', *Journal of Empirical Finance*, pp. 15–102.

Palm, F. (1996): *GARCH Models of Volatility*, forthcoming in: Handbook of Statistics, vol. 14.

Scheicher, M. (1996): *Nonlinear Dynamics: Evidence for a Small Stock Exchange*, Working Paper no. 9607, University of Vienna, Department of Economics.

Silverman, B.U. (1986): *Density Estimation for Statistics and Data Analysis*, Chapman & Hall.

Sola, M. and A. Timmerman (1994): *Fitting the Moments: A Comparison of ARCH and Regime Switching Models for Daily Stock Returns*, mimeo.

F34
P33

21. Foreign Debt Settlements in Bulgaria, Hungary and Poland 1989–1996

Jérôme Sgard

INTRODUCTION

In 1990, the international debate on the support for Central and East European Countries (CEECs) focused largely on financial aid, as a precondition or catalyst for other instruments such as technical assistance and trade liberalization. One proposition, which created much excitement at the time, was the idea of a so–called 'Marshall Plan for Eastern Europe': in a way possibly comparable to that of Western Europe after World War II, it was hoped that a massive transfer of resources over a few years would kick–start reforms and set the transitional economies on a high–growth, converging trajectory, which would open the way for a speedy integration with the EU. Though the total amount of funds made available since then has been substantial, a key difference was soon made plain: more than 80% of total aid to Central Europe since 1990 incurs interests payments close to market terms, whereas only 7% of the funds allocated under the Marshall Plan did so.

As a consequence, most countries have kept tight control on new loan disbursements, and when they have eventually relaxed their objectives in terms of their current account deficits, they have generally given priority to the private sector in funding the capital account. Conversely, in the last years, no country has clearly increased foreign borrowing in the expectation of higher fiscal revenues in the future. In other words, the 'fixed costs' of transition, generally covered by the State, have been mostly financed with domestic savings. In the future, financial constraints will therefore stem from higher public domestic debt as from weak banking systems, rather than from large stocks of public foreign liabilities.

Does this mean that financial aid to CEEC's has been *de facto* limited to standard multilateral programs, *plus* two (successful) convertibility funds in support of the Polish and Czechoslovak currencies? If so, the transition would well prove a clear example in which financial support and public aid has been much less effective than trade liberalization, both in terms of microeconomic adjustment and macro–stabilization. Although it is not the purpose of this paper to settle this latter issue, it shows that the debt and debt–service reduction programs negotiated by Bulgaria and Poland have had indeed a clear positive impact, whether they were negotiated with commercial banks (London Club), or bilateral public creditors (Paris Club). It also highlights the fact that rapid stabilization and adjustment in the Polish case has further increased the benefits of debt forgiveness, while in the Bulgarian case a weak reform process delivered far fewer feedback benefits. However, the comparison with Hungary, which did not renegotiate its large foreign debt, demonstrates the very high costs of this strategy, when compared to its relative benefits. The next section recalls the experience of each country with regard to debt management and its related macro–economic strategy, from the early 1980s till the transition period. The third section presents the broad lines of the London and Paris Club agreements reached by Poland and Bulgaria since 1990; it also assesses the evolution of each country's Brady Bonds on secondary markets since issue. The fourth section tries to assess the macroeconomic impact of each country's debt strategy in terms of aggregate measures of solvency, while the fifth section concludes on the uses of debt forgiveness.

THREE COUNTRIES WITH A HISTORY OF HIGH INDEBTEDNESS

When the transition reforms were started, each country under review clearly showed all the usual patterns of high foreign indebtedness. Hungary had a debt–to–GDP ratio close to 70% in 1990, while Poland and Bulgaria reached levels of 83% and 162%, after the sharp devaluations which accompanied the stabilization programs of 1990 and 1991 respectively (Table 21.1). Though richer in GDP terms, Hungary was reputed to have established a world record of US\$ 2060 foreign debt per capita, against US\$ 1290 for Poland and US\$ 1250 for Bulgaria.[1] Interest due had also stabilized at high levels, in so far as it was paid: Hungary actually transferred 5% of GDP in interest payments in 1990, at a time when Poland should have paid 4.5% and Bulgaria 6.2% (1991).[2]

---

[1] At the same time (1990) per capital debt levels were US\$ 1925 for Argentina, US\$ 1235 for Mexico and US\$ 880 for Turkey.

[2] In 1990, the respective figures were 3% for Argentina, 2.9% for Mexico and 1.8% for Turkey.

Table 21.1. Debt indicators, 1985–1995

Bulgaria	1985	1989	1990	1991	1992	1993	1994	1995 (e)
Foreign debt in US$ million	3,852	10,137	10,890	12,055	12,231	12,325	10,468	9,157
Foreign Debt/GDP	12	21	55	162	141	113	106	71
Interest/Gross Dom. Savings	3.9	9.9	6.2	2.2	11.1	24.5	12.3	.
Interest /Exports of G&S	1.9	7.0	4.0	2.0	4.3	5.7	5.0	5.3
Interest/GDP	1.2	2.7	1.5	0.6	1.8	2.7	2.7	2.8
Interest/ fiscal revenue	na	1.8	2.5	3.1	8.0	9.3	9.4	8.6
Hungary	*1985*	*1989*	*1990*	*1991*	*1992*	*1993*	*1994*	*1995 (e)*
Foreign debt in US$ million	13,957	20,397	21,276	22,624	21,975	24,232	28,019	31,100
Foreign Debt/ GDP	67.7	69.9	64.4	67.9	59.1	63.0	68.0	70.8
Interest/Gross Dom. Savings	18.2	18.4	17.8	25.9	28.9	35.4	32.2	na
Interest /Exports of G&S	11.7	15.3	16.0	14.9	14.0	15.6	16.5	13.6
Interest/GDP	4.9	5.5	5.0	4.9	4.4	4.1	4.7	5.3
Interest/ fiscal revenue	6.6	9.1	7.8	8.4	8.2	6.8	6.5	na
Poland	*1985*	*1989*	*1990*	*1991*	*1992*	*1993*	*1994*	*1995 (e)*
Foreign debt in US$ million	33,307	43,077	49,162	53,585	48,649	45,327	42,160	43,886
Foreign Debt/GDP	46.9	52.4	83.4	70.1	57.7	52.8	44.2	36.6
Interest/Gross Dom. Savings	7.7	2.5	1.7	4.4	6.7	7.2	6.7	na
Interest /Exports of G&S	14.4	6.3	2.0	4.0	6.0	6.6	5.8	5.0
Interest/GDP	2.2	1.1	0.6	0.8	1.1	1.2	1.2	1.0
Interest/ fiscal revenue	5.2	8.5	1.2	1.9	2.9	3.1	2.7	2.2

Note: Interest covers actual payments on the foreign debt.
Source: World Debt Table, national sources.

Although these indices were tending to converge at the beginning of the 1990s, they were the result of very different national experiences and financial strategies in the preceding decade. On the one hand, Bulgaria was a relative newcomer among the highly indebted countries: it had followed a policy of low indebtedness during the 1970s, along with Czechoslovakia and East Germany, and had accumulated most of its foreign debt between 1984 and 1987 (on average +20% of its 1994 GDP per year). Then, shortly before the change of regime in November 1990, it suspended interest payments and entered a long and ill–managed process of negotiations with commercial banks. On average, 33% of interest due, as estimated in 1990, was paid between 1991 and 1994, before a Brady–type, debt–reduction program was signed in April of that year; Paris Club agreements were reached more easily, but concerned only a small fraction of its total foreign exposure.

On the other hand, Hungary and Poland followed a path much closer to the international cycle of high foreign borrowing by LDCs after the first oil–shock, followed by a sharp financial and liquidity crisis in 1982–83, and a painful adjustment process during the following years. Their rapid accumulation of foreign loans was clearly facilitated by the general assumption during the 1970s that 'countries do not go broke', despite ample historical counter evidence. This premise was reputed to be especially strong in the case of Eastern Europe where the Soviet Union was widely expected to bail out any 'satellite country' which could ultimately run into serious financial trouble. In reality, this scenario was rapidly contradicted by events after 1981, as neither Poland nor Romania (not to mention Yugoslavia) ever received any hard–currency support. High indebtedness in the former case, and savage net amortization in the latter, certainly played a role in the economic disintegration of the late 1980s, though it remains to be proved that the no–bail–out decision by the Soviet leaders, say after 1981, was effectively a watershed.

In practice, Poland suspended most payments and asked for debt renegotiation in 1981, during the Solidarity period, and subsequently went through a long series of financial agreements during the 1980s (see Table 21.2). Preferential treatment was given to commercial creditors (London Club) during most of the decade in terms of interest payments, though full payment was never fully resumed. However, until 1989 this eased the way for regular accords, mostly short–term debt–rescheduling and interest capitalization. This policy also contributed to the establishment in 1983 of a bank–based 'revolving short–term agreement' (RSTA), i.e. a rolled–over trade loan which helped finance Poland's foreign trade with the West at a time when it had no access to any other foreign funding, whether private or public; interest on RSTA was duly paid until 1989. In contrast, relations with official bilateral creditors (Paris Club) were completely frozen from the November 1981 military coup till 1985, and they did not fully recover until 1989. At that time, the prospect of a major international aid package in support of the reforms prepared by the new Mazowiecki government drastically changed the incentives. Indeed at the end of that year, the Polish authorities stopped almost all interest payments to private creditors and gave priority to the relationship with bilateral and multilateral public lenders: between 1990 and 1993 commercial banks received around 13% of the US$ 3.2 billion in interest payments due over this period, as estimated in 1989. Serious negotiations with the London Club were then deliberately postponed until late 1993, though the principle of a Brady–type program was admitted as early as 1990.

Although it generally experienced harder financial constraints than its neighbors, Hungary has successfully followed a policy of full debt service up until the present day. Between 1982 and 1984, the Mexican crisis, the end of the East–West *détente* and the payments crisis of Poland, Romania and Yugoslavia thrust it into an intense liquidity crisis, which was further increased by the very short average maturity of its debt. However, it resisted suspension of payments, and implemented a strong macroeconomic adjustment so that access to international credit and capital markets was already regained by 1984. A comprehensive financial strategy was then developed, which in principle has remained unchanged till now: average maturities were lengthened, international reserves were increased when possible, and priority was given to private creditors rather than to multilateral and especially bilateral ones. In this sense, Hungary engineered a successful 'silent rescheduling' between 1985 and 1992 and received large amounts of new money. These results are comparable to those of the 1986–88 Baker Programs, but have been obtained without incurring the heavy costs of a cessation of payments. Most striking, however, is the regular increase since that time of the relative share of bond borrowing, in a move which anticipated the international trends witnessed in the 1990s. Since 1992 almost all sovereign borrowing is bond–denominated, so that the share of bonds in the total debt (55%) is comparable to that of countries which swapped their bank debt against Brady Bonds.[3]

The downside of this strategy is to be found in the real economy. On at least three occasions (1982–83, 1990 and 1995–96) drastic stabilization programs have had to be implemented, so as to reduce domestic absorption and make possible the transfer of revenue necessitated by the payment of interest: since 1980, Hungary has transferred abroad on average 5% of its GDP in interest payments on its public and, increasingly, private foreign debt. In 1989, rumors of an imminent cessation of payments became widespread, as the political transition was accompanied by substantial macroeconomic relaxation. Indeed, this outcome was only avoided due to massive loans from German banks,

---

[3] At the end of 1994, bonds represented 65% of the total long–term foreign debt of Argentina, 58% for Mexico and 25% for Turkey (which did not have a Brady Plan).

guaranteed by the Federal government,[4] and to a short–term bridge–loan by the BIS, in 1990.

This was also the time when it was very often assumed that Hungary would benefit from a Brady–type debt reduction program, parallel to that envisaged for Poland and Bulgaria. However, both the last Communist government and the democratically–elected administration of Mr. Antall repeatedly rejected the option, for the very same reason:[5] a government with long–term foresight should accept the short–term costs of large interest payments and tight demand control, so as to preserve the financial reputation of the country and its easy access to international capital markets. The implication was to make the 1990 macroeconomic adjustment much tougher, as the Antall government imposed a budgetary correction of 2.5% of GDP and a 5.8% cut in the current account balance in 1990, before launching the so–called 'gradualist' transition reforms, a year later.[6]

Though results were rather impressive in 1991 and 1992, a new destabilization brought about a deficit of 10.4% of GDP on the current account in 1994, and of 6.5% of GDP in the budget. Large interest payments on foreign debt appear as the main factor behind the latter imbalance, while the former derives more from non–state sectors. This rapid macroeconomic drift imposed the implementation of a third large stabilization program in 1995, this time by the post–Communist government of Mr Horn. This plan has delivered important results which have helped to shore up the foreign financial position of the country, although it has not suffered as much as in 1990–91. The most symbolic result of this rebuilt financial credibility has certainly been the successful launching of two large international bond issues, in January and

---

[4] At the end of 1989 two large credits totaling DEM 500 million, were granted to the National Bank of Hungary and were then redeemed at a rapid pace, when the country stabilized its overall financial position, despite their long maturity (12 and 22 years). The opening of the Hungarian border with Austria to East German refugees, in autumn 1989, was actually a decisive moment in the process which eventually led, some weeks later, to the fall of the Berlin Wall and to German reunification. This was one of the bases on which strong political and financial relationships between the two countries developed over the following months and years.

[5] The Hungarian–born financier George Soros is generally assumed to have proposed his mediation to the Antall government, so as to pave the way for an orderly debt renegotiation, under the terms of the March 1989 Brady initiative. The personal preferences of Mr Soros, among Hungarian democratic parties, as well as the pressure of right–wing elements in the then parliamentary majority, are often considered as important reasons behind the rejection of his proposal.

[6] By contrast, Poland's 'shock–therapy' in 1990 delivered a budget consolidation of around 6% of GDP and an increase in the current account of 8%, as the 1991 Czech 'velvet transition' translated into a budget slippage of 1.9 GDP points, and a stabilization of 6.3 points in the current account.

February 1995,[7] at a time when most international lending to emerging countries was suspended due to the ongoing Mexican crisis. However, more efforts will be necessary in the years to come, in both the domestic and the foreign sectors, which will probably have new, adverse consequences for growth and living standards.

DEBT REDUCTION: THE EXPERIENCE OF BULGARIA AND POLAND

Technically, the debt reduction programs obtained by Bulgaria and Poland fall clearly under the standard Brady framework as far as their commercial liabilities are concerned, but have taken more diverging forms when it comes to their Paris Club debt (Table 21.2).

The Paris Club Agreements

In March 1991, Poland finalized a two–step, 50% debt–reduction agreement with its official creditors, which was decided in principle at the G7 Paris Summit Meeting, in July 1989.[8] One key prescription of this landmark decision was actually that it would not create a precedent for other middle–income, highly–indebted countries: indeed, since then, only low income countries have seen their public debt being written–off, under *inter alia* the developments of the so–called 'Toronto Initiative' (G7 Summit of June 1988).

The final agreement was signed in March 1991 and had two main characteristics. First, creditors could choose between a reduction in interest rates or the forgiveness of forgiving capital. Five of them opted for the first option, eleven for the second (a special case was made for Japanese loans whose interest due was capitalized through a long–term amortization schedule). The most important creditors at that time were France (18%), Brazil (15%), Austria (13%) Germany (12%) and Canada (11%) (Graziani, 1995). Secondly, the debt reduction would be applied in two steps, the first (30%) taking place in April 1991 and the second (20%) in April 1994. In the interim, interest due to all Paris Club creditors was reduced by 80%, which in practice meant that related payments were almost suspended during the first four years of reform. The subsequent 1994 tranche would however be implemented under two

---

[7] Bonds worth 750 million Austrian Schillings were issued on 24 January; 25 billion yen on 8 February.

[8] Egypt benefited from a comparable offer at the same occasion.

Table 21.2. Debt settlements since 1981

Bulgaria	Poland
1 – Pre-1990 Agreements	**1 – Pre-1990 Agreements**
No negotiation, no service problem.	*Official debt* : 4 agreements : Apr 1981; Jul 1985; Nov 1985; Dec 1987; maturity: 7 to $10^{1/2}$ years. Grace period: 4 to 5 years
	Commercial debt: 7 agreements: Apr 1982; Nov 1982; Nov 1983; Jul 1984; Sep 1986; Jul 1988; Jun 1989; maturity: 5 to 10 years (15 years in 1988); grace: 4 to 5 years (0 in 1988)
2 – Post-1990. Official Debt (Paris Club)	**2 – Post-1990. Official Debt (Paris Club)**
April 1991 $ 573 mat.: 6 yrs+6m. grace: 10 years	February 1990: $ 9.4 bn; maturity: 13yrs+9m.; grace: 8yrs+3m.
December 1992 $ 152 6 yrs+4 m 9 yrs+10m.	April 1991: $ 30.5 bn; 50% debt reduction menu in two steps :
April 1994 $ 200 5 yrs+11m 9 yrs+5m.	04-1991: 80% reduction in interest payments; 30% debt reduction
	04-1994 : 20% reduction. Conditional upon IMF agreement.
3 – Post-1990. Commercial Debt (London Club)	3 options: write-off, interest reduction, or interest capitalization and long-term deferment
July 1994: $8.3 bn. – Brady Plan – total reduction: 48%	**3 – Post-1990. Commercial Debt (London Club)**
a – Capital ($6.2 bn):	Oct. 1994: $ 14.4 bn – Brady Plan – total reduction: 48%
i. Buy-back $0.8 bn price: 0.258c/$	a – Long-term debt ($ 8.9 bn. rescheduled in 1988)
ii. Discount Bonds $3.7 bn price: 0.5c/$ int: lib+13/16	
iii. Par Bonds $1.7 bn price: 100c/$ int:2% to lib+13/16	i. Buy-back $2.13 bn; price: 41c/$
b – Past-due Interests (2.1 bn);	ii. Discount Bonds $5.39 bn; price: 45c/$ int: LIBOR+13/16
i. Write-off $0.2 bn	iii. Par Bonds $0.93 bn; price: 100c/$ int: 2.75 to 5%
ii.Buy-back $0.2 bn price: 0.258c/$	iv. Conversion Bonds $0.39 bn; price: 100c/$ int: 4.5 to 7.5%
iii. PDI Bonds $1.6 bn price: 100c/$ int: LIBOR+13/16	

445

Table 21.2 Debt settlements since 1981 (continued)

Discount Bonds have 30 years maturity (bullet amortization); capital is 100%; collateralized with US Treasury zero coupon bonds;	b – Revolving Short-Term Arrangement ($1.24bn. 1980's trade credit) i. Write-off $ 33 mn. ii. Buy-back $ 0.31 bn; price: 38c/$ iii. Par Bonds $ 0.89 bn; price: 100c/$ int: 2.75 to 5%
Par Bonds have 18 years maturity (8-year grace); interest rates raise from 2% to 3% in 7 years, then serve LIBOR+13/16. 1 year interest collateralized.	c – Past-Due Interest ($ 4.26 bn. accumulated since 1989)
	i.Write-off $ 0.75 bn ii.Buy-back $ 0.77 bn price: 38c/$ iii.PDI Bonds $ 2.67 bn price: 100c/$ int: 3.25 to 7%
	Discount, Par and *RSTA Bonds* have 30-year bullet maturities; the principal is fully collateralized with US Treasury, zero-coupon bonds. No interest collateral. *Conversion Bonds* and *PDI Bonds* have no collateral.

Source: World Debt Table 1996, Malecki (1995), National Bank of Bulgaria (1995).

conditions: the approval by the IMF of current economic policy, and the principle that no other creditor (e.g. London Club) should receive more favorable treatment (i.e. less debt forgiveness). This latter clause actually put a lot of pressure on commercial banks and, in so doing, certainly facilitated the 'quasi–free riding' strategy followed by Poland in the run–up to the Brady Agreement. Indeed, as the eventual result of the London Club negotiations were in large part pre–empted, the Polish party had no clear incentive to bow to the pressures of the commercial banks. Though the history of the relations between private and public creditors since 1982 has been rather complex, the Polish case has certainly been marked by a level of interference only matched by the 'big' Brady programs, of the years 1989–92.[9]

The relations of Bulgaria with the Paris Club have taken a much more conventional course, as the country owed only 10% of its total debt to bilateral public creditors and, possibly, had less geopolitical weight than Poland. Three rather standard agreements were signed by the two parties in April and December 1991, and then in April 1994, which allowed for the capitalization of interest due and rescheduled over a 9–10 year period all amortization with grace periods of around six years in each case (see Table 21.2). This actually allowed for a drastic reduction in Bulgaria's debt service to official creditors: after a total severance of service payments in 1990 and 1991, these amounts averaged only US$ 65 million annually between 1992 and 1994, which is not a tangible amount. The implication is that the financial relief offered was comparable to that obtained by Poland on a fiscal and balance–of–payments basis, though the implicit solvency of the country was not increased. Since 1989, all rescheduled interests have been capitalized so that the total Paris Club debt increased from US$ 910 million to 1460 million by the end of 1994, while the Brady Plan reduced outstanding debt towards commercial bank loans by US$ 2,460 million in the same year.

The Brady Plans

Table 21.2 compares in broad terms the two Brady–type debt reduction agreements, as signed by Poland and Bulgaria with their respective commercial creditors, at a few months' distance in 1994. After each group of creditor banks had chosen between the various options offered in the respective menus, both programs generated the equivalent of a debt reduction of close to 48% on a

---

[9] The debt figures published since then do not allow for the impact of the 1991 agreement on outstanding stocks to be measured directly: the general accord had to be confirmed on a bilateral basis by all 17 creditor countries, some of whom would formally write–down their assets only once, in 1994. The two–option menu also brought some confusion in the interpretation of the figures.

present–value basis.

The Bulgarian plan is a rather standard one which, as usual, discriminates between capital and interest arrears, with the former receiving better treatment than the latter. As for capital, Bulgaria bought back US$ 800 million of its own debt at a discount price close to a quarter to the par. Subsequently, banks could exchange old credits in three ways. First, they could exchange them against *Par Bonds,* which receive non–market interest rates, increasing step–by–step from 2% to LIBOR+13/16 in seven years, and will then remain at this level; capital is fully collateralized with 30–year US Treasury Bills and should be amortized at extinction (bullet amortization). Secondly, *Discount Bonds* were exchanged at 50 cents to the par (against 100 cents in the previous case), but receive market interest rates (LIBOR+13/16): one–year interest payments are collateralized with US T–Bills, but the capital is fully exposed to the risk of a new default. The latter option drained close to 60% of the total stock of liabilities, against 27% for *Par Bonds*, while 13% were bought back. Finally, *Past–Due Interest* could be either written–off, bought back, or exchanged at par against *PDI Bonds* which hold non–market interest rates, rather comparable to that of *Par Bonds,* but with no collateral on either capital or interests.

The Polish Brady plan is built on the same basis but has a more complex structure, as no less than six different categories of bonds have been issued, three of which are partly collateralized, as opposed to only three Bulgarian issues, two of them with collateral. This partially reflects the much larger size of the Polish program, which covered US$ 14.4 billion of old debt, compared with US$ 8.3 billion in the case of Bulgaria. This difference has been reflected since then in the size and activity of the secondary markets. Another important difference is that the debt forgiveness was extended to Poland's interest arrears, which has not been the case in Bulgaria. In practice, three different types of Polish liabilities were differentiated from the start: capital which corresponded to the stock of debt fully restructured in 1988 (62%), past due interest (PDI) accumulated since then (30%), and the RSTA (8%), i.e. the revolving commercial loan established in 1983 (see above). All three categories could be bought back at prices of either 38 or 41 cents per US dollar, or exchanged against *Par Bonds,* with scheduled increases in interest rates converging towards either 5% or 7% (PDI); small shares of the RSTA and of PDI were also written–off. On top of this, capital assets could be exchanged against two other types of securities: *Discount Bonds,* which serve LIBOR+13/16 and were bought at 45 cents to the par; and *Conversion Bonds,* which have two main characteristics. First, they were exchanged at par and bear non–market interest rates which will climb step–by–step to 7.5% after 10 years, a yield notably higher than that offered by alternative *Par Bonds,* so as to reflect the absence of collateral. Secondly, they were associated with the acquisition of uncollateralized *New Money Bonds,* up to 35% of the amounts of old debt converted, receiving LIBOR+13/16. *Par, Discount* and *RSTA Bonds* have collateral on capital only, and maturities of either 30 or 20 years (PDI).

In other words, *Conversion Bonds* are more speculative assets than *Par* and *Discount Bonds;* conversely, the two latter, by design, should be country–risk neutral and are differentiated mostly by their uneven exposure to (US) interest rate risks and by different implications for commercial banks in terms of capital and/or revenue losses.[10]

Market Performances since 1994

Bulgarian and Polish Brady Bonds, as well as Hungarian standard sovereign issues are quoted daily on the international capital markets (secondary trading), which allows for a continuous assessment of their relative creditworthiness, or country risk (see Figure 21.1). On this basis, all countries witnessed a depreciation of their bonds (or increasing yields) over most of 1994, culminating in March 1995 at the peak of the Mexican Peso crisis.[11] Thereafter, yields have fallen steadily, both in absolute levels and as spreads against the US Treasury Bill, a trend witnessed across all major emerging country debt markets. However by the end of March 1996, yields had fallen to levels well below those of the largest Latin American markets, for both Hungary (7.97%) and Poland (9.84%), while in the case of Bulgaria (23.91%) they were still at levels comparable to that reached by Latin Brady Bonds at the heights of the 1995 crisis.[12] This is reflected logically by the market value of bonds, which has remained fairly stable in Bulgaria since 1994, while the Hungarian reference issue has recovered its value of early 1994, after having posted an implicit capital loss of 24% in March 1995. Finally, Polish bonds have appreciated 30% since they were issued in June 1994, reflecting much lower country–risk spreads. This trend accelerated in July 1995 when the country was awarded

---

[10] In all cases of Brady–type debt reduction programs, the choice between *Par* and *Discount Bonds* aims *inter alia* at accommodating the different supervisory and fiscal regulations of banks in different countries. This concerns mostly the writing–down of losses, the constitution of reserves and their different impact on tax payments. In this respect, this partly boils down to the question of which proportion of capital losses incurred by banks on sovereign lending may eventually be transferred to tax payers as opposed to bank shareholders.

[11] The following discussion will rely on the quotation Discount Bonds, whose evolution was tightly correlated to that of other Brady issuings.

[12] By March 1996, yields on Mexican, Brazilian and Argentinian Brady Bonds ranged from 15% to 17%; one year earlier they had reached levels between 22% and 25%. (*Source:* JP Morgan).

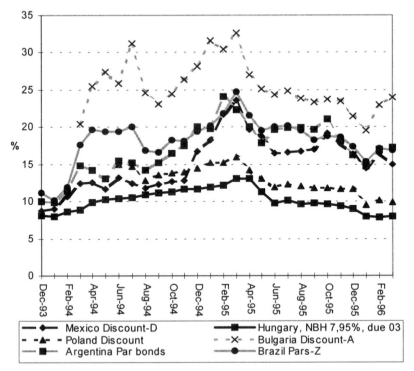

Figure 21.1. Emerging market yields

investment grade rating by a major international notation agency.

The market appraisal of the creditworthiness of the three countries under review is thus sharply contrasted. Bulgarian Bonds, on the one hand, now appear as clearly speculative investments, with a risk premium higher than that of Venezuela or Ecuador, reflecting a substantial anticipated risk of a new suspension of payments in the future. If this outcome were to occur, it would represent the first experience of a default (even if partial) on Brady Bonds, as well as the first open crisis in modern times on a widely–traded, bond–denominated sovereign debt. The range and complexity of the problems at stake would probably make the agreement upon a work–out solution an extremely difficult and costly process, which may have a bearing on Bulgaria's foreign financial relations for a long time.

On the other hand, Poland and Hungary have rapidly become well–established actors in world financial markets, whose capacity to raise funds has steadily increased since the beginning of 1995 and is now clearly superior to that of most Latin American countries, though private international issuing is still limited. While this result was mostly achieved by Hungary during the first years of the 1990s, it has been more recent and spectacular in the case of Poland. Indeed, the (stripped) interest spread of its Brady Bonds against US T–Bills has fallen from 629 basis points in June 1994 to 236 b.p. in March 1996. Morever, a first, international sovereign issue in June 1995 was priced with yields at 185 basis points over the US T–Bills, 24 b.p. *lower* than a highly comparable, Hungarian DEM–issue launched the very same day. At the end of April 1996, an international bond issue by a Polish public bank was priced 88 basis points over US T–Bills, well below Hungarian prices on the primary market.[13]

These impressive results are in sharp contrast with the previous, lengthy period of open conflict with banks creditors, marked by large accumulations of interest arrears and an eventual write–off. The parallel experiences of Hungary and Poland thus confirm what had already been made clear by most Latin American Brady issuers a few years earlier: that the *ex post* cost of a debt write–off is very limited in terms of both access to market and interest spreads.[14] As has also been illustrated by the opposite experience of Bulgaria, developments in the real economy and aggregate financial balances are much more powerful determinants of national creditworthiness over the medium–term. This is further evidenced when the evolution of macroeconomic indicators of solvency are compared over the past five years.

THE IMPACT OF DEBT REDUCTION

Present levels of financial constraints in the three countries under survey allow for a complementary, non–market assessment of their respective financial strategies (Table 21.1). In flow terms, the benefits for Poland and Bulgaria are very clear. Interest payments as a proportion of exports and GDP have remained much lower than in Hungary, though the 1994 debt settlements have had a rather negative impact on *actual* resource transfers, as both countries

---

[13] The substantial difference in yields between the April 1996 primary issue (Bank Handlowy, US$ 100 million, 3 years) and current Brady Bonds quotations is due first to the difference in maturity, and second to the usual underpricing of Brady Bonds on international debt markets, especially when they mix US interest risk and sovereign risk.

[14] W. Cline (1995) estimates the average extra interest spread linked to a debt write–off at 80 basis points.

paid only very small amounts of interest between 1990 and 1993. In this respect, the Brady agreements mostly provided an *ex–post* legal framework for a sharp, unilateral debt–service reduction between 1990 and 1994. In the second half of the 1990s, they will mostly translate into lower, absolute levels of indebtedness, but higher actual service payments in cash–flow terms. Hence, they are doomed to have rather a negative, short–term impact, in terms of their fiscal impact and on real current transactions. The balancing item is thus expected to be more on capital account transactions, and should take the form of higher direct investments and easier access to international capital markets. Indeed, this was rapidly seen to be the case in Poland, where large short–term capital inflows since late 1994 have necessitated heavy sterilization by the Central Bank.

Another point made clear by the Polish and Bulgarian experiences is that the performance of the real economy weighs heavily on the capacity of each country to grow further out of debt, on the basis of debt relief. Though interest payments represent a comparable proportion of exports, sustained recovery in Poland has brought them down to very low levels, when measured as a proportion of GDP. The divergence is even more striking when one assesses their relative pressure on domestic financial resources: since 1991 in Bulgaria, and to an even larger extent in Hungary, the relative burden of the debt service has largely increased due to falling national savings rates. This, in turn, may well be explained, at least partly, by the public debt overhang which may depresses private savings, under standard Ricardian assumptions.[15] This is given further support if the fiscal component is taken into account. In 1995 interest payments represented only 2.7% of total fiscal resources in Poland, against 6.5% in Hungary and 9.4% in Bulgaria, two countries where budget deficits remained high during the later period. Hence, low saving rates and higher fiscal deficits have massively increased the 'leverage effect' of interest payments on the aggregate level of crowding–out, or inflationary pressure.

In order to appraise the evolution of each country's relative indebtedness in more detail, Table 21.3 estimates the direct contribution of six underlying factors to the nominal change observed in the debt–to–GDP ratio, between 1989 and 1994. This is only an arithmetical calculation, which *does not* describe causal relationships, but may give an account of how debt–management strategies and macroeconomic dynamics can interact in the medium–term and produce sharply differentiated adjustment patterns. The two first variables are real growth and the dollar–term appreciation of the GDP (nominal forex exchange on GDP deflator). The four others reflect the

---

[15] Empirically, this hypothesis may well be confirmed in Hungary, where households savings represented only 11.5% of GDP in 1994, against 22% to 24% in Bulgaria (in flow terms).

variations in nominal, outstanding debt, and are based on the stock/flow reconciliation figures published in the *World Debt Tables*: net flows of credits (including interest capitalization), debt forgiveness, cross–currency valuation (reflecting *inter alia* the real depreciation of the dollar against other international currencies), and a residual accounting factor. The relatively large time–span allows for the effects of large fluctuations during the period to be cushioned, so as to highlight the different trajectories over the medium–term.

Table 21.3. Contributions to variations in the debt-to-GDP ratio 1989–1994

	Bulgaria	Hungary	Poland
Debt/ GDP ratio in 1989 and 1994, resp.	21.4 / 106.5	69.9 / 68.0	52.4 / 44.2
change 1989–1994	85.1	-1.9	-8.2
GDP contribution	81.7	-21.9	-11.3
real growth/recession	31.5	10.0	6.0
foreign exchange	50.2	-31.9	-17.3
Debt contribution	3.4	20.0	3.1
net flows on debt	30.5	9.8	11.1
debt forgiveness	-41.8	0	-14.2
cross–currency valuation	3.3	7.5	3.1
residual	11.4	2.7	3.0

A first lesson is that generally the GDP variable has had a much larger impact than the debt term, and that, within it, variations in real exchange rates also tend to weigh more heavily than the real evolutions. This is indeed confirmed by annual data: recoveries in Poland and Hungary have delivered more terms–of–trade benefits than real growth *per se*, and the large fluctuations in the Bulgarian real exchange rate have vastly overshadowed the impact of the long recession and weak ensuing recovery. Though these figures do not account for the indirect impact of debt service reduction on stabilization and growth, they clearly show that debt forgiveness has worked much more as an instrument to strengthen growth potential and underlying solvency than as an accounting device to reduce the nominal level of foreign liabilities. This conclusion confirms that derived from most Latin American countries in the post–Brady era.

This trend is further evidenced by the breakdown of the dynamic of debt. In Bulgaria and Poland, the impact of write–offs has been almost balanced by that of adverse factors, mostly net capital flows and interest capitalizations. This means that on an *ex post* basis debt forgiveness has cushioned the negative impact on capital accounts of the first years of transition, but has not contributed directly, on an accounting basis, to bringing down relative indebtedness to pre–1989 levels. This rule is supported *a contrario* by the case of Hungary, where large current account deficits since 1993 have only been balanced by large gains in the real exchange rate, though this is only true on average, as the latter were mostly accumulated between 1990 and 1992.

In other words, the fact that Hungary did not implement a sharp initial devaluation, contrary to what *all* other reforming economies did in 1990–1991, helped decisively in limiting the strong pressure exerted by foreign debt on its financial balances. On an *ex post* basis, this option was actually validated to some extent by the relatively high growth in exports. But the overall result was only to contain foreign indebtedness at its initial relative level, while, progressively, Poland has proved able to grow out of debt, thanks to both high growth and rapid, real foreign exchange appreciation. Indeed, over 1994 and 1995, total growth in US$–denominated GDP contributed 14.3 points to reducing Poland's ratio of relative indebtedness, against 8.4 points in Hungary. But at the same time, the total debt contributed to a fall of 1.9 points of GDP in the former case, and to an increase of 16.2 points in the latter, due primarily to large current account deficits.[16] These in turn may partly reflect the impact of a large debt overhang on domestic savings rates, as opposed to the Polish where debt forgiveness made the country solvent again and helped in stabilizing the agents' expectations.

CONCLUSION: THE USES OF A DEBT WRITE–OFF

As an hypothesis, previous evidence suggests that three main channels may account for the medium–term impact of debt write–offs in transitional economies. The first one is the standard transfer problem, which has a bearing on the fiscal and domestic saving/investment balances as well as on foreign payments, though by ways which are often indirect and include the behavior of private agents (see Hungary's double deficit in 1994–1995). The second one is the standard Ricardian effect, where a high public debt depresses private savings through the expectation of one type of wealth tax or another (monetization, sharp devaluation, etc). There are strong indices of this factor weighing heavily in Hungary and Poland, though in different directions; the case is much less clear in Bulgaria.

The third possible channel is more specific to transitional economies and

---

[16] Precise accounts of the 1995 dynamics of the debt stock were not available on a comparable basis, at the time of writing.

their strong potential for real foreign exchange appreciation, as witnessed in Central Europe. Though too little work has been done on this remarkable phenomenon (see Halpern and Wyplosz, 1995), it can apparently be linked to two elements: catching–up on excessive real depreciations at the onset of reforms (see the Czech Republic and Poland), and the later appreciation of the real equilibrium exchange rate, due to large efficiency gains delivered by the ongoing microeconomic adjustment (see Hungary and Poland). The crux of the matter is the fact that, in statistical terms, productivity gains are tightly linked to industrial recovery and, apparently, also deliver high levels of self–finance to growing enterprises – that is, all other things being equal, more domestic savings. Microeconomic adjustment would then deliver higher competitiveness and fewer financial constraints, so as to interact dynamically with the above–mentioned Ricardian effect. As a result, the appreciation of the real equilibrium exchange rate eventually delivers large gains in the terms of trade, with the usual Balassa effect on the cost of foreign goods (including capital assets) and transfer payments.

This scenario probably provides a schematic description of the current Polish experience for growing rapidly out of debt. Hungary would then be described as a country which succeeded slightly better than Poland in terms of productivity–increasing, supply–side adjustment (channel 3), but has not been able to reduce the relative weight of large foreign transfers. Hence low savings rates, crippling financial imbalances, lower growth and less real appreciation in the later period. This may suggest that slower productivity gains in a coming, more capital–intensive stage of microeconomic adjustment could translate into a sliding real equilibrium exchange rate, as the pressure of foreign debt would not be balanced by rapid productivity gains. Bulgaria represents the worst–case scenario: the impact of a large comparative reduction of the foreign debt was completely overshadowed by high capital imports (most of all interest capitalization), and, to a larger extent, by the poor performance of the real economy. During the crisis of April–May 1996, the exchange rate was again pushed to extremely low levels, at a time when it is still difficult to identify any clear foundations either for real growth, or real equilibrium appreciation. Under these circumstances, it is difficult to envisage how a new reduction in debt service could clearly make the country more solvent and more able to grow, if decisive macroeconomic and institutional reforms are not implemented.

REFERENCES

Calvo, G., Findlay, R., Koury, P., Braga de Macedo, J. (eds)(1989): *Debt, Stabilization and Development, Essays in Honor of Carlos Diaz–Alejandro*, Basil Blackwell, Oxford.

Cline, W.R. (1995): *International Debt Reconsidered*, The Institute for International Economics, Washington D.C.

Dornbusch, R. (1984): *External Debt, Budget Deficits and Disequilibrium Exchange Rates*, NBER Working Paper no. 1336.

Graziani, G. (1995): *External Debt Burden and Restructuring: the Case of Central and Eastern Europe*, mimeo.

Halpern, L. and C. Wyplosz (1995): *Equilibrium Real Exchange Rate in Transition*, mimeo, 42 pp.

Husain, I. and I. Diwan (1989): *Dealing with the Debt Crisis*, World Bank, Washington D.C.

Krugman, P. (1988): 'Financing versus Forgiving a Debt Overhang', *Journal of Economic Development*, 29 (3).

Malecki, W. (1995): *Poland's External Debt Management during the Transition*, mimeo, Institute of Finance, Warsaw.

Sachs, J.D. (1989): *The Debt Overhang of Developing Countries*, in: G. Calvo *et al.*

Sgard, J. (1995): *The Management of the Hungarian Foreign Debt, the Impact of the No–Write–off Strategy, 1989–1994*, mimeo, Institute of Finance, Warsaw.

Sgard, J. (1996): *Credit Crises and the Role of Banks During Transition: a Five–Country Comparison*, Document de Travail, CEPII, Paris.

ANNEX

Table 21.A. Growth in real gross domestic product (percentage change year-on-year)

	1990	1991	1992	1993	1994	1995	1996ᵉ
Albania	-10	-27.7	-7.2	9.6	9.4	8.9	8.2
Bulgaria	-9.1	-11.7	-7.3	-2.4	1.8	2.1	-10.9
Croatia	-6.9	-19.8	-11.1	-0.9	0.6	1.7	4.2
Czech Republic	-1.2	-11.5	-3.3	0.6	2.7	5.9	4.1
Hungary	-3.5	-11.9	-3.1	-0.6	2.9	1.5	1
Macedonia	-9.9	-12.1	-21.1	-8.4	-4	-1.4	1.1
Poland	-11.6	-7	2.6	3.8	5.2	7	6
Romania	-5.6	-12.9	-8.7	1.5	3.9	7.1	4.1
Slovakia	-2.5	-14.6	-6.5	-3.7	4.9	6.8	6.9
Slovenia	-4.7	-8.9	-5.5	2.8	5.3	4.1	3.1

Note: ᵉ estimate.
Source: EBRD (1997).

Table 21.B. Short-term interest rates (treasury bill rates)(in percentage p.a., end of year)

	1993	1994	1995	1996ᵉ
Albania	.	10	15	20
Bulgaria	59	92	43	477
Croatia	97	14	27	10
Czech Republic (refinancing rate)	12	11	13	14
Hungary	24	32	30	22
Macedonia (liquidity credit rate)	848	66	30	18
Poland	34	27	24	19
Romania	.	.	45	55
Slovakia (money market rate)	16	6	10	15
Slovenia	30	26	19	10

Note: ᵉ estimate.
Source: EBRD (1997), IMF (1997).

Table 21.C. US$ exchange rates (end of year)

	1990	1991	1992	1993	1994	1995	1996ᵉ
Albania	10	25	97	101	95	94	107
Bulgaria	7	21.8	24.5	32.7	66	71	496
Croatia	.	.	0.8	6.56	5.63	5.32	5.54
Czech Republic	.	.	.	30	28	26.6	27.3
Hungary	61.5	75.6	84	100.7	110.7	139.5	164.9
Macedonia	.	.	.	44.5	40.6	38	41.4
Poland	0.95	1.096	1.577	2.134	2.437	2.468	2.876
Romania	34.7	189	460	1276	1767	2578	4.035
Slovakia	.	.	.	33.2	31.3	29.6	30.7
Slovenia	.	56.69	98.7	131.84	126.46	125.99	141.48

Note: ᵉ estimate.
Source: EBRD (1997).

Table 21.D. Inflation (consumer price index)(percentage change year-on-year)

	1991	1992	1993	1994	1995	1996ᵉ
Albania	104	237	31	16	6	17
Bulgaria	339	79	64	122	33	311
Croatia	250	938	1149	-3	4	3
Czech Republic	52	13	18	10	8	9
Hungary	32	22	21	21	28	20
Macedonia	230	1925	230	55	9	0
Poland	60	44	38	29	22	19
Romania	223	199	296	62	28	57
Slovakia	58	9	25	12	7	5
Slovenia	247	93	23	18	9	9

Note: ᵉ estimate.
Source: EBRD (1997).

Table 21.E. General government balances (in per cent of gross domestic product)

	1990	1991	1992	1993	1994	1995	1996ᵉ
Albania	-15	-31	-22	-15	-12	-10	-12
Bulgaria	.	.	-5.2	-10.9	-5.8	-6.4	-13.4
Croatia	.	.	-4	-0.8	1.7	-0.9	-0.5
Czech Republic	.	.	.	2.7	0.8	0.4	-0.2
Hungary	0.4	-2.2	-5.5	-6.8	-8.2	-6.5	-3.5
Macedonia	.	.	-9.6	-13.6	-3.2	-1.3	-0.4
Poland	3.1	-6.7	-6.6	-3.4	-2.8	-3.6	-3.1
Romania	1	3.3	-4.6	-0.4	-1.9	-2.6	-3.9
Slovakia	.	.	.	-7	-1.3	0.1	-1.2
Slovenia	-0.3	2.6	0.2	0.3	-0.2	0	0.3

Note: ᵉ estimate.
Source: EBRD (1997).

Table 21.F. Current account and trade balances (in per cent of gross domestic product, 1996, estimated)

	Current account balance	Merchandise trade balance
Albania	-4.7	-26.7
Bulgaria	1.3	2.4
Croatia	-7.6	-17.2
Czech Republic	-8.1	-10.9
Hungary	-3.8	-5.9
Macedonia	-7.8	-8.6
Poland	-1	-6.1
Romania	-5.9	-4.6
Slovakia	-10.2	-11.1
Slovenia	0.3	-4.6

Source: EBRD (1997).

Table 21.G. Foreign direct investment (net inflows recorded in the balance of payments, in US$, estimated)

	FDI inflows per capita in 1996	Cumulative FDI inflows per capita 1989–1996
Albania	28	93
Bulgaria	12	51
Croatia	73	129
Czech Republic	123	692
Hungary	195	1300
Macedonia	20	38
Poland	71	140
Romania	9	52
Slovakia	33	117
Slovenia	90	372

Source: EBRD (1997).

Table 21.H. Current account and trade balances (in per cent of gross domestic product, 1996, estimated)

	Current account balance	Merchandise trade balance
Albania	-4.7	-26.7
Bulgaria	1.3	2.4
Croatia	-7.6	-17.2
Czech Republic	-8.1	-10.9
Hungary	-3.8	-5.9
Macedonia	-7.8	-8.6
Poland	-1	-6.1
Romania	-5.9	-4.6
Slovakia	-10.2	-11.1
Slovenia	0.3	-4.6

Source: EBRD (1997).

Index

adjustment
  as a function of credibility 275
  under a credible program, and
    program of low credibility 273
advisory projects, in Central and Eastern
    Europe 312–16
Aghion, P. 332
Agrawal, A. 393
Ajayi, R. 393
Albania
  80% rule 16
  adequacy ratios 26
  assets and liabilities 27
  Bank of Albania (BoA) 13, 14–15, 25,
    29
    instruments 15–18
    targets 15
  banking sector 24–8
    regulatory framework and
      supervision 24–6
  banking system 13, 36
  Bankruptcy Law 25–6
  central bank independence 14–15
  Commercial Bank of Albania 21
  commercial banks 16, 17
  consumer price index and inflation 17
  currency exchange 31–3
  current account and trade balances
    459
  Enterprise Restructuring Agency 23
  exchange rate, Lek/US$ exchange rate
    32
  exchange rate policy 22
  exchange rates, US$ exchange rates
    458
  exchanges 28–33
  external finance, sources 33
  foreign aid 34–5
  foreign currency deposits 19–20
  foreign debt 24
  foreign direct investment 460
    (1992-5) 33

  foreign financing, dynamics 35
  general government balances 459
  gross domestic product (GDP) 16, 28
    growth in real gross domestic
      product 457
  inflation 458
  inter-enterprise arrears 28
  interbank money market 21
  interest rate policy 18–20
  interest rates
    (1993-5) 31
    in the bond market 31
    short term 457
    structure 20
  Law on the Banking System 24, 25
  monetary policy 14–22
  National Commercial Bank 21, 24, 28,
    36
  non-performing loans 27–8
  privatization 23–4
  refinancing rates 19
  remuneration rates 20
  reserve requirements 26
  reserves policy 21–2
  Rural Commercial Bank 21, 25, 28,
    36
  Savings Bank 21, 23, 24, 36
  treasury bills 29–31
  two-tier banking system 24–5
Annuar, M. 393
Antal, L. 328, 364
Aoki, M. 323, 332
ARCH model 425
Ariff, M. 393
Asia
  equity markets 393
    extent and liquidity 397
Augmented Dickey Fuller (ADF) test
  420
Austria
  central bank 256
  seigniorage 255, 256, 259, 261, 262,

264, 265
Vienna Stock Exchange 417, 424
Ayada, O. 393

Baer, H.L. 332
bail-outs 271, 274, 275, 280
Baillie, R.T. 430
Balcerowicz, L. 277, 321, 334
Ball, C. 432, 433
banking 3–4
banking sector
  Albania 24–8
  Bulgaria 44–6
  Croatia 75–8
  Czech Republic 93–6, 283–300
  FR Yugoslavia 240–41
  Hungary 111–12
  Macedonia 140–43
  Poland 153–6
  reform 7–8
  Slovakia 187–90
  Slovenia 220–23
banks, by total assets, Europe 298–9
Bartholdy, J. 408
Basle Committee for Banking
  Supervision 93
Bates, D. 417, 425
Batt, J. 329, 330, 334
Begg, D. 251
Belka, M. 340
Bentsen, G. 399
Berglof, E. 332
Binbasioglu, M. 393
Bival, G. 223
Black, F. 417, 418, 421
Blanchard, O.J. 328, 332
Bole, V. 74, 75
Bollerslev, T. 425
Bolton, P. 328
Borak, N. 218
Brada, J.C. 331
Brady Bonds 439, 442
  market performance 449–51
  Poland, market performance 449–51
  see also Bulgarian Brady Bonds
Brady Plans 447–9
Brom, K. 356
Bruand, M. 432, 433
Bruno 321
Buchtikova, A. 351

budget constraints, hardening, and
  privatization 330–31
Bulgaria
  Agrobiznesbank 44
  Bank Consolidation Company 45
  bank crisis 39
  banking sector 44–6
  banks, top five banks 45
  bond markets 53–4
  Brady plan 448
  Bulbank 39
  Bulgarian National Bank (BNB) 39,
    40, 41, 53, 55, 56
    and exchange rate 43
  Central Depository 52
  contributions to variations in the debt-
    to-GDP ratio 453
  current account and trade balances
    459
  debt indicators (1985–95) 440
  debt reduction 444–51
  debt settlements (since 1981) 445–6
  equity markets 50–53
  express issues 55
  external debt 58–64
  financial difficulties 38–9
  financial markets 50–58
  First Agricultural and Investment
    Bank 44
  foreign debt 38
  foreign direct investment 460
  foreign exchange policy 42–4
  general government balances 459
  government securities 54
    term structure 56
  gross domestic product (GDP) 39
    growth in real gross domestic
      product 457
  growth of broad money 40
  and IMF 62
  indebtedness 439–42
  inflation 458
  instruments 41–2
  interest rates 39, 42
    base interest rate 55
    short term 457
  internal credit 41, *41*
  internal debt 55–8
  Kristalbank 44
  Law on Banks and Credit Activity 44

Law on the Bulgarian National Bank
44
Lev/US$ rate 417
London Club debt, restructuring 58
Mineralbank 44
monetary policy 40–46
OTC securities, prices 51
Parva Chastna Banka (First Private
Bank) 44
privatization 46–50
by restitution 46
cash privatization 48–50
legislation on cash privatization
48–9
small scale 46
voucher privatization 47–8
privatization funds 48, 52
Securities and Stock Exchange
Commission (SSEC) 50, 52
State Investment and Development
Bank of Bulgaria (SIDB) 312–13
state owned enterprises 38, 39
stock exchange and OTC traded
securities, prices 52
US$ exchange rates 458
and World Bank 62
ZUNK bonds 55–8
ZUNK market 57
Bulgarian Brady Bonds 49
daily spot prices 62
features 61
market 59–60
market performance 449–51
prices 60–62
rates of return, risk premia, and
ratings 63–4
returns 65
risk rating 59–60
see also DISCs; FLIRBs; IABs

Calvo, G. 251, 274, 277
Campbell, J. 417, 420
Canning, D. 327, 328, 334, 357, 358,
361
Capek, A. 351
Capital Asset Pricing Model (CAPM)
430
capital markets
Central Europe 336
Slovakia 192–203

Carlin, W. 252, 332
CECE index family
case study 387–91
eligible stocks, share type 388
free float factor 389
relevance 389
representation factor 389
CECE indices, key data 390
central bank independence
Albania 14–15
Hungary 266
Romania 266
and seigniorage 263–6
central banking, in Economies in
Transition of Eastern Europe (EITs)
251–69
central banks 2, 6–7
Albania 13, 14–18, 25, 29
appointment procedures 265
Austria 256
balance sheets, analysis 256–7
Bulgaria 39, 40, 41, 53, 55, 56
Croatia 67
Czech Republic 89–90, 91, 93, 287
foreign sector 263
FR Yugoslavia 241, 246–7
Hungary 110–11
legislation 264, 265
relevant to the generation of
seigniorage 269
liabilities and assets (1993) 258
Macedonia 141
Poland 148–50
Romania 153, 163, 164, 169
running expenses 261
Slovakia 185, 187, 210–12
Slovenia 214
see also seigniorage
Central and East European Countries
(CEECs), financial aid 438–9
Central and Eastern Europe
current account and trade balances
459
financial markets 417
foreign direct investment 460
general government balances 459
growth in real gross domestic product
457
inflation 458
markets, local equity indices 387

mutual funds 382
number of banks and brokers in equity
    markets 381
shares, foreign trading places 385
short term interest rates 457
stock market risks, instruments 386-7
US$ exchange rates 458
Central Europe
    equity markets
        distribution of returns 405
        efficiency 392-416
        extent and liquidity 397
        institutional structure 395-401
        financial risks 381-91
        runs tests of weak form efficiency 406
Chlumsky, J. 347
Chobanov, G. 417
Chow, K.V. 402
Claessens, S. 393
Clifton, E. 165
Cline, W. 451
Coffee, J.C. 347, 351
collusion, determinants 275-7
collusive trade credit
    policy implications 277-80
    and stabilization policies 270-82
COMECON 38
contractual obligations, East European
    firms 272
Coricelli, F. 251, 274, 277
Cornelius, P.K. 393
corporate control 393
corporate governance 332
Council of Europe 84
Crane 331
credit and transfer circuits, separation
    278-9
Croatia
    balance of payments 85
        and related indicators 87
    bank supervision 75
    banking legislation 75-6
    banking sector 75-8
        ownership structure 76
    banks, rehabilitation procedure 76
    central bank 67
    Croatian Loan Corporation for
        Reconstruction (HKBO, HBOR)
        313
    Croatian Privatization Fund 78, 79

current account and trade balances
    459
domestic debt 74
and EBRD 84
effect of war 85
Eurobond issue 85
exchange rate of Kuna 70
exchanges 81-3
external finance, sources 83-5
foreign aid 84
foreign direct investment 83, 84, 460
foreign exchange regulation 69
foreign investments throught
    privatization 84
general government balances 459
gross domestic product (GDP) 67, 69
    growth in real gross domestic
        product 457
and IMF 69, 84
inflation 458
interbank Kuna money market 81
interest rate developments 74-5
interest rates 73-4, 77
    and financial ratios 73
    short term 457
international reserves 68
Law on Privatization 81
management and employee buy-outs
    (MEBOs) 78
monetary policy 67-75
National Bank of Croatia 67, 68, 69,
    75, 78
    international reserves 70
    structure of balance sheet 72
NBC bills 73, 78, 82
non-performing assets 75
pension funds 79
privatization 78-81
    results 80
Privredna banka 75, 76
reserve requirements, and share of
    NBC bills in M1 71
Riječka banka 76
shares, most active 88
Slavonska banka 76
Splitska banka 76
US$ exchange rates 458
and World Bank 84
Zagreb Money Market 81-2
Zagreb stock exchange 79-80

monthly trading volume 82–3
Zagrebačka banka 75, 83
Cukierman, A. 265
current account and trade balances,
    Central and Eastern Europe 459
Czech Republic 89
    average interbank depository offer rate
        (PRIBOR) 92
    Bank Council 90
    bank failures 96
    bank supervision 93–5
    banking industry, concentration by
        assets and liabilities 286
    banking legislation 89, 93, 95
    banking sector 93–6, 283–300
        prospects 294–7
        total volume and development of
            credits 293
        two tier banking system 89
    banks
        adequacy of reserves 295
        association with European Union
            299–300
        balance sheets 283
        five largest 284–6
            market shares 285
        market capitalization 297
        privatization prospects 295–7
        rating of Czech banks 288–90
        small and medium sized 286
        specialized banking institutions
            286–8
        specialized private banking
            institutions 288
        total assets 297–8
    budget deficit 326
    capital account 106
    capital inflow 105–6
    capital market development 99
    commercial banking 283
    commercial banks 94
    commercial deposits 292
    Consolidation Bank (KOB) 286–7,
        355
    credit dynamics 293–4
    current account and trade balances
        459
    Czech Capital Information Agency
        (CEKIA) 103
    Czech Crown (CZK) 91

Czech Export Bank 287–8
Czech National Bank 89–90, 91, 93,
    287
Czech-Moravian Guarantee and
    Development Bank (CMZRB)
    313–14
debts, cross country comparison
    (1989) 326
decision-making power of enterprises
    322
deposits 290–92
domestic banks, comparison 95
economic and financial indicators 92
exchange rate 92
exchanges 98–105
external finance, sources 105–6
foreign capital inflow 91
foreign direct investment 460
foreign participation in banks 284
foreign portfolio investment 104
general government balances 459
growth in real gross domestic product
    457
household deposits 291–2
and IMF 91
industrial companies, ownership and
    legal form of structure 321
inflation 458
interest rates
    from primary deposits compared
        with inflation rate 291
    short term 457
international exposure and
    competitiveness 297–300
investment funds 97–8, 100
Investment Privatization Funds 347,
    355, 408–9
macroeconomic stability 325
management privatization proposals
    351–2
market capitalization 396
mass privatization 350–55
monetary policy 89–93
municipal bonds 99
national Property Fund, structure of
    ownership 357
National Property Fund (FNM) 100,
    336, 348, 353, 355, 356
non-performing loans 294
Prague Stock Exchange 98–9, 100,

101
  derivative trading 104
  disclosure requirements 412–16
  selected indicators 105
  trading 102–3
Prague Stock Exchange Index PX50
    101, 103
price indexes 103–4
privatization 96–8, 100, 333, 347–57
  approved projects 350
  of banks 283
  comparison with Poland and
      Hungary 318–70
  importance of funds in first wave
      356
  methods 96–7
  multi-track approach 348–50
  results 97
  role of state 355–7
  of stocks 350
privatization legislation 348
privatization plans compared to
    outcomes 335
RM-System over-the-counter market
    98, 99
Security Register 97, 98, 102, 103
seigniorage 259, 261, 262, 263, 364,
    365, 366
share trading 100
shares, distribution 349
State Bank of Czechoslovakia 283
state led restructuring 352
state sector share 320
stock exchange 399
structure of money aggregate 291
Supervisory State Agency 351
taxation 98, 100
US$ exchange rates 458
voucher privatization 96, 97, 98,
    100–101, 319, 347–8, 349,
    353–5
  efficiency 409–10
  in first privatization wave 354
Czechoslovakia
  macroeconomic conditions before
      economic reform programs 324
  monetary policy 184–5
  subsidies outcome in the first years of
      transition 330
  voucher privatization 4

Dăianu, D. 165, 272
Dankenbring, H. 431
Dardania Bank 25
Dasgupta, S. 393
Dayton Agreement 67, 81
debt management 9–10
debt reduction
  Bulgaria 444–51
  Bulgaria and Poland 444
  impact 451–4
debt settlements since 1981
  Bulgaria 445–6
  Poland 445–6
debt swaps 49
debt write-off, uses 454–5
DeGennaro, R.P. 430
Demski, J.S. 399
Denning, K.C. 402
depoliticization of the economy, and
    privatization 328–9
derivative equity index products 386
derivatives 384, 385
Dewatripont, M. 328
Dinkic, M. 241
direct sales method of privatization 337
directed credit, retreat of state 279–80
discount bonds (DISCs) 49, 58, 59, 61,
    64–5
Dittus, P. 332
Dorsey, T. 74, 76, 77
Drazen, A. 253
Duan, J. 418, 435
Dye, R.A. 399

Earle, J.S. 172, 329, 332, 333
EBRD 175, 204
  and Croatia 84
Ebrill, L. 151
Economies in Transition of Eastern
    Europe (EITs), in central banking
    251–69
Ellman, M. 320, 322, 325, 331
emerging equity markets, efficiency,
    studies 393
emerging market yields 450
Emerging Markets Bond Index Plus
    (EMBI+) 63
  for Bulgarian Bradies 64
Emerson, R. 417
employee or management buy-outs 337

employee ownership 337
  Poland 338, 342–3
Engle, R. 425, 430
equity, and privatization 328
equity markets
  Bulgaria 50–53
  Central and Eastern Europe, number
    of banks and brokers 381
  Central Europe 9
    capitalization 396
    distribution of returns 405
    efficiency 392–416
    institutional structure 395–401
    tests of weak-form efficiency 401–6
  Central Europe and Asia, equity
    markets, extent and liquidity 397
  disclosure 398–9
  emerging equity markets, efficiency,
    studies 393
  Hungary 121–2
equity trading 5
Erb, C. 417
Estrin, S. 319, 320, 322, 324, 325, 328,
    329, 332, 333
Eurobond issue, Croatia 85
Europe, banks by total assets 298–9
European Union
  association with Czech banks 299–300
  integration with East European central
    banks 251
  and Kreditanstalt für Wiederaufbau
    (KfW) 312
European Union aid, and Croatia 84
exchange-related trading 4
exchanges
  Albania 28–33
  Croatia 81–3
  Czech Republic 98–105
  Hungary 118–24
  Slovenia 229–34
exposure management 383
Expotential GARCH (EGARCH) 431,
    432
external finance
  sources
    Albania 33
    Croatia 83–5
    Czech Republic 105–6
    Hungary 124–5
    Poland 161

Romania 179–81
Slovakia 204–8
Slovenia 234–7

Fama, E. 425
Feltham, G.A. 399
Fidrmuc, J. 204, 206, 379
Filer, R.K. 9, 407, 410
financial aid, to Central and East
    European Countries (CEECs) 438–9
financial arrears
  collusive creation 7
  creative collusion 270
financial markets
  Bulgaria 50–58
  Central and Eastern Europe 417
  transition economies 382
financial risks, Central Europe 381–91
financial time series, econometric
    modeling 417
FLIRBs *see* front-loaded, interest-
    reduction bonds
foreign aid
  Albania 34–5
  Croatia 84
foreign debt
  Albania 24
  Bulgaria 38
foreign debt settlements, Bulgaria,
    Hungary and Poland (1989–96)
    438–56
foreign direct investment 333
  Albania 33
  Bulgaria 460
  Central and East European countries
    460
  Croatia 83, 84
  Slovakia 206–8
foreign financial assistance, Slovakia
    204–6
foreign investment, Romania 180
foreign investments through
    privatization, Croatia *84*
foreign investors 3–4
foreign sector central banks 263
foreign trade and foreign assistance,
    Macedonia 139–40
FR Yugoslavia
  Avramovic's program 241, 244
  banking crisis 244

banking legislation 240
banking scandals 243
banking sector 240-41, 243-7
Beogradska Banka 244
central bank 241, 246-7
economic development 239-40
frozen foreign currency savings 246,
    247
GSP 239
inflation 241-3
'inflation rationing' 242-3, 245
Karic Banka 244
National Bank of Yugoslavia 241
front-loaded, interest-reduction bonds
    (FLIRBs) 49, 58, 59, 61, 64
Fry, M.J. 253
Frydman, R. 172, 360

Gabrijelčič, L. 230
GARCH model 418, 425-39
    extensions 430-32
GARCH volatility
    of DAX 429
    of WGI 429
Gdansk surveys 340
Gelb, A. 277, 321, 334
general government balances, Central
    and East European countries 459
Generalized Autoregressive Conditional
    Heteroscedasticity *see* GARCH
Geometric Brownian Motion 418, 425
German Bank for Development 8
German-Polish Association for
    Economic Promotion (AEP) 315
Germany
    bank loans to Hungary 442
    Frankfurt Stock Exchange 9
    Kreditanstalt für Wiederaufbau (KfW)
        301-2
    seigniorage 261, 263
give-away schemes 336
    method of privatization 337
Glan, J. 393
Gligorov, V. 129, 239
Glosten, L. 431
Gomulka, St. 319, 339, 342
Gorden, B. 400
government, role in privatization 368
government revenues, increasing, and
    privatization 330

Gray, Ch. W. 332
Gros, D. 260
growth in real gross domestic product,
    Central and East European
    countries 457

Halpern, L. 455
Ham, J.C. 353
Hamar, J. 359
Hamilton, J. 433
Hanousek, J. 9, 407, 410
Hare, P. 322, 327, 328, 330, 332, 334,
    357, 358, 361
Harrison, P. 435
Harvey, C. 417
Harvey, C.R. 393
hedging tools 383
Hlvavsa, A. 409
Hochreiter, E. 6, 251, 264, 265
Hughes, K. 333, 369
Hungary
    bank bail-outs 112
    banking sector 111-12
        privatization 117
    banks
        market share of groups of banks
            111
        ownership structure 112
        total balance sheet by groups of
            banks 111
    Bokros' Package 109
    Budapest stock exchange 117
        admission conditions 119-20
        main figures 126-8
        markets 121-2
        membership and operation 122-3
        outlook 123
        and privatization 124
    central bank independence 266
    central bank seigniorage 260
    central banks 110-11
    contributions to variations in the debt-
        to-GDP ratio 453
    current account 109
    and trade balances 459
    debt indicators (1985-95) 440
    debt service 442-4
    debts, cross country comparison
        (1989) 326
    derivative markets 122

electricity sector, privatization 117
Employee Share Ownership programs
    362
enterprise councils 322
equity market 121-2
exchanges 118-24
existence loans 362
external finance, sources 124-5
foreign debt servicing 6
foreign debt settlements 438-56
foreign direct investment 460
foreign investment 359
foreign investors 333
Forint, devaluation 110
gas distribution companies,
    privatization 116-17
general government balances 459
gross domestic product (GDP) 109
    growth in real gross domestic
        product 457
Hungarian Investment and
    Development Bank (MBFB) 314
Hungarian Power Companies Ltd
    (MVM) 116
Hungarian Telecommunication
    Company (MATAV) 117
indebtedness 439-444
independence of enterprises 322-3
industrial companies, ownership and
    legal form of structure 321
industrial structure 323-4
inflation 458
macroeconomic conditions before
    economic reform programs 324
macroeconomic developments and
    economic policy 109-11
MEBOs 362
Ministry of Industry and Trade 357
monetary policy 109-10
monetary policy instruments 110
official share index (BUX) 121
ownership structure
    of banks 112
    changes 367
privatization 112-18, 357-67
    comparison with Poland and Czech
        Republic 318-70
    of electricity sector 115-16
    of integrated oil company (MOL)
        115

politicization and evolution 359-63
    revenues 359
    and state 364-5
privatization legislation 113-14, 360,
    361
privatization plans compared to
    outcomes 335
reforms 322
seigniorage 261, 262, 263
shares, distribution 358
short term interest rates 457
Small Investor's Share Program 362
state, and privatization 364-5
State Holding Company (State Asset
    Management company) 336, 362,
    365, 366
state ownership (1992) 365
State Privatization Agency 113, 336,
    364-5, 365
State Privatization and Asset
    Management Company 363
State Privatization and Holding
    Company (SPHC) 114, 361
State Property Agency 361
    and managers 366
state sector share 320
State-Owned Enterprises 113
stock exchange
    regulations related to foreigners 119
    regulatory framework 118
    trading 121
subsidies outcome in the first years of
    transition 330
telecommunications, privatization 117
US$ exchange rates 458
voucher privatization 362

IABs *see* interest arrears bonds
IBCA, rating of Czech banks 290
Ickes, B. 271
illiquidity 270-71, 272, 274
IMF 17, 21, 28, 34, 43, 166, 204, 215
    Article VIII 69
    and Bulgaria 62
    and Croatia 84
    and Czech Republic 91
    and Macedonia 140
indebtedness
    Bulgaria 439-442
    Hungary 439-444

Poland 439–442
inflation, Central and East European
    countries 458
inflation rates 252
insider trading, Central European equity
    markets 400
integrated GARCH (IGARCH) model
    428
inter-firm debt 277
interest arrears bonds (IABs) 58, 59, 61,
    63, 64
interest rate subsidies 262
interest rates
    Albania
        interest rate policy 18–20
        interest rates structure 20
    Bulgaria 42
    Croatia 73–4, 77
        interest rates and financial ratios 73
    Czech Republic 291, 457
    Poland 150
    Romania 166, 262
    Slovenia 186–7, 210
international funding 5–10
International Monetary Fund *see* IMF
involuntary trade credit *see* collusive
    trade credit
Irsch, N. 7
Iwanek, M. 323

Jasinski, P. 319, 339, 342
Jorion, P. 432, 433
JP Morgan 63, 65
jump-diffusion processes 432–4

Kamshad, K.M. 333
Karsai, J. 362
Kazancioglu, N. 393
Kenway, P. 347
Keren, M. 331
Kim, D. 434
Kim, M. 432
King, A.E. 410
Klaus, V. 318, 331
Klein, M. 253
Kletzer, K. 86
Kokoszczyński, R. 148, 150
Kon, S. 434
Kondratowicz, A. 150
Kopint-Datorg 109, 361

Kornai, J. 320, 323, 330, 331
Kotrba, J. 349
Kotzeva, M. 271
Kraft, E. 74, 76, 77
Kranjec, M. 217
Kreditanstalt für Wiederaufbau (KfW)
    301–2
    advisory assistance 311–12
    and European Union 312
Kroch, E. 410

Latin America
    Brady Bonds 60, 451
    equity markets 393
    monthly return 404
Lavigne, M. 328
Lavrač, V. 215
Law for Settling the Non-performing
    Credits *see* ZUNK bonds
Layard, R. 328
Leandowski, J. 318
Leftwich, R. 399
Legros, P. 279
Levene, H. 404
LIBOR 59
Lilien, D. 430
Lipton, D. 318, 328, 329
liquidation method of privatization 337
Ljung-Box test 424
Lo, A. 401, 420, 424
London Club of creditors 58, 85, 439,
    442, 447
Luxembourg Stock Exchange 85

Ma, C.-Y. 410
Macedonia
    Bank Rehabilitation Agency 141
    banking system 140–43
    break-up costs 129
    central bank 141
    current account 139
        and trade balances 459
    discount and interest rates 132
    foreign direct investment 460
    foreign trade and foreign assistance
        139–40
    freezing of foreign currency deposits
        142–3
    general government balances 459
    gross social product (GSP) 130

growth in real gross domestic product 457
and IMF 140
inflation 458
internal instability 129
isolation from main markets 129
Macedonian Central Bank 131, 132
monetary policy 131–3
money supply, growth and inflation dynamics 131
privatization 133–8
privatization legislation 134
privatization process, by sectors 137
production 133
prospects 146
restructuring 138–9
short term interest rates 457
stock exchange 143–5
  membership 143–4
  trading 144–5
Stopanska banka 141, 142
trading partners 140
US\$ exchange rates 458
MacKinlay, A. 424
MacKinlay, C. 401, 420
Madzar, L. 244
Malkiel, B.G. 393
management and employee buy-outs (MEBOs) 4
Croatia 78
Poland 338
management incentive structure 332
Mandelbrot, B. 425
market capitalization 398
market efficiency, tests of semi-strong and strong-form 407–9
market research 383–5
Marshall Plan 438
Marshall Plan aid 301
'Marshall Plan for Eastern Europe' 438
mass privatization *see* voucher privatization
Matits, A. 323
Mayer, C. 252
Mejstrik, M. 347, 355
Merton, R. 418, 432, 434, 435
Meszanos, D. 417
Mexico, Peso crisis 449
Meyhdian, S. 393
Milanovic, B. 328

Milosevic, Slobodan 244
Missong, M. 431
Mitchell, J. 279, 332
mixed ownership 369
Mladek, J. 351
Mohsin, K. 165
MOL (Hungarian national oil and gas industry company) 115
monetary policy 2
Albania 14–22
Bulgaria 40–46
Croatia 67–75
Czech Republic 89–93
Czechoslovakia 184–5
Hungary 109–10
Macedonia 131–3
Poland 149–53
Romania 163–8
Slovakia 184–7, 210–12
Slovenia 214–20
Montenegro *see* FR Yugoslavia
Moody's 59
ratings of Czech banks 289
mutual funds 394
Central and Eastern Europe 382

Nelson, D. 431
Nelson, R.H. 329
Němeček, L. 408
Neumann, M. 253
non-performing loans
Albania 27–8
Bulgaria 55
Czech Republic 294
Nuti, D.M. 323, 328, 331, 333, 336, 337, 338, 343, 345, 346, 347, 367

Offe, C. 329
OMV, Austria 115
option-pricing 417
Orenstein, M. 356
ÖTOB 383, 384, 385, 386, 387
output targets 331

Pagan, A. 417
Pálenik, V. 8, 200, 375, 376, 379
Panas, E. 393
Paris Club 84, 140, 151, 439, 441, 447
agreements 444–7
pension funds, Croatia 79

Perotti, E. 7, 251, 270, 271
PHARE 84
PHARE funds 175
PHARE program 204
Phelps, E.S. 332
Phillips, S. 399
Pistor, K. 355, 356, 369
Poisson jump process 418, 434
Poland
  bank restructuring program 155
  banking legislation 153–4
  banking sector 153–6
  banks
    by ownership structure 154
    market share of major bank groups
      155
  Brady bonds, market perfomance
    449–51
  Brady plan 448
  capital privatization 156
  commercialization (restructuring) 338,
    343–5
  contributions to variations in the debt-
    to-GDP ratio 453
  control of enterprises 323
  current account and trade balances
    459
  DAX 420, 421
    20-day volatility 426
    GARCH volatility 429
    normalized estimated unconditional
      distribution 423
    returns 422
  debt indicators (1985-95) 440
  debt reduction 444–51
  debt renegotiation 441
  debt settlements (since 1981) 445–6
  debt-equity swaps 338
  debts, cross country comparison
    (1989) 326
  direct sales 345–6
  employee ownership 338, 342–3
  equity market 149
  exchange rate 152
  external finance, sources 161
  financial markets 148
  foreign debt settlements 438–56
  foreign direct investment 460
  foreign investment 150–52
  forex regulations 151, 152

  general government balances 459
  growth in real gross domestic product
    457
  guarantee institution for Western
    Poland 315–6
  indebtedness 439–442
  industrial companies, ownership and
    legal form of structure 321
  inflation 458
  interest rate policy 150
  joint stock companies 345
    employment distribution 346
  Law on State Enterprises (1981) 323
  legal reform 324
  macroeconomic conditions before
    economic reform programs 324
  management-employee buy-outs
    (MEBOs) 338, 342, 346
  mass privatization 337, 340–42
  monetary policy 149–53
  National Bank of Poland 148, 149
  National Investment Funds 157, 340,
    342
  open market operations 150
  ownership transformation type
    sector breakdown 344
    size breakdown 344
Polski Bank Rozwoju (PBR) 314–16
privatization 156–8, 333, 337–46
  comparison with Czech Republic and
    Hungary 318–70
  organic privatization 339
  sales revenues 346
  summary of progress 339
  privatization legislation 156, 337, 338,
    342
  privatization plans compared to
    outcomes 335
  privatization schemes, and foreign
    investors 157
  privatization through liquidation' 156,
    338, 340, 342–3
  shares, distribution 343
  short term interest rates 457
  state enterprises, employment
    distribution 345
  state sector, share 320
  stock exchange 158–60
  stock returns, modeling 417–37
  subsidies outcome in the first years of

transition 330
taxation 157–8
US$ exchange rates 458
voucher privatization 156–7, 340–41
Warsaw General Index 419
  20-day volatility 426
  GARCH volatility 429
  normalized estimated unconditional
    distribution 423
  returns 422
Warsaw Stock Exchange 9, 149,
  158–60, 341, 417, 418–20
  index and main market turnover
    160
  list of members 162
  statistical properties of returns
    420–425
  trading 159
  workers councils 323
Portes, R. 251
Portugal, debts, cross country
  comparison (1989) 326
privatization 4, 8
  Albania 23–4
  and Budapest Stock Exchange 124
  and budget constraints 330–31
  Bulgaria 46–50
  comparison of Poland, Czech
    Republic and Hungary 318–70
  Croatia 78–81
  Czech Republic 96–8
  defined 318, 319
  and depoliticizing of the economy
    328–9
  description 334–7
  and equity 328
  give-away schemes 336
  Hungary 112–18
  and increasing government revenues
    330
  Macedonia 133–8
  methods 337
  models 332
  objectives, overview of literature 328
  Poland 156–8, 337–46
  preconditions 320–27
  and restructuring of enterprises 331
  role of government 368–9
  Romania 171–5
  Slovakia 190–92, 208

Slovenia 223–9
  and state assets, appropriation by
    insiders 329–30
  see also voucher privatization
privatization funds, Bulgaria 48
privatization policy, aims 327–34
privatization/efficiency/incentives link
  332
privatization/restructuring link 332
promotional banking 8
promotional banks
  in Central and Eastern Europe 301–17
  constituent principles 306–8
  creation of a national promotional
    bank 310–11
  and the development of small and
    medium sized enterprises (SMEs)
    304–6
  functions 306–8
  refinancing function 309
  risk function 309–10
  Romania 316
Prowse, St. 332
pyramid schemes 3, 243
pyramid structures, Bulgaria 50
Pyun, C. 393

random walk hypothesis 402–4
  variance ratio tests 402
Rapaczynski, A. 172, 360
Rejnuš, O. 207
reserve requirements
  Albania 26
  and seigniorage 266, 267
restitution schemes 336
restructuring
  of enterprises, and privatization 331
  of firms 276
  Macedonia 138–9
Reuters All-Bulgarian Stock Index
  (RABSI) 51, 53
Revesz, T. 322
Riding, A. 408
Rittenberg, L. 400
RM-system
  creation and development 372–6
  Czech Republic 98, 99
  Slovakia 371–80
    continuous auction technique
    375–6

indices 376–8
periodic auction technique 372–5
regional structure 373
results of trading 374
trading safety 378–80
Robins, R. 430
Rohatinski, Ž. 79, 80, 81
Rojec, M. 235
Roland, G. 328
Roldos, J. 86
Romania
  agriculture 165
  bank privatization 170
  bank reserves 169
  bank supervision 169
  banking sector 169–71
  Bucharest Stock Exchange 175–7
    market capitalization and turnover
      178
    share price dynamics 178–9
    trading 177
  capital market 175–9
  central bank 169
  central bank independence 266
  central bank seigniorage 260
  current account deficit 180
  current account and trade balances
    459
  directed credits 164
  exchange rate policy 167
  external debt 181
  external finance, sources 179–81
  foreign direct investment 460
  foreign investment 180
  forex market 167
  general government balances 459
  gross domestic product (GDP) 163
    growth in real gross domestic
      product 457
  imports versus foreign direct
    investment 181
  inflation 458
  interest rate subsidies 262
  interest rates applied by banks 166
  international financing 6
  mass privatization 172–3
    companies in program by branches
      174
  monetary indicators (1996) 167
  monetary policy 163–8

National Bank of Romania 163, 164,
  169
privatization 171–5
  public share offering 172
  sale of assets 172
privatization legislation 171, 173
promotional bank 316
prudential rules 170
RASDAQ 179
real exchange rate and current
    account balance 168
refinancing interest rate and inflation
    rate 165
seigniorage 261, 262, 263
selected macroeconomic indicators
    182–3
short term interest rates 457
US$ exchange rates 458
Ronald, G. 328
Rostowski, J. 271
Rovelli, R. 6, 251, 253, 255
Ryterman, R. 271

Sachs, J. 318, 328, 329
Saje, J. 215
Scheicher, M. 9, 424
Schiendl, G. 9
Schleifer, A. 328, 329, 332
Schmidt, K.M. 328, 332
Schmied, R. 207
Schnitzer 328, 332
Scholes, W. 417, 418, 421
Schroeder Wagg (UK) 362
Schwartz Information Criterion (SIC)
    424
Securities and Stock Exchange
    Commission (SSEC), Bulgaria 50,
    52
securities trading 8–9
Security Register, Czech Republic 97, 98
seigniorage 6–7, 252
  appropriation of central bank
    seigniorage 260, 261–3
  Austria 261, 262, 264
  and central bank independence 263–6
  and central bank legislation 269
  definitions 253–5
  distributed to government 262
  distribution of central bank
    seigniorage 262

earning liabilities 259
foregone seigniorage 262
generation 259-61
Germany 261, 264
Hungary 261, 262, 263
measuring 253-7
and reserve requirements 266, 267
retained 261
Romania 261, 262, 263
semi-strong market efficiency 407-8
Serbia *see* FR Yugoslavia
Sgard, J. 9
Shamsher, M. 393
short term interest rates, Central and
Eastern Europe 457
Siklos, P. 264
Silverman, B.U. 421
Singer, M. 347, 354, 409
Skalicky 353
Slovakia
assets of commercial banks 189
bad debts 190
banking legislation 187-8
banking sector 187-90
bond privatization 191-2
Bratislava Options Exchange, trading
volume 202
Bratislava Stock Exchange 193-4
list of members 213
listed securities 196-8
minimum listing conditions 196
registered securities 198
trading 195
trading volume 198-9
unified average prices 200
capital adequacy 188-9
capital markets 192-203
investors 201
legislation 193
securities traders 200-201
trade volume as a percentage of
GDP 203
central bank 187
credit limits 210
currency basket 211
current account and trade balances
459
equity trading 194-6
exchange rate and foreign exchange
policy 211

exchange rates 185-6
external finance
and foreign debt 205
sources 204-8
foreign direct investment 206-8, 460
foreign financial assistance 204-6
Fund of National Property, bonds 379
futures and options exchanges 201-3
general government balances 459
growth in real gross domestic product
457
inflation 458
interest rate policy 210
interest rates 186-7
short term 457
investment legislation 211-12
isolation 184
management buy-outs 192
monetary policy 184-7, 210-12
money market 203
National Bank of Slovakia 185, 187
instruments of monetary policy
210-12
privatization 190-92, 208
legislation 190
small scale 190
refinancing system 210
reforms 184
reserve requirements 186
RM-system 371-80
SAX index 199-200
Slovak Loan Corporation (SLC) 316
transition to market economy 184
US$ exchange rates 458
voucher privatization 190
wages 206
Slovenia
Bank of Slovenia 214, 215
bills issued 216
banking legislation 214-15, 220, 222,
223
banking sector 220-23
summary balance sheet structure
221
banking supervision 222
banks
ownership 222
top five banks 219
central bank 214
current account and trade balances

459
derivatives exchange 233
economy 214, 237
exchange rates 217–18
exchanges 229–34
    legislation 229–30
external finance, sources 234–7
foreign debt 235, 237
foreign direct investment 235, 460
foreign exchange markets 218
foreign financial assistance by
    international financial institutions
    236
foreign investment
    most important foreign investors
    236
    openness of selected sectors 236
foreign investment legislation 234
general government balances 459
growth in real gross domestic product
    457
inflation 458
interest rate policy 216–17
Ljubljana Stock Exchange 230–34
    listing requirements 227
    market capitalization 235
monetary policy 214–20
new currency 214
privatization 223–9
privatization legislation 224, 225
reserves 220
short term interest rates 457
tax 228–9
US$ exchange rates 458
small and medium sized enterprises
    (SMEs)
    development and promotional banks
    304–6
    funding 302–4
Sola, M. 431
Šonje, V. 74, 76, 77
stabilization policies, and collusive trade
    credit 270–82
Standard & Poor's, evaluation of Czech
    banking sector 288
Stanovik, P. 215
state
    and privatization 368
    retreat from directed credit 279–80
state assets, appropriation by insiders,

and privatization 329
state owned enterprises, Bulgaria 38,
    39
state property, sale 336
Stengos, T. 393
Štiblar, F. 221
stock exchange
    Macedonia 143–5
    and OTC traded securities, prices,
        Bulgaria 52
    Poland 158–60
stock returns, modeling Polish stock
    returns 417–37
Stolin, M.R. 402
strong-form market efficiency 408
Studentized Maximum Modulus (SMM)
    402
Svejnar, J. 347, 353, 354, 409
Szakmáry, D. 124
Szendrei, C. 119

Takla, L. 8, 322, 332, 347, 349
Tandon, K. 393
Terrell, K. 353
Timmerman, A. 431
Tirole, J. 328
Todd, S. 333
'Toronto Initiative' 444
Torous, W. 432, 433
trade arrears 277
trading structure, East European firms
    272
transition, and reform 1
transition economies, financial markets
    382
transition to market economy 301
Turkey, monthly returns 404
Turkowitz, J. 355, 356, 369
two tier banking system 3
    Albania 24–5
    Bulgaria 44
    Czech Republic 89
    Poland 153

Unčovsky, L. 379
Urrutia, J.L. 393, 404
Ury, H.K. 402
US$ exchange rates, Central and Eastern
    Europe 458
US stock markets 424

Uvalic, M. 333

Vandille, G. 260
variance ratio tests of random walk
    hypothesis
    monthly returns variance ratio 402
    weekly returns variance ratio 403
Veselinovič, D. 230
Vickers, J. 319
Vishny 328, 329, 332
Viskanta, T. 417
volatility clustering 424
volatility smile 425
Voszka, E. 365
voucher privatization 336
    Albania 23
    arguments for 328–31
    Bulgaria 47–8
    Czech Republic 96, 97, 98, 100–101,
        319, 347
        efficiency 409–10
    Czechoslovakia 4
    Hungary 362
    Poland 156–7, 340–41
    Romania 171

Slovakia 190–92

Wiengand, H. 7
Winckler, G. 6, 251
Wörgötter, A. 223
World Bank 34, 136, 161, 204
    and Bulgaria 62
    and Croatia 84
World Debt Tables 453
Wyplosz, C. 455
Wyzen, M.L. 129

Yarrow, G. 319
Yugoslavia, National Bank of
    Yugoslavia 68, 74

Zahradnik, P. 7
Zecher, J.R. 399
Zemplinerova, A. 324
ZUNK bonds 49
    BGL and US$ denominated 58
    Bulgaria 55–8
ZUNK market, Bulgaria 57
Zychowicz, E.J. 393, 404